CQ's State Fact Finder

CQ's State Fact Finder 2003

Rankings Across America

Kendra A. Hovey

Harold A. Hovey

CQ PRESS

A Division of Congressional Quarterly Inc.
Washington, D.C.

To the memory of Harold A. Hovey

CQ Press
1255 22nd Street, N.W., Suite 400
Washington, D.C. 20037

(202) 729-1900; toll-free, 1-866-4CQ-PRESS (1-866-427-7737)

www.cqpress.com

∞ The paper used in this publication meets the minimum requirements of the American National Standard for Information Sciences—Permanence of Paper for Printed Library Materials, ANSI Z39.48-1992.

Printed and bound in the United States of America

07 06 05 04 03   5 4 3 2 1

ISBN 1-56802-810-5 (cloth)
ISBN 1-56802-809-1 (paper)
ISSN 1079-7149

Contents

Introduction   **xi**

Finding Information Users Want to Know   **1**

        About Personal Decisions on Where to Live or Visit   1
        About Business Decisions on Where to Locate and Expand   6
        About Government and Public Policy   10

Subject Rankings   **15**

        Population   17
        Economies   37
        Geography   77
        Government   95
        Federal Impacts   119
        Taxes   139
        Revenues and Finances   167
        Education   193
        Health   225
        Crime and Law Enforcement   249
        Transportation   269
        Welfare   283
        Technology   303

State Rankings   **313**

Index   **415**

Detailed Contents of Subject Rankings

Population

A-1   Population and Percentage Distribution, 2001 18
A-2   Percentage Change in Population, 2000-2001 19
A-3   Percentage Change in Population, 1990-2001 20
A-4   Projected Population, 2015, and Population
       Change, 2001-2015 21
A-5   Projected Population for the Year 2025 22
A-6   Population Age 65 and Over and as Percentage of
       Population, 2001.. 23
A-7   Population Age 17 and Under and as Percentage
       of Population, 2000 24
A-8   Median Age, 2000 25
A-9   African American Population and Percentage of
       Population, 2000.. 26
A-10   Hispanic Population and Percentage of
       Population, 2000.. 27
A-11   Population in Poverty, 2001..................................... 28
A-12   Number and Rate of Children in Poverty, 2001 29
A-13   Female Population, 2000 30
A-14   Birth Rates, 2001 31
A-15   Death Rates (age-adjusted), 2000.............................. 32
A-16   Population Density, 2001.. 33
A-17   Legal Immigrants Admitted, FY 2000.......................... 34

Economies

B-1   Personal Income, 2001.. 38
B-2   Gross State Product, Total and Per Capita, 2000 39
B-3   Per Capita Personal Income, 2001 40
B-4   Personal Income from Wages and Salaries, 2001 41
B-5   Average Annual Pay, 2001 42
B-6   Average Hourly Earnings, 2002 43
B-7   Value Added in Manufacturing, 2000 44
B-8   Cost of Living, 2002 45
B-9   Average Annual Pay in Manufacturing, 2001 46
B-10   Average Annual Pay in Retailing, 2001...................... 47
B-11   Labor Force, 2002 48
B-12   Unemployed and Unemployment Rate, 2002 49
B-13   Employment and Employment Rate, 2002 50
B-14   Government Employment, 2002................................. 51
B-15   Manufacturing Employment, 2002............................ 52
B-16   *Fortune* 500 Companies, 2002 53
B-17   *Forbes* 500 Companies, 2002 54
B-18   Tourism Spending, 2000 55
B-19   Exports, 2001.. 56
B-20   Housing Permits, 2001 57
B-21   Percentage Change in Home Prices, 1997-2002 58
B-22   Net Farm Income, 2001... 59
B-23   Financial Institution Assets, 2001 60
B-24   Bankruptcy Filings by Individuals
       and Businesses, 2002 61
B-25   Patents Issued, FY 2001.. 62
B-26   Workers' Compensation Temporary
       Disability Payments, 2002...................................... 63
B-27   Average Unemployment Compensation
       Benefit, 2001 64
B-28   Index of State Economic Momentum,
       September 2002... 65
B-29   Employment Change, 2001-2002 66

B-30　Manufacturing Employment Change, 2001-2002 67
B-31　Home Ownership, 1997-2001 68
B-32　Gambling, 2000 69
B-33　Average Annual Electricity Use Per
　　　　Residential Customer, 2001 70
B-34　Average Cost Per Kilowatt Hour, 2001 71
B-35　New Companies, 2001 72

Geography

C-1　Total Land Area, 2000 78
C-2　Land Owned by Federal Government, 2000 79
C-3　State Park Acreage, FY 2002 80
C-4　State Park Visitors, FY 2002 81
C-5　Percentage of Population Not
　　　　Physically Active, 2001 82
C-6　Hunters with Firearms, 2001 83
C-7　Registered Boats, 2001 84
C-8　State Spending on State Arts Agencies, FY 2002 85
C-9　Energy Consumption, Total and Per Capita, 2000 86
C-10　Toxic Chemical Release, 2000 87
C-11　Hazardous Waste Sites, 2002 88
C-12　Polluted Rivers and Streams, 2000 89
C-13　Expired Surface Water Pollution Discharge
　　　　Permits, 2002 90
C-14　Air Pollution Emissions, 1999 91

Government

D-1　Members of the United States House, 2003 96
D-2　Members of State Legislatures, 2003 97
D-3　State Legislators Per Million Population, 2003 98
D-4　Units of Government, 1997 99
D-5　State Legislator Compensation, 2002 100
D-6　Percentage of Legislators Who Are Female, 2002 101
D-7　Turnover in Legislatures, Post-election 2002 102
D-8　Term Limits (in years), 2002 103
D-9　Legislative Session Length, 2003 104
D-10　Party Control of State Legislatures, 2003 105
D-11　Governor's Power Rating, 2002 106
D-12　Number of Statewide Elected Officials, 2000 107
D-13　State and Local Government Employees, 2001 108
D-14　Average Salaries of State and Local
　　　　Government Employees, 2001 109
D-15　Local Employment, 2001 110
D-16　Local Spending Accountability, FY 2000 111
D-17　Percentage of Eligible Voters Registered,
　　　　November 2002 112
D-18　Percentage of Population Voting,
　　　　November 2002 113
D-19　Statewide Initiatives, 2002 114
D-20　Campaign Costs Per Vote in Most Recent Guber-
　　　　natorial Election, 1998, 1999, 2000, or 2001 115

Federal Impacts

E-1　Federal Spending, Total and Per Capita, FY 2001 120
E-2　Increase in Total Federal Spending,
　　　　FY 1996-2001 121
E-3　Federal Spending on Grants, Total and
　　　　Per Capita, FY 2001 122
E-4　Federal Spending on Procurement, Total
　　　　and Per Capita, FY 2001 123
E-5　Federal Spending on Payments to
　　　　Individuals, FY 2001 124
E-6　Federal Spending on Social Security
　　　　and Medicare, FY 2001 125
E-7　Social Security Benefits Paid, 2000 126
E-8　Federal Spending on Employee Wages
　　　　and Salaries, FY 2001 127
E-9　Federal Grant Spending Per Dollar of State
　　　　Tax Revenue, FY 2000 128
E-10　State and Local General Revenue from
　　　　Federal Government, FY 2000 129
E-11　Federal Tax Burden, Total and Per
　　　　Capita, FY 2002 130
E-12　Federal Spending Per Dollar of Taxes
　　　　Paid, FY 2001 131
E-13　Highway Charges Returned to States, FY 2001 132
E-14　Terms of Trade with the Federal
　　　　Government, FY 2001 133
E-15　Federal Personal Income Taxes, 2000 134
E-16　Federal Share of Medicaid, 2002 and 2003 135

Taxes

F-1　State and Local Tax Revenue, Total and
　　　　as a Percentage of Personal Income, FY 2000 140
F-2　Per Capita State and Local Tax Revenue, FY 2000 141
F-3　State and Local Tax Effort, 1996 142
F-4　State and Local Tax Capacity, 1996 143
F-5　Change in State and Local Taxes,
　　　　FY 1995-2000 144
F-6　Property Taxes, Total and as a Percentage of
　　　　Personal Income, FY 2000 145
F-7　Property Taxes Per Capita, FY 2000 146
F-8　Property Tax Revenue as a Percentage of
　　　　Three-Tax Revenue, FY 2000 147
F-9　Sales Taxes, Total and as a Percentage of
　　　　Personal Income, FY 2000 148
F-10　Sales Taxes Per Capita, FY 2000 149
F-11　Sales Tax Revenue as a Percentage of
　　　　Three-Tax Revenue, FY 2000 150
F-12　Sales Tax Rates and Reach, 2003 151
F-13　Individual Income Taxes, Total and
　　　　as a Percentage of Personal Income, FY 2000 152
F-14　Individual Income Taxes Per Capita, FY 2000 153

F-15 Individual Income Tax Revenue as a
Percentage of Three-Tax Revenue, FY 2000 154

F-16 Highest Personal Income Tax Rate, 2002 155

F-17 Corporate Income Taxes, Total and
Per Capita, FY 2000 156

F-18 Motor Fuel Taxes 157

F-19 Tobacco Taxes 158

F-20 State and Local Taxes on High Income Families,
2001 159

F-21 State and Local Taxes in the Largest
City in Each State, 2001 160

F-22 Progressivity of Major State and Local Taxes, 2001 .. 161

F-23 State Estate Taxes, 2002 162

Revenues and Finances

G-1 State and Local Total Revenue, FY 2000 168

G-2 State and Local General Revenue, FY 2000 169

G-3 State and Local "Own-source" General
Revenue, FY 2000 170

G-4 State and Local Non-tax "Own-source"
Revenue, FY 2000 171

G-5 State and Local Total Expenditures, FY 2000 172

G-6 State and Local General Expenditures, FY 2000 173

G-7 State and Local General Expenditures
Per Capita, FY 2000 174

G-8 Percentage Change in State and Local
Expenditures, FY 1995-2000 175

G-9 State Government General Revenue, FY 2000 176

G-10 State Government General Spending, FY 2000 177

G-11 State Government General Fund
Spending, FY 2001 178

G-12 State and Local Debt, FY 2000 179

G-13 State and Local Debt Related to Revenue,
FY 2000 180

G-14 State and Local Full Faith and Credit Debt,
FY 2000 181

G-15 State Government Bond Ratings, 2002 182

G-16 State Solvency Index, 2002 183

G-17 Assets of State-administered Pension Plans, 2000 ... 184

G-18 State Reserves at the End of FY 2002 185

G-19 State and Local Capital Outlays and
Interest, FY 2000 186

G-20 Index of State Budget Process Quality, 2002 187

G-21 Relative State Spending "Needs," FY 1996 188

G-22 Structural Deficits 189

Education

H-1 Average Proficiency in Math,
Eighth Grade, 2000 194

H-2 Average Proficiency in Science,
Eighth Grade, 2000 195

H-3 Armed Forces Qualification Test Ranks, FY 2000 196

H-4 SAT Scores, 2002 197

H-5 ACT Scores, 2002 198

H-6 Percentage of Population Over 25 with a
High School Diploma, 2000 199

H-7 Students in Private Schools, 1999-2000 200

H-8 High School Completion Rates, 1998-2000 201

H-9 Pupil-Teacher Ratio, 2001-2002 202

H-10 Public School Enrollment, 2001-2002 203

H-11 Public Library Holdings Per Capita, FY 2000 204

H-12 Children with Disabilities, 1999-2000 205

H-13 State and Local Education Spending, FY 2000 206

H-14 State and Local Education Spending as a
Percentage of General Spending, FY 2000 207

H-15 Spending Per Pupil, 2001-2002 208

H-16 Average Teacher Salary, 2001-2002 209

H-17 Sources of School Funds, 2000-2001 210

H-18 State Aid Per Pupil in Average Daily
Attendance, 2001-2002 211

H-19 State and Local Spending for Higher
Education, FY 2000 212

H-20 State and Local Spending for Higher Education
as a Percentage of General Spending,
FY 2000 213

H-21 Public Higher Education Enrollment, 2000 214

H-22 Per Pupil State Support of Higher
Education, 2001-2002 215

H-23 Average Tuition and Fees at Public
Universities, 2000-2001 216

H-24 Average Salary of Associate Professors
at "Flagship" State Universities, 2001-2002 217

H-25 State and Local Education Employees, 2001 218

H-26 Federal Research and Development
Spending, FY 2000 219

H-27 Total Library Operating Expenditures,
FY 2000 220

Health

I-1 Immunization Rates, 2001 226

I-2 Infant Mortality Rates, 2000 227

I-3 State Health Rankings, 2002 228

I-4 Percentage of Non-Elderly Population Without
Health Insurance, 2001 229

I-5 Abortions, 1998 230

I-6 Alcohol Consumption Per Capita, 1999 231

I-7 Percentage of Adult Smokers, 2001 232

I-8 Percentage of Population Obese, 2001 233

I-9 AIDS Cases, 2001 234

I-10 Physicians Per 100,000 Population, 2002 235

I-11 Hospital Beds Per 1,000 Population, 2000 236

I-12 Medicaid Recipients, FY 2000 237

I-13   Medicaid Recipients as a Percentage of Poverty Population, FY 2000 238
I-14   State and Local Spending for Health and Hospitals, FY 2000 239
I-15   State and Local Health and Hospital Spending as a Percentage of General Spending, FY 2000 240
I-16   Per Capita Medicaid Spending, FY 2000 241
I-17   Average Medicaid Spending Per Aged Recipient, FY 2000 242
I-18   Average Medicaid Spending Per Child, FY 2000 243
I-19   Medicare Payment Per Hospital Day, FY 2000 244
I-20   Hospital Expense Per Inpatient Day, 2000 245
I-21   Percentage of Population in Health Maintenance Organizations, 2002 246

Crime and Law Enforcement

J-1   Total Crime Rate, 2001 250
J-2   Violent Crime Rate, 2001 251
J-3   Murder and Rape Rates, 2001 252
J-4   Property Crime Rate, 2001 253
J-5   Motor Vehicle Theft Rate, 2001 254
J-6   Violent Crime Rate Change, 1996-2001 255
J-7   Prisoners, 2001 256
J-8   Change in Prisoners, 1995-2001 257
J-9   Incarceration Rate, 2001 258
J-10   Juvenile Violent Crime Index, 2000 259
J-11   State and Local Law Enforcement Employees, 2001 260
J-12   State and Local Corrections Employees, 2001 261
J-13   State Corrections Spending, FY 2001 262
J-14   Percentage Increase in State Corrections Spending, FY 1999-2001 263
J-15   State and Local Spending for Law Enforcement, FY 2000 264
J-16   State and Local Law Enforcement Spending as a Percentage of General Spending, FY 2000 265

Transportation

K-1   Travel on Interstate Highways, 2001 270
K-2   Percentage of Interstate Mileage in "Unacceptable" Condition, 2001 271
K-3   Deficient Bridges, 2001 272
K-4   Traffic Deaths Per 100 Million Vehicle-miles, 2001 273
K-5   Percentage of Drivers Using Seat Belts, 2001 274
K-6   Vehicle-miles Traveled Per Capita, 2001 275
K-7   Percentage of Workers Using Public Transportation, 2000 276
K-8   Road and Street Miles, 2001 277
K-9   State and Local Highway Employees, 2001 278
K-10   State and Local Public Transit Employees, 2001 279

K-11   State and Local Spending for Highways, FY 2000 280
K-12   State and Local Highway Spending as a Percentage of General Spending, FY 2000 281

Welfare

L-1   Percentage of Births to Unwed Mothers, 2001 284
L-2   Temporary Assistance for Needy Families (TANF) Recipients, Total and as a Percentage of Population, 2001 285
L-3   Food Stamp Recipients, Total and as a Percentage of Population, FY 2001 286
L-4   Supplemental Security Income (SSI) Recipients, Total and as a Percentage of Population, 2001 287
L-5   Change in TANF/AFDC Recipients, FY 1996-2001 288
L-6   Condition of Children Index, 2002 289
L-7   Percentage of Families with Children Headed by a Single Parent, 1998-2000 (three-year average) 290
L-8   Average Monthly TANF Cash Assistance Per Family, FY 2000 291
L-9   Welfare Assistance and Earnings of Three-person TANF Family as a Percentage of Poverty-level Income, 2000 292
L-10   Supplemental Security Income (SSI) State Supplements, 2001 293
L-11   State Income Tax Liability of Typical Family in Poverty, 2001 294
L-12   Child Support Collections, FY 2001 295
L-13   Child Support Collections Per Dollar of Administrative Costs, FY 2001 296
L-14   Children in Foster Care, FY 2000 297
L-15   State and Local Welfare Spending, FY 2000 298
L-16   State and Local Welfare Spending as a Percentage of General Spending, FY 2000 299
L-17   Average Monthly Administrative Costs Per TANF Case, FY 2000 300

Technology

M-1   Percentage of Households with Computers, 2001 304
M-2   Percentage of Households with Internet Access, 2001 305
M-3   Percentage of Zip Codes with Broadband Telecommunications Service, 2001 306
M-4   High-tech Jobs, 2001 307
M-5   Dot.com Domain Names, 2001 308
M-6   State Government Web site Ratings, 2002 309
M-7   Students Per Computer, 2001 310

Introduction

CQ's State Fact Finder is an important information source and analytical tool for any person interested in developments in America's fifty states and the District of Columbia. The series is a valuable reference source for anyone looking to uncover trends in the states, whether a policy expert seeking detailed data or an individual wishing to learn more about today's social, political, and economic currents.

The nation's economy, our population, and the government's actions are constantly changing. These changes affect states differently, so it is important that information be as up to date as possible. To meet this need, CQ Press publishes *State Fact Finder* annually; the 2003 book is the ninth edition.

State Fact Finder 2003 reflects our changing landscape by providing new data for more than 90 percent of the statistics covered in the 2002 edition. It is likely that about 90 percent of the statistics in this edition will be different by the time the next edition is issued early in 2004. Readers can make sure they will receive the next edition as soon as it is published by establishing a standing order with CQ Press. The data in this and previous editions of *State Fact Finder* are also available for purchase in electronic form directly from State Policy Research (614-262-9229).

Many readers will want to use the successive volumes of *State Fact Finder* as valuable tools for identifying trends over time. The tables and statistical concepts in this book are closely comparable with those found in the first edition (1993). They are so comparable in the 1996 through 2002 editions that readers will be able to use them for statistical analyses of changes at the state level.

About This Book

The book was prepared by experts who constantly work with data comparing states to analyze state policy options and to compare states in ways important to policy makers, such as the success of their efforts to promote economic development and the costs and apparent results of their decisions. As a result, this book differs considerably from ordinary compilations of statistics in several important ways.

First, *State Fact Finder* includes many statistics that are not contained in standard statistical reports of government agencies and thus do not appear in compilations of statistics that rely solely on such published reports. For example, many of the tables in the health and welfare sections comparing state programs for low-income people are based on unpublished statistics maintained by agencies that administer these programs. Also, there are tables such as B-28, the Index of State Economic Momentum, and G-21, a comparison of state spending "needs," that reflect original research by State Policy Research.

Second, information from other sources is converted to a basis that makes comparisons meaningful. For example, information on the headquarters of the largest companies in America in Table B-16 includes the number of companies in each state in relation to population as well as the total number of companies.

Third, each table provides a ranking of the states. This makes it easy for readers to see how the state or states that interest them relate to neighboring states and to other states throughout the nation.

Fourth, the volume begins with an essay ("Finding Information Users Want to Know") in which the authors guide readers through the use of the information. This section helps readers understand the scope of information available to them.

Fifth, each of the thirteen chapters in the subject rankings section begins with an outlook brief, two or three paragraphs in length, pointing to emerging trends in that subject area, including issues likely to be on the front-burner in the coming year. For instance, in this 2003 edition of *State Fact Finder*, the brief at the beginning of the government section lists some recent examples of individual states leapfrogging the federal government by setting new policy standards that could potentially affect the entire country. The briefs also address continuing currents in the states. As we enter 2003, these include the still limping economy and budget woes.

Finally, *State Fact Finder* offers carefully documented source notes that follow the tables in each section. These notes list the origins of the statistics in each table and guide readers to additional sources where more information on the same topic can be obtained.

New Technology Chapter

For a second year, *State Fact Finder* includes a separate chapter on technology. Although a few tables on technology data have appeared previously, the authors believe the issue has become so important to states that a consolidated collection of tables is appropriate. Among the tables included are those showing the percentage of households with computers and with Internet access. Other tables show the percentage of zip codes with broadband telecommunications services and the number of high-tech jobs.

About the Publisher

State Fact Finder was first published by Congressional Quarterly Inc. in 1993 as part of CQ's tradition of providing comprehensive, reliable, and focused information about national public policy issues in America. This effort has broadened to include developments and trends in the states in recent years through the publication of such books as *State Fact Finder* and the creation of *Governing*, a magazine covering all aspects of state government.

About the Authors

State Policy Research is known to state government experts everywhere as one of the most reliable and knowledgeable organizations dealing with state-level information. For more than fifteen years State Policy Research published the periodicals *State Policy Reports* and *State Budget & Tax News,* and for a decade it published *States in Profile,* which has now merged into *State Fact Finder.* The organization also provides the tables that appear in *Governing* magazine's annual *State and Local Sourcebook.*

Information Development

Any data book is by definition a work in progress. What is useful one year may be less helpful the next, as new information needs arise. For these and many other reasons, the authors welcome reactions from readers, suggestions for additional information or changes in presentation, and, of course, any corrections or clarifications that come to the readers' attention. These should be directed to Kendra Hovey at State Policy Research. She can be reached by phone at 614-262-9229 or by e-mail at SPR@columbus.rr.com.

Finding Information Users Want to Know

Readers differ in their preferences on many things—from what they value in a place to live to the amount of state government spending they consider appropriate. They will not agree on such subjects as where they should move or which state is governed best.

In this section, rather than imposing personal values as though they were facts by ranking some states as the "best places" to live or do business, the authors have provided guideposts on how to use the tables so that readers can obtain the information they need. Using a question-and-answer format, this section leads readers to groups of tables that can be consulted together to deal with the broad questions, such as which state might have the best schools or the best business opportunities.

The section is divided into three parts, each based on particular types of decisions people use state statistics to make. The first covers personal and family decisions, such as those concerning job opportunities. The second focuses on business decisions, such as where to locate a new plant. The third provides information about the government to assist people in voting and in influencing public policy.

Subject Rankings

This section forms the heart of the book. It is organized into thirteen subject areas that are challenging policy makers throughout the country: population, economies, geography, government, federal impacts, taxes, revenues and finances, education, health, crime and law enforcement, transportation, welfare, and technology. States are listed alphabetically in each table. The information also is presented in rankings that allow a reader to see how each state compares with the others.

Source Notes

The source notes that follow each section are designed to be used in tandem with the subject rankings to understand the specific usefulness of, and any caveats about, the data. The sources for all the statistics in the book are documented so that the calculations can be replicated or expanded upon by those who need more detail than space allows here. These source notes allow the reader to locate other information sources that may be useful.

State Rankings

The state rankings section provides the reader with a composite view of each state. In this section, the editors bring together the state rankings of most of the data included in the volume. This compilation gives readers a quick summary of their states' positions in each subject area.

Index

The index guides readers to topics presented in the various sections of the book.

Introduction to the Data

Rankings: There is nothing magical about rankings, though *State Fact Finder* generally follows the convention of most statisticians by ranking from highest to lowest. Most rankings can be interpreted similarly by reversing them. For example, a table showing tax burdens from highest to lowest can be reversed to show tax burdens from lowest to highest by ranking the fiftieth state first, the forty-ninth state second, and so on.

Data Accuracy: The statistics in this volume vary greatly in their accuracy. Some, such as the land area of states or the number of state legislators, can be measured precisely. Other data, such as birth rates or finances of local governments, are estimates. The source notes generally explain how the data were developed or direct readers to the statistical providers, who usually have available detailed technical papers on their methods.

Ranking Positions and Ties: In preparing this report, the editors worked with data as presented by the statistical source. In presenting the data in tables, figures were rounded to a manageable number of digits (such as by expressing financial data as $24.5 million rather than $24,515,078). As a result, the rankings that are based on detailed data will show one state ranked above another even though they are apparently tied in the data published in the table.

When available, the value shown for the United States reflects the value provided by the original statistical source. Some statistical agencies include U.S. territories such as Puerto Rico in their national total. In these cases, adding the fifty-state total to the District of Columbia total will not yield the exact U.S. total.

Junk Data: Many special interest groups have strong opinions about appropriate policies for governments. They translate these opinions into rankings of which states are "best" in their subject areas of interest, such as protecting the environment, providing mental health services, or keeping a favorable climate for business. Sometimes the resulting statistics themselves are unreliable. Sometimes they combine individually reliable statistics into measures that simply reflect the policy preferences of those who rank the composite results. Such reports are generally not included in *State Fact Finder*, but the editors are familiar with them and are willing to help readers deal with them.

Time Periods: The tables all deal with the specific time periods indicated in the headings. These are normally calendar years. In the case of fiscal data, the time periods are fiscal years that end in the years shown.

District of Columbia: The District of Columbia has a unique status in any statistical compilation. It is not a state in the sense that it has no voting representatives in Congress and is counted as a city, not a state, in all Census Bureau statistics on government finances. However, the Census Bureau does include District residents within the total population of the United States. Federal agencies and private data-gathering organizations differ on how they treat the District, Puerto Rico, the Virgin Islands, and other entities in their statistics.

State Fact Finder presents information for the District of Columbia in each table but does not include it in the state rankings. State Policy Research has consistently avoided including the District for two reasons. First, users of rankings find this inclusion cumbersome to explain, often having to resort to particular explanations of rankings (such as a state being ranked fifth, fourth among states and also behind the District of Columbia). Second, the District is economically and demographically a central city with fiscal and other attributes of most central cities (high taxes, high crime rates, large percentages of the population in poverty and receiving government benefits, and so forth). When ranked along with states, the District often ranks first or last in the tables, distorting other rankings.

Finding Information Users
Want to Know

Most people look at state statistics to answer specific questions related to a decision they need to make but often discover that the statistics they seek do not appear in the reference books they consult. Alternatively, they find some comparisons that seem to be relevant but wonder if they are.

State Fact Finder contains a feature not found in other compilations of data about states. Besides finding tables, readers can consult this section to find a list of frequently asked questions. Under each question they will find information about which statistics in this book should be helpful in trying to find answers, as well as road maps to other statistics that might be useful. Readers sometimes will be informed that the statistics they seek are not available anywhere and why.

This section is divided into three parts, each based on particular types of decisions people use state statistics to make. The first covers personal and family decisions, such as finding the states with the best job opportunities, the best health care, and even the best chances for finding a spouse. The second covers business decisions, such as where to locate a new business or where to find the most productive workers. This section is also useful for investors. The third contains information about government to assist people in their roles as voters and in influencing public policy.

About Personal Decisions on Where to Live or Visit

1. Where is the best place to find a job?

As a general rule, people find it easier to get a job, higher pay, better opportunities for advancement, and better opportunities for building professional practices if they locate in rapidly expanding economies. If they go to places in economic decline they will find few job opportunities and stiff competition to get the positions that do exist.

To find states with rapidly expanding economies, look at measures of recent economic growth, particularly the Index of State Economic Momentum (B-28), population growth (A-3), job growth (B-29, B-30), and projections of future population growth (A-4). The Index (B-28) is especially useful because it summarizes the three elements of economic growth important to job-seekers: population growth, income growth, and increases in the number of jobs.

Growth rates are particularly important if you seek jobs that are inherently related to growth, such as jobs in the construction industry. Because the need for construction relates to *changes* in the need for homes and buildings, there are massive differences between fast- and slow-growing states. For example, in 2000 there were 17 new homes being built for every 1,000 residents of Nevada but only 2 for every 1,000 residents of New York (B-20).

When a state is classified as rapidly growing, this does not necessarily mean that all local areas in the state are growing. For example, the fast growth in Nevada is concentrated in the Las Vegas area. Growth in the Pacific Northwest is occurring along the Pacific Coast between Seattle and Portland, but there are few job opportunities in the eastern parts of Oregon and Washington. To find which areas are growing and in what types of industries and jobs, you can consult local sources, such as state economic development departments, local chambers of commerce, or even friends familiar with the area. For nationwide statistics on growth in metropolitan areas, you can get information on recent job growth from the Bureau of Labor Statistics. Somewhat less current statistics on income and other economic factors are available from the Department of Commerce, including detailed books on major counties called *County Business Patterns*. More general statistics can be found at "State and County Quick-Facts" (quickfacts.census.gov/qfd) on the Census Bureau website.

2. Where will tax burdens be least for me and my family?

The tables in the Taxes section (F) are good guides to average tax burdens. Table F-1 shows what share of personal income goes to state and local taxes in each state. Tables F-6, F-9, and F-13 do this for each of the major taxes: property, sales, and personal income. The range among states is very large. For example, New York governments take 14.1 percent of income in state and local taxes, while governments in Tennessee take only 8.9 percent.

The taxes you actually pay will depend on your circumstances, such as how much property you plan to own in relation to your income. You can see the major differences in Tables F-16 and F-23. For example, Florida and Texas have tax systems that wealthy retirees will like—no income, inheritance, or estate taxes. Young couples without much income will pay heavy sales taxes and find that renters do not share in special property tax breaks for homeowners. For them, states like Oregon, which have no sales tax but steep income taxes, might be a better deal.

The state and local taxes you pay will be a combination of state government taxes, which are uniform throughout entire states, and local taxes. These vary greatly from place to place within a state. There are about 50,000 local governments in the United States with the power to set tax rates and there are 50 states—an average of about 1,000 different local governments in each state.

Depending on where you decide to live, you may find you are paying property taxes that are the sum of individual taxes levied by a county; a municipality or township; a school district; perhaps a second school district, such as a community college or vocational district; and hosts of special districts, such as road districts, transit districts, mosquito control districts, and levee districts—to mention just a few of the possibilities. Local governments in many states also levy sales taxes and a few states have significant local income taxes, such as the steep income taxes of New York City and Philadelphia. All these taxes are reflected in the state averages.

Because of these differences, what you pay will depend on where you live even though state government taxes are uniform in each state. To find local areas with low taxes within a state, look for places that have large business sources of tax revenues combined with small numbers of people to serve. In most metropolitan areas, there are suburbs with concentrations of office buildings, shopping centers, and businesses that have much lower property taxes than those of surrounding areas. Realtors in metropolitan regions will be able to identify them. For property taxes, check the county government where you want to locate. The county officials who collect property taxes will have rate information for each local area.

Most state tax departments, with offices in state capitals and major cities, publish free booklets describing all their state taxes and tax rates.

3. Which state has the best public schools?

To compare how well students do, consider the first five tables in the Education section. Use Tables H-1 and H-2 for overall comparisons, H-3 for students not going to college right away, and H-4 and H-5 for the college preparation programs. You can also use the tables to compare states on measures of what they spend per student (H-15), what they pay teachers (H-16), class sizes (H-9), and more.

Except in Hawaii, all schools are local. Expect to find immense variations within areas in every state; these are as important as the variations from state to state. All state education departments, located in state capitals, keep statistics for each school district on spending and number of teachers and pupils. Because of the No Child Left Behind Act of 2001, soon all states will issue "report cards" comparing district performance measures, such as how students do on standardized tests. You can use these or research locally such indicators as percentage of graduates that go on to college, percentages winning National Merit Scholarships and other awards, and local reputations for good schools.

How well students do depends heavily on how much help and motivation they get at home, not just on what happens at school. Much of the difference among states is caused by differences in the students, not in the schools. This is true for districts within a state as well.

One key is getting a child into the right school, not just the right school district. Some of the best specialized programs, and some of the worst schools, are found in central cities.

If you want to send children to private schools, do not expect much help from government. Many states are considering "voucher" plans that would help with tuition, but such plans are available now only in Florida, Ohio, and Wisconsin, where they mostly serve poor, inner-city children. Arizona, Florida, Illinois, Iowa, Minnesota, and Pennsylvania provide limited income tax breaks if you pay private school tuition.

4. Which state is best for children?

Throughout *State Fact Finder* you will find many tables comparing states on aspects of life important to children, including health, education, crime, and economic opportunity. If you want even more comparisons, detailed ones are available from the Children's Defense Fund (25 E Street, N.W., Washington, D.C. 20001, 202-628-8787, www.childrensdefense.org) and from the Annie E. Casey Foundation (410-547-6600, www.aecf.org) in the annual *Kids Count Data Book.*

Children grow up in small worlds, such as school buildings and neighborhoods, so do not expect to rely totally on facts about states, metropolitan areas, or even individual cities and counties for information important to your child's life. Where your child is within one of these areas is often much more important than which geographical area the child is in. State differences are important in such fields as the quality of education and the possibilities for getting a job.

5. Which is the best state for retirement?

Most people retire within twenty miles of where they lived when they stopped working. For them, finding the right place is more a matter of finding the right house or apartment in the right community than of finding the right state. If you are thinking about retirement in another state, *State Fact Finder* can be helpful, but you will need to go beyond it to make an informed decision.

Do not start with statistics comparing places, unless your overriding concern is minimizing the taxes you will pay. Start with your own preferences. Decide first on how far you are willing to be from your family and old friends and on climate issues, such as whether you want to avoid ice and snow and whether you will like places that do not have changing seasons during the year. Most people will be able to narrow their choices considerably this way.

If you are willing to take the time to look systematically at what is important to you about a place, take a "preference inventory" such as the one found in *Frommer's Retirement Places Rated,* by David Savageau. It will force you to consider whether being able to get a part-time job, see and hear a symphony orchestra, follow a professional sports team, and other items are important to you.

In the tables in *State Fact Finder,* you will see systematic differences among the states in such characteristics

as income and education levels of residents, living costs, crime, and taxes.

There are many books designed to help with retirement decisions. A library or good bookstore should be able to recommend some reference book choices. Some describe places to live and provide information on investments, Medicare, and estate planning. Some deal only with places to retire, often with different emphases, such as health (*The 50 Healthiest Places to Live and Retire in the United States* [1991] by Norman D. Ford), culture and lifetime learning (*Choose a College Town for Retirement* [1999] by Joseph M. Lubow) or specialized retirement areas (Florida, for example, or Hilton Head, South Carolina, but not New York City or any place in Ohio or Illinois.

AARP is a good source for a variety of publications on retirement, including specialized guides on state taxes. One topic of particular interest to retirees is what percentage of income from Social Security is taxed by each state.

6. Which state universities are best?

State Fact Finder contains some important statistics that are relevant when selecting among state university systems. Look for them in Tables H-19 to H-24. State statistics alone cannot pick a university to attend because state systems include everything from community colleges to medical schools. California even has systems within systems. They vary from the University of California, with campuses at Berkeley and elsewhere, which contains some of the finest institutions in the country, to California State University, which enjoys less of a national reputation but has some outstanding specialized programs, to community colleges with diverse and varying strengths and weaknesses.

Students attend schools, not states. Consult guides and ratings on individual schools that contain information on the numbers of students, types of curriculum, costs, and attempted assessments of the quality of students and faculty.

7. Which state has the best cultural attractions and recreation?

Recreational opportunities cannot be adequately measured by statistics. Attempts to do so often are misleading. For example, you will find by far the best ratio of park land to people in Alaska, but much of the state is covered by glaciers that are not fit for hiking or camping. Some fine experiences—the "big sky" of Montana, the bustle of the streets of New York, and the beauty of fall foliage in New England—are not specific places and do not count attendance.

There are fairly good statistics about how many people participate in various sports in each state. Table C-6 is an example. See the notes to this table at the end of the chapter for how to obtain specific information on other sports. Most sports have specialized equipment stores, magazines, and guidebooks that are superior to state statistics for making personal recreational choices. For example, just because there are more golfers and courses per capita in one state than another does not mean you will have trouble finding more than enough courses and players to make foursomes in the lower-ranked states.

Cultural opportunities are listed in the many guidebooks and specialized magazines published in nearly every possible field of interest. Government spending on the arts, shown in Table C-8, is not a useful indicator of the extent or quality of arts in each state. States spend, on average, about $1 per year per capita funding the arts—amounts that are dwarfed by sales revenues, admissions, and donations.

8. Where is the best place to invest in property?

It is hard to pick a winner in a field of losers and hard to pick a loser in a field of winners. You want to pick the right state (and metropolitan area in that state) for your investment.

Nearly everyone interested in owning real estate has heard the old saw about the three keys to real estate investment: location, location, and location. This applies to states and metropolitan areas within states. For example, statistics in Table B-21 from the Office of Federal Housing Enterprise Oversight show that in the five years from 1997 to 2002, the average house in Massachusetts appreciated by 69.8 percent while the average house in New Mexico increased in value by only 15.2 percent. Of course, how much your investment will lose or appreciate depends on the property you buy, whether you pay the right price, and local market conditions.

Real estate prices depend on supply and demand. Supply does not go down much in poor markets—who would tear down a house or office building just because values were dropping? Supply responds to increased demand in good markets, but prices rise because new construction usually costs more than established buildings, prices of lots and construction labor tend to rise, and the most desirable locations generally already have buildings on them.

The best strategy for real estate investment is to pick an area with an expanding economy, where lots of new jobs are being created. Look at the answer to Question 1 (where to find a job) for tips on using *State Fact Finder* to identify those places.

9. Can picking the right states help pick winners in stocks and bonds?

Few economists or investment professionals would suggest picking which company's stocks to buy based on the states in which their headquarters or plants are found. The important questions are how good are the products and how well are they marketed. Some successful companies operate from unlikely places. For example, computer-maker Gateway is based in farm country in South Dakota and apparel seller L. L. Bean is based in rural Maine.

For making things, being in a fast-growing economy is bad news, not good news. In fast-growing economies, it is harder to get and keep good workers, their pay is often higher, and transportation facilities are often congested. Look for strong state and regional economies only when looking for regionally oriented companies that sell products, such as new homes and fast food, directly to consumers.

Most people who buy tax-exempt bonds do so through mutual funds or rely heavily on bond-rating agencies, such as Standard & Poor's and Moody's. Those professional investors rely heavily on the kinds of economic, population, and government statistics used in *State Fact Finder* and analyses of recent fiscal developments presented in publications like *State Policy Reports*. People who buy individual bonds or buy mutual funds of tax-exempt bonds issued from a single state, like those that invest solely in the bonds of New York or California, can use these same statistics.

10. Which state government will interfere least with my freedom?

People occasionally say they would like to live where government interferes less with their daily lives. Government intrusiveness cannot easily be compared because governments often restrict the freedom of some citizens to enhance that of others. The ultimate example is capital punishment, which is the most intrusive concept imaginable for the person being punished but is used in the name of increasing freedom from fear and crime for everyone else. State policies are not necessarily consistent on intrusiveness issues. For example, the states that are most likely to allow you to own weapons without restriction are least likely to let you grow marijuana on your own property for personal consumption.

Some elements of government intrusiveness can be measured. One is taxes, measured by the many comparisons in the Taxes section (F). *State Policy Reports* designed an experimental comparison of tax intrusiveness (Vol. 12, Issue 24, December 1994), giving extra weight to property taxes and counting only taxes paid by households, not businesses. With a national average set at 100, it showed variation from 142 in most-intrusive New York to 32 in least-intrusive Alaska.

Another way to look at intrusiveness is the ratio of state and local government employees to population (D-13). If you find local governments closer to citizens and less intrusive than state governments, look at measures of differences in state and local roles as indicated by public employees (D-15) and revenue raising (D-16).

11. Where are taxes likely to go up/down in the future?

Tax rates are set by state legislatures and local bodies (school boards, city councils, county commissions, etc.). Predicting where taxes will be raised or lowered would appear to be a matter of forecasting the views of those who now serve on or will subsequently be elected to these bodies. The economic and population statistics in *State Fact Finder* provide some excellent clues to future tax rates, as does common sense thinking about why some states have higher taxes than others.

Right now, the states with the lowest taxes on people who live there are the states that get lots of their money from other sources—tourists, oil and gas, and gaming casinos, for example. States amply endowed with these—such as Alaska, Nevada, Texas, and Wyoming—have been able to keep taxes low while still offering extensive government services. Some states have been able to keep taxes on their residents relatively low because they have been able to draw new residents who pay substantial taxes but do not have children in public schools, which is the biggest single cause of state and local spending. Fast-growing states of the Southwest and Florida have been the best examples.

These same states will be under the strongest pressures to raise tax levels in the future. As more people come to them, the amount that their unique resources contribute to revenues *per resident* drops. Furthermore, as time passes, their populations become more like the national averages. For example, the childless young people who flocked to Florida in large numbers to work at tourist at-tractions and to provide health care and other services to retirees are having children in large numbers. Florida has to pay for putting nearly 100,000 additional students in its classrooms every year. California and Texas face similar pressures.

12. Which states have the least/most pollution?

State Fact Finder presents summary statistics on air and water pollution and hazardous waste (C-10 to C-14). More important, the notes to the tables provide leads to where to get more details on local areas. State averages are misleading for people seeking to decide where to live or visit. For example, western cities, like Denver and Salt Lake City, have some of the worst air pollution problems in the nation, but away from urban areas the air in these states is about as pure as you will find. An average for California that lumps downtown Los Angeles with the forests of northern California and the state's deserts will not give an accurate picture of any of these places.

13. Where do I find the best health care?

Because much more money is spent in gathering them, state-by-state statistics on health and health care (section I) are quite comprehensive compared with statistics in other fields. The statistics cover (1) health of average people in a state's population, (2) apparent availability of care, (3) cost of care, and (4) government programs, which are generally oriented to poor people. These statistics suggest strong concentrations of health professionals in northeastern states.

People worried about whether they can find adequate health care for themselves and their family need not be guided by these statistics. Most people are limited to amounts their insurance will pay. Because insurers will not pay for long-distance travel and hotel bills except in rare cases, the doctors capable of performing all types of operations have been locating in the areas across the country where paying patients are found. One result is the development of top-flight facilities across the country, such as the University of Iowa hospital, which serves as a specialized facility for patients throughout that state, and the medical complex around Birmingham, Alabama. There is no reason for anyone to avoid an entire state because of concerns about health care, unless they have a very specialized medical problem. The main limits on health care are primarily those that people accept by their decisions on where to locate within a state. People who seek near-wilderness isolation by buying ranches in Colorado or locating on small islands off the Atlantic

Ocean must accept the consequences of their isolation on the availability of health care.

14. Where will I be safest from crime?

State statistics, and even city statistics, on crime are not much help in looking for a safe place to live. In every state, crime is most prevalent in the low-income areas of central cities. Violent crimes are most prevalent in these areas after dark. Reported crime statistics overstate crime risks for people who do not spend evenings in low-income central city areas. A high crime rate for an entire state says more about the percentage of a state's population living in these areas than about safety in that state's suburban, small town, and rural areas as compared with similar areas in other states.

City and state crime rates are also misleading when used to consider which places are safe to visit on business or recreational trips. All statistics, like crime rates and per capita amounts, that relate a category to population use night-time population—the number of people whose regular beds are in a city or state. States such as Florida, Hawaii, and Nevada have many visitors for vacations and conventions. Cities have day-time commuters and business and vacation travelers. Crime rates in cities and these states are much lower for people at risk than when expressed in relation to the number of people who regularly sleep there.

15. Where is the best place to look for a mate?

People looking for an opposite sex partner can reasonably expect better opportunities in locations where they are outnumbered by persons of the opposite sex (A-13). However, aggregate statistics can be misleading for people under fifty-five looking for a partner about their own age. Because women live longer than men, the states with predominately older populations (A-6) also tend to have high ratios of women to men. Careful research by several women on the Federal Reserve Bank of Boston's research staff found the worst sex ratios (from the standpoint of women seeking men) in older northeastern cities and the states with a high percentage of jobs in health care, government, and financial services, which are disproportionately filled by women. The best ratios, again from the perspective of women seeking men, were in booming western states where economic growth draws large numbers of young men to occupations such as mining and construction.

16. Where can I find the lowest living costs?

State Fact Finder includes the best information in use on comparative living costs (B-8), but the data must be used with care. For reasons appearing in the table notes, these measures are not likely to be accurate for what they try to measure—average living costs—and more accurate data are not likely to be available. Also, there are substantial variations within states. All costs, except state and local taxes, are about the same in midsize cities and rural areas throughout the nation. The major differences are taxes (see section F) and costs related to economic growth (see section B).

In booming communities and states, housing prices soar, wage rates tend to be higher, and ample and growing sales discourage everyone from doctors to corner store owners from engaging in price wars. In depressed communities and slow-growth states (for example, West Virginia and older industrial communities such as Syracuse and St. Louis), the reverse factors are reducing housing costs, wages, and prices.

Different people buy different things, so the costs they experience will differ from averages, often by wide margins. Business travelers experience enormous price differences in what they buy—downtown hotel rooms, rental cars, and meals at restaurants catering to expense-account travelers. Highly paid executives with downtown jobs will find large differentials, particularly if they hope to live within fifteen minutes commuting time of their work. The largest differentials are associated with the size of metropolitan areas, not with states. New York, Chicago, and Los Angeles are expensive places for these people, but Rochester, Joliet, and Fresno are not.

Most people will not see such large differences in living costs. Much of what they buy—cars, furniture, alcoholic beverages and soft drinks, packaged foods, motion pictures and videotapes, books, sports equipment, clothing, and more—is produced long distances away. The prices generally reflect only minor differences in shipping costs among states, except Alaska and Hawaii, where prices are higher. A large part of the housing costs will depend on mortgage rates, which are nearly uniform nationwide. Most will select homes far enough away from congested central cities so that older home prices cannot get too far out of line with what it costs to build new houses, which is about the same nationwide.

About Business Decisions on Where to Locate and Expand

1. Where is the best place to locate a business?

State Fact Finder provides useful statistics for some

kinds of business but not all. Businesses that depend on local customers—from doctors' offices to fast-food franchises—will usually do better in rapidly growing areas. To use *State Fact Finder* to identify these areas, see Question 1 in the previous section. Some local businesses have specialized markets, appealing primarily to clearly defined groups, such as children or the retired. To identify where such populations are large and growing, study the tables in the sections on population and the economy.

Sophisticated investors in consumer-oriented businesses, like franchises, often do extensive market research before committing their money. The same is true for companies deciding how and where to market consumer products from cars to shampoo. The serious researchers are generally looking at geographic detail not found in sources like *State Fact Finder*—zip codes and even streets and census tracts, rather than states or metropolitan areas. They rely on their own publications, most notably *American Demographics*. Many private companies specialize in providing such information and the computer software to use it. These companies advertise in such publications.

Some businesses, such as manufacturing companies, can separate where they produce products from where their consumers are located. Their business often limits their location choices. Mining and oil production companies need to be on top of their raw materials. Manufacturing needs an ample supply of labor and may have special transportation requirements, such as access to a rail line or deep-water port.

Within these parameters, the additional factors that help determine the best location for a business relate to costs—labor costs, state and local taxes, electricity prices, and transportation costs. Every firm, indeed every plant, is different in where it gets supplies, where its customers are located, how much and what kind of energy it uses, and the relative use of labor and machinery. This means the best place to locate depends on the match between the needs of a particular firm and the attractions of a potential plant site.

State Fact Finder contains much useful information to compare business locations. The Population (A) and Economies (B) sections provide information about potential markets for selling products and hiring workers. The Government (D) section offers information about how states are governed. The Taxes (F) and Revenues and Finances (G) sections cover factors associated with each state's tax burdens. Elements of government-provided services that are important to business are discussed in the Education (H) and Transportation (K) sections.

In establishing a business oriented to local economic growth, the important question is what growth *will be*, not what growth was. Most statistics show what it *was*. As the warning about mutual funds goes, "past performance is no guarantee of future results." So, too, for state economic growth.

Future growth will depend on many factors, such as changes in oil prices, federal spending (particularly defense), and how well particular firms and industries (and thus the places where they are located) do in the marketplace. To make predictions on future growth, you can review trend statistics (A-2, B-29, and E-2) or look at the composite Index of State Economic Momentum (B-28). Forecasts can be purchased from firms specializing in forecasting or they can be obtained inexpensively from the Department of Commerce (14th Street and Constitution Avenue, N.W., Washington, D.C. 20230).

2. Which state has the most productive workers?

In their industrial development ads in business magazines, some states try to convince firms to locate within their borders because their workers are more productive. Productivity in this context is an elusive concept. Many experts are not even sure that national figures about changes in worker productivity are right, much less state-by-state numbers on the same subject.

Employers' ideas of a productive worker may vary from situation to situation. For example, software design and advertising place a premium on creativity and originality, so employees that work irregular hours still may be considered highly productive. An assembly line, however, will not work unless all the workers show up at the same time. Having lots of formal schooling may make engineers productive, but experience may be better for those who repair plumbing or who fish for a living.

State Fact Finder has many statistics on factors employers may consider to be signs of productivity, particularly in the Education (H) and Health (I) sections. *State Fact Finder* also includes the statistics usually used to calculate productivity in states (B-7), but such data are misleading for the reasons explained in the notes to the table.

3. Which states have the lowest labor costs?

Most comparisons among states regarding labor costs are based on average annual pay (B-5), as well as annual averages in retailing (B-10) and manufacturing (B-9). However, they will not necessarily be correct for hiring new workers in a particular occupation in a particular location within a state. The wages that must be paid to get competent workers in such a situation will depend upon the supply of labor and the demand for it in that local labor market. Firms looking for low-wage workers should do just the opposite of workers looking for high-paying firms, as discussed in Question 1 of the Personal Decisions section.

The really important statistic is how much work an employer gets from a worker in relation to a dollar paid. That statistic is elusive because productivity per worker is hard to calculate accurately (see Question 2, above). For a sophisticated attempt to calculate this unit labor cost in relation to productivity, see the research presented by Regional Financial Associates (West Chester, Pa.), including *The High Costs of High Costs* (1995).

4. Where will my business pay the least taxes?

State taxes on business are a complex web of interlocking provisions made even more complex because many local governments have separate taxes on business. These combinations have different impacts on different types of business, depending on such factors as how profitable they are; how capital-intensive they are; whether they qualify for state and local economic development incentives; and whether they are organized as proprietorships, partnerships, S (small business) corporations, or C (regular) corporations.

There is no substitute for learning the tax rules for the states and localities where you might operate and applying them to the expected characteristics (payroll, profits, etc.) of the business you plan to start or move. These calculations are so complicated that a major consulting industry has been developed to make them.

State Fact Finder provides some good indicators of the possible results of these calculations. Start with the overall levels of taxes (F-1 to F-3). If these are high, you will pay them somewhere—if not in taxes on your firm, then in taxes on your salary, your house, and what your firm pays for utility services. Next, look at the burdens of the specific taxes important to your operations. If you will have high investments in property (plant and equipment), see Tables F-6 to F-8. If you are concerned about payroll taxes, see Tables F-13 to F-16. If you are concerned about taxes on your sales, see Tables F-9 to F-12.

If yours is a local service business, such as a bakery or retail store, you do not have to worry much about state taxes on your business. Unless you are near a border with another state, your competitors will be paying the same taxes as you. This may not be true with local taxes,

so you have to check them specifically. If yours is a small business, you may not be as worried about some taxes, particularly corporate income and franchise taxes, as large firms. You may be more concerned with certain taxes on individuals, such as income and estate taxes, as shown in Tables F-16 and F-23.

If yours is a nationally oriented business, such as manufacturing, you may be in for some pleasant and unpleasant surprises about taxes on your business. Some states with high overall tax levels, such as New York, are very competitive in taxes on manufacturing. Some states with low taxes on households, particularly those with no taxes on personal incomes, have relatively high taxes on firms. For multistate firms, opening a plant in one state affects corporate income taxes in all the states because of the way corporate income is apportioned among states for tax purposes. For samples of calculations of corporate taxes of different industries in many states, see studies that the accounting firm of KPMG Peat Marwick has prepared for states evaluating their "tax competitiveness." Recent studies have been made for Kentucky, New York, and North Carolina.

5. Which states provide the best incentives to locate in them?

The amounts and types of assistance available from state and local governments in tax breaks, grants, and loans for locating in their jurisdiction depend on the type of business. If your business inherently serves local customers—an auto dealership, restaurant, retail store, or repair business, for example—expect no significant help from these governments. Your new business is not going to increase the wealth or income of the area you serve but rather just move it from those already there and competing for the same business you want. You may get some technical assistance and even loans, but mostly from state and local agencies administering federal small business money. If you pick the right state and right local government within that state, you may get some tax breaks because local communities compete for tax base with other local communities.

If your business will draw money from out-of-state, your business (large or small) will likely be offered major incentives from just about any state. There are so many incentives and the number is growing so fast that directories of them are obsolete the day they are released. Do not try to use national directories of these types. Even if you do, you will miss the deals that states might be willing to tailor to fit your business. Nearly every community of any size and all states employ "developers"—economic development professionals whose mission is to draw employers to their community or state by providing information and administering incentives. These people are eager to provide you with details about sites, taxes, worker availability, and state and local incentives. Look for state agencies with *development* in their titles, and find local agencies through county or city governments or chambers of commerce.

6. Which states have the lowest utility rates?

Statistics comparing state averages of electric rates for various consumers appear in Tables B-34. They are indicative of rate differentials for other fuels as well. In general, the farther you locate from the sources of inexpensive energy (the gas fields of the Southwest and hydroelectric sites), the more expensive energy will be. Taxes make a big difference in what you pay for energy. So do state policies that determine how the total bill is divided between household and industrial uses, as Table B-34 dramatically illustrates.

There are price variations within states among users of differing quantities and among types of industrial service (such as cheaper rates for those who will close their plants on high-use days). Many concessions are made to firms newly locating in an area or who demonstrate they can obtain service from a competitor utility. There is no substitute for checking the prices the local utilities charge.

7. Which states regulate business the least?

There is no statistical way to compare state and local regulation of business across the board because there are so many different ways government regulation touches business operations. There is also great variation in policies among states and local areas. Many of the regulatory differences are not systematic. For example, some southern states have less stringent regulation of workplace conditions while imposing more stringent regulation on how corporations are governed.

8. Where is the transportation system best?

The interstate transportation systems—road, rail, air, and even barge lines—form an interconnected network that reaches every state in some way. Once your products or raw materials reach this network, service is close to uniform until they leave it. For businesses with large shipping requirements, the key aspect is how easily you can connect with the national networks used by your particular business. This varies with geography, not state lines, and is critically dependent on exactly where your site is located relative to rail and other transportation access points. As every driver knows, the quality and capacity of roads depends on exactly which roads you use.

However, there are systematic differences among states. These appear most dramatically in measures of maintenance and construction, the condition of bridges (K-3), and highway pavement (K-2).

9. Which states have pro-business attitudes?

Like the rest of us, business owners and managers have differing needs and differing views of appropriate public policies. For example, a company engaged in a low-technology, labor-intensive activity such as poultry processing is not much concerned with the education of its workers but is highly concerned with pollution control costs, state labor regulations, and taxes. A company engaged in high-tech competition for improved designs of computer chips or software is not as affected by such state regulation or even taxes; it is highly sensitive to how well educated employees are and whether governments offer strong university systems and cultural and recreational opportunities. Thus, a state with relatively high taxes that is accustomed to paying for top-flight schools and state universities will appear anti-business to some business leaders and pro-business to others.

The phrase *business climate* was widely used in the 1980s in discussions of state policies for economic development, regulation, labor laws, and taxes. The statistics were developed by the Grant Thornton accounting firm, based on opinions of which characteristics were important to those manufacturing firms that participated in state manufacturing associations. The state rankings much favored southeastern states with low taxes, low wages, and little business regulation. The influence of these ratings on state policies encouraged the development of counter-statistics, particularly the annual *Development Report Card for the States,* published by the Corporation for Enterprise Development, or CFED (777 North Capitol Street, N.E., Suite 800, Washington D.C. 20002, 202-408-9788), whose sponsors include many unions. As the name implies, the *Report Card* gives letter grades, not aggregate rankings, to reflect the complexity and controversy associated with deciding which state policies are pro-business and which are successful in causing state economic development. The state grades are nearly a flip-flop from the business climate rankings. In the CFED's evaluation, southeastern states tend to have the lowest grades.

The availability of these more sophisticated measures discouraged use of the old business climate rankings, which are no longer published. The term *business climate* has been appropriated by the publishers of the business-oriented quarterly *Site Selection*. Its ranking procedure, associated with the number of new jobs primarily in manufacturing, inherently favors large states over less populous ones. Using the test of which states are drawing the most new work, see Table B-30, which shows growth in manufacturing jobs. Using the test of where firms locate their headquarters, see Tables B-16 and B-17.

10. Which states are the best places to sell business-to-business?

Many companies do not sell to consumers; they sell goods and services to other businesses. Finding firms that might want to buy office supplies, parts, maintenance services, and other business-to-business offerings is different then finding individual consumers (which is discussed in Question 1). The statistics needed for finding business customers are too specialized for this book but exist in abundance from government sources. The Bureau of Labor Statistics in the Department of Labor keeps up-to-date statistics on the number of jobs in each state, with breakdowns by major industry. The Commerce Department keeps detailed data and publishes them on a county level in *County Business Patterns*. The Commerce Department also does major surveys of industries, such as the Census of Manufacturing and the Census of Retail Trade.

State governments have even more detailed information, though some do a better job than others in keeping it current and making it available in usable form. The state agencies that administer unemployment compensation (UC)—typically called the Department of Labor or Employment Services Administration—know details on all private firms because they collect UC payroll taxes from them every quarter. Corporations, from mom-and-pop stores to General Motors, are chartered by states and often need some kind of permit to operate in states where they are not chartered. Secretaries of state are the keepers of these records. Many state economic development departments have detailed statistics on businesses operating in the state, and some publish directories.

About Government and Public Policy

1. Which state is the best managed?

No one has ever found a way to use statistics to determine which states, or for that matter which private companies, are best managed. Bottom-line results—good schools, low taxes, and high and growing business profits—count. But some companies and states face greater challenges than others in achieving them because of circumstances beyond the control of their managers. There are awards for well-managed companies and governments, but these are like civic awards. Who gets them depends on who is on the selection committees, the criteria those particular people think are important, and their personal knowledge of the award candidates.

Somewhat more objective measures of state financial management are available. Bond rating agencies, such as Moody's, assess credit risks (G-15) much like a bank would determine how much to loan a family seeking a mortgage. Like personal credit ratings, these concern only the likelihood that loans will be repaid, not whether the borrower is competent, efficient, or doing the right things.

States can also be compared in financial management practices, such as whether they conform to generally accepted accounting principles and whether they use performance-oriented budgeting. Most experts believe these practices improve the quality of state decisions. These comparisons can be found in Table G-20. For detailed comparisons of such state practices as balanced budget requirements, governors' item-veto powers, and use of stabilization or "rainy day" funds, see the National Association of State Budget Officers' publication, *Budget Processes in the States*.

2. Which state has the fairest tax system?

Fairness in taxes depends entirely on one's perspective about who should bear what share of tax burdens—a specific example of the old maxim, "Where you stand depends on where you sit." The data needed to form opinions are found in Tables F-6 through F-22 in the Taxes section. Included are tables on progressivity of taxes; relative reliance on sales, income, and other tax bases; and tax burdens on high- and low-income households.

A large group of experts and state officials—including governors, legislators, and tax commissioners—have jointly published a study about the elements of good tax systems. *Financing State Government in the 1990s* is available from the National Conference of State Legislatures in Denver or the National Governors' Association in Washington, D.C. The study advocates keeping rates of all taxes as low as possible, given the money to be raised, by avoiding lots of special exemptions and balancing reliance on property, income, and sales tax. Look for balance in percentage of three-tax revenue in Tables F-8, F-11, and F-15.

3. Which states keep the share of taxes paid by business low?

Economists argue that all taxes must reduce some person's income in order to make it available for government. They do not believe that legal abstractions, such as corporations and partnerships, bear the burden of any taxes. Instead, the tax burdens find their way into prices paid by customers, lower wages paid to workers, lower prices paid to suppliers, and lower profits credited to stockholders.

Many people do not agree with this. Public opinion polls usually show that voters would rather see taxes on corporations than taxes they *know* they pay, such as sales taxes and personal income taxes. While many business leaders do not agree with the economists' outlook, others believe it but want to protect everyone involved—stockholders, suppliers, workers, and customers—by avoiding taxes on their businesses. As a result there is a lot of interest in comparing how states distribute tax burdens between businesses and people.

Good data to make such comparisons will never exist because the people who might gather the information, the tax collectors, do not care about it. Most collect the same property tax on houses and stores whether they are owned by occupants, individual landlords, or a corporate landlord. When someone buys a pad of paper and pays sales tax no one asks if they are buying it for grocery lists or for a business project. The family farm is both a business and a home, but most states do not divide the value between the two or make the tax lower or higher if the family is organized as a sole proprietorship, partnership, or corporation.

Consequently, comparisons of states on the share of taxes paid by businesses inherently involve guesswork and arbitrary distinctions, such as calling all severance taxes business taxes and all farm taxes people taxes. The most recent comparison was published in *State Policy Reports* in September 1997. It found business paid the lowest share of state and local taxes in Maryland (25.6 percent) and the highest in Alaska (88.4 percent). These data deliberately are not included in *State Fact Finder*.

4. Which state has the highest taxes?

The three standard measures of tax burdens are found in the first three tables of the Taxes section (F-1, F-2, and F-3). None of them is as good as the other tables in this section for considering what taxes are likely to be on an individual household or business. For those answers, see the answers to Question 2 in the Personal Decisions section and Question 4 in the Business Decisions section.

5. Which state has the best education policies?

People disagree about the best policies in education and other public policy fields. To answer questions like these, there are sporadic publications of evaluations of aggregate policies that rank states, but these simply reflect the policy preferences of the interest group issuing them. The scores and rankings are useful to those who share their biases, misleading to those who do not. *State Fact Finder* provides statistics on education (section H) and lets you decide which ones are most important to you.

6. Which states help the poor the most?

There is much disagreement about what is truly helpful to the poor. For example, some people believe providing welfare cash helps, but others argue that this hurts in the long run because it discourages working and hinders the opportunity to rise out of poverty.

State Fact Finder has many tables on programs for the poor, including food stamps (L-3), Temporary Assistance to Needy Families (L-2, L-9, L-15, and L-16), Medicaid (I-12, I-13, I-16, I-17, and I-18), and school aid for the disadvantaged (H-12), as well as on tax policies affecting low-income households (L-11).

If you want to look further into this question, consult the Center for Budget and Policy Priorities (820 1st Street, N.E., Suite 510, Washington, D.C. 20002, 202-408-1080, www.cbpp.org). This group has analyzed which states are most generous to the poor in their spending and how regressive state and local tax policies are—that is, whether they take away in taxes a larger percentage of the purchasing power of the poor than of the rich.

7. Which states have the best roads?

Comparing state policies on a topic such as education does not work well because different people have different ideas about what constitutes good or bad policy. However, for some services, such as providing well-maintained roads, people generally agree on what is good and bad. Even when people can agree on desirable results (for example, how children should perform on standard reading tests), it is difficult to judge states on these outcomes because so much of the result is determined by factors governments do not control. Because state and local governments maintain their own roads, few extraneous factors are involved.

Highways provide a good example of how services can be compared (see Tables K-2 and K-3). Truckers run their own surveys, which can be found in the special-interest magazine *Overdrive*.

8. Overall, which states use tax dollars in the most cost-effective manner?

For conceptual reasons, this question cannot be answered. Conceptual problems arise because people do not agree on what governments should do and how they should do it. For example, most people would agree that administrative costs for welfare should be kept at a minimum so that all available money can be devoted to real work. Most people would agree that it is bad for society if large numbers of people are allowed to cheat their governments, and most would also agree that welfare recipients should be encouraged to find jobs. These beliefs produce contradictory results when applied to available data, such as costs per case of administering welfare (L-17) and collecting child support (L-13). These costs are lowest if a state does little counseling and does not spend much money checking for fraud. Most people would agree that these consequences are not desireable.

Another example of a conceptual problem is the size of elementary school classes (H-9); some people think really small classes are ideal for all schools, while others believe small classes result in unnecessary spending.

Conceptual problems are not unique to governments. How can a company effectively measure whether its public relations or shareholder relations departments are cost-effective?

Even if conceptual problems could be solved, there are enormous difficulties in collecting the relevant data. For many functions, we do not have good measures of effectiveness. Do you know an effective police officer when you meet one, or an effective state university professor, or an effective state legislator? If you do, can you think how you would apply your effectiveness tests to every police officer, state university professor, or legislator in the nation?

Often, good measures of costs are not available either—at least not ones that are related closely to particular services or outputs of government. This problem is not unique to government. What percentage of the cost of a steer goes with the beef and what percentage with the leather?

Most attempts to measure the cost-effectiveness of government are experimental, usually confined to activities that can be measured fairly easily, such as gathering refuse, maintaining highways, and collecting bills. For more information, see the many useful books by Harry Hatry, published by the Urban Institute (2100 M Street, N.W., Washington, D.C. 20037, 202-833-7200, www.urban.org).

9. Which states have the best government institutions?

Beauty is clearly in the eye of the beholder when it comes to deciding how governments ought to be organized, their policies established, and their leaders selected. Some people have strong preferences on these matters, which are from time to time reflected in comparisons oriented to showing the states with the "best" practices.

For the past thirty years, experts have advocated and states have moved to organizing the executive branches of state government in ways that strengthen the power of governors. These moves include (1) strengthening the veto power, including "line-item" vetoes; (2) reducing the number of executive officials (comptrollers, education superintendents, and insurance commissioners, etc.) selected by elections rather than appointed; (3) increasing the governor's role in preparing and administering budgets; and (4) extending governors' terms by converting two-year terms to four-year terms and allowing governors to run for reelection. Information on these developments and classifications of which states have which practices appear in the Government section (D).

For decades state legislatures were criticized as citadels of corrupt power removed from popular control and unresponsive to the needs of citizens. One major change came with a Supreme Court decision on reapportionment, requiring "one man (or woman), one vote." Now the U.S. Senate is the only governing body in the nation where voting power is not proportional to population. The National Conference of State Legislatures and some business groups and foundations have sponsored research on "modern" legislatures emphasizing (1) longer annual sessions, (2) more staff, and (3) higher legislative pay and expenses. Three such measures of the results appear in Tables D-5, D-8, and D-9.

These ideas have come under considerable criticism recently. Some people saw more staffing and full-time legislators making the field a career as a move toward professionalizing the legislature; others saw this as a recipe for making bureaucrats out of legislators, creating "full-time politicians," and pulling legislators out of touch with the people they represent. One result has been a move to limit the number of terms legislators can serve (D-8), in effect encouraging turnover (D-7).

Surveys show that large numbers of Americans think corruption is common among elected officials at the state and federal levels. There is no statistical way to compare ethics, but laws on conflict of interest and disclosure of personal financial information can be compared. The National Conference of State Legislatures does this, with the organization Common Cause providing a kind of watchdog role.

There is no prevailing doctrine on whether "bigger is better" for business and government. Sometimes the fashion is consolidation—forming conglomerates for business and merging regional governments to reduce the roughly 85,000 different state and local governments. Sometimes the emphasis is decentralization and local control, with spin-offs for business and special districts (for example, downtown revitalization areas, police service districts) and decentralized control of neighborhood schools within large school systems.

One way to look at differing state policy is to compare the ratio of governments to people (D-4). Another approach is to examine the percentage of local government spending that local officials do not have to finance with their own taxes (D-16).

10. Overall, which states have the best policies?

For some people, picking the best policy is simple: the best state is the one with the lowest taxes, or the one that spends the most on schools or taking care of the poor, or that is active in some other area of interest to the person making the judgment.

For most people, this question is too general to be answered meaningfully because opinions differ so markedly on what is "best." Even for a particular person, one state may combine "good" policies on one subject with "bad" policies on another.

One thing is clear: State officials have to play the hands they are dealt, balancing the needs of their population and the tax base available for revenue to meet those needs.

Needs appear in the form of children to be educated (H-10), poor people potentially eligible for services (A-11), and more. Tax bases are apparent from economic differences, as shown in the Economies section (B). State differences are summarized in Table G-21 for spending needs and Table F-3 for tax bases.

By comparing these statistics, some conclusions are pretty obvious. For example, compared with most states, it is easy for Connecticut officials to look good, as the state has both low taxes and high spending in relation to what it does, such as spending per school pupil. The state has a rich tax base and a comparatively small percentage of people needing service. Mississippi faces the exact opposite situation.

11. All things considered, which state is run the best?

Readers are advised not to pay attention to magazine rankings purporting to show which state governments are best, or which states are governed the best by the combination of state and local officials responsible for their policies. You can get a pretty good idea that there is something slippery about these just by comparing results. For example, in the mid-1990s, two financial magazines, *Worth* and *Financial World*, published rankings. One said Wyoming was best and Alaska was second. The other ranked Wyoming forty-third and put Alaska next to last.

The rankings for cities and metropolitan areas are no better than those for states. For a good discussion of the pitfalls involved in such rankings, see "Why Nice Cities Finish Last" in *Governing* magazine (September 1995).

If you must rank states on something, pick some areas where they compete for the same prize, such as jobs (B-29); where residents are judged by the same test (H-3); or where the same objective criteria are being applied, such as tax levels (F-1).

There is widespread agreement on what constitutes a valuable football player or an outstanding actor. This is not true for governments. Many people think those that govern best govern least, but others are looking for good schools, good roads, and quick responses from police and fire departments.

Subject Rankings

Population

A-1	Population and Percentage Distribution, 2001	18
A-2	Percentage Change in Population, 2000-2001	19
A-3	Percentage Change in Population, 1990-2001	20
A-4	Projected Population, 2015, and Population Change, 2001-2015	21
A-5	Projected Population for the Year 2025	22
A-6	Population Age 65 and Over and as Percentage of Population, 2001	23
A-7	Population Age 17 and Under and as Percentage of Population, 2000	24
A-8	Median Age, 2000	25
A-9	African American Population and Percentage of Population, 2000	26
A-10	Hispanic Population and Percentage of Population, 2000	27
A-11	Population in Poverty, 2001	28
A-12	Number and Rate of Children in Poverty, 2001	29
A-13	Female Population, 2000	30
A-14	Birth Rates, 2001	31
A-15	Death Rates (age-adjusted), 2000	32
A-16	Population Density, 2001	33
A-17	Legal Immigrants Admitted, FY 2000	34

In 2001 the nation added an estimated 3.4 million to its population rolls. Nevada's numbers grew the fastest—at a rate of 5.4 percent. Some seventy thousand newcomers from other states accounted for a large chunk of Nevada's growth. Other newly minted Nevadans were the result of so-called natural increase (the relationship between births and deaths) and international migration. Four states—Louisiana, Iowa, West Virginia, and North Dakota—lost residents over the same one-year period.

More people live in California than any other state. The second-most populous state is Texas, followed by New York. Together these three constitute over 25 percent of the nation's total population. Conversely, only 16 percent live in the twenty-five least populous states.

Census population numbers often stir up debate. This is because they are used to allocate federal funds and representation in the U.S. House of Representatives. Although the Census Bureau is reporting better results than in the previous decade, minorities and those in low-income urban areas still tend to be missed in greater proportions. Typically, the Census Bureau runs a second set of numbers adjusting for this "undercount." It did not release these for 2000, however, until forced to by an Oregon federal court of appeals in late 2002. Despite protests by some, the adjustment will have no bearing on federal funding. The effect, if any, on other levels of government depends on the actions and laws of the individual state.

A second debate centers on the Census Bureau's method of measuring poverty. After four years of declines, poverty rates are now rising—1.3 million more people were poor in 2001 than a year earlier. Some contend that the situation may be worse than the numbers reveal. The poverty measure now in use was created in the 1960s, but many—both inside and outside the government—recommend the measure be revamped to better reflect current circumstances. Suggestions include accounting for changing standards of living; mandatory expenses, such as taxes; and other factors—for example, the increasing cost of health insurance.

A-1 Population and Percentage Distribution, 2001

State	Population 2001 (in thousands)	Percentage of national total 2001	Rank by percentage
Alabama	4,464	1.6	23
Alaska	635	0.2	47
Arizona	5,307	1.9	20
Arkansas	2,692	0.9	33
California	34,501	12.1	1
Colorado	4,418	1.6	24
Connecticut	3,425	1.2	29
Delaware	796	0.3	45
Florida	16,397	5.8	4
Georgia	8,384	2.9	10
Hawaii	1,224	0.4	42
Idaho	1,321	0.5	39
Illinois	12,482	4.4	5
Indiana	6,115	2.1	14
Iowa	2,923	1.0	30
Kansas	2,695	0.9	32
Kentucky	4,066	1.4	25
Louisiana	4,465	1.6	22
Maine	1,287	0.5	40
Maryland	5,375	1.9	19
Massachusetts	6,379	2.2	13
Michigan	9,991	3.5	8
Minnesota	4,972	1.7	21
Mississippi	2,858	1.0	31
Missouri	5,630	2.0	17
Montana	904	0.3	44
Nebraska	1,713	0.6	38
Nevada	2,106	0.7	35
New Hampshire	1,259	0.4	41
New Jersey	8,484	3.0	9
New Mexico	1,829	0.6	36
New York	19,011	6.7	3
North Carolina	8,186	2.9	11
North Dakota	634	0.2	48
Ohio	11,374	4.0	7
Oklahoma	3,460	1.2	28
Oregon	3,473	1.2	27
Pennsylvania	12,287	4.3	6
Rhode Island	1,059	0.4	43
South Carolina	4,063	1.4	26
South Dakota	757	0.3	46
Tennessee	5,740	2.0	16
Texas	21,325	7.5	2
Utah	2,270	0.8	34
Vermont	613	0.2	49
Virginia	7,188	2.5	12
Washington	5,988	2.1	15
West Virginia	1,802	0.6	37
Wisconsin	5,402	1.9	18
Wyoming	494	0.2	50
50 States	284,225	99.8	
DC	572	0.2	
United States	284,797	100.0	

Rank in order by percentage

1 California
2 Texas
3 New York
4 Florida
5 Illinois
6 Pennsylvania
7 Ohio
8 Michigan
9 New Jersey
10 Georgia
11 North Carolina
12 Virginia
13 Massachusetts
14 Indiana
15 Washington
16 Tennessee
17 Missouri
18 Wisconsin
19 Maryland
20 Arizona
21 Minnesota
22 Louisiana
23 Alabama
24 Colorado
25 Kentucky
26 South Carolina
27 Oregon
28 Oklahoma
29 Connecticut
30 Iowa
31 Mississippi
32 Kansas
33 Arkansas
34 Utah
35 Nevada
36 New Mexico
37 West Virginia
38 Nebraska
39 Idaho
40 Maine
41 New Hampshire
42 Hawaii
43 Rhode Island
44 Montana
45 Delaware
46 South Dakota
47 Alaska
48 North Dakota
49 Vermont
50 Wyoming

Note: Numbers that appear to be identical are rounded and vary slightly in actual value. The rankings reflect the actual values before rounding. See the introduction for more details.

A-2 Percentage Change in Population, 2000-2001

State	Population 2000 (in thousands)	Percentage change in population 2000-2001	Rank by percentage change
Alabama	4,447	0.39	37
Alaska	627	1.27	18
Arizona	5,131	3.44	2
Arkansas	2,673	0.70	27
California	33,872	1.86	9
Colorado	4,301	2.71	3
Connecticut	3,406	0.57	30
Delaware	784	1.60	12
Florida	15,982	2.59	4
Georgia	8,186	2.41	5
Hawaii	1,212	1.06	20
Idaho	1,294	2.09	7
Illinois	12,419	0.51	34
Indiana	6,080	0.56	31
Iowa	2,926	-0.11	48
Kansas	2,688	0.23	41
Kentucky	4,042	0.59	29
Louisiana	4,469	-0.08	47
Maine	1,275	0.92	22
Maryland	5,296	1.49	16
Massachusetts	6,349	0.48	35
Michigan	9,938	0.53	33
Minnesota	4,919	1.07	19
Mississippi	2,845	0.47	36
Missouri	5,595	0.62	28
Montana	902	0.25	39
Nebraska	1,711	0.12	45
Nevada	1,998	5.40	1
New Hampshire	1,236	1.89	8
New Jersey	8,414	0.83	24
New Mexico	1,819	0.56	32
New York	18,976	0.18	42
North Carolina	8,049	1.70	10
North Dakota	642	-1.21	50
Ohio	11,353	0.18	43
Oklahoma	3,451	0.27	38
Oregon	3,421	1.50	15
Pennsylvania	12,281	0.05	46
Rhode Island	1,048	1.01	21
South Carolina	4,012	1.27	17
South Dakota	755	0.23	40
Tennessee	5,689	0.89	23
Texas	20,852	2.27	6
Utah	2,233	1.64	11
Vermont	609	0.70	26
Virginia	7,079	1.54	14
Washington	5,894	1.59	13
West Virginia	1,808	-0.36	49
Wisconsin	5,364	0.71	25
Wyoming	494	0.13	44
50 States	280,850	1.20	
DC	572	-0.04	
United States	281,422	1.20	

Rank in order by percentage change

1	Nevada
2	Arizona
3	Colorado
4	Florida
5	Georgia
6	Texas
7	Idaho
8	New Hampshire
9	California
10	North Carolina
11	Utah
12	Delaware
13	Washington
14	Virginia
15	Oregon
16	Maryland
17	South Carolina
18	Alaska
19	Minnesota
20	Hawaii
21	Rhode Island
22	Maine
23	Tennessee
24	New Jersey
25	Wisconsin
26	Vermont
27	Arkansas
28	Missouri
29	Kentucky
30	Connecticut
31	Indiana
32	New Mexico
33	Michigan
34	Illinois
35	Massachusetts
36	Mississippi
37	Alabama
38	Oklahoma
39	Montana
40	South Dakota
41	Kansas
42	New York
43	Ohio
44	Wyoming
45	Nebraska
46	Pennsylvania
47	Louisiana
48	Iowa
49	West Virginia
50	North Dakota

Note: Numbers that appear to be identical are rounded and vary slightly in actual value. The rankings reflect the actual values before rounding. See the introduction for more details.

A-3 Percentage Change in Population, 1990-2001

State	Population 1990 (in thousands)	Percentage change in population 1990-2001	Rank by percentage change
Alabama	4,041	10.5	25
Alaska	550	15.4	18
Arizona	3,665	44.8	2
Arkansas	2,351	14.5	19
California	29,760	15.9	17
Colorado	3,294	34.1	3
Connecticut	3,287	4.2	47
Delaware	666	19.5	13
Florida	12,938	26.7	7
Georgia	6,478	29.4	6
Hawaii	1,108	10.5	26
Idaho	1,007	31.2	5
Illinois	11,431	9.2	33
Indiana	5,544	10.3	29
Iowa	2,777	5.3	44
Kansas	2,478	8.8	36
Kentucky	3,685	10.3	28
Louisiana	4,220	5.8	41
Maine	1,228	4.8	46
Maryland	4,781	12.4	23
Massachusetts	6,016	6.0	40
Michigan	9,295	7.5	39
Minnesota	4,375	13.6	20
Mississippi	2,573	11.1	24
Missouri	5,117	10.0	30
Montana	799	13.2	22
Nebraska	1,578	8.5	38
Nevada	1,202	75.2	1
New Hampshire	1,109	13.5	21
New Jersey	7,730	9.8	32
New Mexico	1,515	20.7	12
New York	17,990	5.7	42
North Carolina	6,629	23.5	9
North Dakota	639	-0.7	50
Ohio	10,847	4.9	45
Oklahoma	3,146	10.0	31
Oregon	2,842	22.2	11
Pennsylvania	11,882	3.4	48
Rhode Island	1,003	5.5	43
South Carolina	3,487	16.5	15
South Dakota	696	8.7	37
Tennessee	4,877	17.7	14
Texas	16,987	25.5	8
Utah	1,723	31.7	4
Vermont	563	8.9	35
Virginia	6,187	16.2	16
Washington	4,867	23.0	10
West Virginia	1,793	0.5	49
Wisconsin	4,892	10.4	27
Wyoming	454	9.0	34
50 States	248,103	14.6	
DC	607	-5.8	
United States	248,710	14.5	

Rank in order by percentage change

1. Nevada
2. Arizona
3. Colorado
4. Utah
5. Idaho
6. Georgia
7. Florida
8. Texas
9. North Carolina
10. Washington
11. Oregon
12. New Mexico
13. Delaware
14. Tennessee
15. South Carolina
16. Virginia
17. California
18. Alaska
19. Arkansas
20. Minnesota
21. New Hampshire
22. Montana
23. Maryland
24. Mississippi
25. Alabama
26. Hawaii
27. Wisconsin
28. Kentucky
29. Indiana
30. Missouri
31. Oklahoma
32. New Jersey
33. Illinois
34. Wyoming
35. Vermont
36. Kansas
37. South Dakota
38. Nebraska
39. Michigan
40. Massachusetts
41. Louisiana
42. New York
43. Rhode Island
44. Iowa
45. Ohio
46. Maine
47. Connecticut
48. Pennsylvania
49. West Virginia
50. North Dakota

Note: Numbers that appear to be identical are rounded and vary slightly in actual value. The rankings reflect the actual values before rounding. See the introduction for more details.

A-4 Projected Population, 2015, and Population Change

State	Projected population 2015 (in thousands)	Percentage change in population 2001-2015	Rank by percentage change
Alabama	4,956	11.0	14
Alaska	791	24.6	4
Arizona	5,808	9.4	20
Arkansas	2,922	8.5	25
California	41,373	19.9	6
Colorado	4,833	9.4	21
Connecticut	3,506	2.4	45
Delaware	832	4.5	38
Florida	18,497	12.8	12
Georgia	9,200	9.7	18
Hawaii	1,553	26.8	2
Idaho	1,622	22.8	5
Illinois	12,808	2.6	43
Indiana	6,404	4.7	37
Iowa	2,994	2.4	44
Kansas	2,939	9.1	22
Kentucky	4,231	4.1	39
Louisiana	4,840	8.4	26
Maine	1,362	5.9	34
Maryland	5,862	9.1	23
Massachusetts	6,574	3.1	41
Michigan	9,917	-0.7	50
Minnesota	5,283	6.2	32
Mississippi	3,035	6.2	33
Missouri	6,005	6.7	31
Montana	1,069	18.2	7
Nebraska	1,850	8.0	28
Nevada	2,179	3.5	40
New Hampshire	1,372	9.0	24
New Jersey	8,924	5.2	36
New Mexico	2,300	25.7	3
New York	18,916	-0.5	49
North Carolina	8,840	8.0	27
North Dakota	704	11.0	15
Ohio	11,588	1.9	46
Oklahoma	3,789	9.5	19
Oregon	3,992	14.9	10
Pennsylvania	12,449	1.3	47
Rhode Island	1,070	1.0	48
South Carolina	4,369	7.5	30
South Dakota	840	11.0	13
Tennessee	6,365	10.9	16
Texas	24,280	13.9	11
Utah	2,670	17.6	9
Vermont	662	8.0	29
Virginia	7,921	10.2	17
Washington	7,058	17.9	8
West Virginia	1,851	2.7	42
Wisconsin	5,693	5.4	35
Wyoming	641	29.6	1
50 States	309,539	8.9	
DC	594	3.9	
United States*	310,134	8.9	

Rank in order by percentage change	
1	Wyoming
2	Hawaii
3	New Mexico
4	Alaska
5	Idaho
6	California
7	Montana
8	Washington
9	Utah
10	Oregon
11	Texas
12	Florida
13	South Dakota
14	Alabama
15	North Dakota
16	Tennessee
17	Virginia
18	Georgia
19	Oklahoma
20	Arizona
21	Colorado
22	Kansas
23	Maryland
24	New Hampshire
25	Arkansas
26	Louisiana
27	North Carolina
28	Nebraska
29	Vermont
30	South Carolina
31	Missouri
32	Minnesota
33	Mississippi
34	Maine
35	Wisconsin
36	New Jersey
37	Indiana
38	Delaware
39	Kentucky
40	Nevada
41	Massachusetts
42	West Virginia
43	Illinois
44	Iowa
45	Connecticut
46	Ohio
47	Pennsylvania
48	Rhode Island
49	New York
50	Michigan

Note: Numbers that appear to be identical are rounded and vary slightly in actual value. The rankings reflect the actual values before rounding. See the introduction for more details.

Due to rounding or data sources, the 50-state total plus D.C. may not equal the U.S. total. Please see introduction.

A-5 Projected Population for the Year 2025

State	Estimated 2025 population (in thousands)	Rank
Alabama	5,224	22
Alaska	885	45
Arizona	6,412	17
Arkansas	3,055	32
California	49,285	1
Colorado	5,188	23
Connecticut	3,739	29
Delaware	861	47
Florida	20,710	3
Georgia	9,869	9
Hawaii	1,812	39
Idaho	1,739	40
Illinois	13,440	5
Indiana	6,546	16
Iowa	3,040	33
Kansas	3,108	31
Kentucky	4,314	27
Louisiana	5,133	24
Maine	1,423	42
Maryland	6,274	18
Massachusetts	6,902	14
Michigan	10,078	8
Minnesota	5,510	21
Mississippi	3,142	30
Missouri	6,250	19
Montana	1,121	44
Nebraska	1,930	37
Nevada	2,312	36
New Hampshire	1,439	41
New Jersey	9,558	10
New Mexico	2,612	35
New York	19,830	4
North Carolina	9,349	11
North Dakota	729	48
Ohio	11,744	7
Oklahoma	4,057	28
Oregon	4,349	26
Pennsylvania	12,683	6
Rhode Island	1,141	43
South Carolina	4,645	25
South Dakota	866	46
Tennessee	6,665	15
Texas	27,183	2
Utah	2,883	34
Vermont	678	50
Virginia	8,466	12
Washington	7,808	13
West Virginia	1,845	38
Wisconsin	5,867	20
Wyoming	694	49
50 States	334,393	
DC	655	
United States*	335,050	

Rank in order by population	
1	California
2	Texas
3	Florida
4	New York
5	Illinois
6	Pennsylvania
7	Ohio
8	Michigan
9	Georgia
10	New Jersey
11	North Carolina
12	Virginia
13	Washington
14	Massachusetts
15	Tennessee
16	Indiana
17	Arizona
18	Maryland
19	Missouri
20	Wisconsin
21	Minnesota
22	Alabama
23	Colorado
24	Louisiana
25	South Carolina
26	Oregon
27	Kentucky
28	Oklahoma
29	Connecticut
30	Mississippi
31	Kansas
32	Arkansas
33	Iowa
34	Utah
35	New Mexico
36	Nevada
37	Nebraska
38	West Virginia
39	Hawaii
40	Idaho
41	New Hampshire
42	Maine
43	Rhode Island
44	Montana
45	Alaska
46	South Dakota
47	Delaware
48	North Dakota
49	Wyoming
50	Vermont

Due to rounding or data sources, the 50-state total plus D.C. may not equal the U.S. total. Please see introduction.

A-6 Population Age 65 and Over, 2001

State	Population 65 and over (in thousands)	Percentage of population 65 and over	Rank by percentage
Alabama	584	13.1	20
Alaska	37	5.8	50
Arizona	692	13.0	22
Arkansas	374	13.9	9
California	3,656	10.6	45
Colorado	426	9.6	47
Connecticut	470	13.7	10
Delaware	104	13.1	21
Florida	2,848	17.4	1
Georgia	802	9.6	48
Hawaii	164	13.4	15
Idaho	149	11.3	41
Illinois	1,495	12.0	35
Indiana	753	12.3	29
Iowa	433	14.8	4
Kansas	355	13.2	18
Kentucky	506	12.4	27
Louisiana	517	11.6	39
Maine	185	14.4	7
Maryland	609	11.3	40
Massachusetts	860	13.5	12
Michigan	1,223	12.2	30
Minnesota	597	12.0	34
Mississippi	345	12.1	32
Missouri	754	13.4	14
Montana	122	13.4	13
Nebraska	231	13.5	11
Nevada	235	11.1	44
New Hampshire	150	11.9	36
New Jersey	1,114	13.1	19
New Mexico	217	11.9	37
New York	2,446	12.9	24
North Carolina	985	12.0	33
North Dakota	94	14.8	5
Ohio	1,507	13.3	16
Oklahoma	457	13.2	17
Oregon	442	12.7	26
Pennsylvania	1,908	15.5	2
Rhode Island	152	14.4	6
South Carolina	496	12.2	31
South Dakota	108	14.2	8
Tennessee	712	12.4	28
Texas	2,118	9.9	46
Utah	196	8.6	49
Vermont	78	12.8	25
Virginia	808	11.2	42
Washington	671	11.2	43
West Virginia	276	15.3	3
Wisconsin	704	13.0	23
Wyoming	58	11.8	38
50 States	35,223	12.4	
DC	68	11.9	
United States	35,291	12.4	

Rank in order by percentage	
1	Florida
2	Pennsylvania
3	West Virginia
4	Iowa
5	North Dakota
6	Rhode Island
7	Maine
8	South Dakota
9	Arkansas
10	Connecticut
11	Nebraska
12	Massachusetts
13	Montana
14	Missouri
15	Hawaii
16	Ohio
17	Oklahoma
18	Kansas
19	New Jersey
20	Alabama
21	Delaware
22	Arizona
23	Wisconsin
24	New York
25	Vermont
26	Oregon
27	Kentucky
28	Tennessee
29	Indiana
30	Michigan
31	South Carolina
32	Mississippi
33	North Carolina
34	Minnesota
35	Illinois
36	New Hampshire
37	New Mexico
38	Wyoming
39	Louisiana
40	Maryland
41	Idaho
42	Virginia
43	Washington
44	Nevada
45	California
46	Texas
47	Colorado
48	Georgia
49	Utah
50	Alaska

Note: Numbers that appear to be identical are rounded and vary slightly in actual value. The rankings reflect the actual values before rounding. See the introduction for more details.

A-7 Population Age 17 and Under, 2000

State	Population 17 and under (in thousands)	Percentage of population 17 and under	Rank by percentage
Alabama	1,123	25.3	29
Alaska	191	30.4	2
Arizona	1,367	26.6	10
Arkansas	680	25.4	27
California	9,250	27.3	6
Colorado	1,101	25.6	23
Connecticut	842	24.7	38
Delaware	195	24.8	34
Florida	3,646	22.8	49
Georgia	2,169	26.5	12
Hawaii	296	24.4	42
Idaho	369	28.5	3
Illinois	3,245	26.1	15
Indiana	1,574	25.9	18
Iowa	734	25.1	31
Kansas	713	26.5	11
Kentucky	995	24.6	39
Louisiana	1,220	27.3	7
Maine	301	23.6	47
Maryland	1,356	25.6	22
Massachusetts	1,500	23.6	48
Michigan	2,596	26.1	16
Minnesota	1,287	26.2	14
Mississippi	775	27.3	8
Missouri	1,428	25.5	25
Montana	230	25.5	26
Nebraska	450	26.3	13
Nevada	512	25.6	21
New Hampshire	310	25.0	32
New Jersey	2,088	24.8	35
New Mexico	509	28.0	5
New York	4,690	24.7	37
North Carolina	1,964	24.4	43
North Dakota	161	25.0	33
Ohio	2,888	25.4	28
Oklahoma	892	25.9	19
Oregon	847	24.7	36
Pennsylvania	2,922	23.8	45
Rhode Island	248	23.6	46
South Carolina	1,010	25.2	30
South Dakota	203	26.8	9
Tennessee	1,399	24.6	40
Texas	5,887	28.2	4
Utah	719	32.2	1
Vermont	148	24.2	44
Virginia	1,738	24.6	41
Washington	1,514	25.7	20
West Virginia	402	22.3	50
Wisconsin	1,369	25.5	24
Wyoming	129	26.1	17
50 States	72,179	25.7	
DC	115	20.1	
United States	72,294	25.7	

Rank in order by percentage

1 Utah
2 Alaska
3 Idaho
4 Texas
5 New Mexico
6 California
7 Louisiana
8 Mississippi
9 South Dakota
10 Arizona
11 Kansas
12 Georgia
13 Nebraska
14 Minnesota
15 Illinois
16 Michigan
17 Wyoming
18 Indiana
19 Oklahoma
20 Washington
21 Nevada
22 Maryland
23 Colorado
24 Wisconsin
25 Missouri
26 Montana
27 Arkansas
28 Ohio
29 Alabama
30 South Carolina
31 Iowa
32 New Hampshire
33 North Dakota
34 Delaware
35 New Jersey
36 Oregon
37 New York
38 Connecticut
39 Kentucky
40 Tennessee
41 Virginia
42 Hawaii
43 North Carolina
44 Vermont
45 Pennsylvania
46 Rhode Island
47 Maine
48 Massachusetts
49 Florida
50 West Virginia

Note: Numbers that appear to be identical are rounded and vary slightly in actual value. The rankings reflect the actual values before rounding. See the introduction for more details.

A-8 Median Age, 2000

State	Median age 2000	Rank
Alabama	35.8	26
Alaska	32.4	48
Arizona	34.2	42
Arkansas	36.0	19
California	33.3	46
Colorado	34.3	41
Connecticut	37.4	7
Delaware	36.0	19
Florida	38.7	2
Georgia	33.4	45
Hawaii	36.2	14
Idaho	33.2	47
Illinois	34.7	39
Indiana	35.2	36
Iowa	36.6	11
Kansas	35.2	36
Kentucky	35.9	23
Louisiana	34.0	43
Maine	38.6	3
Maryland	36.0	19
Massachusetts	36.5	12
Michigan	35.5	29
Minnesota	35.4	31
Mississippi	33.8	44
Missouri	36.1	18
Montana	37.5	6
Nebraska	35.3	33
Nevada	35.0	38
New Hampshire	37.1	8
New Jersey	36.7	9
New Mexico	34.6	40
New York	35.9	23
North Carolina	35.3	33
North Dakota	36.2	14
Ohio	36.2	14
Oklahoma	35.5	29
Oregon	36.3	13
Pennsylvania	38.0	4
Rhode Island	36.7	9
South Carolina	35.4	31
South Dakota	35.6	28
Tennessee	35.9	23
Texas	32.3	49
Utah	27.1	50
Vermont	37.7	5
Virginia	35.7	27
Washington	35.3	33
West Virginia	38.9	1
Wisconsin	36.0	19
Wyoming	36.2	14
50 States	n/a	
DC	34.6	
United States	35.3	

Rank in order by age	
1	West Virginia
2	Florida
3	Maine
4	Pennsylvania
5	Vermont
6	Montana
7	Connecticut
8	New Hampshire
9	New Jersey
9	Rhode Island
11	Iowa
12	Massachusetts
13	Oregon
14	Hawaii
14	North Dakota
14	Ohio
14	Wyoming
18	Missouri
19	Arkansas
19	Delaware
19	Maryland
19	Wisconsin
23	Kentucky
23	New York
23	Tennessee
26	Alabama
27	Virginia
28	South Dakota
29	Michigan
29	Oklahoma
31	Minnesota
31	South Carolina
33	Nebraska
33	North Carolina
33	Washington
36	Indiana
36	Kansas
38	Nevada
39	Illinois
40	New Mexico
41	Colorado
42	Arizona
43	Louisiana
44	Mississippi
45	Georgia
46	California
47	Idaho
48	Alaska
49	Texas
50	Utah

Note: Ties in ranking reflect ties in actual values.

A-9 African American Population, 2000

State	African American population of one race ("alone") (in thousands)	African American population alone and of more than one race ("in combination") (in thousands)	In combination population as a percentage of alone and in combination population	Alone and in combination population as a percentage of total population	Rank by percentage of total population
Alabama	1,156	1,169	1.1	26.3	6
Alaska	22	27	19.7	4.3	33
Arizona	159	186	14.4	3.6	36
Arkansas	419	427	1.9	16.0	12
California	2,264	2,513	9.9	7.4	26
Colorado	165	191	13.5	4.4	31
Connecticut	310	339	8.6	10.0	21
Delaware	151	157	4.1	20.1	9
Florida	2,336	2,472	5.5	15.5	14
Georgia	2,350	2,393	1.8	29.2	4
Hawaii	22	33	34.0	2.8	38
Idaho	5	8	32.9	0.6	49
Illinois	1,877	1,938	3.1	15.6	13
Indiana	510	538	5.2	8.8	22
Iowa	62	73	14.7	2.5	39
Kansas	154	171	9.6	6.3	27
Kentucky	296	312	5.1	7.7	24
Louisiana	1,452	1,468	1.1	32.9	2
Maine	7	10	29.2	0.7	47
Maryland	1,477	1,525	3.1	28.8	5
Massachusetts	343	398	13.8	6.3	28
Michigan	1,413	1,475	4.2	14.8	15
Minnesota	172	203	15.4	4.1	34
Mississippi	1,034	1,042	0.8	36.6	1
Missouri	629	655	4.0	11.7	19
Montana	3	4	39.4	0.5	50
Nebraska	69	76	9.6	4.4	32
Nevada	135	151	10.0	7.5	25
New Hampshire	9	12	26.1	1.0	43
New Jersey	1,142	1,212	5.8	14.4	16
New Mexico	34	42	19.0	2.3	40
New York	3,014	3,234	6.8	17.0	10
North Carolina	1,738	1,776	2.2	22.1	7
North Dakota	4	5	27.1	0.8	46
Ohio	1,301	1,373	5.2	12.1	17
Oklahoma	261	285	8.4	8.3	23
Oregon	56	73	23.4	2.1	41
Pennsylvania	1,225	1,289	5.0	10.5	20
Rhode Island	47	58	19.2	5.5	30
South Carolina	1,185	1,201	1.3	29.9	3
South Dakota	5	7	29.9	0.9	45
Tennessee	933	953	2.2	16.8	11
Texas	2,405	2,493	3.5	12.0	18
Utah	18	24	27.6	1.1	42
Vermont	3	4	31.8	0.7	48
Virginia	1,390	1,441	3.5	20.4	8
Washington	190	238	20.2	4.0	35
West Virginia	57	63	8.9	3.5	37
Wisconsin	304	327	6.8	6.1	29
Wyoming	4	5	23.5	1.0	44
50 States	34,315	36,069	n/a	12.8	
DC	343	350	2.0	61.3	
United States	34,658	36,419	4.8	12.9	

Rank in order by percentage of total population	
1	Mississippi
2	Louisiana
3	South Carolina
4	Georgia
5	Maryland
6	Alabama
7	North Carolina
8	Virginia
9	Delaware
10	New York
11	Tennessee
12	Arkansas
13	Illinois
14	Florida
15	Michigan
16	New Jersey
17	Ohio
18	Texas
19	Missouri
20	Pennsylvania
21	Connecticut
22	Indiana
23	Oklahoma
24	Kentucky
25	Nevada
26	California
27	Kansas
28	Massachusetts
29	Wisconsin
30	Rhode Island
31	Colorado
32	Nebraska
33	Alaska
34	Minnesota
35	Washington
36	Arizona
37	West Virginia
38	Hawaii
39	Iowa
40	New Mexico
41	Oregon
42	Utah
43	New Hampshire
44	Wyoming
45	South Dakota
46	North Dakota
47	Maine
48	Vermont
49	Idaho
50	Montana

Note: Numbers that appear to be identical are rounded and vary slightly in actual value. The rankings reflect the actual values before rounding. See the introduction for more details.

A-10 Hispanic Population, 2000

State	Hispanic population (in thousands)	Percentage of total population	Rank by percentage
Alabama	75.8	1.7	42
Alaska	25.9	4.1	28
Arizona	1,295.6	25.3	4
Arkansas	86.9	3.2	32
California	10,966.6	32.4	2
Colorado	735.6	17.1	6
Connecticut	320.3	9.4	11
Delaware	37.3	4.8	24
Florida	2,682.7	16.8	7
Georgia	435.2	5.3	22
Hawaii	87.7	7.2	17
Idaho	101.7	7.9	15
Illinois	1,530.3	12.3	10
Indiana	214.5	3.5	30
Iowa	82.5	2.8	35
Kansas	188.3	7.0	18
Kentucky	59.9	1.5	44
Louisiana	107.7	2.4	36
Maine	9.4	0.7	49
Maryland	227.9	4.3	27
Massachusetts	428.7	6.8	19
Michigan	323.9	3.3	31
Minnesota	143.4	2.9	34
Mississippi	39.6	1.4	46
Missouri	118.6	2.1	39
Montana	18.1	2.0	40
Nebraska	94.4	5.5	21
Nevada	394.0	19.7	5
New Hampshire	20.5	1.7	43
New Jersey	1,117.2	13.3	9
New Mexico	765.4	42.1	1
New York	2,867.6	15.1	8
North Carolina	379.0	4.7	25
North Dakota	7.8	1.2	47
Ohio	217.1	1.9	41
Oklahoma	179.3	5.2	23
Oregon	275.3	8.0	14
Pennsylvania	394.1	3.2	33
Rhode Island	90.8	8.7	13
South Carolina	95.1	2.4	37
South Dakota	10.9	1.4	45
Tennessee	123.8	2.2	38
Texas	6,669.7	32.0	3
Utah	201.6	9.0	12
Vermont	5.5	0.9	48
Virginia	329.5	4.7	26
Washington	441.5	7.5	16
West Virginia	12.3	0.7	50
Wisconsin	192.9	3.6	29
Wyoming	31.7	6.4	20
50 States	35,260.9	12.6	
DC	45.0	7.9	
United States*	35,305.8	12.5	

Due to rounding or data sources, the 50-state total plus D.C. may not equal the U.S. total. Please see introduction.

Rank in order by percentage	
1	New Mexico
2	California
3	Texas
4	Arizona
5	Nevada
6	Colorado
7	Florida
8	New York
9	New Jersey
10	Illinois
11	Connecticut
12	Utah
13	Rhode Island
14	Oregon
15	Idaho
16	Washington
17	Hawaii
18	Kansas
19	Massachusetts
20	Wyoming
21	Nebraska
22	Georgia
23	Oklahoma
24	Delaware
25	North Carolina
26	Virginia
27	Maryland
28	Alaska
29	Wisconsin
30	Indiana
31	Michigan
32	Arkansas
33	Pennsylvania
34	Minnesota
35	Iowa
36	Louisiana
37	South Carolina
38	Tennessee
39	Missouri
40	Montana
41	Ohio
42	Alabama
43	New Hampshire
44	Kentucky
45	South Dakota
46	Mississippi
47	North Dakota
48	Vermont
49	Maine
50	West Virginia

Note: Numbers that appear to be identical are rounded and vary slightly in actual value. The rankings reflect the actual values before rounding. See the introduction for more details.

A-11 Population in Poverty, 2001

State	Population in poverty (in thousands)	Percentage of population in poverty	Rank by percentage
Alabama	696	15.9	6
Alaska	54	8.5	38
Arizona	778	14.6	10
Arkansas	472	17.8	3
California	4,321	12.6	17
Colorado	383	8.7	36
Connecticut	249	7.3	46
Delaware	53	6.7	49
Florida	2,077	12.7	16
Georgia	1,069	12.9	15
Hawaii	138	11.4	22
Idaho	151	11.5	21
Illinois	1,249	10.1	27
Indiana	511	8.5	38
Iowa	212	7.4	44
Kansas	267	10.1	27
Kentucky	503	12.6	17
Louisiana	709	16.2	5
Maine	132	10.3	26
Maryland	385	7.2	47
Massachusetts	561	8.9	35
Michigan	927	9.4	33
Minnesota	361	7.4	44
Mississippi	539	19.3	1
Missouri	537	9.7	29
Montana	119	13.3	14
Nebraska	158	9.4	33
Nevada	152	7.1	48
New Hampshire	81	6.5	50
New Jersey	683	8.1	41
New Mexico	323	18.0	2
New York	2,664	14.2	11
North Carolina	1,013	12.5	19
North Dakota	86	13.8	13
Ohio	1,174	10.5	24
Oklahoma	508	15.1	7
Oregon	408	11.8	20
Pennsylvania	1,158	9.6	31
Rhode Island	100	9.6	31
South Carolina	603	15.1	7
South Dakota	62	8.4	40
Tennessee	802	14.1	12
Texas	3,129	14.9	9
Utah	238	10.5	24
Vermont	59	9.7	29
Virginia	564	8.0	42
Washington	634	10.7	23
West Virginia	291	16.4	4
Wisconsin	423	7.9	43
Wyoming	42	8.7	36
50 States	32,808	11.7	
DC	101	18.2	
United States*	32,907	11.7	

Rank in order by percentage

1	Mississippi
2	New Mexico
3	Arkansas
4	West Virginia
5	Louisiana
6	Alabama
7	Oklahoma
7	South Carolina
9	Texas
10	Arizona
11	New York
12	Tennessee
13	North Dakota
14	Montana
15	Georgia
16	Florida
17	California
17	Kentucky
19	North Carolina
20	Oregon
21	Idaho
22	Hawaii
23	Washington
24	Ohio
24	Utah
26	Maine
27	Illinois
27	Kansas
29	Missouri
29	Vermont
31	Pennsylvania
31	Rhode Island
33	Michigan
33	Nebraska
35	Massachusetts
36	Colorado
36	Wyoming
38	Alaska
38	Indiana
40	South Dakota
41	New Jersey
42	Virginia
43	Wisconsin
44	Iowa
44	Minnesota
46	Connecticut
47	Maryland
48	Nevada
49	Delaware
50	New Hampshire

Note: Ties in ranking reflect ties in actual values.

Due to rounding or data sources, the 50-state total plus D.C. may not equal the U.S. total. Please see introduction.

A-12 Number and Rate of Children in Poverty, 2001

State	Number of persons under 18 in poverty (in thousands)	Percentage in poverty	Rank by percentage
Alabama	263	23.2	3
Alaska	24	12.5	31
Arizona	341	22.3	7
Arkansas	194	28.3	1
California	1,602	16.4	17
Colorado	125	10.6	40
Connecticut	75	9.3	42
Delaware	18	9.3	42
Florida	731	18.8	15
Georgia	449	19.5	13
Hawaii	48	15.9	21
Idaho	60	15.9	21
Illinois	486	15.8	23
Indiana	165	11.3	37
Iowa	54	7.6	49
Kansas	91	14.4	25
Kentucky	170	17.2	16
Louisiana	281	23.1	5
Maine	33	12.4	33
Maryland	108	7.6	49
Massachusetts	162	11.9	36
Michigan	314	13.0	29
Minnesota	96	8.4	45
Mississippi	182	23.2	3
Missouri	180	12.9	30
Montana	36	16.4	17
Nebraska	59	13.5	28
Nevada	52	9.1	44
New Hampshire	23	8.2	47
New Jersey	179	9.6	41
New Mexico	124	25.4	2
New York	902	20.0	12
North Carolina	344	16.4	17
North Dakota	25	19.5	13
Ohio	429	16.2	20
Oklahoma	184	21.4	9
Oregon	130	15.1	24
Pennsylvania	384	14.0	26
Rhode Island	27	11.0	38
South Carolina	230	23.0	6
South Dakota	15	8.2	47
Tennessee	286	20.4	11
Texas	1,303	21.1	10
Utah	90	12.5	31
Vermont	15	12.2	34
Virginia	154	8.4	45
Washington	205	13.7	27
West Virginia	85	22.2	8
Wisconsin	152	12.0	35
Wyoming	13	10.7	39
50 States	11,698	16.3	
DC	34	30.8	
United States*	11,733	16.3	

*Due to rounding or data sources, the 50-state total plus D.C. may not equal the U.S. total. Please see introduction.

Rank in order by percentage	
1	Arkansas
2	New Mexico
3	Alabama
3	Mississippi
5	Louisiana
6	South Carolina
7	Arizona
8	West Virginia
9	Oklahoma
10	Texas
11	Tennessee
12	New York
13	Georgia
13	North Dakota
15	Florida
16	Kentucky
17	California
17	Montana
17	North Carolina
20	Ohio
21	Hawaii
21	Idaho
23	Illinois
24	Oregon
25	Kansas
26	Pennsylvania
27	Washington
28	Nebraska
29	Michigan
30	Missouri
31	Alaska
31	Utah
33	Maine
34	Vermont
35	Wisconsin
36	Massachusetts
37	Indiana
38	Rhode Island
39	Wyoming
40	Colorado
41	New Jersey
42	Connecticut
42	Delaware
44	Nevada
45	Minnesota
45	Virginia
47	New Hampshire
47	South Dakota
49	Iowa
49	Maryland

Note: Ties in ranking reflect ties in actual values.

A-13 Female Population, 2000

State	Female population (in thousands)	Percentage of population	Rank by percentage
Alabama	2,301	51.7	4
Alaska	303	48.3	50
Arizona	2,570	50.1	43
Arkansas	1,369	51.2	19
California	16,997	50.2	40
Colorado	2,135	49.6	48
Connecticut	1,756	51.6	9
Delaware	403	51.4	12
Florida	8,185	51.2	18
Georgia	4,159	50.8	31
Hawaii	603	49.8	46
Idaho	645	49.9	45
Illinois	6,339	51.0	21
Indiana	3,098	51.0	26
Iowa	1,491	50.9	27
Kansas	1,360	50.6	34
Kentucky	2,066	51.1	20
Louisiana	2,306	51.6	8
Maine	655	51.3	16
Maryland	2,739	51.7	7
Massachusetts	3,290	51.8	2
Michigan	5,065	51.0	24
Minnesota	2,484	50.5	35
Mississippi	1,471	51.7	6
Missouri	2,875	51.4	14
Montana	453	50.2	41
Nebraska	868	50.7	32
Nevada	980	49.1	49
New Hampshire	628	50.8	30
New Jersey	4,332	51.5	10
New Mexico	925	50.8	29
New York	9,830	51.8	3
North Carolina	4,107	51.0	22
North Dakota	322	50.1	42
Ohio	5,841	51.4	11
Oklahoma	1,755	50.9	28
Oregon	1,725	50.4	36
Pennsylvania	6,351	51.7	5
Rhode Island	545	52.0	1
South Carolina	2,063	51.4	13
South Dakota	380	50.4	37
Tennessee	2,919	51.3	17
Texas	10,499	50.4	38
Utah	1,114	49.9	44
Vermont	310	51.0	23
Virginia	3,607	51.0	25
Washington	2,960	50.2	39
West Virginia	929	51.4	15
Wisconsin	2,715	50.6	33
Wyoming	245	49.7	47
50 States	143,065	50.9	
DC	303	52.9	
United States	143,368	50.9	

Rank in order by percentage

1 Rhode Island
2 Massachusetts
3 New York
4 Alabama
5 Pennsylvania
6 Mississippi
7 Maryland
8 Louisiana
9 Connecticut
10 New Jersey
11 Ohio
12 Delaware
13 South Carolina
14 Missouri
15 West Virginia
16 Maine
17 Tennessee
18 Florida
19 Arkansas
20 Kentucky
21 Illinois
22 North Carolina
23 Vermont
24 Michigan
25 Virginia
26 Indiana
27 Iowa
28 Oklahoma
29 New Mexico
30 New Hampshire
31 Georgia
32 Nebraska
33 Wisconsin
34 Kansas
35 Minnesota
36 Oregon
37 South Dakota
38 Texas
39 Washington
40 California
41 Montana
42 North Dakota
43 Arizona
44 Utah
45 Idaho
46 Hawaii
47 Wyoming
48 Colorado
49 Nevada
50 Alaska

Note: Numbers that appear to be identical are rounded and vary slightly in actual value. The rankings reflect the actual values before rounding. See the introduction for more details.

A-14 Birth Rates, 2001

State	Births per 1,000 population	Rank
Alabama	13.7	31
Alaska	16.0	6
Arizona	17.2	3
Arkansas	14.3	20
California	15.5	9
Colorado	15.9	8
Connecticut	12.7	41
Delaware	13.9	29
Florida	13.2	37
Georgia	16.5	4
Hawaii	14.5	17
Idaho	16.0	6
Illinois	15.0	14
Indiana	14.4	19
Iowa	13.1	38
Kansas	14.5	17
Kentucky	13.6	33
Louisiana	15.3	11
Maine	10.9	49
Maryland	14.2	21
Massachusetts	13.0	39
Michigan	13.4	36
Minnesota	13.9	29
Mississippi	15.1	12
Missouri	13.7	31
Montana	12.3	44
Nebraska	14.8	15
Nevada	16.1	5
New Hampshire	11.9	47
New Jersey	14.0	24
New Mexico	15.4	10
New York	14.0	24
North Carolina	15.1	12
North Dakota	12.2	45
Ohio	14.0	24
Oklahoma	14.8	15
Oregon	13.5	35
Pennsylvania	12.2	45
Rhode Island	12.7	41
South Carolina	14.1	22
South Dakota	14.1	22
Tennessee	14.0	24
Texas	17.5	2
Utah	21.8	1
Vermont	10.6	50
Virginia	14.0	24
Washington	13.6	33
West Virginia	11.4	48
Wisconsin	12.9	40
Wyoming	12.7	41
50 States	n/a	
DC	14.7	
United States	14.5	

Rank in order by rate

1	Utah
2	Texas
3	Arizona
4	Georgia
5	Nevada
6	Alaska
6	Idaho
8	Colorado
9	California
10	New Mexico
11	Louisiana
12	Mississippi
12	North Carolina
14	Illinois
15	Nebraska
15	Oklahoma
17	Hawaii
17	Kansas
19	Indiana
20	Arkansas
21	Maryland
22	South Carolina
22	South Dakota
24	New Jersey
24	New York
24	Ohio
24	Tennessee
24	Virginia
29	Delaware
29	Minnesota
31	Alabama
31	Missouri
33	Kentucky
33	Washington
35	Oregon
36	Michigan
37	Florida
38	Iowa
39	Massachusetts
40	Wisconsin
41	Connecticut
41	Rhode Island
41	Wyoming
44	Montana
45	North Dakota
45	Pennsylvania
47	New Hampshire
48	West Virginia
49	Maine
50	Vermont

Note: Ties in ranking reflect ties in actual values.

A-15 Death Rates (age-adjusted), 2000

State	Deaths per 1,000 population	Rank
Alabama	1,013.3	4
Alaska	861.4	24
Arizona	844.0	29
Arkansas	1,001.7	8
California	765.7	49
Colorado	788.4	45
Connecticut	797.5	44
Delaware	920.2	16
Florida	828.8	34
Georgia	1,002.5	7
Hawaii	666.7	50
Idaho	811.7	39
Illinois	876.9	23
Indiana	936.4	13
Iowa	802.4	42
Kansas	851.9	28
Kentucky	1,004.8	6
Louisiana	1,020.1	2
Maine	887.4	22
Maryland	911.6	17
Massachusetts	818.1	37
Michigan	892.7	21
Minnesota	766.0	48
Mississippi	1,074.1	1
Missouri	928.1	14
Montana	843.1	30
Nebraska	798.4	43
Nevada	951.4	12
New Hampshire	837.1	31
New Jersey	853.1	27
New Mexico	836.1	32
New York	808.6	40
North Carolina	963.9	11
North Dakota	766.4	47
Ohio	922.5	15
Oklahoma	986.8	10
Oregon	834.3	33
Pennsylvania	903.6	18
Rhode Island	827.2	35
South Carolina	994.6	9
South Dakota	813.2	38
Tennessee	1,019.9	3
Texas	895.8	20
Utah	786.1	46
Vermont	854.3	26
Virginia	899.9	19
Washington	806.6	41
West Virginia	1,012.5	5
Wisconsin	826.6	36
Wyoming	860.4	25
50 States	n/a	
DC	1,043.3	
United States	872.0	

Rank in order by rate	
1	Mississippi
2	Louisiana
3	Tennessee
4	Alabama
5	West Virginia
6	Kentucky
7	Georgia
8	Arkansas
9	South Carolina
10	Oklahoma
11	North Carolina
12	Nevada
13	Indiana
14	Missouri
15	Ohio
16	Delaware
17	Maryland
18	Pennsylvania
19	Virginia
20	Texas
21	Michigan
22	Maine
23	Illinois
24	Alaska
25	Wyoming
26	Vermont
27	New Jersey
28	Kansas
29	Arizona
30	Montana
31	New Hampshire
32	New Mexico
33	Oregon
34	Florida
35	Rhode Island
36	Wisconsin
37	Massachusetts
38	South Dakota
39	Idaho
40	New York
41	Washington
42	Iowa
43	Nebraska
44	Connecticut
45	Colorado
46	Utah
47	North Dakota
48	Minnesota
49	California
50	Hawaii

A-16 Population Density, 2001

State	Persons per square mile	Rank
Alabama	88	26
Alaska	1	50
Arizona	47	36
Arkansas	52	34
California	221	12
Colorado	43	37
Connecticut	707	4
Delaware	407	6
Florida	304	8
Georgia	145	18
Hawaii	191	13
Idaho	16	44
Illinois	225	11
Indiana	170	16
Iowa	52	33
Kansas	33	40
Kentucky	102	23
Louisiana	103	22
Maine	42	38
Maryland	550	5
Massachusetts	814	3
Michigan	176	15
Minnesota	62	31
Mississippi	61	32
Missouri	82	27
Montana	6	48
Nebraska	22	42
Nevada	19	43
New Hampshire	140	19
New Jersey	1,144	1
New Mexico	15	45
New York	403	7
North Carolina	168	17
North Dakota	9	47
Ohio	278	9
Oklahoma	50	35
Oregon	36	39
Pennsylvania	274	10
Rhode Island	1,013	2
South Carolina	135	21
South Dakota	10	46
Tennessee	139	20
Texas	81	28
Utah	28	41
Vermont	66	30
Virginia	182	14
Washington	90	25
West Virginia	75	29
Wisconsin	99	24
Wyoming	5	49
50 States	80	
DC	9,374	
United States	81	

Rank in order by density	
1	New Jersey
2	Rhode Island
3	Massachusetts
4	Connecticut
5	Maryland
6	Delaware
7	New York
8	Florida
9	Ohio
10	Pennsylvania
11	Illinois
12	California
13	Hawaii
14	Virginia
15	Michigan
16	Indiana
17	North Carolina
18	Georgia
19	New Hampshire
20	Tennessee
21	South Carolina
22	Louisiana
23	Kentucky
24	Wisconsin
25	Washington
26	Alabama
27	Missouri
28	Texas
29	West Virginia
30	Vermont
31	Minnesota
32	Mississippi
33	Iowa
34	Arkansas
35	Oklahoma
36	Arizona
37	Colorado
38	Maine
39	Oregon
40	Kansas
41	Utah
42	Nebraska
43	Nevada
44	Idaho
45	New Mexico
46	South Dakota
47	North Dakota
48	Montana
49	Wyoming
50	Alaska

A-17 Legal Immigrants Admitted, FY 2000

State	Legal immigrants admitted	Percentage of total legal immigrants admitted	Rank by number of legal immigrants
Alabama	1,904	0.2	39
Alaska	1,374	0.2	42
Arizona	11,980	1.4	14
Arkansas	1,596	0.2	40
California	217,753	25.6	1
Colorado	8,216	1.0	20
Connecticut	11,346	1.3	15
Delaware	1,570	0.2	41
Florida	98,391	11.6	3
Georgia	14,778	1.7	13
Hawaii	6,056	0.7	22
Idaho	1,922	0.2	38
Illinois	36,180	4.3	6
Indiana	4,128	0.5	28
Iowa	3,052	0.4	31
Kansas	4,582	0.5	27
Kentucky	2,989	0.4	33
Louisiana	3,016	0.4	32
Maine	1,133	0.1	43
Maryland	17,705	2.1	11
Massachusetts	23,483	2.8	7
Michigan	16,773	2.0	12
Minnesota	8,671	1.0	18
Mississippi	1,083	0.1	44
Missouri	6,053	0.7	23
Montana	493	0.1	47
Nebraska	2,230	0.3	36
Nevada	7,827	0.9	21
New Hampshire	2,001	0.2	37
New Jersey	40,013	4.7	5
New Mexico	3,973	0.5	29
New York	106,061	12.5	2
North Carolina	9,251	1.1	17
North Dakota	420	0.0	49
Ohio	9,263	1.1	16
Oklahoma	4,586	0.5	26
Oregon	8,543	1.0	19
Pennsylvania	18,148	2.1	10
Rhode Island	2,526	0.3	34
South Carolina	2,267	0.3	35
South Dakota	465	0.1	48
Tennessee	4,882	0.6	25
Texas	63,840	7.5	4
Utah	3,710	0.4	30
Vermont	810	0.1	45
Virginia	20,087	2.4	8
Washington	18,486	2.2	9
West Virginia	573	0.1	46
Wisconsin	5,057	0.6	24
Wyoming	248	0.0	50
50 States	841,494	99.0	
DC	2,542	0.3	
United States*	849,807	100.0	

Rank in order by number

1 California
2 New York
3 Florida
4 Texas
5 New Jersey
6 Illinois
7 Massachusetts
8 Virginia
9 Washington
10 Pennsylvania
11 Maryland
12 Michigan
13 Georgia
14 Arizona
15 Connecticut
16 Ohio
17 North Carolina
18 Minnesota
19 Oregon
20 Colorado
21 Nevada
22 Hawaii
23 Missouri
24 Wisconsin
25 Tennessee
26 Oklahoma
27 Kansas
28 Indiana
29 New Mexico
30 Utah
31 Iowa
32 Louisiana
33 Kentucky
34 Rhode Island
35 South Carolina
36 Nebraska
37 New Hampshire
38 Idaho
39 Alabama
40 Arkansas
41 Delaware
42 Alaska
43 Maine
44 Mississippi
45 Vermont
46 West Virginia
47 Montana
48 South Dakota
49 North Dakota
50 Wyoming

Due to rounding or data sources, the 50-state total plus D.C. may not equal the U.S. total. Please see introduction.

Source Notes for Population (Section A)

A-1 Population and Percentage Distribution, 2001: The U.S. population is counted once every decade in years ending in zero. The last such count was in 2000. For all other years, the Census Bureau prepares estimates for July 1 of each year. The 2001 estimates were released on December 27, 2001 as Table ST-2001EST-01-Time Series of State Population Estimates: April 1, 2000 to July 1, 2001 and are available on the Bureau's website (www.census.gov). Outside experts and the Census Bureau agree that the census undercounts the nation's population and that this undercount tends to be concentrated in low-income areas in major cities. The understatement of population is greatest for these communities and the states that contain them. Because population estimates are used to determine representation in Congress and how much state and local governments get from federal aid programs, some states and cities have gone to court seeking to force the federal government to use more correct estimates. In the past, the Census Bureau successfully resisted these challenges because, while it agrees the official count is inaccurate, it did not know what data might be substituted for that count.

A-2 Percentage Change in Population, 2000-2001: From the same source as Table A-1, this table shows population change over one year.

A-3 Percentage Change in Population, 1990-2001: The 1990 population data shown on this table are from the 1990 census, reflecting the count as of April 1, 1990.

A-4 Projected Population, 2015, and Population Change, 2001-2015: The population projections for 2015 were made by the Census Bureau and are available on their website (www.census.gov). See Table A-1 for the 2001 population numbers used to calculate the projected change over time. The Census Bureau is scheduled to release updated state population projections in March of 2003. More recent national *only* projections were released in 2000. These numbers project a U.S. population of 312,268,000 in 2015, and 337,815,000 in 2025. Many private market research and economic forecasting firms also make population projections. The projections reflect recent trends, so western states are predicted to gain population rapidly while the slowest growth appears in the Northeast and Midwest. Generally, projections for short periods are quite reliable because they are based on events that are predictable for large groups, such as the percentage of persons who will die each year and the percentage of women of childbearing age who will have babies. Over longer periods, more guesswork is involved. Major economic shifts can be caused by changes in defense spending, fluctuations in oil and gas prices, and success or failure of particular firms or industries. Those shifts affect migration of workers and ultimately where they have children and die.

A-5 Projected Population for the Year 2025: See notes to Table A-4.

A-6 Population Age 65 and Over and as Percentage of Population, 2001: This Census Bureau estimate is available on the Bureau's website (see notes to Table A-1). Two kinds of states have the largest percentage of elderly citizens. First, there are states, like Florida and Arkansas, that draw large numbers of retirees from other states. Second, there are states with slow population growth, such as Pennsylvania, that lose many of their working-age younger people through migration to other states.

A-7 Population Age 17 and Under and as Percentage of Population, 2000: This count, from the 2000 census and issued in September of 2001, shows the flip side of the high concentrations of elderly citizens shown in Table A-6. The highest-ranking states, typified by Utah, have a large percentage of adults of childbearing age and high birth rates. Citing delays and hindrances, the Census Bureau cancelled the release of state population statistics by characteristics such as age, sex, and race for 2001.

A-8 Median Age, 2000: In each state, half the population was older than the age shown, while half was younger. This statistic, available on the Census Bureau's website (see notes to Table A-1) is a way to capture age differences among states in a single number for each state. The rankings are based on unrounded numbers. Citing delays and hindrances, the Census Bureau cancelled the release of state population statistics by characteristics such as age, sex, and race for 2001.

A-9 African American Population and Percentage of Population, 2000: The Census Bureau identifies six race categories: White; Black or African American; American Indian and Alaska Native; Asian; Native Hawaiian and Other Pacific Islander; and "some other race" (write-in answer). "Hispanic" is not considered a race by the Census Bureau, so Hispanics are asked to classify themselves using the above six race categories. The 2000 census marked the first year respondents were able to check one or more boxes identifying race. Thus, this *State Fact Finder* table presents two ways of counting the African American population. The first column shows the number of people who classify themselves as African American only (or, in Census Bureau terminology, "the alone population"). The second column also includes those who identify as African American only, but added in are those who identified as African American and some other race or races as well (the "alone" or "in combination" population). The numbers in the second column are used to determine African Americans as a percentage of the total population, which is presented in the fourth column and the ranking table.

The values in the third column show what percentage of the alone and combined African American population (second column) identify as being of two or more races. Nationally, 4.8 percent of African Americans classify themselves as black plus some other race or races. This percentage varies significantly between states, however. The percentage jumps to 39.4 in Montana and dips to 0.8 in Mississippi.

These data come from a Census 2000 Brief, "The Black Population: 2000," released in August, 2001 and available on the Census Bureau's website (see notes to Table A-1). Counts for other federally recognized racial groups are available from the Census Bureau. The "undercount" (see notes to Table A-1) means that statistics probably undercount African Americans and Hispanics. Citing delays and hindrances, the Census Bureau cancelled the release of state population statistics by characteristics such as age, sex, and race for 2001.

A-10 Hispanic Population and Percentage of Population, 2000: See notes to Table A-9. While the census theoretically accounts for every resident in the country, illegal immigrants (many of whom are Hispanic) have an understandable fear of being identified by any government agency. Therefore, the count of this group is probably not very accurate. The data come from the Census Bureau website (see notes to Table A-1). Citing delays and hindrances, the Census Bureau cancelled the release of state population statistics by characteristics such as age, sex, and race for 2001.

A-11 Population in Poverty, 2001: The federal government has a uniform definition of the income families need to avoid poverty. The amount considered necessary varies with family size but not with rural or urban location or from state to state. The income used to calculate whether households are living in poverty does not include the value of non-cash benefits, such as medical care, provided to the poor under government programs. The estimates shown are from the Census Bureau website (see notes to Table A-1). They are based in part on monthly household surveys of a small sample of the nation's population, not a full count. They reflect possible sampling errors, particularly for less populous states.

A-12 Number and Rate of Children in Poverty, 2001: These statistics are available on the Census Bureau's website (see notes to Table A-1). They were made available on September 23, 2002, and are subject to the same caveats as similar data for persons of all ages in Table A-11. The percentage of children in poverty exceeds the percentage of all persons in poverty because households with children are often headed by a parent or parents in their early earning years, and the income needed to avoid the poverty standard is higher for families with children than for adults without children. Children not related to heads of households, such as foster children, are not included in this count.

A-13 Female Population, 2000: More than half of newly born children are male, but women tend to outlive men. The result is about equal numbers of each in the population as a whole, but disproportionate numbers of women in states with more aged population (see Table A-8). These data come from the Census Bureau website (see notes to Table A-1). Citing delays and hindrances, the Census Bureau cancelled the release of state population statistics by characteristics such as age, sex, and race for 2001.

A-14 Birth Rates, 2001: These data show that 14.5 children are born each year for every 1,000 people. The birth rate is nearly 67.2 per 1,000 when only women of childbearing age are considered. The data come from the National Center for Health Statistics publication, *National Vital Statistics Report* (Vol. 50, No. 10, June 6, 2002) available on the Center for Disease Control's website (www.cdc.gov). See notes to Table A-15 below.

A-15 Death Rates (age-adjusted), 2000: Raw death rates, like raw birth rates (births related to population), are highly sensitive to the age distribution of a state's population. A state with large numbers of older persons will tend to have lower raw birth rates and higher death rates. The National Center for Health Statistics makes special calculations adjusting deaths for age and births for the numbers of women of childbearing age (called fertility rates).

State Fact Finder illustrates both approaches by using raw rates for births (Table A-14) and adjusted rates for deaths. Data showing raw rates for deaths are, like the age-adjusted death rates shown, available from the National Center for Health Statistics publication, *National Vital Statistics Reports*, Vol. 50, No. 15, September 16, 2002. This source also provides technical notes indicating exactly how adjustments are made. The notes also explain how a changed population standard in data year 1999 makes these rates not directly comparable to those of previous years. This table is indicating that, on average, people living in Mississippi die sooner than those in Hawaii.

A-16 Population Density, 2001: This table is calculated by taking the land area estimate from the 2000 census, available on the Census Bureau's website (see notes to A-1) and relating it to the 2001 population. The result is a rough measure of urban-rural characteristics of each state and is often cited as a proxy for possible crowding. However, in many states much of the land area is unusable for settlement because of lack of water, extraordinarily low or high elevation, and other factors. Consequently, much of the population of a low-density state may in fact be densely packed in a few small areas.

A-17 Legal Immigrants Admitted, FY 2000: These statistics, showing immigrants admitted by state of intended residence, are from the *2000 Statistical Yearbook of the Immigration and Naturalization Service* (www.ins.usdoj.gov).

Economies

B-1	Personal Income, 2001	38
B-2	Gross State Product, Total and Per Capita, 2000	39
B-3	Per Capita Personal Income, 2001	40
B-4	Personal Income from Wages and Salaries, 2001	41
B-5	Average Annual Pay, 2001	42
B-6	Average Hourly Earnings, 2002	43
B-7	Value Added in Manufacturing, 2000	44
B-8	Cost of Living, 2002	45
B-9	Average Annual Pay in Manufacturing, 2001	46
B-10	Average Annual Pay in Retailing, 2001	47
B-11	Labor Force, 2002	48
B-12	Unemployed and Unemployment Rate, 2002	49
B-13	Employment and Employment Rate, 2002	50
B-14	Government Employment, 2002	51
B-15	Manufacturing Employment, 2002	52
B-16	*Fortune* 500 Companies, 2002	53
B-17	*Forbes* 500 Companies, 2002	54
B-18	Tourism Spending, 2000	55
B-19	Exports, 2001	56
B-20	Housing Permits, 2001	57
B-21	Percentage Change in Home Prices, 1997-2002	58
B-22	Net Farm Income, 2001	59
B-23	Financial Institution Assets, 2001	60
B-24	Bankruptcy Filings by Individuals and Businesses, 2002	61
B-25	Patents Issued, FY 2001	62
B-26	Workers' Compensation Temporary Disability Payments, 2002	63
B-27	Average Unemployment Compensation Benefit, 2001	64
B-28	Index of State Economic Momentum, September 2002	65
B-29	Employment Change, 2001-2002	66
B-30	Manufacturing Employment Change, 2001-2002	67
B-31	Home Ownership, 1997-2001	68
B-32	Gambling, 2000	69
B-33	Average Annual Electricity Use Per Residential Customer, 2001	70
B-34	Average Cost Per Kilowatt Hour, 2001	71
B-35	New Companies, 2001	72

When the economy began faltering in 2001, few predicted that two years later we would still be wondering: how long and how bad? At the beginning of 2003 we are a country still waiting for that collective sigh of relief. Though newspaper headlines and experts spot recovery on the horizon one day and signs of a new slump the next, the official arbiter of the economy—the Business Cycle Dating Committee of the National Bureau of Economic Research—is likely to announce the end of the recession only after most of the country has already felt it. The committee watches for a sustained trough in economic activity by studying monthly measures of income, production and employment. Because of possible revisions to the economic data and the risk of the slump resuming, the committee waits for many months after an apparent trough to issue its judgment. It was December 1992 before the committee announced that the country's previous economic slump had leveled off in March 1991.

In the meantime, although productivity and consumer spending numbers offer some hope, the stock market remains a nail-biter, business investment is still sluggish, and personal income gains slight. Unemployment rates shrunk slightly over the summer of 2002 but inched up again in the fall, and most state governments have spent the last two fiscal years scrambling for revenues. To add to all this bad news are fears of a bust in the housing market. The major warning sign: Price increases that far exceed inflation. But on this issue analysts disagree. Many find evidence that, unlike the bubble in the stock market, this one will not burst. While it is true that housing prices are unlikely to continue to appreciate at today's unsustainable rates, they are also unlikely to dip under inflation either. In any case, although the effects of the recession have been spread somewhat evenly across the country, a faltering housing and construction industry would likely be more acutely painful in those metropolitan areas that have recently experienced the most gains.

To help the economy along the federal government passed an economic stimulus package mid-year 2002. But from the perspective of state officials the benefits did little to outweigh the costs.

B-1 Personal Income, 2001

Rank in order by $

1 California
2 New York
3 Texas
4 Florida
5 Illinois
6 Pennsylvania
7 Ohio
8 New Jersey
9 Michigan
10 Massachusetts
11 Georgia
12 Virginia
13 North Carolina
14 Washington
15 Maryland
16 Indiana
17 Minnesota
18 Missouri
19 Wisconsin
20 Tennessee
21 Colorado
22 Connecticut
23 Arizona
24 Alabama
25 Louisiana
26 Kentucky
27 South Carolina
28 Oregon
29 Oklahoma
30 Iowa
31 Kansas
32 Nevada
33 Mississippi
34 Arkansas
35 Utah
36 Nebraska
37 New Hampshire
38 New Mexico
39 West Virginia
40 Hawaii
41 Maine
42 Idaho
43 Rhode Island
44 Delaware
45 Montana
46 South Dakota
47 Alaska
48 Vermont
49 North Dakota
50 Wyoming

State	Personal income $ (in millions)	Rank
Alabama	109,773	24
Alaska	19,641	47
Arizona	137,314	23
Arkansas	61,613	34
California	1,128,256	1
Colorado	147,860	21
Connecticut	145,341	22
Delaware	25,853	44
Florida	474,626	4
Georgia	240,896	11
Hawaii	35,510	40
Idaho	32,525	42
Illinois	412,200	5
Indiana	169,885	16
Iowa	79,893	30
Kansas	76,973	31
Kentucky	101,326	26
Louisiana	109,560	25
Maine	34,384	41
Maryland	189,142	15
Massachusetts	248,202	10
Michigan	297,609	9
Minnesota	164,589	17
Mississippi	62,163	33
Missouri	158,906	18
Montana	21,673	45
Nebraska	49,489	36
Nevada	62,966	32
New Hampshire	42,986	37
New Jersey	326,723	8
New Mexico	42,354	38
New York	684,774	2
North Carolina	225,234	13
North Dakota	16,434	49
Ohio	327,745	7
Oklahoma	86,750	29
Oregon	97,814	28
Pennsylvania	377,461	6
Rhode Island	31,995	43
South Carolina	101,110	27
South Dakota	20,174	46
Tennessee	154,911	20
Texas	609,489	3
Utah	54,884	35
Vermont	17,531	48
Virginia	233,107	12
Washington	191,763	14
West Virginia	41,230	39
Wisconsin	158,116	19
Wyoming	14,544	50
50 States	8,655,296	
DC	22,959	
United States	8,678,255	

B-2 Gross State Product, Total and Per Capita, 2000

State	Gross state product $ (in millions)	Per capita $	Rank per capita
Alabama	119,921	26,966	45
Alaska	27,747	44,258	4
Arizona	156,303	30,465	36
Arkansas	67,724	25,333	47
California	1,344,623	39,698	7
Colorado	167,918	39,039	9
Connecticut	159,288	46,773	1
Delaware	36,336	46,371	2
Florida	472,105	29,539	39
Georgia	296,142	36,175	16
Hawaii	42,364	34,967	20
Idaho	37,031	28,619	41
Illinois	467,284	37,626	11
Indiana	192,195	31,608	30
Iowa	89,600	30,619	35
Kansas	85,063	31,641	29
Kentucky	118,508	29,321	40
Louisiana	137,700	30,812	32
Maine	35,981	28,222	44
Maryland	186,108	35,138	18
Massachusetts	284,934	44,878	3
Michigan	325,384	32,740	26
Minnesota	184,766	37,558	12
Mississippi	67,315	23,664	49
Missouri	178,845	31,964	28
Montana	21,777	24,138	48
Nebraska	56,072	32,766	25
Nevada	74,745	37,405	13
New Hampshire	47,708	38,605	10
New Jersey	363,089	43,151	5
New Mexico	54,364	29,886	38
New York	799,202	42,115	6
North Carolina	281,741	35,002	19
North Dakota	18,283	28,469	42
Ohio	372,640	32,823	24
Oklahoma	91,773	26,596	46
Oregon	118,637	34,675	22
Pennsylvania	403,985	32,895	23
Rhode Island	36,453	34,773	21
South Carolina	113,377	28,259	43
South Dakota	23,192	30,724	33
Tennessee	178,362	31,351	31
Texas	742,274	35,598	17
Utah	68,549	30,696	34
Vermont	18,411	30,240	37
Virginia	261,355	36,922	15
Washington	219,937	37,315	14
West Virginia	42,271	23,376	50
Wisconsin	173,478	32,343	27
Wyoming	19,294	39,074	8
50 States	9,882,154	35,187	
DC	59,397	103,830	
United States*	9,941,552	35,326	

	Rank in order per capita
1	Connecticut
2	Delaware
3	Massachusetts
4	Alaska
5	New Jersey
6	New York
7	California
8	Wyoming
9	Colorado
10	New Hampshire
11	Illinois
12	Minnesota
13	Nevada
14	Washington
15	Virginia
16	Georgia
17	Texas
18	Maryland
19	North Carolina
20	Hawaii
21	Rhode Island
22	Oregon
23	Pennsylvania
24	Ohio
25	Nebraska
26	Michigan
27	Wisconsin
28	Missouri
29	Kansas
30	Indiana
31	Tennessee
32	Louisiana
33	South Dakota
34	Utah
35	Iowa
36	Arizona
37	Vermont
38	New Mexico
39	Florida
40	Kentucky
41	Idaho
42	North Dakota
43	South Carolina
44	Maine
45	Alabama
46	Oklahoma
47	Arkansas
48	Montana
49	Mississippi
50	West Virginia

Due to rounding or data sources, the 50-state total plus D.C. may not equal the U.S. total. Please see introduction.

B-3 Per Capita Personal Income, 2001

State	Per capita personal income $	Rank
Alabama	24,589	43
Alaska	30,936	14
Arizona	25,872	38
Arkansas	22,887	48
California	32,702	10
Colorado	33,470	7
Connecticut	42,435	1
Delaware	32,472	11
Florida	28,947	22
Georgia	28,733	25
Hawaii	29,002	21
Idaho	24,621	42
Illinois	33,023	9
Indiana	27,783	31
Iowa	27,331	33
Kansas	28,565	28
Kentucky	24,923	40
Louisiana	24,535	44
Maine	26,723	35
Maryland	35,188	5
Massachusetts	38,907	2
Michigan	29,788	18
Minnesota	33,101	8
Mississippi	21,750	50
Missouri	28,226	29
Montana	23,963	46
Nebraska	28,886	23
Nevada	29,897	17
New Hampshire	34,138	6
New Jersey	38,509	3
New Mexico	23,155	47
New York	36,019	4
North Carolina	27,514	32
North Dakota	25,902	37
Ohio	28,816	24
Oklahoma	25,071	39
Oregon	28,165	30
Pennsylvania	30,720	15
Rhode Island	30,215	16
South Carolina	24,886	41
South Dakota	26,664	36
Tennessee	26,988	34
Texas	28,581	27
Utah	24,180	45
Vermont	28,594	26
Virginia	32,431	12
Washington	32,025	13
West Virginia	22,881	49
Wisconsin	29,270	20
Wyoming	29,416	19
50 States	n/a	
DC	40,150	
United States	30,472	

Rank in order per capita

1	Connecticut
2	Massachusetts
3	New Jersey
4	New York
5	Maryland
6	New Hampshire
7	Colorado
8	Minnesota
9	Illinois
10	California
11	Delaware
12	Virginia
13	Washington
14	Alaska
15	Pennsylvania
16	Rhode Island
17	Nevada
18	Michigan
19	Wyoming
20	Wisconsin
21	Hawaii
22	Florida
23	Nebraska
24	Ohio
25	Georgia
26	Vermont
27	Texas
28	Kansas
29	Missouri
30	Oregon
31	Indiana
32	North Carolina
33	Iowa
34	Tennessee
35	Maine
36	South Dakota
37	North Dakota
38	Arizona
39	Oklahoma
40	Kentucky
41	South Carolina
42	Idaho
43	Alabama
44	Louisiana
45	Utah
46	Montana
47	New Mexico
48	Arkansas
49	West Virginia
50	Mississippi

B-4 Personal Income from Wages and Salaries, 2001

State	Wages and salaries $ (in millions)	As percentage of personal income	Rank by percentage
Alabama	59,028	53.8	35
Alaska	11,325	57.7	14
Arizona	78,736	57.3	18
Arkansas	32,524	52.8	38
California	647,222	57.4	17
Colorado	88,434	59.8	7
Connecticut	81,164	55.8	25
Delaware	16,466	63.7	1
Florida	239,379	50.4	44
Georgia	144,367	59.9	6
Hawaii	19,885	56.0	23
Idaho	16,861	51.8	43
Illinois	240,650	58.4	10
Indiana	95,207	56.0	22
Iowa	43,267	54.2	32
Kansas	42,667	55.4	26
Kentucky	55,860	55.1	29
Louisiana	58,069	53.0	37
Maine	17,975	52.3	40
Maryland	98,791	52.2	41
Massachusetts	153,635	61.9	2
Michigan	173,309	58.2	12
Minnesota	99,764	60.6	4
Mississippi	31,005	49.9	46
Missouri	90,852	57.2	19
Montana	10,465	48.3	50
Nebraska	27,328	55.2	27
Nevada	37,022	58.8	9
New Hampshire	22,533	52.4	39
New Jersey	178,439	54.6	30
New Mexico	23,044	54.4	31
New York	411,556	60.1	5
North Carolina	129,670	57.6	15
North Dakota	8,856	53.9	33
Ohio	188,245	57.4	16
Oklahoma	43,749	50.4	45
Oregon	55,157	56.4	21
Pennsylvania	203,375	53.9	34
Rhode Island	16,595	51.9	42
South Carolina	55,779	55.2	28
South Dakota	10,049	49.8	48
Tennessee	86,643	55.9	24
Texas	355,124	58.3	11
Utah	33,792	61.6	3
Vermont	9,407	53.7	36
Virginia	137,840	59.1	8
Washington	110,856	57.8	13
West Virginia	20,132	48.8	49
Wisconsin	89,663	56.7	20
Wyoming	7,251	49.9	47
50 States	4,909,012	56.7	
DC	39,103	170.3	
United States	4,948,115	57.0	

Rank in order by percentage

1 Delaware
2 Massachusetts
3 Utah
4 Minnesota
5 New York
6 Georgia
7 Colorado
8 Virginia
9 Nevada
10 Illinois
11 Texas
12 Michigan
13 Washington
14 Alaska
15 North Carolina
16 Ohio
17 California
18 Arizona
19 Missouri
20 Wisconsin
21 Oregon
22 Indiana
23 Hawaii
24 Tennessee
25 Connecticut
26 Kansas
27 Nebraska
28 South Carolina
29 Kentucky
30 New Jersey
31 New Mexico
32 Iowa
33 North Dakota
34 Pennsylvania
35 Alabama
36 Vermont
37 Louisiana
38 Arkansas
39 New Hampshire
40 Maine
41 Maryland
42 Rhode Island
43 Idaho
44 Florida
45 Oklahoma
46 Mississippi
47 Wyoming
48 South Dakota
49 West Virginia
50 Montana

Note: Numbers that appear to be identical are rounded and vary slightly in actual value. The rankings reflect the actual values before rounding. See the introduction for more details.

B-5 Average Annual Pay, 2001

State	Average annual pay $	Rank		Rank in order by $
Alabama	30,090	33	1	Connecticut
Alaska	36,140	14	2	New York
Arizona	33,408	20	3	Massachusetts
Arkansas	27,258	46	4	New Jersey
California	41,358	5	5	California
Colorado	37,950	9	6	Illinois
Connecticut	46,963	1	7	Delaware
Delaware	38,434	7	8	Maryland
Florida	31,551	28	9	Colorado
Georgia	35,114	17	10	Washington
Hawaii	31,250	30	11	Michigan
Idaho	27,765	45	12	Virginia
Illinois	39,058	6	13	Minnesota
Indiana	31,778	26	14	Alaska
Iowa	28,840	38	15	Texas
Kansas	30,153	32	16	New Hampshire
Kentucky	30,017	35	17	Georgia
Louisiana	29,134	37	18	Pennsylvania
Maine	28,815	39	19	Rhode Island
Maryland	38,237	8	20	Arizona
Massachusetts	44,976	3	21	Ohio
Michigan	37,387	11	22	Oregon
Minnesota	36,585	13	23	Nevada
Mississippi	25,919	47	24	Missouri
Missouri	32,422	24	25	North Carolina
Montana	25,194	50	26	Indiana
Nebraska	28,375	41	27	Wisconsin
Nevada	33,122	23	28	Florida
New Hampshire	35,479	16	29	Tennessee
New Jersey	44,285	4	30	Hawaii
New Mexico	28,698	40	31	Vermont
New York	46,664	2	32	Kansas
North Carolina	32,026	25	33	Alabama
North Dakota	25,707	48	34	Utah
Ohio	33,280	21	35	Kentucky
Oklahoma	28,020	43	36	South Carolina
Oregon	33,203	22	37	Louisiana
Pennsylvania	34,976	18	38	Iowa
Rhode Island	33,592	19	39	Maine
South Carolina	29,253	36	40	New Mexico
South Dakota	25,600	49	41	Nebraska
Tennessee	31,491	29	42	Wyoming
Texas	36,039	15	43	Oklahoma
Utah	30,074	34	44	West Virginia
Vermont	30,240	31	45	Idaho
Virginia	36,716	12	46	Arkansas
Washington	37,475	10	47	Mississippi
West Virginia	27,982	44	48	North Dakota
Wisconsin	31,556	27	49	South Dakota
Wyoming	28,025	42	50	Montana
50 States	n/a			
DC	56,024			
United States	36,214			

B-6 Average Hourly Earnings, 2002

State	Average hourly earnings $	Rank
Alabama	13.28	42
Alaska	18.35	2
Arizona	13.91	36
Arkansas	12.86	44
California	15.01	25
Colorado	15.80	15
Connecticut	16.21	10
Delaware	16.73	5
Florida	13.36	41
Georgia	13.00	43
Hawaii	14.07	34
Idaho	15.78	16
Illinois	14.67	29
Indiana	16.70	6
Iowa	15.36	23
Kansas	15.89	13
Kentucky	15.48	22
Louisiana	16.16	11
Maine	15.85	14
Maryland	16.31	8
Massachusetts	15.69	17
Michigan	20.27	1
Minnesota	15.59	19
Mississippi	12.59	47
Missouri	15.51	21
Montana	14.30	32
Nebraska	13.67	37
Nevada	14.79	27
New Hampshire	13.66	38
New Jersey	15.99	12
New Mexico	14.45	31
New York	15.12	24
North Carolina	13.56	40
North Dakota	12.73	45
Ohio	17.32	4
Oklahoma	13.93	35
Oregon	16.28	9
Pennsylvania	14.96	26
Rhode Island	12.31	48
South Carolina	11.80	49
South Dakota	11.79	50
Tennessee	13.65	39
Texas	12.66	46
Utah	14.29	33
Vermont	14.50	30
Virginia	14.72	28
Washington	18.05	3
West Virginia	15.53	20
Wisconsin	15.67	18
Wyoming	16.61	7
50 States	n/a	
DC	15.75	
United States	15.28	

Rank in order by $	
1	Michigan
2	Alaska
3	Washington
4	Ohio
5	Delaware
6	Indiana
7	Wyoming
8	Maryland
9	Oregon
10	Connecticut
11	Louisiana
12	New Jersey
13	Kansas
14	Maine
15	Colorado
16	Idaho
17	Massachusetts
18	Wisconsin
19	Minnesota
20	West Virginia
21	Missouri
22	Kentucky
23	Iowa
24	New York
25	California
26	Pennsylvania
27	Nevada
28	Virginia
29	Illinois
30	Vermont
31	New Mexico
32	Montana
33	Utah
34	Hawaii
35	Oklahoma
36	Arizona
37	Nebraska
38	New Hampshire
39	Tennessee
40	North Carolina
41	Florida
42	Alabama
43	Georgia
44	Arkansas
45	North Dakota
46	Texas
47	Mississippi
48	Rhode Island
49	South Carolina
50	South Dakota

B-7 Value Added in Manufacturing, 2000

State	Value added $ (in millions)	Per capita $	Rank per capita
Alabama	29,998	6,746	29
Alaska	1,169	1,865	49
Arizona	29,259	5,703	37
Arkansas	21,329	7,978	16
California	242,667	7,164	26
Colorado	20,206	4,698	41
Connecticut	27,536	8,085	15
Delaware	6,021	7,684	19
Florida	41,919	2,623	46
Georgia	61,169	7,472	23
Hawaii	1,353	1,116	50
Idaho	14,229	10,997	4
Illinois	102,040	8,216	13
Indiana	78,202	12,861	1
Iowa	31,002	10,594	5
Kansas	20,869	7,763	18
Kentucky	32,795	8,114	14
Louisiana	28,258	6,323	32
Maine	8,680	6,808	28
Maryland	18,455	3,484	44
Massachusetts	48,638	7,661	20
Michigan	96,411	9,701	7
Minnesota	43,007	8,742	9
Mississippi	17,893	6,290	33
Missouri	41,083	7,343	24
Montana	1,687	1,869	48
Nebraska	12,377	7,233	25
Nevada	4,529	2,267	47
New Hampshire	10,350	8,375	12
New Jersey	52,185	6,202	34
New Mexico	10,176	5,594	38
New York	85,467	4,504	42
North Carolina	92,463	11,487	3
North Dakota	2,419	3,766	43
Ohio	117,972	10,391	6
Oklahoma	18,198	5,274	39
Oregon	26,838	7,844	17
Pennsylvania	92,512	7,533	21
Rhode Island	6,223	5,936	35
South Carolina	35,324	8,805	8
South Dakota	5,308	7,032	27
Tennessee	47,651	8,376	11
Texas	134,088	6,431	30
Utah	13,174	5,899	36
Vermont	5,140	8,443	10
Virginia	53,191	7,514	22
Washington	37,443	6,353	31
West Virginia	8,503	4,702	40
Wisconsin	63,684	11,873	2
Wyoming	1,462	2,961	45
50 States	2,002,551	7,130	
DC	98	171	
United States	2,002,649	7,116	

Rank in order per capita	
1	Indiana
2	Wisconsin
3	North Carolina
4	Idaho
5	Iowa
6	Ohio
7	Michigan
8	South Carolina
9	Minnesota
10	Vermont
11	Tennessee
12	New Hampshire
13	Illinois
14	Kentucky
15	Connecticut
16	Arkansas
17	Oregon
18	Kansas
19	Delaware
20	Massachusetts
21	Pennsylvania
22	Virginia
23	Georgia
24	Missouri
25	Nebraska
26	California
27	South Dakota
28	Maine
29	Alabama
30	Texas
31	Washington
32	Louisiana
33	Mississippi
34	New Jersey
35	Rhode Island
36	Utah
37	Arizona
38	New Mexico
39	Oklahoma
40	West Virginia
41	Colorado
42	New York
43	North Dakota
44	Maryland
45	Wyoming
46	Florida
47	Nevada
48	Montana
49	Alaska
50	Hawaii

B-8 Cost of Living, 2002

State	Cost of living index	Rank by index
Alabama	92.4	40
Alaska	126.1	5
Arizona	97.0	25
Arkansas	90.1	45
California	122.0	6
Colorado	101.2	15
Connecticut	131.0	4
Delaware	101.7	13
Florida	98.0	21
Georgia	91.9	42
Hawaii	139.5	2
Idaho	96.8	27
Illinois	102.9	10
Indiana	94.5	32
Iowa	95.0	30
Kansas	94.7	31
Kentucky	92.6	39
Louisiana	95.5	29
Maine	n/a	n/a
Maryland	94.1	33
Massachusetts	132.2	3
Michigan	99.0	19
Minnesota	102.4	11
Mississippi	93.0	37
Missouri	93.5	35
Montana	97.5	23
Nebraska	93.1	36
Nevada	108.1	8
New Hampshire	n/a	n/a
New Jersey	143.9	1
New Mexico	101.8	12
New York	121.0	7
North Carolina	97.0	25
North Dakota	93.9	34
Ohio	97.7	22
Oklahoma	91.7	44
Oregon	104.2	9
Pennsylvania	100.8	16
Rhode Island	n/a	n/a
South Carolina	98.8	20
South Dakota	97.4	24
Tennessee	89.0	46
Texas	91.8	43
Utah	92.7	38
Vermont	n/a	n/a
Virginia	100.4	18
Washington	101.7	13
West Virginia	92.0	41
Wisconsin	95.9	28
Wyoming	100.8	16
50 States	n/a	
DC	133.2	
United States	100.0	

Rank in order by index	
1	New Jersey
2	Hawaii
3	Massachusetts
4	Connecticut
5	Alaska
6	California
7	New York
8	Nevada
9	Oregon
10	Illinois
11	Minnesota
12	New Mexico
13	Delaware
13	Washington
15	Colorado
16	Pennsylvania
16	Wyoming
18	Virginia
19	Michigan
20	South Carolina
21	Florida
22	Ohio
23	Montana
24	South Dakota
25	Arizona
25	North Carolina
27	Idaho
28	Wisconsin
29	Louisiana
30	Iowa
31	Kansas
32	Indiana
33	Maryland
34	North Dakota
35	Missouri
36	Nebraska
37	Mississippi
38	Utah
39	Kentucky
40	Alabama
41	West Virginia
42	Georgia
43	Texas
44	Oklahoma
45	Arkansas
46	Tennessee

Note: Ties in ranking reflect ties in actual values.

B-9 Average Annual Pay in Manufacturing, 2001

State	Average annual pay in manufacturing $	Rank
Alabama	34,609	41
Alaska	30,187	46
Arizona	48,021	6
Arkansas	29,869	48
California	51,298	4
Colorado	47,544	8
Connecticut	55,706	1
Delaware	43,691	15
Florida	37,984	30
Georgia	37,003	34
Hawaii	30,062	47
Idaho	37,715	31
Illinois	43,789	14
Indiana	42,097	18
Iowa	37,234	32
Kansas	39,245	23
Kentucky	38,065	28
Louisiana	41,909	19
Maine	36,448	38
Maryland	47,170	9
Massachusetts	54,455	2
Michigan	49,660	5
Minnesota	42,481	17
Mississippi	29,416	50
Missouri	38,964	26
Montana	32,925	43
Nebraska	32,483	44
Nevada	39,477	22
New Hampshire	44,709	11
New Jersey	51,612	3
New Mexico	38,214	27
New York	44,510	12
North Carolina	37,097	33
North Dakota	31,616	45
Ohio	42,738	16
Oklahoma	34,323	42
Oregon	44,058	13
Pennsylvania	41,439	20
Rhode Island	36,757	36
South Carolina	35,878	40
South Dakota	29,836	49
Tennessee	36,933	35
Texas	46,233	10
Utah	36,298	39
Vermont	41,366	21
Virginia	38,021	29
Washington	47,558	7
West Virginia	39,091	25
Wisconsin	39,219	24
Wyoming	36,671	37
50 States	n/a	
DC	63,872	
United States	42,975	

Rank in order by $

1 Connecticut
2 Massachusetts
3 New Jersey
4 California
5 Michigan
6 Arizona
7 Washington
8 Colorado
9 Maryland
10 Texas
11 New Hampshire
12 New York
13 Oregon
14 Illinois
15 Delaware
16 Ohio
17 Minnesota
18 Indiana
19 Louisiana
20 Pennsylvania
21 Vermont
22 Nevada
23 Kansas
24 Wisconsin
25 West Virginia
26 Missouri
27 New Mexico
28 Kentucky
29 Virginia
30 Florida
31 Idaho
32 Iowa
33 North Carolina
34 Georgia
35 Tennessee
36 Rhode Island
37 Wyoming
38 Maine
39 Utah
40 South Carolina
41 Alabama
42 Oklahoma
43 Montana
44 Nebraska
45 North Dakota
46 Alaska
47 Hawaii
48 Arkansas
49 South Dakota
50 Mississippi

B-10 Average Annual Pay in Retailing, 2001

State	Average annual pay in retailing $	Rank
Alabama	19,889	35
Alaska	23,689	11
Arizona	24,398	7
Arkansas	17,670	50
California	27,644	1
Colorado	23,846	10
Connecticut	27,043	2
Delaware	21,689	21
Florida	22,645	15
Georgia	22,499	16
Hawaii	21,977	19
Idaho	20,221	32
Illinois	22,839	14
Indiana	19,704	37
Iowa	18,870	41
Kansas	19,595	38
Kentucky	19,060	39
Louisiana	18,771	42
Maine	19,837	36
Maryland	24,012	9
Massachusetts	24,791	5
Michigan	21,672	22
Minnesota	21,074	27
Mississippi	18,000	48
Missouri	20,368	31
Montana	18,450	44
Nebraska	18,403	45
Nevada	25,200	4
New Hampshire	23,162	13
New Jersey	26,841	3
New Mexico	20,732	30
New York	24,253	8
North Carolina	21,200	24
North Dakota	18,199	46
Ohio	21,175	25
Oklahoma	19,007	40
Oregon	22,384	17
Pennsylvania	21,153	26
Rhode Island	21,985	18
South Carolina	20,755	29
South Dakota	18,117	47
Tennessee	21,956	20
Texas	23,521	12
Utah	20,215	33
Vermont	20,825	28
Virginia	21,310	23
Washington	24,771	6
West Virginia	17,731	49
Wisconsin	19,963	34
Wyoming	18,693	43
50 States	n/a	
DC	25,743	
United States	22,670	

Rank in order by $

1. California
2. Connecticut
3. New Jersey
4. Nevada
5. Massachusetts
6. Washington
7. Arizona
8. New York
9. Maryland
10. Colorado
11. Alaska
12. Texas
13. New Hampshire
14. Illinois
15. Florida
16. Georgia
17. Oregon
18. Rhode Island
19. Hawaii
20. Tennessee
21. Delaware
22. Michigan
23. Virginia
24. North Carolina
25. Ohio
26. Pennsylvania
27. Minnesota
28. Vermont
29. South Carolina
30. New Mexico
31. Missouri
32. Idaho
33. Utah
34. Wisconsin
35. Alabama
36. Maine
37. Indiana
38. Kansas
39. Kentucky
40. Oklahoma
41. Iowa
42. Louisiana
43. Wyoming
44. Montana
45. Nebraska
46. North Dakota
47. South Dakota
48. Mississippi
49. West Virginia
50. Arkansas

B-11 Labor Force, 2002

State	Labor force (in thousands)	Labor force as percentage of population	Rank by percentage
Alabama	2,152	48.2	41
Alaska	334	52.6	15
Arizona	2,499	47.1	46
Arkansas	1,289	47.9	43
California	17,536	50.8	26
Colorado	2,371	53.7	11
Connecticut	1,720	50.2	29
Delaware	413	51.8	21
Florida	7,799	47.6	44
Georgia	4,231	50.5	27
Hawaii	596	48.7	39
Idaho	686	52.0	18
Illinois	6,242	50.0	33
Indiana	3,156	51.6	23
Iowa	1,630	55.8	5
Kansas	1,456	54.0	9
Kentucky	1,991	49.0	37
Louisiana	2,009	45.0	49
Maine	684	53.2	13
Maryland	2,904	54.0	10
Massachusetts	3,381	53.0	14
Michigan	5,144	51.5	24
Minnesota	2,851	57.3	1
Mississippi	1,302	45.6	48
Missouri	2,941	52.2	17
Montana	469	51.9	20
Nebraska	952	55.6	6
Nevada	1,046	49.7	35
New Hampshire	714	56.7	3
New Jersey	4,258	50.2	31
New Mexico	860	47.0	47
New York	8,995	47.3	45
North Carolina	3,970	48.5	40
North Dakota	339	53.4	12
Ohio	5,894	51.8	22
Oklahoma	1,689	48.8	38
Oregon	1,805	52.0	19
Pennsylvania	6,110	49.7	34
Rhode Island	508	48.0	42
South Carolina	2,010	49.5	36
South Dakota	409	54.1	8
Tennessee	2,876	50.1	32
Texas	10,738	50.4	28
Utah	1,140	50.2	30
Vermont	347	56.6	4
Virginia	3,778	52.6	16
Washington	3,082	51.5	25
West Virginia	809	44.9	50
Wisconsin	3,066	56.8	2
Wyoming	272	54.9	7
50 States	143,448	50.5	
DC	270	47.3	
United States	143,718	50.5	

Rank in order by percentage	
1	Minnesota
2	Wisconsin
3	New Hampshire
4	Vermont
5	Iowa
6	Nebraska
7	Wyoming
8	South Dakota
9	Kansas
10	Maryland
11	Colorado
12	North Dakota
13	Maine
14	Massachusetts
15	Alaska
16	Virginia
17	Missouri
18	Idaho
19	Oregon
20	Montana
21	Delaware
22	Ohio
23	Indiana
24	Michigan
25	Washington
26	California
27	Georgia
28	Texas
29	Connecticut
30	Utah
31	New Jersey
32	Tennessee
33	Illinois
34	Pennsylvania
35	Nevada
36	South Carolina
37	Kentucky
38	Oklahoma
39	Hawaii
40	North Carolina
41	Alabama
42	Rhode Island
43	Arkansas
44	Florida
45	New York
46	Arizona
47	New Mexico
48	Mississippi
49	Louisiana
50	West Virginia

Note: Numbers that appear to be identical are rounded and vary slightly in actual value. The rankings reflect the actual values before rounding. See the introduction for more details.

B-12 Unemployed and Unemployment Rate, 2002

State	Unemployed (in thousands)	Unemployment rate (percentage of labor force unemployed)	Rank by rate
Alabama	121.8	5.7	14
Alaska	24.9	7.5	1
Arizona	142.6	5.7	13
Arkansas	64.4	5.0	29
California	1107.6	6.3	5
Colorado	122.6	5.2	24
Connecticut	70.3	4.1	38
Delaware	16.8	4.1	39
Florida	401.4	5.1	25
Georgia	197.2	4.7	33
Hawaii	25.1	4.2	36
Idaho	37.6	5.5	17
Illinois	395.4	6.3	4
Indiana	157.8	5.0	28
Iowa	63.1	3.9	46
Kansas	66.6	4.6	34
Kentucky	103.8	5.2	21
Louisiana	118.6	5.9	10
Maine	27.8	4.1	40
Maryland	116.6	4.0	41
Massachusetts	175.8	5.2	23
Michigan	298.1	5.8	12
Minnesota	114.3	4.0	42
Mississippi	76.3	5.9	11
Missouri	140.5	4.8	31
Montana	18.3	3.9	44
Nebraska	32.7	3.4	49
Nevada	51.1	4.9	30
New Hampshire	32.1	4.5	35
New Jersey	227.1	5.3	19
New Mexico	52.1	6.1	8
New York	500.6	5.6	15
North Carolina	243.5	6.1	6
North Dakota	11.9	3.5	48
Ohio	325.8	5.5	16
Oklahoma	70.2	4.2	37
Oregon	122.1	6.8	3
Pennsylvania	318.6	5.2	22
Rhode Island	25.6	5.0	27
South Carolina	107.4	5.3	18
South Dakota	10.5	2.6	50
Tennessee	136.9	4.8	32
Texas	656.5	6.1	7
Utah	60.6	5.3	20
Vermont	13.9	4.0	43
Virginia	146.9	3.9	45
Washington	228.1	7.4	2
West Virginia	49.0	6.1	9
Wisconsin	154.9	5.1	26
Wyoming	10.5	3.9	47
50 States	**7793.9**	**5.4**	
DC	16.2	6.0	
United States	**7810.1**	**5.4**	

Rank in order by rate

1. Alaska
2. Washington
3. Oregon
4. Illinois
5. California
6. North Carolina
7. Texas
8. New Mexico
9. West Virginia
10. Louisiana
11. Mississippi
12. Michigan
13. Arizona
14. Alabama
15. New York
16. Ohio
17. Idaho
18. South Carolina
19. New Jersey
20. Utah
21. Kentucky
22. Pennsylvania
23. Massachusetts
24. Colorado
25. Florida
26. Wisconsin
27. Rhode Island
28. Indiana
29. Arkansas
30. Nevada
31. Missouri
32. Tennessee
33. Georgia
34. Kansas
35. New Hampshire
36. Hawaii
37. Oklahoma
38. Connecticut
39. Delaware
40. Maine
41. Maryland
42. Minnesota
43. Vermont
44. Montana
45. Virginia
46. Iowa
47. Wyoming
48. North Dakota
49. Nebraska
50. South Dakota

Note: Numbers that appear to be identical are rounded and vary slightly in actual value. The rankings reflect the actual values before rounding. See the introduction for more details.

B-13 Employment and Employment Rate, 2002

State	Employed (in thousands)	Employment rate (percentage of labor force employed)	Rank by rate
Alabama	2,030	94.3	37
Alaska	309	92.5	50
Arizona	2,356	94.3	38
Arkansas	1,224	95.0	22
California	16,428	93.7	46
Colorado	2,248	94.8	27
Connecticut	1,650	95.9	13
Delaware	396	95.9	12
Florida	7,397	94.9	26
Georgia	4,034	95.3	18
Hawaii	571	95.8	15
Idaho	649	94.5	34
Illinois	5,847	93.7	47
Indiana	2,998	95.0	23
Iowa	1,567	96.1	5
Kansas	1,390	95.4	17
Kentucky	1,887	94.8	30
Louisiana	1,891	94.1	41
Maine	656	95.9	11
Maryland	2,787	96.0	10
Massachusetts	3,206	94.8	28
Michigan	4,846	94.2	39
Minnesota	2,737	96.0	9
Mississippi	1,226	94.1	40
Missouri	2,800	95.2	20
Montana	451	96.1	7
Nebraska	919	96.6	2
Nevada	995	95.1	21
New Hampshire	682	95.5	16
New Jersey	4,030	94.7	32
New Mexico	807	93.9	43
New York	8,494	94.4	36
North Carolina	3,727	93.9	45
North Dakota	327	96.5	3
Ohio	5,568	94.5	35
Oklahoma	1,618	95.8	14
Oregon	1,682	93.2	48
Pennsylvania	5,791	94.8	29
Rhode Island	483	95.0	24
South Carolina	1,903	94.7	33
South Dakota	399	97.4	1
Tennessee	2,739	95.2	19
Texas	10,082	93.9	44
Utah	1,079	94.7	31
Vermont	333	96.0	8
Virginia	3,631	96.1	6
Washington	2,853	92.6	49
West Virginia	760	93.9	42
Wisconsin	2,911	94.9	25
Wyoming	261	96.1	4
50 States	135,654	94.6	
DC	254	94.0	
United States	135,908	94.6	

Rank in order by rate

1. South Dakota
2. Nebraska
3. North Dakota
4. Wyoming
5. Iowa
6. Virginia
7. Montana
8. Vermont
9. Minnesota
10. Maryland
11. Maine
12. Delaware
13. Connecticut
14. Oklahoma
15. Hawaii
16. New Hampshire
17. Kansas
18. Georgia
19. Tennessee
20. Missouri
21. Nevada
22. Arkansas
23. Indiana
24. Rhode Island
25. Wisconsin
26. Florida
27. Colorado
28. Massachusetts
29. Pennsylvania
30. Kentucky
31. Utah
32. New Jersey
33. South Carolina
34. Idaho
35. Ohio
36. New York
37. Alabama
38. Arizona
39. Michigan
40. Mississippi
41. Louisiana
42. West Virginia
43. New Mexico
44. Texas
45. North Carolina
46. California
47. Illinois
48. Oregon
49. Washington
50. Alaska

Note: Numbers that appear to be identical are rounded and vary slightly in actual value. The rankings reflect the actual values before rounding. See the introduction for more details.

B-14 Government Employment, 2002

State	Government employment (in thousands)	Percentage of total employment	Rank by percentage
Alabama	357	18.8	15
Alaska	81	27.4	1
Arizona	380	17.0	28
Arkansas	195	17.0	27
California	2,458	16.8	30
Colorado	355	16.2	32
Connecticut	249	14.9	38
Delaware	57	13.6	47
Florida	1,051	14.5	41
Georgia	611	15.8	34
Hawaii	117	21.3	6
Idaho	112	19.9	8
Illinois	836	14.1	44
Indiana	415	14.3	43
Iowa	249	16.9	29
Kansas	254	18.6	16
Kentucky	317	17.2	23
Louisiana	379	19.6	11
Maine	105	17.2	24
Maryland	465	18.9	14
Massachusetts	428	13.1	48
Michigan	700	15.4	35
Minnesota	404	15.3	36
Mississippi	244	21.6	5
Missouri	426	15.9	33
Montana	84	21.3	7
Nebraska	157	17.3	21
Nevada	130	12.1	50
New Hampshire	85	13.7	45
New Jersey	604	15.1	37
New Mexico	193	25.3	3
New York	1,494	17.5	19
North Carolina	646	16.6	31
North Dakota	75	22.7	4
Ohio	802	14.6	40
Oklahoma	299	19.7	10
Oregon	270	17.1	26
Pennsylvania	730	13.0	49
Rhode Island	66	13.6	46
South Carolina	321	17.5	20
South Dakota	75	19.8	9
Tennessee	401	14.9	39
Texas	1,627	17.3	22
Utah	196	18.4	17
Vermont	51	17.1	25
Virginia	628	18.0	18
Washington	512	19.5	12
West Virginia	141	19.4	13
Wisconsin	411	14.5	42
Wyoming	63	25.5	2
50 States	21,302	16.3	
DC	222	34.1	
United States	21,524	16.4	

Rank in order by percentage	
1	Alaska
2	Wyoming
3	New Mexico
4	North Dakota
5	Mississippi
6	Hawaii
7	Montana
8	Idaho
9	South Dakota
10	Oklahoma
11	Louisiana
12	Washington
13	West Virginia
14	Maryland
15	Alabama
16	Kansas
17	Utah
18	Virginia
19	New York
20	South Carolina
21	Nebraska
22	Texas
23	Kentucky
24	Maine
25	Vermont
26	Oregon
27	Arkansas
28	Arizona
29	Iowa
30	California
31	North Carolina
32	Colorado
33	Missouri
34	Georgia
35	Michigan
36	Minnesota
37	New Jersey
38	Connecticut
39	Tennessee
40	Ohio
41	Florida
42	Wisconsin
43	Indiana
44	Illinois
45	New Hampshire
46	Rhode Island
47	Delaware
48	Massachusetts
49	Pennsylvania
50	Nevada

Note: Numbers that appear to be identical are rounded and vary slightly in actual value. The rankings reflect the actual values before rounding. See the introduction for more details.

B-15 Manufacturing Employment, 2002

State	Manufacturing employment (in thousands)	Percentage of total employment	Rank by percentage
Alabama	327	17.2	8
Alaska	14	4.6	47
Arizona	193	8.6	40
Arkansas	227	19.7	4
California	1,804	12.3	27
Colorado	184	8.4	41
Connecticut	240	14.3	20
Delaware	54	13.0	24
Florida	443	6.1	44
Georgia	539	13.9	21
Hawaii	18	3.2	50
Idaho	71	12.7	25
Illinois	881	14.9	16
Indiana	620	21.4	1
Iowa	246	16.8	11
Kansas	200	14.6	18
Kentucky	299	16.3	12
Louisiana	178	9.2	39
Maine	75	12.3	28
Maryland	171	6.9	43
Massachusetts	399	12.2	29
Michigan	906	19.9	3
Minnesota	403	15.2	14
Mississippi	207	18.3	5
Missouri	359	13.4	23
Montana	24	5.9	45
Nebraska	113	12.4	26
Nevada	46	4.3	48
New Hampshire	99	15.9	13
New Jersey	421	10.5	35
New Mexico	41	5.3	46
New York	790	9.2	38
North Carolina	702	18.0	7
North Dakota	25	7.6	42
Ohio	998	18.1	6
Oklahoma	174	11.5	32
Oregon	227	14.3	19
Pennsylvania	845	15.0	15
Rhode Island	67	13.9	22
South Carolina	314	17.1	10
South Dakota	43	11.5	31
Tennessee	464	17.2	9
Texas	999	10.6	34
Utah	120	11.3	33
Vermont	44	14.8	17
Virginia	357	10.2	36
Washington	303	11.5	30
West Virginia	73	10.1	37
Wisconsin	570	20.1	2
Wyoming	11	4.3	49
50 States	16,923	13.0	
DC	11	1.7	
United States	16,934	12.9	

Rank in order by percentage

1 Indiana
2 Wisconsin
3 Michigan
4 Arkansas
5 Mississippi
6 Ohio
7 North Carolina
8 Alabama
9 Tennessee
10 South Carolina
11 Iowa
12 Kentucky
13 New Hampshire
14 Minnesota
15 Pennsylvania
16 Illinois
17 Vermont
18 Kansas
19 Oregon
20 Connecticut
21 Georgia
22 Rhode Island
23 Missouri
24 Delaware
25 Idaho
26 Nebraska
27 California
28 Maine
29 Massachusetts
30 Washington
31 South Dakota
32 Oklahoma
33 Utah
34 Texas
35 New Jersey
36 Virginia
37 West Virginia
38 New York
39 Louisiana
40 Arizona
41 Colorado
42 North Dakota
43 Maryland
44 Florida
45 Montana
46 New Mexico
47 Alaska
48 Nevada
49 Wyoming
50 Hawaii

Note: Numbers that appear to be identical are rounded and vary slightly in actual value. The rankings reflect the actual values before rounding. See the introduction for more details.

B-16 *Fortune* 500 Companies, 2002

State	Number of *Fortune* 500 companies	*Fortune* 500 companies per million population	Rank per million
Alabama	7	1.6	25
Alaska	n/a	n/a	n/a
Arizona	4	0.8	32
Arkansas	5	1.9	19
California	56	1.6	24
Colorado	6	1.4	26
Connecticut	13	3.8	1
Delaware	3	3.8	2
Florida	11	0.7	35
Georgia	14	1.7	23
Hawaii	n/a	n/a	n/a
Idaho	4	3.0	4
Illinois	36	2.9	6
Indiana	5	0.8	31
Iowa	2	0.7	34
Kansas	2	0.7	33
Kentucky	5	1.2	29
Louisiana	1	0.2	40
Maine	n/a	n/a	n/a
Maryland	7	1.3	28
Massachusetts	13	2.0	15
Michigan	22	2.2	11
Minnesota	16	3.2	3
Mississippi	1	0.3	38
Missouri	12	2.1	13
Montana	n/a	n/a	n/a
Nebraska	5	2.9	5
Nevada	4	1.9	17
New Hampshire	n/a	n/a	n/a
New Jersey	21	2.5	8
New Mexico	n/a	n/a	n/a
New York	51	2.7	7
North Carolina	14	1.7	22
North Dakota	n/a	n/a	n/a
Ohio	28	2.5	9
Oklahoma	6	1.7	21
Oregon	2	0.6	36
Pennsylvania	26	2.1	14
Rhode Island	2	1.9	18
South Carolina	1	0.2	39
South Dakota	1	1.3	27
Tennessee	7	1.2	30
Texas	46	2.2	12
Utah	1	0.4	37
Vermont	n/a	n/a	n/a
Virginia	16	2.2	10
Washington	11	1.8	20
West Virginia	n/a	n/a	n/a
Wisconsin	11	2.0	16
Wyoming	n/a	n/a	n/a
50 States	498	1.8	
DC	2	3.5	
United States	500	1.8	

Rank in order per million

1. Connecticut
2. Delaware
3. Minnesota
4. Idaho
5. Nebraska
6. Illinois
7. New York
8. New Jersey
9. Ohio
10. Virginia
11. Michigan
12. Texas
13. Missouri
14. Pennsylvania
15. Massachusetts
16. Wisconsin
17. Nevada
18. Rhode Island
19. Arkansas
20. Washington
21. Oklahoma
22. North Carolina
23. Georgia
24. California
25. Alabama
26. Colorado
27. South Dakota
28. Maryland
29. Kentucky
30. Tennessee
31. Indiana
32. Arizona
33. Kansas
34. Iowa
35. Florida
36. Oregon
37. Utah
38. Mississippi
39. South Carolina
40. Louisiana

Note: Numbers that appear to be identical are rounded and vary slightly in actual value. The rankings reflect the actual values before rounding. See the introduction for more details.

B-17 *Forbes* 500 Companies, 2002

State	Number of *Forbes* 500 companies	*Forbes* 500 companies per million companies	Rank per million
Alabama	11	2.5	24
Alaska	0	n/a	n/a
Arizona	8	1.5	37
Arkansas	5	1.9	30
California	110	3.2	15
Colorado	15	3.4	13
Connecticut	23	6.7	1
Delaware	5	6.3	2
Florida	22	1.3	41
Georgia	17	2.0	27
Hawaii	2	1.6	35
Idaho	4	3.0	17
Illinois	50	4.0	6
Indiana	12	2.0	28
Iowa	5	1.7	33
Kansas	5	1.9	31
Kentucky	6	1.5	38
Louisiana	6	1.3	40
Maine	2	1.6	36
Maryland	14	2.6	22
Massachusetts	28	4.4	4
Michigan	29	2.9	19
Minnesota	22	4.4	3
Mississippi	4	1.4	39
Missouri	20	3.6	10
Montana	0	n/a	n/a
Nebraska	5	2.9	18
Nevada	5	2.4	25
New Hampshire	1	0.8	44
New Jersey	31	3.7	8
New Mexico	3	1.6	34
New York	81	4.3	5
North Carolina	16	2.0	29
North Dakota	2	3.2	16
Ohio	41	3.6	9
Oklahoma	12	3.5	11
Oregon	2	0.6	45
Pennsylvania	42	3.4	12
Rhode Island	3	2.8	20
South Carolina	4	1.0	43
South Dakota	2	2.6	21
Tennessee	10	1.7	32
Texas	70	3.3	14
Utah	3	1.3	42
Vermont	0	n/a	n/a
Virginia	27	3.8	7
Washington	15	2.5	23
West Virginia	1	0.6	46
Wisconsin	12	2.2	26
Wyoming	0	n/a	n/a
50 States	813	2.9	
DC	6	10.5	
United States*	824	2.9	

Rank in order per million

1. Connecticut
2. Delaware
3. Minnesota
4. Massachusetts
5. New York
6. Illinois
7. Virginia
8. New Jersey
9. Ohio
10. Missouri
11. Oklahoma
12. Pennsylvania
13. Colorado
14. Texas
15. California
16. North Dakota
17. Idaho
18. Nebraska
19. Michigan
20. Rhode Island
21. South Dakota
22. Maryland
23. Washington
24. Alabama
25. Nevada
26. Wisconsin
27. Georgia
28. Indiana
29. North Carolina
30. Arkansas
31. Kansas
32. Tennessee
33. Iowa
34. New Mexico
35. Hawaii
36. Maine
37. Arizona
38. Kentucky
39. Mississippi
40. Louisiana
41. Florida
42. Utah
43. South Carolina
44. New Hampshire
45. Oregon
46. West Virginia

Note: Numbers that appear to be identical are rounded and vary slightly in actual value. The rankings reflect the actual values before rounding. See the introduction for more details.

Due to rounding or data sources, the 50-state total plus D.C. may not equal the U.S. total. Please see introduction.

B-18 Tourism Spending, 2000

State	Tourism spending $ (in millions)	Percentage of U.S. total	Per capita $	Rank per capita
Alabama	5,291	0.9	1,190	47
Alaska	1,543	0.3	2,462	6
Arizona	10,606	1.9	2,067	14
Arkansas	3,845	0.7	1,438	40
California	78,134	13.8	2,307	8
Colorado	10,190	1.8	2,369	7
Connecticut	6,967	1.2	2,046	15
Delaware	1,141	0.2	1,456	39
Florida	59,848	10.5	3,745	3
Georgia	15,482	2.7	1,891	20
Hawaii	15,115	2.7	12,476	1
Idaho	2,310	0.4	1,785	26
Illinois	23,705	4.2	1,909	19
Indiana	6,701	1.2	1,102	49
Iowa	4,470	0.8	1,528	36
Kansas	3,686	0.6	1,371	41
Kentucky	5,331	0.9	1,319	43
Louisiana	9,018	1.6	2,018	16
Maine	2,122	0.4	1,664	32
Maryland	8,793	1.5	1,660	33
Massachusetts	13,158	2.3	2,072	12
Michigan	12,793	2.3	1,287	45
Minnesota	8,401	1.5	1,708	31
Mississippi	5,047	0.9	1,774	27
Missouri	9,790	1.7	1,750	28
Montana	2,064	0.4	2,288	9
Nebraska	2,717	0.5	1,588	35
Nevada	22,434	4.0	11,227	2
New Hampshire	2,616	0.5	2,117	11
New Jersey	15,683	2.8	1,864	23
New Mexico	3,910	0.7	2,150	10
New York	39,281	6.9	2,070	13
North Carolina	12,810	2.3	1,591	34
North Dakota	1,201	0.2	1,871	22
Ohio	13,571	2.4	1,195	46
Oklahoma	3,938	0.7	1,141	48
Oregon	5,912	1.0	1,728	29
Pennsylvania	15,954	2.8	1,299	44
Rhode Island	1,531	0.3	1,461	38
South Carolina	7,372	1.3	1,838	24
South Dakota	1,442	0.3	1,910	18
Tennessee	10,314	1.8	1,813	25
Texas	36,014	6.3	1,727	30
Utah	4,205	0.7	1,883	21
Vermont	1,531	0.3	2,515	5
Virginia	13,673	2.4	1,932	17
Washington	8,994	1.6	1,526	37
West Virginia	1,749	0.3	967	50
Wisconsin	7,124	1.3	1,328	42
Wyoming	1,626	0.3	3,294	4
50 States	561,155	98.9	1,998	
DC	6,336	1.1	11,075	
United States	567,491	100.0	2,017	

Rank in order per capita	
1	Hawaii
2	Nevada
3	Florida
4	Wyoming
5	Vermont
6	Alaska
7	Colorado
8	California
9	Montana
10	New Mexico
11	New Hampshire
12	Massachusetts
13	New York
14	Arizona
15	Connecticut
16	Louisiana
17	Virginia
18	South Dakota
19	Illinois
20	Georgia
21	Utah
22	North Dakota
23	New Jersey
24	South Carolina
25	Tennessee
26	Idaho
27	Mississippi
28	Missouri
29	Oregon
30	Texas
31	Minnesota
32	Maine
33	Maryland
34	North Carolina
35	Nebraska
36	Iowa
37	Washington
38	Rhode Island
39	Delaware
40	Arkansas
41	Kansas
42	Wisconsin
43	Kentucky
44	Pennsylvania
45	Michigan
46	Ohio
47	Alabama
48	Oklahoma
49	Indiana
50	West Virginia

State	Exports $ (millions)	Exports per capita $	Rank per capita
Alabama	7,570	1,696	27
Alaska	2,418	3,809	4
Arizona	12,514	2,358	15
Arkansas	2,911	1,081	42
California	106,777	3,095	7
Colorado	6,126	1,387	36
Connecticut	8,610	2,514	10
Delaware	1,985	2,493	11
Florida	27,185	1,658	28
Georgia	14,644	1,747	26
Hawaii	370	302	50
Idaho	2,122	1,606	30
Illinois	30,434	2,438	13
Indiana	14,365	2,349	16
Iowa	4,660	1,594	31
Kansas	5,005	1,857	25
Kentucky	9,048	2,226	18
Louisiana	16,589	3,715	5
Maine	1,813	1,409	35
Maryland	4,975	926	44
Massachusetts	17,490	2,742	8
Michigan	32,366	3,240	6
Minnesota	10,524	2,117	20
Mississippi	3,557	1,245	38
Missouri	6,173	1,097	41
Montana	489	540	49
Nebraska	2,702	1,577	32
Nevada	1,423	676	48
New Hampshire	2,401	1,907	24
New Jersey	18,946	2,233	17
New Mexico	1,405	768	47
New York	42,172	2,218	19
North Carolina	16,799	2,052	21
North Dakota	806	1,271	37
Ohio	27,095	2,382	14
Oklahoma	2,661	769	46
Oregon	8,900	2,563	9
Pennsylvania	17,433	1,419	34
Rhode Island	1,269	1,198	40
South Carolina	9,956	2,450	12
South Dakota	595	786	45
Tennessee	11,320	1,972	22
Texas	94,995	4,455	3
Utah	3,506	1,545	33
Vermont	2,830	4,617	2
Virginia	11,631	1,618	29
Washington	34,929	5,833	1
West Virginia	2,241	1,244	39
Wisconsin	10,489	1,942	23
Wyoming	503	1,018	43
50 States	677,726	2,384	
DC	1,034	1,808	
United States*	730,897	2,566	

	Rank in order per capita
1	Washington
2	Vermont
3	Texas
4	Alaska
5	Louisiana
6	Michigan
7	California
8	Massachusetts
9	Oregon
10	Connecticut
11	Delaware
12	South Carolina
13	Illinois
14	Ohio
15	Arizona
16	Indiana
17	New Jersey
18	Kentucky
19	New York
20	Minnesota
21	North Carolina
22	Tennessee
23	Wisconsin
24	New Hampshire
25	Kansas
26	Georgia
27	Alabama
28	Florida
29	Virginia
30	Idaho
31	Iowa
32	Nebraska
33	Utah
34	Pennsylvania
35	Maine
36	Colorado
37	North Dakota
38	Mississippi
39	West Virginia
40	Rhode Island
41	Missouri
42	Arkansas
43	Wyoming
44	Maryland
45	South Dakota
46	Oklahoma
47	New Mexico
48	Nevada
49	Montana
50	Hawaii

Due to rounding or data sources, the 50-state total plus D.C. may not equal the U.S. total. Please see introduction.

B-20 Housing Permits, 2001

State	Housing permits	Permits per 10,000 population	Rank per 10,000
Alabama	17,706	39.7	36
Alaska	2,939	46.3	27
Arizona	62,496	117.8	3
Arkansas	10,407	38.7	38
California	146,739	42.5	34
Colorado	55,007	124.5	2
Connecticut	9,290	27.1	46
Delaware	4,814	60.5	17
Florida	167,035	101.9	5
Georgia	93,059	111.0	4
Hawaii	4,790	39.1	37
Idaho	11,820	89.5	7
Illinois	54,839	43.9	31
Indiana	39,117	64.0	15
Iowa	13,085	44.8	29
Kansas	14,530	53.9	22
Kentucky	17,685	43.5	33
Louisiana	15,653	35.1	41
Maine	6,492	50.5	24
Maryland	29,059	54.1	21
Massachusetts	17,034	26.7	47
Michigan	50,139	50.2	25
Minnesota	34,131	68.7	13
Mississippi	9,908	34.7	42
Missouri	24,739	43.9	30
Montana	2,604	28.8	45
Nebraska	8,198	47.9	26
Nevada	36,125	171.5	1
New Hampshire	6,624	52.6	23
New Jersey	28,267	33.3	44
New Mexico	9,989	54.6	20
New York	45,542	24.0	48
North Carolina	82,030	100.2	6
North Dakota	2,687	42.4	35
Ohio	49,931	43.9	32
Oklahoma	12,352	35.7	40
Oregon	21,322	61.4	16
Pennsylvania	41,403	33.7	43
Rhode Island	2,407	22.7	49
South Carolina	30,133	74.2	9
South Dakota	4,455	58.9	18
Tennessee	32,370	56.4	19
Texas	150,342	70.5	11
Utah	18,887	83.2	8
Vermont	2,747	44.8	28
Virginia	52,860	73.5	10
Washington	38,345	64.0	14
West Virginia	3,947	21.9	50
Wisconsin	37,773	69.9	12
Wyoming	1,907	38.6	39
50 States	1,635,780	57.6	
DC	896	15.7	
United States	1,636,676	57.5	

Rank in order per 10,000 population

1	Nevada
2	Colorado
3	Arizona
4	Georgia
5	Florida
6	North Carolina
7	Idaho
8	Utah
9	South Carolina
10	Virginia
11	Texas
12	Wisconsin
13	Minnesota
14	Washington
15	Indiana
16	Oregon
17	Delaware
18	South Dakota
19	Tennessee
20	New Mexico
21	Maryland
22	Kansas
23	New Hampshire
24	Maine
25	Michigan
26	Nebraska
27	Alaska
28	Vermont
29	Iowa
30	Missouri
31	Illinois
32	Ohio
33	Kentucky
34	California
35	North Dakota
36	Alabama
37	Hawaii
38	Arkansas
39	Wyoming
40	Oklahoma
41	Louisiana
42	Mississippi
43	Pennsylvania
44	New Jersey
45	Montana
46	Connecticut
47	Massachusetts
48	New York
49	Rhode Island
50	West Virginia

Note: Numbers that appear to be identical are rounded and vary slightly in actual value. The rankings reflect the actual values before rounding. See the introduction for more details.

B-21 Percentage Change in Home Prices, 1997-2002

State	Percentage change in price	Rank
Alabama	23.18	41
Alaska	25.12	36
Arizona	34.38	19
Arkansas	20.48	46
California	63.25	3
Colorado	50.96	5
Connecticut	43.40	11
Delaware	34.78	16
Florida	43.62	10
Georgia	37.21	15
Hawaii	17.88	48
Idaho	19.48	47
Illinois	29.71	25
Indiana	22.89	43
Iowa	26.71	29
Kansas	31.88	20
Kentucky	25.93	31
Louisiana	25.80	32
Maine	48.52	8
Maryland	34.70	17
Massachusetts	69.78	1
Michigan	37.46	13
Minnesota	56.92	4
Mississippi	23.90	39
Missouri	31.88	20
Montana	25.20	35
Nebraska	24.42	38
Nevada	22.85	44
New Hampshire	65.91	2
New Jersey	47.74	9
New Mexico	15.23	50
New York	50.67	7
North Carolina	26.39	30
North Dakota	21.32	45
Ohio	27.17	28
Oklahoma	27.54	26
Oregon	24.68	37
Pennsylvania	27.37	27
Rhode Island	50.82	6
South Carolina	30.27	23
South Dakota	25.56	33
Tennessee	23.43	40
Texas	31.79	22
Utah	16.81	49
Vermont	37.46	14
Virginia	38.38	12
Washington	34.68	18
West Virginia	23.11	42
Wisconsin	30.02	24
Wyoming	25.36	34
50 States	n/a	
DC	71.24	
United States	38.71	

Rank in order by percentage

1	Massachusetts
2	New Hampshire
3	California
4	Minnesota
5	Colorado
6	Rhode Island
7	New York
8	Maine
9	New Jersey
10	Florida
11	Connecticut
12	Virginia
13	Michigan
14	Vermont
15	Georgia
16	Delaware
17	Maryland
18	Washington
19	Arizona
20	Kansas
20	Missouri
22	Texas
23	South Carolina
24	Wisconsin
25	Illinois
26	Oklahoma
27	Pennsylvania
28	Ohio
29	Iowa
30	North Carolina
31	Kentucky
32	Louisiana
33	South Dakota
34	Wyoming
35	Montana
36	Alaska
37	Oregon
38	Nebraska
39	Mississippi
40	Tennessee
41	Alabama
42	West Virginia
43	Indiana
44	Nevada
45	North Dakota
46	Arkansas
47	Idaho
48	Hawaii
49	Utah
50	New Mexico

Note: Ties in ranking reflect ties in actual values.

B-22 Net Farm Income, 2001

State	Net farm income $ (in thousands)	Net farm income per capita $	Rank by total income
Alabama	1,581,452	354	8
Alaska	10,144	16	49
Arizona	1,003,699	189	16
Arkansas	1,399,823	520	10
California	3,768,764	109	2
Colorado	989,681	224	17
Connecticut	144,018	42	41
Delaware	217,857	274	37
Florida	2,166,133	132	5
Georgia	2,298,556	274	4
Hawaii	93,897	77	44
Idaho	1,147,092	868	13
Illinois	1,418,739	114	9
Indiana	964,199	158	19
Iowa	1,946,475	666	6
Kansas	958,188	356	20
Kentucky	1,229,695	302	11
Louisiana	418,095	94	33
Maine	82,397	64	45
Maryland	521,901	97	31
Massachusetts	27,327	4	47
Michigan	190,607	19	39
Minnesota	695,508	140	26
Mississippi	1,111,748	389	14
Missouri	909,969	162	22
Montana	303,919	336	35
Nebraska	1,610,282	940	7
Nevada	119,231	57	43
New Hampshire	12,594	10	48
New Jersey	188,837	22	40
New Mexico	819,647	448	24
New York	802,820	42	25
North Carolina	3,201,148	391	3
North Dakota	586,777	925	30
Ohio	1,049,230	92	15
Oklahoma	922,482	267	21
Oregon	265,856	77	36
Pennsylvania	968,555	79	18
Rhode Island	5,542	5	50
South Carolina	684,031	168	27
South Dakota	1,217,697	1,609	12
Tennessee	510,788	89	32
Texas	4,288,138	201	1
Utah	394,636	174	34
Vermont	136,045	222	42
Virginia	600,139	83	29
Washington	620,758	104	28
West Virginia	47,703	26	46
Wisconsin	888,360	164	23
Wyoming	199,756	404	38
50 States	45,740,933	161	
DC	n/a	n/a	
United States	45,740,933	161	

Rank in order by total income

1 Texas
2 California
3 North Carolina
4 Georgia
5 Florida
6 Iowa
7 Nebraska
8 Alabama
9 Illinois
10 Arkansas
11 Kentucky
12 South Dakota
13 Idaho
14 Mississippi
15 Ohio
16 Arizona
17 Colorado
18 Pennsylvania
19 Indiana
20 Kansas
21 Oklahoma
22 Missouri
23 Wisconsin
24 New Mexico
25 New York
26 Minnesota
27 South Carolina
28 Washington
29 Virginia
30 North Dakota
31 Maryland
32 Tennessee
33 Louisiana
34 Utah
35 Montana
36 Oregon
37 Delaware
38 Wyoming
39 Michigan
40 New Jersey
41 Connecticut
42 Vermont
43 Nevada
44 Hawaii
45 Maine
46 West Virginia
47 Massachusetts
48 New Hampshire
49 Alaska
50 Rhode Island

B-23 Financial Institution Assets, 2001

State	Total assets $ (in millions)	Per capita assets $	Rank per capita
Alabama	192,023	43,012	8
Alaska	6,606	10,405	43
Arizona	44,138	8,316	47
Arkansas	31,570	11,727	38
California	768,139	22,264	16
Colorado	50,895	11,521	39
Connecticut	51,056	14,907	29
Delaware	188,692	237,001	1
Florida	88,808	5,416	49
Georgia	183,537	21,892	18
Hawaii	29,990	24,494	14
Idaho	3,649	2,762	50
Illinois	476,309	38,159	9
Indiana	127,758	20,893	19
Iowa	52,312	17,896	23
Kansas	48,451	17,981	22
Kentucky	58,661	14,429	32
Louisiana	47,499	10,637	40
Maine	16,323	12,686	36
Maryland	57,130	10,629	41
Massachusetts	185,248	29,039	11
Michigan	175,175	17,534	24
Minnesota	110,454	22,214	17
Mississippi	36,417	12,742	35
Missouri	76,712	13,626	34
Montana	14,363	15,881	26
Nebraska	46,608	27,205	13
Nevada	35,617	16,912	25
New Hampshire	35,450	28,153	12
New Jersey	121,955	14,374	33
New Mexico	18,698	10,222	44
New York	1,496,542	78,718	4
North Carolina	962,553	117,581	3
North Dakota	19,654	30,978	10
Ohio	550,688	48,418	7
Oklahoma	52,985	15,313	27
Oregon	20,203	5,817	48
Pennsylvania	273,578	22,265	15
Rhode Island	207,626	196,073	2
South Carolina	33,901	8,344	46
South Dakota	52,181	68,968	5
Tennessee	105,961	18,460	21
Texas	199,342	9,348	45
Utah	133,158	58,665	6
Vermont	8,989	14,662	31
Virginia	106,824	14,862	30
Washington	72,542	12,115	37
West Virginia	19,072	10,584	42
Wisconsin	103,370	19,136	20
Wyoming	7,383	14,933	28
50 States	7,806,795	27,467	
DC	691	1,208	
United States*	7,868,249	27,628	

Rank in order per capita	
1	Delaware
2	Rhode Island
3	North Carolina
4	New York
5	South Dakota
6	Utah
7	Ohio
8	Alabama
9	Illinois
10	North Dakota
11	Massachusetts
12	New Hampshire
13	Nebraska
14	Hawaii
15	Pennsylvania
16	California
17	Minnesota
18	Georgia
19	Indiana
20	Wisconsin
21	Tennessee
22	Kansas
23	Iowa
24	Michigan
25	Nevada
26	Montana
27	Oklahoma
28	Wyoming
29	Connecticut
30	Virginia
31	Vermont
32	Kentucky
33	New Jersey
34	Missouri
35	Mississippi
36	Maine
37	Washington
38	Arkansas
39	Colorado
40	Louisiana
41	Maryland
42	West Virginia
43	Alaska
44	New Mexico
45	Texas
46	South Carolina
47	Arizona
48	Oregon
49	Florida
50	Idaho

Due to rounding or data sources, the 50-state total plus D.C. may not equal the U.S. total. Please see introduction.

B-24 Bankruptcy Filings by Individuals and Businesses, 2002

State	Bankruptcy petitions	Petitions per 1,000 residents	Rank per 1,000
Alabama	39,099	8.76	4
Alaska	1,454	2.29	50
Arizona	26,265	4.95	24
Arkansas	21,572	8.01	7
California	152,601	4.42	30
Colorado	18,856	4.27	32
Connecticut	11,387	3.32	46
Delaware	4,079	5.12	23
Florida	88,085	5.37	21
Georgia	71,518	8.53	5
Hawaii	4,977	4.06	37
Idaho	8,389	6.35	14
Illinois	76,418	6.12	16
Indiana	49,792	8.14	6
Iowa	11,205	3.83	38
Kansas	13,947	5.18	22
Kentucky	26,363	6.48	12
Louisiana	26,960	6.04	17
Maine	4,552	3.54	44
Maryland	35,294	6.57	11
Massachusetts	17,205	2.70	49
Michigan	48,416	4.85	26
Minnesota	18,815	3.78	39
Mississippi	22,153	7.75	8
Missouri	31,228	5.55	20
Montana	3,962	4.38	31
Nebraska	7,213	4.21	34
Nevada	18,458	8.76	3
New Hampshire	3,904	3.10	47
New Jersey	41,322	4.87	25
New Mexico	8,668	4.74	28
New York	68,660	3.61	41
North Carolina	34,402	4.20	35
North Dakota	2,128	3.35	45
Ohio	72,910	6.41	13
Oklahoma	23,258	6.72	10
Oregon	23,470	6.76	9
Pennsylvania	52,239	4.25	33
Rhode Island	4,804	4.54	29
South Carolina	14,820	3.65	40
South Dakota	2,731	3.61	42
Tennessee	61,364	10.69	1
Texas	76,956	3.61	43
Utah	20,120	8.86	2
Vermont	1,748	2.85	48
Virginia	41,629	5.79	18
Washington	37,406	6.25	15
West Virginia	10,167	5.64	19
Wisconsin	22,635	4.19	36
Wyoming	2,394	4.84	27
50 States	1,487,998	5.24	
DC	2,556	4.47	
United States*	1,504,806	5.28	

Rank in order per 1,000 residents

1 Tennessee
2 Utah
3 Nevada
4 Alabama
5 Georgia
6 Indiana
7 Arkansas
8 Mississippi
9 Oregon
10 Oklahoma
11 Maryland
12 Kentucky
13 Ohio
14 Idaho
15 Washington
16 Illinois
17 Louisiana
18 Virginia
19 West Virginia
20 Missouri
21 Florida
22 Kansas
23 Delaware
24 Arizona
25 New Jersey
26 Michigan
27 Wyoming
28 New Mexico
29 Rhode Island
30 California
31 Montana
32 Colorado
33 Pennsylvania
34 Nebraska
35 North Carolina
36 Wisconsin
37 Hawaii
38 Iowa
39 Minnesota
40 South Carolina
41 New York
42 South Dakota
43 Texas
44 Maine
45 North Dakota
46 Connecticut
47 New Hampshire
48 Vermont
49 Massachusetts
50 Alaska

Note: Numbers that appear to be identical are rounded and vary slightly in actual value. The rankings reflect the actual values before rounding. See the introduction for more details.

*Due to rounding or data sources, the 50-state total plus D.C. may not equal the U.S. total. Please see introduction.

B-25 Patents Issued, FY 2001

State	Patents issued	Patents per 100,000 population	Rank per 100,000
Alabama	456	10.2	45
Alaska	57	9.0	47
Arizona	1,843	34.7	19
Arkansas	249	9.2	46
California	21,469	62.2	5
Colorado	2,168	49.1	10
Connecticut	2,138	62.4	4
Delaware	436	54.8	8
Florida	3,282	20.0	28
Georgia	1,672	19.9	29
Hawaii	104	8.5	49
Idaho	1,716	129.9	1
Illinois	4,516	36.2	16
Indiana	1,709	27.9	26
Iowa	845	28.9	24
Kansas	403	15.0	39
Kentucky	580	14.3	40
Louisiana	576	12.9	42
Maine	158	12.3	43
Maryland	1,629	30.3	23
Massachusetts	4,048	63.5	3
Michigan	4,419	44.2	11
Minnesota	3,027	60.9	6
Mississippi	207	7.2	50
Missouri	994	17.7	33
Montana	155	17.1	35
Nebraska	267	15.6	38
Nevada	410	19.5	30
New Hampshire	715	56.8	7
New Jersey	4,424	52.1	9
New Mexico	385	21.0	27
New York	7,334	38.6	14
North Carolina	2,296	28.0	25
North Dakota	107	16.9	36
Ohio	4,112	36.2	17
Oklahoma	637	18.4	31
Oregon	1,508	43.4	12
Pennsylvania	4,013	32.7	21
Rhode Island	343	32.4	22
South Carolina	651	16.0	37
South Dakota	90	11.9	44
Tennessee	1,005	17.5	34
Texas	6,980	32.7	20
Utah	809	35.6	18
Vermont	505	82.4	2
Virginia	1,287	17.9	32
Washington	2,229	37.2	15
West Virginia	154	8.5	48
Wisconsin	2,334	43.2	13
Wyoming	66	13.3	41
50 States	101,517	35.7	
DC	75	13.1	
United States*	101,619	35.7	

Rank in order per 100,000 population	
1	Idaho
2	Vermont
3	Massachusetts
4	Connecticut
5	California
6	Minnesota
7	New Hampshire
8	Delaware
9	New Jersey
10	Colorado
11	Michigan
12	Oregon
13	Wisconsin
14	New York
15	Washington
16	Illinois
17	Ohio
18	Utah
19	Arizona
20	Texas
21	Pennsylvania
22	Rhode Island
23	Maryland
24	Iowa
25	North Carolina
26	Indiana
27	New Mexico
28	Florida
29	Georgia
30	Nevada
31	Oklahoma
32	Virginia
33	Missouri
34	Tennessee
35	Montana
36	North Dakota
37	South Carolina
38	Nebraska
39	Kansas
40	Kentucky
41	Wyoming
42	Louisiana
43	Maine
44	South Dakota
45	Alabama
46	Arkansas
47	Alaska
48	West Virginia
49	Hawaii
50	Mississippi

Note: Numbers that appear to be identical are rounded and vary slightly in actual value. The rankings reflect the actual values before rounding. See the introduction for more details.

Due to rounding or data sources, the 50-state total plus D.C. may not equal the U.S. total. Please see introduction.

B-26 Workers' Compensation Temporary Disability Payments, 2002

State	Maximum weekly benefit $	Rank
Alabama	549.00	29
Alaska	762.00	9
Arizona	374.01	49
Arkansas	425.00	44
California	490.00	37
Colorado	645.96	16
Connecticut	887.00	5
Delaware	469.10	41
Florida	594.00	22
Georgia	400.00	46
Hawaii	564.00	25
Idaho	473.40	38
Illinois	972.12	3
Indiana	508.00	35
Iowa	1,069.00	1
Kansas	417.00	45
Kentucky	550.66	27
Louisiana	398.00	48
Maine	471.76	40
Maryland	668.00	12
Massachusetts	890.94	4
Michigan	644.00	18
Minnesota	750.00	10
Mississippi	322.90	50
Missouri	628.90	20
Montana	454.00	43
Nebraska	528.00	31
Nevada	580.72	24
New Hampshire	997.50	2
New Jersey	629.00	19
New Mexico	516.89	33
New York	400.00	46
North Carolina	654.00	14
North Dakota	516.00	34
Ohio	628.00	21
Oklahoma	473.00	39
Oregon	857.85	6
Pennsylvania	662.00	13
Rhode Island	682.00	11
South Carolina	549.42	28
South Dakota	468.00	42
Tennessee	581.00	23
Texas	533.00	30
Utah	554.00	26
Vermont	827.00	8
Virginia	645.00	17
Washington	851.28	7
West Virginia	506.49	36
Wisconsin	647.00	15
Wyoming	527.00	32
50 States	n/a	
DC	966.08	
United States	n/a	

Rank in order by $	
1	Iowa
2	New Hampshire
3	Illinois
4	Massachusetts
5	Connecticut
6	Oregon
7	Washington
8	Vermont
9	Alaska
10	Minnesota
11	Rhode Island
12	Maryland
13	Pennsylvania
14	North Carolina
15	Wisconsin
16	Colorado
17	Virginia
18	Michigan
19	New Jersey
20	Missouri
21	Ohio
22	Florida
23	Tennessee
24	Nevada
25	Hawaii
26	Utah
27	Kentucky
28	South Carolina
29	Alabama
30	Texas
31	Nebraska
32	Wyoming
33	New Mexico
34	North Dakota
35	Indiana
36	West Virginia
37	California
38	Idaho
39	Oklahoma
40	Maine
41	Delaware
42	South Dakota
43	Montana
44	Arkansas
45	Kansas
46	Georgia
46	New York
48	Louisiana
49	Arizona
50	Mississippi

Note: Ties in ranking reflect ties in actual values.

B-27 Average Unemployment Compensation Benefit, 2001

State	Average weekly UC benefit $	Rank
Alabama	164.17	49
Alaska	193.01	45
Arizona	172.74	47
Arkansas	220.10	33
California	172.01	48
Colorado	291.47	6
Connecticut	277.09	9
Delaware	220.71	32
Florida	223.24	31
Georgia	228.42	28
Hawaii	296.97	5
Idaho	223.46	30
Illinois	268.68	11
Indiana	243.98	19
Iowa	249.57	16
Kansas	260.89	12
Kentucky	234.32	25
Louisiana	193.94	43
Maine	215.83	35
Maryland	235.27	23
Massachusetts	334.72	1
Michigan	260.73	13
Minnesota	306.73	4
Mississippi	162.99	50
Missouri	200.49	40
Montana	194.19	42
Nebraska	204.80	38
Nevada	228.46	27
New Hampshire	240.59	22
New Jersey	308.91	3
New Mexico	193.23	44
New York	268.99	10
North Carolina	248.00	17
North Dakota	218.17	34
Ohio	247.65	18
Oklahoma	227.88	29
Oregon	255.97	14
Pennsylvania	281.52	8
Rhode Island	289.12	7
South Carolina	205.88	37
South Dakota	189.91	46
Tennessee	197.81	41
Texas	241.35	21
Utah	252.84	15
Vermont	232.93	26
Virginia	234.63	24
Washington	311.27	2
West Virginia	202.14	39
Wisconsin	241.71	20
Wyoming	215.31	36
50 States	n/a	
DC	261.56	
United States	238.07	

Rank in order by $	
1	Massachusetts
2	Washington
3	New Jersey
4	Minnesota
5	Hawaii
6	Colorado
7	Rhode Island
8	Pennsylvania
9	Connecticut
10	New York
11	Illinois
12	Kansas
13	Michigan
14	Oregon
15	Utah
16	Iowa
17	North Carolina
18	Ohio
19	Indiana
20	Wisconsin
21	Texas
22	New Hampshire
23	Maryland
24	Virginia
25	Kentucky
26	Vermont
27	Nevada
28	Georgia
29	Oklahoma
30	Idaho
31	Florida
32	Delaware
33	Arkansas
34	North Dakota
35	Maine
36	Wyoming
37	South Carolina
38	Nebraska
39	West Virginia
40	Missouri
41	Tennessee
42	Montana
43	Louisiana
44	New Mexico
45	Alaska
46	South Dakota
47	Arizona
48	California
49	Alabama
50	Mississippi

B-28 Index of State Economic Momentum, September 2002

State	Index of state economic momentum September 2002	Rank
Alabama	-0.19	39
Alaska	1.67	2
Arizona	0.93	6
Arkansas	0.49	13
California	0.15	29
Colorado	-0.46	42
Connecticut	-0.78	47
Delaware	0.52	12
Florida	1.44	5
Georgia	0.28	24
Hawaii	0.38	18
Idaho	0.41	16
Illinois	-0.94	49
Indiana	-0.56	44
Iowa	-0.44	41
Kansas	0.02	33
Kentucky	0.71	9
Louisiana	0.02	32
Maine	0.62	10
Maryland	0.35	19
Massachusetts	-1.02	50
Michigan	-0.56	45
Minnesota	-0.10	36
Mississippi	0.45	15
Missouri	-0.36	40
Montana	0.74	8
Nebraska	-0.17	38
Nevada	2.39	1
New Hampshire	0.38	17
New Jersey	0.02	34
New Mexico	1.58	3
New York	-0.88	48
North Carolina	0.17	28
North Dakota	0.49	14
Ohio	-0.47	43
Oklahoma	0.76	7
Oregon	-0.15	37
Pennsylvania	-0.65	46
Rhode Island	0.32	21
South Carolina	0.08	30
South Dakota	0.08	31
Tennessee	0.32	22
Texas	0.33	20
Utah	0.31	23
Vermont	0.26	25
Virginia	0.59	11
Washington	0.23	26
West Virginia	0.01	35
Wisconsin	0.22	27
Wyoming	1.57	4
50 States	0.00	
DC	0.27	
United States	0.00	

Rank in order by index	
1	Nevada
2	Alaska
3	New Mexico
4	Wyoming
5	Florida
6	Arizona
7	Oklahoma
8	Montana
9	Kentucky
10	Maine
11	Virginia
12	Delaware
13	Arkansas
14	North Dakota
15	Mississippi
16	Idaho
17	New Hampshire
18	Hawaii
19	Maryland
20	Texas
21	Rhode Island
22	Tennessee
23	Utah
24	Georgia
25	Vermont
26	Washington
27	Wisconsin
28	North Carolina
29	California
30	South Carolina
31	South Dakota
32	Louisiana
33	Kansas
34	New Jersey
35	West Virginia
36	Minnesota
37	Oregon
38	Nebraska
39	Alabama
40	Missouri
41	Iowa
42	Colorado
43	Ohio
44	Indiana
45	Michigan
46	Pennsylvania
47	Connecticut
48	New York
49	Illinois
50	Massachusetts

Note: Numbers that appear to be identical are rounded and vary slightly in actual value. The rankings reflect the actual values before rounding. See the introduction for more details.

B-29 Employment Change, 2001-2002

State	Change in number of jobs July 2001-2002 (in thousands)	Percentage change in employment	Rank by percentage change
Alabama	-20.4	-1.07	38
Alaska	1.8	0.58	7
Arizona	-25.6	-1.15	40
Arkansas	-3.7	-0.32	20
California	-58.2	-0.40	21
Colorado	-52.3	-2.33	50
Connecticut	-7.7	-0.46	24
Delaware	-2.6	-0.61	26
Florida	27.5	0.39	10
Georgia	-91.6	-2.32	49
Hawaii	-5.6	-1.02	37
Idaho	-4.3	-0.75	32
Illinois	-88.3	-1.46	44
Indiana	-36.1	-1.24	41
Iowa	-6.3	-0.43	22
Kansas	5.7	0.42	9
Kentucky	17.2	0.95	2
Louisiana	-13.1	-0.68	29
Maine	1.0	0.16	13
Maryland	-38.3	-1.55	45
Massachusetts	-46.2	-1.39	43
Michigan	-39.3	-0.87	34
Minnesota	-17.8	-0.66	28
Mississippi	-2.4	-0.21	17
Missouri	-53.4	-1.97	48
Montana	3.1	0.79	4
Nebraska	-4.9	-0.54	25
Nevada	14.2	1.35	1
New Hampshire	1.2	0.19	12
New Jersey	-18.3	-0.45	23
New Mexico	6.1	0.81	3
New York	-78.0	-0.90	35
North Carolina	-11.3	-0.29	19
North Dakota	-0.2	-0.06	15
Ohio	-53.1	-0.95	36
Oklahoma	9.9	0.66	6
Oregon	-9.9	-0.62	27
Pennsylvania	-61.7	-1.08	39
Rhode Island	3.2	0.67	5
South Carolina	-13.2	-0.72	30
South Dakota	0.1	0.03	14
Tennessee	-2.2	-0.08	16
Texas	-70.3	-0.74	31
Utah	-17.6	-1.64	46
Vermont	-0.7	-0.24	18
Virginia	-27.4	-0.78	33
Washington	-49.8	-1.84	47
West Virginia	-9.2	-1.25	42
Wisconsin	10.9	0.38	11
Wyoming	1.1	0.43	8
50 States	-938.0	-0.72	
DC	-4.2	-0.63	
United States	-942.2	-0.72	

Rank in order by percentage change

1	Nevada
2	Kentucky
3	New Mexico
4	Montana
5	Rhode Island
6	Oklahoma
7	Alaska
8	Wyoming
9	Kansas
10	Florida
11	Wisconsin
12	New Hampshire
13	Maine
14	South Dakota
15	North Dakota
16	Tennessee
17	Mississippi
18	Vermont
19	North Carolina
20	Arkansas
21	California
22	Iowa
23	New Jersey
24	Connecticut
25	Nebraska
26	Delaware
27	Oregon
28	Minnesota
29	Louisiana
30	South Carolina
31	Texas
32	Idaho
33	Virginia
34	Michigan
35	New York
36	Ohio
37	Hawaii
38	Alabama
39	Pennsylvania
40	Arizona
41	Indiana
42	West Virginia
43	Massachusetts
44	Illinois
45	Maryland
46	Utah
47	Washington
48	Missouri
49	Georgia
50	Colorado

B-30 Manufacturing Employment Change, 2001-2002

State	Change in number of manufacturing jobs July 2001-2002 (in thousands)	Percentage change in manufacturing employment	Rank by percentage change
Alabama	-10.6	-3.14	23
Alaska	-0.9	-4.13	29
Arizona	-14.7	-7.00	49
Arkansas	-10.8	-4.51	37
California	-83.1	-4.35	33
Colorado	-12.8	-6.43	48
Connecticut	-10.9	-4.34	32
Delaware	-0.9	-1.62	9
Florida	-20.7	-4.45	36
Georgia	-10.6	-1.94	11
Hawaii	-0.2	-1.11	4
Idaho	-4.8	-6.29	47
Illinois	-20.2	-2.24	16
Indiana	-19.6	-3.05	21
Iowa	-5.0	-1.98	13
Kansas	-7.8	-3.78	27
Kentucky	-5.9	-1.94	12
Louisiana	-5.5	-3.01	20
Maine	-4.9	-6.06	46
Maryland	-6.9	-3.85	28
Massachusetts	-18.0	-4.32	31
Michigan	-19.9	-2.17	15
Minnesota	-13.4	-3.17	24
Mississippi	-3.0	-1.42	8
Missouri	-17.5	-4.67	39
Montana	-0.2	-0.83	3
Nebraska	-5.0	-4.23	30
Nevada	-0.2	-0.43	2
New Hampshire	-2.5	-2.45	18
New Jersey	-24.8	-5.56	43
New Mexico	-0.6	-1.39	5
New York	-41.6	-4.96	40
North Carolina	-27.1	-3.73	26
North Dakota	-0.1	-0.39	1
Ohio	-21.4	-2.10	14
Oklahoma	-2.5	-1.40	7
Oregon	-6.8	-2.83	19
Pennsylvania	-40.3	-4.52	38
Rhode Island	-0.9	-1.39	6
South Carolina	-16.5	-4.98	41
South Dakota	-2.6	-5.60	45
Tennessee	-8.2	-1.74	10
Texas	-46.6	-4.42	35
Utah	-7.1	-5.59	44
Vermont	-2.5	-5.25	42
Virginia	-11.4	-3.11	22
Washington	-29.1	-8.52	50
West Virginia	-3.4	-4.40	34
Wisconsin	-13.3	-2.26	17
Wyoming	-0.4	-3.60	25
50 States	**-643.7**	**-3.65**	
DC	-0.3	-2.65	
United States	**-644.0**	**-3.65**	

Rank in order by percentage change

1	North Dakota
2	Nevada
3	Montana
4	Hawaii
5	New Mexico
6	Rhode Island
7	Oklahoma
8	Mississippi
9	Delaware
10	Tennessee
11	Georgia
12	Kentucky
13	Iowa
14	Ohio
15	Michigan
16	Illinois
17	Wisconsin
18	New Hampshire
19	Oregon
20	Louisiana
21	Indiana
22	Virginia
23	Alabama
24	Minnesota
25	Wyoming
26	North Carolina
27	Kansas
28	Maryland
29	Alaska
30	Nebraska
31	Massachusetts
32	Connecticut
33	California
34	West Virginia
35	Texas
36	Florida
37	Arkansas
38	Pennsylvania
39	Missouri
40	New York
41	South Carolina
42	Vermont
43	New Jersey
44	Utah
45	South Dakota
46	Maine
47	Idaho
48	Colorado
49	Arizona
50	Washington

Note: Numbers that appear to be identical are rounded and vary slightly in actual value. The rankings reflect the actual values before rounding. See the introduction for more details.

B-31 Home Ownership, 1997-2001

State	Home ownership rate (as percentage)	Rank
Alabama	73.08	12
Alaska	66.32	39
Arizona	65.94	40
Arkansas	67.82	35
California	56.54	48
Colorado	66.84	38
Connecticut	69.66	26
Delaware	71.84	14
Florida	67.80	36
Georgia	70.66	22
Hawaii	54.06	49
Idaho	71.48	17
Illinois	68.10	33
Indiana	73.96	10
Iowa	74.10	9
Kansas	68.08	34
Kentucky	74.26	8
Louisiana	67.00	37
Maine	75.78	3
Maryland	69.88	25
Massachusetts	60.88	46
Michigan	75.70	4
Minnesota	75.82	2
Mississippi	74.68	6
Missouri	72.46	13
Montana	69.04	31
Nebraska	69.56	29
Nevada	62.98	44
New Hampshire	68.84	32
New Jersey	64.68	41
New Mexico	71.60	15
New York	53.10	50
North Carolina	71.12	18
North Dakota	69.58	28
Ohio	70.58	23
Oklahoma	70.78	20
Oregon	63.96	43
Pennsylvania	74.28	7
Rhode Island	60.14	47
South Carolina	76.08	1
South Dakota	69.66	26
Tennessee	70.80	19
Texas	62.92	45
Utah	73.20	11
Vermont	69.16	30
Virginia	71.60	15
Washington	64.52	42
West Virginia	75.30	5
Wisconsin	70.68	21
Wyoming	70.38	24
50 States	n/a	
DC	41.48	
United States	66.80	

Rank in order by rate

1	South Carolina
2	Minnesota
3	Maine
4	Michigan
5	West Virginia
6	Mississippi
7	Pennsylvania
8	Kentucky
9	Iowa
10	Indiana
11	Utah
12	Alabama
13	Missouri
14	Delaware
15	New Mexico
15	Virginia
17	Idaho
18	North Carolina
19	Tennessee
20	Oklahoma
21	Wisconsin
22	Georgia
23	Ohio
24	Wyoming
25	Maryland
26	Connecticut
26	South Dakota
28	North Dakota
29	Nebraska
30	Vermont
31	Montana
32	New Hampshire
33	Illinois
34	Kansas
35	Arkansas
36	Florida
37	Louisiana
38	Colorado
39	Alaska
40	Arizona
41	New Jersey
42	Washington
43	Oregon
44	Nevada
45	Texas
46	Massachusetts
47	Rhode Island
48	California
49	Hawaii
50	New York

Note: Ties in ranking reflect ties in actual values.

B-32 Gambling, 2000

State	Gambling gross revenue $ (in millions)	Per capita gambling revenue	Rank by total revenue
Alabama	58	13	41
Alaska	54	86	42
Arizona	196	38	33
Arkansas	52	19	43
California	2,629	78	6
Colorado	869	202	18
Connecticut	418	123	28
Delaware	576	735	22
Florida	1,618	101	10
Georgia	1,063	130	16
Hawaii	0	0	n/a
Idaho	45	34	44
Illinois	2,680	216	5
Indiana	2,049	337	8
Iowa	1,004	343	17
Kansas	127	47	36
Kentucky	507	125	25
Louisiana	2,194	491	7
Maine	104	81	38
Maryland	747	141	19
Massachusetts	1,347	212	12
Michigan	1,706	172	9
Minnesota	422	86	27
Mississippi	2,685	944	4
Missouri	1,262	226	13
Montana	302	335	29
Nebraska	120	70	37
Nevada	9,632	4,820	1
New Hampshire	158	128	35
New Jersey	5,451	648	2
New Mexico	161	89	34
New York	2,739	144	3
North Carolina	8	1	47
North Dakota	76	119	39
Ohio	1,199	106	14
Oklahoma	62	18	40
Oregon	607	178	21
Pennsylvania	1,134	92	15
Rhode Island	298	285	30
South Carolina	422	105	26
South Dakota	275	364	31
Tennessee	0	0	n/a
Texas	1,364	65	11
Utah	0	0	n/a
Vermont	34	57	45
Virginia	523	74	24
Washington	659	112	20
West Virginia	525	290	23
Wisconsin	241	45	32
Wyoming	8	16	46
50 States	50,411	179	
DC	117	205	
United States	50,528	180	

Rank in order by total revenue	
1	Nevada
2	New Jersey
3	New York
4	Mississippi
5	Illinois
6	California
7	Louisiana
8	Indiana
9	Michigan
10	Florida
11	Texas
12	Massachusetts
13	Missouri
14	Ohio
15	Pennsylvania
16	Georgia
17	Iowa
18	Colorado
19	Maryland
20	Washington
21	Oregon
22	Delaware
23	West Virginia
24	Virginia
25	Kentucky
26	South Carolina
27	Minnesota
28	Connecticut
29	Montana
30	Rhode Island
31	South Dakota
32	Wisconsin
33	Arizona
34	New Mexico
35	New Hampshire
36	Kansas
37	Nebraska
38	Maine
39	North Dakota
40	Oklahoma
41	Alabama
42	Alaska
43	Arkansas
44	Idaho
45	Vermont
46	Wyoming
47	North Carolina

Note: Numbers that appear to be identical are rounded and vary slightly in actual value. The rankings reflect the actual values before rounding. See the introduction for more details.

B-33 Annual Electricity Use Per Residential Customer, 2001

State	Average annual kwh use per residential customer	Rank
Alabama	14,270	5
Alaska	8,084	38
Arizona	12,925	11
Arkansas	12,649	14
California	6,227	49
Colorado	7,998	39
Connecticut	8,602	37
Delaware	10,963	25
Florida	13,761	7
Georgia	12,751	12
Hawaii	7,502	42
Idaho	12,665	13
Illinois	8,711	34
Indiana	11,382	24
Iowa	9,975	29
Kansas	10,529	27
Kentucky	13,248	8
Louisiana	14,600	2
Maine	6,182	50
Maryland	12,357	17
Massachusetts	6,943	44
Michigan	7,678	41
Minnesota	9,331	33
Mississippi	14,326	3
Missouri	12,233	18
Montana	9,608	30
Nebraska	11,709	22
Nevada	11,633	23
New Hampshire	6,935	45
New Jersey	7,973	40
New Mexico	6,811	46
New York	6,505	47
North Carolina	12,586	15
North Dakota	11,989	19
Ohio	10,361	28
Oklahoma	12,972	10
Oregon	11,985	20
Pennsylvania	9,514	32
Rhode Island	6,495	48
South Carolina	13,859	6
South Dakota	10,870	26
Tennessee	15,266	1
Texas	14,290	4
Utah	8,689	35
Vermont	7,087	43
Virginia	13,191	9
Washington	12,546	16
West Virginia	11,866	21
Wisconsin	8,650	36
Wyoming	9,589	31
50 States	n/a	
DC	8,454	
United States	10,535	

Rank in order by average use

1	Tennessee
2	Louisiana
3	Mississippi
4	Texas
5	Alabama
6	South Carolina
7	Florida
8	Kentucky
9	Virginia
10	Oklahoma
11	Arizona
12	Georgia
13	Idaho
14	Arkansas
15	North Carolina
16	Washington
17	Maryland
18	Missouri
19	North Dakota
20	Oregon
21	West Virginia
22	Nebraska
23	Nevada
24	Indiana
25	Delaware
26	South Dakota
27	Kansas
28	Ohio
29	Iowa
30	Montana
31	Wyoming
32	Pennsylvania
33	Minnesota
34	Illinois
35	Utah
36	Wisconsin
37	Connecticut
38	Alaska
39	Colorado
40	New Jersey
41	Michigan
42	Hawaii
43	Vermont
44	Massachusetts
45	New Hampshire
46	New Mexico
47	New York
48	Rhode Island
49	California
50	Maine

B-34 Average Cost Per Kilowatt Hour, 2001

State	Average cost for industrial customer (cents per kwh)	Average cost for residential customer (cents per kwh)	Residential cost as percentage of industrial cost	Rank by residential as percentage of industrial
Alabama	3.9	7.1	181.6	12
Alaska	7.7	12.2	157.3	36
Arizona	5.3	8.3	158.6	35
Arkansas	4.5	7.7	171.7	19
California	7.7	11.7	152.3	38
Colorado	4.4	7.5	169.2	21
Connecticut	7.6	10.9	142.5	43
Delaware	3.9	8.6	219.3	2
Florida	5.4	8.6	159.3	34
Georgia	4.3	7.8	180.6	14
Hawaii	11.7	16.3	139.9	44
Idaho	3.6	6.1	167.9	23
Illinois	4.1	8.7	211.1	3
Indiana	3.8	6.9	181.1	13
Iowa	4.2	8.4	201.4	4
Kansas	4.6	7.7	166.7	28
Kentucky	3.1	5.5	178.2	15
Louisiana	5.5	7.9	144.2	42
Maine	8.5	9.0	105.9	50
Maryland	4.0	7.7	189.8	7
Massachusetts	9.1	12.4	135.2	47
Michigan	5.0	8.3	163.6	31
Minnesota	4.5	7.6	167.8	24
Mississippi	4.5	7.4	165.2	29
Missouri	4.5	6.9	154.4	37
Montana	4.2	6.8	163.8	30
Nebraska	3.7	6.5	174.9	17
Nevada	6.5	9.0	138.1	45
New Hampshire	9.1	12.5	137.2	46
New Jersey	7.2	10.5	146.4	40
New Mexico	5.4	8.8	162.5	32
New York	4.9	13.9	281.4	1
North Carolina	4.7	8.2	172.1	18
North Dakota	3.9	6.5	167.6	25
Ohio	4.7	8.2	176.0	16
Oklahoma	4.2	7.2	169.5	20
Oregon	4.4	6.5	147.2	39
Pennsylvania	5.1	9.5	186.8	9
Rhode Island	9.4	12.1	129.1	49
South Carolina	3.9	7.8	200.7	5
South Dakota	4.4	7.5	169.0	22
Tennessee	4.4	6.4	145.8	41
Texas	5.3	8.8	166.8	27
Utah	3.6	6.7	187.7	8
Vermont	7.9	12.6	159.4	33
Virginia	4.2	7.7	185.1	11
Washington	4.6	6.0	129.4	48
West Virginia	3.7	6.3	167.6	26
Wisconsin	4.2	7.9	185.5	10
Wyoming	3.4	6.6	193.6	6
50 States	n/a	n/a	n/a	
DC	2.8	7.5	265.0	
United States	4.8	8.5	176.2	

Rank in order by percentage	
1	New York
2	Delaware
3	Illinois
4	Iowa
5	South Carolina
6	Wyoming
7	Maryland
8	Utah
9	Pennsylvania
10	Wisconsin
11	Virginia
12	Alabama
13	Indiana
14	Georgia
15	Kentucky
16	Ohio
17	Nebraska
18	North Carolina
19	Arkansas
20	Oklahoma
21	Colorado
22	South Dakota
23	Idaho
24	Minnesota
25	North Dakota
26	West Virginia
27	Texas
28	Kansas
29	Mississippi
30	Montana
31	Michigan
32	New Mexico
33	Vermont
34	Florida
35	Arizona
36	Alaska
37	Missouri
38	California
39	Oregon
40	New Jersey
41	Tennessee
42	Louisiana
43	Connecticut
44	Hawaii
45	Nevada
46	New Hampshire
47	Massachusetts
48	Washington
49	Rhode Island
50	Maine

Note: Numbers that appear to be identical are rounded and vary slightly in actual value. The rankings reflect the actual values before rounding. See the introduction for more details.

B-35 New Companies, 2001

State	New companies	New companies per 1,000 employees	Rank per 1,000
Alabama	10,060	4.9	38
Alaska	2,438	8.1	11
Arizona	14,541	6.3	22
Arkansas	3,990	3.4	50
California	128,885	7.8	13
Colorado	24,730	11.2	2
Connecticut	9,074	5.5	31
Delaware	3,352	8.3	8
Florida	60,370	8.3	9
Georgia	23,211	5.9	28
Hawaii	3,811	6.6	21
Idaho	5,534	8.5	7
Illinois	28,426	4.7	40
Indiana	13,903	4.7	44
Iowa	5,659	3.7	49
Kansas	7,026	5.3	33
Kentucky	8,713	4.7	43
Louisiana	9,816	5.1	34
Maine	4,667	7.1	18
Maryland	20,072	7.4	16
Massachusetts	18,166	5.7	30
Michigan	23,060	4.7	41
Minnesota	12,700	4.7	42
Mississippi	6,164	5.0	36
Missouri	14,360	5.1	35
Montana	3,608	8.1	10
Nebraska	4,419	4.9	39
Nevada	8,864	9.1	6
New Hampshire	4,398	6.6	20
New Jersey	36,747	9.2	5
New Mexico	5,753	7.2	17
New York	62,730	7.5	14
North Carolina	22,436	5.9	27
North Dakota	1,419	4.3	46
Ohio	22,951	4.1	48
Oklahoma	9,940	6.2	23
Oregon	13,246	7.9	12
Pennsylvania	33,497	5.8	29
Rhode Island	3,547	7.4	15
South Carolina	11,372	6.2	24
South Dakota	1,953	5.0	37
Tennessee	16,488	6.1	25
Texas	53,271	5.4	32
Utah	10,745	10.1	3
Vermont	2,226	6.9	19
Virginia	21,371	6.0	26
Washington	39,641	14.1	1
West Virginia	3,691	4.7	45
Wisconsin	12,025	4.2	47
Wyoming	2,558	9.8	4
50 States	**871,624**	**6.5**	
DC	4,090	15.7	
United States*	**881,296**	**6.5**	

Due to rounding or data sources, the 50-state total plus D.C. may not equal the U.S. total. Please see introduction.

Rank in order per 1,000 employees	
1	Washington
2	Colorado
3	Utah
4	Wyoming
5	New Jersey
6	Nevada
7	Idaho
8	Delaware
9	Florida
10	Montana
11	Alaska
12	Oregon
13	California
14	New York
15	Rhode Island
16	Maryland
17	New Mexico
18	Maine
19	Vermont
20	New Hampshire
21	Hawaii
22	Arizona
23	Oklahoma
24	South Carolina
25	Tennessee
26	Virginia
27	North Carolina
28	Georgia
29	Pennsylvania
30	Massachusetts
31	Connecticut
32	Texas
33	Kansas
34	Louisiana
35	Missouri
36	Mississippi
37	South Dakota
38	Alabama
39	Nebraska
40	Illinois
41	Michigan
42	Minnesota
43	Kentucky
44	Indiana
45	West Virginia
46	North Dakota
47	Wisconsin
48	Ohio
49	Iowa
50	Arkansas

Note: Numbers that appear to be identical are rounded and vary slightly in actual value. The rankings reflect the actual values before rounding. See the introduction for more details.

Source Notes for Economies (Section B)

B-1 Personal Income, 2001: These data reflect income of residents of each state, including pensions, dividends, interest, and rent as well as amounts received from employers as wages and salaries. These estimates are made by the Department of Commerce each quarter. The calendar year 2000 estimates were released on September 23, 2002, and are available on the Department's website (www.bea.doc.gov).

B-2 Gross State Product, Total and Per Capita, 2000: The gross state product is the state counterpart of the gross national product (now called the gross domestic product). This is the single best measure of the size of a state's economy. It is the sum of all the value of production of goods and services. While estimates of national data are released on a current basis, state-by-state estimates are made by the Department of Commerce only with a substantial lag. These 2000 data were released in June 2002 and come from the same source as Table B-1.

B-3 Per Capita Personal Income, 2001: These data, from the same source as Table B-1, reflect personal income in relation to population. They are a common measure of the relative affluence of each state. The data are also used to determine what percentage the federal government pays of each state's Medicaid costs.

B-4 Personal Income from Wages and Salaries, 2001: These data show the portion of personal income that comes from wages and salaries. The data on origins of personal income were released by the Department of Commerce Bureau of Economic Analysis (BEA) on September 23, 2002. They are available on the BEA website (www.bea.doc.gov). The percentages, calculated for *State Fact Finder*, indicate relative reliance of states' economies on current work, as distinct from investments and government payments.

B-5 Average Annual Pay, 2001: These data reflect the average pay of workers in each state. They are prepared by the Department of Labor and available on-line at www.bls.gov. They were released September 24, 2002.

B-6 Average Hourly Earnings, 2002: These data are often used to compare wage costs of the states. They are prepared by the Department of Labor monthly and released in the publication *Employment and Earnings*. These June 2002 data appeared in the September 2002 edition. These data only cover production workers, excluding service and retailing employees as well as government employees.

B-7 Value Added in Manufacturing, 2000: This table measures the value that is added by manufacturing operations in each state. Value added is calculated by subtracting the value of inputs to production from the value of the outputs. For example, the value of manufacturing a car is the value of the car minus the value of components, such as engines, purchased to manufacture it. These data are from the Census Bureau's *2000 Annual Survey of Manufacturers (M00(AS)-3)*, issued March 2002. Value added per worker can be calculated from this report. This per worker statistic is sometimes used to compare the productivity of state work forces but is a misleading statistic because capital investments in machinery make massive contributions to adding values in highly automated operations such as chemical manufacturing.

B-8 Cost of Living, 2002: The federal government has not attempted to produce measures that compare living costs since the 1980s and, even then, provided the data only for selected large metropolitan areas, not states. Some researchers periodically try to produce such indices, but they are of doubtful statistical validity. The one shown is from the Missouri Economic Research and Information Center and is based on voluntary surveys of chambers of commerce taken by ACCRA, a non-profit economic and community development research organization.

B-9 Average Annual Pay in Manufacturing, 2001: This is the manufacturing component of the data described for Table B-5, from the same source. States with many jobs in high-wage industries, like chemical or vehicle manufacturing, rank highest.

B-10 Average Annual Pay in Retailing, 2001: This is the retailing component of the data described for Table B-5, from the same source. Because most retailing jobs are entry-level positions requiring little experience or formal training, these data are a good measure of the costs of obtaining new workers in the states.

B-11 Labor Force, 2002: About 143.7 million people, 51 percent of Americans, are either working or looking for work but not working (unemployed). These two groups make up the labor force. The rest of the population are not in the labor force because they are retired, too young to work, disabled, or have opted not to work. This group includes "discouraged workers" who indicate that they would like to work but have given up hope of finding a job.

The labor force data are available on the website of the Bureau of Labor Statistics (www.bls.gov). They are also available in their monthly publication *Regional and State Area Employment and Unemployment* released on October 22, 2002, with preliminary estimates for September. The data are seasonally adjusted to make month-to-month comparisons possible despite fluctuations associated with time of the year such as hiring by retail stores for the December holiday season and summertime hiring of students. The 2001 population estimates come from the Census Bureau (see Table A-1). Labor force as a percentage of population varies among states because of differences in the percentage of population at working age and the percentage of people who want to work—the labor force participation rate.

B-12 Unemployed and Unemployment Rate, 2002: The estimates of persons unemployed and the unemployment rate (percentage of labor force unemployed) are from the same source as Table B-11. See notes to Table B-13 for an explanation of why the national unemployment rate shown in the table (5.4 percent) differs from the national value (5.6 percent) reported for September in the Bureau of Labor Statistics' October release, *The Employment Situation: 2002.*

B-13 Employment and Employment Rate, 2002: The Bureau of Labor Statistics faces a perpetual dilemma in presenting statistics on employment and unemployment. It must make national unemployment estimates based on a survey of households in which people are asked whether they are looking for work. This *household survey* also provides the national estimate of the people who are employed. But the sample is too small to provide reliable estimates of employment for less populous states. To provide estimates for those states, the Bureau obtains monthly reports from employers, called the *establishment survey*. The national totals from the two different surveys often diverge by hundreds of thousands of workers. Periodically, the Bureau "benchmarks" the totals and revises past estimates to make them consistent.

To make the matter even more complicated, the Bureau attempts in various complex ways to use the results of one survey to guide estimating procedures for the other. How this is done is explained in detail in various technical publications available from the Bureau. The net effect harmonizes the results of the two approaches better for large states than small ones. For example, the employment in Wyoming implicit in the Bureau's estimates is the labor force (Table B-11) minus the unemployed (Table B-12)—261,000— but the employment published in a different table in the report (see notes to Table B-11) is 247,000. For Table B-13, *State Fact Finder* uses the implicit estimate so that employment plus unemployment sum to the labor force for each state. The employment rate is the relationship between the employment shown and the labor force on Table B-11.

Because *State Fact Finder* contains many tables relying on employment data for individual states, it uses the best employment estimates available, those from the establishment survey, in Table B-14 and other tables showing state-by-state details of employment.

B-14 Government Employment, 2002: This table, from the same source as Table B-11, uses seasonally adjusted data from the establishment survey (see notes to Table B-13 on differences between the household and establishment surveys) which were made available by the Bureau of Labor Statistics on October 22, 2002, with preliminary estimates for September. The employment reported on this table includes federal, state, and local employees.

These Bureau of Labor Statistics data on government employment covering 2002 are more current than data provided by the Census Bureau. The latest Census Bureau data, published in 2002, cover information on March 2001 payrolls. But the Census Bureau data are used often in *State Fact Finder* because the Bureau of Labor Statistics data do not include such details as how much employees are paid and the type of service (for example, education, transportation) they provide.

B-15 Manufacturing Employment, 2002: These data are comparable to those shown in Table B-14, but cover manufacturing.

B-16 *Fortune* 500 Companies, 2002: Two major business magazines—*Fortune* and *Forbes*—provide annual listings of the largest companies in America, using somewhat different criteria. This table reflects the list as published in *Fortune* (April 15, 2002). Because large states tend to have the most large companies, the rankings are based on a calculation of the representation of these companies' headquarters in each state in relation to population of that state.

B-17 *Forbes* 500 Companies, 2002: This table is the counterpart of Table B-16. This listing was published in *Forbes* magazine (April 15, 2002). Because *Forbes* uses four separate criteria for its listings, 824 American companies are included in the "500" list.

B-18 Tourism Spending, 2000: The travel industry is a major factor in the economies of all states and a dominant factor in a few. However, data on it are elusive. Many trips combine business and pleasure, so separating tourism from business is difficult. Other trips combine an activity, such as coming home for the holidays, with a tourist activity, such as visiting a museum. Restaurants and gift shops do not normally know whether their customers are tourists or local customers. Consequently, estimates of tourism spending have more guesswork than most of the statistics in *State Fact Finder*. The 2000 data shown in the table are the most up-to-date. They are prepared by the Travel Industry Association of America and are published in *Tourism Works for America, 11th Annual Edition 2002.*

B-19 Exports, 2001: National estimates of exports are made quarterly by the Department of Commerce to develop estimates of gross domestic product and balance of payments with other nations. Relatively current estimates by state are also made by the Commerce Department but are of doubtful reliability because of data-gathering limitations and conceptual problems. For example, does a shipment from a New York port of a product from an Ohio plant of items made from components from Ohio and Mississippi contained in boxes produced in South Carolina constitute an export from New York, Ohio, or somewhere else? The data shown came from the Census Bureau's website (www.census.gov) on July 23, 2002.

B-20 Housing Permits, 2001: No state-by-state system exists to report completion of single-family houses and apartment and condominium units, but there are good data on the issuance of permits for such construction. Although some builders obtain permits and then don't build, permits are expensive so most permits are followed by construction. The data shown were compiled by the National Association of Home Builders and are available on its website (www.nahb.com). The relationship to population shows which states have rapidly growing populations and which are more stagnant.

B-21 Percentage Change in Home Prices, 1997-2002: Most people are interested in changes in housing prices because of the implications for a specific existing home—usually the one they own. The data often cited in the media, which come from realtors' sales records, come from averages of homes sold. As a result, they include large percentages of new (and typically larger, better equipped, and more expensive) homes in fast-growing states. A preferable way to measure price changes is to examine prices for successive sales of the same homes. This has recently become possible with improvements in computing capacity and the increasing importance of secondary mortgage lenders, who buy massive numbers of mortgages from banks and other lenders. The data in the table reflect this approach.

The information comes from *House Price Index Second Quarter 2002* published by the Office of Federal Housing Enterprise Oversight and available on its website (www.ofheo.gov).

B-22 Net Farm Income, 2001: These data reflect the net income derived from farming—the value of farm sales minus the cost of production. They are estimates made by the Department of Agriculture and are available on its website (www.ers.usda.gov). The *State Fact Finder* calculation of per capita amounts provides a basis for comparing the importance of agriculture to the economies of each state.

B-23 Financial Institution Assets, 2001: This table shows total assets of banks, trust companies, and savings institutions. These data, from the Federal Deposit Insurance Corporation's *Statistics on Banking: 2001*, provide a good measure of the importance of banking in each state. However, they provide no indication of the wealth of individuals in a state as deposits flow freely across state lines. States that have successfully tried to draw financial institutions, like Delaware and South Dakota, show large per capita amounts, as do regional banking centers, such as the Boston banks that serve customers throughout New England.

B-24 Bankruptcy Filings by Individuals and Businesses, 2002: These data show how new bankruptcy cases (mostly individuals rather than businesses) were distributed among the states. These data cover the twelve-month period ending March 31, 2002, and come from the website of the Administrative Office of the U.S. Courts (www.uscourts.gov).

B-25 Patents Issued, FY 2001: The U.S. Patent Office issued 101,619 new patents in FY 2001 to residents (both corporations and individuals) in the states shown. When related to population, this statistic is often used to compare states in the degree to which they are on the forefront of new technology. The data come from the United States Patent and Trademark Office and are available on its website (www.uspto.gov) as *Performance and Accountability Report Fiscal Year 2001*. Because patent applications are often made by or for companies, headquarters of companies (for example, DuPont in Delaware and 3M in Minnesota) affect the results.

B-26 Workers' Compensation Temporary Disability Payments, 2002: All states maintain a program that provides compensation for workers who are injured on the job. These programs differ massively from state to state in how much money is paid for certain injuries, how hard it is to prove disability and its relationship to the job, and how employers are forced to pay program costs. These differences, set by state policy, are not captured by aggregate statistics on workers' compensation costs because some industries (like construction and logging) are inherently more hazardous than others (like banking), so state-by-state costs will vary with the mix of industries. This table compares one major dimension of benefit generosity/parsimony, the maximum payment per month to a worker who is temporarily unable to work because of a job-related injury. The data come from the Department of Labor publication dated January 2002, *State Workers' Compensation Laws.*

B-27 Average Unemployment Compensation Benefit, 2001: All states maintain a federally supervised program of unemployment compensation. States have wide discretion in determining how large unemployment compensation payments will be, how long they will last, and how costs are distributed among employers. This table from the website of the Department of Labor Employment and Training Administration (ows.doleta.gov) shows the average weekly benefit paid in each state.

B-28 Index of State Economic Momentum, September 2002: Each quarter *State Policy Reports* publishes its Index of State Economic Momentum, a statistic created by State Policy Research to compare the recent economic performance of each state in relation to the national average. A state growing at the national average rate would show an index of 0.0 while one growing roughly 1.0 percent faster would show an index of 1.0. Negative numbers show states lagging behind national average growth. The index combines (with equal weights) the most recent known one-year changes in (1) employment, (2) personal income, and (3) population.

B-29 Employment Change, 2001-2002: This table uses Department of Labor data from July 2001 and 2002 (not seasonally adjusted) to show the change in the number of jobs in each state. The data, from the Bureau of Labor Statistics website (www.bls.gov), are one component of the state economic momentum index shown in Table B-28.

B-30 Manufacturing Employment Change, 2001-2002: This table uses Department of Labor (see source for Table B-29) data from July 2001 to July 2002 (not seasonally adjusted) to show the states experiencing job loss and those experiencing job growth in manufacturing. These data are released monthly and revised often, but differences in state economic performance tend to persist from month to month.

B-31 Home Ownership, 1997-2001: These data show the percentage of households living in homes they own. The data come from the *Housing Vacancy Survey*, available on the Census website (www.census.gov). These are estimates based on Census surveys averaged over five years. Because of the relatively small samples, the margin of error for less populous states is relatively large.

B-32 Gambling, 2000: Legal gambling establishments in the United States grossed over $50.5 billion in 2000—$180 per person, including people who do not gamble at all. The distribution of these revenues among the states is shown in the table, reflecting estimates made by Christiansen Capital Advisors.

These statistics dealing with the revenues of gaming establishments provide one indication of the amount of gambling activity. However, they should not be confused with amounts bet. While gamblers lose, on average, about 50 cents for every dollar spent on state lotteries and 20 cents for every dollar at horse tracks, they lose only about 2 cents of what they bet at casino table games and about 5 cents at slot machines. So, the same dollar is, in effect, bet many times before it is lost. Christiansen Capital Advisors has much more detailed estimates of gambling by state and type of gambling, as well as information on gambling taxes and revenues of gambling establishments.

B-33 Average Annual Electricity Use Per Residential Customer, 2001: These data from the Edison Electric Institute(EEI) show differences in electricity use among the states. The results are heavily influenced by the relative importance of heating and air conditioning and the mix of fuels used for heating. EEI warns that these data are not strictly comparable to data for earlier years published in its *Statistical Yearbook*. Unlike previous years, 2001 data include data for retail customers serviced by alternative power suppliers.

B-34 Average Cost Per Kilowatt Hour, 2001: These data also come from the Edison Electric Institute (see source for Table B-33), which maintains additional details on other years, types of consumers, and more. The data have many uses. The cost per kilowatt hour permits comparisons among states of electricity costs for households and businesses. The residential rate as a percentage of industrial rate is a useful indicator of the extent to which state regulatory policy (which controls rates charged by private companies) is tilted toward providing low industrial rates to stimulate economic development or low residential rates to keep prices low for voter/consumers at the potential expense of loss of industry. Based on costs of service, industrial users should pay less because they are cheaper per kilowatt to bill and often agree to have service curtailed when there is a shortage of power. See source for Table B-33 for information to consider when comparing 2001 data to Edison Electric Institute data from previous years.

B-35 New Companies, 2001: These data show the number of companies that applied for new account numbers from state employment services. These data were made available to *State Fact Finder* by Tom Stengle of the Department of Labor Unemployment Insurance Service in an e-mail dated October 18, 2002. *State Fact Finder* then related these numbers to the total number of workers in each state. These employment numbers are annual averages and were released on the Bureau of Labor Statistics' website (www.bls.gov) on February 22, 2002.

Geography

C-1	Total Land Area, 2000	78
C-2	Land Owned by Federal Government, 2000	79
C-3	State Park Acreage, FY 2002	80
C-4	State Park Visitors, FY 2002	81
C-5	Percentage of Population Not Physically Active, 2001	82
C-6	Hunters with Firearms, 2001	83
C-7	Registered Boats, 2001	84
C-8	State Spending on State Arts Agencies, FY 2002	85
C-9	Energy Consumption, Total and Per Capita, 2000	86
C-10	Toxic Chemical Release, 2000	87
C-11	Hazardous Waste Sites, 2002	88
C-12	Polluted Rivers and Streams, 2000	89
C-13	Expired Surface Water Pollution Discharge Permits, 2002	90
C-14	Air Pollution Emissions, 1999	91

The sagging economy and talk of war left little room for action on an energy bill already mired in controversy. The 108th Congress and the Bush administration may take up the debate over dependence on fossil fuels again in 2003. But while energy policy stalled at the federal level, states didn't wait idly by. Many states, especially those in the West, are moving forward with programs geared toward greater reliance on renewable energy.

Forty-four states have some form of renewable energy program in place. Thirty-nine states offer tax deductions, credits, or exemptions. Twelve states require that a percentage of a utility's generating capacity be derived from renewable resources and three other states have set timelines for this rule to go into effect. In addition, fifteen states have public benefit funds that support research and development, energy efficiency and low-income assistance.

When gas and coal prices mount, so does interest in renewables, which include hydroelectric, solar, geothermal, and wind power, as well as alcohol fuels. But according to a survey by the National Conference of State Legislatures, states are also developing renewable power in response to consumer demand for it and increased energy needs. Renewable energy is also seen as a tool for rural economic development, a hedge against fuel price volatility, and a means to improve air quality.

One state that has combined economic development with support of alternative energy is Michigan. There, Governor John Engler unveiled plans to turn the auto-industry state into the "world headquarters of the alternative energy industry." Called NextEnergy, his program, among other things, encourages companies working on alternative energy technologies, including fuel cells, to locate in Michigan.

Other big environmental moves at the state level include new pollution controls in New Hampshire and legislation in California limiting greenhouse gas emissions from automobile exhaust. If it survives court challenge, California's law could spearhead changes across the nation.

C-1 Total Land Area, 2000

State	Land area (in square miles)	Rank
Alabama	50,744	28
Alaska	571,951	1
Arizona	113,635	6
Arkansas	52,068	27
California	155,959	3
Colorado	103,718	8
Connecticut	4,845	48
Delaware	1,954	49
Florida	53,927	26
Georgia	57,906	21
Hawaii	6,423	47
Idaho	82,747	11
Illinois	55,584	24
Indiana	35,867	38
Iowa	55,869	23
Kansas	81,815	13
Kentucky	39,728	36
Louisiana	43,562	33
Maine	30,862	39
Maryland	9,774	42
Massachusetts	7,840	45
Michigan	56,804	22
Minnesota	79,610	14
Mississippi	46,907	31
Missouri	68,886	18
Montana	145,552	4
Nebraska	76,872	15
Nevada	109,826	7
New Hampshire	8,968	44
New Jersey	7,417	46
New Mexico	121,356	5
New York	47,214	30
North Carolina	48,711	29
North Dakota	68,976	17
Ohio	40,948	35
Oklahoma	68,667	19
Oregon	95,997	10
Pennsylvania	44,817	32
Rhode Island	1,045	50
South Carolina	30,110	40
South Dakota	75,885	16
Tennessee	41,217	34
Texas	261,797	2
Utah	82,144	12
Vermont	9,250	43
Virginia	39,594	37
Washington	66,544	20
West Virginia	24,078	41
Wisconsin	54,310	25
Wyoming	97,100	9
50 States	3,537,380	
DC	61	
United States	3,537,441	

Rank in order by square mile

1. Alaska
2. Texas
3. California
4. Montana
5. New Mexico
6. Arizona
7. Nevada
8. Colorado
9. Wyoming
10. Oregon
11. Idaho
12. Utah
13. Kansas
14. Minnesota
15. Nebraska
16. South Dakota
17. North Dakota
18. Missouri
19. Oklahoma
20. Washington
21. Georgia
22. Michigan
23. Iowa
24. Illinois
25. Wisconsin
26. Florida
27. Arkansas
28. Alabama
29. North Carolina
30. New York
31. Mississippi
32. Pennsylvania
33. Louisiana
34. Tennessee
35. Ohio
36. Kentucky
37. Virginia
38. Indiana
39. Maine
40. South Carolina
41. West Virginia
42. Maryland
43. Vermont
44. New Hampshire
45. Massachusetts
46. New Jersey
47. Hawaii
48. Connecticut
49. Delaware
50. Rhode Island

C-2 Land Owned by Federal Government, 2000

State	Total acres of federally owned land (in thousands)	Percentage of land federally owned	Rank by total acres
Alabama	1,326	4.1	29
Alaska	220,852	60.4	1
Arizona	32,379	44.5	6
Arkansas	3,410	10.1	17
California	47,889	47.8	3
Colorado	24,108	36.3	11
Connecticut	14	0.5	49
Delaware	16	1.2	48
Florida	4,599	13.2	14
Georgia	2,027	5.4	23
Hawaii	639	15.6	37
Idaho	33,106	62.5	5
Illinois	590	1.6	38
Indiana	510	2.2	39
Iowa	230	0.6	42
Kansas	674	1.3	35
Kentucky	1,447	5.7	28
Louisiana	1,199	4.2	31
Maine	173	0.9	44
Maryland	166	2.6	45
Massachusetts	71	1.4	47
Michigan	4,076	11.2	16
Minnesota	4,217	8.2	15
Mississippi	1,672	5.5	26
Missouri	4,798	10.8	13
Montana	27,428	29.4	9
Nebraska	651	1.3	36
Nevada	58,319	83.0	2
New Hampshire	759	13.2	33
New Jersey	124	2.6	46
New Mexico	26,572	34.2	10
New York	222	0.7	43
North Carolina	1,989	6.3	24
North Dakota	2,316	5.2	19
Ohio	441	1.7	40
Oklahoma	1,666	3.8	27
Oregon	32,356	52.5	7
Pennsylvania	717	2.5	34
Rhode Island	4	0.5	50
South Carolina	1,110	5.7	32
South Dakota	3,120	6.4	18
Tennessee	2,115	7.9	22
Texas	2,307	1.4	20
Utah	34,001	64.5	4
Vermont	375	6.3	41
Virginia	2,280	8.9	21
Washington	12,176	28.5	12
West Virginia	1,222	7.9	30
Wisconsin	1,819	5.2	25
Wyoming	31,070	49.8	8
50 States	635,346	28.0	
DC	9	23.2	
United States	635,355	28.0	

Rank in order by total acres

1 Alaska
2 Nevada
3 California
4 Utah
5 Idaho
6 Arizona
7 Oregon
8 Wyoming
9 Montana
10 New Mexico
11 Colorado
12 Washington
13 Missouri
14 Florida
15 Minnesota
16 Michigan
17 Arkansas
18 South Dakota
19 North Dakota
20 Texas
21 Virginia
22 Tennessee
23 Georgia
24 North Carolina
25 Wisconsin
26 Mississippi
27 Oklahoma
28 Kentucky
29 Alabama
30 West Virginia
31 Louisiana
32 South Carolina
33 New Hampshire
34 Pennsylvania
35 Kansas
36 Nebraska
37 Hawaii
38 Illinois
39 Indiana
40 Ohio
41 Vermont
42 Iowa
43 New York
44 Maine
45 Maryland
46 New Jersey
47 Massachusetts
48 Delaware
49 Connecticut
50 Rhode Island

C-3 State Park Acreage, FY 2002

State	State park acreage	Acreage per 1,000 population	Rank by total acreage
Alabama	49,710	11.1	41
Alaska	3,291,121	5,183.7	1
Arizona	58,491	11.0	39
Arkansas	50,375	18.7	40
California	1,416,221	41.0	2
Colorado	431,435	97.7	6
Connecticut	184,990	54.0	17
Delaware	21,395	26.9	48
Florida	571,212	34.8	5
Georgia	78,942	9.4	32
Hawaii	27,627	22.6	46
Idaho	42,917	32.5	43
Illinois	287,376	23.0	11
Indiana	178,665	29.2	18
Iowa	63,171	21.6	37
Kansas	32,300	12.0	45
Kentucky	43,508	10.7	42
Louisiana	37,329	8.4	44
Maine	93,634	72.8	29
Maryland	258,757	48.1	13
Massachusetts	290,601	45.6	9
Michigan	351,264	35.2	8
Minnesota	258,316	52.0	14
Mississippi	24,287	8.5	47
Missouri	138,357	24.6	21
Montana	65,182	72.1	36
Nebraska	134,230	78.3	22
Nevada	132,523	62.9	23
New Hampshire	78,849	62.6	33
New Jersey	357,805	42.2	7
New Mexico	90,693	49.6	30
New York	1,158,450	60.9	3
North Carolina	167,837	20.5	19
North Dakota	18,750	29.6	49
Ohio	204,445	18.0	15
Oklahoma	71,579	20.7	34
Oregon	94,937	27.3	28
Pennsylvania	288,795	23.5	10
Rhode Island	8,748	8.3	50
South Carolina	80,459	19.8	31
South Dakota	102,069	134.9	27
Tennessee	142,797	24.9	20
Texas	593,139	27.8	4
Utah	114,236	50.3	26
Vermont	68,677	112.0	35
Virginia	62,006	8.6	38
Washington	262,345	43.8	12
West Virginia	195,584	108.5	16
Wisconsin	132,238	24.5	24
Wyoming	121,170	245.1	25
50 States	13,029,544	45.8	
DC	n/a	n/a	
United States	13,029,544	45.8	

Rank in order by total acreage	
1	Alaska
2	California
3	New York
4	Texas
5	Florida
6	Colorado
7	New Jersey
8	Michigan
9	Massachusetts
10	Pennsylvania
11	Illinois
12	Washington
13	Maryland
14	Minnesota
15	Ohio
16	West Virginia
17	Connecticut
18	Indiana
19	North Carolina
20	Tennessee
21	Missouri
22	Nebraska
23	Nevada
24	Wisconsin
25	Wyoming
26	Utah
27	South Dakota
28	Oregon
29	Maine
30	New Mexico
31	South Carolina
32	Georgia
33	New Hampshire
34	Oklahoma
35	Vermont
36	Montana
37	Iowa
38	Virginia
39	Arizona
40	Arkansas
41	Alabama
42	Kentucky
43	Idaho
44	Louisiana
45	Kansas
46	Hawaii
47	Mississippi
48	Delaware
49	North Dakota
50	Rhode Island

C-4 State Park Visitors, FY 2002

State	State park total visitors (in thousands)	Visitors per capita	Rank per capita
Alabama	5,456	1.2	45
Alaska	3,662	5.8	7
Arizona	2,516	0.5	49
Arkansas	7,746	2.9	22
California	80,306	2.3	27
Colorado	10,528	2.4	26
Connecticut	7,453	2.2	29
Delaware	3,189	4.0	15
Florida	18,133	1.1	46
Georgia	15,348	1.8	34
Hawaii	18,665	15.2	1
Idaho	2,430	1.8	33
Illinois	44,064	3.5	16
Indiana	17,595	2.9	21
Iowa	15,203	5.2	10
Kansas	7,485	2.8	23
Kentucky	7,831	1.9	31
Louisiana	1,970	0.4	50
Maine	2,281	1.8	37
Maryland	9,838	1.8	35
Massachusetts	12,282	1.9	32
Michigan	25,499	2.6	25
Minnesota	8,343	1.7	39
Mississippi	4,236	1.5	41
Missouri	17,892	3.2	17
Montana	1,340	1.5	42
Nebraska	9,898	5.8	6
Nevada	3,425	1.6	40
New Hampshire	6,689	5.3	8
New Jersey	15,064	1.8	36
New Mexico	4,003	2.2	28
New York	55,529	2.9	20
North Carolina	11,995	1.5	43
North Dakota	1,104	1.7	38
Ohio	59,369	5.2	9
Oklahoma	15,125	4.4	14
Oregon	39,758	11.4	2
Pennsylvania	36,436	3.0	18
Rhode Island	6,351	6.0	5
South Carolina	8,763	2.2	30
South Dakota	7,568	10.0	3
Tennessee	28,821	5.0	11
Texas	17,540	0.8	48
Utah	6,296	2.8	24
Vermont	820	1.3	44
Virginia	6,011	0.8	47
Washington	47,774	8.0	4
West Virginia	8,026	4.5	13
Wisconsin	15,994	3.0	19
Wyoming	2,372	4.8	12
50 States	766,021	2.7	
DC	n/a	n/a	
United States	766,021	2.7	

Rank in order per capita

1. Hawaii
2. Oregon
3. South Dakota
4. Washington
5. Rhode Island
6. Nebraska
7. Alaska
8. New Hampshire
9. Ohio
10. Iowa
11. Tennessee
12. Wyoming
13. West Virginia
14. Oklahoma
15. Delaware
16. Illinois
17. Missouri
18. Pennsylvania
19. Wisconsin
20. New York
21. Indiana
22. Arkansas
23. Kansas
24. Utah
25. Michigan
26. Colorado
27. California
28. New Mexico
29. Connecticut
30. South Carolina
31. Kentucky
32. Massachusetts
33. Idaho
34. Georgia
35. Maryland
36. New Jersey
37. Maine
38. North Dakota
39. Minnesota
40. Nevada
41. Mississippi
42. Montana
43. North Carolina
44. Vermont
45. Alabama
46. Florida
47. Virginia
48. Texas
49. Arizona
50. Louisiana

Note: Numbers that appear to be identical are rounded and vary slightly in actual value. The rankings reflect the actual values before rounding. See the introduction for more details.

C-5 Percentage of Population Not Physically Active, 2001

State	Percentage reporting not to be physically active	Rank
Alabama	31.2	9
Alaska	21.1	40
Arizona	21.9	37
Arkansas	31.5	7
California	26.6	16
Colorado	19.2	46
Connecticut	24.0	30
Delaware	25.7	25
Florida	27.7	11
Georgia	27.3	13
Hawaii	18.9	47
Idaho	21.0	41
Illinois	26.5	18
Indiana	26.2	21
Iowa	25.9	23
Kansas	26.7	15
Kentucky	33.4	3
Louisiana	35.6	1
Maine	23.2	32
Maryland	24.2	29
Massachusetts	22.8	35
Michigan	23.4	31
Minnesota	17.1	48
Mississippi	33.4	3
Missouri	27.5	12
Montana	21.9	37
Nebraska	31.4	8
Nevada	22.6	36
New Hampshire	19.5	45
New Jersey	26.6	16
New Mexico	25.8	24
New York	28.7	10
North Carolina	26.4	19
North Dakota	23.2	32
Ohio	26.2	21
Oklahoma	32.8	5
Oregon	20.8	42
Pennsylvania	24.7	28
Rhode Island	24.9	27
South Carolina	26.4	19
South Dakota	25.4	26
Tennessee	35.1	2
Texas	27.1	14
Utah	16.5	50
Vermont	20.3	44
Virginia	23.2	32
Washington	17.1	48
West Virginia	31.7	6
Wisconsin	20.7	43
Wyoming	21.2	39
50 States	n/a	
DC	24.2	
United States	25.8	

Rank in order by percentage

1	Louisiana
2	Tennessee
3	Kentucky
3	Mississippi
5	Oklahoma
6	West Virginia
7	Arkansas
8	Nebraska
9	Alabama
10	New York
11	Florida
12	Missouri
13	Georgia
14	Texas
15	Kansas
16	California
16	New Jersey
18	Illinois
19	North Carolina
19	South Carolina
21	Indiana
21	Ohio
23	Iowa
24	New Mexico
25	Delaware
26	South Dakota
27	Rhode Island
28	Pennsylvania
29	Maryland
30	Connecticut
31	Michigan
32	Maine
32	North Dakota
32	Virginia
35	Massachusetts
36	Nevada
37	Arizona
37	Montana
39	Wyoming
40	Alaska
41	Idaho
42	Oregon
43	Wisconsin
44	Vermont
45	New Hampshire
46	Colorado
47	Hawaii
48	Minnesota
48	Washington
50	Utah

Note: Ties in ranking reflect ties in actual values.

C-6 Hunters with Firearms, 2001

State	Hunters with firearms (in thousands)	Percentage of population	Rank by percentage
Alabama	562	12.6	9
Alaska	n/a	n/a	n/a
Arizona	394	7.4	23
Arkansas	492	18.3	3
California	1,273	3.7	42
Colorado	409	9.3	20
Connecticut	165	4.8	36
Delaware	n/a	n/a	n/a
Florida	621	3.8	41
Georgia	394	4.7	37
Hawaii	n/a	n/a	n/a
Idaho	222	16.8	4
Illinois	560	4.5	39
Indiana	499	8.2	22
Iowa	289	9.9	17
Kansas	147	5.5	34
Kentucky	485	11.9	10
Louisiana	518	11.6	11
Maine	75	5.8	30
Maryland	77	1.4	46
Massachusetts	181	2.8	43
Michigan	1,018	10.2	15
Minnesota	571	11.5	13
Mississippi	369	12.9	7
Missouri	650	11.5	12
Montana	57	6.3	29
Nebraska	217	12.7	8
Nevada	149	7.1	25
New Hampshire	80	6.4	28
New Jersey	201	2.4	45
New Mexico	51	2.8	44
New York	1,102	5.8	31
North Carolina	468	5.7	33
North Dakota	84	13.2	6
Ohio	739	6.5	27
Oklahoma	251	7.3	24
Oregon	339	9.8	18
Pennsylvania	1,306	10.6	14
Rhode Island	n/a	n/a	n/a
South Carolina	205	5.0	35
South Dakota	76	10.0	16
Tennessee	261	4.5	38
Texas	1,236	5.8	32
Utah	156	6.9	26
Vermont	121	19.7	2
Virginia	617	8.6	21
Washington	250	4.2	40
West Virginia	367	20.4	1
Wisconsin	791	14.6	5
Wyoming	48	9.7	19
50 States	19,143	6.7	
DC	n/a	n/a	
United States*	19,173	6.7	

Due to rounding or data sources, the 50-state total plus D.C. may not equal the U.S. total. Please see introduction.

Rank in order by percentage

1	West Virginia
2	Vermont
3	Arkansas
4	Idaho
5	Wisconsin
6	North Dakota
7	Mississippi
8	Nebraska
9	Alabama
10	Kentucky
11	Louisiana
12	Missouri
13	Minnesota
14	Pennsylvania
15	Michigan
16	South Dakota
17	Iowa
18	Oregon
19	Wyoming
20	Colorado
21	Virginia
22	Indiana
23	Arizona
24	Oklahoma
25	Nevada
26	Utah
27	Ohio
28	New Hampshire
29	Montana
30	Maine
31	New York
32	Texas
33	North Carolina
34	Kansas
35	South Carolina
36	Connecticut
37	Georgia
38	Tennessee
39	Illinois
40	Washington
41	Florida
42	California
43	Massachusetts
44	New Mexico
45	New Jersey
46	Maryland

Note: Numbers that appear to be identical are rounded and vary slightly in actual value. The rankings reflect the actual values before rounding. See the introduction for more details.

C-7 Registered Boats, 2001

State	Registered boats	Registered boats per 1,000 population	Rank by total number of boats
Alabama	262,016	59	17
Alaska	41,110	65	46
Arizona	129,863	24	30
Arkansas	199,713	74	25
California	957,463	28	2
Colorado	104,476	24	33
Connecticut	105,362	31	32
Delaware	47,486	60	44
Florida	902,964	55	3
Georgia	327,026	39	14
Hawaii	13,903	11	50
Idaho	81,932	62	36
Illinois	396,848	32	9
Indiana	218,180	36	22
Iowa	210,841	72	23
Kansas	102,755	38	34
Kentucky	171,273	42	28
Louisiana	322,779	72	15
Maine	119,243	93	31
Maryland	197,005	37	26
Massachusetts	146,475	23	29
Michigan	1,003,947	100	1
Minnesota	826,048	166	4
Mississippi	300,970	105	16
Missouri	335,521	60	13
Montana	50,808	56	43
Nebraska	74,653	44	38
Nevada	61,122	29	40
New Hampshire	99,520	79	35
New Jersey	206,562	24	24
New Mexico	36,127	20	47
New York	526,190	28	7
North Carolina	353,560	43	12
North Dakota	51,483	81	41
Ohio	414,658	36	8
Oklahoma	229,454	66	21
Oregon	195,636	56	27
Pennsylvania	359,525	29	11
Rhode Island	41,314	39	45
South Carolina	382,072	94	10
South Dakota	51,226	68	42
Tennessee	256,670	45	19
Texas	621,244	29	5
Utah	79,586	35	37
Vermont	33,988	55	48
Virginia	240,509	33	20
Washington	260,335	43	18
West Virginia	63,061	35	39
Wisconsin	575,920	107	6
Wyoming	27,221	55	49
50 States	12,817,643	45	
DC	1,984	3	
United States*	12,884,166	45	

Rank in order by total number	
1	Michigan
2	California
3	Florida
4	Minnesota
5	Texas
6	Wisconsin
7	New York
8	Ohio
9	Illinois
10	South Carolina
11	Pennsylvania
12	North Carolina
13	Missouri
14	Georgia
15	Louisiana
16	Mississippi
17	Alabama
18	Washington
19	Tennessee
20	Virginia
21	Oklahoma
22	Indiana
23	Iowa
24	New Jersey
25	Arkansas
26	Maryland
27	Oregon
28	Kentucky
29	Massachusetts
30	Arizona
31	Maine
32	Connecticut
33	Colorado
34	Kansas
35	New Hampshire
36	Idaho
37	Utah
38	Nebraska
39	West Virginia
40	Nevada
41	North Dakota
42	South Dakota
43	Montana
44	Delaware
45	Rhode Island
46	Alaska
47	New Mexico
48	Vermont
49	Wyoming
50	Hawaii

Due to rounding or data sources, the 50-state total plus D.C. may not equal the U.S. total. Please see introduction.

C-8 State Spending on State Arts Agencies, FY 2002

State	State spending for the arts $ (in thousands)	Per capita $	Rank per capita
Alabama	5,705	1.28	18
Alaska	457	0.72	33
Arizona	4,140	0.78	28
Arkansas	1,180	0.44	45
California	43,399	1.26	19
Colorado	1,860	0.42	46
Connecticut	12,201	3.56	2
Delaware	1,658	2.08	10
Florida	32,833	2.00	11
Georgia	5,180	0.62	38
Hawaii	6,370	5.20	1
Idaho	1,017	0.77	30
Illinois	19,569	1.57	13
Indiana	3,673	0.60	40
Iowa	1,598	0.55	41
Kansas	1,655	0.61	39
Kentucky	3,972	0.98	24
Louisiana	5,196	1.16	20
Maine	822	0.64	37
Maryland	13,554	2.52	8
Massachusetts	19,145	3.00	3
Michigan	26,934	2.70	5
Minnesota	13,118	2.64	7
Mississippi	2,122	0.74	31
Missouri	8,917	1.58	12
Montana	332	0.37	47
Nebraska	1,441	0.84	27
Nevada	1,427	0.68	36
New Hampshire	651	0.52	42
New Jersey	22,740	2.68	6
New Mexico	1,969	1.08	22
New York	51,494	2.71	4
North Carolina	5,986	0.73	32
North Dakota	491	0.77	29
Ohio	14,669	1.29	17
Oklahoma	4,475	1.29	16
Oregon	1,214	0.35	48
Pennsylvania	14,000	1.14	21
Rhode Island	2,538	2.40	9
South Carolina	4,177	1.03	23
South Dakota	520	0.69	34
Tennessee	1,893	0.33	49
Texas	5,744	0.27	50
Utah	3,015	1.33	15
Vermont	564	0.92	25
Virginia	4,880	0.68	35
Washington	2,896	0.48	43
West Virginia	2,527	1.40	14
Wisconsin	2,576	0.48	44
Wyoming	426	0.86	26
50 States	388,921	1.37	
DC	1,760	3.08	
United States*	411,382	1.44	

Rank in order per capita	
1	Hawaii
2	Connecticut
3	Massachusetts
4	New York
5	Michigan
6	New Jersey
7	Minnesota
8	Maryland
9	Rhode Island
10	Delaware
11	Florida
12	Missouri
13	Illinois
14	West Virginia
15	Utah
16	Oklahoma
17	Ohio
18	Alabama
19	California
20	Louisiana
21	Pennsylvania
22	New Mexico
23	South Carolina
24	Kentucky
25	Vermont
26	Wyoming
27	Nebraska
28	Arizona
29	North Dakota
30	Idaho
31	Mississippi
32	North Carolina
33	Alaska
34	South Dakota
35	Virginia
36	Nevada
37	Maine
38	Georgia
39	Kansas
40	Indiana
41	Iowa
42	New Hampshire
43	Washington
44	Wisconsin
45	Arkansas
46	Colorado
47	Montana
48	Oregon
49	Tennessee
50	Texas

Note: Numbers that appear to be identical are rounded and vary slightly in actual value. The rankings reflect the actual values before rounding. See the introduction for more details.

Due to rounding or data sources, the 50-state total plus D.C. may not equal the U.S. total. Please see introduction.

C-9 Energy Consumption, Total and Per Capita, 2000

State	Energy consumption (in trillion BTUs)	BTUs per capita	Rank per capita
Alabama	2,494.6	560,950	9
Alaska	639.4	1,019,887	3
Arizona	1,767.9	344,577	35
Arkansas	1,209.1	452,271	15
California	7,864.3	232,179	48
Colorado	1,381.3	321,138	39
Connecticut	820.7	240,988	45
Delaware	281.3	358,984	30
Florida	4,337.5	271,393	44
Georgia	3,035.0	370,734	27
Hawaii	283.9	234,330	46
Idaho	452.3	349,549	34
Illinois	4,790.8	385,755	25
Indiana	3,435.4	564,988	8
Iowa	1,279.5	437,238	16
Kansas	1,311.2	487,722	11
Kentucky	2,240.6	554,361	10
Louisiana	3,984.2	891,524	4
Maine	392.6	307,940	40
Maryland	1,451.5	274,050	43
Massachusetts	1,397.8	220,157	49
Michigan	3,359.0	337,980	37
Minnesota	1,816.5	369,246	28
Mississippi	1,177.2	413,828	20
Missouri	2,026.9	362,256	29
Montana	561.7	622,593	6
Nebraska	746.9	436,461	17
Nevada	766.8	383,734	26
New Hampshire	379.3	306,930	41
New Jersey	2,527.1	300,332	42
New Mexico	853.3	469,092	13
New York	4,438.5	233,895	47
North Carolina	2,847.6	353,769	33
North Dakota	658.8	1,025,849	2
Ohio	4,438.6	390,958	24
Oklahoma	1,632.8	473,186	12
Oregon	1,211.1	353,978	32
Pennsylvania	4,905.0	399,396	22
Rhode Island	203.5	194,120	50
South Carolina	1,872.0	466,599	14
South Dakota	295.8	391,869	23
Tennessee	2,331.2	409,753	21
Texas	12,788.7	613,313	7
Utah	942.4	422,001	18
Vermont	208.2	341,969	36
Virginia	2,308.5	326,128	38
Washington	2,480.3	420,809	19
West Virginia	1,457.7	806,097	5
Wisconsin	1,912.9	356,640	31
Wyoming	820.6	1,661,867	1
50 States	106,819.8	380,345	
DC	104.5	182,673	
United States*	106,925.1	379,946	

Due to rounding or data sources, the 50-state total plus D.C. may not equal the U.S. total. Please see introduction.

Rank in order per capita

1. Wyoming
2. North Dakota
3. Alaska
4. Louisiana
5. West Virginia
6. Montana
7. Texas
8. Indiana
9. Alabama
10. Kentucky
11. Kansas
12. Oklahoma
13. New Mexico
14. South Carolina
15. Arkansas
16. Iowa
17. Nebraska
18. Utah
19. Washington
20. Mississippi
21. Tennessee
22. Pennsylvania
23. South Dakota
24. Ohio
25. Illinois
26. Nevada
27. Georgia
28. Minnesota
29. Missouri
30. Delaware
31. Wisconsin
32. Oregon
33. North Carolina
34. Idaho
35. Arizona
36. Vermont
37. Michigan
38. Virginia
39. Colorado
40. Maine
41. New Hampshire
42. New Jersey
43. Maryland
44. Florida
45. Connecticut
46. Hawaii
47. New York
48. California
49. Massachusetts
50. Rhode Island

C-10 Toxic Chemical Release, 2000

State	Toxic chemical release in pounds (in thousands)	Per capita release in pounds	Rank per capita
Alabama	150,637	33.9	12
Alaska	535,489	854.1	1
Arizona	744,720	145.2	4
Arkansas	51,434	19.2	22
California	75,609	2.2	46
Colorado	30,601	7.1	39
Connecticut	8,747	2.6	45
Delaware	13,601	17.4	25
Florida	143,573	9.0	36
Georgia	122,209	14.9	26
Hawaii	1,274	1.1	49
Idaho	76,668	59.3	7
Illinois	150,341	12.1	32
Indiana	204,097	33.6	13
Iowa	43,426	14.8	27
Kansas	38,347	14.3	29
Kentucky	101,431	25.1	16
Louisiana	154,523	34.6	11
Maine	10,597	8.3	38
Maryland	45,194	8.5	37
Massachusetts	12,997	2.0	47
Michigan	140,190	14.1	30
Minnesota	33,003	6.7	40
Mississippi	81,083	28.5	15
Missouri	130,957	23.4	19
Montana	122,149	135.4	5
Nebraska	30,061	17.6	24
Nevada	1,008,270	504.6	2
New Hampshire	6,161	5.0	42
New Jersey	29,010	3.4	43
New Mexico	125,209	68.8	6
New York	60,536	3.2	44
North Carolina	157,280	19.5	21
North Dakota	24,200	37.7	10
Ohio	283,020	24.9	17
Oklahoma	33,003	9.6	34
Oregon	82,160	24.0	18
Pennsylvania	225,913	18.4	23
Rhode Island	1,276	1.2	48
South Carolina	79,369	19.8	20
South Dakota	9,606	12.7	31
Tennessee	162,856	28.6	14
Texas	301,519	14.5	28
Utah	955,942	428.1	3
Vermont	402	0.7	50
Virginia	82,194	11.6	33
Washington	31,708	5.4	41
West Virginia	97,714	54.0	8
Wisconsin	49,679	9.3	35
Wyoming	21,131	42.8	9
50 States	7,081,115	25.2	
DC	66	0.1	
United States*	7,100,731	25.2	

Rank in order per capita	
1	Alaska
2	Nevada
3	Utah
4	Arizona
5	Montana
6	New Mexico
7	Idaho
8	West Virginia
9	Wyoming
10	North Dakota
11	Louisiana
12	Alabama
13	Indiana
14	Tennessee
15	Mississippi
16	Kentucky
17	Ohio
18	Oregon
19	Missouri
20	South Carolina
21	North Carolina
22	Arkansas
23	Pennsylvania
24	Nebraska
25	Delaware
26	Georgia
27	Iowa
28	Texas
29	Kansas
30	Michigan
31	South Dakota
32	Illinois
33	Virginia
34	Oklahoma
35	Wisconsin
36	Florida
37	Maryland
38	Maine
39	Colorado
40	Minnesota
41	Washington
42	New Hampshire
43	New Jersey
44	New York
45	Connecticut
46	California
47	Massachusetts
48	Rhode Island
49	Hawaii
50	Vermont

Due to rounding or data sources, the 50-state total plus D.C. may not equal the U.S. total. Please see introduction.

C-11 Hazardous Waste Sites, 2002

State	Hazardous waste sites #	Rank
Alabama	15	25
Alaska	7	44
Arizona	10	40
Arkansas	12	34
California	99	2
Colorado	17	22
Connecticut	16	23
Delaware	16	23
Florida	52	6
Georgia	15	25
Hawaii	3	46
Idaho	10	40
Illinois	45	8
Indiana	29	14
Iowa	14	29
Kansas	12	34
Kentucky	14	29
Louisiana	15	25
Maine	13	31
Maryland	19	20
Massachusetts	32	12
Michigan	69	5
Minnesota	24	17
Mississippi	4	45
Missouri	23	18
Montana	15	25
Nebraska	11	38
Nevada	1	49
New Hampshire	19	20
New Jersey	116	1
New Mexico	13	31
New York	91	4
North Carolina	27	15
North Dakota	0	50
Ohio	33	11
Oklahoma	11	38
Oregon	12	34
Pennsylvania	97	3
Rhode Island	12	34
South Carolina	25	16
South Dakota	2	47
Tennessee	13	31
Texas	41	9
Utah	21	19
Vermont	9	42
Virginia	30	13
Washington	48	7
West Virginia	9	42
Wisconsin	40	10
Wyoming	2	47
50 States	1,283	
DC	1	
United States*	1,296	

Due to rounding or data sources, the 50-state total plus D.C. may not equal the U.S. total. Please see introduction.

Rank in order by #	
1	New Jersey
2	California
3	Pennsylvania
4	New York
5	Michigan
6	Florida
7	Washington
8	Illinois
9	Texas
10	Wisconsin
11	Ohio
12	Massachusetts
13	Virginia
14	Indiana
15	North Carolina
16	South Carolina
17	Minnesota
18	Missouri
19	Utah
20	Maryland
20	New Hampshire
22	Colorado
23	Connecticut
23	Delaware
25	Alabama
25	Georgia
25	Louisiana
25	Montana
29	Iowa
29	Kentucky
31	Maine
31	New Mexico
31	Tennessee
34	Arkansas
34	Kansas
34	Oregon
34	Rhode Island
38	Nebraska
38	Oklahoma
40	Arizona
40	Idaho
42	Vermont
42	West Virginia
44	Alaska
45	Mississippi
46	Hawaii
47	South Dakota
47	Wyoming
49	Nevada
50	North Dakota

Note: Ties in ranking reflect ties in actual values.

C-12 Polluted Rivers and Streams, 2000

State	Percentage of EPA-surveyed river and stream miles that are polluted	EPA-surveyed river and stream miles as a percentage of total river and stream miles	Rank by percentage polluted
Alabama	73.4	3.4	5
Alaska	36.5	0.4	30
Arizona	24.3	3.2	39
Arkansas	14.5	9.3	47
California	82.9	11.9	2
Colorado	3.0	39.0	49
Connecticut	32.3	20.7	32
Delaware	70.4	100.0	7
Florida	31.0	19.6	34
Georgia	59.9	14.2	14
Hawaii	68.5	100.0	9
Idaho	47.5	15.0	23
Illinois	50.3	17.9	18
Indiana	24.1	49.2	40
Iowa	29.8	8.9	36
Kansas	81.3	13.6	3
Kentucky	37.2	20.2	28
Louisiana	89.3	11.1	1
Maine	2.3	100.0	50
Maryland	37.3	98.0	27
Massachusetts	64.8	18.2	10
Michigan	23.8	25.5	41
Minnesota	69.3	12.4	8
Mississippi	72.3	17.8	6
Missouri	47.8	41.6	22
Montana	75.0	6.5	4
Nebraska	57.8	7.8	15
Nevada	60.9	1.1	13
New Hampshire	16.6	24.6	45
New Jersey	63.3	4.1	11
New Mexico	62.4	3.9	12
New York	37.1	5.6	29
North Carolina	6.7	100.0	48
North Dakota	48.3	27.5	21
Ohio	45.5	28.3	25
Oklahoma	54.3	17.9	16
Oregon	23.3	46.5	42
Pennsylvania	20.5	42.7	44
Rhode Island	33.5	46.9	31
South Carolina	26.0	51.7	38
South Dakota	49.9	35.9	19
Tennessee	31.0	39.8	33
Texas	30.1	7.9	35
Utah	26.9	12.2	37
Vermont	21.4	76.9	43
Virginia	48.6	18.6	20
Washington	53.6	100.0	17
West Virginia	46.0	35.8	24
Wisconsin	42.6	42.8	26
Wyoming	15.3	2.7	46
50 States	**38.3**	**18.8**	
DC	**100.0**	**98.5**	
United States	**38.7**	**19.0**	

Rank in order by percentage polluted	
1	Louisiana
2	California
3	Kansas
4	Montana
5	Alabama
6	Mississippi
7	Delaware
8	Minnesota
9	Hawaii
10	Massachusetts
11	New Jersey
12	New Mexico
13	Nevada
14	Georgia
15	Nebraska
16	Oklahoma
17	Washington
18	Illinois
19	South Dakota
20	Virginia
21	North Dakota
22	Missouri
23	Idaho
24	West Virginia
25	Ohio
26	Wisconsin
27	Maryland
28	Kentucky
29	New York
30	Alaska
31	Rhode Island
32	Connecticut
33	Tennessee
34	Florida
35	Texas
36	Iowa
37	Utah
38	South Carolina
39	Arizona
40	Indiana
41	Michigan
42	Oregon
43	Vermont
44	Pennsylvania
45	New Hampshire
46	Wyoming
47	Arkansas
48	North Carolina
49	Colorado
50	Maine

Note: Numbers that appear to be identical are rounded and vary slightly in actual value. The rankings reflect the actual values before rounding. See the introduction for more details.

C-13 Expired Surface Water Pollution Discharge Permits, 2002

State	Percentage of major facilities with expired Clean Water Act permits	Rank
Alabama	3.7	44
Alaska	6.7	40
Arizona	4.0	43
Arkansas	13.5	32
California	22.2	20
Colorado	33.3	10
Connecticut	14.2	30
Delaware	26.1	18
Florida	15.6	28
Georgia	1.2	48
Hawaii	18.2	24
Idaho	8.8	37
Illinois	17.3	26
Indiana	44.0	6
Iowa	15.5	29
Kansas	1.7	47
Kentucky	4.6	42
Louisiana	54.2	2
Maine	27.6	15
Maryland	19.4	23
Massachusetts	26.6	17
Michigan	17.4	25
Minnesota	48.8	4
Mississippi	11.6	34
Missouri	31.8	12
Montana	37.2	8
Nebraska	53.6	3
Nevada	30.0	14
New Hampshire	16.7	27
New Jersey	38.5	7
New Mexico	8.6	38
New York	3.7	44
North Carolina	32.5	11
North Dakota	0.0	49
Ohio	27.2	16
Oklahoma	5.3	41
Oregon	66.7	1
Pennsylvania	24.6	19
Rhode Island	12.0	33
South Carolina	30.3	13
South Dakota	13.8	31
Tennessee	7.7	39
Texas	20.5	22
Utah	0.0	49
Vermont	2.9	46
Virginia	20.7	21
Washington	45.3	5
West Virginia	34.4	9
Wisconsin	9.7	36
Wyoming	11.5	35
50 States	n/a	
DC	50.0	
United States	22.0	

Rank in order by percentage

1 Oregon
2 Louisiana
3 Nebraska
4 Minnesota
5 Washington
6 Indiana
7 New Jersey
8 Montana
9 West Virginia
10 Colorado
11 North Carolina
12 Missouri
13 South Carolina
14 Nevada
15 Maine
16 Ohio
17 Massachusetts
18 Delaware
19 Pennsylvania
20 California
21 Virginia
22 Texas
23 Maryland
24 Hawaii
25 Michigan
26 Illinois
27 New Hampshire
28 Florida
29 Iowa
30 Connecticut
31 South Dakota
32 Arkansas
33 Rhode Island
34 Mississippi
35 Wyoming
36 Wisconsin
37 Idaho
38 New Mexico
39 Tennessee
40 Alaska
41 Oklahoma
42 Kentucky
43 Arizona
44 Alabama
44 New York
46 Vermont
47 Kansas
48 Georgia
49 North Dakota
49 Utah

Note: Ties in ranking reflect ties in actual values.

C-14 Air Pollution Emissions, 1999

State	Emissions in short tons (in thousands)	Per capita	Rank by total emissions
Alabama	4,906	1.1	12
Alaska	3,166	5.1	24
Arizona	3,517	0.7	21
Arkansas	2,396	0.9	32
California	11,792	0.4	2
Colorado	2,714	0.7	29
Connecticut	1,356	0.4	41
Delaware	453	0.6	48
Florida	9,415	0.6	3
Georgia	7,144	0.9	5
Hawaii	567	0.5	47
Idaho	1,822	1.5	36
Illinois	7,003	0.6	6
Indiana	5,619	0.9	10
Iowa	2,482	0.9	30
Kansas	2,781	1.0	28
Kentucky	3,614	0.9	19
Louisiana	4,325	1.0	15
Maine	1,040	0.8	44
Maryland	2,180	0.4	35
Massachusetts	2,437	0.4	31
Michigan	6,272	0.6	9
Minnesota	3,724	0.8	17
Mississippi	2,924	1.1	27
Missouri	4,208	0.8	16
Montana	1,478	1.7	39
Nebraska	1,760	1.1	37
Nevada	1,169	0.6	43
New Hampshire	797	0.7	46
New Jersey	2,989	0.4	26
New Mexico	2,388	1.4	33
New York	6,299	0.3	8
North Carolina	5,467	0.7	11
North Dakota	1,405	2.2	40
Ohio	8,494	0.8	4
Oklahoma	3,273	1.0	23
Oregon	3,541	1.1	20
Pennsylvania	6,579	0.5	7
Rhode Island	378	0.4	50
South Carolina	3,163	0.8	25
South Dakota	895	1.2	45
Tennessee	4,597	0.8	13
Texas	13,615	0.7	1
Utah	1,635	0.8	38
Vermont	450	0.8	49
Virginia	4,330	0.6	14
Washington	3,702	0.6	18
West Virginia	2,371	1.3	34
Wisconsin	3,494	0.7	22
Wyoming	1,303	2.7	42
50 States	183,431	0.7	
DC	131	0.3	
United States*	183,561	0.7	

Rank in order by total emissions	
1	Texas
2	California
3	Florida
4	Ohio
5	Georgia
6	Illinois
7	Pennsylvania
8	New York
9	Michigan
10	Indiana
11	North Carolina
12	Alabama
13	Tennessee
14	Virginia
15	Louisiana
16	Missouri
17	Minnesota
18	Washington
19	Kentucky
20	Oregon
21	Arizona
22	Wisconsin
23	Oklahoma
24	Alaska
25	South Carolina
26	New Jersey
27	Mississippi
28	Kansas
29	Colorado
30	Iowa
31	Massachusetts
32	Arkansas
33	New Mexico
34	West Virginia
35	Maryland
36	Idaho
37	Nebraska
38	Utah
39	Montana
40	North Dakota
41	Connecticut
42	Wyoming
43	Nevada
44	Maine
45	South Dakota
46	New Hampshire
47	Hawaii
48	Delaware
49	Vermont
50	Rhode Island

Due to rounding or data sources, the 50-state total plus D.C. may not equal the U.S. total. Please see introduction.

Source Notes for Geography (Section C)

C-1 Total Land Area, 2000: This statistic comes from the 2000 census and is prepared by the geography division of the Census Bureau. It can be combined with population statistics to calculate the population "density" of each state (see Table A-16).

C-2 Land Owned by Federal Government, 2000: The federal government owns land for its buildings, military installations, and other facilities in every state, but these holdings are not major factors in the land use patterns of most states. The federal government also owns massive areas as part of the National Park Service and the Forest Service, and public lands managed by the U.S. Department of the Interior, primarily arid lands in Western states. These federal land holdings, measured in land area—not land usefulness—are more than half of the land in some states. The data are maintained by the individual federal agencies that own the land, and they are compiled in the U.S. General Services Administration's annual publication, *Inventory Report on Real Property Owned by the United States Throughout the World.* The next report, to be released in the spring of 2003, will cover FY 2002.

C-3 State Park Acreage, FY 2002: These statistics show the acres of state parks and the number of acres of state parks per one thousand people. The data are for the year ending June 30, 2002. They come from the National Association of State Park Directors (www.naspd.org). The ratio was calculated by *State Fact Finder.*

C-4 State Park Visitors, FY 2002: State park agencies make estimates of the number of visitors to state parks maintained by the National Association of State Park Directors (see source for Table C-3). *State Fact Finder* related these visits to population using Census data. The data can be viewed as indicating that the average person visits a state park about 2.7 times a year.

C-5 Percentage of Population Not Physically Active, 2001: There are few reliable data on a state level on the participation of citizens in various forms of recreational activities, as no one maintains records of who hikes, plays tennis, or fishes except when they use facilities requiring admission. These data are from a survey of the Centers for Disease Control and Prevention (CDC). The data reflect the percentage of those surveyed who answered "no" to the question "During the past month, did you participate in any leisure time physical activity?" The numbers are available on the CDC website (www.cdc.gov) as "2001 BRFSS Summary Prevalence Report."

C-6 Hunters with Firearms, 2001: These data show the sharp differences among states in the use of firearms for hunting—statistics highly relevant to debates over use and control of firearms. Note that the participant for the state listed is a resident of that state even though they may not have hunted in that state. That is, a hunter with firearms in Texas is a resident of Texas even though he or she may have hunted in Louisiana. Estimates by state are made by the National Sporting Goods Association (Mt. Prospect, Illinois 60056) for all major recreation activities.

C-7 Registered Boats, 2001: All states require registration of motorboats and some require registration of other boats, such as canoes and sailboats. These data, collected from state authorities by the U.S. Coast Guard, show the number of registered boats and the relationship between the number of boats and population. The data come from the Consumer Affairs and Analysis Branch of the U.S. Coast Guard and were provided to *State Fact Finder* by e-mail on October 10, 2002.

C-8 State Spending on State Arts Agencies, FY 2002: Each of the fifty states and six jurisdictional governments supports an arts agency as the primary means of funding the arts and encouraging cultural participation. These agencies receive the bulk of their funding from state level legislative appropriations, with additional support from the National Endowment for the Arts and other sources (governmental, private, and earned). This table measures legislative support for state arts agencies in FY 2002. The National Assembly of State Arts Agencies collects and publishes this information and provided it to *State Fact Finder* via e-mail November 4, 2002.

C-9 Energy Consumption, Total and Per Capita, 2000: At the time of the "energy crisis" of the 1970s, the federal government established a Department of Energy (DOE) and a vast data collection mechanism covering production and consumption of all forms of energy, including coal, oil, gas, and nuclear power. This table from the Energy Information Administration (EIA) of the DOE shows total energy consumption and relates it to the population of each state.

These data show consumption by all users, including businesses, by the state where energy is used, not necessarily where it was produced. States with relatively small populations and intensive energy use for mining and petrochemical manufacturing show the largest use. The EIA has detailed data by state on sources of energy and use in categories, such as residential and industrial. For those users interested in comparisons over time, this 2000 data is not comparable to data in previous editions of *State Fact Finder.* This is because it does not include energy from ethanol or wood and waste. Data from these sources was not available at the time of publication. When EIA compiles and releases consumption numbers for these renewable energy sources, the data will be posted on the EIA website (www.eia.doe.gov). The EIA also publishes an annual report, *State Energy Data Report,* with detailed information regarding energy consumption and prices.

C-10 Toxic Chemical Release, 2000: The U.S. Environmental Protection Agency (EPA) requires detailed reporting of what it defines as "toxic" chemical releases into the atmosphere. These data, from the *2000 Toxics Release Inventory*, available on the EPA website (www.epa.gov), are frequently cited by the media as indicators of health risks and air pollution in particular states. They are of little value for this purpose. The effects of releases in a particular state often are not felt in that state because they are carried to an adjacent state or the oceans. High totals are generally associated with a few plants whose owners argue that their releases are not hazardous to health.

C-11 Hazardous Waste Sites, 2002: This table shows the number of sites the Environmental Protection Agency (EPA) has designated for cleanup under the Superfund program. The program and the designations are highly controversial, but the data are often cited as indicators of the relative prevalence of hazardous waste problems in particular states. The data are available on the EPA website (www.epa.gov/superfund).

C-12 Polluted Rivers and Streams, 2000: Under federal water pollution laws, each state reports to the Environmental Protection Agency (EPA) on the status of its rivers, specifically whether they are safe for fishing (and eating the catch) and swimming. The EPA compiles this data in its biannual publication *National Water Quality Inventory: Report to Congress*. These data are printed in the 2000 report that was released in 2002. The percentages reflect not the total number of rivers and streams in a state but the total number that were surveyed. Nationwide, 19 percent of 3.7 million river and stream miles were surveyed in 2000. Impairment refers to reduced "aquatic life support."

This table and other available measures of the pollution of rivers are not particularly useful for many purposes. At this point, states are unable to survey all their bodies of water and thus tend to monitor areas with suspected problems. In addition, any compilation of river-miles includes many stretches in remote locations that are of little use for swimming or fishing because of inaccessibility, low flows, few fish, and insufficient depth for swimming. There is no statistic that allows comparing states on a basis more reflective of the extent to which pollution prevents safe fishing and swimming in relation to the fishing and swimming that would occur if there were no pollution at all.

C-13 Expired Surface Water Pollution Discharge Permits, 2002: Through the Clean Water Act a system of permits was created. These permits are issued to factories, utilities, sewage treatment plants, and any other private or public entity that releases pollutants into the nation's waters. The purpose is to regulate and reduce pollution discharges. Permits come up for renewal at least every five years, at which time new requirements for pollution reduction or better treatment technologies are generally required. This table based on data from the Environmental Protection Agency's National Pollutant Discharge Elimination System (NPDES) and available on their website (www.cfpub.epa.gov/npdes) provides a measure of the permit backlog in each state. Environmental groups argue that while permits remain in limbo, a water pollution program cannot be operated effectively. The EPA has put forth the goal of reducing backlog to 10 percent (the amount determined by the EPA to be acceptable) by the end of 2004.

C-14 Air Pollution Emissions, 1999: Despite many years and millions of dollars put into efforts to measure air pollution on a state-by-state basis, no satisfactory method has been found to develop a summary measure. There are many problems. Air pollution affects people where they breathe, so for some purposes the relevant measure is what's in the ambient air, but there is little interest in measuring air quality in places with few or no people like mountains and deserts. So, such measures focus on metropolitan areas, not states. Within each state, there are dramatic differences in pollution levels associated with such factors as proximity to prevailing winds and pollution sources and elevation.

Air pollution can only be controlled where it originates, so measurement related to enforcement concentrates on place of origin, which is often not the same as the state where people are affected. Airborne pollutants don't recognize state lines, so the relevant concept is airsheds, not states.

State Fact Finder developed this table primarily to lead users to the vast quantities of data available. The table reflects added estimates of short tons of pollution emissions in each state for five pollutants — carbon monoxide, nitrogen oxide, volatile organic compounds, sulfur dioxide, and particulate matter. The per capita calculation is provided only as a subject of possible interest. The ranking based on total tons of emissions is not a proxy for the seriousness of air pollution to the residents of the states listed and not a recognized measure of how effectively states control pollution.

The data on each pollutant by state and major causes (for example, transportation, farming, utility operation) come from the Emission Factor and Inventory Group at the Environmental Protection Agency Office of Air Quality Planning and Standards. This office and its publication *National Air Pollutant Emission Trends* are good sources for other information useful to readers interested in comparing air pollution emissions of the various states.

Government

D-1	Members of the United States House, 2003	96
D-2	Members of State Legislatures, 2003	97
D-3	State Legislators Per Million Population, 2003	98
D-4	Units of Government, 1997	99
D-5	State Legislator Compensation, 2002	100
D-6	Percentage of Legislators Who Are Female, 2002	101
D-7	Turnover in Legislatures, Post-election 2002	102
D-8	Term Limits (in years), 2002	103
D-9	Legislative Session Length, 2003	104
D-10	Party Control of State Legislatures, 2003	105
D-11	Governor's Power Rating, 2002	106
D-12	Number of Statewide Elected Officials, 2000	107
D-13	State and Local Government Employees, 2001	108
D-14	Average Salaries of State and Local Government Employees, 2001	109
D-15	Local Employment, 2001	110
D-16	Local Spending Accountability, FY 2000	111
D-17	Percentage of Eligible Voters Registered, November 2002	112
D-18	Percentage of Population Voting, November 2002	113
D-19	Statewide Initiatives and Popular Referenda, 2002	114
D-20	Campaign Costs Per Vote in Most Recent Gubernatorial Election, 1998, 1999, 2000, or 2001	115

Is there a growing trend in state government? Peter Harkness, publisher of *Governing* magazine, hinted at one in 2002: "The news has been offering up stories that, taken by themselves, are unusual. When you consider the trend these stories are defining, it's extraordinary." The stories:

- New York's attorney general tackles securities fraud, several other attorneys general follow in his footsteps.
- California, a state that accounts for 12 percent of the nation's auto and truck sales, sets new standards to reduce tailpipe emissions of greenhouse gases.
- Refusing to accept the U.S. Justice Department's settlement with Microsoft, nine states challenge the deal in court. After losing, one state—Massachusetts—presses on with an appeal.
- Nine states challenge the Bush administration's relaxation of air pollution laws.

Should states oversee Wall Street? Should one state set policy standards for the nation? The issues are debatable, but in the end, says Harkness, "you're still left with the fact that all of this is going on, that New York has taken the lead on regulating the securities industry" and "that California may change our national global warming and fuel-efficiency policies."

Another example of a state leapfrogging federal action is Georgia. Long before President Bush signed the "Help America Vote Act" the Peach State replaced every antiquated voting machine with modern equipment.

In fact, no state wanted to be "the next Florida." Across the country states introduced 1,555 election reform bills, covering everything from bans on punch cards to registration rules to the very methods used to count votes. All but eight states passed some kind of reform in 2000 or 2001. Twenty-one states legislated changes to update or replace outmoded voting standards and equipment, and sixteen states revisited their recount procedures. In the end, despite a close gubernatorial race in Alabama and legislative control in five states that hinged on a recount, states skirted controversy in the mid-term elections—elections that decided thirty-six governors and over six thousand state legislative seats.

D-1 Members of the United States House, 2003

State	Number of House members	Change from 1990 census	Rank
Alabama	7	0	22
Alaska	1	0	44
Arizona	8	+2	18
Arkansas	4	0	31
California	53	+1	1
Colorado	7	+1	22
Connecticut	5	-1	27
Delaware	1	0	44
Florida	25	+2	4
Georgia	13	+2	9
Hawaii	2	0	39
Idaho	2	0	39
Illinois	19	-1	5
Indiana	9	-1	14
Iowa	5	0	27
Kansas	4	0	31
Kentucky	6	0	25
Louisiana	7	0	22
Maine	2	0	39
Maryland	8	0	18
Massachusetts	10	0	13
Michigan	15	-1	8
Minnesota	8	0	18
Mississippi	4	-1	31
Missouri	9	0	14
Montana	1	0	44
Nebraska	3	0	34
Nevada	3	+1	34
New Hampshire	2	0	39
New Jersey	13	0	9
New Mexico	3	0	34
New York	29	-2	3
North Carolina	13	+1	9
North Dakota	1	0	44
Ohio	18	-1	7
Oklahoma	5	-1	27
Oregon	5	0	27
Pennsylvania	19	-2	5
Rhode Island	2	0	39
South Carolina	6	0	25
South Dakota	1	0	44
Tennessee	9	0	14
Texas	32	+2	2
Utah	3	0	34
Vermont	1	0	44
Virginia	11	0	12
Washington	9	0	14
West Virginia	3	0	34
Wisconsin	8	-1	18
Wyoming	1	0	44
50 States	435		
DC	n/a		
United States	435		

Rank in order by

1	California
2	Texas
3	New York
4	Florida
5	Illinois
5	Pennsylvania
7	Ohio
8	Michigan
9	Georgia
9	New Jersey
9	North Carolina
12	Virginia
13	Massachusetts
14	Indiana
14	Missouri
14	Tennessee
14	Washington
18	Arizona
18	Maryland
18	Minnesota
18	Wisconsin
22	Alabama
22	Colorado
22	Louisiana
25	Kentucky
25	South Carolina
27	Connecticut
27	Iowa
27	Oklahoma
27	Oregon
31	Arkansas
31	Kansas
31	Mississippi
34	Nebraska
34	Nevada
34	New Mexico
34	Utah
34	West Virginia
39	Hawaii
39	Idaho
39	Maine
39	New Hampshire
39	Rhode Island
44	Alaska
44	Delaware
44	Montana
44	North Dakota
44	South Dakota
44	Vermont
44	Wyoming

Note: Ties in ranking reflect ties in actual values.

D-2 Members of State Legislatures, 2003

State	Senate members	House members	Total members	Rank by total members
Alabama	35	105	140	27
Alaska	20	40	60	49
Arizona	30	60	90	43
Arkansas	35	100	135	30
California	40	80	120	35
Colorado	35	65	100	42
Connecticut	36	151	187	9
Delaware	21	41	62	48
Florida	40	120	160	18
Georgia	56	180	236	3
Hawaii	25	51	76	46
Idaho	35	70	105	39
Illinois	59	118	177	13
Indiana	50	100	150	19
Iowa	50	100	150	19
Kansas	40	125	165	17
Kentucky	38	100	138	29
Louisiana	39	105	144	25
Maine	35	151	186	10
Maryland	47	141	188	8
Massachusetts	40	160	200	6
Michigan	38	110	148	23
Minnesota	67	134	201	5
Mississippi	52	122	174	14
Missouri	34	163	197	7
Montana	50	100	150	19
Nebraska	49	n/a	49	50
Nevada	21	42	63	47
New Hampshire	24	400	424	1
New Jersey	40	80	120	35
New Mexico	42	70	112	38
New York	62	150	212	4
North Carolina	50	120	170	15
North Dakota	47	94	141	26
Ohio	33	99	132	32
Oklahoma	48	101	149	22
Oregon	30	60	90	43
Pennsylvania	50	203	253	2
Rhode Island	38	75	113	37
South Carolina	46	124	170	15
South Dakota	35	70	105	39
Tennessee	33	99	132	32
Texas	31	150	181	11
Utah	29	75	104	41
Vermont	30	150	180	12
Virginia	40	100	140	27
Washington	49	98	147	24
West Virginia	34	100	134	31
Wisconsin	33	99	132	32
Wyoming	30	60	90	43
50 States	1,971	5,411	7,382	
DC	n/a	n/a	n/a	
United States	1,971	5,411	7,382	

Rank in order by total members	
1	New Hampshire
2	Pennsylvania
3	Georgia
4	New York
5	Minnesota
6	Massachusetts
7	Missouri
8	Maryland
9	Connecticut
10	Maine
11	Texas
12	Vermont
13	Illinois
14	Mississippi
15	North Carolina
15	South Carolina
17	Kansas
18	Florida
19	Indiana
19	Iowa
19	Montana
22	Oklahoma
23	Michigan
24	Washington
25	Louisiana
26	North Dakota
27	Alabama
27	Virginia
29	Kentucky
30	Arkansas
31	West Virginia
32	Ohio
32	Tennessee
32	Wisconsin
35	California
35	New Jersey
37	Rhode Island
38	New Mexico
39	Idaho
39	South Dakota
41	Utah
42	Colorado
43	Arizona
43	Oregon
43	Wyoming
46	Hawaii
47	Nevada
48	Delaware
49	Alaska
50	Nebraska

Note: Ties in ranking reflect ties in actual values.

D-3 State Legislators Per Million Population, 2003

State	Legislators per million population	Rank
Alabama	31	28
Alaska	95	9
Arizona	17	42
Arkansas	50	19
California	3	50
Colorado	23	38
Connecticut	55	17
Delaware	78	11
Florida	10	48
Georgia	28	32
Hawaii	62	13
Idaho	79	10
Illinois	14	44
Indiana	25	35
Iowa	51	18
Kansas	61	14
Kentucky	34	26
Louisiana	32	27
Maine	145	6
Maryland	35	25
Massachusetts	31	29
Michigan	15	43
Minnesota	40	23
Mississippi	61	16
Missouri	35	24
Montana	166	5
Nebraska	29	31
Nevada	30	30
New Hampshire	337	1
New Jersey	14	45
New Mexico	61	15
New York	11	47
North Carolina	21	39
North Dakota	222	3
Ohio	12	46
Oklahoma	43	21
Oregon	26	33
Pennsylvania	21	40
Rhode Island	107	8
South Carolina	42	22
South Dakota	139	7
Tennessee	23	37
Texas	8	49
Utah	46	20
Vermont	294	2
Virginia	19	41
Washington	25	34
West Virginia	74	12
Wisconsin	24	36
Wyoming	182	4
50 States	26	
DC	n/a	
United States	26	

Rank in order per million population

1 New Hampshire
2 Vermont
3 North Dakota
4 Wyoming
5 Montana
6 Maine
7 South Dakota
8 Rhode Island
9 Alaska
10 Idaho
11 Delaware
12 West Virginia
13 Hawaii
14 Kansas
15 New Mexico
16 Mississippi
17 Connecticut
18 Iowa
19 Arkansas
20 Utah
21 Oklahoma
22 South Carolina
23 Minnesota
24 Missouri
25 Maryland
26 Kentucky
27 Louisiana
28 Alabama
29 Massachusetts
30 Nevada
31 Nebraska
32 Georgia
33 Oregon
34 Washington
35 Indiana
36 Wisconsin
37 Tennessee
38 Colorado
39 North Carolina
40 Pennsylvania
41 Virginia
42 Arizona
43 Michigan
44 Illinois
45 New Jersey
46 Ohio
47 New York
48 Florida
49 Texas
50 California

Note: Numbers that appear to be identical are rounded and vary slightly in actual value. The rankings reflect the actual values before rounding. See the introduction for more details.

D-4 Units of Government, 1997

State	Number of government units	Units per 10,000 population	Rank per 10,000 population
Alabama	1,132	2.6	32
Alaska	176	2.9	30
Arizona	638	1.4	42
Arkansas	1,517	6.0	13
California	4,608	1.4	40
Colorado	1,870	4.8	20
Connecticut	584	1.8	37
Delaware	337	4.6	22
Florida	1,082	0.7	48
Georgia	1,345	1.8	36
Hawaii	20	0.2	50
Idaho	1,148	9.5	8
Illinois	6,836	5.7	15
Indiana	3,199	5.5	16
Iowa	1,877	6.6	11
Kansas	3,951	15.2	4
Kentucky	1,367	3.5	25
Louisiana	468	1.1	46
Maine	833	6.7	10
Maryland	421	0.8	47
Massachusetts	862	1.4	41
Michigan	2,776	2.8	31
Minnesota	3,502	7.5	9
Mississippi	937	3.4	26
Missouri	3,417	6.3	12
Montana	1,145	13.0	6
Nebraska	2,895	17.5	3
Nevada	206	1.2	44
New Hampshire	576	4.9	19
New Jersey	1,422	1.8	38
New Mexico	882	5.1	18
New York	3,414	1.9	35
North Carolina	953	1.3	43
North Dakota	2,759	43.0	1
Ohio	3,598	3.2	29
Oklahoma	1,800	5.4	17
Oregon	1,494	4.6	21
Pennsylvania	5,071	4.2	23
Rhode Island	120	1.2	45
South Carolina	717	1.9	34
South Dakota	1,811	24.5	2
Tennessee	941	1.8	39
Texas	4,701	2.4	33
Utah	684	3.3	27
Vermont	692	11.8	7
Virginia	484	0.7	49
Washington	1,813	3.2	28
West Virginia	705	3.9	24
Wisconsin	3,060	5.9	14
Wyoming	655	13.6	5
50 States	87,501	3.3	
DC	2	0.0	
United States*	87,504	3.3	

Rank in order per 10,000 population	
1	North Dakota
2	South Dakota
3	Nebraska
4	Kansas
5	Wyoming
6	Montana
7	Vermont
8	Idaho
9	Minnesota
10	Maine
11	Iowa
12	Missouri
13	Arkansas
14	Wisconsin
15	Illinois
16	Indiana
17	Oklahoma
18	New Mexico
19	New Hampshire
20	Colorado
21	Oregon
22	Delaware
23	Pennsylvania
24	West Virginia
25	Kentucky
26	Mississippi
27	Utah
28	Washington
29	Ohio
30	Alaska
31	Michigan
32	Alabama
33	Texas
34	South Carolina
35	New York
36	Georgia
37	Connecticut
38	New Jersey
39	Tennessee
40	California
41	Massachusetts
42	Arizona
43	North Carolina
44	Nevada
45	Rhode Island
46	Louisiana
47	Maryland
48	Florida
49	Virginia
50	Hawaii

Note: Numbers that appear to be identical are rounded and vary slightly in actual value. The rankings reflect the actual values before rounding. See the introduction for more details.

Due to rounding or data sources, the 50-state total plus D.C. may not equal the U.S. total. Please see introduction.

D-5 State Legislator Compensation, 2002

State	Salary $	Per diem during session $	Rank by salary
Alabama	1,000	2,280/month	48
Alaska	24,012	161/day	20
Arizona	24,000	35-60/day	21
Arkansas	12,769	95/day	32
California	99,000	121/day	1
Colorado	30,000	45-99/day	17
Connecticut	28,000	0	18
Delaware	33,400	0	11
Florida	27,900	99/day	19
Georgia	16,200	128/day	26
Hawaii	32,000	10-80/day	13
Idaho	15,646	38-99/day	28
Illinois	55,788	85/day	5
Indiana	11,600	112/day	34
Iowa	20,758	65-86/day	22
Kansas	7,088	85/day	43
Kentucky	16,029	93.50/day	27
Louisiana	16,800	116/day	24
Maine	9,270	70/day	39
Maryland	31,509	126/day	15
Massachusetts	50,123	10-100/day	7
Michigan	77,400	12,000/year	3
Minnesota	31,140	56-66/day	16
Mississippi	10,000	85/day	38
Missouri	31,561	72/day	14
Montana	5,603	58/day	45
Nebraska	12,000	30-85/day	33
Nevada	7,800	federal rate	41
New Hampshire	100	0	49
New Jersey	49,000	0	8
New Mexico	0	145/day	50
New York	79,500	varies	2
North Carolina	13,951	104/day	31
North Dakota	10,767	900/month	36
Ohio	51,674	0	6
Oklahoma	38,400	103/day	10
Oregon	15,396	85/day	29
Pennsylvania	61,890	124/day	4
Rhode Island	11,236	0	35
South Carolina	10,400	95/day	37
South Dakota	6,000	110/day	44
Tennessee	16,500	124/day	25
Texas	7,200	124/day	42
Utah	3,360	117/day	46
Vermont	9,112	87-32/day	40
Virginia	18,000	115/day	23
Washington	32,064	82/day	12
West Virginia	15,000	115/day	30
Wisconsin	44,333	88/day	9
Wyoming	2,875	80/day	47
50 States (average)	24,703	n/a	
DC	92,500	0	
United States (average)	26,032	n/a	

Rank in order by salary

1 California
2 New York
3 Michigan
4 Pennsylvania
5 Illinois
6 Ohio
7 Massachusetts
8 New Jersey
9 Wisconsin
10 Oklahoma
11 Delaware
12 Washington
13 Hawaii
14 Missouri
15 Maryland
16 Minnesota
17 Colorado
18 Connecticut
19 Florida
20 Alaska
21 Arizona
22 Iowa
23 Virginia
24 Louisiana
25 Tennessee
26 Georgia
27 Kentucky
28 Idaho
29 Oregon
30 West Virginia
31 North Carolina
32 Arkansas
33 Nebraska
34 Indiana
35 Rhode Island
36 North Dakota
37 South Carolina
38 Mississippi
39 Maine
40 Vermont
41 Nevada
42 Texas
43 Kansas
44 South Dakota
45 Montana
46 Utah
47 Wyoming
48 Alabama
49 New Hampshire
50 New Mexico

D-6 Percentage of Legislators Who Are Female, 2002

State	Percentage of female legislators	Rank
Alabama	7.9	50
Alaska	20.0	32
Arizona	35.6	2
Arkansas	14.1	45
California	28.3	13
Colorado	34.0	5
Connecticut	30.5	8
Delaware	25.8	17
Florida	23.8	21
Georgia	21.2	30
Hawaii	25.0	19
Idaho	27.6	15
Illinois	26.6	16
Indiana	17.3	36
Iowa	22.0	28
Kansas	32.1	6
Kentucky	10.9	47
Louisiana	16.0	39
Maine	29.6	10
Maryland	30.9	7
Massachusetts	25.5	18
Michigan	22.3	26
Minnesota	29.4	11
Mississippi	12.6	46
Missouri	23.4	23
Montana	24.0	20
Nebraska	20.4	31
Nevada	34.9	3
New Hampshire	29.0	12
New Jersey	15.8	41
New Mexico	30.4	9
New York	22.3	26
North Carolina	18.8	34
North Dakota	17.0	37
Ohio	22.0	28
Oklahoma	10.1	49
Oregon	34.4	4
Pennsylvania	14.2	44
Rhode Island	22.7	25
South Carolina	10.6	48
South Dakota	16.2	38
Tennessee	15.9	40
Texas	19.3	33
Utah	23.1	24
Vermont	28.3	13
Virginia	15.7	42
Washington	38.8	1
West Virginia	18.7	35
Wisconsin	23.5	22
Wyoming	15.6	43
50 States	22.6	
DC	n/a	
United States	22.6	

Rank in order by percentage

1. Washington
2. Arizona
3. Nevada
4. Oregon
5. Colorado
6. Kansas
7. Maryland
8. Connecticut
9. New Mexico
10. Maine
11. Minnesota
12. New Hampshire
13. California
13. Vermont
15. Idaho
16. Illinois
17. Delaware
18. Massachusetts
19. Hawaii
20. Montana
21. Florida
22. Wisconsin
23. Missouri
24. Utah
25. Rhode Island
26. Michigan
26. New York
28. Iowa
28. Ohio
30. Georgia
31. Nebraska
32. Alaska
33. Texas
34. North Carolina
35. West Virginia
36. Indiana
37. North Dakota
38. South Dakota
39. Louisiana
40. Tennessee
41. New Jersey
42. Virginia
43. Wyoming
44. Pennsylvania
45. Arkansas
46. Mississippi
47. Kentucky
48. South Carolina
49. Oklahoma
50. Alabama

Note: Ties in ranking reflect ties in actual values.

D-7 Turnover in Legislatures, Post-election 2002

State	Percentage of new legislators	Rank
Alabama	22.1	28
Alaska	36.7	8
Arizona	55.6	2
Arkansas	37.8	7
California	32.5	11
Colorado	24.0	25
Connecticut	16.6	34
Delaware	14.5	37
Florida	26.9	20
Georgia	27.5	19
Hawaii	25.0	23
Idaho	33.3	10
Illinois	24.9	24
Indiana	12.0	41
Iowa	38.7	5
Kansas	17.0	33
Kentucky	10.9	44
Louisiana	n/a	n/a
Maine	42.5	4
Maryland	31.4	15
Massachusetts	11.0	43
Michigan	56.8	1
Minnesota	31.8	13
Mississippi	n/a	n/a
Missouri	51.8	3
Montana	30.7	16
Nebraska	14.3	38
Nevada	31.7	14
New Hampshire	35.4	9
New Jersey	n/a	n/a
New Mexico	9.8	46
New York	12.7	40
North Carolina	30.6	17
North Dakota	13.1	39
Ohio	20.5	29
Oklahoma	16.1	35
Oregon	26.7	21
Pennsylvania	10.7	45
Rhode Island	32.0	12
South Carolina	11.8	42
South Dakota	38.1	6
Tennessee	19.7	30
Texas	23.2	26
Utah	17.3	31
Vermont	25.6	22
Virginia	n/a	n/a
Washington	17.0	32
West Virginia	22.4	27
Wisconsin	15.9	36
Wyoming	27.8	18
50 States	23.9	
DC	n/a	
United States	23.9	

Rank in order by percentage

1 Michigan
2 Arizona
3 Missouri
4 Maine
5 Iowa
6 South Dakota
7 Arkansas
8 Alaska
9 New Hampshire
10 Idaho
11 California
12 Rhode Island
13 Minnesota
14 Nevada
15 Maryland
16 Montana
17 North Carolina
18 Wyoming
19 Georgia
20 Florida
21 Oregon
22 Vermont
23 Hawaii
24 Illinois
25 Colorado
26 Texas
27 West Virginia
28 Alabama
29 Ohio
30 Tennessee
31 Utah
32 Washington
33 Kansas
34 Connecticut
35 Oklahoma
36 Wisconsin
37 Delaware
38 Nebraska
39 North Dakota
40 New York
41 Indiana
42 South Carolina
43 Massachusetts
44 Kentucky
45 Pennsylvania
46 New Mexico

Note: Numbers that appear to be identical are rounded and vary slightly in actual value. The rankings reflect the actual values before rounding. See the introduction for more details.

D-8 Term Limits (in years), 2002

State	Consecutive term limits Governor	Consecutive term limits House	Consecutive term limits Senate	Rank by House members
Alabama	8	n/a	n/a	n/a
Alaska	8	n/a	n/a	n/a
Arizona	8	8	8	6
Arkansas	8	6	8	15
California	8	6	8	15
Colorado	8	8	8	6
Connecticut	n/a	n/a	n/a	n/a
Delaware	8	n/a	n/a	n/a
Florida	8	8	8	6
Georgia	8	n/a	n/a	n/a
Hawaii	8	n/a	n/a	n/a
Idaho	8	n/a	n/a	n/a
Illinois	n/a	n/a	n/a	n/a
Indiana	8	n/a	n/a	n/a
Iowa	n/a	n/a	n/a	n/a
Kansas	8	n/a	n/a	n/a
Kentucky	8	n/a	n/a	n/a
Louisiana	8	12	12	1
Maine	8	8	8	6
Maryland	8	n/a	n/a	n/a
Massachusetts	n/a	n/a	n/a	n/a
Michigan	8	6	8	15
Minnesota	n/a	n/a	n/a	n/a
Mississippi	8	n/a	n/a	n/a
Missouri	8	8	8	6
Montana	8	8	8	6
Nebraska	8	unicameral	8	6
Nevada	8	12	12	1
New Hampshire	n/a	n/a	n/a	n/a
New Jersey	8	n/a	n/a	n/a
New Mexico	8	n/a	n/a	n/a
New York	n/a	n/a	n/a	n/a
North Carolina	8	n/a	n/a	n/a
North Dakota	n/a	n/a	n/a	n/a
Ohio	8	8	8	6
Oklahoma	8	12	12	1
Oregon	8	n/a	n/a	n/a
Pennsylvania	8	n/a	n/a	n/a
Rhode Island	8	n/a	n/a	n/a
South Carolina	8	n/a	n/a	n/a
South Dakota	8	8	8	6
Tennessee	8	n/a	n/a	n/a
Texas	n/a	n/a	n/a	n/a
Utah	12	12	12	1
Vermont	n/a	n/a	n/a	n/a
Virginia	4	n/a	n/a	n/a
Washington	n/a	n/a	n/a	n/a
West Virginia	8	n/a	n/a	n/a
Wisconsin	n/a	n/a	n/a	n/a
Wyoming	8	12	12	1
50 States	n/a	n/a	n/a	
DC	n/a	n/a	n/a	
United States	n/a	n/a ·	n/a	

Rank in order by House members

1	Louisiana
1	Nevada
1	Oklahoma
1	Utah
1	Wyoming
6	Arizona
6	Colorado
6	Florida
6	Maine
6	Missouri
6	Montana
6	Nebraska
6	Ohio
6	South Dakota
15	Arkansas
15	California
15	Michigan

Note: Ties in ranking reflect ties in actual values.

D-9 Legislative Session Length, 2003

State	Legislative length in calendar days #	Rank
Alabama	105	24
Alaska	121	16
Arizona	99	26
Arkansas	60	36
California	288	1
Colorado	120	17
Connecticut	148	9
Delaware	168	4
Florida	60	36
Georgia	62	35
Hawaii	113	21
Idaho	75	33
Illinois	no limit	n/a
Indiana	107	22
Iowa	99	26
Kansas	99	26
Kentucky	83	32
Louisiana	85	31
Maine	197	2
Maryland	90	29
Massachusetts	no limit	n/a
Michigan	no limit	n/a
Minnesota	133	13
Mississippi	90	29
Missouri	143	10
Montana	106	23
Nebraska	151	8
Nevada	120	17
New Hampshire	165	6
New Jersey	no limit	n/a
New Mexico	60	36
New York	no limit	n/a
North Carolina	160	7
North Dakota	114	20
Ohio	no limit	n/a
Oklahoma	117	19
Oregon	184	3
Pennsylvania	no limit	n/a
Rhode Island	166	5
South Carolina	143	10
South Dakota	67	34
Tennessee	128	14
Texas	140	12
Utah	45	42
Vermont	128	14
Virginia	47	41
Washington	105	24
West Virginia	60	36
Wisconsin	no limit	n/a
Wyoming	53	40
50 States	n/a	
DC	no limit	
United States	n/a	

Rank in order by

1 California
2 Maine
3 Oregon
4 Delaware
5 Rhode Island
6 New Hampshire
7 North Carolina
8 Nebraska
9 Connecticut
10 Missouri
10 South Carolina
12 Texas
13 Minnesota
14 Tennessee
14 Vermont
16 Alaska
17 Colorado
17 Nevada
19 Oklahoma
20 North Dakota
21 Hawaii
22 Indiana
23 Montana
24 Alabama
24 Washington
26 Arizona
26 Iowa
26 Kansas
29 Maryland
29 Mississippi
31 Louisiana
32 Kentucky
33 Idaho
34 South Dakota
35 Georgia
36 Arkansas
36 Florida
36 New Mexico
36 West Virginia
40 Wyoming
41 Virginia
42 Utah

Note: Ties in ranking reflect ties in actual values.

D-10 Party Control of State Legislatures, 2003

State	Democrats in legislature	Republicans in legislature	Legislative control	Percentage of members Republican	Rank by percentage Republican
Alabama	89	51	D	36.4	41
Alaska	21	38	R	63.3	10
Arizona	34	56	R	62.2	12
Arkansas	97	38	D	28.1	46
California	74	46	D	38.3	40
Colorado	45	55	R	55.0	22
Connecticut	115	72	D	38.5	39
Delaware	25	37	S	59.7	13
Florida	53	107	R	66.9	7
Georgia	133	102	S	43.2	35
Hawaii	56	20	D	26.3	47
Idaho	23	82	R	78.1	1
Illinois	98	79	D	44.6	34
Indiana	69	81	S	54.0	25
Iowa	67	83	R	55.3	21
Kansas	55	110	R	66.7	8
Kentucky	82	56	S	40.6	36
Louisiana	97	47	D	32.6	42
Maine	98	84	D	45.2	33
Maryland	131	57	D	30.3	44
Massachusetts	170	29	D	14.5	49
Michigan	63	85	R	57.4	17
Minnesota	87	113	S	56.2	18
Mississippi	119	51	D	29.3	45
Missouri	87	110	R	55.8	19
Montana	68	82	R	54.7	23
Nebraska	n/a	n/a	n/a	n/a	n/a
Nevada	32	31	S	49.2	26
New Hampshire	125	299	R	70.5	4
New Jersey	64	56	S	46.7	29
New Mexico	66	45	D	40.2	37
New York	128	84	S	39.6	38
North Carolina	87	83	S	48.8	27
North Dakota	44	97	R	68.8	6
Ohio	48	84	R	63.6	9
Oklahoma	81	68	D	45.6	31
Oregon	40	50	S	55.6	20
Pennsylvania	115	138	R	54.5	24
Rhode Island	95	17	D	15.0	48
South Carolina	72	98	R	57.6	15
South Dakota	30	74	R	70.5	5
Tennessee	72	60	D	45.5	32
Texas	74	107	R	59.1	14
Utah	26	78	R	75.0	2
Vermont	89	84	S	46.7	30
Virginia	50	88	R	62.9	11
Washington	76	71	S	48.3	28
West Virginia	92	42	D	31.3	43
Wisconsin	56	76	R	57.6	16
Wyoming	25	65	R	72.2	3
50 States	3,643	3,666	16 D, 21 R, 12 S	49.7	
DC	n/a	n/a		n/a	
United States	3,643	3,666		49.7	

Rank in order by percentage Republican	
1	Idaho
2	Utah
3	Wyoming
4	New Hampshire
5	South Dakota
6	North Dakota
7	Florida
8	Kansas
9	Ohio
10	Alaska
11	Virginia
12	Arizona
13	Delaware
14	Texas
15	South Carolina
16	Wisconsin
17	Michigan
18	Minnesota
19	Missouri
20	Oregon
21	Iowa
22	Colorado
23	Montana
24	Pennsylvania
25	Indiana
26	Nevada
27	North Carolina
28	Washington
29	New Jersey
30	Vermont
31	Oklahoma
32	Tennessee
33	Maine
34	Illinois
35	Georgia
36	Kentucky
37	New Mexico
38	New York
39	Connecticut
40	California
41	Alabama
42	Louisiana
43	West Virginia
44	Maryland
45	Mississippi
46	Arkansas
47	Hawaii
48	Rhode Island
49	Massachusetts

Note: Numbers that appear to be identical are rounded and vary slightly in actual value. The rankings reflect the actual values before rounding. See the introduction for more details.

D-11 Governor's Power Rating, 2002

State	Power rating	Rank
Alabama	2.8	47
Alaska	4.1	2
Arizona	3.2	34
Arkansas	3.1	41
California	3.5	24
Colorado	3.9	5
Connecticut	3.6	18
Delaware	3.5	24
Florida	3.6	18
Georgia	3.0	43
Hawaii	3.6	18
Idaho	3.5	24
Illinois	3.8	10
Indiana	2.9	46
Iowa	3.5	24
Kansas	3.3	30
Kentucky	3.5	24
Louisiana	3.1	41
Maine	3.6	18
Maryland	3.7	12
Massachusetts	3.6	18
Michigan	3.6	18
Minnesota	3.7	12
Mississippi	3.2	34
Missouri	3.2	34
Montana	3.7	12
Nebraska	3.8	10
Nevada	3.0	43
New Hampshire	3.2	34
New Jersey	3.9	5
New Mexico	3.7	12
New York	4.1	2
North Carolina	2.7	48
North Dakota	3.9	5
Ohio	3.9	5
Oklahoma	3.3	30
Oregon	3.3	30
Pennsylvania	3.7	12
Rhode Island	2.6	49
South Carolina	3.0	43
South Dakota	3.7	12
Tennessee	3.9	5
Texas	3.2	34
Utah	4.2	1
Vermont	2.5	50
Virginia	3.2	34
Washington	3.4	29
West Virginia	4.1	2
Wisconsin	3.3	30
Wyoming	3.2	34
50 States	3.5	
DC	n/a	
United States	3.5	

Rank in order by rating

1	Utah
2	Alaska
2	New York
2	West Virginia
5	Colorado
5	New Jersey
5	North Dakota
5	Ohio
5	Tennessee
10	Illinois
10	Nebraska
12	Maryland
12	Minnesota
12	Montana
12	New Mexico
12	Pennsylvania
12	South Dakota
18	Connecticut
18	Florida
18	Hawaii
18	Maine
18	Massachusetts
18	Michigan
24	California
24	Delaware
24	Idaho
24	Iowa
24	Kentucky
29	Washington
30	Kansas
30	Oklahoma
30	Oregon
30	Wisconsin
34	Arizona
34	Mississippi
34	Missouri
34	New Hampshire
34	Texas
34	Virginia
34	Wyoming
41	Arkansas
41	Louisiana
43	Georgia
43	Nevada
43	South Carolina
46	Indiana
47	Alabama
48	North Carolina
49	Rhode Island
50	Vermont

Note: Ties in ranking reflect ties in actual values.

D-12 Number of Statewide Elected Officials, 2000

State	Elected officials #	Rank
Alabama	9	4
Alaska	2	45
Arizona	6	21
Arkansas	6	21
California	8	9
Colorado	5	35
Connecticut	6	21
Delaware	6	21
Florida	10	2
Georgia	9	4
Hawaii	2	45
Idaho	7	16
Illinois	9	4
Indiana	8	9
Iowa	7	16
Kansas	7	16
Kentucky	8	9
Louisiana	8	9
Maine	1	48
Maryland	4	40
Massachusetts	6	21
Michigan	4	40
Minnesota	4	40
Mississippi	8	9
Missouri	6	21
Montana	7	16
Nebraska	6	21
Nevada	6	21
New Hampshire	1	48
New Jersey	1	48
New Mexico	7	16
New York	4	40
North Carolina	10	2
North Dakota	12	1
Ohio	5	35
Oklahoma	8	9
Oregon	6	21
Pennsylvania	5	35
Rhode Island	5	35
South Carolina	9	4
South Dakota	6	21
Tennessee	2	45
Texas	6	21
Utah	5	35
Vermont	6	21
Virginia	3	44
Washington	9	4
West Virginia	6	21
Wisconsin	6	21
Wyoming	8	9
50 States	n/a	
DC	n/a	
United States	n/a	

Rank in order by #	
1	North Dakota
2	Florida
2	North Carolina
4	Alabama
4	Georgia
4	Illinois
4	South Carolina
4	Washington
9	California
9	Indiana
9	Kentucky
9	Louisiana
9	Mississippi
9	Oklahoma
9	Wyoming
16	Idaho
16	Iowa
16	Kansas
16	Montana
16	New Mexico
21	Arizona
21	Arkansas
21	Connecticut
21	Delaware
21	Massachusetts
21	Missouri
21	Nebraska
21	Nevada
21	Oregon
21	South Dakota
21	Texas
21	Vermont
21	West Virginia
21	Wisconsin
35	Colorado
35	Ohio
35	Pennsylvania
35	Rhode Island
35	Utah
40	Maryland
40	Michigan
40	Minnesota
40	New York
44	Virginia
45	Alaska
45	Hawaii
45	Tennessee
48	Maine
48	New Hampshire
48	New Jersey

Note: Ties in ranking reflect ties in actual values.

D-13 State and Local Government Employees, 2001

State	Government employees #	Per 10,000 population	Rank per 10,000 population
Alabama	268,440	601	12
Alaska	49,553	780	2
Arizona	251,745	474	48
Arkansas	151,069	561	23
California	1,735,142	503	44
Colorado	234,095	530	38
Connecticut	182,354	532	35
Delaware	45,758	575	18
Florida	803,175	490	47
Georgia	459,259	548	27
Hawaii	69,230	565	21
Idaho	76,076	576	17
Illinois	616,153	494	46
Indiana	324,447	531	37
Iowa	176,084	602	10
Kansas	170,771	634	6
Kentucky	227,713	560	24
Louisiana	280,139	627	7
Maine	74,661	580	15
Maryland	279,013	519	41
Massachusetts	332,556	521	40
Michigan	499,493	500	45
Minnesota	280,665	564	22
Mississippi	192,963	675	3
Missouri	305,853	543	28
Montana	53,302	589	13
Nebraska	112,072	654	5
Nevada	87,074	413	50
New Hampshire	65,689	522	39
New Jersey	459,066	541	29
New Mexico	120,517	659	4
New York	1,178,230	620	8
North Carolina	463,555	566	20
North Dakota	38,201	602	11
Ohio	607,482	534	33
Oklahoma	199,819	577	16
Oregon	179,221	516	42
Pennsylvania	540,725	440	49
Rhode Island	57,016	538	31
South Carolina	237,408	584	14
South Dakota	40,739	538	30
Tennessee	305,583	532	36
Texas	1,209,448	567	19
Utah	126,274	556	25
Vermont	36,968	603	9
Virginia	397,420	553	26
Washington	306,955	513	43
West Virginia	96,534	536	32
Wisconsin	288,252	534	34
Wyoming	40,449	818	1
50 States	15,334,406	540	
DC	44,518	779	
United States	15,378,924	540	

Rank in order by 10,000 population

1. Wyoming
2. Alaska
3. Mississippi
4. New Mexico
5. Nebraska
6. Kansas
7. Louisiana
8. New York
9. Vermont
10. Iowa
11. North Dakota
12. Alabama
13. Montana
14. South Carolina
15. Maine
16. Oklahoma
17. Idaho
18. Delaware
19. Texas
20. North Carolina
21. Hawaii
22. Minnesota
23. Arkansas
24. Kentucky
25. Utah
26. Virginia
27. Georgia
28. Missouri
29. New Jersey
30. South Dakota
31. Rhode Island
32. West Virginia
33. Ohio
34. Wisconsin
35. Connecticut
36. Tennessee
37. Indiana
38. Colorado
39. New Hampshire
40. Massachusetts
41. Maryland
42. Oregon
43. Washington
44. California
45. Michigan
46. Illinois
47. Florida
48. Arizona
49. Pennsylvania
50. Nevada

Note: Numbers that appear to be identical are rounded and vary slightly in actual value. The rankings reflect the actual values before rounding. See the introduction for more details.

D-14 Average Salaries of State and Local Government Employees, 2001

State	Average salary $	Rank
Alabama	31,936	36
Alaska	45,103	5
Arizona	35,394	22
Arkansas	28,711	49
California	49,646	1
Colorado	39,220	15
Connecticut	45,110	4
Delaware	38,197	18
Florida	34,761	23
Georgia	32,596	33
Hawaii	36,019	20
Idaho	31,119	42
Illinois	39,765	13
Indiana	33,401	28
Iowa	34,665	24
Kansas	32,178	34
Kentucky	30,793	45
Louisiana	29,612	47
Maine	31,974	35
Maryland	42,334	10
Massachusetts	42,362	9
Michigan	41,142	11
Minnesota	39,872	12
Mississippi	27,184	50
Missouri	31,921	37
Montana	31,074	43
Nebraska	32,693	31
Nevada	43,619	6
New Hampshire	34,381	25
New Jersey	48,208	2
New Mexico	31,017	44
New York	46,687	3
North Carolina	33,347	29
North Dakota	32,633	32
Ohio	37,052	19
Oklahoma	29,964	46
Oregon	38,833	17
Pennsylvania	39,700	14
Rhode Island	43,385	7
South Carolina	31,299	39
South Dakota	29,471	48
Tennessee	31,603	38
Texas	32,812	30
Utah	33,740	27
Vermont	33,841	26
Virginia	35,491	21
Washington	43,111	8
West Virginia	31,210	41
Wisconsin	38,905	16
Wyoming	31,292	40
50 States	38,414	
DC	47,050	
United States	38,439	

Rank in order by $

1 California
2 New Jersey
3 New York
4 Connecticut
5 Alaska
6 Nevada
7 Rhode Island
8 Washington
9 Massachusetts
10 Maryland
11 Michigan
12 Minnesota
13 Illinois
14 Pennsylvania
15 Colorado
16 Wisconsin
17 Oregon
18 Delaware
19 Ohio
20 Hawaii
21 Virginia
22 Arizona
23 Florida
24 Iowa
25 New Hampshire
26 Vermont
27 Utah
28 Indiana
29 North Carolina
30 Texas
31 Nebraska
32 North Dakota
33 Georgia
34 Kansas
35 Maine
36 Alabama
37 Missouri
38 Tennessee
39 South Carolina
40 Wyoming
41 West Virginia
42 Idaho
43 Montana
44 New Mexico
45 Kentucky
46 Oklahoma
47 Louisiana
48 South Dakota
49 Arkansas
50 Mississippi

D-15 Local Employment, 2001

State	Number of local employees	Local share of state and local employees %	Rank by percentage
Alabama	184,132	68.6	31
Alaska	25,616	51.7	48
Arizona	186,560	74.1	9
Arkansas	99,839	66.1	37
California	1,362,464	78.5	3
Colorado	166,767	71.2	20
Connecticut	116,154	63.7	41
Delaware	21,434	46.8	49
Florida	615,623	76.6	6
Georgia	338,079	73.6	10
Hawaii	14,340	20.7	50
Idaho	52,861	69.5	28
Illinois	486,311	78.9	1
Indiana	237,838	73.3	12
Iowa	121,366	68.9	29
Kansas	126,718	74.2	8
Kentucky	150,807	66.2	36
Louisiana	186,220	66.5	35
Maine	53,117	71.1	22
Maryland	187,725	67.3	34
Massachusetts	237,297	71.4	19
Michigan	358,118	71.7	17
Minnesota	205,077	73.1	13
Mississippi	136,182	70.6	24
Missouri	213,290	69.7	27
Montana	33,913	63.6	42
Nebraska	79,365	70.8	23
Nevada	63,918	73.4	11
New Hampshire	46,769	71.2	21
New Jersey	322,174	70.2	25
New Mexico	72,678	60.3	45
New York	926,131	78.6	2
North Carolina	333,864	72.0	16
North Dakota	22,303	58.4	47
Ohio	468,114	77.1	5
Oklahoma	135,115	67.6	32
Oregon	125,048	69.8	26
Pennsylvania	386,907	71.6	18
Rhode Island	36,871	64.7	39
South Carolina	156,189	65.8	38
South Dakota	27,470	67.4	33
Tennessee	222,902	72.9	14
Texas	940,811	77.8	4
Utah	74,204	58.8	46
Vermont	23,302	63.0	44
Virginia	273,899	68.9	30
Washington	195,823	63.8	40
West Virginia	61,186	63.4	43
Wisconsin	218,824	75.9	7
Wyoming	29,291	72.4	15
50 States	11,161,006	72.8	
DC	44,518	100.0	
United States	11,205,524	72.9	

Rank in order by percentage	
1	Illinois
2	New York
3	California
4	Texas
5	Ohio
6	Florida
7	Wisconsin
8	Kansas
9	Arizona
10	Georgia
11	Nevada
12	Indiana
13	Minnesota
14	Tennessee
15	Wyoming
16	North Carolina
17	Michigan
18	Pennsylvania
19	Massachusetts
20	Colorado
21	New Hampshire
22	Maine
23	Nebraska
24	Mississippi
25	New Jersey
26	Oregon
27	Missouri
28	Idaho
29	Iowa
30	Virginia
31	Alabama
32	Oklahoma
33	South Dakota
34	Maryland
35	Louisiana
36	Kentucky
37	Arkansas
38	South Carolina
39	Rhode Island
40	Washington
41	Connecticut
42	Montana
43	West Virginia
44	Vermont
45	New Mexico
46	Utah
47	North Dakota
48	Alaska
49	Delaware
50	Hawaii

Note: Numbers that appear to be identical are rounded and vary slightly in actual value. The rankings reflect the actual values before rounding. See the introduction for more details.

D-16 Local Spending Accountability, FY 2000

State	Percentage of local spending raised by local government	Rank
Alabama	56.9	38
Alaska	56.6	39
Arizona	58.2	35
Arkansas	49.3	46
California	55.3	41
Colorado	73.5	3
Connecticut	66.5	15
Delaware	53.1	45
Florida	69.9	7
Georgia	70.8	6
Hawaii	81.2	1
Idaho	58.6	33
Illinois	63.4	24
Indiana	65.5	16
Iowa	61.6	28
Kansas	64.5	18
Kentucky	55.8	40
Louisiana	64.1	22
Maine	69.3	9
Maryland	73.5	2
Massachusetts	59.5	31
Michigan	48.5	48
Minnesota	54.3	43
Mississippi	54.6	42
Missouri	67.0	14
Montana	64.3	20
Nebraska	71.2	5
Nevada	59.4	32
New Hampshire	69.7	8
New Jersey	69.0	10
New Mexico	43.0	50
New York	68.8	11
North Carolina	57.4	37
North Dakota	58.6	34
Ohio	63.9	23
Oklahoma	62.0	27
Oregon	57.9	36
Pennsylvania	59.5	30
Rhode Island	71.5	4
South Carolina	65.0	17
South Dakota	68.1	12
Tennessee	62.9	26
Texas	67.4	13
Utah	64.1	21
Vermont	43.4	49
Virginia	63.2	25
Washington	64.5	19
West Virginia	54.2	44
Wisconsin	49.0	47
Wyoming	60.7	29
50 States	62.2	
DC	77.3	
United States	62.3	

Rank in order by percentage

1 Hawaii
2 Maryland
3 Colorado
4 Rhode Island
5 Nebraska
6 Georgia
7 Florida
8 New Hampshire
9 Maine
10 New Jersey
11 New York
12 South Dakota
13 Texas
14 Missouri
15 Connecticut
16 Indiana
17 South Carolina
18 Kansas
19 Washington
20 Montana
21 Utah
22 Louisiana
23 Ohio
24 Illinois
25 Virginia
26 Tennessee
27 Oklahoma
28 Iowa
29 Wyoming
30 Pennsylvania
31 Massachusetts
32 Nevada
33 Idaho
34 North Dakota
35 Arizona
36 Oregon
37 North Carolina
38 Alabama
39 Alaska
40 Kentucky
41 California
42 Mississippi
43 Minnesota
44 West Virginia
45 Delaware
46 Arkansas
47 Wisconsin
48 Michigan
49 Vermont
50 New Mexico

Note: Numbers that appear to be identical are rounded and vary slightly in actual value. The rankings reflect the actual values before rounding. See the introduction for more details.

D-17 Percentage of Eligible Voters Registered, November 2002

State	Percentage of registered voters	Rank
Alabama	71.7	38
Alaska	110.5	1
Arizona	59.9	43
Arkansas	80.0	26
California	69.7	40
Colorado	89.9	9
Connecticut	83.8	19
Delaware	89.0	11
Florida	80.6	25
Georgia	60.7	42
Hawaii	82.0	24
Idaho	72.5	37
Illinois	79.2	28
Indiana	93.6	5
Iowa	90.2	8
Kansas	82.2	23
Kentucky	85.0	18
Louisiana	88.5	14
Maine	n/a	n/a
Maryland	71.6	39
Massachusetts	86.1	16
Michigan	95.6	3
Minnesota	88.5	13
Mississippi	n/a	n/a
Missouri	89.3	10
Montana	94.2	4
Nebraska	n/a	n/a
Nevada	58.6	44
New Hampshire	76.0	33
New Jersey	77.2	32
New Mexico	74.6	35
New York	85.3	17
North Carolina	82.4	21
North Dakota	n/a	n/a
Ohio	86.8	15
Oklahoma	82.4	22
Oregon	73.8	36
Pennsylvania	n/a	n/a
Rhode Island	88.7	12
South Carolina	78.8	29
South Dakota	95.9	2
Tennessee	77.4	30
Texas	91.9	7
Utah	83.6	20
Vermont	92.6	6
Virginia	79.7	27
Washington	75.1	34
West Virginia	77.2	31
Wisconsin	n/a	n/a
Wyoming	68.3	41
50 States	n/a	
DC	75.9	
United States	80.7	

Rank in order by percentage

1 Alaska
2 South Dakota
3 Michigan
4 Montana
5 Indiana
6 Vermont
7 Texas
8 Iowa
9 Colorado
10 Missouri
11 Delaware
12 Rhode Island
13 Minnesota
14 Louisiana
15 Ohio
16 Massachusetts
17 New York
18 Kentucky
19 Connecticut
20 Utah
21 North Carolina
22 Oklahoma
23 Kansas
24 Hawaii
25 Florida
26 Arkansas
27 Virginia
28 Illinois
29 South Carolina
30 Tennessee
31 West Virginia
32 New Jersey
33 New Hampshire
34 Washington
35 New Mexico
36 Oregon
37 Idaho
38 Alabama
39 Maryland
40 California
41 Wyoming
42 Georgia
43 Arizona
44 Nevada

Note: Numbers that appear to be identical are rounded and vary slightly in actual value. The rankings reflect the actual values before rounding. See the introduction for more details.

D-18 Percentage of Population Voting, November 2002

State	Percentage voting	Rank
Alabama	41.6	24
Alaska	55.5	3
Arizona	33.0	47
Arkansas	40.8	26
California	34.4	42
Colorado	43.9	20
Connecticut	42.9	22
Delaware	39.8	29
Florida	44.2	18
Georgia	33.2	45
Hawaii	46.3	13
Idaho	43.9	21
Illinois	39.9	28
Indiana	34.4	43
Iowa	47.3	12
Kansas	42.5	23
Kentucky	36.3	39
Louisiana	39.4	32
Maine	53.4	4
Maryland	44.7	17
Massachusetts	47.6	11
Michigan	44.7	16
Minnesota	62.6	1
Mississippi	32.9	48
Missouri	45.6	14
Montana	50.0	7
Nebraska	39.5	31
Nevada	33.9	44
New Hampshire	49.2	10
New Jersey	35.0	40
New Mexico	38.1	36
New York	34.7	41
North Carolina	38.2	35
North Dakota	49.9	9
Ohio	38.7	33
Oklahoma	41.2	25
Oregon	50.0	8
Pennsylvania	39.7	30
Rhode Island	44.0	19
South Carolina	36.6	38
South Dakota	61.3	2
Tennessee	38.6	34
Texas	33.1	46
Utah	37.1	37
Vermont	50.0	6
Virginia	28.6	50
Washington	40.2	27
West Virginia	31.3	49
Wisconsin	45.1	15
Wyoming	52.5	5
50 States	n/a	
DC	30.1	
United States	39.2	

Rank in order by percentage	
1	Minnesota
2	South Dakota
3	Alaska
4	Maine
5	Wyoming
6	Vermont
7	Montana
8	Oregon
9	North Dakota
10	New Hampshire
11	Massachusetts
12	Iowa
13	Hawaii
14	Missouri
15	Wisconsin
16	Michigan
17	Maryland
18	Florida
19	Rhode Island
20	Colorado
21	Idaho
22	Connecticut
23	Kansas
24	Alabama
25	Oklahoma
26	Arkansas
27	Washington
28	Illinois
29	Delaware
30	Pennsylvania
31	Nebraska
32	Louisiana
33	Ohio
34	Tennessee
35	North Carolina
36	New Mexico
37	Utah
38	South Carolina
39	Kentucky
40	New Jersey
41	New York
42	California
43	Indiana
44	Nevada
45	Georgia
46	Texas
47	Arizona
48	Mississippi
49	West Virginia
50	Virginia

Note: Numbers that appear to be identical are rounded and vary slightly in actual value. The rankings reflect the actual values before rounding. See the introduction for more details.

D-19 Statewide Initiatives and Popular Referenda, 2002

State	Number of initiatives	Initiatives approved by voters	Rank by number of initiatives
Alabama	0	n/a	n/a
Alaska	2	1	9
Arizona	4	1	4
Arkansas	2	0	9
California	4	2	4
Colorado	5	1	2
Connecticut	0	n/a	n/a
Delaware	0	n/a	n/a
Florida	5	5	2
Georgia	0	n/a	n/a
Hawaii	0	n/a	n/a
Idaho	2	2	9
Illinois	0	n/a	n/a
Indiana	0	n/a	n/a
Iowa	0	n/a	n/a
Kansas	0	n/a	n/a
Kentucky	0	n/a	n/a
Louisiana	0	n/a	n/a
Maine	0	n/a	n/a
Maryland	0	n/a	n/a
Massachusetts	2	1	9
Michigan	3	1	6
Minnesota	0	n/a	n/a
Mississippi	0	n/a	n/a
Missouri	2	0	9
Montana	3	2	6
Nebraska	0	n/a	n/a
Nevada	2	1	9
New Hampshire	0	n/a	n/a
New Jersey	0	n/a	n/a
New Mexico	0	n/a	n/a
New York	0	n/a	n/a
North Carolina	0	n/a	n/a
North Dakota	2	1	9
Ohio	1	0	17
Oklahoma	1	1	17
Oregon	7	3	1
Pennsylvania	0	n/a	n/a
Rhode Island	0	n/a	n/a
South Carolina	0	n/a	n/a
South Dakota	2	0	9
Tennessee	0	n/a	n/a
Texas	0	n/a	n/a
Utah	1	0	17
Vermont	0	n/a	n/a
Virginia	0	n/a	n/a
Washington	3	3	6
West Virginia	0	n/a	n/a
Wisconsin	0	n/a	n/a
Wyoming	0	n/a	n/a
50 States	53	25	
DC	n/a	n/a	
United States	53	25	

Rank in order by

1	Oregon
2	Colorado
2	Florida
4	Arizona
4	California
6	Michigan
6	Montana
6	Washington
9	Alaska
9	Arkansas
9	Idaho
9	Massachusetts
9	Missouri
9	Nevada
9	North Dakota
9	South Dakota
17	Ohio
17	Oklahoma
17	Utah

Note: Ties in ranking reflect ties in actual values.

D-20 Campaign Costs Per Vote in Most Recent Gubernatorial Election, 1998, 1999, 2000, or 2001

State	Number of candidates and election year	Winning party and margin of victory %	Partisan shift (yes or no) and type of race (incumbent or open seat)	Cost per vote $	Rank by cost per vote
Alabama	9 in 1998	D-16	Y-I*[1]	18.35	4
Alaska	13 in 1998	D-34	N-I	12.04	10
Arizona	6 in 1998	R-25	N-I	3.67	43
Arkansas	4 in 1998	R-21	N-I	4.92	34
California	17 in 1998	D-20	Y-O	16.09	8
Colorado	6 in 1998	R-1	Y-O	2.95	46
Connecticut	5 in 1998	R-28	N-I	6.98	29
Delaware	4 in 2000	D-19	N-O	9.78	16
Florida	2 in 1998	R-10	Y-O	3.29	45
Georgia	11 in 1998	D-9	N-O	21.51	2
Hawaii	12 in 1998	D-1	N-I	19.27	3
Idaho	7 in 1998	R-39	N-O	4.75	36
Illinois	9 in 1998	R-4	N-O	7.82	26
Indiana	4 in 2000	D-14	N-I	8.45	21
Iowa	8 in 1998	D-5	Y-O	8.84	19
Kansas	6 in 1998	R-50	N-I	3.95	42
Kentucky	4 in 1999	D-39	N-I	2.49	50
Louisiana	13 in 1999	R-32	N-I	5.51	33
Maine	8 in 1998	In-40	N-I	2.59	49
Maryland	6 in 1998	D-12	N-I	7.24	28
Massachusetts	6 in 1998	R-4	N-I	10.42	13
Michigan	5 in 1998	R-24	N-I	4.69	38
Minnesota	11 in 1998	Rf-3	Y-O	4.55	39
Mississippi	11 in 1999	D-1	Y-O	11.47	11
Missouri	10 in 2000	D-1	N-O	8.37	22
Montana	6 in 2000	R-4	N-O	11.46	12
Nebraska	9 in 1998	R-8	Y-O	16.93	6
Nevada	16 in 1998	R-10	Y-O	24.89	1
New Hampshire	9 in 2000	D-5	N-I	8.29	23
New Jersey	11 in 2001	D-15	Y-O	16.44	7
New Mexico	8 in 1998	R-10	N-I	12.77	9
New York	12 in 1998	R-23	N-I	8.80	20
North Carolina	14 in 2000	D-6	N-O	9.77	17
North Dakota	4 in 2000	R-10	N-O	8.12	24
Ohio	4 in 1998	R-5	N-O	7.55	27
Oklahoma	4 in 1998	R-17	N-I	3.66	44
Oregon	12 in 1998	D-33	N-I	4.90	35
Pennsylvania	6 in 1998	R-27	N-I	4.52	40
Rhode Island	5 in 1998	R-9	N-I	10.29	14
South Carolina	4 in 1998	D-8	Y-I*[1]	9.28	18
South Dakota	4 in 1998	R-31	N-I	5.68	31
Tennessee	14 in 1998	R-40	N-I	5.63	32
Texas	5 in 1998	R-38	N-I	6.78	30
Utah	4 in 2000	R-14	N-I	2.92	47
Vermont	10 in 2000	D-12	N-I	7.85	25
Virginia	4 in 2001	D-5	Y-O	17.93	5
Washington	6 in 2000	D-19	N-I	2.71	48
West Virginia	15 in 2000	D-3	Y-I*[1]	10.28	15
Wisconsin	8 in 1998	R-21	N-I	4.27	41
Wyoming	5 in 1998	R-16	N-I	4.70	37
50 States (average)	8	16.8	n/a	8.73	
DC	n/a	n/a	n/a	n/a	
United States (average)	8	16.8	n/a	8.73	

[1] incumbent did not win

Rank in order by cost per vote

1 Nevada
2 Georgia
3 Hawaii
4 Alabama
5 Virginia
6 Nebraska
7 New Jersey
8 California
9 New Mexico
10 Alaska
11 Mississippi
12 Montana
13 Massachusetts
14 Rhode Island
15 West Virginia
16 Delaware
17 North Carolina
18 South Carolina
19 Iowa
20 New York
21 Indiana
22 Missouri
23 New Hampshire
24 North Dakota
25 Vermont
26 Illinois
27 Ohio
28 Maryland
29 Connecticut
30 Texas
31 South Dakota
32 Tennessee
33 Louisiana
34 Arkansas
35 Oregon
36 Idaho
37 Wyoming
38 Michigan
39 Minnesota
40 Pennsylvania
41 Wisconsin
42 Kansas
43 Arizona
44 Oklahoma
45 Florida
46 Colorado
47 Utah
48 Washington
49 Maine
50 Kentucky

Source Notes for Government (Section D)

D-1 Members of the United States House, 2003: Each state is allocated two senators and representation in the House of Representatives based on population, as determined by the census, which is taken in every year ending in zero (for example, 2000 and 2010).

The data in the table list the number of representatives as of 2002, based on unadjusted population numbers (see notes to Table A-1) from the 2000 census. Reapportionment of the 435 house seats resulted in gains in some western and southern states and loses in some northeastern and midwestern states. This allocation will prevail until seats are reapportioned based on the results of the 2010 census.

D-2 Members of State Legislatures, 2003: Like the Congress, state legislatures—except Nebraska's one-house legislature—have an upper and lower house, generally called senates and assemblies. These data come from the organization of legislators nationwide, the National Conference of State Legislatures.

D-3 State Legislators Per Million Population, 2003: Some small population states, like New Hampshire, have large legislatures. Some large states, like California, have relatively small ones. This table highlights the differences by relating the number of legislators (see Table D-2) to the most recent population estimates (see Table A-1).

D-4 Units of Government, 1997: There are more than eighty thousand units of government in the United States, including counties, cities, towns, townships, school districts, and special districts that provide water, maintain sewage systems, build and maintain roads, control mosquitoes, and more. There are so many that they are only counted every five years in the Census Bureau's Census of Governments, the most recent of which was in 1997. The data are available on the Census Bureau website (www.census.gov) as *Volume 1, Government Organization 1997*.

D-5 State Legislator Compensation, 2002: These data show the major sources of cash compensation of legislators, annual salaries and per diem amounts. The data are drawn from the National Conference of State Legislatures' website (www.ncsl.org).

Comparisons of legislative pay from state to state are nearly impossible. Some states pay their legislators like most employers pay their employees—a regular salary plus reimbursement of employment-related travel expenses while on official business away from the normal place of work. In addition, because most legislators live in their districts, they are paid expenses when staying overnight in the state capitol. Some states compensate legislators at a per diem rate, often adding an expense allowance that can exceed expenses actually incurred. Additionally, some legislatures provide extra pay for committee chairpersons

and legislative leaders. Pensions for legislative service are nonexistent or negligible in some states, while pension and other benefits, such as employer-paid health care, are an important part of legislative compensation in other states.

D-6 Percentage of Legislators Who Are Female, 2002: The percentage of legislators who are women passed 20 percent in 1993 from less than 10 percent in the 1970s and less than 5 percent in the 1960s. The percentages for each state were calculated by the Center for the American Woman and Politics, Eagleton Institute of Politics, at Rutgers University and are available on their website (www.rci.rutgers.edu).

D-7 Turnover in Legislatures, Post-election 2002: This table, from Tim Storey of the National Conference of State Legislatures, shows the percentage of new state legislators taking office after the 2002 elections.

Turnover after the 2002 elections was particularly high. In some states, newly drawn political maps eliminated legislative seats, and in some cases, pitted incumbent against incumbent. Rhode Island is the extreme case—it lost 25 percent of its legislative seats in redistricting. Term limits account for a great deal of the turnover, especially in those states where the term limit laws kicked in for the first time in 2002. In Michigan, for instance, the senate lost 76 percent of its members before the first vote of the general election was even cast.

D-8 Term Limits (in years), 2002: This table, from the website of U.S. Term Limits (www.termlimits.org), a national group favoring term limit laws, shows the maximum number of consecutive years governors and legislators can serve. The states shown with no limits allow elected officials to serve as long as voters approve. The states are ranked, with many ties, somewhat arbitrarily. Those with the longest allowable terms for members of their lower house are ranked highest.

In 2001, Oregon's law was successfully challenged in the courts and in February 2002, the Idaho legislature repealed that state's legislative term limit law.

D-9 Legislative Session Length, 2003: Many states have constitutional limits on the length of time the legislature meets in its regular sessions. Those shown in the table are calendar days (for example, a sixty-day limit would be about two months). Many of the states with short sessions exercise the option of having special sessions called by the legislative leadership or governor. These data are available on the website of the National Conference of State Legislatures (www.ncsl.org).

It is difficult to compare the varying practices of the states. While most meet annually, some meet biannually, and some meet throughout the year.

D-10 Party Control of State Legislatures, 2003: These data, developed by the National Conference of State Legislatures shortly after the November 2002 election, show the party affiliation of legislators taking office in 2003. The states are ranked by the percentage of Republicans (reading top to bottom) or Democrats (bottom to top) in the combined legislative houses. S represents a split in party control.

D-11 Governor's Power Rating, 2002: This table presents the results of an update of the on-going study by Dr. Thad Beyle of the University of North Carolina at Chapel Hill, included in *Politics in the American States: A Comparative Analysis* published by CQ Press. The ranking is based on six measures of institutional power — tenure, appointment power, the number of other statewide elected officials, budget power, veto power, and party control. Those interested in more detailed data on this and earlier studies of the governor's powers should visit Dr. Thad Beyle's website (www.unc.edu/~beyle).

D-12 Number of Statewide Elected Officials, 2000: The federal pattern of holding nationwide elections for only the chief executive and running mate (president and vice president) is not followed by the states. States often elect the attorneys general, secretaries of state, comptrollers, treasurers, and auditors. The count in the table, from the Council of State Government's *The Book of the States 2001-02*, excludes judges, who are also elected in many states. *The Book of the States* is a biannual publication.

D-13 State and Local Government Employees, 2001: These statistics, from the Census Bureau's count of public employees available on the Census Bureau's website (www.census.gov), express the full-time equivalent of part-time workers plus full-time workers in state and local governments and relate the totals to population.

D-14 Average Salaries of State and Local Government Employees, 2001: These statistics, from the same source as Table D-13, show annual average state and local government salaries, which were obtained by dividing compensation in March 2001 by the number of employees in 2001 and multiplying by twelve.

D-15 Local Employment, 2001: The count of local employees identified is substantially larger than the number of state employees. The table shows the percentage of local employees. See Table D-13 for the source of these data.

D-16 Local Spending Accountability, FY 2000: Since 1970 there has been a massive growth in both federal and state aid to local governments. As a result, local officials finance over one-third of what they spend with money they do not raise by their own local taxes and fees. Critics say this encourages government spending to be excessive because the elected officials who spend the money do not have to account to taxpayers for raising it. The Wisconsin Taxpayers Association has dubbed this difference "the accountability gap." The table shows a measure of this gap, as calculated by State Policy Research using data from the Census Bureau (see source note to Table F-1 for important details). The numbers reflect the percentage of their spending local officials raised.

D-17 Percentage of Eligible Voters Registered, November 2002: These statistics, available for 44 states and the District of Columbia, were compiled from each state's chief election officer by the Committee for the Study of the American Electorate (CSAE), a non-partisan, non-profit research organization based in Washington D.C. The table shows the best available data on the percentage of persons presumably eligible to vote in each state, based on the voting age population in relation to the number who have complied with that state's requirements to vote.

Presumably the 111 percent of registered voters in Alaska is a fiction. According to CSAE, "in any given election the official registration figures provided by the states are inaccurate." This is because registration rolls often contain the names of people who have died or have moved. As part of the Moter-Voter law, states are required to maintain those who have moved or died on the registration rolls for at least two federal elections, though the names can be moved to an inactive list. The accuracy of a state's registration count is related to the practices of a state's election administration—specifically, how often and how thorough the state conducts a so-called list cleaning.

At the time of publication, November 2002 registration data was unreported for Maine, Mississippi, Nebraska, and Pennsylvania. Data are not available for North Dakota because the state has no voter registration. Wisconsin has election day registration at the polls.

D-18 Percentage of Population Voting, November 2002: Not all persons legally old enough to vote actually do so. The table shows the percentage of eligible U.S citizens who voted in the elections of November 2002. It comes from the Committee for the Study of the American Electorate (CSAE), which notes that as of December 19, 2002, the figures are final and official, except for Indiana, Ohio and West Virginia. For a detailed and highly readable account of the methodology for counting voters see CSAE's November 8, 2002 release: "Turnout Modestly Higher, Democrats in Deep Doo-Doo, Many Questions Emerge."

D-19 Statewide Initiatives and Popular Referenda, 2002: In most states, voters select candidates to make policy for them as legislators but never vote directly on policy except when changes in the state constitution are being made. Some states allow "direct democracy," including allowing voters to put up a measure for popular vote by collecting a minimum number of signatures (voter initiatives). This tabulation shows the number of such initiatives on state ballots in the November 2002 election.

The numbers reflect (1) whether initiatives are permitted in the state; (2) the difficulty of putting measures on the ballot, as affected by the number for signatures required and other factors in the constitutions of each state; and (3) voter interest in making state policy by this direct democracy approach.

These statistics come from a compilation of ballot measure results from the Initiative and Referendum Institute (www.iandrinstitute.org) and ballotwatch.org.

D-20 Campaign Costs Per Vote in Most Recent Gubernatorial Election, 1998, 1999, 2000, or 2001: This table was created by Thad Beyle (Department of Political Science, UNC at Chapel Hill, NC 27599-3265) and Jennifer M. Jensen (Department of Political Science, University of Albany-SUNY, Albany, NY 12222). The authors compiled data from the specific agency in each state that regulates elections and campaign finances. The result is a measure of the gubernatorial campaign costs (converted to 2001 dollars) in each state per vote in each state. Variables that have potential effects on these costs are also presented in this table. These variables include (1) the number of candidates seeking office, (2) the election year, (3) the party that won the office, (4) by what margin of victory, (5) whether or not the election resulted in a partisan shift, (6) whether or not an incumbent was seeking reelection, and (7) whether or not the incumbent won. Anyone interested in more detailed data on these elections should visit the co-author's website (www.unc.edu/~beyle).

Federal Impacts

E-1	Federal Spending, Total and Per Capita, FY 2001	120
E-2	Increase in Total Federal Spending, FY 1996-2001	121
E-3	Federal Spending on Grants, Total and Per Capita, FY 2001	122
E-4	Federal Spending on Procurement, Total and Per Capita, FY 2001	123
E-5	Federal Spending on Payments to Individuals, FY 2001	124
E-6	Federal Spending on Social Security and Medicare, FY 2001	125
E-7	Social Security Benefits Paid, 2000	126
E-8	Federal Spending on Employee Wages and Salaries, FY 2001	127
E-9	Federal Grant Spending Per Dollar of State Tax Revenue, FY 2000	128
E-10	State and Local General Revenue from Federal Government, FY 2000	129
E-11	Federal Tax Burden, Total and Per Capita, FY 2002	130
E-12	Federal Spending Per Dollar of Taxes Paid, FY 2001	131
E-13	Highway Charges Returned to States, FY 2001	132
E-14	Terms of Trade with the Federal Government, FY 2001	133
E-15	Federal Personal Income Taxes, 2000	134
E-16	Federal Share of Medicaid, 2002 and 2003	135

Federal spending in the states takes many forms—everything from Social Security checks for eligible residents to large payments for highway construction to paychecks for postal workers. But for varying reasons some states receive more than others. Expressed per capita, Maine residents get $1,340 more in federal dollars than their New Hampshire neighbors.

During times of fiscal strain it becomes imperative for states to make the most of available federal funds. To help, Washington D.C.-based Federal Funds Information for States (FFIS) compiled the following list of questions state officials should be asking themselves:

- Are we applying for competitive grants?
- Are we influencing authorization bills by entering into formula debates?
- Are we taking advantage of new funding made available to states, such as Homeland Security?
- Are we lobbying for programs to be funded?
- Are we lobbying for programs to be funded at authorized levels?
- Are we spending all of our federal funds such as those available for State Children's Health Insurance Program (SCHIP) and Temporary Assistance for Needy Families (TANF)?
- Are we applying and qualifying for bonus funds?
- Are we electing state options to, for instance, expand services and draw on enhanced federal matching rates?
- Are we monitoring, not just federal funding, but federal actions?
- Are we maximizing federal Medicaid dollars?

In past years states were able to squeeze additional federal funding out of the Medicaid program. This loophole is now being phased out. In addition, trends show that payments directly to individuals through Social Security, Medicare, and Medicaid, for example, are growing at a faster rate than so-called discretionary spending, which is dolled out annually at rates determined by the federal government.

These trends, according to FFIS, will challenge state officials who will need to be "even more assertive in their quest for federal funds."

E-1 Federal Spending, Total and Per Capita, FY 2001

State	Total federal spending $ (in millions)	Per capita federal spending $	Rank per capita
Alabama	31,700	7,101	10
Alaska	6,403	10,085	1
Arizona	30,376	5,723	32
Arkansas	16,632	6,178	25
California	188,517	5,464	36
Colorado	24,345	5,511	35
Connecticut	22,742	6,640	15
Delaware	4,246	5,333	40
Florida	99,998	6,099	28
Georgia	47,320	5,644	34
Hawaii	9,722	7,940	6
Idaho	7,529	5,699	33
Illinois	65,036	5,210	44
Indiana	32,166	5,260	43
Iowa	17,401	5,953	31
Kansas	16,699	6,197	24
Kentucky	25,835	6,355	21
Louisiana	27,816	6,229	23
Maine	8,180	6,357	20
Maryland	48,164	8,960	5
Massachusetts	44,179	6,925	14
Michigan	51,632	5,168	45
Minnesota	24,935	5,015	46
Mississippi	20,212	7,072	11
Missouri	39,191	6,961	12
Montana	6,618	7,317	8
Nebraska	10,771	6,287	22
Nevada	9,624	4,570	50
New Hampshire	6,314	5,014	47
New Jersey	46,240	5,450	37
New Mexico	16,587	9,068	4
New York	116,366	6,121	27
North Carolina	44,557	5,443	38
North Dakota	5,948	9,375	3
Ohio	61,705	5,425	39
Oklahoma	22,672	6,552	17
Oregon	18,401	5,299	41
Pennsylvania	79,310	6,455	18
Rhode Island	6,989	6,600	16
South Carolina	24,675	6,073	30
South Dakota	5,807	7,675	7
Tennessee	36,758	6,404	19
Texas	112,530	5,277	42
Utah	11,377	5,012	48
Vermont	3,734	6,090	29
Virginia	71,257	9,914	2
Washington	36,903	6,163	26
West Virginia	12,541	6,960	13
Wisconsin	26,645	4,933	49
Wyoming	3,584	7,249	9
50 States	1,708,889	6,012	
DC	30,941	54,109	
United States*	1,778,884	6,246	

Rank in order per capita

1. Alaska
2. Virginia
3. North Dakota
4. New Mexico
5. Maryland
6. Hawaii
7. South Dakota
8. Montana
9. Wyoming
10. Alabama
11. Mississippi
12. Missouri
13. West Virginia
14. Massachusetts
15. Connecticut
16. Rhode Island
17. Oklahoma
18. Pennsylvania
19. Tennessee
20. Maine
21. Kentucky
22. Nebraska
23. Louisiana
24. Kansas
25. Arkansas
26. Washington
27. New York
28. Florida
29. Vermont
30. South Carolina
31. Iowa
32. Arizona
33. Idaho
34. Georgia
35. Colorado
36. California
37. New Jersey
38. North Carolina
39. Ohio
40. Delaware
41. Oregon
42. Texas
43. Indiana
44. Illinois
45. Michigan
46. Minnesota
47. New Hampshire
48. Utah
49. Wisconsin
50. Nevada

Due to rounding or data sources, the 50-state total plus D.C. may not equal the U.S. total. Please see introduction.

E-2 Increase in Total Federal Spending, FY 1996-2001

State	Total federal spending FY 1996 $ (in millions)	Percentage increase in federal spending	Rank by percentage increase
Alabama	23,548	34.6	14
Alaska	4,378	46.3	3
Arizona	21,951	38.4	8
Arkansas	12,164	36.7	10
California	156,075	20.8	47
Colorado	20,011	21.7	45
Connecticut	18,142	25.4	35
Delaware	3,408	24.6	38
Florida	79,614	25.6	34
Georgia	34,857	35.8	12
Hawaii	7,990	21.7	44
Idaho	5,489	37.2	9
Illinois	51,586	26.1	33
Indiana	24,250	32.6	22
Iowa	13,415	29.7	28
Kansas	12,359	35.1	13
Kentucky	19,742	30.9	25
Louisiana	22,048	26.2	32
Maine	6,819	20.0	49
Maryland	37,110	29.8	27
Massachusetts	36,136	22.3	41
Michigan	39,633	30.3	26
Minnesota	18,994	31.3	24
Mississippi	15,184	33.1	20
Missouri	35,321	11.0	50
Montana	4,972	33.1	21
Nebraska	7,591	41.9	5
Nevada	7,514	28.1	31
New Hampshire	5,049	25.1	36
New Jersey	38,467	20.2	48
New Mexico	12,141	36.6	11
New York	95,798	21.5	46
North Carolina	33,370	33.5	19
North Dakota	3,605	65.0	1
Ohio	50,601	21.9	43
Oklahoma	16,843	34.6	15
Oregon	14,246	29.2	30
Pennsylvania	64,610	22.8	40
Rhode Island	5,718	22.2	42
South Carolina	18,354	34.4	16
South Dakota	3,867	50.2	2
Tennessee	27,520	33.6	18
Texas	86,783	29.7	29
Utah	8,153	39.5	7
Vermont	2,784	34.1	17
Virginia	50,688	40.6	6
Washington	29,563	24.8	37
West Virginia	10,066	24.6	39
Wisconsin	20,095	32.6	23
Wyoming	2,504	43.1	4
50 States	1,341,126	27.4	
DC	22,678	36.4	
United States*	1,396,673	27.4	

Rank in order by percentage increase	
1	North Dakota
2	South Dakota
3	Alaska
4	Wyoming
5	Nebraska
6	Virginia
7	Utah
8	Arizona
9	Idaho
10	Arkansas
11	New Mexico
12	Georgia
13	Kansas
14	Alabama
15	Oklahoma
16	South Carolina
17	Vermont
18	Tennessee
19	North Carolina
20	Mississippi
21	Montana
22	Indiana
23	Wisconsin
24	Minnesota
25	Kentucky
26	Michigan
27	Maryland
28	Iowa
29	Texas
30	Oregon
31	Nevada
32	Louisiana
33	Illinois
34	Florida
35	Connecticut
36	New Hampshire
37	Washington
38	Delaware
39	West Virginia
40	Pennsylvania
41	Massachusetts
42	Rhode Island
43	Ohio
44	Hawaii
45	Colorado
46	New York
47	California
48	New Jersey
49	Maine
50	Missouri

Note: Numbers that appear to be identical are rounded and vary slightly in actual value. The rankings reflect the actual values before rounding. See the introduction for more details.

Due to rounding or data sources, the 50-state total plus D.C. may not equal the U.S. total. Please see introduction.

E-3 Federal Spending on Grants, Total and Per Capita, FY 2001

State	Federal grants to state and local governments $ (in millions)	Per capita federal grants to state and local government $	Rank per capita
Alabama	5,298	1,187	26
Alaska	2,314	3,645	1
Arizona	5,190	978	43
Arkansas	3,448	1,281	16
California	39,797	1,153	28
Colorado	3,916	886	47
Connecticut	4,364	1,274	17
Delaware	892	1,120	31
Florida	13,666	833	48
Georgia	7,929	946	46
Hawaii	1,514	1,237	20
Idaho	1,505	1,139	29
Illinois	11,883	952	45
Indiana	5,850	957	44
Iowa	3,079	1,053	36
Kansas	2,721	1,010	40
Kentucky	5,100	1,254	18
Louisiana	6,173	1,382	15
Maine	1,905	1,481	13
Maryland	7,586	1,411	14
Massachusetts	9,718	1,523	10
Michigan	10,887	1,090	33
Minnesota	5,260	1,058	35
Mississippi	4,246	1,486	12
Missouri	6,865	1,219	22
Montana	1,665	1,841	5
Nebraska	2,054	1,199	24
Nevada	1,442	685	50
New Hampshire	1,288	1,023	38
New Jersey	8,478	999	41
New Mexico	3,586	1,960	4
New York	32,897	1,730	7
North Carolina	9,122	1,114	32
North Dakota	1,284	2,024	3
Ohio	11,762	1,034	37
Oklahoma	4,119	1,190	25
Oregon	4,308	1,240	19
Pennsylvania	14,847	1,208	23
Rhode Island	1,607	1,518	11
South Carolina	4,730	1,164	27
South Dakota	1,254	1,657	8
Tennessee	7,027	1,224	21
Texas	21,675	1,016	39
Utah	2,244	989	42
Vermont	1,069	1,744	6
Virginia	5,908	822	49
Washington	6,794	1,135	30
West Virginia	2,971	1,649	9
Wisconsin	5,843	1,082	34
Wyoming	1,213	2,453	2
50 States	330,293	1,162	
DC	4,020	7,030	
United States*	338,977	1,190	

Rank in order per capita

1. Alaska
2. Wyoming
3. North Dakota
4. New Mexico
5. Montana
6. Vermont
7. New York
8. South Dakota
9. West Virginia
10. Massachusetts
11. Rhode Island
12. Mississippi
13. Maine
14. Maryland
15. Louisiana
16. Arkansas
17. Connecticut
18. Kentucky
19. Oregon
20. Hawaii
21. Tennessee
22. Missouri
23. Pennsylvania
24. Nebraska
25. Oklahoma
26. Alabama
27. South Carolina
28. California
29. Idaho
30. Washington
31. Delaware
32. North Carolina
33. Michigan
34. Wisconsin
35. Minnesota
36. Iowa
37. Ohio
38. New Hampshire
39. Texas
40. Kansas
41. New Jersey
42. Utah
43. Arizona
44. Indiana
45. Illinois
46. Georgia
47. Colorado
48. Florida
49. Virginia
50. Nevada

Due to rounding or data sources, the 50-state total plus D.C. may not equal the U.S. total. Please see introduction.

E-4 Federal Spending on Procurement, FY 2001

State	Total spending on procurement $ (in millions)	Per capita procurement spending $	Rank per capita
Alabama	5,204	1,166	8
Alaska	1,130	1,780	4
Arizona	5,260	991	12
Arkansas	692	257	49
California	28,949	839	17
Colorado	4,468	1,011	11
Connecticut	4,734	1,382	5
Delaware	148	186	50
Florida	8,859	540	27
Georgia	7,382	880	16
Hawaii	1,467	1,198	6
Idaho	1,197	906	15
Illinois	4,135	331	43
Indiana	2,734	447	34
Iowa	897	307	45
Kansas	1,383	513	30
Kentucky	2,759	679	21
Louisiana	2,625	588	25
Maine	674	524	28
Maryland	10,736	1,997	3
Massachusetts	6,851	1,074	9
Michigan	3,378	338	41
Minnesota	2,049	412	36
Mississippi	1,863	652	22
Missouri	6,741	1,197	7
Montana	371	410	37
Nebraska	447	261	48
Nevada	1,041	494	31
New Hampshire	655	520	29
New Jersey	4,158	490	32
New Mexico	5,122	2,800	2
New York	6,168	324	44
North Carolina	3,154	385	39
North Dakota	280	441	35
Ohio	5,124	451	33
Oklahoma	2,212	639	23
Oregon	959	276	47
Pennsylvania	6,788	552	26
Rhode Island	392	370	40
South Carolina	3,155	777	18
South Dakota	301	398	38
Tennessee	5,811	1,012	10
Texas	15,649	734	19
Utah	2,084	918	13
Vermont	391	638	24
Virginia	26,935	3,747	1
Washington	5,480	915	14
West Virginia	527	292	46
Wisconsin	1,817	336	42
Wyoming	341	690	20
50 States	215,677	759	
DC	10,263	17,948	
United States*	246,219	865	

Rank in order per capita

1 Virginia
2 New Mexico
3 Maryland
4 Alaska
5 Connecticut
6 Hawaii
7 Missouri
8 Alabama
9 Massachusetts
10 Tennessee
11 Colorado
12 Arizona
13 Utah
14 Washington
15 Idaho
16 Georgia
17 California
18 South Carolina
19 Texas
20 Wyoming
21 Kentucky
22 Mississippi
23 Oklahoma
24 Vermont
25 Louisiana
26 Pennsylvania
27 Florida
28 Maine
29 New Hampshire
30 Kansas
31 Nevada
32 New Jersey
33 Ohio
34 Indiana
35 North Dakota
36 Minnesota
37 Montana
38 South Dakota
39 North Carolina
40 Rhode Island
41 Michigan
42 Wisconsin
43 Illinois
44 New York
45 Iowa
46 West Virginia
47 Oregon
48 Nebraska
49 Arkansas
50 Delaware

Due to rounding or data sources, the 50-state total plus D.C. may not equal the U.S. total. Please see introduction.

E-5 Federal Spending on Payments to Individuals, FY 2001

State	Total federal payments to individuals $ (in millions)	Per capita federal payments to individuals $	Rank per capita
Alabama	18,303	4,100	11
Alaska	1,546	2,435	49
Arizona	17,009	3,205	39
Arkansas	11,314	4,203	10
California	101,914	2,954	46
Colorado	12,094	2,738	48
Connecticut	12,269	3,582	24
Delaware	2,779	3,490	29
Florida	69,058	4,212	9
Georgia	25,078	2,991	44
Hawaii	4,217	3,444	30
Idaho	4,074	3,084	42
Illinois	42,765	3,426	31
Indiana	21,462	3,510	28
Iowa	12,396	4,241	6
Kansas	10,728	3,981	13
Kentucky	15,172	3,732	19
Louisiana	16,708	3,742	18
Maine	4,793	3,725	20
Maryland	20,920	3,892	15
Massachusetts	24,395	3,824	17
Michigan	34,217	3,425	32
Minnesota	15,721	3,162	41
Mississippi	12,377	4,331	4
Missouri	22,122	3,930	14
Montana	3,871	4,280	5
Nebraska	7,216	4,212	8
Nevada	6,121	2,906	47
New Hampshire	3,855	3,062	43
New Jersey	29,822	3,515	25
New Mexico	6,131	3,352	33
New York	69,180	3,639	22
North Carolina	26,779	3,271	36
North Dakota	3,750	5,911	1
Ohio	39,968	3,514	26
Oklahoma	13,290	3,841	16
Oregon	11,541	3,323	34
Pennsylvania	51,912	4,225	7
Rhode Island	4,241	4,005	12
South Carolina	14,265	3,511	27
South Dakota	3,652	4,827	2
Tennessee	20,985	3,656	21
Texas	63,102	2,959	45
Utah	5,284	2,328	50
Vermont	1,954	3,187	40
Virginia	26,069	3,627	23
Washington	19,684	3,287	35
West Virginia	8,038	4,461	3
Wisconsin	17,359	3,213	38
Wyoming	1,594	3,224	37
50 States	993,094	3,494	
DC	4,012	7,016	
United States*	1,005,613	3,531	

	Rank in order per capita
1	North Dakota
2	South Dakota
3	West Virginia
4	Mississippi
5	Montana
6	Iowa
7	Pennsylvania
8	Nebraska
9	Florida
10	Arkansas
11	Alabama
12	Rhode Island
13	Kansas
14	Missouri
15	Maryland
16	Oklahoma
17	Massachusetts
18	Louisiana
19	Kentucky
20	Maine
21	Tennessee
22	New York
23	Virginia
24	Connecticut
25	New Jersey
26	Ohio
27	South Carolina
28	Indiana
29	Delaware
30	Hawaii
31	Illinois
32	Michigan
33	New Mexico
34	Oregon
35	Washington
36	North Carolina
37	Wyoming
38	Wisconsin
39	Arizona
40	Vermont
41	Minnesota
42	Idaho
43	New Hampshire
44	Georgia
45	Texas
46	California
47	Nevada
48	Colorado
49	Alaska
50	Utah

Note: Numbers that appear to be identical are rounded and vary slightly in actual value. The rankings reflect the actual values before rounding. See the introduction for more details.

Due to rounding or data sources, the 50-state total plus D.C. may not equal the U.S. total. Please see introduction.

E-6 Federal Spending on Social Security and Medicare, FY 2001

State	Total Social Security and Medicare spending $ (in millions)	Per capita spending $	Rank per capita
Alabama	12,886	2,886	7
Alaska	754	1,187	50
Arizona	12,063	2,273	35
Arkansas	7,538	2,800	9
California	74,715	2,166	38
Colorado	7,894	1,787	48
Connecticut	9,937	2,901	6
Delaware	2,054	2,580	21
Florida	53,007	3,233	3
Georgia	17,066	2,036	44
Hawaii	2,648	2,163	39
Idaho	2,677	2,026	45
Illinois	31,148	2,495	24
Indiana	15,617	2,554	22
Iowa	7,769	2,658	19
Kansas	6,778	2,515	23
Kentucky	11,326	2,786	10
Louisiana	12,162	2,724	14
Maine	3,432	2,668	18
Maryland	12,197	2,269	36
Massachusetts	18,583	2,913	4
Michigan	27,713	2,774	12
Minnesota	10,705	2,153	41
Mississippi	7,769	2,718	15
Missouri	15,563	2,764	13
Montana	2,186	2,416	28
Nebraska	3,989	2,328	33
Nevada	4,237	2,012	46
New Hampshire	2,871	2,280	34
New Jersey	23,556	2,776	11
New Mexico	3,830	2,094	43
New York	53,961	2,838	8
North Carolina	19,451	2,376	31
North Dakota	1,557	2,454	26
Ohio	30,654	2,695	16
Oklahoma	8,968	2,592	20
Oregon	8,224	2,368	32
Pennsylvania	40,382	3,287	2
Rhode Island	3,080	2,909	5
South Carolina	9,957	2,451	27
South Dakota	1,808	2,390	30
Tennessee	15,357	2,675	17
Texas	41,504	1,946	47
Utah	3,388	1,493	49
Vermont	1,473	2,402	29
Virginia	15,205	2,115	42
Washington	12,900	2,154	40
West Virginia	6,222	3,453	1
Wisconsin	13,283	2,459	25
Wyoming	1,085	2,194	37
50 States	713,130	2,509	
DC	1,425	2,492	
United States*	720,703	2,531	

Rank in order per capita	
1	West Virginia
2	Pennsylvania
3	Florida
4	Massachusetts
5	Rhode Island
6	Connecticut
7	Alabama
8	New York
9	Arkansas
10	Kentucky
11	New Jersey
12	Michigan
13	Missouri
14	Louisiana
15	Mississippi
16	Ohio
17	Tennessee
18	Maine
19	Iowa
20	Oklahoma
21	Delaware
22	Indiana
23	Kansas
24	Illinois
25	Wisconsin
26	North Dakota
27	South Carolina
28	Montana
29	Vermont
30	South Dakota
31	North Carolina
32	Oregon
33	Nebraska
34	New Hampshire
35	Arizona
36	Maryland
37	Wyoming
38	California
39	Hawaii
40	Washington
41	Minnesota
42	Virginia
43	New Mexico
44	Georgia
45	Idaho
46	Nevada
47	Texas
48	Colorado
49	Utah
50	Alaska

Due to rounding or data sources, the 50-state total plus D.C. may not equal the U.S. total. Please see introduction.

E-7 Social Security Benefits Paid, 2000

State	Social Security amounts paid $ (in thousands)	Number of recipients	Average monthly benefit $	Rank by average benefit
Alabama	585,492	825,773	709	43
Alaska	39,340	54,331	724	41
Arizona	624,375	795,936	784	16
Arkansas	365,138	523,588	697	48
California	3,281,762	4,208,926	780	20
Colorado	403,003	534,196	754	30
Connecticut	496,011	577,972	858	2
Delaware	107,476	132,368	812	6
Florida	2,482,741	3,195,615	777	21
Georgia	801,606	1,101,028	728	39
Hawaii	141,807	183,802	772	24
Idaho	146,680	195,695	750	31
Illinois	1,497,924	1,840,206	814	5
Indiana	805,822	999,089	807	7
Iowa	419,552	541,304	775	22
Kansas	348,729	440,531	792	13
Kentucky	520,425	739,585	704	47
Louisiana	492,834	711,631	693	49
Maine	177,490	250,724	708	44
Maryland	568,804	724,544	785	15
Massachusetts	831,434	1,060,613	784	17
Michigan	1,355,199	1,646,864	823	3
Minnesota	570,592	739,824	771	25
Mississippi	344,721	514,300	670	50
Missouri	761,447	1,008,424	755	29
Montana	116,707	157,443	741	33
Nebraska	217,602	285,555	762	27
Nevada	227,841	286,981	794	12
New Hampshire	158,694	199,781	794	11
New Jersey	1,161,715	1,348,996	861	1
New Mexico	195,426	277,262	705	45
New York	2,463,489	3,007,120	819	4
North Carolina	999,447	1,351,121	740	35
North Dakota	82,520	114,627	720	42
Ohio	1,496,027	1,912,006	782	18
Oklahoma	437,302	594,155	736	37
Oregon	444,389	562,381	790	14
Pennsylvania	1,888,992	2,356,051	802	9
Rhode Island	150,709	192,680	782	19
South Carolina	505,183	688,569	734	38
South Dakota	95,867	136,227	704	46
Tennessee	720,825	991,029	727	40
Texas	1,943,502	2,634,620	738	36
Utah	185,445	241,086	769	26
Vermont	78,963	104,476	756	28
Virginia	774,388	1,036,281	747	32
Washington	679,676	844,367	805	8
West Virginia	291,510	393,593	741	34
Wisconsin	720,423	901,712	799	10
Wyoming	58,835	76,116	773	23
50 States	34,265,881	44,241,104	775	
DC	48,924	73,703	664	
United States*	34,848,868	45,414,762	767	

Due to rounding or data sources, the 50-state total plus D.C. may not equal the U.S. total. Please see introduction.

Rank in order by average benefit

1. New Jersey
2. Connecticut
3. Michigan
4. New York
5. Illinois
6. Delaware
7. Indiana
8. Washington
9. Pennsylvania
10. Wisconsin
11. New Hampshire
12. Nevada
13. Kansas
14. Oregon
15. Maryland
16. Arizona
17. Massachusetts
18. Ohio
19. Rhode Island
20. California
21. Florida
22. Iowa
23. Wyoming
24. Hawaii
25. Minnesota
26. Utah
27. Nebraska
28. Vermont
29. Missouri
30. Colorado
31. Idaho
32. Virginia
33. Montana
34. West Virginia
35. North Carolina
36. Texas
37. Oklahoma
38. South Carolina
39. Georgia
40. Tennessee
41. Alaska
42. North Dakota
43. Alabama
44. Maine
45. New Mexico
46. South Dakota
47. Kentucky
48. Arkansas
49. Louisiana
50. Mississippi

Note: Numbers that appear to be identical are rounded and vary slightly in actual value. The rankings reflect the actual values before rounding. See the introduction for more details.

E-8 Federal Spending on Employee Wages and Salaries, FY 2001

State	Total federal spending on wages and salaries $ (in millions)	Per capita spending on wages and salaries $	Rank per capita
Alabama	2,895	648	19
Alaska	1,414	2,227	1
Arizona	2,917	550	28
Arkansas	1,178	438	41
California	17,858	518	31
Colorado	3,868	876	9
Connecticut	1,375	401	45
Delaware	428	538	29
Florida	8,415	513	33
Georgia	6,931	827	10
Hawaii	2,525	2,062	2
Idaho	753	570	25
Illinois	6,252	501	36
Indiana	2,121	347	48
Iowa	1,029	352	47
Kansas	1,866	692	16
Kentucky	2,805	690	17
Louisiana	2,310	517	32
Maine	808	628	20
Maryland	8,921	1,660	4
Massachusetts	3,214	504	35
Michigan	3,150	315	49
Minnesota	1,904	383	46
Mississippi	1,725	604	24
Missouri	3,463	615	22
Montana	711	786	13
Nebraska	1,053	615	23
Nevada	1,019	484	37
New Hampshire	516	410	44
New Jersey	3,782	446	40
New Mexico	1,747	955	6
New York	8,122	427	42
North Carolina	5,502	672	18
North Dakota	634	999	5
Ohio	4,851	427	43
Oklahoma	3,050	881	7
Oregon	1,592	458	39
Pennsylvania	5,763	469	38
Rhode Island	747	705	15
South Carolina	2,526	622	21
South Dakota	600	793	12
Tennessee	2,935	511	34
Texas	12,104	568	26
Utah	1,765	778	14
Vermont	319	520	30
Virginia	12,345	1,718	3
Washington	4,945	826	11
West Virginia	1,005	558	27
Wisconsin	1,626	301	50
Wyoming	435	880	8
50 States	169,819	597	
DC	12,646	22,115	
United States*	188,075	660	

	Rank in order per capita
1	Alaska
2	Hawaii
3	Virginia
4	Maryland
5	North Dakota
6	New Mexico
7	Oklahoma
8	Wyoming
9	Colorado
10	Georgia
11	Washington
12	South Dakota
13	Montana
14	Utah
15	Rhode Island
16	Kansas
17	Kentucky
18	North Carolina
19	Alabama
20	Maine
21	South Carolina
22	Missouri
23	Nebraska
24	Mississippi
25	Idaho
26	Texas
27	West Virginia
28	Arizona
29	Delaware
30	Vermont
31	California
32	Louisiana
33	Florida
34	Tennessee
35	Massachusetts
36	Illinois
37	Nevada
38	Pennsylvania
39	Oregon
40	New Jersey
41	Arkansas
42	New York
43	Ohio
44	New Hampshire
45	Connecticut
46	Minnesota
47	Iowa
48	Indiana
49	Michigan
50	Wisconsin

Due to rounding or data sources, the 50-state total plus D.C. may not equal the U.S. total. Please see introduction.

E-9 Federal Grant Spending Per Dollar of State Tax Revenue, FY 2000

State	Federal aid per dollar of state tax revenue $	Rank
Alabama	0.74	8
Alaska	0.84	3
Arizona	0.51	26
Arkansas	0.56	21
California	0.40	40
Colorado	0.46	34
Connecticut	0.33	48
Delaware	0.37	43
Florida	0.40	41
Georgia	0.47	30
Hawaii	0.34	46
Idaho	0.45	35
Illinois	0.41	36
Indiana	0.47	31
Iowa	0.51	25
Kansas	0.49	29
Kentucky	0.56	20
Louisiana	0.73	9
Maine	0.58	18
Maryland	0.39	42
Massachusetts	0.34	47
Michigan	0.40	38
Minnesota	0.33	49
Mississippi	0.71	10
Missouri	0.61	14
Montana	0.84	4
Nebraska	0.52	24
Nevada	0.27	50
New Hampshire	0.59	17
New Jersey	0.40	39
New Mexico	0.57	19
New York	0.63	13
North Carolina	0.53	23
North Dakota	0.83	5
Ohio	0.50	28
Oklahoma	0.51	27
Oregon	0.78	6
Pennsylvania	0.47	33
Rhode Island	0.54	22
South Carolina	0.64	12
South Dakota	0.84	2
Tennessee	0.77	7
Texas	0.60	15
Utah	0.47	32
Vermont	0.59	16
Virginia	0.34	45
Washington	0.41	37
West Virginia	0.71	11
Wisconsin	0.37	44
Wyoming	0.88	1
50 States	**0.48**	
DC	n/a	
United States	**0.48**	

Rank in order by $

1	Wyoming
2	South Dakota
3	Alaska
4	Montana
5	North Dakota
6	Oregon
7	Tennessee
8	Alabama
9	Louisiana
10	Mississippi
11	West Virginia
12	South Carolina
13	New York
14	Missouri
15	Texas
16	Vermont
17	New Hampshire
18	Maine
19	New Mexico
20	Kentucky
21	Arkansas
22	Rhode Island
23	North Carolina
24	Nebraska
25	Iowa
26	Arizona
27	Oklahoma
28	Ohio
29	Kansas
30	Georgia
31	Indiana
32	Utah
33	Pennsylvania
34	Colorado
35	Idaho
36	Illinois
37	Washington
38	Michigan
39	New Jersey
40	California
41	Florida
42	Maryland
43	Delaware
44	Wisconsin
45	Virginia
46	Hawaii
47	Massachusetts
48	Connecticut
49	Minnesota
50	Nevada

Note: Numbers that appear to be identical are rounded and vary slightly in actual value. The rankings reflect the actual values before rounding. See the introduction for more details.

E-10 State and Local General Revenue from Federal Government, FY 2000

State	Total general revenue from federal government $ (in millions)	Percentage of revenue from federal government	Rank by percentage
Alabama	5,087	24.2	11
Alaska	1,411	15.6	45
Arizona	4,475	19.6	22
Arkansas	2,823	24.4	10
California	38,476	18.5	31
Colorado	3,711	15.8	44
Connecticut	3,674	15.9	42
Delaware	830	16.0	41
Florida	11,718	15.4	46
Georgia	7,070	17.8	35
Hawaii	1,294	18.2	34
Idaho	1,150	18.9	28
Illinois	10,791	16.8	39
Indiana	5,169	17.4	37
Iowa	2,885	19.1	26
Kansas	2,482	18.5	29
Kentucky	4,595	23.7	13
Louisiana	5,070	22.7	14
Maine	1,630	21.9	17
Maryland	4,609	15.9	43
Massachusetts	6,439	16.8	38
Michigan	10,331	18.3	33
Minnesota	4,769	15.4	47
Mississippi	3,528	26.0	4
Missouri	5,628	21.7	18
Montana	1,306	26.9	3
Nebraska	1,710	19.0	27
Nevada	1,233	12.9	50
New Hampshire	1,062	18.5	32
New Jersey	7,883	15.3	48
New Mexico	2,398	23.8	12
New York	29,249	20.3	20
North Carolina	9,051	22.0	16
North Dakota	1,126	28.8	1
Ohio	10,933	18.5	30
Oklahoma	3,181	20.3	21
Oregon	5,233	25.0	8
Pennsylvania	12,498	19.3	25
Rhode Island	1,196	20.8	19
South Carolina	4,377	22.2	15
South Dakota	869	24.9	9
Tennessee	6,321	25.5	6
Texas	18,576	19.4	23
Utah	2,172	19.4	24
Vermont	903	25.8	5
Virginia	5,010	14.1	49
Washington	5,828	17.4	36
West Virginia	2,489	27.5	2
Wisconsin	5,059	16.5	40
Wyoming	891	25.1	7
50 States	290,202	18.9	
DC	1,748	30.5	
United States	291,950	18.9	

Rank in order by percentage	
1	North Dakota
2	West Virginia
3	Montana
4	Mississippi
5	Vermont
6	Tennessee
7	Wyoming
8	Oregon
9	South Dakota
10	Arkansas
11	Alabama
12	New Mexico
13	Kentucky
14	Louisiana
15	South Carolina
16	North Carolina
17	Maine
18	Missouri
19	Rhode Island
20	New York
21	Oklahoma
22	Arizona
23	Texas
24	Utah
25	Pennsylvania
26	Iowa
27	Nebraska
28	Idaho
29	Kansas
30	Ohio
31	California
32	New Hampshire
33	Michigan
34	Hawaii
35	Georgia
36	Washington
37	Indiana
38	Massachusetts
39	Illinois
40	Wisconsin
41	Delaware
42	Connecticut
43	Maryland
44	Colorado
45	Alaska
46	Florida
47	Minnesota
48	New Jersey
49	Virginia
50	Nevada

Note: Numbers that appear to be identical are rounded and vary slightly in actual value. The rankings reflect the actual values before rounding. See the introduction for more details.

E-11 Federal Tax Burden, Total and Per Capita, FY 2002

State	Federal tax burden total $ (in millions)	Federal tax burden per capita $	Rank per capita
Alabama	22,660	5,041	42
Alaska	4,189	6,474	20
Arizona	30,706	5,801	33
Arkansas	12,648	4,679	48
California	266,867	7,738	10
Colorado	34,404	7,771	9
Connecticut	39,021	11,461	1
Delaware	5,784	7,258	14
Florida	111,934	6,836	17
Georgia	53,223	6,344	23
Hawaii	6,877	5,517	36
Idaho	6,684	4,948	43
Illinois	97,221	7,814	7
Indiana	36,931	6,021	29
Iowa	16,872	5,765	34
Kansas	16,666	6,157	26
Kentucky	20,764	5,100	40
Louisiana	21,601	4,823	46
Maine	6,999	5,441	37
Maryland	42,018	7,792	8
Massachusetts	60,345	9,479	3
Michigan	68,168	6,852	16
Minnesota	37,059	7,444	11
Mississippi	12,246	4,271	50
Missouri	33,957	6,014	30
Montana	4,459	4,829	45
Nebraska	10,519	6,108	28
Nevada	15,321	7,298	13
New Hampshire	10,365	8,205	6
New Jersey	80,843	9,548	2
New Mexico	8,736	4,686	47
New York	158,846	8,419	4
North Carolina	48,388	5,905	31
North Dakota	3,340	5,199	38
Ohio	69,553	6,110	27
Oklahoma	16,835	4,857	44
Oregon	21,582	6,168	25
Pennsylvania	83,440	6,791	18
Rhode Island	7,065	6,728	19
South Carolina	21,064	5,192	39
South Dakota	4,349	5,673	35
Tennessee	33,563	5,804	32
Texas	136,717	6,402	22
Utah	11,587	5,046	41
Vermont	3,822	6,186	24
Virginia	53,496	7,416	12
Washington	50,165	8,307	5
West Virginia	7,854	4,337	49
Wisconsin	34,928	6,449	21
Wyoming	3,632	7,146	15
50 States	1,966,313	6,918	
DC	5,542	9,830	
United States	1,971,855	6,918	

Rank in order per capita	
1	Connecticut
2	New Jersey
3	Massachusetts
4	New York
5	Washington
6	New Hampshire
7	Illinois
8	Maryland
9	Colorado
10	California
11	Minnesota
12	Virginia
13	Nevada
14	Delaware
15	Wyoming
16	Michigan
17	Florida
18	Pennsylvania
19	Rhode Island
20	Alaska
21	Wisconsin
22	Texas
23	Georgia
24	Vermont
25	Oregon
26	Kansas
27	Ohio
28	Nebraska
29	Indiana
30	Missouri
31	North Carolina
32	Tennessee
33	Arizona
34	Iowa
35	South Dakota
36	Hawaii
37	Maine
38	North Dakota
39	South Carolina
40	Kentucky
41	Utah
42	Alabama
43	Idaho
44	Oklahoma
45	Montana
46	Louisiana
47	New Mexico
48	Arkansas
49	West Virginia
50	Mississippi

E-12 Federal Spending Per Dollar of Taxes Paid, FY 2001

State	Spending per dollar of taxes paid $	Rank
Alabama	1.53	8
Alaska	1.63	6
Arizona	1.12	25
Arkansas	1.45	11
California	0.82	44
Colorado	0.82	43
Connecticut	0.67	49
Delaware	0.86	39
Florida	1.05	31
Georgia	1.01	33
Hawaii	1.54	7
Idaho	1.24	19
Illinois	0.78	46
Indiana	0.99	35
Iowa	1.17	21
Kansas	1.14	24
Kentucky	1.38	14
Louisiana	1.42	13
Maine	1.31	15
Maryland	1.26	18
Massachusetts	0.84	41
Michigan	0.86	38
Minnesota	0.81	45
Mississippi	1.78	3
Missouri	1.29	17
Montana	1.67	5
Nebraska	1.17	22
Nevada	0.76	47
New Hampshire	0.71	48
New Jersey	0.67	50
New Mexico	2.08	1
New York	0.83	42
North Carolina	1.06	30
North Dakota	1.95	2
Ohio	1.01	32
Oklahoma	1.48	10
Oregon	1.00	34
Pennsylvania	1.07	29
Rhode Island	1.11	27
South Carolina	1.30	16
South Dakota	1.50	9
Tennessee	1.20	20
Texas	0.92	36
Utah	1.11	28
Vermont	1.12	26
Virginia	1.45	12
Washington	0.84	40
West Virginia	1.73	4
Wisconsin	0.89	37
Wyoming	1.14	23
50 States	n/a	
DC	5.73	
United States	1.00	

Rank in order by $

1	New Mexico
2	North Dakota
3	Mississippi
4	West Virginia
5	Montana
6	Alaska
7	Hawaii
8	Alabama
9	South Dakota
10	Oklahoma
11	Arkansas
12	Virginia
13	Louisiana
14	Kentucky
15	Maine
16	South Carolina
17	Missouri
18	Maryland
19	Idaho
20	Tennessee
21	Iowa
22	Nebraska
23	Wyoming
24	Kansas
25	Arizona
26	Vermont
27	Rhode Island
28	Utah
29	Pennsylvania
30	North Carolina
31	Florida
32	Ohio
33	Georgia
34	Oregon
35	Indiana
36	Texas
37	Wisconsin
38	Michigan
39	Delaware
40	Washington
41	Massachusetts
42	New York
43	Colorado
44	California
45	Minnesota
46	Illinois
47	Nevada
48	New Hampshire
49	Connecticut
50	New Jersey

Note: Numbers that appear to be identical are rounded and vary slightly in actual value. The rankings reflect the actual values before rounding. See the introduction for more details.

State	Percentage of charges returned to states	Rank
Alabama	152	14
Alaska	911	1
Arizona	113	40
Arkansas	156	13
California	116	32
Colorado	109	44
Connecticut	182	12
Delaware	203	9
Florida	108	46
Georgia	105	49
Hawaii	352	2
Idaho	197	10
Illinois	111	42
Indiana	114	39
Iowa	136	24
Kansas	133	25
Kentucky	115	35
Louisiana	108	45
Maine	116	34
Maryland	142	18
Massachusetts	115	36
Michigan	112	41
Minnesota	124	30
Mississippi	149	16
Missouri	117	31
Montana	292	5
Nebraska	129	27
Nevada	142	19
New Hampshire	141	21
New Jersey	109	43
New Mexico	138	22
New York	151	15
North Carolina	115	37
North Dakota	323	4
Ohio	106	48
Oklahoma	107	47
Oregon	138	23
Pennsylvania	145	17
Rhode Island	278	6
South Carolina	116	33
South Dakota	334	3
Tennessee	114	38
Texas	103	50
Utah	125	29
Vermont	239	8
Virginia	142	20
Washington	129	28
West Virginia	268	7
Wisconsin	132	26
Wyoming	183	11
50 States	n/a	
DC	465	
United States	128	

Rank in order by percentage

1	Alaska
2	Hawaii
3	South Dakota
4	North Dakota
5	Montana
6	Rhode Island
7	West Virginia
8	Vermont
9	Delaware
10	Idaho
11	Wyoming
12	Connecticut
13	Arkansas
14	Alabama
15	New York
16	Mississippi
17	Pennsylvania
18	Maryland
19	Nevada
20	Virginia
21	New Hampshire
22	New Mexico
23	Oregon
24	Iowa
25	Kansas
26	Wisconsin
27	Nebraska
28	Washington
29	Utah
30	Minnesota
31	Missouri
32	California
33	South Carolina
34	Maine
35	Kentucky
36	Massachusetts
37	North Carolina
38	Tennessee
39	Indiana
40	Arizona
41	Michigan
42	Illinois
43	New Jersey
44	Colorado
45	Louisiana
46	Florida
47	Oklahoma
48	Ohio
49	Georgia
50	Texas

Note: Numbers that appear to be identical are rounded and vary slightly in actual value. The rankings reflect the actual values before rounding. See the introduction for more details.

E-14 Terms of Trade with the Federal Government, FY 2001

State	Federal grants to state and local governments $ (in millions)	Terms of trade, ratio of federal grants to federal taxes paid	Rank by ratio
Alabama	5,298	1.38	15
Alaska	2,314	3.22	1
Arizona	5,190	1.01	30
Arkansas	3,448	1.61	11
California	39,797	0.88	40
Colorado	3,916	0.67	46
Connecticut	4,364	0.66	47
Delaware	892	0.91	38
Florida	13,666	0.72	44
Georgia	7,929	0.89	39
Hawaii	1,514	1.28	19
Idaho	1,505	1.32	18
Illinois	11,883	0.72	45
Indiana	5,850	0.93	37
Iowa	3,079	1.08	27
Kansas	2,721	0.96	33
Kentucky	5,100	1.45	13
Louisiana	6,173	1.69	9
Maine	1,905	1.61	12
Maryland	7,586	1.06	28
Massachusetts	9,718	0.95	34
Michigan	10,887	0.94	36
Minnesota	5,260	0.84	41
Mississippi	4,246	2.05	6
Missouri	6,865	1.19	22
Montana	1,665	2.23	4
Nebraska	2,054	1.15	25
Nevada	1,442	0.56	50
New Hampshire	1,288	0.73	43
New Jersey	8,478	0.61	49
New Mexico	3,586	2.47	2
New York	32,897	1.21	21
North Carolina	9,122	1.12	26
North Dakota	1,284	2.28	3
Ohio	11,762	0.99	31
Oklahoma	4,119	1.44	14
Oregon	4,308	1.19	23
Pennsylvania	14,847	1.04	29
Rhode Island	1,607	1.34	16
South Carolina	4,730	1.33	17
South Dakota	1,254	1.71	8
Tennessee	7,027	1.24	20
Texas	21,675	0.94	35
Utah	2,244	1.15	24
Vermont	1,069	1.67	10
Virginia	5,908	0.65	48
Washington	6,794	0.80	42
West Virginia	2,971	2.23	5
Wisconsin	5,843	0.99	32
Wyoming	1,213	1.98	7
50 States	330,293	0.99	
DC	4,020	4.26	
United States*	338,977	1.01	

Rank in order by ratio	
1	Alaska
2	New Mexico
3	North Dakota
4	Montana
5	West Virginia
6	Mississippi
7	Wyoming
8	South Dakota
9	Louisiana
10	Vermont
11	Arkansas
12	Maine
13	Kentucky
14	Oklahoma
15	Alabama
16	Rhode Island
17	South Carolina
18	Idaho
19	Hawaii
20	Tennessee
21	New York
22	Missouri
23	Oregon
24	Utah
25	Nebraska
26	North Carolina
27	Iowa
28	Maryland
29	Pennsylvania
30	Arizona
31	Ohio
32	Wisconsin
33	Kansas
34	Massachusetts
35	Texas
36	Michigan
37	Indiana
38	Delaware
39	Georgia
40	California
41	Minnesota
42	Washington
43	New Hampshire
44	Florida
45	Illinois
46	Colorado
47	Connecticut
48	Virginia
49	New Jersey
50	Nevada

Note: Numbers that appear to be identical are rounded and vary slightly in actual value. The rankings reflect the actual values before rounding. See the introduction for more details.

*Due to rounding or data sources, the 50-state total plus D.C. may not equal the U.S. total. Please see introduction.

E-15 Federal Personal Income Taxes, 2000

State	Federal tax liability $ (in millions)	Federal tax liability per capita $	Rank per capita		Rank in order per capita
Alabama	9.93	2,233	43	1	Connecticut
Alaska	2.17	3,466	17	2	Massachusetts
Arizona	14.73	2,872	28	3	New Jersey
Arkansas	5.37	2,010	47	4	New Hampshire
California	152.74	4,509	5	5	California
Colorado	19.00	4,418	8	6	Washington
Connecticut	23.44	6,882	1	7	New York
Delaware	2.88	3,676	15	8	Colorado
Florida	58.50	3,660	16	9	Illinois
Georgia	25.70	3,140	22	10	Maryland
Hawaii	3.28	2,708	34	11	Nevada
Idaho	3.09	2,390	38	12	Wyoming
Illinois	51.18	4,121	9	13	Virginia
Indiana	17.11	2,814	30	14	Minnesota
Iowa	7.32	2,500	37	15	Delaware
Kansas	7.88	2,930	26	16	Florida
Kentucky	9.07	2,245	42	17	Alaska
Louisiana	9.75	2,183	45	18	Texas
Maine	3.35	2,625	35	19	Pennsylvania
Maryland	21.71	4,099	10	20	Michigan
Massachusetts	37.63	5,926	2	21	Rhode Island
Michigan	32.84	3,304	20	22	Georgia
Minnesota	18.42	3,744	14	23	Wisconsin
Mississippi	4.96	1,744	49	24	Oregon
Missouri	15.95	2,851	29	25	Vermont
Montana	1.91	2,116	46	26	Kansas
Nebraska	4.80	2,807	31	27	Ohio
Nevada	8.09	4,046	11	28	Arizona
New Hampshire	5.91	4,785	4	29	Missouri
New Jersey	45.78	5,440	3	30	Indiana
New Mexico	2.85	1,568	50	31	Nebraska
New York	83.85	4,419	7	32	North Carolina
North Carolina	22.24	2,763	32	33	Tennessee
North Dakota	1.45	2,254	41	34	Hawaii
Ohio	32.91	2,899	27	35	Maine
Oklahoma	7.55	2,187	44	36	South Dakota
Oregon	10.23	2,990	24	37	Iowa
Pennsylvania	40.80	3,322	19	38	Idaho
Rhode Island	3.45	3,293	21	39	Utah
South Carolina	9.24	2,303	40	40	South Carolina
South Dakota	1.96	2,595	36	41	North Dakota
Tennessee	15.43	2,712	33	42	Kentucky
Texas	70.57	3,384	18	43	Alabama
Utah	5.19	2,326	39	44	Oklahoma
Vermont	1.81	2,973	25	45	Louisiana
Virginia	27.00	3,814	13	46	Montana
Washington	26.15	4,437	6	47	Arkansas
West Virginia	3.28	1,813	48	48	West Virginia
Wisconsin	16.52	3,081	23	49	Mississippi
Wyoming	1.90	3,842	12	50	New Mexico
50 States	1,008.89	3,592			
DC	2.96	5,178			
United States*	1,019.93	3,624			

Due to rounding or data sources, the 50-state total plus D.C. may not equal the U.S. total. Please see introduction.

E-16 Federal Share of Medicaid, 2002 and 2003

State	2002 federal cost-sharing percentages for Medicaid %	2003 federal cost-sharing percentages for Medicaid %	Rank by 2003
Alabama	70.45	70.60	9
Alaska	57.38	58.27	33
Arizona	64.98	67.25	14
Arkansas	72.64	74.28	4
California	51.40	50.00	39
Colorado	50.00	50.00	39
Connecticut	50.00	50.00	39
Delaware	50.00	50.00	39
Florida	56.43	58.83	29
Georgia	59.00	59.60	27
Hawaii	56.34	58.77	31
Idaho	71.02	70.96	8
Illinois	50.00	50.00	39
Indiana	62.04	61.97	21
Iowa	62.86	63.50	18
Kansas	60.20	60.15	25
Kentucky	69.94	69.89	11
Louisiana	70.30	71.28	6
Maine	66.58	66.22	15
Maryland	50.00	50.00	39
Massachusetts	50.00	50.00	39
Michigan	56.36	55.42	34
Minnesota	50.00	50.00	39
Mississippi	76.09	76.62	1
Missouri	61.06	61.23	23
Montana	72.83	72.96	5
Nebraska	59.55	59.52	28
Nevada	50.00	52.39	37
New Hampshire	50.00	50.00	39
New Jersey	50.00	50.00	39
New Mexico	73.04	74.56	3
New York	50.00	50.00	39
North Carolina	61.46	62.56	19
North Dakota	69.87	68.36	13
Ohio	58.78	58.83	29
Oklahoma	70.43	70.56	10
Oregon	59.20	60.16	24
Pennsylvania	54.65	54.69	36
Rhode Island	52.45	55.40	35
South Carolina	69.34	69.81	12
South Dakota	65.93	65.29	16
Tennessee	63.64	64.59	17
Texas	60.17	59.99	26
Utah	70.00	71.24	7
Vermont	63.06	62.41	20
Virginia	51.45	50.53	38
Washington	50.37	50.00	39
West Virginia	75.27	75.04	2
Wisconsin	58.57	58.43	32
Wyoming	61.97	61.32	22
50 States	n/a	n/a	
DC	70.00	70.00	
United States	n/a	n/a	

Rank in order by 2003 percentage

1	Mississippi
2	West Virginia
3	New Mexico
4	Arkansas
5	Montana
6	Louisiana
7	Utah
8	Idaho
9	Alabama
10	Oklahoma
11	Kentucky
12	South Carolina
13	North Dakota
14	Arizona
15	Maine
16	South Dakota
17	Tennessee
18	Iowa
19	North Carolina
20	Vermont
21	Indiana
22	Wyoming
23	Missouri
24	Oregon
25	Kansas
26	Texas
27	Georgia
28	Nebraska
29	Florida
29	Ohio
31	Hawaii
32	Wisconsin
33	Alaska
34	Michigan
35	Rhode Island
36	Pennsylvania
37	Nevada
38	Virginia
39	California
39	Colorado
39	Connecticut
39	Delaware
39	Illinois
39	Maryland
39	Massachusetts
39	Minnesota
39	New Hampshire
39	New Jersey
39	New York
39	Washington

Note: Ties in ranking reflect ties in actual values.

Source Notes for Federal Impacts (Section E)

E-1 Federal Spending, Total and Per Capita, FY 2001: The federal government affects state economies and state finances through its massive spending, accounting for nearly one-quarter of all economic activity in the United States. The primary components of that spending are grants to state and local governments; payments to individuals, such as Social Security; wages and salaries of federal employees; and purchases of goods and services, such as weapons for the Defense Department.

Details of where these funds are spent are compiled by federal agencies and summarized by the Census Bureau in *Consolidated Federal Funds Report for Fiscal Year 2001*. Many tables in this section reflect the latest version of this report, covering federal spending in fiscal 2001, which for the federal government ended in September 2001.

This table reflects total federal spending of nearly $1.8 trillion, along with the results of dividing each state's total by its population to permit meaningful comparisons among states. The federal figures exclude certain forms of federal spending that cannot reasonably be associated with particular states, primarily interest on the federal debt and money spent in other countries.

E-2 Increase in Total Federal Spending, FY 1996-FY 2001: This table uses the Census Bureau reports for federal fiscal years 1996 and 2001 to show the percentage change in total federal spending in each state over a five-year period. The data come from the federal report described in the notes to Table E-1.

E-3 Federal Spending on Grants, Total and Per Capita, FY 2001: This table reflects the federal spending for grants that help state and local governments finance welfare, Medicaid, highway construction, and other activities. The data come from the federal report described in the notes to Table E-1.

E-4 Federal Spending on Procurement, Total and Per Capita, FY 2001: This table reflects the federal spending for purchases ranging from tanks and space shuttles to gasoline for federal vehicles. The data come from the federal report described in the notes to Table E-1.

E-5 Federal Spending on Payments to Individuals, FY 2001: This table reflects the federal spending for payments to individuals. The primary components are Social Security pensions, Medicare payments to health care providers, pensions for retired federal workers, and food stamps. The data come from the federal report described in the notes to Table E-1.

E-6 Federal Spending on Social Security and Medicare, FY 2001: This table reflects the federal spending for Social Security pensions and Medicare payments to health care providers. This spending is a part of the total covered by Table E-5. The per capita amounts suggest the massive impact that this flow of funds has among states. While revenues from payroll taxes are concentrated in states that are showing strong economic growth, states with slower growth (primarily those in the Northeast) receive large portions of personal income from these retirement-related federal payments and private pensions. The data come from the federal report described in the notes to Table E-1.

E-7 Social Security Benefits Paid, 2000: This table provides another perspective on Social Security payments, using tabulations for December 2000 payments prepared by the Social Security Administration and available on the SSA website (www.ssa.gov).

This agency can provide additional details on benefits paid in each state, such as the amounts paid to retired workers, to deceased workers' beneficiaries, and to workers and their families based on disability. Besides the amounts paid and number of recipient households, the table shows the average benefit per household. This amount is appreciably higher in states where salaries have been high (such as in the Northeast) than where they have been low (such as in the South).

E-8 Federal Spending on Employee Wages and Salaries, FY 2001: This table reflects the federal spending on payments for salaries of civilian and military federal employees. The largest amounts are found in states with major federal installations, such as military bases. Because the Postal Service is included and some agencies, such as the Department of Agriculture, which operate in every state, even states without major installations show substantial federal spending. The data come from the federal report described in the notes to Table E-1.

E-9 Federal Grant Spending Per Dollar of State Tax Revenue, FY 2000: Most federal grant spending is now concentrated on state-administered programs, such as welfare and Medicaid. The amounts are substantial when compared with the amount that states raise from state taxes, as shown by the table, which relates the amounts provided by federal grants to the amounts states raised from taxes. The data for fiscal 2000 are from "State Government Finances," available on the Census Bureau website (www.census.gov).

E-10 State and Local General Revenue from Federal Government, FY 2000: These data, covering both state and local government, show the amount of federal aid contributing to "general revenue" as defined by the Census Bureau in its annual survey of government finances. It excludes certain trust funds, such as unemployment insurance, but includes others, such as those used for highway construction. The data are calculated from the Census Bureau's "State and Local Government Finances: 1999-2000" available on the Census Bureau website (www.census.gov).

E-11 Federal Tax Burden, Total and Per Capita, FY 2002: This table shows where the burdens of federal taxes fell in federal fiscal year 2002. The data come from the Tax Foundation's *Special Report* (July 2002, No. 116), which uses formulas to spread the burden of certain taxes, such as the corporate income tax, among states and actual data from federal tax collectors to show the sources of major tax revenues, such as those from personal income and payroll taxes.

E-12 Federal Spending Per Dollar of Taxes Paid, FY 2001: These data relate how much taxpayers in each state pay in federal taxes to the amounts the federal government spends in each state. The information comes from calculations by the Tax Foundation using allocations of tax burdens (see Table E-11) and the Census Bureau report on federal spending (see Table E-1).

Many states get more than a dollar back in federal spending for every dollar sent to the federal government in taxes. This occurs primarily in states where federal installations and/or purchasing is concentrated. Because a substantial portion of federal spending is financed by borrowing (deficit spending), the nationwide total would show more money returned as spending than paid as taxes, so the Tax Foundation adjusted spending to eliminate the deficit-financed portion.

E-13 Highway Charges Returned to States, FY 2001: Federal spending for highways is financed by special user charges, such as federal taxes on gasoline and diesel fuel. Some states, such as Alaska and Hawaii, receive much more federal highway aid than federal user charges collected in their states. Others, which highway officials call "donor states," usually receive less than a dollar of aid from every dollar in federal highway taxes collected within their boundaries. According to the data from the Federal Highway Administration no states were donors in 2001. Some states will appear as particularly large "donee states" because of expansive interstate projects underway in a particular period. Which states should "donate" how much is a subject of perpetual controversy in the Congress. The controversy spawns many different ways to measure the federal redistribution of highway revenues.

In FY 2001, federal collections of highway user charges were about $26.9 billion while allocations of spending authority to states were about $34.5 billion. Federal spending for highways is financed by special "user charges," such as federal taxes on gasoline and diesel fuel.

This table is parallel to Table E-12 but covers only highway spending. It was developed by the Federal Highway Administration and is published in *2001 Highway Statistics*. Data from this book and earlier editions of *Highway Statistics* are available on the FHWA website (www.fhwa.dot.gov).

E-14 Terms of Trade with the Federal Government, FY 2001: This table was developed by State Policy Research to show the relationship between amounts paid by taxpayers in each state to the federal grants to state and local government financed by their federal taxes. The table shows federal grants, identical to the amounts shown in Table E-3. Because all grants, even those paid currently out of money the federal government raises by borrowing, are ultimately paid for by taxpayers, the total federal tax revenue to pay for grants was stipulated as equal to the grants for the fifty states and the District of Columbia.

To determine how this tax burden to pay for grants was distributed among states, the total tax burden for grants was allocated based on the percentage of all federal taxes paid by citizens and corporations in each state, using the Tax Foundation's logic (also used to prepare Table E-11). The result is that the sum of grants and of taxes are identical for the fifty states plus the District of Columbia.

However, the amounts are by no means equal for individual states. States with relatively high personal incomes (and thus federal tax liabilities) but low grants will show ratios below one. Conceptually, for example, 0.95 can be considered as getting 95 cents back in grants for every dollar in federal taxes paid, or a 95 percent return. Conversely, states with lower incomes and high grants will show a ratio above one.

E-15 Federal Personal Income Taxes, 2000: This table shows how much households in each state were required to pay in federal income taxes on their income during 2000, as reported in tax returns filed in early 2001. The data are from the Internal Revenue Service as reported in the *SOI Bulletin* (Vol. 21, No. 4, Spring 2002).

E-16 Federal Share of Medicaid, 2002 and 2003: The federal grants to states for Medicaid are based on multiplying the total costs of these programs by the federal cost-sharing percentages shown in the table. The formula used to determine each state's share provides the largest federal shares for the states with the lowest per capita incomes. A special rule overrides the calculation for more affluent states, so no state has less than 50 percent of these costs paid by the federal government. The percentages were published in Federal Funds Information for States' *Issue Brief 02-50*, released September 24, 2002.

Federal welfare reform legislation, enacted in 1996, was partially implemented at the option of the states during late 1996 and early 1997. Effective in October of 1997, the block grants established under the legislation became fully effective based on federal spending patterns from fiscal year 1994. However, under the block grants, the federal government no longer shares in additional welfare costs with matching money.

Taxes

F-1	State and Local Tax Revenue, Total and as a Percentage of Personal Income, FY 2000	140
F-2	Per Capita State and Local Tax Revenue, FY 2000	141
F-3	State and Local Tax Effort, 1996	142
F-4	State and Local Tax Capacity, 1996	143
F-5	Change in State and Local Taxes, FY 1995-2000	144
F-6	Property Taxes, Total and as a Percentage of Personal Income, FY 2000	145
F-7	Property Taxes Per Capita, FY 2000	146
F-8	Property Tax Revenue as a Percentage of Three-Tax Revenue, FY 2000	147
F-9	Sales Taxes, Total and as a Percentage of Personal Income, FY 2000	148
F-10	Sales Taxes Per Capita, FY 2000	149
F-11	Sales Tax Revenue as a Percentage of Three-Tax Revenue, FY 2000	150
F-12	Sales Tax Rates and Reach, 2003	151
F-13	Individual Income Taxes, Total and as a Percentage of Personal Income, FY 2000	152
F-14	Individual Income Taxes Per Capita, FY 2000	153
F-15	Individual Income Tax Revenue as a Percentage of Three-Tax Revenue, FY 2000	154
F-16	Highest Personal Income Tax Rate, 2002	155
F-17	Corporate Income Taxes, Total and Per Capita, FY 2000	156
F-18	Motor Fuel Taxes	157
F-19	Tobacco Taxes	158
F-20	State and Local Taxes on High Income Families, 2001	159
F-21	State and Local Taxes in the Largest City in Each State, 2001	160
F-22	Progressivity of Major State and Local Taxes, 2001	161
F-23	State Estate Taxes, 2002	162

Tax collections dwindled in fiscal year 2002, which for most states ended June 30 of that year. According to the National Association of State Budget Officers, sales taxes were 3.2 percent under estimates, personal income taxes were off by a significant 12.8 percent, and corporate income taxes were 21.5 percent lower than expected. Modest tax increases were not sufficient to close the resulting budget gaps. Instead states cut spending and relied on a variety of short-term fixes.

In fiscal year 2003, states are responding to continued financial hard times with larger tax increases—adding a potential $8.3 billion to revenues. As in fiscal year 2002, states looked first to two so-called "sin" taxes—cigarette and tobacco taxes. Nineteen states increased these rates—hoping to bring in an estimated $2.9 billion. Eleven states raised their sales taxes, for an anticipated increase of $1.4 billion in funds. Personal income taxes were cut in eleven states, while five states raised them. The expected result is a net gain of $1 billion. Massachusetts—which delayed a decrease in rates, changed personal exemptions, and restored the tax on capital gains—accounted for almost 96 percent of the net increase. Eight states raised corporate income taxes to the tune of $1.2 billion—65 percent of which was the result of actions in New Jersey.

A survey of state fiscal offices conducted by the National Conference of State Legislatures reports that as of November 2002 revenues were coming in under estimates in thirty-three states. Mid-year adjustments are sure to come, with states again debating taxes, spending and the use of reserve funds.

One way states are trying to protect their budgets is by avoiding the fiscal consequences of the phase-out of the federal estate tax. Although the tax affects a relatively small number of wealthy taxpayers, it has a billion dollar effect on the states. In fiscal year 2001 states collected $5.7 billion from a credit against the federal estate tax. They are scheduled to gradually lose this revenue source until it is eliminated in tax year 2005. One way to prevent this is to "decouple." For most states this means legislative action that severs the link between the state tax code and the changes in the federal tax code. Seventeen states and the District of Columbia are currently decoupled.

F-1 State and Local Tax Revenue, FY 2000

State	State and local taxes $ (in millions)	State and local taxes as a percentage of personal income	Rank by percentage
Alabama	9,415	9.4	48
Alaska	2,312	13.1	3
Arizona	13,334	11.1	21
Arkansas	5,961	10.5	38
California	120,068	12.1	10
Colorado	13,216	10.3	42
Connecticut	15,651	12.1	9
Delaware	2,619	11.3	19
Florida	41,937	10.0	44
Georgia	23,254	10.9	28
Hawaii	4,102	12.6	6
Idaho	3,294	11.5	15
Illinois	40,256	10.7	36
Indiana	16,363	10.5	37
Iowa	8,091	11.0	24
Kansas	7,616	10.7	34
Kentucky	10,172	11.1	22
Louisiana	10,887	10.9	29
Maine	4,262	13.8	2
Maryland	18,290	10.9	30
Massachusetts	24,042	11.0	27
Michigan	31,474	11.4	17
Minnesota	18,173	12.4	7
Mississippi	6,299	11.0	25
Missouri	14,314	9.9	45
Montana	2,132	11.0	26
Nebraska	4,973	11.0	23
Nevada	5,825	10.4	41
New Hampshire	3,278	8.8	50
New Jersey	32,838	11.3	18
New Mexico	4,801	12.6	5
New York	86,868	14.1	1
North Carolina	21,440	10.8	31
North Dakota	1,768	12.0	11
Ohio	34,239	11.2	20
Oklahoma	8,251	10.7	33
Oregon	9,412	10.5	39
Pennsylvania	36,581	10.7	35
Rhode Island	3,412	11.7	14
South Carolina	9,543	10.4	40
South Dakota	1,736	9.5	47
Tennessee	12,431	8.9	49
Texas	52,227	9.7	46
Utah	5,873	11.8	13
Vermont	1,876	12.2	8
Virginia	21,083	10.3	43
Washington	18,734	10.7	32
West Virginia	4,362	11.5	16
Wisconsin	18,547	13.0	4
Wyoming	1,505	11.9	12
50 States	869,135	11.2	
DC	3,216	15.5	
United States	872,351	11.2	

Rank in order by percentage

1. New York
2. Maine
3. Alaska
4. Wisconsin
5. New Mexico
6. Hawaii
7. Minnesota
8. Vermont
9. Connecticut
10. California
11. North Dakota
12. Wyoming
13. Utah
14. Rhode Island
15. Idaho
16. West Virginia
17. Michigan
18. New Jersey
19. Delaware
20. Ohio
21. Arizona
22. Kentucky
23. Nebraska
24. Iowa
25. Mississippi
26. Montana
27. Massachusetts
28. Georgia
29. Louisiana
30. Maryland
31. North Carolina
32. Washington
33. Oklahoma
34. Kansas
35. Pennsylvania
36. Illinois
37. Indiana
38. Arkansas
39. Oregon
40. South Carolina
41. Nevada
42. Colorado
43. Virginia
44. Florida
45. Missouri
46. Texas
47. South Dakota
48. Alabama
49. Tennessee
50. New Hampshire

Note: Numbers that appear to be identical are rounded and vary slightly in actual value. The rankings reflect the actual values before rounding. See the introduction for more details.

F-2 Per Capita State and Local Tax Revenue, FY 2000

State	State and local taxes per capita $	State taxes per capita $	Local taxes per capita $	Rank by state and local taxes per capita
Alabama	2,117	1,448	669	50
Alaska	3,687	2,270	1,417	6
Arizona	2,599	1,579	1,020	36
Arkansas	2,230	1,822	408	47
California	3,545	2,474	1,070	7
Colorado	3,073	1,645	1,428	18
Connecticut	4,595	2,986	1,609	1
Delaware	3,340	2,720	621	12
Florida	2,624	1,553	1,071	35
Georgia	2,841	1,651	1,190	25
Hawaii	3,384	2,751	633	10
Idaho	2,546	1,837	709	38
Illinois	3,241	1,835	1,406	14
Indiana	2,691	1,662	1,029	30
Iowa	2,765	1,772	993	27
Kansas	2,833	1,804	1,030	26
Kentucky	2,517	1,904	613	39
Louisiana	2,436	1,457	979	41
Maine	3,343	2,087	1,256	11
Maryland	3,454	1,955	1,498	9
Massachusetts	3,787	2,544	1,243	4
Michigan	3,167	2,290	877	16
Minnesota	3,694	2,712	983	5
Mississippi	2,214	1,656	558	48
Missouri	2,558	1,532	1,026	37
Montana	2,363	1,564	799	45
Nebraska	2,906	1,742	1,164	24
Nevada	2,915	1,860	1,055	23
New Hampshire	2,652	1,372	1,280	32
New Jersey	3,903	2,157	1,746	3
New Mexico	2,639	2,058	581	33
New York	4,578	2,199	2,378	2
North Carolina	2,664	1,903	761	31
North Dakota	2,754	1,826	928	28
Ohio	3,016	1,733	1,283	20
Oklahoma	2,391	1,692	699	43
Oregon	2,751	1,738	1,013	29
Pennsylvania	2,979	1,829	1,149	21
Rhode Island	3,256	1,942	1,314	13
South Carolina	2,379	1,591	788	44
South Dakota	2,299	1,228	1,071	46
Tennessee	2,185	1,360	825	49
Texas	2,505	1,315	1,189	40
Utah	2,630	1,782	848	34
Vermont	3,080	2,435	644	17
Virginia	2,978	1,787	1,192	22
Washington	3,178	2,132	1,046	15
West Virginia	2,413	1,849	564	42
Wisconsin	3,458	2,344	1,113	8
Wyoming	3,046	1,951	1,095	19
50 States	3,095	1,922	1,173	
DC	5,622	0	5,622	
United States	3,100	1,918	1,182	

Rank in order by state and local taxes per capita	
1	Connecticut
2	New York
3	New Jersey
4	Massachusetts
5	Minnesota
6	Alaska
7	California
8	Wisconsin
9	Maryland
10	Hawaii
11	Maine
12	Delaware
13	Rhode Island
14	Illinois
15	Washington
16	Michigan
17	Vermont
18	Colorado
19	Wyoming
20	Ohio
21	Pennsylvania
22	Virginia
23	Nevada
24	Nebraska
25	Georgia
26	Kansas
27	Iowa
28	North Dakota
29	Oregon
30	Indiana
31	North Carolina
32	New Hampshire
33	New Mexico
34	Utah
35	Florida
36	Arizona
37	Missouri
38	Idaho
39	Kentucky
40	Texas
41	Louisiana
42	West Virginia
43	Oklahoma
44	South Carolina
45	Montana
46	South Dakota
47	Arkansas
48	Mississippi
49	Tennessee
50	Alabama

F-3 State and Local Tax Effort, 1996

State	Tax effort %	Rank
Alabama	83	43
Alaska	116	4
Arizona	93	28
Arkansas	92	29
California	101	15
Colorado	82	44
Connecticut	115	5
Delaware	90	32
Florida	90	32
Georgia	95	26
Hawaii	104	9
Idaho	92	29
Illinois	97	25
Indiana	88	39
Iowa	98	24
Kansas	99	20
Kentucky	99	20
Louisiana	86	41
Maine	113	7
Maryland	100	16
Massachusetts	104	9
Michigan	100	16
Minnesota	113	7
Mississippi	102	12
Missouri	87	40
Montana	79	45
Nebraska	99	20
Nevada	73	50
New Hampshire	74	48
New Jersey	114	6
New Mexico	102	12
New York	141	1
North Carolina	94	27
North Dakota	89	35
Ohio	100	16
Oklahoma	92	29
Oregon	85	42
Pennsylvania	102	12
Rhode Island	117	2
South Carolina	89	35
South Dakota	79	45
Tennessee	79	45
Texas	90	32
Utah	89	35
Vermont	100	16
Virginia	89	35
Washington	104	9
West Virginia	99	20
Wisconsin	117	3
Wyoming	74	48
50 States	n/a	
DC	141	
United States	100	

Rank in order by tax effort	
1	New York
2	Rhode Island
3	Wisconsin
4	Alaska
5	Connecticut
6	New Jersey
7	Maine
7	Minnesota
9	Hawaii
9	Massachusetts
9	Washington
12	Mississippi
12	New Mexico
12	Pennsylvania
15	California
16	Maryland
16	Michigan
16	Ohio
16	Vermont
20	Kansas
20	Kentucky
20	Nebraska
20	West Virginia
24	Iowa
25	Illinois
26	Georgia
27	North Carolina
28	Arizona
29	Arkansas
29	Idaho
29	Oklahoma
32	Delaware
32	Florida
32	Texas
35	North Dakota
35	South Carolina
35	Utah
35	Virginia
39	Indiana
40	Missouri
41	Louisiana
42	Oregon
43	Alabama
44	Colorado
45	Montana
45	South Dakota
45	Tennessee
48	New Hampshire
48	Wyoming
50	Nevada

Note: Ties in ranking reflect ties in actual values.

F-4 State and Local Tax Capacity, 1996

State	Tax capacity %	Rank
Alabama	83	47
Alaska	127	3
Arizona	94	34
Arkansas	81	48
California	103	16
Colorado	114	10
Connecticut	129	2
Delaware	121	5
Florida	100	19
Georgia	96	29
Hawaii	120	6
Idaho	90	40
Illinois	110	11
Indiana	97	24
Iowa	97	24
Kansas	96	29
Kentucky	84	45
Louisiana	88	42
Maine	89	41
Maryland	108	13
Massachusetts	116	8
Michigan	98	23
Minnesota	107	14
Mississippi	72	50
Missouri	97	24
Montana	99	20
Nebraska	99	20
Nevada	141	1
New Hampshire	118	7
New Jersey	116	8
New Mexico	85	43
New York	109	12
North Carolina	92	35
North Dakota	97	24
Ohio	96	29
Oklahoma	84	45
Oregon	103	16
Pennsylvania	95	32
Rhode Island	91	38
South Carolina	85	43
South Dakota	95	32
Tennessee	92	35
Texas	91	38
Utah	92	35
Vermont	99	20
Virginia	101	18
Washington	104	15
West Virginia	78	49
Wisconsin	97	24
Wyoming	127	3
50 States	n/a	
DC	126	
United States	100	

Rank in order by tax capacity

1	Nevada
2	Connecticut
3	Alaska
3	Wyoming
5	Delaware
6	Hawaii
7	New Hampshire
8	Massachusetts
8	New Jersey
10	Colorado
11	Illinois
12	New York
13	Maryland
14	Minnesota
15	Washington
16	California
16	Oregon
18	Virginia
19	Florida
20	Montana
20	Nebraska
20	Vermont
23	Michigan
24	Indiana
24	Iowa
24	Missouri
24	North Dakota
24	Wisconsin
29	Georgia
29	Kansas
29	Ohio
32	Pennsylvania
32	South Dakota
34	Arizona
35	North Carolina
35	Tennessee
35	Utah
38	Rhode Island
38	Texas
40	Idaho
41	Maine
42	Louisiana
43	New Mexico
43	South Carolina
45	Kentucky
45	Oklahoma
47	Alabama
48	Arkansas
49	West Virginia
50	Mississippi

Note: Ties in ranking reflect ties in actual values.

F-5 Change in State and Local Taxes, FY 1995-2000

State	Percentage change in state and local taxes	Percentage change per capita	Change as a percentage of personal income	Rank by percentage change in state and local taxes
Alabama	29.2	23.6	-2.7	31
Alaska	-14.2	-17.3	-31.2	50
Arizona	37.9	13.4	-10.5	8
Arkansas	36.0	26.4	-1.2	11
California	47.9	37.9	4.8	3
Colorado	51.2	31.7	-3.6	1
Connecticut	29.6	24.6	-4.4	29
Delaware	35.1	23.5	-5.3	13
Florida	31.4	16.5	-5.4	24
Georgia	45.8	28.3	-2.4	5
Hawaii	13.0	10.7	-1.9	49
Idaho	37.4	23.4	0.2	9
Illinois	29.9	23.8	-4.6	26
Indiana	28.1	22.3	-3.9	32
Iowa	15.5	12.1	-10.3	48
Kansas	25.3	19.6	-6.7	41
Kentucky	25.4	19.8	-7.4	40
Louisiana	36.4	32.5	3.8	10
Maine	39.3	35.5	9.1	6
Maryland	31.5	25.2	-2.5	22
Massachusetts	32.8	27.1	-6.4	18
Michigan	34.3	29.1	2.0	16
Minnesota	31.6	23.3	-9.0	21
Mississippi	31.5	24.6	-3.2	23
Missouri	25.2	19.1	-5.8	42
Montana	20.3	16.0	-5.6	47
Nebraska	26.7	21.2	-5.0	35
Nevada	48.3	13.6	-8.3	2
New Hampshire	26.0	17.0	-9.3	38
New Jersey	25.8	18.8	-4.7	39
New Mexico	32.7	22.9	-1.7	19
New York	21.8	16.4	-7.7	46
North Carolina	34.9	20.5	-6.2	15
North Dakota	26.3	26.1	1.6	37
Ohio	27.7	25.4	-3.2	34
Oklahoma	30.1	23.6	-3.2	25
Oregon	29.8	19.1	-8.5	28
Pennsylvania	22.4	20.3	-4.6	44
Rhode Island	29.6	22.4	-2.6	30
South Carolina	35.2	23.8	-4.1	12
South Dakota	24.4	20.1	-4.1	43
Tennessee	32.1	22.0	-5.2	20
Texas	35.0	21.2	-9.1	14
Utah	46.2	27.8	-3.4	4
Vermont	29.9	24.8	-1.5	27
Virginia	38.1	29.1	-0.6	7
Washington	26.5	16.5	-12.9	36
West Virginia	22.1	23.4	0.4	45
Wisconsin	27.9	22.1	-5.0	33
Wyoming	32.9	29.2	1.8	17
50 States	32.1	23.3	-4.2	
DC	31.9	27.7	11.1	
United States	32.1	23.3	-4.2	

Rank in order by percentage change

1 Colorado
2 Nevada
3 California
4 Utah
5 Georgia
6 Maine
7 Virginia
8 Arizona
9 Idaho
10 Louisiana
11 Arkansas
12 South Carolina
13 Delaware
14 Texas
15 North Carolina
16 Michigan
17 Wyoming
18 Massachusetts
19 New Mexico
20 Tennessee
21 Minnesota
22 Maryland
23 Mississippi
24 Florida
25 Oklahoma
26 Illinois
27 Vermont
28 Oregon
29 Connecticut
30 Rhode Island
31 Alabama
32 Indiana
33 Wisconsin
34 Ohio
35 Nebraska
36 Washington
37 North Dakota
38 New Hampshire
39 New Jersey
40 Kentucky
41 Kansas
42 Missouri
43 South Dakota
44 Pennsylvania
45 West Virginia
46 New York
47 Montana
48 Iowa
49 Hawaii
50 Alaska

Note: Numbers that appear to be identical are rounded and vary slightly in actual value. The rankings reflect the actual values before rounding. See the introduction for more details.

F-6 Property Taxes, FY 2000

State	Property taxes $ (in millions)	Property taxes as a percentage of personal income	Rank by percentage
Alabama	1,340	1.33	50
Alaska	761	4.30	7
Arizona	3,906	3.24	22
Arkansas	966	1.70	46
California	26,235	2.65	35
Colorado	3,680	2.88	32
Connecticut	5,407	4.19	8
Delaware	382	1.65	48
Florida	14,098	3.36	21
Georgia	5,932	2.79	34
Hawaii	603	1.85	44
Idaho	867	3.03	28
Illinois	14,511	3.84	12
Indiana	5,552	3.57	14
Iowa	2,599	3.54	16
Kansas	2,173	3.05	27
Kentucky	1,722	1.87	43
Louisiana	1,742	1.74	45
Maine	1,598	5.19	2
Maryland	4,809	2.86	33
Massachusetts	7,643	3.48	17
Michigan	9,499	3.43	20
Minnesota	4,565	3.10	26
Mississippi	1,462	2.55	38
Missouri	3,405	2.36	39
Montana	908	4.67	5
Nebraska	1,549	3.44	19
Nevada	1,437	2.56	37
New Hampshire	2,028	5.43	1
New Jersey	14,449	4.99	4
New Mexico	620	1.63	49
New York	25,202	4.09	9
North Carolina	4,607	2.32	40
North Dakota	527	3.57	15
Ohio	9,544	3.12	24
Oklahoma	1,303	1.69	47
Oregon	2,789	3.11	25
Pennsylvania	10,067	2.93	29
Rhode Island	1,360	4.67	6
South Carolina	2,680	2.93	30
South Dakota	632	3.44	18
Tennessee	2,887	2.06	42
Texas	19,817	3.68	13
Utah	1,303	2.63	36
Vermont	782	5.09	3
Virginia	5,986	2.92	31
Washington	5,493	3.14	23
West Virginia	855	2.26	41
Wisconsin	5,689	3.98	11
Wyoming	513	4.05	10
50 States	248,485	3.20	
DC	693	3.35	
United States	249,178	3.20	

Rank in order by percentage	
1	New Hampshire
2	Maine
3	Vermont
4	New Jersey
5	Montana
6	Rhode Island
7	Alaska
8	Connecticut
9	New York
10	Wyoming
11	Wisconsin
12	Illinois
13	Texas
14	Indiana
15	North Dakota
16	Iowa
17	Massachusetts
18	South Dakota
19	Nebraska
20	Michigan
21	Florida
22	Arizona
23	Washington
24	Ohio
25	Oregon
26	Minnesota
27	Kansas
28	Idaho
29	Pennsylvania
30	South Carolina
31	Virginia
32	Colorado
33	Maryland
34	Georgia
35	California
36	Utah
37	Nevada
38	Mississippi
39	Missouri
40	North Carolina
41	West Virginia
42	Tennessee
43	Kentucky
44	Hawaii
45	Louisiana
46	Arkansas
47	Oklahoma
48	Delaware
49	New Mexico
50	Alabama

Note: Numbers that appear to be identical are rounded and vary slightly in actual value. The rankings reflect the actual values before rounding. See the introduction for more details.

F-7 Property Taxes Per Capita, FY 2000

State	Property tax per capita $	Rank
Alabama	301	50
Alaska	1,214	8
Arizona	761	32
Arkansas	361	48
California	775	31
Colorado	856	23
Connecticut	1,588	3
Delaware	488	43
Florida	882	22
Georgia	725	33
Hawaii	497	42
Idaho	670	35
Illinois	1,168	10
Indiana	913	18
Iowa	888	21
Kansas	809	30
Kentucky	426	45
Louisiana	390	46
Maine	1,254	7
Maryland	908	19
Massachusetts	1,204	9
Michigan	956	14
Minnesota	928	17
Mississippi	514	40
Missouri	609	37
Montana	1,007	13
Nebraska	905	20
Nevada	719	34
New Hampshire	1,641	2
New Jersey	1,717	1
New Mexico	341	49
New York	1,328	4
North Carolina	572	39
North Dakota	821	27
Ohio	841	25
Oklahoma	377	47
Oregon	815	29
Pennsylvania	820	28
Rhode Island	1,297	5
South Carolina	668	36
South Dakota	838	26
Tennessee	507	41
Texas	950	15
Utah	584	38
Vermont	1,284	6
Virginia	846	24
Washington	932	16
West Virginia	473	44
Wisconsin	1,061	11
Wyoming	1,038	12
50 States	885	
DC	1,211	
United States	885	

Rank in order per capita

1	New Jersey
2	New Hampshire
3	Connecticut
4	New York
5	Rhode Island
6	Vermont
7	Maine
8	Alaska
9	Massachusetts
10	Illinois
11	Wisconsin
12	Wyoming
13	Montana
14	Michigan
15	Texas
16	Washington
17	Minnesota
18	Indiana
19	Maryland
20	Nebraska
21	Iowa
22	Florida
23	Colorado
24	Virginia
25	Ohio
26	South Dakota
27	North Dakota
28	Pennsylvania
29	Oregon
30	Kansas
31	California
32	Arizona
33	Georgia
34	Nevada
35	Idaho
36	South Carolina
37	Missouri
38	Utah
39	North Carolina
40	Mississippi
41	Tennessee
42	Hawaii
43	Delaware
44	West Virginia
45	Kentucky
46	Louisiana
47	Oklahoma
48	Arkansas
49	New Mexico
50	Alabama

F-8 Property Tax Revenue as a Percentage of Three-Tax Revenue, FY 2000

State	Property tax as a percentage of three-tax revenue	Rank
Alabama	16.6	48
Alaska	72.9	2
Arizona	31.8	26
Arkansas	17.9	47
California	24.9	40
Colorado	30.3	30
Connecticut	37.5	13
Delaware	26.3	37
Florida	38.8	12
Georgia	27.5	36
Hawaii	15.8	49
Idaho	29.9	31
Illinois	40.8	11
Indiana	37.2	14
Iowa	36.0	16
Kansas	31.4	27
Kentucky	19.4	45
Louisiana	18.2	46
Maine	41.3	10
Maryland	29.0	32
Massachusetts	35.0	20
Michigan	35.0	19
Minnesota	28.5	34
Mississippi	25.8	39
Missouri	26.0	38
Montana	51.3	3
Nebraska	35.1	18
Nevada	28.6	33
New Hampshire	76.5	1
New Jersey	48.3	4
New Mexico	15.8	50
New York	33.0	23
North Carolina	24.2	41
North Dakota	36.6	15
Ohio	30.4	29
Oklahoma	19.5	44
Oregon	35.8	17
Pennsylvania	33.3	22
Rhode Island	42.6	8
South Carolina	31.1	28
South Dakota	42.0	9
Tennessee	27.8	35
Texas	42.7	7
Utah	24.2	42
Vermont	46.0	6
Virginia	31.9	25
Washington	32.4	24
West Virginia	23.4	43
Wisconsin	33.5	21
Wyoming	46.8	5
50 States	32.4	
DC	25.0	
United States	32.4	

Rank in order by percentage

1 New Hampshire
2 Alaska
3 Montana
4 New Jersey
5 Wyoming
6 Vermont
7 Texas
8 Rhode Island
9 South Dakota
10 Maine
11 Illinois
12 Florida
13 Connecticut
14 Indiana
15 North Dakota
16 Iowa
17 Oregon
18 Nebraska
19 Michigan
20 Massachusetts
21 Wisconsin
22 Pennsylvania
23 New York
24 Washington
25 Virginia
26 Arizona
27 Kansas
28 South Carolina
29 Ohio
30 Colorado
31 Idaho
32 Maryland
33 Nevada
34 Minnesota
35 Tennessee
36 Georgia
37 Delaware
38 Missouri
39 Mississippi
40 California
41 North Carolina
42 Utah
43 West Virginia
44 Oklahoma
45 Kentucky
46 Louisiana
47 Arkansas
48 Alabama
49 Hawaii
50 New Mexico

Note: Numbers that appear to be identical are rounded and vary slightly in actual value. The rankings reflect the actual values before rounding. See the introduction for more details.

F-9 Sales Taxes, FY 2000

State	State and local sales taxes $ (in millions)	State and local taxes as a percentage of personal income	Rank by percentage
Alabama	4,586	4.57	17
Alaska	284	1.60	47
Arizona	6,070	5.04	10
Arkansas	2,947	5.19	9
California	39,695	4.00	24
Colorado	4,848	3.79	28
Connecticut	5,054	3.92	25
Delaware	298	1.28	49
Florida	22,264	5.30	7
Georgia	9,298	4.37	18
Hawaii	2,141	6.56	2
Idaho	1,070	3.74	30
Illinois	13,376	3.54	36
Indiana	5,113	3.29	39
Iowa	2,698	3.67	32
Kansas	2,886	4.05	20
Kentucky	3,686	4.01	23
Louisiana	6,227	6.23	5
Maine	1,195	3.88	26
Maryland	4,622	2.75	44
Massachusetts	5,156	2.35	45
Michigan	9,906	3.57	35
Minnesota	5,909	4.02	22
Mississippi	3,202	5.59	6
Missouri	5,833	4.04	21
Montana	346	1.78	46
Nebraska	1,690	3.75	29
Nevada	3,586	6.39	4
New Hampshire	556	1.49	48
New Jersey	8,229	2.84	43
New Mexico	2,434	6.40	3
New York	22,465	3.64	33
North Carolina	7,201	3.62	34
North Dakota	714	4.83	14
Ohio	10,353	3.39	38
Oklahoma	3,234	4.20	19
Oregon	912	1.02	50
Pennsylvania	10,837	3.16	40
Rhode Island	1,004	3.45	37
South Carolina	3,480	3.80	27
South Dakota	874	4.76	15
Tennessee	7,316	5.22	8
Texas	26,579	4.94	11
Utah	2,430	4.90	12
Vermont	485	3.15	41
Virginia	5,970	2.92	42
Washington	11,481	6.56	1
West Virginia	1,836	4.85	13
Wisconsin	5,331	3.73	31
Wyoming	583	4.61	16
50 States	308,290	3.97	
DC	1,000	4.83	
United States	309,290	3.97	

Rank in order by percentage

1 Washington
2 Hawaii
3 New Mexico
4 Nevada
5 Louisiana
6 Mississippi
7 Florida
8 Tennessee
9 Arkansas
10 Arizona
11 Texas
12 Utah
13 West Virginia
14 North Dakota
15 South Dakota
16 Wyoming
17 Alabama
18 Georgia
19 Oklahoma
20 Kansas
21 Missouri
22 Minnesota
23 Kentucky
24 California
25 Connecticut
26 Maine
27 South Carolina
28 Colorado
29 Nebraska
30 Idaho
31 Wisconsin
32 Iowa
33 New York
34 North Carolina
35 Michigan
36 Illinois
37 Rhode Island
38 Ohio
39 Indiana
40 Pennsylvania
41 Vermont
42 Virginia
43 New Jersey
44 Maryland
45 Massachusetts
46 Montana
47 Alaska
48 New Hampshire
49 Delaware
50 Oregon

Note: Numbers that appear to be identical are rounded and vary slightly in actual value. The rankings reflect the actual values before rounding. See the introduction for more details.

F-10 Sales Taxes Per Capita, FY 2000

State	Sales taxes per capita $	Rank per capita
Alabama	1,031	25
Alaska	452	46
Arizona	1,183	12
Arkansas	1,103	20
California	1,172	14
Colorado	1,127	17
Connecticut	1,484	4
Delaware	380	49
Florida	1,393	6
Georgia	1,136	16
Hawaii	1,767	3
Idaho	827	43
Illinois	1,077	22
Indiana	841	42
Iowa	922	34
Kansas	1,074	23
Kentucky	912	35
Louisiana	1,393	5
Maine	937	32
Maryland	873	39
Massachusetts	812	44
Michigan	997	27
Minnesota	1,201	10
Mississippi	1,126	18
Missouri	1,042	24
Montana	383	48
Nebraska	988	29
Nevada	1,795	2
New Hampshire	449	47
New Jersey	978	30
New Mexico	1,338	7
New York	1,184	11
North Carolina	895	37
North Dakota	1,112	19
Ohio	912	36
Oklahoma	937	33
Oregon	267	50
Pennsylvania	882	38
Rhode Island	958	31
South Carolina	867	40
South Dakota	1,157	15
Tennessee	1,286	8
Texas	1,275	9
Utah	1,088	21
Vermont	796	45
Virginia	843	41
Washington	1,948	1
West Virginia	1,016	26
Wisconsin	994	28
Wyoming	1,181	13
50 States	1,098	
DC	1,748	
United States	1,099	

Rank in order per capita

1	Washington
2	Nevada
3	Hawaii
4	Connecticut
5	Louisiana
6	Florida
7	New Mexico
8	Tennessee
9	Texas
10	Minnesota
11	New York
12	Arizona
13	Wyoming
14	California
15	South Dakota
16	Georgia
17	Colorado
18	Mississippi
19	North Dakota
20	Arkansas
21	Utah
22	Illinois
23	Kansas
24	Missouri
25	Alabama
26	West Virginia
27	Michigan
28	Wisconsin
29	Nebraska
30	New Jersey
31	Rhode Island
32	Maine
33	Oklahoma
34	Iowa
35	Kentucky
36	Ohio
37	North Carolina
38	Pennsylvania
39	Maryland
40	South Carolina
41	Virginia
42	Indiana
43	Idaho
44	Massachusetts
45	Vermont
46	Alaska
47	New Hampshire
48	Montana
49	Delaware
50	Oregon

Note: Numbers that appear to be identical are rounded and vary slightly in actual value. The rankings reflect the actual values before rounding. See the introduction for more details.

F-11 Sales Tax Revenue as a Percentage of Three-Tax Revenue, FY 2000

State	Sales taxes as a percentage of three-tax revenue	Rank
Alabama	56.7	9
Alaska	27.1	45
Arizona	49.5	16
Arkansas	54.8	12
California	37.6	28
Colorado	39.9	24
Connecticut	35.0	34
Delaware	20.5	48
Florida	61.2	6
Georgia	43.1	20
Hawaii	56.2	11
Idaho	36.9	31
Illinois	37.7	27
Indiana	34.2	35
Iowa	37.3	29
Kansas	41.7	21
Kentucky	41.6	22
Louisiana	65.2	4
Maine	30.9	40
Maryland	27.9	43
Massachusetts	23.6	46
Michigan	36.5	32
Minnesota	36.9	30
Mississippi	56.5	10
Missouri	44.6	19
Montana	19.5	49
Nebraska	38.3	25
Nevada	71.4	1
New Hampshire	21.0	47
New Jersey	27.5	44
New Mexico	61.8	5
New York	29.4	41
North Carolina	37.9	26
North Dakota	49.6	15
Ohio	33.0	36
Oklahoma	48.5	17
Oregon	11.7	50
Pennsylvania	35.9	33
Rhode Island	31.5	38
South Carolina	40.4	23
South Dakota	58.0	7
Tennessee	70.5	2
Texas	57.3	8
Utah	45.1	18
Vermont	28.5	42
Virginia	31.8	37
Washington	67.6	3
West Virginia	50.2	14
Wisconsin	31.4	39
Wyoming	53.2	13
50 States	**40.2**	
DC	36.1	
United States	**40.2**	

Rank in order percentage	
1	Nevada
2	Tennessee
3	Washington
4	Louisiana
5	New Mexico
6	Florida
7	South Dakota
8	Texas
9	Alabama
10	Mississippi
11	Hawaii
12	Arkansas
13	Wyoming
14	West Virginia
15	North Dakota
16	Arizona
17	Oklahoma
18	Utah
19	Missouri
20	Georgia
21	Kansas
22	Kentucky
23	South Carolina
24	Colorado
25	Nebraska
26	North Carolina
27	Illinois
28	California
29	Iowa
30	Minnesota
31	Idaho
32	Michigan
33	Pennsylvania
34	Connecticut
35	Indiana
36	Ohio
37	Virginia
38	Rhode Island
39	Wisconsin
40	Maine
41	New York
42	Vermont
43	Maryland
44	New Jersey
45	Alaska
46	Massachusetts
47	New Hampshire
48	Delaware
49	Montana
50	Oregon

Note: Numbers that appear to be identical are rounded and vary slightly in actual value. The rankings reflect the actual values before rounding. See the introduction for more details.

F-12 Sales Tax Rates and Reach, 2003

State	State sales tax rate 2003 %	Number of services subject to sales tax 1996	Estimated losses from failure to tax e-commerce 2001 $ (in millions)	Rank by sales tax rate
Alabama	4.00	32	177.4	37
Alaska	n/a	1	n/a	n/a
Arizona	5.60	57	231.1	17
Arkansas	5.13	65	143.8	18
California	6.00	13	1,750.0	9
Colorado	2.90	14	200.7	45
Connecticut	6.00	87	190.5	9
Delaware	n/a	142	n/a	n/a
Florida	6.00	64	932.2	9
Georgia	4.00	34	439.0	37
Hawaii	4.00	157	105.1	37
Idaho	5.00	29	44.4	19
Illinois	6.25	17	532.9	7
Indiana	5.00	22	215.5	19
Iowa	5.00	94	111.8	19
Kansas	4.90	76	134.4	32
Kentucky	6.00	26	158.7	9
Louisiana	4.00	58	302.6	37
Maine	5.00	27	43.1	19
Maryland	5.00	39	194.4	19
Massachusetts	5.00	20	200.6	19
Michigan	6.00	29	502.9	9
Minnesota	6.50	61	270.6	4
Mississippi	7.00	70	136.5	1
Missouri	4.23	28	261.6	36
Montana	n/a	19	n/a	n/a
Nebraska	5.00	49	70.9	19
Nevada	6.50	11	126.3	4
New Hampshire	n/a	11	n/a	n/a
New Jersey	6.00	50	337.8	9
New Mexico	5.00	152	129.1	19
New York	4.00	74	1,052.9	37
North Carolina	4.50	28	293.4	34
North Dakota	5.00	25	26.4	19
Ohio	5.00	52	446.7	19
Oklahoma	4.50	32	202.8	34
Oregon	n/a	0	n/a	n/a
Pennsylvania	6.00	61	446.4	9
Rhode Island	7.00	28	36.8	1
South Carolina	5.00	32	153.4	19
South Dakota	4.00	141	39.4	37
Tennessee	7.00	71	362.3	1
Texas	6.25	78	1,162.1	7
Utah	4.75	54	104.5	33
Vermont	5.00	23	21.0	19
Virginia	3.50	18	238.5	44
Washington	6.50	152	416.5	4
West Virginia	6.00	110	70.1	9
Wisconsin	5.00	69	213.5	19
Wyoming	4.00	63	26.1	37
50 States	n/a	n/a	13,256.4	
DC	5.75	63	36.7	
United States	median=5.00	164	13,293.1	

Rank in order by rate

1	Mississippi
1	Rhode Island
1	Tennessee
4	Minnesota
4	Nevada
4	Washington
7	Illinois
7	Texas
9	California
9	Connecticut
9	Florida
9	Kentucky
9	Michigan
9	New Jersey
9	Pennsylvania
9	West Virginia
17	Arizona
18	Arkansas
19	Idaho
19	Indiana
19	Iowa
19	Maine
19	Maryland
19	Massachusetts
19	Nebraska
19	New Mexico
19	North Dakota
19	Ohio
19	South Carolina
19	Vermont
19	Wisconsin
32	Kansas
33	Utah
34	North Carolina
34	Oklahoma
36	Missouri
37	Alabama
37	Georgia
37	Hawaii
37	Louisiana
37	New York
37	South Dakota
37	Wyoming
44	Virginia
45	Colorado

Note: Ties in ranking reflect ties in actual values.

F-13 Individual Income Taxes, FY 2000

State	Individual income tax $ (in millions)	Income tax as a percentage of personal income	Rank by percentage
Alabama	2,159	2.15	36
Alaska	0	n/a	n/a
Arizona	2,292	1.90	38
Arkansas	1,470	2.59	32
California	39,575	3.99	6
Colorado	3,637	2.84	20
Connecticut	3,974	3.08	17
Delaware	775	3.34	13
Florida	0	n/a	n/a
Georgia	6,365	2.99	18
Hawaii	1,064	3.26	16
Idaho	965	3.38	12
Illinois	7,637	2.02	37
Indiana	4,268	2.75	24
Iowa	1,928	2.62	29
Kansas	1,862	2.61	30
Kentucky	3,448	3.75	8
Louisiana	1,582	1.58	40
Maine	1,077	3.49	11
Maryland	7,155	4.26	3
Massachusetts	9,042	4.12	5
Michigan	7,730	2.79	22
Minnesota	5,547	3.77	7
Mississippi	1,007	1.76	39
Missouri	3,850	2.67	27
Montana	516	2.66	28
Nebraska	1,174	2.60	31
Nevada	0	n/a	n/a
New Hampshire	66	0.18	42
New Jersey	7,238	2.50	34
New Mexico	881	2.32	35
New York	28,640	4.64	1
North Carolina	7,210	3.62	10
North Dakota	199	1.34	41
Ohio	11,451	3.75	9
Oklahoma	2,135	2.77	23
Oregon	4,097	4.57	2
Pennsylvania	9,284	2.71	25
Rhode Island	829	2.85	19
South Carolina	2,446	2.67	26
South Dakota	0	n/a	n/a
Tennessee	180	0.13	43
Texas	0	n/a	n/a
Utah	1,651	3.33	15
Vermont	432	2.81	21
Virginia	6,829	3.34	14
Washington	0	n/a	n/a
West Virginia	966	2.55	33
Wisconsin	5,952	4.17	4
Wyoming	0	n/a	n/a
50 States	210,584	2.71	
DC	1,077	5.21	
United States	211,661	2.72	

Rank in order by percentage

1. New York
2. Oregon
3. Maryland
4. Wisconsin
5. Massachusetts
6. California
7. Minnesota
8. Kentucky
9. Ohio
10. North Carolina
11. Maine
12. Idaho
13. Delaware
14. Virginia
15. Utah
16. Hawaii
17. Connecticut
18. Georgia
19. Rhode Island
20. Colorado
21. Vermont
22. Michigan
23. Oklahoma
24. Indiana
25. Pennsylvania
26. South Carolina
27. Missouri
28. Montana
29. Iowa
30. Kansas
31. Nebraska
32. Arkansas
33. West Virginia
34. New Jersey
35. New Mexico
36. Alabama
37. Illinois
38. Arizona
39. Mississippi
40. Louisiana
41. North Dakota
42. New Hampshire
43. Tennessee

Note: Numbers that appear to be identical are rounded and vary slightly in actual value. The rankings reflect the actual values before rounding. See the introduction for more details.

F-14 Individual Income Taxes Per Capita, FY 2000

State	Income taxes per capita $	Rank per capita
Alabama	486	36
Alaska	0	n/a
Arizona	447	38
Arkansas	550	34
California	1,168	5
Colorado	846	16
Connecticut	1,167	6
Delaware	988	10
Florida	0	n/a
Georgia	777	20
Hawaii	878	13
Idaho	746	22
Illinois	615	31
Indiana	702	25
Iowa	659	29
Kansas	693	26
Kentucky	853	15
Louisiana	354	39
Maine	845	17
Maryland	1,351	3
Massachusetts	1,424	2
Michigan	778	19
Minnesota	1,128	7
Mississippi	354	40
Missouri	688	27
Montana	572	33
Nebraska	686	28
Nevada	0	n/a
New Hampshire	53	42
New Jersey	860	14
New Mexico	484	37
New York	1,509	1
North Carolina	896	12
North Dakota	309	41
Ohio	1,009	9
Oklahoma	619	30
Oregon	1,198	4
Pennsylvania	756	21
Rhode Island	791	18
South Carolina	610	32
South Dakota	0	n/a
Tennessee	32	43
Texas	0	n/a
Utah	740	23
Vermont	709	24
Virginia	965	11
Washington	0	n/a
West Virginia	534	35
Wisconsin	1,110	8
Wyoming	0	n/a
50 States	750	
DC	1,883	
United States	752	

Rank in order per capita	
1	New York
2	Massachusetts
3	Maryland
4	Oregon
5	California
6	Connecticut
7	Minnesota
8	Wisconsin
9	Ohio
10	Delaware
11	Virginia
12	North Carolina
13	Hawaii
14	New Jersey
15	Kentucky
16	Colorado
17	Maine
18	Rhode Island
19	Michigan
20	Georgia
21	Pennsylvania
22	Idaho
23	Utah
24	Vermont
25	Indiana
26	Kansas
27	Missouri
28	Nebraska
29	Iowa
30	Oklahoma
31	Illinois
32	South Carolina
33	Montana
34	Arkansas
35	West Virginia
36	Alabama
37	New Mexico
38	Arizona
39	Louisiana
40	Mississippi
41	North Dakota
42	New Hampshire
43	Tennessee

Note: Numbers that appear to be identical are rounded and vary slightly in actual value. The rankings reflect the actual values before rounding. See the introduction for more details.

F-15 Individual Income Tax Revenue as a Percentage of Three-Tax Revenue, FY 2000

State	Income tax as a percentage of three-tax revenue	Rank
Alabama	26.7	29
Alaska	n/a	n/a
Arizona	18.7	38
Arkansas	27.3	27
California	37.5	8
Colorado	29.9	17
Connecticut	27.5	26
Delaware	53.3	1
Florida	n/a	n/a
Georgia	29.5	18
Hawaii	27.9	24
Idaho	33.3	13
Illinois	21.5	37
Indiana	28.6	21
Iowa	26.7	30
Kansas	26.9	28
Kentucky	38.9	5
Louisiana	16.6	40
Maine	27.8	25
Maryland	43.1	3
Massachusetts	41.4	4
Michigan	28.5	22
Minnesota	34.6	12
Mississippi	17.8	39
Missouri	29.4	19
Montana	29.2	20
Nebraska	26.6	31
Nevada	n/a	n/a
New Hampshire	2.5	42
New Jersey	24.2	35
New Mexico	22.4	36
New York	37.5	7
North Carolina	37.9	6
North Dakota	13.8	41
Ohio	36.5	9
Oklahoma	32.0	14
Oregon	52.5	2
Pennsylvania	30.8	15
Rhode Island	26.0	33
South Carolina	28.4	23
South Dakota	n/a	n/a
Tennessee	1.7	43
Texas	n/a	n/a
Utah	30.7	16
Vermont	25.4	34
Virginia	36.4	10
Washington	n/a	n/a
West Virginia	26.4	32
Wisconsin	35.1	11
Wyoming	n/a	n/a
50 States	27.4	
DC	38.9	
United States	27.5	

Rank in order by percentage

1 Delaware
2 Oregon
3 Maryland
4 Massachusetts
5 Kentucky
6 North Carolina
7 New York
8 California
9 Ohio
10 Virginia
11 Wisconsin
12 Minnesota
13 Idaho
14 Oklahoma
15 Pennsylvania
16 Utah
17 Colorado
18 Georgia
19 Missouri
20 Montana
21 Indiana
22 Michigan
23 South Carolina
24 Hawaii
25 Maine
26 Connecticut
27 Arkansas
28 Kansas
29 Alabama
30 Iowa
31 Nebraska
32 West Virginia
33 Rhode Island
34 Vermont
35 New Jersey
36 New Mexico
37 Illinois
38 Arizona
39 Mississippi
40 Louisiana
41 North Dakota
42 New Hampshire
43 Tennessee

Note: Numbers that appear to be identical are rounded and vary slightly in actual value. The rankings reflect the actual values before rounding. See the introduction for more details.

F-16 Highest Personal Income Tax Rate, 2002

State	Highest rate %	Rank
Alabama	3.02	39
Alaska	no tax	n/a
Arizona	5.04	31
Arkansas	7.00	12
California	9.30	3
Colorado	4.63	34
Connecticut	4.50	35
Delaware	5.95	25
Florida	no tax	n/a
Georgia	6.00	22
Hawaii	8.50	6
Idaho	7.80	10
Illinois	3.00	40
Indiana	3.40	38
Iowa	5.42	30
Kansas	6.45	20
Kentucky	6.00	22
Louisiana	3.62	37
Maine	8.50	6
Maryland	4.80	33
Massachusetts	5.85	26
Michigan	4.20	36
Minnesota	7.85	9
Mississippi	5.00	32
Missouri	6.00	22
Montana	6.64	18
Nebraska	6.68	17
Nevada	no tax	n/a
New Hampshire	no tax	n/a
New Jersey	6.37	21
New Mexico	8.20	8
New York	6.85	14
North Carolina	8.75	5
North Dakota	5.54	29
Ohio	7.50	11
Oklahoma	6.75	15
Oregon	9.00	4
Pennsylvania	2.80	41
Rhode Island	9.90	1
South Carolina	7.00	12
South Dakota	no tax	n/a
Tennessee	no tax	n/a
Texas	no tax	n/a
Utah	5.61	28
Vermont	9.50	2
Virginia	5.75	27
Washington	no tax	n/a
West Virginia	6.50	19
Wisconsin	6.75	15
Wyoming	no tax	n/a
50 States	n/a	
DC	9.50	
United States	n/a	

Rank in order by percentage

1	Rhode Island
2	Vermont
3	California
4	Oregon
5	North Carolina
6	Hawaii
6	Maine
8	New Mexico
9	Minnesota
10	Idaho
11	Ohio
12	Arkansas
12	South Carolina
14	New York
15	Oklahoma
15	Wisconsin
17	Nebraska
18	Montana
19	West Virginia
20	Kansas
21	New Jersey
22	Georgia
22	Kentucky
22	Missouri
25	Delaware
26	Massachusetts
27	Virginia
28	Utah
29	North Dakota
30	Iowa
31	Arizona
32	Mississippi
33	Maryland
34	Colorado
35	Connecticut
36	Michigan
37	Louisiana
38	Indiana
39	Alabama
40	Illinois
41	Pennsylvania

Note: Ties in ranking reflect ties in actual values.

F-17 Corporate Income Taxes, Total and Per Capita, FY 2000

State	Corporate income taxes $ (in millions)	Corporate income taxes per capita $	Rank per capita
Alabama	243	55	44
Alaska	438	699	1
Arizona	523	102	22
Arkansas	237	89	25
California	6,639	196	7
Colorado	335	78	32
Connecticut	427	125	14
Delaware	240	307	3
Florida	1,183	74	35
Georgia	712	87	27
Hawaii	75	62	39
Idaho	126	97	24
Illinois	2,261	182	8
Indiana	925	152	11
Iowa	215	73	36
Kansas	272	101	23
Kentucky	306	76	34
Louisiana	222	50	45
Maine	150	118	18
Maryland	431	81	29
Massachusetts	1,306	206	6
Michigan	2,382	240	5
Minnesota	803	163	9
Mississippi	228	80	30
Missouri	265	47	46
Montana	100	111	19
Nebraska	140	82	28
Nevada	0	n/a	n/a
New Hampshire	312	253	4
New Jersey	1,347	160	10
New Mexico	159	88	26
New York	6,047	319	2
North Carolina	1,197	149	12
North Dakota	78	122	15
Ohio	631	56	43
Oklahoma	194	56	42
Oregon	407	119	17
Pennsylvania	1,697	138	13
Rhode Island	75	71	38
South Carolina	227	57	41
South Dakota	45	60	40
Tennessee	614	108	20
Texas	0	n/a	n/a
Utah	174	78	33
Vermont	44	73	37
Virginia	566	80	31
Washington	0	n/a	n/a
West Virginia	218	120	16
Wisconsin	578	108	21
Wyoming	0	n/a	n/a
50 States	35,798	127	
DC	261	457	
United States	36,059	128	

Rank in order per capita	
1	Alaska
2	New York
3	Delaware
4	New Hampshire
5	Michigan
6	Massachusetts
7	California
8	Illinois
9	Minnesota
10	New Jersey
11	Indiana
12	North Carolina
13	Pennsylvania
14	Connecticut
15	North Dakota
16	West Virginia
17	Oregon
18	Maine
19	Montana
20	Tennessee
21	Wisconsin
22	Arizona
23	Kansas
24	Idaho
25	Arkansas
26	New Mexico
27	Georgia
28	Nebraska
29	Maryland
30	Mississippi
31	Virginia
32	Colorado
33	Utah
34	Kentucky
35	Florida
36	Iowa
37	Vermont
38	Rhode Island
39	Hawaii
40	South Dakota
41	South Carolina
42	Oklahoma
43	Ohio
44	Alabama
45	Louisiana
46	Missouri

Note: Numbers that appear to be identical are rounded and vary slightly in actual value. The rankings reflect the actual values before rounding. See the introduction for more details.

F-18 Motor Fuel Taxes

State	Gasoline tax 2002 cents/gallons	Motor fuel taxes FY 2000 $ (in millions)	Fuel taxes as a percentage of personal income	Rank by gas tax
Alabama	18.00	552	0.55	35
Alaska	8.00	42	0.24	49
Arizona	18.00	593	0.49	35
Arkansas	21.70	389	0.68	21
California	18.00	3,041	0.31	35
Colorado	22.00	544	0.43	17
Connecticut	25.00	543	0.42	8
Delaware	23.00	104	0.45	14
Florida	13.90	2,154	0.51	48
Georgia	7.50	632	0.30	50
Hawaii	16.00	135	0.41	43
Idaho	26.00	209	0.73	5
Illinois	19.30	1,545	0.41	31
Indiana	15.00	700	0.45	45
Iowa	20.00	346	0.47	26
Kansas	21.00	356	0.50	23
Kentucky	16.40	440	0.48	42
Louisiana	20.00	549	0.55	26
Maine	22.00	181	0.59	17
Maryland	23.50	652	0.39	13
Massachusetts	21.00	653	0.30	23
Michigan	19.00	1,075	0.39	32
Minnesota	20.00	608	0.41	26
Mississippi	18.40	427	0.74	34
Missouri	17.05	698	0.48	40
Montana	27.00	188	0.97	3
Nebraska	25.40	279	0.62	6
Nevada	24.00	325	0.58	11
New Hampshire	19.00	117	0.31	32
New Jersey	14.50	506	0.17	46
New Mexico	18.00	233	0.61	35
New York	22.60	522	0.08	16
North Carolina	24.45	1,067	0.54	10
North Dakota	21.00	111	0.75	23
Ohio	22.00	1,414	0.46	17
Oklahoma	17.00	403	0.52	41
Oregon	24.00	485	0.54	11
Pennsylvania	26.60	764	0.22	4
Rhode Island	29.00	131	0.45	1
South Carolina	16.00	370	0.40	43
South Dakota	22.00	125	0.68	17
Tennessee	21.40	788	0.56	22
Texas	20.00	2,689	0.50	26
Utah	24.75	330	0.67	9
Vermont	20.00	61	0.39	26
Virginia	17.50	815	0.40	39
Washington	23.00	776	0.44	14
West Virginia	25.35	240	0.63	7
Wisconsin	27.30	916	0.64	2
Wyoming	14.00	81	0.64	47
50 States	n/a	30,905	0.40	
DC	20.00	34	0.17	
United States	n/a	30,939	0.40	

Rank in order by gas tax	
1	Rhode Island
2	Wisconsin
3	Montana
4	Pennsylvania
5	Idaho
6	Nebraska
7	West Virginia
8	Connecticut
9	Utah
10	North Carolina
11	Nevada
11	Oregon
13	Maryland
14	Delaware
14	Washington
16	New York
17	Colorado
17	Maine
17	Ohio
17	South Dakota
21	Arkansas
22	Tennessee
23	Kansas
23	Massachusetts
23	North Dakota
26	Iowa
26	Louisiana
26	Minnesota
26	Texas
26	Vermont
31	Illinois
32	Michigan
32	New Hampshire
34	Mississippi
35	Alabama
35	Arizona
35	California
35	New Mexico
39	Virginia
40	Missouri
41	Oklahoma
42	Kentucky
43	Hawaii
43	South Carolina
45	Indiana
46	New Jersey
47	Wyoming
48	Florida
49	Alaska
50	Georgia

Note: Ties in ranking reflect ties in actual values.

F-19 Tobacco Taxes

State	Cigarette tax rate 2003 cents/pack	Tobacco taxes FY 2000 $ (in millions)	Tobacco taxes as a percentage of personal income	Rank by tax rate
Alabama	16.5	80.6	0.08	44
Alaska	100.0	52.8	0.30	10
Arizona	58.0	162.9	0.14	21
Arkansas	31.5	92.9	0.16	33
California	87.0	1,216.6	0.12	16
Colorado	20.0	68.2	0.05	38
Connecticut	111.0	129.0	0.10	9
Delaware	24.0	26.7	0.12	35
Florida	33.9	442.5	0.11	31
Georgia	12.0	87.0	0.04	45
Hawaii	120.0	42.3	0.13	8
Idaho	28.0	28.8	0.10	34
Illinois	98.0	534.4	0.14	14
Indiana	55.5	88.3	0.06	22
Iowa	36.0	97.0	0.13	28
Kansas	70.0	52.9	0.07	18
Kentucky	3.0	17.0	0.02	49
Louisiana	36.0	89.9	0.09	28
Maine	100.0	74.9	0.24	10
Maryland	100.0	210.0	0.13	10
Massachusetts	151.0	279.9	0.13	1
Michigan	125.0	604.7	0.22	7
Minnesota	48.0	186.0	0.13	25
Mississippi	18.0	56.4	0.10	40
Missouri	17.0	130.0	0.09	42
Montana	18.0	13.8	0.07	40
Nebraska	64.0	46.3	0.10	20
Nevada	35.0	64.7	0.12	30
New Hampshire	52.0	94.6	0.25	24
New Jersey	150.0	399.8	0.14	2
New Mexico	21.0	24.2	0.06	37
New York	150.0	699.4	0.11	2
North Carolina	5.0	42.0	0.02	48
North Dakota	44.0	22.8	0.15	26
Ohio	55.0	295.2	0.10	23
Oklahoma	23.0	74.8	0.10	36
Oregon	128.0	189.8	0.21	6
Pennsylvania	100.0	324.3	0.09	10
Rhode Island	132.0	59.7	0.21	5
South Carolina	7.0	29.7	0.03	47
South Dakota	33.0	19.1	0.10	32
Tennessee	20.0	82.8	0.06	38
Texas	41.0	532.2	0.10	27
Utah	69.5	48.3	0.10	19
Vermont	93.0	25.5	0.17	15
Virginia	2.5	48.4	0.02	50
Washington	142.5	277.3	0.16	4
West Virginia	17.0	32.3	0.09	42
Wisconsin	77.0	257.9	0.18	17
Wyoming	12.0	10.7	0.08	45
50 States	n/a	8,567.6	0.11	
DC	65.0	17.2	0.08	
United States	48.0	8,584.8	0.11	

Rank in order by tax rate	
1	Massachusetts
2	New Jersey
2	New York
4	Washington
5	Rhode Island
6	Oregon
7	Michigan
8	Hawaii
9	Connecticut
10	Alaska
10	Maine
10	Maryland
10	Pennsylvania
14	Illinois
15	Vermont
16	California
17	Wisconsin
18	Kansas
19	Utah
20	Nebraska
21	Arizona
22	Indiana
23	Ohio
24	New Hampshire
25	Minnesota
26	North Dakota
27	Texas
28	Iowa
28	Louisiana
30	Nevada
31	Florida
32	South Dakota
33	Arkansas
34	Idaho
35	Delaware
36	Oklahoma
37	New Mexico
38	Colorado
38	Tennessee
40	Mississippi
40	Montana
42	Missouri
42	West Virginia
44	Alabama
45	Georgia
45	Wyoming
47	South Carolina
48	North Carolina
49	Kentucky
50	Virginia

Note: Ties in ranking reflect ties in actual values.

F-20 State and Local Taxes on High Income Families, 2001

State	Taxes for family with $150,000/year income $	Percentage of income	Rank by $
Alabama	12,314	8.2	37
Alaska	5,805	3.9	49
Arizona	13,757	9.2	33
Arkansas	14,430	9.6	24
California	18,740	12.5	7
Colorado	10,459	7.0	42
Connecticut	28,859	19.2	1
Delaware	12,108	8.1	38
Florida	6,927	4.6	47
Georgia	17,466	11.6	11
Hawaii	14,338	9.6	25
Idaho	15,075	10.1	21
Illinois	14,621	9.7	23
Indiana	11,683	7.8	39
Iowa	20,448	13.6	4
Kansas	12,916	8.6	34
Kentucky	16,608	11.1	15
Louisiana	12,862	8.6	35
Maine	19,202	12.8	6
Maryland	17,166	11.4	13
Massachusetts	13,798	9.2	32
Michigan	17,850	11.9	10
Minnesota	18,605	12.4	9
Mississippi	14,049	9.4	28
Missouri	13,938	9.3	29
Montana	13,937	9.3	30
Nebraska	15,477	10.3	20
Nevada	6,582	4.4	48
New Hampshire	10,912	7.3	41
New Jersey	22,954	15.3	2
New Mexico	14,803	9.9	22
New York	20,335	13.6	5
North Carolina	15,557	10.4	19
North Dakota	11,505	7.7	40
Ohio	16,322	10.9	16
Oklahoma	13,900	9.3	31
Oregon	16,923	11.3	14
Pennsylvania	18,642	12.4	8
Rhode Island	21,792	14.5	3
South Carolina	15,748	10.5	18
South Dakota	7,035	4.7	46
Tennessee	8,540	5.7	45
Texas	8,568	5.7	44
Utah	14,303	9.5	26
Vermont	15,859	10.6	17
Virginia	12,620	8.4	36
Washington	9,497	6.3	43
West Virginia	14,229	9.5	27
Wisconsin	17,247	11.5	12
Wyoming	5,321	3.5	50
50 States	n/a	n/a	
DC	17,215	11.5	
United States	14,507	9.7	

Rank in order by $

1. Connecticut
2. New Jersey
3. Rhode Island
4. Iowa
5. New York
6. Maine
7. California
8. Pennsylvania
9. Minnesota
10. Michigan
11. Georgia
12. Wisconsin
13. Maryland
14. Oregon
15. Kentucky
16. Ohio
17. Vermont
18. South Carolina
19. North Carolina
20. Nebraska
21. Idaho
22. New Mexico
23. Illinois
24. Arkansas
25. Hawaii
26. Utah
27. West Virginia
28. Mississippi
29. Missouri
30. Montana
31. Oklahoma
32. Massachusetts
33. Arizona
34. Kansas
35. Louisiana
36. Virginia
37. Alabama
38. Delaware
39. Indiana
40. North Dakota
41. New Hampshire
42. Colorado
43. Washington
44. Texas
45. Tennessee
46. South Dakota
47. Florida
48. Nevada
49. Alaska
50. Wyoming

F-21 State and Local Taxes in the Largest City in Each State, 2001

State	Taxes for family with $50,000/year income $	Percentage of income	Rank by $
Alabama	4,185	8.4	25
Alaska	2,187	4.4	49
Arizona	3,837	7.7	33
Arkansas	4,085	8.2	28
California	4,240	8.5	23
Colorado	2,793	5.6	45
Connecticut	8,459	16.9	1
Delaware	3,453	6.9	40
Florida	2,216	4.4	48
Georgia	5,049	10.1	14
Hawaii	4,107	8.2	27
Idaho	3,715	7.4	36
Illinois	4,816	9.6	15
Indiana	3,826	7.7	34
Iowa	6,004	12.0	5
Kansas	3,224	6.4	41
Kentucky	5,118	10.2	12
Louisiana	3,480	7.0	38
Maine	5,266	10.5	9
Maryland	5,549	11.1	8
Massachusetts	4,328	8.7	21
Michigan	5,619	11.2	6
Minnesota	5,564	11.1	7
Mississippi	3,797	7.6	35
Missouri	4,334	8.7	20
Montana	3,170	6.3	42
Nebraska	4,190	8.4	24
Nevada	2,404	4.8	47
New Hampshire	3,999	8.0	29
New Jersey	7,380	14.8	2
New Mexico	3,901	7.8	30
New York	5,170	10.3	11
North Carolina	4,449	8.9	18
North Dakota	3,554	7.1	37
Ohio	4,594	9.2	16
Oklahoma	4,115	8.2	26
Oregon	5,071	10.1	13
Pennsylvania	6,623	13.2	3
Rhode Island	6,476	13.0	4
South Carolina	4,250	8.5	22
South Dakota	2,557	5.1	46
Tennessee	3,044	6.1	43
Texas	3,020	6.0	44
Utah	4,581	9.2	17
Vermont	4,369	8.7	19
Virginia	3,879	7.8	31
Washington	3,460	6.9	39
West Virginia	3,841	7.7	32
Wisconsin	5,188	10.4	10
Wyoming	1,782	3.6	50
50 States	n/a	n/a	
DC	4,933	9.9	
United States	4,299	8.6	

Rank in order by $

1. Connecticut
2. New Jersey
3. Pennsylvania
4. Rhode Island
5. Iowa
6. Michigan
7. Minnesota
8. Maryland
9. Maine
10. Wisconsin
11. New York
12. Kentucky
13. Oregon
14. Georgia
15. Illinois
16. Ohio
17. Utah
18. North Carolina
19. Vermont
20. Missouri
21. Massachusetts
22. South Carolina
23. California
24. Nebraska
25. Alabama
26. Oklahoma
27. Hawaii
28. Arkansas
29. New Hampshire
30. New Mexico
31. Virginia
32. West Virginia
33. Arizona
34. Indiana
35. Mississippi
36. Idaho
37. North Dakota
38. Louisiana
39. Washington
40. Delaware
41. Kansas
42. Montana
43. Tennessee
44. Texas
45. Colorado
46. South Dakota
47. Nevada
48. Florida
49. Alaska
50. Wyoming

F-22 Progressivity of Major State and Local Taxes, 2001

State	Progressivity index %	Rank by most progressive to least
Alabama	106.5	42
Alaska	124.5	50
Arizona	72.2	20
Arkansas	75.4	26
California	68.1	14
Colorado	62.1	8
Connecticut	90.6	39
Delaware	73.9	23
Florida	84.0	34
Georgia	68.1	14
Hawaii	73.6	22
Idaho	43.9	1
Illinois	89.6	37
Indiana	93.9	40
Iowa	76.7	28
Kansas	54.2	5
Kentucky	80.8	31
Louisiana	50.5	2
Maine	65.6	11
Maryland	58.9	7
Massachusetts	70.5	19
Michigan	87.5	35
Minnesota	68.5	16
Mississippi	63.7	9
Missouri	82.0	32
Montana	53.5	4
Nebraska	69.6	17
Nevada	121.4	49
New Hampshire	118.0	46
New Jersey	99.0	41
New Mexico	64.5	10
New York	52.9	3
North Carolina	70.2	18
North Dakota	90.3	38
Ohio	76.3	27
Oklahoma	78.7	29
Oregon	80.7	30
Pennsylvania	89.0	36
Rhode Island	72.6	21
South Carolina	55.3	6
South Dakota	118.8	48
Tennessee	116.7	45
Texas	107.6	43
Utah	74.0	24
Vermont	67.0	13
Virginia	82.6	33
Washington	118.1	47
West Virginia	75.0	25
Wisconsin	66.0	12
Wyoming	108.5	44
50 States	n/a	
DC	61.4	
United States	79.9	

Rank in order by percentage	
1	Idaho
2	Louisiana
3	New York
4	Montana
5	Kansas
6	South Carolina
7	Maryland
8	Colorado
9	Mississippi
10	New Mexico
11	Maine
12	Wisconsin
13	Vermont
14	California
14	Georgia
16	Minnesota
17	Nebraska
18	North Carolina
19	Massachusetts
20	Arizona
21	Rhode Island
22	Hawaii
23	Delaware
24	Utah
25	West Virginia
26	Arkansas
27	Ohio
28	Iowa
29	Oklahoma
30	Oregon
31	Kentucky
32	Missouri
33	Virginia
34	Florida
35	Michigan
36	Pennsylvania
37	Illinois
38	North Dakota
39	Connecticut
40	Indiana
41	New Jersey
42	Alabama
43	Texas
44	Wyoming
45	Tennessee
46	New Hampshire
47	Washington
48	South Dakota
49	Nevada
50	Alaska

Note: Ties in ranking reflect ties in actual values.

F-23 State Estate Taxes, 2002

State	Type of state death tax 2002	State revenue "picked-up" from the federal estate tax FY 2001 $ (in millions)	Per capita state revenue from the federal estate tax $	Rank per capita
Alabama	Pick-up	45.80	10.26	39
Alaska	Pick-up	2.70	4.25	47
Arizona	Pick-up	74.65	14.07	29
Arkansas	Pick-up	26.10	9.70	41
California	Pick-up	934.00	27.07	8
Colorado	Pick-up	82.60	18.70	17
Connecticut	Inheritance	68.00	19.85	14
Delaware	Pick-up	41.20	51.75	1
Florida	Pick-up	767.10	46.78	2
Georgia	Pick-up	127.50	15.21	24
Hawaii	Pick-up	17.50	14.29	27
Idaho	Pick-up	41.40	31.34	5
Illinois	Pick-up	361.00	28.92	6
Indiana	Inheritance	29.00	4.74	45
Iowa	Inheritance	38.50	13.17	32
Kansas	Pick-up	41.20	15.29	23
Kentucky	Inheritance	45.10	11.09	37
Louisiana	Inheritance	20.30	4.55	46
Maine	Pick-up	30.60	23.78	10
Maryland	Inheritance	103.40	19.24	15
Massachusetts	Pick-up	203.30	31.87	4
Michigan	Pick-up	155.30	15.54	22
Minnesota	Pick-up	53.00	10.66	38
Mississippi	Pick-up	27.60	9.66	42
Missouri	Pick-up	156.80	27.85	7
Montana	Pick-up	10.10	11.17	36
Nebraska	Inheritance	27.90	16.28	20
Nevada	Pick-up	42.50	20.18	13
New Hampshire	Inheritance	24.00	19.06	16
New Jersey	Inheritance	202.00	23.81	9
New Mexico	Pick-up	25.30	13.83	30
New York	Pick-up	720.00	37.87	3
North Carolina	Pick-up	123.10	15.04	26
North Dakota	Pick-up	5.30	8.35	43
Ohio	Estate	35.00	3.08	48
Oklahoma	Estate	0.00	0.00	50
Oregon	Pick-up	43.70	12.58	33
Pennsylvania	Inheritance	60.00	4.88	44
Rhode Island	Pick-up	22.00	20.78	11
South Carolina	Pick-up	49.00	12.06	34
South Dakota	Pick-up	8.60	11.37	35
Tennessee	Inheritance	9.60	1.67	49
Texas	Pick-up	322.40	15.12	25
Utah	Pick-up	30.50	13.44	31
Vermont	Pick-up	12.70	20.71	12
Virginia	Pick-up	125.00	17.39	19
Washington	Pick-up	107.10	17.89	18
West Virginia	Pick-up	17.50	9.71	40
Wisconsin	Pick-up	77.00	14.25	28
Wyoming	Pick-up	7.90	15.98	21
50 States	n/a	5,601.85	19.71	
DC	Pick-up	51.50	90.06	
United States*	n/a	5,653.40	19.85	

Rank in order per capita

1 Delaware
2 Florida
3 New York
4 Massachusetts
5 Idaho
6 Illinois
7 Missouri
8 California
9 New Jersey
10 Maine
11 Rhode Island
12 Vermont
13 Nevada
14 Connecticut
15 Maryland
16 New Hampshire
17 Colorado
18 Washington
19 Virginia
20 Nebraska
21 Wyoming
22 Michigan
23 Kansas
24 Georgia
25 Texas
26 North Carolina
27 Hawaii
28 Wisconsin
29 Arizona
30 New Mexico
31 Utah
32 Iowa
33 Oregon
34 South Carolina
35 South Dakota
36 Montana
37 Kentucky
38 Minnesota
39 Alabama
40 West Virginia
41 Arkansas
42 Mississippi
43 North Dakota
44 Pennsylvania
45 Indiana
46 Louisiana
47 Alaska
48 Ohio
49 Tennessee
50 Oklahoma

Due to rounding or data sources, the 50-state total plus D.C. may not equal the U.S. total. Please see introduction.

Source Notes for Taxes (Section F)

F-1 State and Local Tax Revenue, Total and as a Percentage of Personal Income, FY 2000: This is the most common definition of the tax burdens of state and local governments. It is the tax component of "general revenue" used by the Census Bureau in its annual survey of government finances. It excludes taxes used to finance certain trust funds, such as unemployment insurance taxes, but includes other earmarked revenues, such as gasoline tax revenues for highway construction. Tax revenues are related to personal income as a common proxy for tax base or "ability to pay."

For decades, state officials, media, scholars, taxpayer groups, and others have been comparing tax burdens and spending patterns of states using data published by the Census Bureau in its annual volume *Governmental Finances*. These data were also republished in many secondary sources such as *Significant Features of Fiscal Federalism*, published by the Advisory Commission on Intergovernmental Relations; *Statistical Abstract of the United States*, published by the Census Bureau and U.S. Government Printing Office; and other secondary sources.

The Census Bureau and other federal statistical agencies have been responding to tight budgets by limiting the number of their printed publications and analyses, both statistical and narrative, of the data they produce. This has allowed them to concentrate their resources on what only they can do—collecting and refining the underlying data. Beginning with the data for 1993, the Census Bureau has stopped publishing state and local fiscal data in printed reports such as *Governmental Finances*, making them available only electronically. Also the Bureau has discontinued making popular analytical calculations such as those comparing taxes and spending with personal income and population. This change and budget restrictions have eliminated some secondary sources, such as *Significant Features*.

Anyone with access to the Internet, computer capability, and the ability to unzip and download the Census data can make calculations such as taxes as a percentage of personal income and per capita spending on particular state and/or local functions. However, not everyone has these capabilities, and those that do can produce different data unless they are careful to follow particular complex conventions covering such matters as which concepts of taxing and spending to use, which revision of often-revised government data to use, and which years of population and personal income estimates to use.

No government agency, including the Census Bureau, will certify the resulting differing numbers as the appropriate ones or vouch for their accuracy in applying past concepts for calculating them. However, many users will demand that comparative numbers be consistent from user to user, from year to year, and from state to state. As a result, some publications are becoming more authoritative than others. Congressional Quarterly Inc., in conjunction with State Policy Research, Inc., is committed to publishing these comparative data annually in such widely used publications as *State Fact Finder, State Policy Reports*, and *Governing* magazine. It is likely that these sources, which are using identical data, will become the standard sources for most users.

All of the tables in *State Fact Finder* which rely on Census Bureau data covering government finances in 2000 use the same conventions, based on past practices of the Census Bureau. The underlying data on tax revenues and spending come from the Census Bureau website (www.census.gov). These data reflect fiscal information for varying government fiscal years ending in 2000, which for most states is a fiscal year ending on June 30, 2000, and for many local governments is a fiscal year ending on December 31, 2000.

Following the historical practice of the Census Bureau not to use revised personal income and population numbers, the personal income numbers used for comparison with these fiscal data are calendar year data for 1999 representing the original 1999 estimates released by the Bureau of Economic Analysis. The population data used to calculate per capita amounts are estimates for July 1, 2000, as originally released by the Census Bureau in 2001.

The data on tax burdens and spending in relation to personal income and per capita are comparable with those of prior years, as published by the Census Bureau and secondary sources, to exactly the degree that Census data for earlier years have been comparable. Data for any year are not recalculated. While underlying data on government revenues and spending are not normally revised, the Census Bureau and Bureau of Economic Analysis do re-estimate historical estimates of population and personal income.

F-2 Per Capita State and Local Tax Revenue, FY 2000: This table relates total tax revenue to population, providing another measure of relative tax burdens (see Table F-1). It also shows the division of tax revenues between state and local governments in each state.

F-3 State and Local Tax Effort, FY 1996: The revenue-raising ability of states and their local governments varies markedly among the states. For example, Alaska and Texas get massive revenues by taxing oil and gas, and Nevada gets large revenues from taxing casino gambling, but most states get no revenue from these sources. What states will collect from particular tax rates applied to property, sales, and income is higher in states with more affluent citizens. Because of these differences, the revenue collected (see Tables F-1 and F-2) is not a good indicator of how high tax rates are in each state.

A more appropriate way to compare the relative burden of state and local taxes, or what is often called "tax effort," is to consider what each state would raise if it and its local governments applied national average tax rates to their own tax bases. Unfortunately, this methodology, known as the "representative tax system," is tedious and expensive to apply. The Advisory Commission on Intergovernmental Relations historically did this work but stopped with the 1991 calculations. The commission was phased out in 1996, and no one had stepped forward to do the work until recently, when a report, based on the FY 1994 Census data on state and local finances, was issued by the Federal Reserve Bank of Boston. Robert Tannenwald, the author of that report and assistant vice president and economist at the Federal Reserve Bank of Boston, has published a second report with statistics for FY 1996. "Fiscal Disparity Among the States Revisited" is the source for the FY 1996 tax effort statistics shown in this table.

The values reflect differences in tax effort. For example, New York state and local governments have taxes that raise 41 percent more than would be raised if tax rates in that state were equal to the national average.

While the best available data on tax effort and tax capacity are those appearing in Tables F-3 and F-4, they must be used with caution. For states which are quite close to the national average and to each other, the results are not what statisticians call "robust." The measurements of tax base and tax revenues are quite reliable, but not so reliable that they prevent a point or two difference in the index from potentially being explained by errors. Also the differences in tax rates associated with small differences in tax effort are likely to be too small to affect decisions of households and businesses. Finally, the data are for FY 1996, while decisions made today are in FY 2003. The relevant data, which are unavailable, would reflect changes already made and others already underway.

So, for example, the differences among Kansas (99), Iowa (98), and Michigan (100) and among Georgia (95), Arizona (93), and North Carolina (94) cannot appropriately be used as an argument for changing public policy in those states. This being said, large differences among the states and extreme differences from the national average permit substantial conclusions about differing state policies and their effects.

F-4 State and Local Tax Capacity, FY 1996: The representative tax system (see notes to Table F-3) also permits a comparison of the tax base, or fiscal capacity, of individual states. This is presented in what can be viewed either as percentages of the national average or as index numbers. Either way, the table indicates, for example, that if it applied national average tax rates, Alabama would raise only 83 percent of the amount that those same rates would in the average state. For reasons indicated in the notes to Table F-3, these data are not available for any year more recent than 1996.

F-5 Change in State and Local Taxes, FY 1995-2000: In the five years covered by the table, the Census Bureau reports for each year indicate that state and local tax revenues have increased by just over 32 percent. However, growth has been much faster in some states than others. See Table F-1 for the source for 2000 figures; 1995 numbers come from *State Fact Finder 1999*.

The table shows increases in state and local taxes as would be expected because the nation's population has been growing and prices have increased due to inflation. Predictably, the increases tend to be largest in states where population and government workloads, such as children in public schools, have grown most rapidly, such as Nevada. However, on average, tax burdens (taxes in relation to personal income) have declined.

F-6 Property Taxes, Total and as a Percentage of Personal Income, FY 2000: This and subsequent tables deal with the total revenues raised by particular state and local taxes. They start with the revenues from those taxes as indicated by Census Bureau data (see notes to Table F-1). Those revenues are then related to both population and personal income to provide the two most common measures of the levels, or burdens, of those taxes in each state.

F-7 Property Taxes Per Capita, FY 2000: See notes to Table F-6.

F-8 Property Tax Revenue as a Percentage of Three-Tax Revenue, FY 2000: Some people feel that their total state and local taxes are too high, while others may not be sure about total tax burdens but feel that a particular revenue source, such as property taxes, is too heavily used in their state. This table, using Census data (see notes to Table F-1), relates the amount raised from taxing property with the amounts raised from the other two major tax bases—sales and income.

F-9 Sales Taxes, Total and as a Percentage of Personal Income, FY 2000: All states, including those which do not have state sales taxes, show some sales tax revenues. The Census Bureau counts as sales tax revenues both revenues from sales taxes levied on sales of most goods and special excise taxes on particular goods, such as tobacco and alcoholic beverages. See notes to Table F-6.

F-10 Sales Taxes Per Capita, FY 2000: See notes to Tables F-6 and F-9.

F-11 Sales Tax Revenue as a Percentage of Three-Tax Revenue, FY 2000: See notes to Tables F-8 and F-9.

F-12 Sales Tax Rates and Reach, 2003: Many of the "goods" of today's economy are beyond the reach of the sales tax as it is currently structured. For instance, cars and clothing are taxed, but services such as barbering and landscaping generally are not. Neither are out-of-state mail order or e-commerce purchases. Because of the limited reach of the sales tax, without rate hikes sales tax collections would fall.

Many experts suggest that the sales tax would be fairer and a more productive revenue source if it applied equally to both goods *and* services; bricks-and-mortar *and* Internet shopping. A current debate centers around how to extend the reach of the sales tax, if indeed it should be extended at all. This table provides three elements relevant to that debate. The first column of information shows each states' statewide sales tax rate at the beginning of 2003 (localities may levy additional taxes). The second column shows the number of services covered in 1996 by the sales tax in each state. The table includes states, such as Oregon, that have no general sales tax and ones, such as Alaska, that may have special excise taxes on a few services. With the exception of Nebraska which broadened its sales tax base in 2002 by adding services such as security, pest control, car washing, towing and computer software training, since 1996 there has been little change in sales tax of services in the states. This count, along with the sales tax rates, was compiled by the Federation of Tax Administrators (FTA) and is available on its website (www.taxadmin.org).

The third column shows the estimated state and local revenue losses from e-commerce in 2001. The data come from a study conducted by two economists, Dr. Donald Bruce and Dr. William F. Fox, at the Center for Business and Economic Research (CBER) at the University of Tennessee. The study is titled "State and Local Sales Tax Revenue Losses from E-Commerce: Updated Estimates" and is available on the CBER website (cber.bus.utk.edu/ecomm/ecom0901.pdf). For general information on the efforts of some states to simplify and unify the sales tax consult the Streamlined Sales Tax Project.

F-13 Individual Income Taxes, Total and as a Percentage of Personal Income, FY 2000: Some states which do not tax personal income from wages and salaries do have taxes based on income from other sources, such as dividends, interest, rent, and capital gains. Revenues from all these taxes appear in the table. For the source, see notes to Table F-6.

F-14 Individual Income Taxes Per Capita, FY 2000: See notes to Tables F-6 and F-13.

F-15 Individual Income Tax Revenue as a Percentage of Three-Tax Revenue, FY 2000: See notes to Tables F-8 and F-13.

F-16 Highest Personal Income Tax Rate, 2002: While some states have no income tax at all, the rates paid by high-income households in a few others states can go as high as nine percent. This table, developed by State Policy Research from compilations of state tax laws published by CCH, Inc., shows the highest state personal income tax rates. A few states use low flat-rate income taxes with few deductions and exemptions, so the same rate is applicable to all taxable income. Most states use a graduated rate schedule. In most of the states showing the highest rates in the table, this "marginal" or "top bracket" rate is paid only on income exceeding a threshold of $100,000 or more.

The rates shown were those in effect in December 2002 on income earned in 2002, to be reported on tax returns filed in early 2003.

F-17 Corporate Income Taxes, Total and Per Capita, FY 2000: See notes to Table F-6. This table is now the best of many unsatisfactory ways of comparing corporate income taxes in the fifty states. However, since 2000 states have made more changes in corporate income taxes (tax base, tax rates, tax credits) than in any other single tax affecting business.

Because of the widespread use of special tax credits for investment, research and development, job expansion, and other purposes and because of differences among states in how much income of multistate corporations is attributed to the taxing state, comparisons of corporate income tax rates are not particularly meaningful.

The most appropriate way to compare corporate income taxes of states is to make calculations of tax liability for individual hypothetical corporations. Such calculations reflect the different state definitions of the tax base, different tax rates, and different tax credits as well as different characteristics of firms in particular industries which affect tax liability. These calculations are complex because taxes levied by one state depend in part on taxes levied by other states. Such calculations have been made in special studies prepared for individual states, but they are typically made only for those ten to twenty states that the requesting state considers to be its major competitors in economic development.

F-18 Motor Fuel Taxes: States tax motor fuels, such as gasoline and diesel fuel, mostly to provide funds for road construction and maintenance. The table shows the tax rate on gasoline from a special compilation prepared by the Federation of Tax Administrators (FTA), covering rates in effect January 1, 2002. This statistic is available on the FTA website (www.taxadmin.org). The table also includes total state and local revenues from motor fuel taxes in fiscal 2000, compiled by the Census Bureau and available on its website (see notes to Table F-1). *State Fact Finder* related those revenues to personal income.

F-19 Tobacco Taxes: These data come from the same sources as those of Table F-18 but cover cigarette and related tobacco taxes. Almost half of the states increased cigarette excise taxes in 2002. The rates shown on the table were in effect January of 2003. Two states—Kansas and Vermont—are scheduled to increase rates a second time in mid-year 2003. Hawaii has scheduled a tax rate increase for July 2004.

F-20 State and Local Taxes on High Income Families, 2001: The amounts shown are the liability to be faced by a hypothetical family with an adjusted yearly gross income of $150,000. The estimates are based on taxes incurred in the largest city in each state, as calculated by the District of Columbia Department of Finance and Revenue in *Tax Rates and Tax Burdens in the District of Columbia: A Nationwide Comparison*, an unpublished report issued in August 2002. The calculations for each state's largest city are not necessarily representative of statewide averages.

F-21 State and Local Taxes in the Largest City in Each State, 2001: These data show the costs of state and local taxes in the largest city in each state to typical families with incomes of $50,000. The calculations for each state's largest city are not necessarily representative of statewide averages. For the source of the data see the notes to Table F-20.

F-22 Progressivity of Major State and Local Taxes, 2001: These data compare the tax burdens as a percentage of income on households of two income levels ($25,000 and $150,000), using data from the analysis described in the notes to Table F-21. Low numbers indicate that the percentage paid by higher-income households is significantly higher than the percentage paid by low-income households, making the state and local tax structure "progressive." States with no personal income tax and high reliance on sales and property taxes, such as Nevada, have tax systems that can be called regressive. Their progressivity percentages over one hundred indicate that poorer households pay a larger percentage of their income on state and local taxes than do higher-income households.

F-23 State Estate Taxes, 2002: The federal government levies taxes on the estates of persons when they die. State governments also tax estates either directly by taxing the amount left to heirs (estate taxes) or by taxing the amounts received by particular heirs (inheritance taxes). Some of the state tax liability is allowed by the federal government as a 100 percent credit against federal taxes owed. This means that states can levy taxes up to the amount of the credit without making taxpayers pay more, so all states levy such "pick-up" taxes. Some states levy additional taxes, though the trend has been to eliminate the extra taxes out of fear that they encourage affluent older residents to move to other states. The table shows which states levy these extra taxes and the type of tax they used in 2002. Connecticut, Louisiana and New Hampshire are in the process of phasing out their inheritance taxes.

The table also shows how much revenue the states collected from pick-up taxes—$5.7 billion in FY 2001—and ranks this amount per capita. These data show how the phase out and eventual repeal of the federal estate tax will effect state budgets. The revenue numbers, plus a discussion of how states can avoid losing this income, are found in a report from the Center on Budget and Policy Priorities titled, "States Can Retain Their Estate Taxes Even as the Federal Estate Tax is Phased Out" available on their website (www.cbpp.org).

Revenues and Finances

G-1	State and Local Total Revenue, FY 2000	168
G-2	State and Local General Revenue, FY 2000	169
G-3	State and Local "Own-source" General Revenue, FY 2000	170
G-4	State and Local Non-tax "Own-source" Revenue, FY 2000	171
G-5	State and Local Total Expenditures, FY 2000	172
G-6	State and Local General Expenditures, FY 2000	173
G-7	State and Local General Expenditures Per Capita, FY 2000	174
G-8	Percentage Change in State and Local Expenditures, FY 1995-2000	175
G-9	State Government General Revenue, FY 2000	176
G-10	State Government General Spending, FY 2000	177
G-11	State Government General Fund Spending, FY 2001	178
G-12	State and Local Debt, FY 2000	179
G-13	State and Local Debt Related to Revenue, FY 2000	180
G-14	State and Local Full Faith and Credit Debt, FY 2000	181
G-15	State Government Bond Ratings, 2002	182
G-16	State Solvency Index, 2002	183
G-17	Assets of State-administered Pension Plans, 2000	184
G-18	State Reserves at the End of FY 2002	185
G-19	State and Local Capital Outlays and Interest, FY 2000	186
G-20	Index of State Budget Process Quality, 2002	187
G-21	Relative State Spending "Needs," FY 1996	188
G-22	Structural Deficits	189

"Bleak," "anemic," "in crisis," and "dire" are some of the words used to describe the fiscal condition of the states at the start of 2003. In terms of economic activity, the recent recession has been relatively mild, so why has it hit state governments so hard? The economic bubble that burst in 2001 and the mediocre growth that followed dramatically reduced state revenues while the falling stock market all but dried up robust capital gains taxes. Unlike the federal government and individuals, states cannot plug budget holes with credit. Almost every state is required to balance its budget before the end of its fiscal year.

All these factors are pressuring the states. But economic activity always moves through periods of growth and decline. Why then did states not prepare better for a downturn when they had the chance? One answer is that they did—just not enough. Rainy day funds are proving insufficient to see states through this fiscal crisis. Another answer is that states exacerbated their problem by enacting *permanent* tax cuts during *temporary* good times. Conversely, some critics accuse the states of overspending. Still others suggest that better methods of forecasting revenues might have improved current conditions in the fifty states.

There is yet another explanation for the current financial woes faced by many states: structural problems. Unlike cyclical events, such as recession, structural problems reflect such intractable issues as ballooning healthcare costs—especially Medicaid—and out-of-date tax systems. More and more of the economic activity of today's service-oriented economy are beyond the reach of taxes, leaving states with less and less revenue.

Whether or not these structural problems are addressed, states will have to figure out how to provide and pay for basic services. In 2002 states used up a lot of their short-term options: increases in "sin" taxes and some fees, use of one-time funds (such as tobacco settlement money), hiring freezes, layoffs, and a variety of nips and tucks—from eliminating the Film Commissioner in Ohio to reducing funding for youth violence prevention programs in Colorado. Mid-way through fiscal year 2003, thirty-three states reported revenues under projections. In January 2003, expect leaders to make the difficult budgeting choices they were able to avoid in fiscal year 2002.

G-1 State and Local Total Revenue, FY 2000

State	Total revenue $ (in millions)	Per capita total revenue $	Total revenue as a percentage of personal income	Rank per capita
Alabama	25,726	5,785	25.6	42
Alaska	10,525	16,787	59.5	1
Arizona	27,778	5,414	23.1	48
Arkansas	13,833	5,175	24.4	50
California	270,380	7,982	27.3	6
Colorado	29,603	6,883	23.1	19
Connecticut	25,828	7,583	20.0	10
Delaware	6,224	7,938	26.8	7
Florida	92,402	5,782	22.0	43
Georgia	49,310	6,024	23.2	33
Hawaii	8,488	7,004	26.0	17
Idaho	7,590	5,866	26.6	38
Illinois	80,695	6,498	21.4	25
Indiana	32,716	5,381	21.1	49
Iowa	17,220	5,885	23.4	37
Kansas	16,235	6,040	22.8	32
Kentucky	25,200	6,235	27.4	30
Louisiana	27,109	6,066	27.1	31
Maine	8,554	6,709	27.7	21
Maryland	33,949	6,410	20.2	26
Massachusetts	46,103	7,261	21.0	12
Michigan	70,112	7,055	25.3	15
Minnesota	38,785	7,885	26.4	8
Mississippi	16,672	5,860	29.1	39
Missouri	31,635	5,654	21.9	45
Montana	5,643	6,256	29.0	28
Nebraska	11,650	6,809	25.9	20
Nevada	11,885	5,948	21.2	35
New Hampshire	6,948	5,621	18.6	46
New Jersey	62,331	7,408	21.5	11
New Mexico	13,073	7,187	34.4	13
New York	188,907	9,955	30.6	3
North Carolina	50,542	6,279	25.4	27
North Dakota	4,495	7,002	30.4	18
Ohio	80,074	7,053	26.2	16
Oklahoma	18,760	5,436	24.3	47
Oregon	28,644	8,373	32.0	4
Pennsylvania	80,546	6,559	23.5	24
Rhode Island	7,427	7,087	25.5	14
South Carolina	23,467	5,849	25.6	40
South Dakota	4,277	5,666	23.3	44
Tennessee	33,625	5,910	24.0	36
Texas	120,666	5,787	22.4	41
Utah	14,954	6,697	30.1	22
Vermont	4,019	6,599	26.1	23
Virginia	44,175	6,240	21.6	29
Washington	46,372	7,868	26.5	9
West Virginia	10,760	5,951	28.4	34
Wisconsin	43,003	8,017	30.1	5
Wyoming	7,030	14,231	55.5	2
50 States	1,935,945	6,893	24.9	
DC	6,383	11,159	30.9	
United States	1,942,328	6,902	25.0	

Rank in order per capita

1 Alaska
2 Wyoming
3 New York
4 Oregon
5 Wisconsin
6 California
7 Delaware
8 Minnesota
9 Washington
10 Connecticut
11 New Jersey
12 Massachusetts
13 New Mexico
14 Rhode Island
15 Michigan
16 Ohio
17 Hawaii
18 North Dakota
19 Colorado
20 Nebraska
21 Maine
22 Utah
23 Vermont
24 Pennsylvania
25 Illinois
26 Maryland
27 North Carolina
28 Montana
29 Virginia
30 Kentucky
31 Louisiana
32 Kansas
33 Georgia
34 West Virginia
35 Nevada
36 Tennessee
37 Iowa
38 Idaho
39 Mississippi
40 South Carolina
41 Texas
42 Alabama
43 Florida
44 South Dakota
45 Missouri
46 New Hampshire
47 Oklahoma
48 Arizona
49 Indiana
50 Arkansas

G-2 State and Local General Revenue, FY 2000

State	General revenue $ (in millions)	Per capita general revenue $	General revenue as a percentage of personal income	Rank per capita
Alabama	21,012	4,725	20.9	41
Alaska	9,042	14,421	51.1	1
Arizona	22,863	4,456	19.0	48
Arkansas	11,582	4,333	20.4	50
California	208,373	6,152	21.0	7
Colorado	23,436	5,449	18.3	21
Connecticut	23,108	6,785	17.9	4
Delaware	5,203	6,637	22.4	5
Florida	75,865	4,747	18.1	40
Georgia	39,690	4,849	18.6	36
Hawaii	7,092	5,851	21.7	12
Idaho	6,077	4,696	21.3	42
Illinois	64,420	5,187	17.1	26
Indiana	29,749	4,893	19.1	35
Iowa	15,134	5,172	20.6	27
Kansas	13,391	4,982	18.8	33
Kentucky	19,423	4,805	21.1	37
Louisiana	22,342	4,999	22.4	32
Maine	7,440	5,835	24.1	13
Maryland	29,076	5,490	17.3	19
Massachusetts	38,295	6,032	17.4	11
Michigan	56,415	5,677	20.3	16
Minnesota	30,957	6,293	21.1	6
Mississippi	13,590	4,777	23.7	39
Missouri	25,905	4,630	18.0	44
Montana	4,856	5,384	25.0	22
Nebraska	9,021	5,272	20.0	23
Nevada	9,592	4,801	17.1	38
New Hampshire	5,755	4,656	15.4	43
New Jersey	51,504	6,121	17.8	9
New Mexico	10,062	5,532	26.5	18
New York	143,901	7,583	23.3	2
North Carolina	41,131	5,110	20.7	28
North Dakota	3,914	6,096	26.5	10
Ohio	59,017	5,198	19.3	25
Oklahoma	15,698	4,549	20.4	47
Oregon	20,969	6,130	23.4	8
Pennsylvania	64,615	5,261	18.8	24
Rhode Island	5,748	5,484	19.7	20
South Carolina	19,727	4,917	21.6	34
South Dakota	3,491	4,623	19.0	45
Tennessee	24,824	4,363	17.7	49
Texas	95,539	4,582	17.7	46
Utah	11,208	5,019	22.6	29
Vermont	3,497	5,742	22.8	14
Virginia	35,434	5,005	17.3	31
Washington	33,426	5,671	19.1	17
West Virginia	9,055	5,008	23.9	30
Wisconsin	30,572	5,699	21.4	15
Wyoming	3,554	7,195	28.1	3
50 States	1,535,590	5,468	19.8	
DC	5,732	10,022	27.7	
United States	1,541,322	5,477	19.8	

Rank in order per capita	
1	Alaska
2	New York
3	Wyoming
4	Connecticut
5	Delaware
6	Minnesota
7	California
8	Oregon
9	New Jersey
10	North Dakota
11	Massachusetts
12	Hawaii
13	Maine
14	Vermont
15	Wisconsin
16	Michigan
17	Washington
18	New Mexico
19	Maryland
20	Rhode Island
21	Colorado
22	Montana
23	Nebraska
24	Pennsylvania
25	Ohio
26	Illinois
27	Iowa
28	North Carolina
29	Utah
30	West Virginia
31	Virginia
32	Louisiana
33	Kansas
34	South Carolina
35	Indiana
36	Georgia
37	Kentucky
38	Nevada
39	Mississippi
40	Florida
41	Alabama
42	Idaho
43	New Hampshire
44	Missouri
45	South Dakota
46	Texas
47	Oklahoma
48	Arizona
49	Tennessee
50	Arkansas

G-3 State and Local "Own-source" General Revenue, FY 2000

State	"Own-source" general revenue $ (in millions)	Per capita "Own-source" general revenue $	"Own-source" general revenue as a percentage of personal income	Rank per capita
Alabama	15,925	3,581	15.9	46
Alaska	7,631	12,171	43.1	1
Arizona	18,388	3,584	15.3	45
Arkansas	8,759	3,277	15.4	49
California	169,897	5,016	17.1	9
Colorado	19,724	4,586	15.4	16
Connecticut	19,435	5,706	15.1	3
Delaware	4,373	5,577	18.9	4
Florida	64,146	4,014	15.3	32
Georgia	32,620	3,985	15.3	34
Hawaii	5,798	4,784	17.8	10
Idaho	4,927	3,807	17.2	38
Illinois	53,629	4,318	14.2	20
Indiana	24,580	4,043	15.8	31
Iowa	12,249	4,186	16.7	27
Kansas	10,909	4,058	15.3	29
Kentucky	14,828	3,668	16.1	41
Louisiana	17,272	3,865	17.3	36
Maine	5,810	4,556	18.8	17
Maryland	24,466	4,620	14.6	14
Massachusetts	31,856	5,017	14.5	8
Michigan	46,084	4,637	16.6	13
Minnesota	26,188	5,324	17.8	6
Mississippi	10,062	3,537	17.6	47
Missouri	20,277	3,624	14.1	44
Montana	3,551	3,936	18.3	35
Nebraska	7,310	4,273	16.2	22
Nevada	8,359	4,184	14.9	28
New Hampshire	4,692	3,796	12.6	39
New Jersey	43,622	5,184	15.1	7
New Mexico	7,664	4,213	20.2	26
New York	114,653	6,042	18.6	2
North Carolina	32,080	3,986	16.1	33
North Dakota	2,788	4,343	18.9	18
Ohio	48,084	4,235	15.7	25
Oklahoma	12,517	3,627	16.2	43
Oregon	15,736	4,600	17.6	15
Pennsylvania	52,117	4,244	15.2	24
Rhode Island	4,551	4,343	15.6	19
South Carolina	15,351	3,826	16.8	37
South Dakota	2,621	3,472	14.3	48
Tennessee	18,503	3,252	13.2	50
Texas	76,964	3,691	14.3	40
Utah	9,036	4,046	18.2	30
Vermont	2,594	4,259	16.9	23
Virginia	30,424	4,298	14.9	21
Washington	27,599	4,682	15.8	12
West Virginia	6,565	3,631	17.3	42
Wisconsin	25,513	4,756	17.9	11
Wyoming	2,664	5,392	21.0	5
50 States	1,245,388	4,434	16.0	
DC	3,985	6,966	19.3	
United States	1,249,373	4,439	16.1	

Rank in order per capita

1 Alaska
2 New York
3 Connecticut
4 Delaware
5 Wyoming
6 Minnesota
7 New Jersey
8 Massachusetts
9 California
10 Hawaii
11 Wisconsin
12 Washington
13 Michigan
14 Maryland
15 Oregon
16 Colorado
17 Maine
18 North Dakota
19 Rhode Island
20 Illinois
21 Virginia
22 Nebraska
23 Vermont
24 Pennsylvania
25 Ohio
26 New Mexico
27 Iowa
28 Nevada
29 Kansas
30 Utah
31 Indiana
32 Florida
33 North Carolina
34 Georgia
35 Montana
36 Louisiana
37 South Carolina
38 Idaho
39 New Hampshire
40 Texas
41 Kentucky
42 West Virginia
43 Oklahoma
44 Missouri
45 Arizona
46 Alabama
47 Mississippi
48 South Dakota
49 Arkansas
50 Tennessee

Note: Numbers that appear to be identical are rounded and vary slightly in actual value. The rankings reflect the actual values before rounding. See the introduction for more details.

G-4 State and Local Non-tax "Own-source" Revenue, FY 2000

State	Non-tax "own-source" revenue $ (in millions)	Per capita non-tax "own-source" revenue $	Non-tax "own-source" revenue as a percentage of personal income	Rank per capita
Alabama	6,510	1,464	6.5	14
Alaska	5,320	8,484	30.0	1
Arizona	5,054	985	4.2	50
Arkansas	2,798	1,047	4.9	49
California	49,830	1,471	5.0	11
Colorado	6,508	1,513	5.1	9
Connecticut	3,784	1,111	2.9	44
Delaware	1,754	2,237	7.6	3
Florida	22,209	1,390	5.3	20
Georgia	9,367	1,144	4.4	42
Hawaii	1,696	1,399	5.2	19
Idaho	1,632	1,261	5.7	30
Illinois	13,373	1,077	3.5	46
Indiana	8,217	1,351	5.3	22
Iowa	4,158	1,421	5.7	17
Kansas	3,292	1,225	4.6	33
Kentucky	4,655	1,152	5.1	41
Louisiana	6,385	1,429	6.4	16
Maine	1,547	1,214	5.0	36
Maryland	6,177	1,166	3.7	40
Massachusetts	7,814	1,231	3.6	32
Michigan	14,610	1,470	5.3	12
Minnesota	8,015	1,629	5.5	5
Mississippi	3,762	1,322	6.6	23
Missouri	5,963	1,066	4.1	48
Montana	1,419	1,573	7.3	8
Nebraska	2,337	1,366	5.2	21
Nevada	2,534	1,268	4.5	28
New Hampshire	1,414	1,144	3.8	43
New Jersey	10,784	1,282	3.7	27
New Mexico	2,863	1,574	7.5	7
New York	27,784	1,464	4.5	13
North Carolina	10,640	1,322	5.3	24
North Dakota	1,020	1,589	6.9	6
Ohio	13,846	1,220	4.5	34
Oklahoma	4,266	1,236	5.5	31
Oregon	6,324	1,849	7.1	4
Pennsylvania	15,536	1,265	4.5	29
Rhode Island	1,139	1,087	3.9	45
South Carolina	5,808	1,448	6.3	15
South Dakota	886	1,173	4.8	39
Tennessee	6,072	1,067	4.3	47
Texas	24,737	1,186	4.6	37
Utah	3,163	1,416	6.4	18
Vermont	718	1,179	4.7	38
Virginia	9,341	1,320	4.6	25
Washington	8,865	1,504	5.1	10
West Virginia	2,203	1,218	5.8	35
Wisconsin	6,966	1,299	4.9	26
Wyoming	1,159	2,346	9.2	2
50 States	376,253	1,340	4.8	
DC	769	1,344	3.7	
United States	377,022	1,340	4.8	

Rank in order per capita	
1	Alaska
2	Wyoming
3	Delaware
4	Oregon
5	Minnesota
6	North Dakota
7	New Mexico
8	Montana
9	Colorado
10	Washington
11	California
12	Michigan
13	New York
14	Alabama
15	South Carolina
16	Louisiana
17	Iowa
18	Utah
19	Hawaii
20	Florida
21	Nebraska
22	Indiana
23	Mississippi
24	North Carolina
25	Virginia
26	Wisconsin
27	New Jersey
28	Nevada
29	Pennsylvania
30	Idaho
31	Oklahoma
32	Massachusetts
33	Kansas
34	Ohio
35	West Virginia
36	Maine
37	Texas
38	Vermont
39	South Dakota
40	Maryland
41	Kentucky
42	Georgia
43	New Hampshire
44	Connecticut
45	Rhode Island
46	Illinois
47	Tennessee
48	Missouri
49	Arkansas
50	Arizona

Note: Numbers that appear to be identical are rounded and vary slightly in actual value. The rankings reflect the actual values before rounding. See the introduction for more details.

G-5 State and Local Total Expenditures, FY 2000

State	Total expenditures $ (in millions)	Per capita total expenditures $	Total expenditures as a percentage of personal income	Rank per capita
Alabama	25,319	5,694	25.2	30
Alaska	8,628	13,760	48.7	1
Arizona	27,293	5,319	22.7	39
Arkansas	12,245	4,581	21.6	50
California	236,645	6,986	23.9	9
Colorado	26,173	6,085	20.5	21
Connecticut	24,011	7,050	18.6	6
Delaware	5,153	6,573	22.2	11
Florida	84,301	5,275	20.1	42
Georgia	43,517	5,316	20.4	40
Hawaii	8,254	6,810	25.3	10
Idaho	6,404	4,949	22.4	48
Illinois	74,727	6,017	19.8	23
Indiana	31,250	5,140	20.1	44
Iowa	17,275	5,904	23.5	25
Kansas	14,419	5,364	20.3	38
Kentucky	21,473	5,312	23.3	41
Louisiana	25,018	5,598	25.0	33
Maine	7,652	6,002	24.8	24
Maryland	30,598	5,778	18.2	28
Massachusetts	44,362	6,987	20.2	8
Michigan	61,506	6,189	22.2	16
Minnesota	35,424	7,201	24.1	4
Mississippi	15,379	5,405	26.8	36
Missouri	27,953	4,996	19.4	46
Montana	4,983	5,525	25.6	35
Nebraska	10,831	6,330	24.0	14
Nevada	11,230	5,621	20.0	32
New Hampshire	6,222	5,034	16.6	45
New Jersey	54,590	6,488	18.9	12
New Mexico	11,195	6,154	29.4	19
New York	171,858	9,057	27.9	2
North Carolina	46,135	5,732	23.2	29
North Dakota	4,041	6,294	27.4	15
Ohio	68,418	6,026	22.4	22
Oklahoma	15,962	4,625	20.7	49
Oregon	24,086	7,041	26.9	7
Pennsylvania	75,624	6,158	22.0	18
Rhode Island	6,432	6,138	22.1	20
South Carolina	23,436	5,841	25.6	27
South Dakota	3,760	4,980	20.5	47
Tennessee	32,010	5,627	22.8	31
Texas	109,634	5,258	20.4	43
Utah	13,044	5,842	26.3	26
Vermont	3,766	6,183	24.5	17
Virginia	38,092	5,381	18.6	37
Washington	41,794	7,091	23.9	5
West Virginia	9,990	5,526	26.4	34
Wisconsin	34,559	6,443	24.2	13
Wyoming	3,743	7,577	29.6	3
50 States	1,740,416	6,197	22.4	
DC	6,527	11,411	31.6	
United States	1,746,943	6,208	22.4	

Rank in order per capita

1. Alaska
2. New York
3. Wyoming
4. Minnesota
5. Washington
6. Connecticut
7. Oregon
8. Massachusetts
9. California
10. Hawaii
11. Delaware
12. New Jersey
13. Wisconsin
14. Nebraska
15. North Dakota
16. Michigan
17. Vermont
18. Pennsylvania
19. New Mexico
20. Rhode Island
21. Colorado
22. Ohio
23. Illinois
24. Maine
25. Iowa
26. Utah
27. South Carolina
28. Maryland
29. North Carolina
30. Alabama
31. Tennessee
32. Nevada
33. Louisiana
34. West Virginia
35. Montana
36. Mississippi
37. Virginia
38. Kansas
39. Arizona
40. Georgia
41. Kentucky
42. Florida
43. Texas
44. Indiana
45. New Hampshire
46. Missouri
47. South Dakota
48. Idaho
49. Oklahoma
50. Arkansas

G-6 State and Local General Expenditures, FY 2000

State	General expenditures $ (in millions)	General expenditures as a percentage of personal income	Rank by percentage
Alabama	22,062	22.0	16
Alaska	7,600	42.9	1
Arizona	23,262	19.3	27
Arkansas	11,057	19.5	26
California	195,767	19.7	24
Colorado	22,527	17.6	41
Connecticut	21,420	16.6	47
Delaware	4,691	20.2	23
Florida	75,290	17.9	37
Georgia	38,078	17.9	38
Hawaii	7,291	22.3	12
Idaho	5,828	20.4	21
Illinois	64,403	17.0	45
Indiana	28,740	18.5	34
Iowa	15,563	21.2	19
Kansas	12,884	18.1	35
Kentucky	19,020	20.7	20
Louisiana	22,277	22.3	13
Maine	6,955	22.6	9
Maryland	27,446	16.3	48
Massachusetts	37,770	17.2	44
Michigan	54,750	19.7	25
Minnesota	31,166	21.2	18
Mississippi	13,932	24.3	5
Missouri	24,818	17.2	43
Montana	4,523	23.3	6
Nebraska	8,406	18.7	33
Nevada	9,755	17.4	42
New Hampshire	5,664	15.2	50
New Jersey	47,231	16.3	49
New Mexico	10,099	26.6	2
New York	140,020	22.7	8
North Carolina	40,434	20.3	22
North Dakota	3,674	24.9	4
Ohio	57,649	18.9	31
Oklahoma	13,767	17.9	39
Oregon	20,161	22.5	10
Pennsylvania	65,871	19.2	28
Rhode Island	5,560	19.1	30
South Carolina	20,260	22.1	15
South Dakota	3,444	18.8	32
Tennessee	25,272	18.0	36
Texas	95,762	17.8	40
Utah	11,013	22.2	14
Vermont	3,446	22.4	11
Virginia	34,727	17.0	46
Washington	33,475	19.1	29
West Virginia	8,711	23.0	7
Wisconsin	30,762	21.5	17
Wyoming	3,330	26.3	3
50 States	1,497,616	19.3	
DC	5,152	24.9	
United States	1,502,768	19.3	

Rank in order by percentage

1 Alaska
2 New Mexico
3 Wyoming
4 North Dakota
5 Mississippi
6 Montana
7 West Virginia
8 New York
9 Maine
10 Oregon
11 Vermont
12 Hawaii
13 Louisiana
14 Utah
15 South Carolina
16 Alabama
17 Wisconsin
18 Minnesota
19 Iowa
20 Kentucky
21 Idaho
22 North Carolina
23 Delaware
24 California
25 Michigan
26 Arkansas
27 Arizona
28 Pennsylvania
29 Washington
30 Rhode Island
31 Ohio
32 South Dakota
33 Nebraska
34 Indiana
35 Kansas
36 Tennessee
37 Florida
38 Georgia
39 Oklahoma
40 Texas
41 Colorado
42 Nevada
43 Missouri
44 Massachusetts
45 Illinois
46 Virginia
47 Connecticut
48 Maryland
49 New Jersey
50 New Hampshire

Note: Numbers that appear to be identical are rounded and vary slightly in actual value. The rankings reflect the actual values before rounding. See the introduction for more details.

G-7 State and Local General Expenditures Per Capita, FY 2000

State	State and local general expenditure per capita $	State general expenditure per capita $	Local general expenditure per capita $	Rank by state and local general expenditure per capita
Alabama	4,961	2,359	2,602	30
Alaska	12,121	7,887	4,234	1
Arizona	4,534	1,771	2,763	45
Arkansas	4,137	2,335	1,802	49
California	5,780	2,032	3,748	10
Colorado	5,238	2,042	3,196	22
Connecticut	6,289	3,374	2,914	5
Delaware	5,983	3,899	2,084	7
Florida	4,711	1,778	2,933	39
Georgia	4,652	1,944	2,708	41
Hawaii	6,016	4,800	1,216	6
Idaho	4,504	2,134	2,370	46
Illinois	5,186	2,001	3,185	23
Indiana	4,727	2,048	2,679	38
Iowa	5,319	2,498	2,821	20
Kansas	4,793	2,055	2,739	37
Kentucky	4,706	2,701	2,005	40
Louisiana	4,985	2,475	2,510	29
Maine	5,455	3,088	2,366	18
Maryland	5,182	2,441	2,742	24
Massachusetts	5,949	3,242	2,707	8
Michigan	5,509	2,194	3,315	17
Minnesota	6,336	2,717	3,619	4
Mississippi	4,897	2,391	2,507	34
Missouri	4,436	2,021	2,415	48
Montana	5,014	2,843	2,171	28
Nebraska	4,913	2,309	2,604	32
Nevada	4,883	1,561	3,322	35
New Hampshire	4,582	2,291	2,292	43
New Jersey	5,613	2,320	3,293	15
New Mexico	5,552	3,045	2,507	16
New York	7,379	2,600	4,778	2
North Carolina	5,024	2,229	2,795	27
North Dakota	5,722	3,082	2,640	12
Ohio	5,078	2,045	3,033	25
Oklahoma	3,989	1,755	2,234	50
Oregon	5,893	2,700	3,194	9
Pennsylvania	5,364	2,489	2,875	19
Rhode Island	5,305	3,158	2,147	21
South Carolina	5,050	2,589	2,460	26
South Dakota	4,561	2,357	2,204	44
Tennessee	4,442	2,014	2,428	47
Texas	4,592	1,833	2,760	42
Utah	4,932	2,677	2,254	31
Vermont	5,659	3,507	2,152	14
Virginia	4,906	2,186	2,719	33
Washington	5,680	2,643	3,036	13
West Virginia	4,818	2,838	1,981	36
Wisconsin	5,735	2,290	3,445	11
Wyoming	6,740	2,866	3,874	3
50 States	5,333	2,270	3,062	
DC	9,007	n/a	9,007	
United States	5,340	2,266	3,074	

Rank in order by state and local per capita	
1	Alaska
2	New York
3	Wyoming
4	Minnesota
5	Connecticut
6	Hawaii
7	Delaware
8	Massachusetts
9	Oregon
10	California
11	Wisconsin
12	North Dakota
13	Washington
14	Vermont
15	New Jersey
16	New Mexico
17	Michigan
18	Maine
19	Pennsylvania
20	Iowa
21	Rhode Island
22	Colorado
23	Illinois
24	Maryland
25	Ohio
26	South Carolina
27	North Carolina
28	Montana
29	Louisiana
30	Alabama
31	Utah
32	Nebraska
33	Virginia
34	Mississippi
35	Nevada
36	West Virginia
37	Kansas
38	Indiana
39	Florida
40	Kentucky
41	Georgia
42	Texas
43	New Hampshire
44	South Dakota
45	Arizona
46	Idaho
47	Tennessee
48	Missouri
49	Arkansas
50	Oklahoma

G-8 Percentage Change in State and Local Expenditures, FY 1995-2000

State	Percentage change	Rank
Alabama	40.2	9
Alaska	21.5	45
Arizona	46.7	3
Arkansas	37.9	14
California	34.6	18
Colorado	43.7	6
Connecticut	26.0	40
Delaware	34.3	20
Florida	30.2	31
Georgia	30.9	29
Hawaii	8.6	50
Idaho	34.4	19
Illinois	32.2	25
Indiana	35.9	17
Iowa	30.1	32
Kansas	26.1	39
Kentucky	39.3	12
Louisiana	19.6	46
Maine	33.8	21
Maryland	29.5	33
Massachusetts	26.5	38
Michigan	31.9	26
Minnesota	31.0	27
Mississippi	44.6	4
Missouri	39.7	11
Montana	27.9	34
Nebraska	26.5	37
Nevada	51.6	1
New Hampshire	25.6	41
New Jersey	11.9	49
New Mexico	37.0	16
New York	18.0	47
North Carolina	47.4	2
North Dakota	32.9	23
Ohio	30.9	28
Oklahoma	22.6	42
Oregon	39.7	10
Pennsylvania	30.8	30
Rhode Island	14.7	48
South Carolina	41.8	7
South Dakota	22.2	43
Tennessee	32.6	24
Texas	40.9	8
Utah	43.7	5
Vermont	37.8	15
Virginia	38.3	13
Washington	26.7	36
West Virginia	22.0	44
Wisconsin	33.3	22
Wyoming	27.0	35
50 States	31.2	
DC	19.7	
United States	31.1	

Rank in order by percentage

1 Nevada
2 North Carolina
3 Arizona
4 Mississippi
5 Utah
6 Colorado
7 South Carolina
8 Texas
9 Alabama
10 Oregon
11 Missouri
12 Kentucky
13 Virginia
14 Arkansas
15 Vermont
16 New Mexico
17 Indiana
18 California
19 Idaho
20 Delaware
21 Maine
22 Wisconsin
23 North Dakota
24 Tennessee
25 Illinois
26 Michigan
27 Minnesota
28 Ohio
29 Georgia
30 Pennsylvania
31 Florida
32 Iowa
33 Maryland
34 Montana
35 Wyoming
36 Washington
37 Nebraska
38 Massachusetts
39 Kansas
40 Connecticut
41 New Hampshire
42 Oklahoma
43 South Dakota
44 West Virginia
45 Alaska
46 Louisiana
47 New York
48 Rhode Island
49 New Jersey
50 Hawaii

Note: Numbers that appear to be identical are rounded and vary slightly in actual value. The rankings reflect the actual values before rounding. See the introduction for more details.

G-9 State Government General Revenue, FY 2000

State	State government general revenue $ (in millions)	State government general revenue per capita $	Rank per capita
Alabama	14,117	3,174	37
Alaska	7,330	11,691	1
Arizona	14,724	2,870	45
Arkansas	9,118	3,411	25
California	135,782	4,009	14
Colorado	12,925	3,005	43
Connecticut	16,232	4,766	5
Delaware	4,333	5,526	2
Florida	41,665	2,607	50
Georgia	23,395	2,858	46
Hawaii	5,729	4,727	6
Idaho	4,202	3,248	33
Illinois	38,759	3,121	40
Indiana	18,857	3,101	41
Iowa	9,892	3,381	29
Kansas	8,561	3,185	36
Kentucky	14,648	3,624	21
Louisiana	14,872	3,328	31
Maine	5,274	4,136	13
Maryland	17,956	3,391	27
Massachusetts	27,418	4,319	10
Michigan	39,491	3,974	15
Minnesota	20,971	4,263	11
Mississippi	9,636	3,387	28
Missouri	16,486	2,946	44
Montana	3,496	3,876	19
Nebraska	5,706	3,335	30
Nevada	5,473	2,739	48
New Hampshire	3,876	3,136	38
New Jersey	32,237	3,831	20
New Mexico	7,888	4,336	9
New York	84,765	4,467	7
North Carolina	27,762	3,449	23
North Dakota	2,798	4,358	8
Ohio	36,166	3,186	35
Oklahoma	10,783	3,125	39
Oregon	14,406	4,211	12
Pennsylvania	41,700	3,395	26
Rhode Island	4,106	3,918	17
South Carolina	13,317	3,319	32
South Dakota	2,282	3,022	42
Tennessee	15,928	2,800	47
Texas	55,312	2,653	49
Utah	7,697	3,447	24
Vermont	2,943	4,833	3
Virginia	22,715	3,209	34
Washington	21,254	3,606	22
West Virginia	7,032	3,889	18
Wisconsin	21,183	3,949	16
Wyoming	2,357	4,770	4
50 States	985,556	3,509	
DC	n/a	n/a	
United States	985,556	3,509	

Rank in order per capita

1	Alaska
2	Delaware
3	Vermont
4	Wyoming
5	Connecticut
6	Hawaii
7	New York
8	North Dakota
9	New Mexico
10	Massachusetts
11	Minnesota
12	Oregon
13	Maine
14	California
15	Michigan
16	Wisconsin
17	Rhode Island
18	West Virginia
19	Montana
20	New Jersey
21	Kentucky
22	Washington
23	North Carolina
24	Utah
25	Arkansas
26	Pennsylvania
27	Maryland
28	Mississippi
29	Iowa
30	Nebraska
31	Louisiana
32	South Carolina
33	Idaho
34	Virginia
35	Ohio
36	Kansas
37	Alabama
38	New Hampshire
39	Oklahoma
40	Illinois
41	Indiana
42	South Dakota
43	Colorado
44	Missouri
45	Arizona
46	Georgia
47	Tennessee
48	Nevada
49	Texas
50	Florida

G-10 State Government General Spending, FY 2000

State	State government general spending $ (in millions)	State government general spending per capita	Rank per capita
Alabama	14,400	3,238	32
Alaska	5,972	9,525	1
Arizona	15,284	2,979	40
Arkansas	8,967	3,354	28
California	134,204	3,962	12
Colorado	12,485	2,903	43
Connecticut	14,856	4,362	7
Delaware	3,913	4,991	3
Florida	42,486	2,658	48
Georgia	23,092	2,821	45
Hawaii	5,975	4,930	4
Idaho	4,039	3,121	38
Illinois	36,895	2,971	41
Indiana	19,188	3,156	36
Iowa	10,520	3,595	20
Kansas	8,376	3,116	39
Kentucky	14,197	3,512	25
Louisiana	14,783	3,308	30
Maine	4,850	3,804	17
Maryland	17,281	3,263	31
Massachusetts	26,821	4,225	10
Michigan	39,004	3,925	13
Minnesota	20,975	4,264	8
Mississippi	10,049	3,532	24
Missouri	15,837	2,831	44
Montana	3,325	3,686	19
Nebraska	5,537	3,236	33
Nevada	5,369	2,687	47
New Hampshire	3,884	3,143	37
New Jersey	28,160	3,347	29
New Mexico	7,985	4,390	6
New York	80,617	4,248	9
North Carolina	27,242	3,384	27
North Dakota	2,569	4,001	11
Ohio	36,144	3,184	35
Oklahoma	9,146	2,650	49
Oregon	13,155	3,845	15
Pennsylvania	41,937	3,415	26
Rhode Island	3,987	3,805	16
South Carolina	14,195	3,538	23
South Dakota	2,228	2,951	42
Tennessee	15,822	2,781	46
Texas	54,452	2,611	50
Utah	7,956	3,563	22
Vermont	3,068	5,037	2
Virginia	22,609	3,194	34
Washington	21,951	3,724	18
West Virginia	6,490	3,590	21
Wisconsin	20,645	3,849	14
Wyoming	2,254	4,563	5
50 States	965,174	3,444	
DC	n/a	n/a	
United States	965,174	3,437	

	Rank in order per capita
1	Alaska
2	Vermont
3	Delaware
4	Hawaii
5	Wyoming
6	New Mexico
7	Connecticut
8	Minnesota
9	New York
10	Massachusetts
11	North Dakota
12	California
13	Michigan
14	Wisconsin
15	Oregon
16	Rhode Island
17	Maine
18	Washington
19	Montana
20	Iowa
21	West Virginia
22	Utah
23	South Carolina
24	Mississippi
25	Kentucky
26	Pennsylvania
27	North Carolina
28	Arkansas
29	New Jersey
30	Louisiana
31	Maryland
32	Alabama
33	Nebraska
34	Virginia
35	Ohio
36	Indiana
37	New Hampshire
38	Idaho
39	Kansas
40	Arizona
41	Illinois
42	South Dakota
43	Colorado
44	Missouri
45	Georgia
46	Tennessee
47	Nevada
48	Florida
49	Oklahoma
50	Texas

G-11 State Government General Fund Spending, FY 2001

State	State government general fund spending $ (in millions)	As a percentage of personal income	Rank by percentage
Alabama	15,390	14.0	17
Alaska	n/a	n/a	n/a
Arizona	17,351	12.6	25
Arkansas	11,133	18.1	4
California	137,655	12.2	28
Colorado	12,703	8.6	46
Connecticut	18,953	13.0	20
Delaware	5,417	21.0	2
Florida	52,390	11.0	36
Georgia	24,889	10.3	43
Hawaii	7,277	20.5	3
Idaho	3,984	12.2	26
Illinois	37,657	9.1	45
Indiana	17,767	10.5	41
Iowa	12,288	15.4	10
Kansas	8,850	11.5	34
Kentucky	16,849	16.6	8
Louisiana	15,961	14.6	14
Maine	5,269	15.3	11
Maryland	20,481	10.8	37
Massachusetts	30,107	12.1	29
Michigan	37,952	12.8	22
Minnesota	20,832	12.7	24
Mississippi	9,726	15.6	9
Missouri	16,653	10.5	40
Montana	3,104	14.3	15
Nebraska	6,058	12.2	27
Nevada	4,780	7.6	49
New Hampshire	3,425	8.0	48
New Jersey	32,267	9.9	44
New Mexico	10,794	25.5	1
New York	79,753	11.6	33
North Carolina	26,958	12.0	31
North Dakota	2,297	14.0	18
Ohio	42,296	12.9	21
Oklahoma	11,979	13.8	19
Oregon	17,033	17.4	7
Pennsylvania	40,694	10.8	38
Rhode Island	4,873	15.2	12
South Carolina	14,450	14.3	16
South Dakota	2,353	11.7	32
Tennessee	17,434	11.3	35
Texas	52,356	8.6	47
Utah	6,977	12.7	23
Vermont	2,665	15.2	13
Virginia	24,218	10.4	42
Washington	23,061	12.0	30
West Virginia	7,442	18.0	5
Wisconsin	28,092	17.8	6
Wyoming	1,546	10.6	39
50 States	1,024,439	11.8	
DC	n/a	n/a	
United States	1,024,439	11.8	

Rank in order by percentage

1 New Mexico
2 Delaware
3 Hawaii
4 Arkansas
5 West Virginia
6 Wisconsin
7 Oregon
8 Kentucky
9 Mississippi
10 Iowa
11 Maine
12 Rhode Island
13 Vermont
14 Louisiana
15 Montana
16 South Carolina
17 Alabama
18 North Dakota
19 Oklahoma
20 Connecticut
21 Ohio
22 Michigan
23 Utah
24 Minnesota
25 Arizona
26 Idaho
27 Nebraska
28 California
29 Massachusetts
30 Washington
31 North Carolina
32 South Dakota
33 New York
34 Kansas
35 Tennessee
36 Florida
37 Maryland
38 Pennsylvania
39 Wyoming
40 Missouri
41 Indiana
42 Virginia
43 Georgia
44 New Jersey
45 Illinois
46 Colorado
47 Texas
48 New Hampshire
49 Nevada

Note: Numbers that appear to be identical are rounded and vary slightly in actual value. The rankings reflect the actual values before rounding. See the introduction for more details.

G-12 State and Local Debt, FY 2000

State	State and local debt $ (in millions)	State and local debt per capita $	State and local debt as a percentage of personal income	Rank per capita
Alabama	16,799	3,778	16.7	39
Alaska	7,257	11,573	41.0	1
Arizona	23,599	4,599	19.6	26
Arkansas	7,829	2,929	13.8	48
California	177,920	5,253	17.9	18
Colorado	23,199	5,394	18.1	17
Connecticut	23,495	6,898	18.2	4
Delaware	4,585	5,848	19.8	11
Florida	78,495	4,911	18.7	19
Georgia	29,948	3,658	14.1	41
Hawaii	7,909	6,526	24.2	8
Idaho	3,430	2,650	12.0	49
Illinois	67,573	5,441	17.9	16
Indiana	19,869	3,268	12.8	45
Iowa	7,310	2,498	9.9	50
Kansas	10,440	3,884	14.7	38
Kentucky	23,420	5,794	25.4	12
Louisiana	17,980	4,023	18.0	35
Maine	5,845	4,585	19.0	27
Maryland	23,830	4,500	14.2	29
Massachusetts	55,163	8,689	25.1	3
Michigan	47,195	4,749	17.0	23
Minnesota	27,409	5,572	18.6	14
Mississippi	8,519	2,994	14.9	47
Missouri	19,286	3,447	13.4	43
Montana	3,798	4,210	19.5	33
Nebraska	6,648	3,885	14.8	37
Nevada	13,235	6,624	23.6	5
New Hampshire	7,041	5,696	18.8	13
New Jersey	50,315	5,980	17.4	9
New Mexico	7,652	4,207	20.1	34
New York	177,550	9,357	28.8	2
North Carolina	29,114	3,617	14.6	42
North Dakota	2,781	4,331	18.8	32
Ohio	42,087	3,707	13.8	40
Oklahoma	11,409	3,306	14.8	44
Oregon	15,607	4,562	17.4	28
Pennsylvania	73,325	5,971	21.4	10
Rhode Island	6,878	6,563	23.6	7
South Carolina	18,671	4,654	20.4	25
South Dakota	3,289	4,356	17.9	31
Tennessee	18,377	3,230	13.1	46
Texas	100,175	4,804	18.6	20
Utah	12,394	5,551	25.0	15
Vermont	2,839	4,662	18.5	24
Virginia	31,546	4,456	15.4	30
Washington	38,697	6,566	22.1	6
West Virginia	7,094	3,924	18.7	36
Wisconsin	25,563	4,766	17.9	22
Wyoming	2,368	4,793	18.7	21
50 States	1,446,753	5,151	18.6	
DC	5,062	8,850	24.5	
United States	1,451,815	5,159	18.7	

Rank in order per capita

1	Alaska
2	New York
3	Massachusetts
4	Connecticut
5	Nevada
6	Washington
7	Rhode Island
8	Hawaii
9	New Jersey
10	Pennsylvania
11	Delaware
12	Kentucky
13	New Hampshire
14	Minnesota
15	Utah
16	Illinois
17	Colorado
18	California
19	Florida
20	Texas
21	Wyoming
22	Wisconsin
23	Michigan
24	Vermont
25	South Carolina
26	Arizona
27	Maine
28	Oregon
29	Maryland
30	Virginia
31	South Dakota
32	North Dakota
33	Montana
34	New Mexico
35	Louisiana
36	West Virginia
37	Nebraska
38	Kansas
39	Alabama
40	Ohio
41	Georgia
42	North Carolina
43	Missouri
44	Oklahoma
45	Indiana
46	Tennessee
47	Mississippi
48	Arkansas
49	Idaho
50	Iowa

G-13 State and Local Debt Related to Revenue, FY 2000

State	State and local debt as a percentage of general revenue	Rank
Alabama	65.3	32
Alaska	68.9	25
Arizona	85.0	10
Arkansas	56.6	43
California	65.8	31
Colorado	78.4	18
Connecticut	91.0	9
Delaware	73.7	20
Florida	84.9	11
Georgia	60.7	37
Hawaii	93.2	5
Idaho	45.2	48
Illinois	83.7	12
Indiana	60.7	38
Iowa	42.4	49
Kansas	64.3	33
Kentucky	92.9	6
Louisiana	66.3	29
Maine	68.3	26
Maryland	70.2	24
Massachusetts	119.7	1
Michigan	67.3	27
Minnesota	70.7	22
Mississippi	51.1	47
Missouri	61.0	35
Montana	67.3	28
Nebraska	57.1	42
Nevada	111.4	2
New Hampshire	101.3	3
New Jersey	80.7	16
New Mexico	58.5	40
New York	94.0	4
North Carolina	57.6	41
North Dakota	61.9	34
Ohio	52.6	46
Oklahoma	60.8	36
Oregon	54.5	45
Pennsylvania	91.0	8
Rhode Island	92.6	7
South Carolina	79.6	17
South Dakota	76.9	19
Tennessee	54.7	44
Texas	83.0	14
Utah	82.9	15
Vermont	70.6	23
Virginia	71.4	21
Washington	83.5	13
West Virginia	65.9	30
Wisconsin	59.4	39
Wyoming	33.7	50
50 States	74.7	
DC	79.3	
United States	74.7	

Rank in order by percentage	
1	Massachusetts
2	Nevada
3	New Hampshire
4	New York
5	Hawaii
6	Kentucky
7	Rhode Island
8	Pennsylvania
9	Connecticut
10	Arizona
11	Florida
12	Illinois
13	Washington
14	Texas
15	Utah
16	New Jersey
17	South Carolina
18	Colorado
19	South Dakota
20	Delaware
21	Virginia
22	Minnesota
23	Vermont
24	Maryland
25	Alaska
26	Maine
27	Michigan
28	Montana
29	Louisiana
30	West Virginia
31	California
32	Alabama
33	Kansas
34	North Dakota
35	Missouri
36	Oklahoma
37	Georgia
38	Indiana
39	Wisconsin
40	New Mexico
41	North Carolina
42	Nebraska
43	Arkansas
44	Tennessee
45	Oregon
46	Ohio
47	Mississippi
48	Idaho
49	Iowa
50	Wyoming

Note: Numbers that appear to be identical are rounded and vary slightly in actual value. The rankings reflect the actual values before rounding. See the introduction for more details.

G-14 State and Local Full Faith and Credit Debt, FY 2000

State	Full faith and credit debt $ (in millions)	Per capita $	As a percentage of personal income	Rank per capita
Alabama	6,072	1,365	6.0	29
Alaska	2,145	3,422	12.1	5
Arizona	8,753	1,706	7.3	20
Arkansas	1,992	745	3.5	43
California	44,667	1,319	4.5	33
Colorado	8,080	1,879	6.3	16
Connecticut	14,809	4,348	11.5	2
Delaware	1,364	1,740	5.9	18
Florida	13,382	837	3.2	40
Georgia	10,274	1,255	4.8	34
Hawaii	5,270	4,348	16.1	1
Idaho	789	610	2.8	45
Illinois	33,822	2,723	9.0	9
Indiana	3,271	538	2.1	49
Iowa	2,919	998	4.0	38
Kansas	3,929	1,462	5.5	25
Kentucky	2,287	566	2.5	48
Louisiana	5,936	1,328	5.9	32
Maine	1,744	1,368	5.7	28
Maryland	11,493	2,170	6.8	13
Massachusetts	22,767	3,586	10.4	4
Michigan	16,583	1,669	6.0	21
Minnesota	14,076	2,862	9.6	8
Mississippi	4,520	1,589	7.9	23
Missouri	5,370	960	3.7	39
Montana	585	649	3.0	44
Nebraska	1,711	1,000	3.8	37
Nevada	7,923	3,965	14.1	3
New Hampshire	1,995	1,614	5.3	22
New Jersey	16,803	1,997	5.8	15
New Mexico	2,120	1,166	5.6	36
New York	63,242	3,333	10.3	6
North Carolina	9,701	1,205	4.9	35
North Dakota	512	797	3.5	41
Ohio	15,230	1,341	5.0	31
Oklahoma	1,963	569	2.5	47
Oregon	7,543	2,205	8.4	12
Pennsylvania	28,329	2,307	8.3	11
Rhode Island	1,867	1,782	6.4	17
South Carolina	6,916	1,724	7.6	19
South Dakota	588	779	3.2	42
Tennessee	8,226	1,446	5.9	26
Texas	42,817	2,053	8.0	14
Utah	3,003	1,345	6.1	30
Vermont	965	1,584	6.3	24
Virginia	10,184	1,439	5.0	27
Washington	17,922	3,041	10.2	7
West Virginia	711	393	1.9	50
Wisconsin	13,968	2,604	9.8	10
Wyoming	298	603	2.4	46
50 States	511,436	1,821	6.6	
DC	3,719	6,501	18.0	
United States	515,155	1,831	6.6	

Rank in order per capita	
1	Hawaii
2	Connecticut
3	Nevada
4	Massachusetts
5	Alaska
6	New York
7	Washington
8	Minnesota
9	Illinois
10	Wisconsin
11	Pennsylvania
12	Oregon
13	Maryland
14	Texas
15	New Jersey
16	Colorado
17	Rhode Island
18	Delaware
19	South Carolina
20	Arizona
21	Michigan
22	New Hampshire
23	Mississippi
24	Vermont
25	Kansas
26	Tennessee
27	Virginia
28	Maine
29	Alabama
30	Utah
31	Ohio
32	Louisiana
33	California
34	Georgia
35	North Carolina
36	New Mexico
37	Nebraska
38	Iowa
39	Missouri
40	Florida
41	North Dakota
42	South Dakota
43	Arkansas
44	Montana
45	Idaho
46	Wyoming
47	Oklahoma
48	Kentucky
49	Indiana
50	West Virginia

Note: Numbers that appear to be identical are rounded and vary slightly in actual value. The rankings reflect the actual values before rounding. See the introduction for more details.

G-15 State Government Bond Ratings, 2002

State	State bond ratings	Rank
Alabama	Aa3	4
Alaska	Aa2	3
Arizona	no general obligation debt	n/a
Arkansas	Aa2	3
California	A1	5
Colorado	no general obligation debt	n/a
Connecticut	Aa2	3
Delaware	Aaa	1
Florida	Aa2	3
Georgia	Aaa	1
Hawaii	Aa3	4
Idaho	no general obligation debt	n/a
Illinois	Aa2	3
Indiana	no general obligation debt	n/a
Iowa	no general obligation debt	n/a
Kansas	no general obligation debt	n/a
Kentucky	no general obligation debt	n/a
Louisiana	A2	6
Maine	Aa2	3
Maryland	Aaa	1
Massachusetts	Aa2	3
Michigan	Aaa	1
Minnesota	Aaa	1
Mississippi	Aa3	4
Missouri	Aaa	1
Montana	Aa3	4
Nebraska	no general obligation debt	n/a
Nevada	Aa2	3
New Hampshire	Aa2	3
New Jersey	Aa2	3
New Mexico	Aa1	2
New York	A2	6
North Carolina	Aa1	2
North Dakota	no general obligation debt	n/a
Ohio	Aa1	2
Oklahoma	Aa3	4
Oregon	Aa2	3
Pennsylvania	Aa2	3
Rhode Island	Aa3	4
South Carolina	Aaa	1
South Dakota	no general obligation debt	n/a
Tennessee	Aa2	3
Texas	Aa1	2
Utah	Aaa	1
Vermont	Aa1	2
Virginia	Aaa	1
Washington	Aa1	2
West Virginia	Aa3	4
Wisconsin	Aa3	4
Wyoming	no general obligation debt	n/a
50 States	n/a	
DC	Baa3	
United States	n/a	

Rank in order by rating

1	Delaware
1	Georgia
1	Maryland
1	Michigan
1	Minnesota
1	Missouri
1	South Carolina
1	Utah
1	Virginia
2	New Mexico
2	North Carolina
2	Ohio
2	Texas
2	Vermont
2	Washington
3	Alaska
3	Arkansas
3	Connecticut
3	Florida
3	Illinois
3	Maine
3	Massachusetts
3	Nevada
3	New Hampshire
3	New Jersey
3	Oregon
3	Pennsylvania
3	Tennessee
4	Alabama
4	Hawaii
4	Mississippi
4	Montana
4	Oklahoma
4	Rhode Island
4	West Virginia
4	Wisconsin
5	California
6	Louisiana
6	New York

Note: Ties in ranking reflect ties in actual values.

G-16 State Solvency Index, 2002

State	State solvency index	Rank by index
Alabama	-287	33
Alaska	52,945	1
Arizona	1,608	13
Arkansas	188	25
California	1,675	10
Colorado	1,533	14
Connecticut	-2,840	50
Delaware	2,576	5
Florida	1,620	12
Georgia	1,417	17
Hawaii	-2,578	48
Idaho	986	20
Illinois	-1,593	45
Indiana	-8	29
Iowa	628	22
Kansas	-374	34
Kentucky	-65	30
Louisiana	-1,189	41
Maine	-1,285	43
Maryland	-421	35
Massachusetts	-2,772	49
Michigan	1,345	19
Minnesota	1,363	18
Mississippi	-858	38
Missouri	186	26
Montana	1,956	8
Nebraska	38	27
Nevada	-1,193	42
New Hampshire	-720	36
New Jersey	1,459	16
New Mexico	7,556	3
New York	28	28
North Carolina	1,995	7
North Dakota	2,700	4
Ohio	522	23
Oklahoma	-1,369	44
Oregon	-890	39
Pennsylvania	1,650	11
Rhode Island	-2,415	46
South Carolina	-1,107	40
South Dakota	912	21
Tennessee	396	24
Texas	1,891	9
Utah	-186	31
Vermont	-789	37
Virginia	1,477	15
Washington	-245	32
West Virginia	-2,448	47
Wisconsin	2,519	6
Wyoming	9,034	2
50 States	797	
DC	n/a	
United States	797	

Rank in order by index

1	Alaska
2	Wyoming
3	New Mexico
4	North Dakota
5	Delaware
6	Wisconsin
7	North Carolina
8	Montana
9	Texas
10	California
11	Pennsylvania
12	Florida
13	Arizona
14	Colorado
15	Virginia
16	New Jersey
17	Georgia
18	Minnesota
19	Michigan
20	Idaho
21	South Dakota
22	Iowa
23	Ohio
24	Tennessee
25	Arkansas
26	Missouri
27	Nebraska
28	New York
29	Indiana
30	Kentucky
31	Utah
32	Washington
33	Alabama
34	Kansas
35	Maryland
36	New Hampshire
37	Vermont
38	Mississippi
39	Oregon
40	South Carolina
41	Louisiana
42	Nevada
43	Maine
44	Oklahoma
45	Illinois
46	Rhode Island
47	West Virginia
48	Hawaii
49	Massachusetts
50	Connecticut

G-17 Assets of State-administered Pension Plans, 2000

State	Total assets $ (in millions)	Total membership #	Average assets per member	Rank by average
Alabama	22,733	247,766	91,753	38
Alaska	11,337	61,099	185,559	5
Arizona	31,097	314,261	98,954	33
Arkansas	13,523	121,109	111,661	23
California	376,114	1,824,276	206,171	1
Colorado	25,720	280,184	91,797	37
Connecticut	20,884	147,176	141,899	14
Delaware	6,115	40,134	152,363	11
Florida	83,411	686,011	121,589	20
Georgia	43,182	564,254	76,530	42
Hawaii	8,420	232,297	36,248	49
Idaho	7,360	60,490	121,671	19
Illinois	88,101	851,240	103,497	31
Indiana	18,241	365,723	49,877	48
Iowa	20,237	251,931	80,328	41
Kansas	10,621	177,963	59,681	45
Kentucky	23,627	242,165	97,567	36
Louisiana	27,698	282,946	97,891	35
Maine	7,570	53,022	142,765	13
Maryland	44,409	266,507	166,635	8
Massachusetts	43,122	327,548	131,652	17
Michigan	75,772	448,224	169,050	7
Minnesota	45,366	450,674	100,662	32
Mississippi	17,158	259,919	66,012	44
Missouri	39,907	275,188	145,018	12
Montana	5,635	75,988	74,159	43
Nebraska	7,258	82,513	87,964	39
Nevada	14,348	86,510	165,854	9
New Hampshire	4,615	44,007	104,872	29
New Jersey	56,733	459,111	123,571	18
New Mexico	14,519	133,669	108,621	27
New York	242,911	1,196,615	202,999	2
North Carolina	57,551	494,158	116,463	21
North Dakota	2,787	104,333	26,712	50
Ohio	112,517	1,086,938	103,518	30
Oklahoma	15,988	161,983	98,700	34
Oregon	21,997	203,494	108,097	28
Pennsylvania	98,361	510,576	192,647	3
Rhode Island	7,251	38,914	186,326	4
South Carolina	19,395	354,271	54,745	46
South Dakota	5,948	44,739	132,938	16
Tennessee	30,210	226,467	133,396	15
Texas	140,924	1,279,606	110,130	26
Utah	13,058	113,955	114,585	22
Vermont	2,496	29,051	85,926	40
Virginia	48,749	440,579	110,648	24
Washington	51,522	323,665	159,183	10
West Virginia	4,172	80,548	51,790	47
Wisconsin	69,669	383,828	181,512	6
Wyoming	3,922	35,481	110,534	25
50 States	2,164,263	16,823,106	128,648	
DC	4,380	11,069	395,736	
United States*	2,168,643	16,833,698	128,827	

Rank in order by average

1. California
2. New York
3. Pennsylvania
4. Rhode Island
5. Alaska
6. Wisconsin
7. Michigan
8. Maryland
9. Nevada
10. Washington
11. Delaware
12. Missouri
13. Maine
14. Connecticut
15. Tennessee
16. South Dakota
17. Massachusetts
18. New Jersey
19. Idaho
20. Florida
21. North Carolina
22. Utah
23. Arkansas
24. Virginia
25. Wyoming
26. Texas
27. New Mexico
28. Oregon
29. New Hampshire
30. Ohio
31. Illinois
32. Minnesota
33. Arizona
34. Oklahoma
35. Louisiana
36. Kentucky
37. Colorado
38. Alabama
39. Nebraska
40. Vermont
41. Iowa
42. Georgia
43. Montana
44. Mississippi
45. Kansas
46. South Carolina
47. West Virginia
48. Indiana
49. Hawaii
50. North Dakota

*Due to rounding or data sources, the 50-state total plus D.C. may not equal the U.S. total. Please see introduction.

G-18 State Reserves at the End of FY 2002

State	Balances as a percentage of expenditures	Rank
Alabama	5.3	14
Alaska	104.6	1
Arizona	0.8	38
Arkansas	0.0	48
California	0.1	47
Colorado	2.5	29
Connecticut	0.0	48
Delaware	19.6	2
Florida	n/a	n/a
Georgia	7.9	8
Hawaii	5.0	16
Idaho	2.7	27
Illinois	2.0	32
Indiana	2.8	26
Iowa	5.0	16
Kansas	0.3	43
Kentucky	0.3	43
Louisiana	4.0	23
Maine	1.3	35
Maryland	7.8	9
Massachusetts	5.3	14
Michigan	4.1	21
Minnesota	6.7	11
Mississippi	3.0	24
Missouri	4.1	21
Montana	6.0	13
Nebraska	6.4	12
Nevada	12.0	4
New Hampshire	2.7	27
New Jersey	0.5	40
New Mexico	8.5	6
New York	2.5	29
North Carolina	0.2	46
North Dakota	8.4	7
Ohio	2.5	29
Oklahoma	2.9	25
Oregon	0.5	40
Pennsylvania	0.7	39
Rhode Island	4.3	20
South Carolina	1.0	37
South Dakota	12.9	3
Tennessee	1.1	36
Texas	7.6	10
Utah	0.3	45
Vermont	1.5	34
Virginia	5.0	16
Washington	4.4	19
West Virginia	9.0	5
Wisconsin	0.5	40
Wyoming	1.6	33
50 States	n/a	
DC	n/a	
United States	3.5	

Rank in order by percentage

1	Alaska
2	Delaware
3	South Dakota
4	Nevada
5	West Virginia
6	New Mexico
7	North Dakota
8	Georgia
9	Maryland
10	Texas
11	Minnesota
12	Nebraska
13	Montana
14	Alabama
14	Massachusetts
16	Hawaii
16	Iowa
16	Virginia
19	Washington
20	Rhode Island
21	Michigan
21	Missouri
23	Louisiana
24	Mississippi
25	Oklahoma
26	Indiana
27	Idaho
27	New Hampshire
29	Colorado
29	New York
29	Ohio
32	Illinois
33	Wyoming
34	Vermont
35	Maine
36	Tennessee
37	South Carolina
38	Arizona
39	Pennsylvania
40	New Jersey
40	Oregon
40	Wisconsin
43	Kansas
43	Kentucky
43	Utah
46	North Carolina
47	California
48	Arkansas
48	Connecticut

Note: Ties in ranking reflect ties in actual values.

G-19 State and Local Capital Outlays and Interest, FY 2000

State	Outlays and interest per capita $	Capital outlays per capita $	Interest per capita $	Rank by outlays and interest per capita
Alabama	896	705	191	34
Alaska	2,757	2,021	736	1
Arizona	1,112	839	273	14
Arkansas	630	485	144	50
California	1,009	738	271	26
Colorado	1,239	928	310	11
Connecticut	1,083	678	405	16
Delaware	1,146	777	369	13
Florida	1,085	801	285	15
Georgia	1,062	870	192	20
Hawaii	1,341	853	488	7
Idaho	763	619	144	46
Illinois	1,074	764	310	19
Indiana	835	666	170	42
Iowa	952	818	134	29
Kansas	843	650	193	41
Kentucky	1,047	709	337	22
Louisiana	856	633	224	37
Maine	733	471	262	47
Maryland	973	691	282	27
Massachusetts	1,456	999	457	4
Michigan	932	701	231	31
Minnesota	1,247	945	303	10
Mississippi	854	685	169	39
Missouri	850	663	187	40
Montana	854	608	246	38
Nebraska	1,253	1,042	211	8
Nevada	1,427	1,124	302	5
New Hampshire	795	479	316	43
New Jersey	857	589	269	36
New Mexico	1,020	792	229	25
New York	1,563	988	576	2
North Carolina	915	706	209	33
North Dakota	1,252	1,016	236	9
Ohio	947	749	198	30
Oklahoma	788	603	185	45
Oregon	1,035	762	273	24
Pennsylvania	959	619	339	28
Rhode Island	726	399	327	48
South Carolina	1,046	787	259	23
South Dakota	1,057	828	229	21
Tennessee	930	766	165	32
Texas	1,076	802	273	18
Utah	1,182	880	302	12
Vermont	672	405	267	49
Virginia	861	597	264	35
Washington	1,356	1,019	337	6
West Virginia	790	554	236	44
Wisconsin	1,077	811	266	17
Wyoming	1,561	1,286	276	3
50 States	1,055	769	286	
DC	2,171	1,735	437	
United States	1,057	771	286	

Rank in order per capita

1 Alaska
2 New York
3 Wyoming
4 Massachusetts
5 Nevada
6 Washington
7 Hawaii
8 Nebraska
9 North Dakota
10 Minnesota
11 Colorado
12 Utah
13 Delaware
14 Arizona
15 Florida
16 Connecticut
17 Wisconsin
18 Texas
19 Illinois
20 Georgia
21 South Dakota
22 Kentucky
23 South Carolina
24 Oregon
25 New Mexico
26 California
27 Maryland
28 Pennsylvania
29 Iowa
30 Ohio
31 Michigan
32 Tennessee
33 North Carolina
34 Alabama
35 Virginia
36 New Jersey
37 Louisiana
38 Montana
39 Mississippi
40 Missouri
41 Kansas
42 Indiana
43 New Hampshire
44 West Virginia
45 Oklahoma
46 Idaho
47 Maine
48 Rhode Island
49 Vermont
50 Arkansas

G-20 Index of State Budget Process Quality, 2002

State	Index of state budget process quality	Rank
Alabama	56.9	40
Alaska	49.0	45
Arizona	48.6	46
Arkansas	52.0	42
California	60.5	35
Colorado	73.7	14
Connecticut	72.4	15
Delaware	67.0	21
Florida	76.0	13
Georgia	93.0	1
Hawaii	77.0	12
Idaho	37.9	47
Illinois	81.2	3
Indiana	29.9	49
Iowa	72.2	16
Kansas	59.0	39
Kentucky	65.5	26
Louisiana	80.5	6
Maine	62.0	31
Maryland	77.1	11
Massachusetts	79.2	7
Michigan	81.4	2
Minnesota	80.8	5
Mississippi	60.3	37
Missouri	70.9	18
Montana	66.0	24
Nebraska	64.0	28
Nevada	71.0	17
New Hampshire	27.5	50
New Jersey	77.5	9
New Mexico	78.0	8
New York	68.4	20
North Carolina	53.0	41
North Dakota	60.4	36
Ohio	60.6	34
Oklahoma	69.0	19
Oregon	66.8	22
Pennsylvania	65.7	25
Rhode Island	77.3	10
South Carolina	62.7	29
South Dakota	66.4	23
Tennessee	61.5	32
Texas	62.7	29
Utah	81.2	3
Vermont	37.7	48
Virginia	52.0	42
Washington	61.1	33
West Virginia	59.6	38
Wisconsin	51.9	44
Wyoming	64.2	27
50 States	64.6	
DC	n/a	
United States	64.6	

Rank in order by index	
1	Georgia
2	Michigan
3	Illinois
3	Utah
5	Minnesota
6	Louisiana
7	Massachusetts
8	New Mexico
9	New Jersey
10	Rhode Island
11	Maryland
12	Hawaii
13	Florida
14	Colorado
15	Connecticut
16	Iowa
17	Nevada
18	Missouri
19	Oklahoma
20	New York
21	Delaware
22	Oregon
23	South Dakota
24	Montana
25	Pennsylvania
26	Kentucky
27	Wyoming
28	Nebraska
29	South Carolina
29	Texas
31	Maine
32	Tennessee
33	Washington
34	Ohio
35	California
36	North Dakota
37	Mississippi
38	West Virginia
39	Kansas
40	Alabama
41	North Carolina
42	Arkansas
42	Virginia
44	Wisconsin
45	Alaska
46	Arizona
47	Idaho
48	Vermont
49	Indiana
50	New Hampshire

Note: Ties in ranking reflect ties in actual values.

G-21 Relative State Spending "Needs," FY 1996

State	Additional spending needed to meet national average %	Rank by least "need" to most
Alabama	4	41
Alaska	2	38
Arizona	5	45
Arkansas	0	30
California	10	48
Colorado	-10	8
Connecticut	2	38
Delaware	-11	4
Florida	-4	24
Georgia	4	41
Hawaii	-10	8
Idaho	0	30
Illinois	1	33
Indiana	-8	12
Iowa	-11	4
Kansas	-5	18
Kentucky	1	33
Louisiana	9	47
Maine	-12	2
Maryland	-5	18
Massachusetts	-7	14
Michigan	1	33
Minnesota	-6	16
Mississippi	10	48
Missouri	-8	12
Montana	-2	29
Nebraska	-12	2
Nevada	-6	16
New Hampshire	-16	1
New Jersey	-5	18
New Mexico	15	50
New York	4	41
North Carolina	-5	18
North Dakota	-4	24
Ohio	-3	28
Oklahoma	4	41
Oregon	-9	11
Pennsylvania	-7	14
Rhode Island	-11	4
South Carolina	1	33
South Dakota	-4	24
Tennessee	2	38
Texas	8	46
Utah	-5	18
Vermont	-10	8
Virginia	-4	24
Washington	-5	18
West Virginia	0	30
Wisconsin	-11	4
Wyoming	1	33
50 States	n/a	
DC	26	
United States	0	

Rank in order by percentage

1	New Hampshire
2	Maine
2	Nebraska
4	Delaware
4	Iowa
4	Rhode Island
4	Wisconsin
8	Colorado
8	Hawaii
8	Vermont
11	Oregon
12	Indiana
12	Missouri
14	Massachusetts
14	Pennsylvania
16	Minnesota
16	Nevada
18	Kansas
18	Maryland
18	New Jersey
18	North Carolina
18	Utah
18	Washington
24	Florida
24	North Dakota
24	South Dakota
24	Virginia
28	Ohio
29	Montana
30	Arkansas
30	Idaho
30	West Virginia
33	Illinois
33	Kentucky
33	Michigan
33	South Carolina
33	Wyoming
38	Alaska
38	Connecticut
38	Tennessee
41	Alabama
41	Georgia
41	New York
41	Oklahoma
45	Arizona
46	Texas
47	Louisiana
48	California
48	Mississippi
50	New Mexico

Note: Ties in ranking reflect ties in actual values.

G-22 Structural Deficits

State	Projected state surplus or shortfall as a percentage of baseline revenues	Rank
Alabama	-4.8	31
Alaska	-16.4	49
Arizona	-10.5	44
Arkansas	-2.3	21
California	-2.8	23
Colorado	-7.0	38
Connecticut	0.4	6
Delaware	-3.0	25
Florida	-8.8	42
Georgia	-6.5	35
Hawaii	-15.1	48
Idaho	-13.2	47
Illinois	-0.4	13
Indiana	-5.7	33
Iowa	2.7	1
Kansas	-1.9	18
Kentucky	0.5	5
Louisiana	-2.5	22
Maine	0.1	9
Maryland	-7.1	39
Massachusetts	0.0	11
Michigan	0.4	6
Minnesota	0.1	9
Mississippi	-2.0	19
Missouri	-1.8	17
Montana	-5.7	33
Nebraska	1.5	2
Nevada	-18.3	50
New Hampshire	-8.2	41
New Jersey	-3.3	26
New Mexico	-12.0	46
New York	0.3	8
North Carolina	-3.7	27
North Dakota	0.9	3
Ohio	0.9	3
Oklahoma	-2.1	20
Oregon	-0.1	12
Pennsylvania	-1.3	14
Rhode Island	-2.9	24
South Carolina	-4.6	29
South Dakota	-5.0	32
Tennessee	-9.1	43
Texas	-7.8	40
Utah	-4.3	28
Vermont	-4.6	29
Virginia	-6.8	37
Washington	-6.7	36
West Virginia	-1.4	15
Wisconsin	-1.5	16
Wyoming	-10.6	45
50 States	n/a	
DC	n/a	
United States	-3.8	

Rank in order by percentage

1	Iowa
2	Nebraska
3	North Dakota
3	Ohio
5	Kentucky
6	Connecticut
6	Michigan
8	New York
9	Maine
9	Minnesota
11	Massachusetts
12	Oregon
13	Illinois
14	Pennsylvania
15	West Virginia
16	Wisconsin
17	Missouri
18	Kansas
19	Mississippi
20	Oklahoma
21	Arkansas
22	Louisiana
23	California
24	Rhode Island
25	Delaware
26	New Jersey
27	North Carolina
28	Utah
29	South Carolina
29	Vermont
31	Alabama
32	South Dakota
33	Indiana
33	Montana
35	Georgia
36	Washington
37	Virginia
38	Colorado
39	Maryland
40	Texas
41	New Hampshire
42	Florida
43	Tennessee
44	Arizona
45	Wyoming
46	New Mexico
47	Idaho
48	Hawaii
49	Alaska
50	Nevada

Note: Ties in ranking reflect ties in actual values.

Source Notes for Revenues and Finances (Section G)

G-1 State and Local Total Revenue, FY 2000: This table and many others in this section of *State Fact Finder* rely on analysis of data collected by the Census Bureau for FY 2000. For sources of the fiscal data and the population and personal income estimates used to build the tables, see the extensive note associated with Table F-1.

Total revenue, shown in this table, is the most inclusive definition of the financial size of state and local governments used by the Census Bureau in its annual survey of government finances. It includes utilities run by state and local governments and many categories of trust funds. Such funds typically collect revenues, such as unemployment insurance taxes, for a particular purpose, such as paying unemployment compensation benefits, and are not commingled with other public funds. The revenues included come from state and local taxes, fees such as hospital charges and university tuition, and from the federal government.

G-2 State and Local General Revenue, FY 2000: From the same source as Table F-1, this table relates general revenue to population and personal income in each state. Because general revenue eliminates difficult to compare proprietary functions, such as utility and trust fund revenues, it allows for more appropriate state-by-state comparisons.

G-3 State and Local "Own-source" General Revenue, FY 2000: These data reflect the concept often used to measure the fiscal burdens associated with state and local activity. Revenues from federal aid are excluded, along with the revenues of trust funds and utilities. For source see the notes to Table F-1.

G-4 State and Local Non-tax "Own-source" Revenue, FY 2000: The principal sources of non-tax revenues are (1) fees related to use of state facilities and services, such as those charged by public hospitals and universities, and (2) interest earned on money held by governments in anticipation of spending. For source see the notes to Table F-1.

G-5 State and Local Total Expenditures, FY 2000: This is the spending counterpart of the revenues shown on Table G-1. For source see the notes to Table F-1.

G-6 State and Local General Expenditures, FY 2000: This concept of "general" spending (see notes to Table G-2) is the most appropriate for comparing spending among states. For source see the notes to Table F-1.

G-7 State and Local General Expenditures Per Capita, FY 2000: This table relates general expenditures to population with separate totals for state governments and local governments. State aid to local governments is included only when local officials spend the resources, to avoid double counting. For source see the notes to Table F-1.

G-8 Percentage Change in State and Local Expenditures, FY 1995-2000: This statistic shows the differences among states in the five-year growth of state and local spending. The changes shown are not adjusted for factors that might account for some of the differences in growth rates, such as growth in population and other factors affecting needs for government services. FY 1995 data come from the Census Bureau and are published in *State Fact Finder 1999*. See source for Table F-1 for FY 2000 data.

G-9 State Government General Revenue, FY 2000: Unlike Tables G-1 through G-8, these data deal with state governments alone, not state and local governments combined. They are from the 2000 version of "State Government Finances," available on the Census Bureau website (www.census.gov).

For most purposes, comparisons of finances among states need to include state and local revenues and spending because of major differences in the division of state and local responsibilities between states. For example, New York local governments pay nearly half of all state and local welfare costs, but local governments in most other states have almost no responsibility for paying these costs. Comparisons of states alone would make New York spending look artificially small. In Hawaii, the state alone pays for schools, while in other states local governments pay half these costs. Comparisons of states alone would make Hawaii's spending look artificially large.

However, comparisons of state governments alone are useful for those attempting to evaluate state officeholders and aspirants and for discussions of state government spending priorities and tax burdens.

This table and Table G-10 show "general" revenues and expenditures, a less inclusive measure than "total" expenditures. The difference is primarily associated with enterprises run by some state governments and not others, particularly liquor sales monopolies run by about a third of the states and the electric power marketing operations run by a few states. State impacts on utility services and liquor prices and sales are similar from state to state but some states achieve them by directly managing these functions. Because huge amounts of money are involved, inclusion of these operations in state comparisons would artificially distort the spending comparisons, so the concepts of general expenditures and general revenues exclude them.

G-10 State Government General Spending, FY 2000: See notes to Table G-9.

G-11 State Government General Fund Spending, FY 2001: These data reflect other estimates of state government spending. They come from a survey of state executive branch budget offices reported in the *2001 State Expenditure Report* by the National Association of State Budget Officers (NASBO). They reflect state fiscal 2001 definitions.

The year ended on June 30, 2001, for forty-six states, while one state ended the fiscal year in the spring and three ended in the fall.

The NASBO report differs from Census Bureau reports in many ways. The Census Bureau reports include all funds, while the NASBO report covers primarily funds subject to appropriation by legislatures and therefore for most states excludes funds of quasi-independent entities such as toll highway authorities. The Census Bureau does not distinguish among funds within state government, while the NASBO report presents data separately for state general funds, federal funds, and other state funds. The data shown in the table reflect the total of all reported funds. The NASBO data use different definitions of spending categories than do the Census Bureau data. See the notes for Table G-9 on the hazards of considering state spending without also considering local spending.

G-12 State and Local Debt, FY 2000: These data, from the Census Bureau (see notes to Table F-1), reflect the total debt of all state and local governments at the end of fiscal 2000, including debt of special authorities.

G-13 State and Local Debt Related to Revenue, FY 2000: This table relates total debt (see Table G-12) to total revenue (see Table G-1). Consequently, it offers a measure of how state and local budgets are strained by the costs of paying principal and interest on past obligations.

G-14 State and Local Full Faith and Credit Debt, FY 2000: These data reflect the component of total debt (see Table G-12) that is backed by the "full faith and credit" of the governments that issued the debt. This debt, commonly known as "general obligation" debt, is backed by all revenue sources of the issuing government. The debt not included in these totals, often known as revenue bonds, is backed only by specified revenues, not general taxes.

G-15 State Government Bond Ratings, 2002: Because thousands of individual state and local governments issue bonds, purchasers such as individuals and mutual funds find it difficult to analyze the risks associated with each individual issue. As a result, three rating agencies (Fitch, Moody's, and Standard & Poor's) evaluate the quality of individual bond issues. The ratings of revenue bonds are unique to the bonds and the revenue sources that back them. The ratings of general obligation bonds shown in this table are reflections of the fiscal soundness of state governments overall. As a result, they affect perceptions of fiscal soundness of states by voters as well as by potential bond purchasers.

The ratings shown come from Moody's and are dated August 26, 2002. Ratings from the other two agencies would show about the same ranking of states. Moody's system considers Aaa highest, followed by Aa1, Aa2, Aa3, A1, A2, and so on, down to lower ratings, which are awarded to

some local governments but no states, which are generally considered good credit risks. Some states have so little general obligation debt that they have no recent ratings and therefore are not ranked in this table. While there is no clearly appropriate way to insert them in the rankings, many of these states have strong credit and would rank above many of the states shown in the rankings.

G-16 State Solvency Index, 2002: While state financial reports and Census Bureau data provide substantial detail about state finances, they do not provide answers to some common sense questions about state financial status. One of these questions is equivalent to "net worth," a fundamental concept in viewing the finances of individuals and companies. This table reflects a special study created by State Policy Research, Inc., using data from a variety of dates as close to late 2002 as possible. See *State Policy Reports* (Vol. 20, #20) for more on the Solvency Index.

Conceptually, the number shown is an answer to the question: If each state were to cease operations tomorrow and pay off all debts (including pension promises to employees), how much money would be left over? For some states, the answer is that nothing would be left. Instead, they would have to levy a special assessment on each citizen (the amounts shown as negative numbers) in order to cease operations. Some states, particularly Alaska with its large reserves built from oil revenues, would have money left over that could be distributed to taxpayers. The calculations exclude the value of physical assets, such as state park lands, trucks, and computers.

G-17 Assets of State-administered Pension Plans, 2000: States run pension plans for their own employees and, in most states, for teachers, city workers, and other local employees as well. To be considered actuarially sound, these plans must have built up enough assets from contributions of employees and their government employers to be able to cover the amounts needed to pay retired workers plus current workers when they retire. How much this amounts to depends on many factors, such as the exact benefits promised and the life expectancy of workers. There is no substitute for actuarial studies of each plan for determining the right amount each plan should have to cover future obligations.

This table shows the assets of state-administered plans and the persons who are considered members of these plans—retirees and active workers accruing retirement benefits. Dividing these two numbers produces average assets per member, which is a rough measure of the relative solvency of the public pension plans in each state. The data come from the Census Bureau website (www.census.gov).

G-18 State Reserves at the End of FY 2002: These data reflect the projected cash reserves of state governments as they finished fiscal year 2002, generally in the summer of 2002.

These reserves come in two primary forms—balances (equivalent to the balances people show in their checkbooks) and "rainy day" or stabilization funds (formal reserves, somewhat akin to the savings accounts maintained by individuals). The data come from a survey of state budget officers by the National Association of State Budget Officers (NASBO) published in November 2002, titled *The Fiscal Survey of States*, and available on the NASBO website (www.nasbo.org).

Relating balances to spending provides a basis for comparisons among states of different sizes and financial responsibilities. Nationwide, this table indicates that states have enough in reserve to pay their normal bills for about 3.5 percent of their fiscal years, or roughly twelve days, with no additional revenue coming in.

Halfway through FY 2003 two-thirds of the states were pessimistic that revenues would meet projections. By the end of the fiscal year the balances shown in this table are bound to be reduced. Yet, the percentages show the extent of reserves as states headed into the fiscally troubled new fiscal year.

G-19 State and Local Capital Outlays and Interest, FY 2000:
This table, from the same source as Table F-1, shows per capita amounts of spending in fiscal 2000 for interest and capital outlays. The outlays reflect the pace of activity in financing new facilities, such as roads and schools. The interest reflects the extent to which taxpayers of each state are seeing their tax funds used to pay interest on past spending, normally borrowing to finance capital outlays.

G-20 Index of State Budget Process Quality, 2002:
Experts in public administration and budgeting generally agree on criteria of best budgeting practices, such as considering the impacts of spending and tax decisions over a longer period than one year. The numbers shown in the table are scores, with a perfect score being 100, developed by State Policy Research by comparing these criteria with actual state budget practices, as reported by the National Association of State Budget Officers in its special report *Budget Processes in the States* (January 2002).

G-21 Relative State Spending "Needs," FY 1996:
Individual states have quite different population characteristics, as shown by many of the tables in *State Fact Finder*. For example, school-age children are an extraordinarily large proportion of the population of Utah, but a smaller-than-average proportion of Pennsylvania's population. As a result, some states would have higher per capita spending than others, even if all states spent identical amounts per pupil, had identical welfare payments, and identical levels of other services. These differences are important to consider in viewing differences in per capita spending among states.

The table was created by Robert Tannenwald of the Federal Reserve Bank of Boston and published in "Fiscal Disparity Among the States Revisited." Tannenwald calculated what state and local governments in each state would have to spend if they applied national average spending (for example, spending per pupil) to their own particular mix of population using government services. For example, to match national average spending patterns, Louisiana would have to spend nine percent more than the national average. Why? Because the state has extra burdens associated with large percentages of welfare recipients and school children.

These data are conceptually similar to concepts of tax capacity shown in Table F-4. Together, these data reflect a consistent pattern of strains that circumstances put on taxpayers and decision makers of individual states. More affluent states, such as Connecticut, often combine above-average tax bases with below-average spending needs while less affluent states, like Mississippi, show the reverse.

G-22 Structural Deficits:
Even with their current prosperity, many state officials worry about *structural* deficits—long-term shortfalls because revenues from current taxes will be insufficient to cover the spending needed to maintain current programs. If such deficits exist, they would be obscured by extraordinary performance of the economy and tax collections, but would be magnified by *cyclical* deficits during any economic downturn.

This table shows the result of subtracting projected spending from projected revenues three years from now. A budget gap or structural deficit is indicated by all the negative results. A value of zero indicates that state and local governments could cover the future costs of their current policies, including adjustments for inflation and workload changes, with revenues from their current tax system, with no change in tax rates or the definition of bases. A positive value means covering costs with money left.

The data were prepared by State Policy Research, Inc., and are published in *The Outlook for State and Local Finances* (National Education Association, 1998).

Education

H-1	Average Proficiency in Math, Eighth Grade, 2000	194
H-2	Average Proficiency in Science, Eighth Grade, 2000	195
H-3	Armed Forces Qualification Test Ranks, FY 2000	196
H-4	SAT Scores, 2002	197
H-5	ACT Scores, 2002	198
H-6	Percentage of Population Over 25 with a High School Diploma, 2000	199
H-7	Students in Private Schools, 1999-2000	200
H-8	High School Completion Rates, 1998-2000	201
H-9	Pupil-Teacher Ratio, 2001-2002	202
H-10	Public School Enrollment, 2001-2002	203
H-11	Public Library Holdings Per Capita, FY 2000	204
H-12	Children with Disabilities, 1999-2000	205
H-13	State and Local Education Spending, FY 2000	206
H-14	State and Local Education Spending as a Percentage of General Spending, FY 2000	207
H-15	Spending Per Pupil, 2001-2002	208
H-16	Average Teacher Salary, 2001-2002	209
H-17	Sources of School Funds, 2000-2001	210
H-18	State Aid Per Pupil in Average Daily Attendance, 2001-2002	211
H-19	State and Local Spending for Higher Education, FY 2000	212
H-20	State and Local Spending for Higher Education as a Percentage of General Spending, FY 2000	213
H-21	Public Higher Education Enrollment, 2000	214
H-22	Per Pupil State Support of Higher Education, 2001-2002	215
H-23	Average Tuition and Fees at Public Universities, 2000-2001	216
H-24	Average Salary of Associate Professors at "Flagship" State Universities, 2001-2002	217
H-25	State and Local Education Employees, 2001	218
H-26	Federal Research and Development Spending, FY 2000	219
H-27	Total Library Operating Expenditures, FY 2000	220

The latest federal education reform legislation—The No Child Left Behind Act of 2001 (NCLB)—was signed into law in early 2002. In brief, it requires states to:

- Assess student performance in math and reading through annual standardized testing,
- Release test results and annual report cards for schools,
- Hire teachers qualified by federal standards, and
- Allow students to transfer out of "failing" schools into better performing ones.

Though local governments raise the biggest chunk of funds for schools through property taxes, states and the federal government kick in as well. As a result of NCLB, federal funding will now come with strings attached. A certain result for the states will be a widely expanded federal role in the schools. This can be beneficial as new federal incentives and resources become available, but also demanding as states struggle to meet federal demands. It is a "tall order," according to the Education Commission on the States— "States will have their hands full deciding not just how to comply with the new law, but how to take maximum advantage of its potential to improve student achievement."

The law has its supporters and detractors. It is praised for implementing national accountability standards. Some argue, however, that the federal policy has the potential to effectively abandon failing schools rather than fixing them—leaving behind those students who for whatever reason do not opt to exercise school choice.

It's no big surprise that universities are feeling the fiscal pinch. Because of the perceived ability to pass costs on to students and their families through tuition hikes, higher education is usually the first casualty of stressed state budgets. University systems are responding with hiring freezes and spending cuts.

H-1 Average Proficiency in Math, Eighth Grade, 2000

State	Average math score	Rank
Alabama	262	34
Alaska	n/a	n/a
Arizona	271	27
Arkansas	261	36
California	262	34
Colorado	n/a	n/a
Connecticut	282	10
Delaware	n/a	n/a
Florida	n/a	n/a
Georgia	266	30
Hawaii	263	32
Idaho	278	14
Illinois	277	16
Indiana	283	5
Iowa	n/a	n/a
Kansas	284	3
Kentucky	272	25
Louisiana	259	38
Maine	284	3
Maryland	276	19
Massachusetts	283	5
Michigan	278	14
Minnesota	288	1
Mississippi	254	39
Missouri	274	23
Montana	287	2
Nebraska	281	11
Nevada	268	29
New Hampshire	n/a	n/a
New Jersey	n/a	n/a
New Mexico	260	37
New York	276	19
North Carolina	280	13
North Dakota	283	5
Ohio	283	5
Oklahoma	272	25
Oregon	281	11
Pennsylvania	n/a	n/a
Rhode Island	273	24
South Carolina	266	30
South Dakota	n/a	n/a
Tennessee	263	32
Texas	275	21
Utah	275	21
Vermont	283	5
Virginia	277	16
Washington	n/a	n/a
West Virginia	271	27
Wisconsin	n/a	n/a
Wyoming	277	16
50 States	n/a	
DC	234	
United States	274	

Rank in order by score

1	Minnesota
2	Montana
3	Kansas
3	Maine
5	Indiana
5	Massachusetts
5	North Dakota
5	Ohio
5	Vermont
10	Connecticut
11	Nebraska
11	Oregon
13	North Carolina
14	Idaho
14	Michigan
16	Illinois
16	Virginia
16	Wyoming
19	Maryland
19	New York
21	Texas
21	Utah
23	Missouri
24	Rhode Island
25	Kentucky
25	Oklahoma
27	Arizona
27	West Virginia
29	Nevada
30	Georgia
30	South Carolina
32	Hawaii
32	Tennessee
34	Alabama
34	California
36	Arkansas
37	New Mexico
38	Louisiana
39	Mississippi

Note: Ties in ranking reflect ties in actual values.

H-2 Average Proficiency in Science, Eighth Grade, 2000

State	Reading score	Rank
Alabama	141	33
Alaska	n/a	n/a
Arizona	146	26
Arkansas	143	30
California	132	37
Colorado	n/a	n/a
Connecticut	154	15
Delaware	n/a	n/a
Florida	n/a	n/a
Georgia	144	28
Hawaii	132	37
Idaho	159	8
Illinois	150	19
Indiana	156	11
Iowa	n/a	n/a
Kansas	n/a	n/a
Kentucky	152	17
Louisiana	136	35
Maine	160	6
Maryland	149	22
Massachusetts	161	2
Michigan	156	11
Minnesota	160	6
Mississippi	134	36
Missouri	156	11
Montana	165	1
Nebraska	157	10
Nevada	143	30
New Hampshire	n/a	n/a
New Jersey	n/a	n/a
New Mexico	140	34
New York	149	22
North Carolina	147	25
North Dakota	161	2
Ohio	161	2
Oklahoma	149	22
Oregon	154	15
Pennsylvania	n/a	n/a
Rhode Island	150	19
South Carolina	142	32
South Dakota	n/a	n/a
Tennessee	146	26
Texas	144	28
Utah	155	14
Vermont	161	2
Virginia	152	17
Washington	n/a	n/a
West Virginia	150	19
Wisconsin	n/a	n/a
Wyoming	158	9
50 States	n/a	
DC	n/a	
United States	149	

Rank in order by score

1	Montana
2	Massachusetts
2	North Dakota
2	Ohio
2	Vermont
6	Maine
6	Minnesota
8	Idaho
9	Wyoming
10	Nebraska
11	Indiana
11	Michigan
11	Missouri
14	Utah
15	Connecticut
15	Oregon
17	Kentucky
17	Virginia
19	Illinois
19	Rhode Island
19	West Virginia
22	Maryland
22	New York
22	Oklahoma
25	North Carolina
26	Arizona
26	Tennessee
28	Georgia
28	Texas
30	Arkansas
30	Nevada
32	South Carolina
33	Alabama
34	New Mexico
35	Louisiana
36	Mississippi
37	California
37	Hawaii

Note: Ties in ranking reflect ties in actual values.

State	AFQT rank	Rank
Alabama	56.6	44
Alaska	62.6	9
Arizona	60.0	23
Arkansas	56.5	45
California	57.7	38
Colorado	62.3	12
Connecticut	59.0	28
Delaware	58.1	36
Florida	58.6	30
Georgia	56.4	46
Hawaii	55.0	48
Idaho	62.2	13
Illinois	58.6	30
Indiana	61.9	16
Iowa	63.0	5
Kansas	60.8	19
Kentucky	56.9	42
Louisiana	54.8	49
Maine	62.2	13
Maryland	57.7	38
Massachusetts	60.2	21
Michigan	59.4	25
Minnesota	63.1	3
Mississippi	53.3	50
Missouri	59.3	27
Montana	62.6	9
Nebraska	61.8	17
Nevada	60.5	20
New Hampshire	64.0	2
New Jersey	57.5	40
New Mexico	57.4	41
New York	58.2	35
North Carolina	58.4	33
North Dakota	63.1	3
Ohio	59.7	24
Oklahoma	58.6	30
Oregon	63.0	5
Pennsylvania	60.1	22
Rhode Island	58.9	29
South Carolina	55.6	47
South Dakota	62.4	11
Tennessee	59.4	25
Texas	58.4	33
Utah	62.1	15
Vermont	62.9	8
Virginia	58.0	37
Washington	63.0	5
West Virginia	56.7	43
Wisconsin	64.1	1
Wyoming	61.1	18
50 States	58.8	
DC	52.3	
United States	58.8	

Rank in order by rank	
1	Wisconsin
2	New Hampshire
3	Minnesota
3	North Dakota
5	Iowa
5	Oregon
5	Washington
8	Vermont
9	Alaska
9	Montana
11	South Dakota
12	Colorado
13	Idaho
13	Maine
15	Utah
16	Indiana
17	Nebraska
18	Wyoming
19	Kansas
20	Nevada
21	Massachusetts
22	Pennsylvania
23	Arizona
24	Ohio
25	Michigan
25	Tennessee
27	Missouri
28	Connecticut
29	Rhode Island
30	Florida
30	Illinois
30	Oklahoma
33	North Carolina
33	Texas
35	New York
36	Delaware
37	Virginia
38	California
38	Maryland
40	New Jersey
41	New Mexico
42	Kentucky
43	West Virginia
44	Alabama
45	Arkansas
46	Georgia
47	South Carolina
48	Hawaii
49	Louisiana
50	Mississippi

Note: Ties in ranking reflect ties in actual values.

H-4 SAT Scores, 2002

State	Average SAT score	Percentage of graduates tested	Rank by score
Alabama	n/a	n/a	n/a
Alaska	1,035	52	5
Arizona	1,043	36	3
Arkansas	n/a	n/a	n/a
California	1,013	52	11
Colorado	n/a	n/a	n/a
Connecticut	1,018	83	9
Delaware	1,002	69	16
Florida	995	57	21
Georgia	980	65	24
Hawaii	1,008	53	13
Idaho	n/a	n/a	n/a
Illinois	n/a	n/a	n/a
Indiana	1,001	62	17
Iowa	n/a	n/a	n/a
Kansas	n/a	n/a	n/a
Kentucky	n/a	n/a	n/a
Louisiana	n/a	n/a	n/a
Maine	1,005	69	15
Maryland	1,020	67	8
Massachusetts	1,028	81	6
Michigan	n/a	n/a	n/a
Minnesota	n/a	n/a	n/a
Mississippi	n/a	n/a	n/a
Missouri	n/a	n/a	n/a
Montana	n/a	n/a	n/a
Nebraska	n/a	n/a	n/a
Nevada	n/a	n/a	n/a
New Hampshire	1,038	73	4
New Jersey	1,011	82	12
New Mexico	n/a	n/a	n/a
New York	1,000	79	18
North Carolina	998	67	19
North Dakota	n/a	n/a	n/a
Ohio	n/a	n/a	n/a
Oklahoma	n/a	n/a	n/a
Oregon	1,052	56	2
Pennsylvania	998	72	19
Rhode Island	1,007	73	14
South Carolina	981	59	23
South Dakota	n/a	n/a	n/a
Tennessee	n/a	n/a	n/a
Texas	991	55	22
Utah	n/a	n/a	n/a
Vermont	1,022	69	7
Virginia	1,016	68	10
Washington	1,054	54	1
West Virginia	n/a	n/a	n/a
Wisconsin	n/a	n/a	n/a
Wyoming	n/a	n/a	n/a
50 States	n/a	n/a	
DC	953	76	
United States	1,020	46	

Rank in order by score

1. Washington
2. Oregon
3. Arizona
4. New Hampshire
5. Alaska
6. Massachusetts
7. Vermont
8. Maryland
9. Connecticut
10. Virginia
11. California
12. New Jersey
13. Hawaii
14. Rhode Island
15. Maine
16. Delaware
17. Indiana
18. New York
19. North Carolina
19. Pennsylvania
21. Florida
22. Texas
23. South Carolina
24. Georgia

Note: Ties in ranking reflect ties in actual values.

H-5 ACT Scores, 2002

State	ACT composite scores	Percentage of graduates tested	Rank by score
Alabama	20.1	71	19
Alaska	n/a	n/a	n/a
Arizona	n/a	n/a	n/a
Arkansas	20.2	72	18
California	n/a	n/a	n/a
Colorado	20.1	99	19
Connecticut	n/a	n/a	n/a
Delaware	n/a	n/a	n/a
Florida	n/a	n/a	n/a
Georgia	n/a	n/a	n/a
Hawaii	n/a	n/a	n/a
Idaho	21.2	57	14
Illinois	20.1	99	19
Indiana	n/a	n/a	n/a
Iowa	22.0	66	3
Kansas	21.6	76	6
Kentucky	20.0	72	22
Louisiana	19.6	79	25
Maine	n/a	n/a	n/a
Maryland	n/a	n/a	n/a
Massachusetts	n/a	n/a	n/a
Michigan	21.3	68	12
Minnesota	22.1	65	2
Mississippi	18.6	84	26
Missouri	21.5	68	7
Montana	21.7	52	4
Nebraska	21.7	72	4
Nevada	21.3	36	12
New Hampshire	n/a	n/a	n/a
New Jersey	n/a	n/a	n/a
New Mexico	20.0	63	22
New York	n/a	n/a	n/a
North Carolina	n/a	n/a	n/a
North Dakota	21.2	78	14
Ohio	21.4	62	8
Oklahoma	20.5	69	16
Oregon	n/a	n/a	n/a
Pennsylvania	n/a	n/a	n/a
Rhode Island	n/a	n/a	n/a
South Carolina	n/a	n/a	n/a
South Dakota	21.4	71	8
Tennessee	20.0	79	22
Texas	n/a	n/a	n/a
Utah	21.4	66	8
Vermont	n/a	n/a	n/a
Virginia	n/a	n/a	n/a
Washington	n/a	n/a	n/a
West Virginia	20.3	61	17
Wisconsin	22.2	68	1
Wyoming	21.4	64	8
50 States	n/a	n/a	
DC	n/a	n/a	
United States	20.8	39	

Rank in order by score

1	Wisconsin
2	Minnesota
3	Iowa
4	Montana
4	Nebraska
6	Kansas
7	Missouri
8	Ohio
8	South Dakota
8	Utah
8	Wyoming
12	Michigan
12	Nevada
14	Idaho
14	North Dakota
16	Oklahoma
17	West Virginia
18	Arkansas
19	Alabama
19	Colorado
19	Illinois
22	Kentucky
22	New Mexico
22	Tennessee
25	Louisiana
26	Mississippi

Note: Ties in ranking reflect ties in actual values.

H-6 Percentage of Population Over 25 with a High School Diploma, 2000

State	High school graduates %	Rank by percentage
Alabama	77.5	49
Alaska	90.4	5
Arizona	85.1	31
Arkansas	81.7	40
California	81.2	42
Colorado	89.7	9
Connecticut	88.2	13
Delaware	86.1	25
Florida	84.0	34
Georgia	82.6	37
Hawaii	87.4	17
Idaho	86.2	23
Illinois	85.5	29
Indiana	84.6	33
Iowa	89.7	9
Kansas	88.1	14
Kentucky	78.7	48
Louisiana	80.8	43
Maine	89.3	12
Maryland	85.7	27
Massachusetts	85.1	31
Michigan	86.2	23
Minnesota	90.8	3
Mississippi	80.3	44
Missouri	86.6	21
Montana	89.6	11
Nebraska	90.4	5
Nevada	82.8	36
New Hampshire	88.1	14
New Jersey	87.3	18
New Mexico	82.2	39
New York	82.5	38
North Carolina	79.2	46
North Dakota	85.5	29
Ohio	87.0	19
Oklahoma	86.1	25
Oregon	88.1	14
Pennsylvania	85.7	27
Rhode Island	81.3	41
South Carolina	83.0	35
South Dakota	91.8	1
Tennessee	79.9	45
Texas	79.2	46
Utah	90.7	4
Vermont	90.0	7
Virginia	86.6	21
Washington	91.8	1
West Virginia	77.1	50
Wisconsin	86.7	20
Wyoming	90.0	7
50 States	n/a	
DC	83.2	
United States	84.1	

Rank in order by percentage

1	South Dakota
1	Washington
3	Minnesota
4	Utah
5	Alaska
5	Nebraska
7	Vermont
7	Wyoming
9	Colorado
9	Iowa
11	Montana
12	Maine
13	Connecticut
14	Kansas
14	New Hampshire
14	Oregon
17	Hawaii
18	New Jersey
19	Ohio
20	Wisconsin
21	Missouri
21	Virginia
23	Idaho
23	Michigan
25	Delaware
25	Oklahoma
27	Maryland
27	Pennsylvania
29	Illinois
29	North Dakota
31	Arizona
31	Massachusetts
33	Indiana
34	Florida
35	South Carolina
36	Nevada
37	Georgia
38	New York
39	New Mexico
40	Arkansas
41	Rhode Island
42	California
43	Louisiana
44	Mississippi
45	Tennessee
46	North Carolina
46	Texas
48	Kentucky
49	Alabama
50	West Virginia

Note: Ties in ranking reflect ties in actual values.

H-7 Students in Private Schools, 1999-2000

State	Private school enrollment	As a percentage of total enrollment	Rank by percentage
Alabama	73,352	9.1	26
Alaska	6,172	4.3	46
Arizona	44,060	4.9	44
Arkansas	26,424	5.6	40
California	619,067	9.4	23
Colorado	52,142	6.9	36
Connecticut	70,058	11.2	15
Delaware	22,779	16.7	1
Florida	290,872	10.9	16
Georgia	116,407	7.6	33
Hawaii	32,193	14.8	4
Idaho	10,209	4.0	48
Illinois	299,871	12.9	10
Indiana	105,533	9.7	21
Iowa	49,565	9.1	27
Kansas	43,113	8.4	28
Kentucky	75,084	10.6	17
Louisiana	138,135	15.5	3
Maine	18,287	8.0	30
Maryland	144,131	14.5	5
Massachusetts	132,154	12.0	14
Michigan	179,579	9.5	22
Minnesota	92,795	9.7	20
Mississippi	51,369	9.3	25
Missouri	122,387	12.0	13
Montana	8,711	5.2	42
Nebraska	42,141	12.8	11
Nevada	13,926	4.1	47
New Hampshire	23,383	10.2	19
New Jersey	198,631	13.7	8
New Mexico	23,055	6.6	38
New York	475,942	14.3	6
North Carolina	96,262	7.2	34
North Dakota	7,148	5.8	39
Ohio	254,494	12.3	12
Oklahoma	31,276	4.8	45
Oregon	45,352	7.7	32
Pennsylvania	339,484	15.7	2
Rhode Island	24,738	13.7	7
South Carolina	55,612	7.8	31
South Dakota	9,364	6.8	37
Tennessee	93,680	9.4	24
Texas	227,645	5.4	41
Utah	12,614	2.6	49
Vermont	12,170	10.4	18
Virginia	100,171	8.1	29
Washington	76,885	7.1	35
West Virginia	15,895	5.2	43
Wisconsin	139,455	13.7	9
Wyoming	2,221	2.4	50
50 States	5,145,994	10.0	
DC	16,690	17.8	
United States	5,162,684	10.0	

Rank in order by percentage

1 Delaware
2 Pennsylvania
3 Louisiana
4 Hawaii
5 Maryland
6 New York
7 Rhode Island
8 New Jersey
9 Wisconsin
10 Illinois
11 Nebraska
12 Ohio
13 Missouri
14 Massachusetts
15 Connecticut
16 Florida
17 Kentucky
18 Vermont
19 New Hampshire
20 Minnesota
21 Indiana
22 Michigan
23 California
24 Tennessee
25 Mississippi
26 Alabama
27 Iowa
28 Kansas
29 Virginia
30 Maine
31 South Carolina
32 Oregon
33 Georgia
34 North Carolina
35 Washington
36 Colorado
37 South Dakota
38 New Mexico
39 North Dakota
40 Arkansas
41 Texas
42 Montana
43 West Virginia
44 Arizona
45 Oklahoma
46 Alaska
47 Nevada
48 Idaho
49 Utah
50 Wyoming

Note: Numbers that appear to be identical are rounded and vary slightly in actual value. The rankings reflect the actual values before rounding. See the introduction for more details.

H-8 High School Completion Rates, 1998-2000

State	Percentage of 18 to 24 year-olds completing high school	Rank
Alabama	81.6	46
Alaska	93.3	3
Arizona	73.5	50
Arkansas	84.1	39
California	82.5	42
Colorado	81.6	46
Connecticut	91.7	8
Delaware	91.0	11
Florida	84.6	38
Georgia	83.5	40
Hawaii	91.8	7
Idaho	86.4	31
Illinois	87.1	29
Indiana	89.4	20
Iowa	90.8	13
Kansas	90.4	15
Kentucky	86.2	33
Louisiana	82.1	45
Maine	94.5	1
Maryland	87.4	26
Massachusetts	90.9	12
Michigan	89.2	21
Minnesota	91.9	6
Mississippi	82.3	43
Missouri	92.6	4
Montana	91.1	10
Nebraska	91.3	9
Nevada	77.9	49
New Hampshire	85.1	36
New Jersey	90.1	16
New Mexico	83.0	41
New York	86.3	32
North Carolina	86.1	34
North Dakota	94.4	2
Ohio	87.7	25
Oklahoma	85.7	35
Oregon	82.3	43
Pennsylvania	89.0	22
Rhode Island	87.9	24
South Carolina	85.1	36
South Dakota	92.0	5
Tennessee	89.0	22
Texas	79.4	48
Utah	90.0	17
Vermont	90.8	13
Virginia	87.3	28
Washington	87.4	26
West Virginia	89.6	19
Wisconsin	90.0	17
Wyoming	86.5	30
50 States	n/a	
DC	88.0	
United States	85.7	

Rank in order by percentage	
1	Maine
2	North Dakota
3	Alaska
4	Missouri
5	South Dakota
6	Minnesota
7	Hawaii
8	Connecticut
9	Nebraska
10	Montana
11	Delaware
12	Massachusetts
13	Iowa
13	Vermont
15	Kansas
16	New Jersey
17	Utah
17	Wisconsin
19	West Virginia
20	Indiana
21	Michigan
22	Pennsylvania
22	Tennessee
24	Rhode Island
25	Ohio
26	Maryland
26	Washington
28	Virginia
29	Illinois
30	Wyoming
31	Idaho
32	New York
33	Kentucky
34	North Carolina
35	Oklahoma
36	New Hampshire
36	South Carolina
38	Florida
39	Arkansas
40	Georgia
41	New Mexico
42	California
43	Mississippi
43	Oregon
45	Louisiana
46	Alabama
46	Colorado
48	Texas
49	Nevada
50	Arizona

Note: Ties in ranking reflect ties in actual values.

H-9 Pupil-Teacher Ratio, 2001-2002

State	Pupils per teacher in public K-12 schools	Rank by ratio
Alabama	15.1	25
Alaska	16.9	12
Arizona	21.1	1
Arkansas	14.6	32
California	20.8	3
Colorado	17.1	11
Connecticut	13.7	39
Delaware	15.2	23
Florida	18.2	7
Georgia	15.8	18
Hawaii	16.5	14
Idaho	17.5	9
Illinois	15.9	17
Indiana	16.7	13
Iowa	14.0	38
Kansas	14.2	36
Kentucky	16.5	14
Louisiana	14.6	32
Maine	12.9	47
Maryland	16.1	16
Massachusetts	17.9	8
Michigan	17.2	10
Minnesota	14.8	30
Mississippi	15.8	18
Missouri	13.7	39
Montana	14.6	32
Nebraska	13.7	39
Nevada	19.0	5
New Hampshire	14.5	35
New Jersey	13.0	45
New Mexico	15.2	23
New York	13.6	44
North Carolina	15.8	18
North Dakota	13.7	39
Ohio	15.1	25
Oklahoma	15.0	27
Oregon	18.9	6
Pennsylvania	15.4	22
Rhode Island	12.2	49
South Carolina	15.0	27
South Dakota	13.7	39
Tennessee	15.6	21
Texas	14.7	31
Utah	21.1	1
Vermont	11.5	50
Virginia	12.7	48
Washington	19.6	4
West Virginia	14.1	37
Wisconsin	14.9	29
Wyoming	13.0	45
50 States	n/a	
DC	14.0	
United States	16.0	

Rank in order by ratio

1	Arizona
1	Utah
3	California
4	Washington
5	Nevada
6	Oregon
7	Florida
8	Massachusetts
9	Idaho
10	Michigan
11	Colorado
12	Alaska
13	Indiana
14	Hawaii
14	Kentucky
16	Maryland
17	Illinois
18	Georgia
18	Mississippi
18	North Carolina
21	Tennessee
22	Pennsylvania
23	Delaware
23	New Mexico
25	Alabama
25	Ohio
27	Oklahoma
27	South Carolina
29	Wisconsin
30	Minnesota
31	Texas
32	Arkansas
32	Louisiana
32	Montana
35	New Hampshire
36	Kansas
37	West Virginia
38	Iowa
39	Connecticut
39	Missouri
39	Nebraska
39	North Dakota
39	South Dakota
44	New York
45	New Jersey
45	Wyoming
47	Maine
48	Virginia
49	Rhode Island
50	Vermont

Note: Ties in ranking reflect ties in actual values.

H-10 Public School Enrollment, 2001-2002

State	Enrollment (in thousands)	As a percentage of total population	Rank by percentage
Alabama	726	16.3	32
Alaska	134	21.2	1
Arizona	918	17.3	13
Arkansas	446	16.6	26
California	6,141	17.8	6
Colorado	742	16.8	20
Connecticut	570	16.6	21
Delaware	115	14.5	50
Florida	2,496	15.2	45
Georgia	1,471	17.5	8
Hawaii	185	15.1	46
Idaho	246	18.6	4
Illinois	2,069	16.6	24
Indiana	996	16.3	30
Iowa	486	16.6	22
Kansas	468	17.4	11
Kentucky	631	15.5	43
Louisiana	730	16.4	29
Maine	206	16.0	36
Maryland	864	16.1	35
Massachusetts	973	15.3	44
Michigan	1,735	17.4	12
Minnesota	858	17.3	14
Mississippi	492	17.2	15
Missouri	890	15.8	40
Montana	152	16.8	19
Nebraska	284	16.6	25
Nevada	357	16.9	17
New Hampshire	212	16.8	18
New Jersey	1,342	15.8	41
New Mexico	320	17.5	9
New York	2,840	14.9	47
North Carolina	1,322	16.1	33
North Dakota	111	17.5	10
Ohio	1,805	15.9	38
Oklahoma	622	18.0	5
Oregon	552	15.9	37
Pennsylvania	1,822	14.8	49
Rhode Island	158	14.9	48
South Carolina	670	16.5	27
South Dakota	126	16.6	23
Tennessee	908	15.8	39
Texas	4,147	19.4	3
Utah	478	21.1	2
Vermont	101	16.5	28
Virginia	1,158	16.1	34
Washington	1,028	17.2	16
West Virginia	282	15.7	42
Wisconsin	879	16.3	31
Wyoming	88	17.8	7
50 States	47,348	16.7	
DC	68	12.0	
United States	47,416	16.6	

Rank in order by percentage	
1	Alaska
2	Utah
3	Texas
4	Idaho
5	Oklahoma
6	California
7	Wyoming
8	Georgia
9	New Mexico
10	North Dakota
11	Kansas
12	Michigan
13	Arizona
14	Minnesota
15	Mississippi
16	Washington
17	Nevada
18	New Hampshire
19	Montana
20	Colorado
21	Connecticut
22	Iowa
23	South Dakota
24	Illinois
25	Nebraska
26	Arkansas
27	South Carolina
28	Vermont
29	Louisiana
30	Indiana
31	Wisconsin
32	Alabama
33	North Carolina
34	Virginia
35	Maryland
36	Maine
37	Oregon
38	Ohio
39	Tennessee
40	Missouri
41	New Jersey
42	West Virginia
43	Kentucky
44	Massachusetts
45	Florida
46	Hawaii
47	New York
48	Rhode Island
49	Pennsylvania
50	Delaware

Note: Numbers that appear to be identical are rounded and vary slightly in actual value. The rankings reflect the actual values before rounding. See the introduction for more details.

H-11 Public Library Holdings Per Capita, FY 2000

State	Holdings per capita	Rank per capita
Alabama	2.0	41
Alaska	3.5	19
Arizona	1.8	48
Arkansas	2.2	36
California	1.9	45
Colorado	2.6	32
Connecticut	4.3	9
Delaware	2.2	36
Florida	1.8	48
Georgia	1.9	45
Hawaii	2.7	27
Idaho	3.2	21
Illinois	3.8	17
Indiana	4.2	11
Iowa	4.0	14
Kansas	4.7	6
Kentucky	2.0	41
Louisiana	2.4	34
Maine	4.9	3
Maryland	3.0	23
Massachusetts	4.9	3
Michigan	2.9	25
Minnesota	3.2	21
Mississippi	2.0	41
Missouri	4.8	5
Montana	3.0	23
Nebraska	4.0	14
Nevada	2.2	36
New Hampshire	4.5	8
New Jersey	3.7	18
New Mexico	2.7	27
New York	4.6	7
North Carolina	2.0	41
North Dakota	3.9	16
Ohio	4.2	11
Oklahoma	2.2	36
Oregon	2.7	27
Pennsylvania	2.3	35
Rhode Island	4.1	13
South Carolina	2.1	40
South Dakota	4.3	9
Tennessee	1.8	48
Texas	1.9	45
Utah	2.6	32
Vermont	5.1	1
Virginia	2.7	27
Washington	2.9	25
West Virginia	2.7	27
Wisconsin	3.4	20
Wyoming	5.0	2
50 States	n/a	
DC	4.2	
United States	2.9	

Rank in order per capita

1	Vermont
2	Wyoming
3	Maine
3	Massachusetts
5	Missouri
6	Kansas
7	New York
8	New Hampshire
9	Connecticut
9	South Dakota
11	Indiana
11	Ohio
13	Rhode Island
14	Iowa
14	Nebraska
16	North Dakota
17	Illinois
18	New Jersey
19	Alaska
20	Wisconsin
21	Idaho
21	Minnesota
23	Maryland
23	Montana
25	Michigan
25	Washington
27	Hawaii
27	New Mexico
27	Oregon
27	Virginia
27	West Virginia
32	Colorado
32	Utah
34	Louisiana
35	Pennsylvania
36	Arkansas
36	Delaware
36	Nevada
36	Oklahoma
40	South Carolina
41	Alabama
41	Kentucky
41	Mississippi
41	North Carolina
45	California
45	Georgia
45	Texas
48	Arizona
48	Florida
48	Tennessee

Note: Ties in ranking reflect ties in actual values.

H-12 Children with Disabilities, 1999-2000

State	Children with disabilities #	Percentage of public school enrollment	Rank by percentage
Alabama	99,763	13.7	24
Alaska	17,495	12.8	32
Arizona	93,336	10.7	49
Arkansas	60,864	14.3	18
California	640,815	10.6	50
Colorado	76,948	10.9	48
Connecticut	74,722	13.5	27
Delaware	16,287	14.3	16
Florida	356,198	15.0	11
Georgia	164,374	11.6	46
Hawaii	22,964	12.4	39
Idaho	29,112	11.9	43
Illinois	291,221	14.3	17
Indiana	151,599	15.3	8
Iowa	71,970	14.4	14
Kansas	60,036	12.8	33
Kentucky	91,537	14.4	15
Louisiana	96,632	13.6	25
Maine	35,139	16.0	6
Maryland	111,711	13.2	29
Massachusetts	165,013	16.9	3
Michigan	213,404	12.5	37
Minnesota	107,942	12.6	35
Mississippi	62,359	12.5	36
Missouri	134,950	15.1	9
Montana	19,039	12.1	42
Nebraska	42,577	14.8	12
Nevada	35,703	10.9	47
New Hampshire	28,597	13.7	23
New Jersey	214,330	16.6	4
New Mexico	52,346	16.1	5
New York	434,347	15.1	10
North Carolina	173,067	13.8	22
North Dakota	13,612	12.2	41
Ohio	236,200	12.9	31
Oklahoma	83,149	13.1	30
Oregon	73,531	13.5	26
Pennsylvania	231,175	12.7	34
Rhode Island	29,895	19.1	1
South Carolina	103,153	15.9	7
South Dakota	16,246	12.4	38
Tennessee	126,732	13.9	20
Texas	493,850	12.3	40
Utah	55,389	11.6	45
Vermont	14,073	13.3	28
Virginia	161,298	14.2	19
Washington	116,235	11.6	44
West Virginia	50,314	17.3	2
Wisconsin	121,209	13.8	21
Wyoming	13,307	14.5	13
50 States	6,185,765	13.2	
DC	9,348	13.2	
United States	6,195,113	13.2	

Rank in order by percentage

1	Rhode Island
2	West Virginia
3	Massachusetts
4	New Jersey
5	New Mexico
6	Maine
7	South Carolina
8	Indiana
9	Missouri
10	New York
11	Florida
12	Nebraska
13	Wyoming
14	Iowa
15	Kentucky
16	Delaware
17	Illinois
18	Arkansas
19	Virginia
20	Tennessee
21	Wisconsin
22	North Carolina
23	New Hampshire
24	Alabama
25	Louisiana
26	Oregon
27	Connecticut
28	Vermont
29	Maryland
30	Oklahoma
31	Ohio
32	Alaska
33	Kansas
34	Pennsylvania
35	Minnesota
36	Mississippi
37	Michigan
38	South Dakota
39	Hawaii
40	Texas
41	North Dakota
42	Montana
43	Idaho
44	Washington
45	Utah
46	Georgia
47	Nevada
48	Colorado
49	Arizona
50	California

Note: Numbers that appear to be identical are rounded and vary slightly in actual value. The rankings reflect the actual values before rounding. See the introduction for more details.

H-13 State and Local Education Spending, FY 2000

State	Education spending $ (in millions)	Education spending per capita	Education spending as a percentage of personal income	Rank per capita
Alabama	7,768	1,747	7.7	36
Alaska	1,761	2,808	9.9	1
Arizona	7,871	1,534	6.5	46
Arkansas	4,198	1,570	7.4	45
California	63,559	1,876	6.4	22
Colorado	7,904	1,838	6.2	24
Connecticut	6,722	1,974	5.2	12
Delaware	1,715	2,188	7.4	5
Florida	22,826	1,428	5.4	50
Georgia	14,768	1,804	6.9	29
Hawaii	1,854	1,530	5.7	47
Idaho	2,132	1,648	7.5	41
Illinois	22,728	1,830	6.0	25
Indiana	11,450	1,883	7.4	20
Iowa	5,964	2,038	8.1	10
Kansas	4,884	1,817	6.9	27
Kentucky	6,374	1,577	6.9	44
Louisiana	7,185	1,608	7.2	43
Maine	2,228	1,747	7.2	35
Maryland	10,055	1,899	6.0	16
Massachusetts	11,445	1,803	5.2	30
Michigan	22,484	2,262	8.1	3
Minnesota	10,283	2,090	7.0	9
Mississippi	4,818	1,694	8.4	37
Missouri	9,224	1,649	6.4	40
Montana	1,641	1,819	8.4	26
Nebraska	3,267	1,909	7.2	15
Nevada	3,020	1,512	5.4	48
New Hampshire	2,059	1,666	5.5	39
New Jersey	18,788	2,233	6.5	4
New Mexico	3,696	2,032	9.7	11
New York	40,630	2,141	6.6	7
North Carolina	14,164	1,760	7.1	33
North Dakota	1,255	1,954	8.5	14
Ohio	20,612	1,816	6.7	28
Oklahoma	5,836	1,691	7.6	38
Oregon	6,448	1,885	7.2	19
Pennsylvania	23,256	1,894	6.8	18
Rhode Island	1,857	1,772	6.4	32
South Carolina	7,126	1,776	7.8	31
South Dakota	1,218	1,613	6.6	42
Tennessee	8,369	1,471	6.0	49
Texas	39,217	1,881	7.3	21
Utah	4,233	1,896	8.5	17
Vermont	1,330	2,185	8.7	6
Virginia	13,132	1,855	6.4	23
Washington	11,565	1,962	6.6	13
West Virginia	3,171	1,754	8.4	34
Wisconsin	11,427	2,130	8.0	8
Wyoming	1,125	2,277	8.9	2
50 States	520,643	1,854	6.7	
DC	969	1,695	4.7	
United States	521,612	1,853	6.7	

Rank in order per capita

1	Alaska
2	Wyoming
3	Michigan
4	New Jersey
5	Delaware
6	Vermont
7	New York
8	Wisconsin
9	Minnesota
10	Iowa
11	New Mexico
12	Connecticut
13	Washington
14	North Dakota
15	Nebraska
16	Maryland
17	Utah
18	Pennsylvania
19	Oregon
20	Indiana
21	Texas
22	California
23	Virginia
24	Colorado
25	Illinois
26	Montana
27	Kansas
28	Ohio
29	Georgia
30	Massachusetts
31	South Carolina
32	Rhode Island
33	North Carolina
34	West Virginia
35	Maine
36	Alabama
37	Mississippi
38	Oklahoma
39	New Hampshire
40	Missouri
41	Idaho
42	South Dakota
43	Louisiana
44	Kentucky
45	Arkansas
46	Arizona
47	Hawaii
48	Nevada
49	Tennessee
50	Florida

H-14 State and Local Education Spending as a Percentage of General Spending, FY 2000

State	Education spending as a percentage of general spending	Rank by percentage
Alabama	35.2	27
Alaska	23.2	50
Arizona	33.8	34
Arkansas	38.0	11
California	32.5	40
Colorado	35.1	29
Connecticut	31.4	44
Delaware	36.6	19
Florida	30.3	46
Georgia	38.8	7
Hawaii	25.4	49
Idaho	36.6	18
Illinois	35.3	26
Indiana	39.8	4
Iowa	38.3	10
Kansas	37.9	12
Kentucky	33.5	36
Louisiana	32.3	41
Maine	32.0	42
Maryland	36.6	16
Massachusetts	30.3	47
Michigan	41.1	2
Minnesota	33.0	39
Mississippi	34.6	31
Missouri	37.2	14
Montana	36.3	22
Nebraska	38.9	6
Nevada	31.0	45
New Hampshire	36.4	21
New Jersey	39.8	5
New Mexico	36.6	17
New York	29.0	48
North Carolina	35.0	30
North Dakota	34.2	33
Ohio	35.8	23
Oklahoma	42.4	1
Oregon	32.0	43
Pennsylvania	35.3	25
Rhode Island	33.4	37
South Carolina	35.2	28
South Dakota	35.4	24
Tennessee	33.1	38
Texas	41.0	3
Utah	38.4	9
Vermont	38.6	8
Virginia	37.8	13
Washington	34.5	32
West Virginia	36.4	20
Wisconsin	37.1	15
Wyoming	33.8	35
50 States	34.8	
DC	18.8	
United States	34.7	

Rank in order by percentage

1. Oklahoma
2. Michigan
3. Texas
4. Indiana
5. New Jersey
6. Nebraska
7. Georgia
8. Vermont
9. Utah
10. Iowa
11. Arkansas
12. Kansas
13. Virginia
14. Missouri
15. Wisconsin
16. Maryland
17. New Mexico
18. Idaho
19. Delaware
20. West Virginia
21. New Hampshire
22. Montana
23. Ohio
24. South Dakota
25. Pennsylvania
26. Illinois
27. Alabama
28. South Carolina
29. Colorado
30. North Carolina
31. Mississippi
32. Washington
33. North Dakota
34. Arizona
35. Wyoming
36. Kentucky
37. Rhode Island
38. Tennessee
39. Minnesota
40. California
41. Louisiana
42. Maine
43. Oregon
44. Connecticut
45. Nevada
46. Florida
47. Massachusetts
48. New York
49. Hawaii
50. Alaska

Note: Numbers that appear to be identical are rounded and vary slightly in actual value. The rankings reflect the actual values before rounding. See the introduction for more details.

H-15 Spending Per Pupil, 2001-2002

State	Spending per pupil $	Rank
Alabama	5,210	47
Alaska	9,447	6
Arizona	5,084	48
Arkansas	5,684	46
California	6,816	28
Colorado	6,659	34
Connecticut	10,825	3
Delaware	9,677	5
Florida	6,254	40
Georgia	7,620	19
Hawaii	6,676	33
Idaho	5,965	42
Illinois	8,906	10
Indiana	7,866	16
Iowa	6,691	32
Kansas	6,806	29
Kentucky	7,047	25
Louisiana	6,140	41
Maine	8,945	9
Maryland	7,652	18
Massachusetts	9,831	4
Michigan	7,461	20
Minnesota	8,397	12
Mississippi	5,699	44
Missouri	6,639	35
Montana	7,130	24
Nebraska	6,782	30
Nevada	5,813	43
New Hampshire	7,152	23
New Jersey	10,869	2
New Mexico	6,705	31
New York	11,021	1
North Carolina	6,364	39
North Dakota	4,374	50
Ohio	7,204	21
Oklahoma	6,436	37
Oregon	7,856	17
Pennsylvania	8,070	14
Rhode Island	9,394	7
South Carolina	7,012	26
South Dakota	6,574	36
Tennessee	5,693	45
Texas	6,850	27
Utah	4,674	49
Vermont	9,248	8
Virginia	6,371	38
Washington	7,157	22
West Virginia	8,245	13
Wisconsin	8,617	11
Wyoming	7,873	15
50 States	n/a	
DC	13,078	
United States	7,463	

Rank in order by $

1 New York
2 New Jersey
3 Connecticut
4 Massachusetts
5 Delaware
6 Alaska
7 Rhode Island
8 Vermont
9 Maine
10 Illinois
11 Wisconsin
12 Minnesota
13 West Virginia
14 Pennsylvania
15 Wyoming
16 Indiana
17 Oregon
18 Maryland
19 Georgia
20 Michigan
21 Ohio
22 Washington
23 New Hampshire
24 Montana
25 Kentucky
26 South Carolina
27 Texas
28 California
29 Kansas
30 Nebraska
31 New Mexico
32 Iowa
33 Hawaii
34 Colorado
35 Missouri
36 South Dakota
37 Oklahoma
38 Virginia
39 North Carolina
40 Florida
41 Louisiana
42 Idaho
43 Nevada
44 Mississippi
45 Tennessee
46 Arkansas
47 Alabama
48 Arizona
49 Utah
50 North Dakota

H-16 Average Teacher Salary, 2001-2002

State	Average teacher salary $	Rank
Alabama	39,268	27
Alaska	49,418	9
Arizona	39,973	25
Arkansas	37,140	40
California	53,870	1
Colorado	40,222	24
Connecticut	53,551	2
Delaware	48,363	11
Florida	39,275	26
Georgia	44,073	16
Hawaii	42,615	20
Idaho	37,482	37
Illinois	50,000	7
Indiana	44,195	15
Iowa	38,230	33
Kansas	36,673	42
Kentucky	37,847	35
Louisiana	34,505	46
Maine	37,300	39
Maryland	46,200	12
Massachusetts	49,054	10
Michigan	52,037	4
Minnesota	43,330	19
Mississippi	32,800	48
Missouri	37,904	34
Montana	34,379	47
Nebraska	36,236	44
Nevada	44,738	14
New Hampshire	38,911	31
New Jersey	51,186	5
New Mexico	36,440	43
New York	53,081	3
North Carolina	41,991	22
North Dakota	31,709	49
Ohio	44,029	17
Oklahoma	34,744	45
Oregon	46,039	13
Pennsylvania	50,599	6
Rhode Island	49,758	8
South Carolina	38,943	30
South Dakota	31,295	50
Tennessee	38,554	32
Texas	39,232	29
Utah	37,414	38
Vermont	39,240	28
Virginia	41,262	23
Washington	43,474	18
West Virginia	36,751	41
Wisconsin	42,232	21
Wyoming	37,841	36
50 States	n/a	
DC	47,049	
United States	44,499	

Rank in order by $	
1	California
2	Connecticut
3	New York
4	Michigan
5	New Jersey
6	Pennsylvania
7	Illinois
8	Rhode Island
9	Alaska
10	Massachusetts
11	Delaware
12	Maryland
13	Oregon
14	Nevada
15	Indiana
16	Georgia
17	Ohio
18	Washington
19	Minnesota
20	Hawaii
21	Wisconsin
22	North Carolina
23	Virginia
24	Colorado
25	Arizona
26	Florida
27	Alabama
28	Vermont
29	Texas
30	South Carolina
31	New Hampshire
32	Tennessee
33	Iowa
34	Missouri
35	Kentucky
36	Wyoming
37	Idaho
38	Utah
39	Maine
40	Arkansas
41	West Virginia
42	Kansas
43	New Mexico
44	Nebraska
45	Oklahoma
46	Louisiana
47	Montana
48	Mississippi
49	North Dakota
50	South Dakota

H-17 Sources of School Funds, 2000-2001

State	Percentage from federal	Percentage from state	Percentage from local	Rank by percentage local
Alabama	10.3	63.4	26.2	43
Alaska	12.5	63.5	23.9	45
Arizona	6.2	52.9	40.9	29
Arkansas	8.2	62.2	29.6	38
California	9.6	61.1	29.4	39
Colorado	5.1	41.2	53.7	9
Connecticut	5.0	41.5	53.5	10
Delaware	8.2	66.9	25.0	44
Florida	8.9	48.4	42.6	24
Georgia	6.4	47.6	46.0	19
Hawaii	8.4	89.8	1.8	50
Idaho	7.2	60.0	32.8	34
Illinois	8.0	30.8	61.1	2
Indiana	5.2	52.2	42.6	24
Iowa	4.9	52.6	42.5	26
Kansas	6.3	62.5	31.2	35
Kentucky	7.7	62.9	29.4	39
Louisiana	11.7	48.6	39.8	30
Maine	7.3	47.9	44.8	20
Maryland	4.8	36.9	58.3	5
Massachusetts	5.4	45.3	49.4	16
Michigan	4.5	74.1	21.4	48
Minnesota	4.8	59.3	35.9	31
Mississippi	14.1	55.2	30.7	36
Missouri	7.1	37.1	55.8	6
Montana	11.1	44.9	44.1	21
Nebraska	5.5	40.7	53.8	8
Nevada	4.9	30.2	64.9	1
New Hampshire	4.3	44.1	51.7	11
New Jersey	3.0	37.3	59.8	3
New Mexico	13.2	74.1	12.6	49
New York	6.8	45.9	47.3	17
North Carolina	7.7	70.6	21.8	46
North Dakota	11.7	38.4	50.0	14
Ohio	6.0	43.3	50.8	12
Oklahoma	10.2	59.1	30.7	36
Oregon	6.9	57.3	35.8	32
Pennsylvania	5.2	40.4	54.4	7
Rhode Island	4.1	37.4	58.5	4
South Carolina	7.9	50.5	41.6	27
South Dakota	9.8	40.3	49.9	15
Tennessee	9.5	46.9	43.7	22
Texas	9.1	43.8	47.2	18
Utah	7.5	58.3	34.2	33
Vermont	6.0	72.3	21.8	46
Virginia	5.7	43.8	50.6	13
Washington	7.9	64.3	27.8	42
West Virginia	11.4	60.1	28.5	41
Wisconsin	4.8	54.0	41.3	28
Wyoming	8.4	48.8	42.8	23
50 States	n/a	n/a	n/a	
DC	12.0	n/a	88.0	
United States	7.3	50.2	42.5	

Rank in order by percentage local

1	Nevada
2	Illinois
3	New Jersey
4	Rhode Island
5	Maryland
6	Missouri
7	Pennsylvania
8	Nebraska
9	Colorado
10	Connecticut
11	New Hampshire
12	Ohio
13	Virginia
14	North Dakota
15	South Dakota
16	Massachusetts
17	New York
18	Texas
19	Georgia
20	Maine
21	Montana
22	Tennessee
23	Wyoming
24	Florida
24	Indiana
26	Iowa
27	South Carolina
28	Wisconsin
29	Arizona
30	Louisiana
31	Minnesota
32	Oregon
33	Utah
34	Idaho
35	Kansas
36	Mississippi
36	Oklahoma
38	Arkansas
39	California
39	Kentucky
41	West Virginia
42	Washington
43	Alabama
44	Delaware
45	Alaska
46	North Carolina
46	Vermont
48	Michigan
49	New Mexico
50	Hawaii

Note: Ties in ranking reflect ties in actual values.

H-18 State Aid Per Pupil in Average Daily Attendance, 2001-2002

State	State aid per pupil $ (in thousands)	Rank
Alabama	4,086	30
Alaska	6,921	4
Arizona	3,477	40
Arkansas	3,983	33
California	5,163	17
Colorado	3,369	42
Connecticut	5,043	19
Delaware	7,478	3
Florida	3,529	39
Georgia	4,509	23
Hawaii	8,995	1
Idaho	4,341	25
Illinois	3,264	44
Indiana	5,290	15
Iowa	4,166	28
Kansas	5,564	11
Kentucky	5,050	18
Louisiana	3,648	36
Maine	4,574	22
Maryland	3,321	43
Massachusetts	5,222	16
Michigan	6,342	5
Minnesota	6,164	7
Mississippi	3,640	37
Missouri	3,135	46
Montana	4,090	29
Nebraska	3,120	47
Nevada	2,229	50
New Hampshire	3,939	34
New Jersey	4,268	26
New Mexico	6,309	6
New York	5,561	12
North Carolina	5,647	8
North Dakota	2,720	49
Ohio	4,365	24
Oklahoma	4,077	32
Oregon	5,586	10
Pennsylvania	4,190	27
Rhode Island	3,595	38
South Carolina	4,840	21
South Dakota	2,838	48
Tennessee	3,195	45
Texas	3,420	41
Utah	3,731	35
Vermont	8,053	2
Virginia	4,083	31
Washington	5,525	14
West Virginia	5,620	9
Wisconsin	5,526	13
Wyoming	5,027	20
50 States	4,517	
DC	n/a	
United States	4,510	

Rank in order by $

1. Hawaii
2. Vermont
3. Delaware
4. Alaska
5. Michigan
6. New Mexico
7. Minnesota
8. North Carolina
9. West Virginia
10. Oregon
11. Kansas
12. New York
13. Wisconsin
14. Washington
15. Indiana
16. Massachusetts
17. California
18. Kentucky
19. Connecticut
20. Wyoming
21. South Carolina
22. Maine
23. Georgia
24. Ohio
25. Idaho
26. New Jersey
27. Pennsylvania
28. Iowa
29. Montana
30. Alabama
31. Virginia
32. Oklahoma
33. Arkansas
34. New Hampshire
35. Utah
36. Louisiana
37. Mississippi
38. Rhode Island
39. Florida
40. Arizona
41. Texas
42. Colorado
43. Maryland
44. Illinois
45. Tennessee
46. Missouri
47. Nebraska
48. South Dakota
49. North Dakota
50. Nevada

H-19 State and Local Spending for Higher Education, FY 2000

State	Higher education spending $ (in millions)	Per capita $	As a percentage of personal income	Rank per capita
Alabama	2,374	534	2.4	21
Alaska	375	598	2.1	12
Arizona	2,469	481	2.1	30
Arkansas	1,241	464	2.2	32
California	18,010	532	1.8	22
Colorado	2,514	584	2.0	15
Connecticut	1,196	351	0.9	46
Delaware	554	707	2.4	4
Florida	5,067	317	1.2	50
Georgia	3,363	411	1.6	39
Hawaii	689	569	2.1	16
Idaho	630	487	2.2	28
Illinois	5,050	407	1.3	41
Indiana	3,618	595	2.3	14
Iowa	2,032	694	2.8	5
Kansas	1,667	620	2.3	9
Kentucky	2,033	503	2.2	26
Louisiana	1,960	439	2.0	35
Maine	463	363	1.5	45
Maryland	2,892	546	1.7	20
Massachusetts	2,104	331	1.0	47
Michigan	6,850	689	2.5	6
Minnesota	2,613	531	1.8	23
Mississippi	1,562	549	2.7	19
Missouri	2,282	408	1.6	40
Montana	479	531	2.5	24
Nebraska	1,082	632	2.4	7
Nevada	657	329	1.2	48
New Hampshire	464	376	1.2	44
New Jersey	3,484	414	1.2	38
New Mexico	1,409	774	3.7	1
New York	6,095	321	1.0	49
North Carolina	4,492	558	2.3	18
North Dakota	461	718	3.1	3
Ohio	5,077	447	1.7	34
Oklahoma	1,782	516	2.3	25
Oregon	2,039	596	2.3	13
Pennsylvania	5,107	416	1.5	37
Rhode Island	401	383	1.4	43
South Carolina	1,944	484	2.1	29
South Dakota	305	404	1.7	42
Tennessee	2,379	418	1.7	36
Texas	9,795	470	1.8	31
Utah	1,631	731	3.3	2
Vermont	371	610	2.4	10
Virginia	3,502	495	1.7	27
Washington	3,334	566	1.9	17
West Virginia	837	463	2.2	33
Wisconsin	3,228	602	2.3	11
Wyoming	310	628	2.5	8
50 States	134,272	478	1.7	
DC	80	141	0.4	
United States	134,352	477	1.7	

Rank in order per capita

1. New Mexico
2. Utah
3. North Dakota
4. Delaware
5. Iowa
6. Michigan
7. Nebraska
8. Wyoming
9. Kansas
10. Vermont
11. Wisconsin
12. Alaska
13. Oregon
14. Indiana
15. Colorado
16. Hawaii
17. Washington
18. North Carolina
19. Mississippi
20. Maryland
21. Alabama
22. California
23. Minnesota
24. Montana
25. Oklahoma
26. Kentucky
27. Virginia
28. Idaho
29. South Carolina
30. Arizona
31. Texas
32. Arkansas
33. West Virginia
34. Ohio
35. Louisiana
36. Tennessee
37. Pennsylvania
38. New Jersey
39. Georgia
40. Missouri
41. Illinois
42. South Dakota
43. Rhode Island
44. New Hampshire
45. Maine
46. Connecticut
47. Massachusetts
48. Nevada
49. New York
50. Florida

Note: Numbers that appear to be identical are rounded and vary slightly in actual value. The rankings reflect the actual values before rounding. See the introduction for more details.

H-20 State and Local Spending for Higher Education as a Percentage of General Spending, FY 2000

State	Higher education spending as a percentage of general spending	Rank
Alabama	10.8	17
Alaska	4.9	49
Arizona	10.6	19
Arkansas	11.2	11
California	9.2	32
Colorado	11.2	13
Connecticut	5.6	47
Delaware	11.8	10
Florida	6.7	44
Georgia	8.8	35
Hawaii	9.5	29
Idaho	10.8	15
Illinois	7.8	40
Indiana	12.6	7
Iowa	13.1	3
Kansas	12.9	5
Kentucky	10.7	18
Louisiana	8.8	37
Maine	6.7	46
Maryland	10.5	21
Massachusetts	5.6	48
Michigan	12.5	9
Minnesota	8.4	38
Mississippi	11.2	12
Missouri	9.2	33
Montana	10.6	20
Nebraska	12.9	6
Nevada	6.7	45
New Hampshire	8.2	39
New Jersey	7.4	42
New Mexico	14.0	2
New York	4.4	50
North Carolina	11.1	14
North Dakota	12.6	8
Ohio	8.8	36
Oklahoma	12.9	4
Oregon	10.1	24
Pennsylvania	7.8	41
Rhode Island	7.2	43
South Carolina	9.6	28
South Dakota	8.9	34
Tennessee	9.4	30
Texas	10.2	23
Utah	14.8	1
Vermont	10.8	16
Virginia	10.1	25
Washington	10.0	26
West Virginia	9.6	27
Wisconsin	10.5	22
Wyoming	9.3	31
50 States	9.0	
DC	1.6	
United States	8.9	

Rank in order by percentage

1. Utah
2. New Mexico
3. Iowa
4. Oklahoma
5. Kansas
6. Nebraska
7. Indiana
8. North Dakota
9. Michigan
10. Delaware
11. Arkansas
12. Mississippi
13. Colorado
14. North Carolina
15. Idaho
16. Vermont
17. Alabama
18. Kentucky
19. Arizona
20. Montana
21. Maryland
22. Wisconsin
23. Texas
24. Oregon
25. Virginia
26. Washington
27. West Virginia
28. South Carolina
29. Hawaii
30. Tennessee
31. Wyoming
32. California
33. Missouri
34. South Dakota
35. Georgia
36. Ohio
37. Louisiana
38. Minnesota
39. New Hampshire
40. Illinois
41. Pennsylvania
42. New Jersey
43. Rhode Island
44. Florida
45. Nevada
46. Maine
47. Connecticut
48. Massachusetts
49. Alaska
50. New York

Note: Numbers that appear to be identical are rounded and vary slightly in actual value. The rankings reflect the actual values before rounding. See the introduction for more details.

H-21 Public Higher Education Enrollment, 2000

State	Higher education enrollment #	As a percentage of total population	Rank
Alabama	207,435	4.7	11
Alaska	26,559	4.2	25
Arizona	284,522	5.5	6
Arkansas	101,775	3.8	34
California	1,927,771	5.7	3
Colorado	222,227	5.2	9
Connecticut	101,027	3.0	47
Delaware	34,194	4.4	21
Florida	556,912	3.5	41
Georgia	271,755	3.3	42
Hawaii	44,579	3.7	36
Idaho	53,751	4.2	29
Illinois	534,155	4.3	23
Indiana	240,023	3.9	32
Iowa	135,008	4.6	15
Kansas	159,976	6.0	1
Kentucky	151,973	3.8	35
Louisiana	189,213	4.2	26
Maine	40,662	3.2	44
Maryland	227,969	4.3	22
Massachusetts	183,248	2.9	49
Michigan	467,861	4.7	10
Minnesota	218,617	4.4	18
Mississippi	125,355	4.4	20
Missouri	201,509	3.6	39
Montana	37,387	4.1	30
Nebraska	88,531	5.2	8
Nevada	83,120	4.2	28
New Hampshire	35,870	2.9	48
New Jersey	266,921	3.2	45
New Mexico	101,450	5.6	5
New York	588,390	3.1	46
North Carolina	329,422	4.1	31
North Dakota	36,014	5.6	4
Ohio	411,161	3.6	38
Oklahoma	153,699	4.5	17
Oregon	154,756	4.5	16
Pennsylvania	339,229	2.8	50
Rhode Island	38,458	3.7	37
South Carolina	155,519	3.9	33
South Dakota	34,857	4.6	14
Tennessee	202,530	3.6	40
Texas	896,534	4.3	24
Utah	123,046	5.5	7
Vermont	20,021	3.3	43
Virginia	313,780	4.4	19
Washington	273,928	4.6	13
West Virginia	76,136	4.2	27
Wisconsin	249,737	4.7	12
Wyoming	28,715	5.8	2
50 States	11,747,287	4.2	
DC	5,499	1.0	
United States	11,752,786	4.2	

Rank in order by percentage

1 Kansas
2 Wyoming
3 California
4 North Dakota
5 New Mexico
6 Arizona
7 Utah
8 Nebraska
9 Colorado
10 Michigan
11 Alabama
12 Wisconsin
13 Washington
14 South Dakota
15 Iowa
16 Oregon
17 Oklahoma
18 Minnesota
19 Virginia
20 Mississippi
21 Delaware
22 Maryland
23 Illinois
24 Texas
25 Alaska
26 Louisiana
27 West Virginia
28 Nevada
29 Idaho
30 Montana
31 North Carolina
32 Indiana
33 South Carolina
34 Arkansas
35 Kentucky
36 Hawaii
37 Rhode Island
38 Ohio
39 Missouri
40 Tennessee
41 Florida
42 Georgia
43 Vermont
44 Maine
45 New Jersey
46 New York
47 Connecticut
48 New Hampshire
49 Massachusetts
50 Pennsylvania

Note: Numbers that appear to be identical are rounded and vary slightly in actual value. The rankings reflect the actual values before rounding. See the introduction for more details.

H-22 Per Pupil State Support of Higher Education, 2001-2002

State	Per pupil support $	Rank
Alabama	5,381	27
Alaska	7,713	2
Arizona	3,339	49
Arkansas	6,420	8
California	4,911	38
Colorado	3,525	48
Connecticut	7,542	3
Delaware	5,534	23
Florida	5,067	35
Georgia	6,254	10
Hawaii	7,832	1
Idaho	6,154	11
Illinois	5,471	26
Indiana	5,504	25
Iowa	6,149	12
Kansas	4,473	43
Kentucky	7,137	5
Louisiana	5,273	32
Maine	5,900	18
Maryland	5,691	20
Massachusetts	5,511	24
Michigan	4,859	39
Minnesota	6,324	9
Mississippi	6,429	7
Missouri	5,208	33
Montana	4,005	46
Nebraska	5,933	16
Nevada	4,173	44
New Hampshire	3,000	50
New Jersey	6,725	6
New Mexico	6,024	14
New York	6,074	13
North Carolina	7,415	4
North Dakota	5,595	22
Ohio	5,364	29
Oklahoma	5,367	28
Oregon	4,619	41
Pennsylvania	5,999	15
Rhode Island	4,549	42
South Carolina	5,766	19
South Dakota	4,073	45
Tennessee	5,299	31
Texas	5,660	21
Utah	4,946	37
Vermont	3,656	47
Virginia	5,359	30
Washington	5,016	36
West Virginia	5,149	34
Wisconsin	4,777	40
Wyoming	5,918	17
50 States	5,418	
DC	n/a	
United States	5,415	

Rank in order by $	
1	Hawaii
2	Alaska
3	Connecticut
4	North Carolina
5	Kentucky
6	New Jersey
7	Mississippi
8	Arkansas
9	Minnesota
10	Georgia
11	Idaho
12	Iowa
13	New York
14	New Mexico
15	Pennsylvania
16	Nebraska
17	Wyoming
18	Maine
19	South Carolina
20	Maryland
21	Texas
22	North Dakota
23	Delaware
24	Massachusetts
25	Indiana
26	Illinois
27	Alabama
28	Oklahoma
29	Ohio
30	Virginia
31	Tennessee
32	Louisiana
33	Missouri
34	West Virginia
35	Florida
36	Washington
37	Utah
38	California
39	Michigan
40	Wisconsin
41	Oregon
42	Rhode Island
43	Kansas
44	Nevada
45	South Dakota
46	Montana
47	Vermont
48	Colorado
49	Arizona
50	New Hampshire

H-23 Average Tuition and Fees at Public Universities, 2000-2001

State	Average in-state tuition and fees $	Rank
Alabama	2,987	28
Alaska	2,936	34
Arizona	2,346	47
Arkansas	3,006	27
California	2,561	43
Colorado	2,980	29
Connecticut	4,543	10
Delaware	4,797	5
Florida	2,365	45
Georgia	2,698	38
Hawaii	2,974	30
Idaho	2,627	40
Illinois	4,177	13
Indiana	3,785	18
Iowa	3,158	24
Kansas	2,637	39
Kentucky	2,898	35
Louisiana	2,773	37
Maine	4,259	12
Maryland	4,778	6
Massachusetts	4,003	16
Michigan	4,626	9
Minnesota	4,024	15
Mississippi	2,967	31
Missouri	3,878	17
Montana	3,076	26
Nebraska	3,097	25
Nevada	2,349	46
New Hampshire	6,455	2
New Jersey	5,607	4
New Mexico	2,626	41
New York	4,062	14
North Carolina	2,299	48
North Dakota	2,938	33
Ohio	4,740	7
Oklahoma	2,257	49
Oregon	3,650	20
Pennsylvania	5,918	3
Rhode Island	4,512	11
South Carolina	4,684	8
South Dakota	3,486	22
Tennessee	2,950	32
Texas	2,803	36
Utah	2,244	50
Vermont	7,134	1
Virginia	3,723	19
Washington	3,604	21
West Virginia	2,548	44
Wisconsin	3,414	23
Wyoming	2,575	42
50 States	n/a	
DC	2,070	
United States	3,506	

Rank in order by $	
1	Vermont
2	New Hampshire
3	Pennsylvania
4	New Jersey
5	Delaware
6	Maryland
7	Ohio
8	South Carolina
9	Michigan
10	Connecticut
11	Rhode Island
12	Maine
13	Illinois
14	New York
15	Minnesota
16	Massachusetts
17	Missouri
18	Indiana
19	Virginia
20	Oregon
21	Washington
22	South Dakota
23	Wisconsin
24	Iowa
25	Nebraska
26	Montana
27	Arkansas
28	Alabama
29	Colorado
30	Hawaii
31	Mississippi
32	Tennessee
33	North Dakota
34	Alaska
35	Kentucky
36	Texas
37	Louisiana
38	Georgia
39	Kansas
40	Idaho
41	New Mexico
42	Wyoming
43	California
44	West Virginia
45	Florida
46	Nevada
47	Arizona
48	North Carolina
49	Oklahoma
50	Utah

H-24 Average Salary of Associate Professors at "Flagship" State Universities, 2001-2002

State	Associate professor average salary $ (in thousands)	Rank
Alabama	55.0	44
Alaska	54.2	45
Arizona	62.8	25
Arkansas	58.8	35
California	73.2	5
Colorado	65.4	16
Connecticut	74.5	2
Delaware	70.0	10
Florida	62.4	27
Georgia	63.0	24
Hawaii	60.6	31
Idaho	55.8	42
Illinois	69.9	11
Indiana	64.0	18
Iowa	63.7	20
Kansas	59.6	33
Kentucky	60.5	32
Louisiana	56.9	39
Maine	56.5	40
Maryland	74.4	3
Massachusetts	70.5	8
Michigan	76.3	1
Minnesota	69.2	12
Mississippi	52.1	46
Missouri	63.9	19
Montana	51.8	48
Nebraska	62.8	25
Nevada	65.9	14
New Hampshire	63.1	23
New Jersey	74.0	4
New Mexico	58.4	37
New York	64.4	17
North Carolina	72.2	6
North Dakota	51.6	49
Ohio	63.5	21
Oklahoma	58.5	36
Oregon	55.4	43
Pennsylvania	66.5	13
Rhode Island	62.2	28
South Carolina	61.8	30
South Dakota	51.1	50
Tennessee	62.1	29
Texas	63.5	21
Utah	59.0	34
Vermont	57.5	38
Virginia	71.2	7
Washington	65.5	15
West Virginia	56.3	41
Wisconsin	70.2	9
Wyoming	52.1	46
50 States	62.7	
DC	71.1	
United States	62.8	

Rank in order by $

1 Michigan
2 Connecticut
3 Maryland
4 New Jersey
5 California
6 North Carolina
7 Virginia
8 Massachusetts
9 Wisconsin
10 Delaware
11 Illinois
12 Minnesota
13 Pennsylvania
14 Nevada
15 Washington
16 Colorado
17 New York
18 Indiana
19 Missouri
20 Iowa
21 Ohio
21 Texas
23 New Hampshire
24 Georgia
25 Arizona
25 Nebraska
27 Florida
28 Rhode Island
29 Tennessee
30 South Carolina
31 Hawaii
32 Kentucky
33 Kansas
34 Utah
35 Arkansas
36 Oklahoma
37 New Mexico
38 Vermont
39 Louisiana
40 Maine
41 West Virginia
42 Idaho
43 Oregon
44 Alabama
45 Alaska
46 Mississippi
46 Wyoming
48 Montana
49 North Dakota
50 South Dakota

Note: Ties in ranking reflect ties in actual values.

H-25 State and Local Education Employees, 2001

State	Education employees #	Per 10,000 population	Rank per 10,000 population
Alabama	99,076	222	32
Alaska	19,388	305	2
Arizona	99,730	188	45
Arkansas	67,473	251	9
California	649,903	188	44
Colorado	86,179	195	43
Connecticut	83,006	242	16
Delaware	15,802	198	42
Florida	307,911	188	46
Georgia	209,169	249	10
Hawaii	25,519	208	38
Idaho	30,599	232	28
Illinois	255,142	204	40
Indiana	135,039	221	33
Iowa	69,723	239	22
Kansas	70,627	262	7
Kentucky	104,300	257	8
Louisiana	107,579	241	19
Maine	35,585	277	4
Maryland	110,472	206	39
Massachusetts	148,060	232	27
Michigan	211,577	212	36
Minnesota	121,894	245	14
Mississippi	76,526	268	5
Missouri	127,171	226	30
Montana	22,180	245	13
Nebraska	42,637	249	11
Nevada	30,850	146	50
New Hampshire	30,716	244	15
New Jersey	202,001	238	23
New Mexico	44,150	241	18
New York	456,462	240	20
North Carolina	177,802	217	34
North Dakota	14,436	228	29
Ohio	242,077	213	35
Oklahoma	85,341	247	12
Oregon	64,395	185	47
Pennsylvania	218,430	178	48
Rhode Island	25,592	242	17
South Carolina	94,590	233	26
South Dakota	17,974	238	25
Tennessee	116,532	203	41
Texas	570,981	268	6
Utah	47,749	210	37
Vermont	18,550	303	3
Virginia	170,822	238	24
Washington	94,676	158	49
West Virginia	43,039	239	21
Wisconsin	120,679	223	31
Wyoming	15,597	315	1
50 States	6,235,708	219	
DC	11,110	194	
United States	6,246,818	219	

Rank in order per 10,000 population

1 Wyoming
2 Alaska
3 Vermont
4 Maine
5 Mississippi
6 Texas
7 Kansas
8 Kentucky
9 Arkansas
10 Georgia
11 Nebraska
12 Oklahoma
13 Montana
14 Minnesota
15 New Hampshire
16 Connecticut
17 Rhode Island
18 New Mexico
19 Louisiana
20 New York
21 West Virginia
22 Iowa
23 New Jersey
24 Virginia
25 South Dakota
26 South Carolina
27 Massachusetts
28 Idaho
29 North Dakota
30 Missouri
31 Wisconsin
32 Alabama
33 Indiana
34 North Carolina
35 Ohio
36 Michigan
37 Utah
38 Hawaii
39 Maryland
40 Illinois
41 Tennessee
42 Delaware
43 Colorado
44 California
45 Arizona
46 Florida
47 Oregon
48 Pennsylvania
49 Washington
50 Nevada

Note: Numbers that appear to be identical are rounded and vary slightly in actual value. The rankings reflect the actual values before rounding. See the introduction for more details.

H-26 Federal Research and Development Spending, FY 2000

State	Federal R&D spending $ (in thousands)	Federal R&D spending per capita $	Rank per capita
Alabama	1,614,901	363	7
Alaska	146,777	234	12
Arizona	1,121,701	219	15
Arkansas	116,333	44	50
California	14,082,960	416	5
Colorado	1,369,733	318	9
Connecticut	806,228	237	11
Delaware	69,867	89	39
Florida	2,216,206	139	25
Georgia	2,632,186	322	8
Hawaii	209,737	173	18
Idaho	216,928	168	19
Illinois	1,404,613	113	34
Indiana	506,326	83	40
Iowa	267,038	91	38
Kansas	223,493	83	41
Kentucky	203,851	50	49
Louisiana	249,045	56	46
Maine	249,812	196	16
Maryland	8,684,796	1,640	1
Massachusetts	4,145,472	653	4
Michigan	975,052	98	37
Minnesota	781,132	159	21
Mississippi	394,585	139	24
Missouri	890,597	159	20
Montana	95,025	105	35
Nebraska	98,491	58	45
Nevada	263,897	132	27
New Hampshire	356,873	289	10
New Jersey	1,937,769	230	13
New Mexico	2,130,504	1,171	2
New York	2,927,523	154	23
North Carolina	1,062,536	132	28
North Dakota	64,051	100	36
Ohio	1,799,136	158	22
Oklahoma	185,121	54	47
Oregon	468,167	137	26
Pennsylvania	2,357,552	192	17
Rhode Island	418,037	399	6
South Carolina	248,988	62	44
South Dakota	38,803	51	48
Tennessee	734,406	129	30
Texas	2,671,790	128	31
Utah	285,968	128	32
Vermont	72,030	118	33
Virginia	4,842,811	684	3
Washington	1,329,466	226	14
West Virginia	235,677	130	29
Wisconsin	420,839	78	42
Wyoming	35,059	71	43
50 States	68,659,888	244	
DC	2,374,647	4,151	
United States*	71,261,475	253	

Rank in order per capita	
1	Maryland
2	New Mexico
3	Virginia
4	Massachusetts
5	California
6	Rhode Island
7	Alabama
8	Georgia
9	Colorado
10	New Hampshire
11	Connecticut
12	Alaska
13	New Jersey
14	Washington
15	Arizona
16	Maine
17	Pennsylvania
18	Hawaii
19	Idaho
20	Missouri
21	Minnesota
22	Ohio
23	New York
24	Mississippi
25	Florida
26	Oregon
27	Nevada
28	North Carolina
29	West Virginia
30	Tennessee
31	Texas
32	Utah
33	Vermont
34	Illinois
35	Montana
36	North Dakota
37	Michigan
38	Iowa
39	Delaware
40	Indiana
41	Kansas
42	Wisconsin
43	Wyoming
44	South Carolina
45	Nebraska
46	Louisiana
47	Oklahoma
48	South Dakota
49	Kentucky
50	Arkansas

Note: Numbers that appear to be identical are rounded and vary slightly in actual value. The rankings reflect the actual values before rounding. See the introduction for more details.

Due to rounding or data sources, the 50-state total plus D.C. may not equal the U.S. total. Please see introduction.

H-27 Total Library Operating Expenditures, FY 2000

State	Library spending $ (in thousands)	Library spending per capita	Rank per capita
Alabama	63,088	14.2	44
Alaska	22,652	36.1	4
Arizona	106,947	20.8	26
Arkansas	33,036	12.4	49
California	754,642	22.3	24
Colorado	138,247	32.1	9
Connecticut	129,971	38.2	3
Delaware	13,382	17.1	37
Florida	319,902	20.0	28
Georgia	135,794	16.6	38
Hawaii	22,378	18.5	33
Idaho	22,763	17.6	35
Illinois	408,625	32.9	8
Indiana	208,518	34.3	5
Iowa	66,108	22.6	23
Kansas	68,110	25.3	18
Kentucky	64,989	16.1	40
Louisiana	89,880	20.1	27
Maine	25,056	19.7	30
Maryland	169,633	32.0	10
Massachusetts	195,447	30.8	12
Michigan	250,351	25.2	19
Minnesota	141,171	28.7	14
Mississippi	33,191	11.7	50
Missouri	122,515	21.9	25
Montana	13,590	15.1	42
Nebraska	33,648	19.7	29
Nevada	46,255	23.1	22
New Hampshire	32,311	26.1	17
New Jersey	287,717	34.2	6
New Mexico	26,448	14.5	43
New York	775,826	40.9	2
North Carolina	137,877	17.1	36
North Dakota	7,973	12.4	47
Ohio	538,177	47.4	1
Oklahoma	52,806	15.3	41
Oregon	104,039	30.4	13
Pennsylvania	233,556	19.0	32
Rhode Island	32,403	30.9	11
South Carolina	71,154	17.7	34
South Dakota	12,506	16.6	39
Tennessee	70,500	12.4	48
Texas	287,678	13.8	45
Utah	54,289	24.3	21
Vermont	11,914	19.6	31
Virginia	174,490	24.7	20
Washington	200,791	34.1	7
West Virginia	23,326	12.9	46
Wisconsin	153,424	28.6	15
Wyoming	13,618	27.6	16
50 States	7,002,712	24.9	
DC	25,196	44.0	
United States	7,027,908	25.0	

Rank in order per capita	
1	Ohio
2	New York
3	Connecticut
4	Alaska
5	Indiana
6	New Jersey
7	Washington
8	Illinois
9	Colorado
10	Maryland
11	Rhode Island
12	Massachusetts
13	Oregon
14	Minnesota
15	Wisconsin
16	Wyoming
17	New Hampshire
18	Kansas
19	Michigan
20	Virginia
21	Utah
22	Nevada
23	Iowa
24	California
25	Missouri
26	Arizona
27	Louisiana
28	Florida
29	Nebraska
30	Maine
31	Vermont
32	Pennsylvania
33	Hawaii
34	South Carolina
35	Idaho
36	North Carolina
37	Delaware
38	Georgia
39	South Dakota
40	Kentucky
41	Oklahoma
42	Montana
43	New Mexico
44	Alabama
45	Texas
46	West Virginia
47	North Dakota
48	Tennessee
49	Arkansas
50	Mississippi

Note: Numbers that appear to be identical are rounded and vary slightly in actual value. The rankings reflect the actual values before rounding. See the introduction for more details.

Source Notes for Education (Section H)

H-1 Average Proficiency in Math, Eighth Grade, 2000: These statistics reflect scores on national tests administered to eighth graders to determine their ability to deal with basic concepts of mathematics. Because some states choose different assessment methods, only thirty-nine states participated in this study. The statistics are representative of those being developed through the National Assessment of Educational Progress, as administered by the U.S. Department of Education and cooperating states. They were printed in the *NAEP 2000 Mathematics Report Card.*

Statistics comparing the educational achievements of students in individual states, school districts, and schools are a response to the widespread criticism that taxpayers and parents have few ways to assess how well schools are educating children. Many states have established their own tests and print comparisons, often called "report cards," among school districts and schools within the state. Supporters of these statistics and tests argue that it is much more appropriate to compare results in education programs than the common statistics that just compare costs, such as how much is spent per pupil. Statistics on test results measure achievement of pupils, not that of teachers or school systems. Experts disagree on the relative influence of factors affecting student achievement, but all agree that it is heavily influenced by such out-of-school factors as early childhood training in the home, children's physical and mental health, and participation of parents in the educational process.

H-2 Average Proficiency in Science, Eighth Grade, 2000: These data are comparable to those shown in Table H-1, except they cover science. Through the National Assessment of Educational Progress, the Department of Education conducts mathematics, reading, and science assessments every other year on different timelines. *State Fact Finder* will publish the most recent assessment statistics available. These statistics, while not available for all states (see notes to Table H-1), come from the *NAEP 2000 Science Report Card.*

H-3 Armed Forces Qualification Test Ranks, FY 2000: Many employers test potential employees to determine their suitability for work, as indicated by such factors as ability to read and understand instructions and perform simple calculations. One of the most widely used tests is offered nationwide to persons seeking to enlist in the armed forces. These data reflect average scores of test-takers in the period from October 1999 to the end of September 2000. These data are prepared by the Department of Defense and published annually, along with other information about persons in uniform, in *Population Representation in the Military Services.*

The Defense Department, which does not want to become an arbitrator of which states prepare students best for jobs, tries to discourage the use of these results to rank states. Regardless, the results provide the best single measure of performance of high school graduates being tested by an employer using criteria approximating aptitude for work.

H-4 SAT Scores, 2002: College-bound students are generally required to take an achievement test to gain admission to the college or university of their choice. There are two major tests used for this purpose, the Scholastic Aptitude Test (SAT), which is administered by the College Board (www.collegeboard.org), and the ACT test, which is administered by the American College Testing Program (www.act.org). Both organizations seek to discourage the use of their test scores as a way to compare education systems of states, but they are commonly used because of the lack of other comparisons indicating how well states and individual school districts and schools compare in meeting these standards for college admissions. The test scores are presented here and in Table H-5, with neither table including all states. Each state's results are given only for the test that is most often taken in that state. Failure to sort in this way would produce highly misleading results. For example, many southern states rely primarily on the ACT, but their students who seek admission to exclusive private universities in the Northeast and California must take the SAT. As a result, the SAT is taken by a small fraction of high school graduates, but those who take it score extraordinarily high.

H-5 ACT Scores, 2002: See notes to Table H-4.

H-6 Percentage of Population Over 25 with a High School Diploma, 2000: These data reflect the percentage of the total population over age twenty-five that has a high school degree. Because each generation of Americans has, on average, attended school longer than its predecessors, the states with the highest ranks tend to be those with the fastest growth and thus youngest population. The data, from the Census Bureau website (www.census.gov), should be updated in early 2003.

H-7 Students in Private Schools, 1999-2000: Just over five million students in kindergarten through the twelfth grade attend private schools. The private enrollment statistics were released in August 2001 by the Department of Education, National Center for Education Statistics (NCES). The data are posted on the NCES website (nces.ed.gov). Public enrollment statistics are gathered every two years as part of the National Education Association's Private School Survey (PSS).

H-8 High School Completion Rates, 1998-2000: An average over a three year period shows that, nationwide, 85.7 percent of eighteen- to twenty-four-year-olds have graduated from high school. Subtracting this figure from a 100 percent graduation rate suggests a "dropout" rate of 14.3 percent.

This approach is one of several ways of comparing dropout rates among the states. The Department of Education has produced a dropout rate statistic that relies on a count of dropouts. Currently only thirty-seven states have reliable data that use this concept. The data printed here are from the Census Bureau and are available in a Department of Education, National Center for Education Statistics report titled *Dropout Rates in the United States: 2000*, released on the NCES website (nces.ed.gov) on November 15, 2001.

H-9 Pupil-Teacher Ratio, 2001-2002: Small classes are generally believed to be more beneficial to students than large ones, so pupil-teacher ratios are commonly used as a proxy measure of educational quality. The statistic shows a ratio lower than typical class sizes because some specialized teachers, such as those teaching art or special education, are included. These data come from the National Education Association's *Rankings and Estimates Update* released in November of 2002.

For these and other commonly used educational statistics comparing states, there are three primary sources: the Department of Education, the National Education Association (NEA), and the American Federation of Teachers (which, like the NEA, represents teachers). These organizations produce somewhat different data, using different concepts and different schedules. However, the rankings of states on any particular indicator are about the same regardless of the source used.

H-10 Public School Enrollment, 2001-2002: These statistics show how the nation's 47.4 million public school pupils are distributed among the states. The comparison with each state's population is a rough indicator of the differences among states in the financial burdens of providing free public education. The data come from the National Education Association's November 2002 report *Rankings and Estimates Update*.

H-11 Public Library Holdings Per Capita, FY 2000: These data, from *Public Libraries Survey, FY 2000* published by the National Center of Educational Statistics, relate the holdings of books (and related materials) to the population of each state. Nationally, public libraries hold about three books for every person. The reports exclude significant sources of reading materials not in public libraries, such as collections of private and university libraries and certain public school systems.

H-12 Children with Disabilities, 1999-2000: A substantial percentage of the nation's public school students are given special financing by state and federal programs because of something unique about them. The table reflects a Department of Education count of students in the 1999-2000 school year classified as disabled or receiving extra school money because of poverty. These data come from the Department of Education, Office of Special Education Programs, Data Analysis System (www.ed.gov).

H-13 State and Local Education Spending, FY 2000: This table relates spending data to population and personal income in each state. The data come from the Census Bureau's electronic publication "State and Local Government Finance Estimates, by State," available on the Census website (www.census.gov). Population numbers, also from the census, are as of July 1, 2000, and personal income numbers are from the Department of Commerce. Based on census historical practices, *State Fact Finder* used calendar year 1999 numbers. See notes to Table F-1 for more extensive information on the source of the data.

H-14 State and Local Education Spending as a Percentage of General Spending, FY 2000: This table, from the same source as Table H-13, shows the relative importance of education spending in state and local budgets. It is derived by comparing this spending with total "general" spending. General spending includes essentially all other spending, except municipal electric and other utilities and trust funds, such as those for workers' compensation.

H-15 Spending Per Pupil, 2001-2002: This table, from the same source as Table H-9, shows spending in public schools for operations (excluding capital outlays) in relation to the number of pupils enrolled.

H-16 Average Teacher Salary, 2001-2002: These average salary calculations, from the same source as Table H-9, show the average gross wage of teachers, not including special pay for leading student activities or teaching in summer sessions.

H-17 Sources of School Funds, 2000-2001: Except in a few states, federal aid covers less than 12 percent of public school costs. State and local governments divide the remainder in proportions that vary considerably from state to state, as shown in the table. The data come from the National Education Association's *Rankings and Estimates*.

H-18 State Aid Per Pupil in Average Daily Attendance, 2001-2002: These data, calculated from statistics in the National Education Association's 2002 release *Rankings and Estimates* and the November 2002 update, show the amount each state government spends on supporting local public schools, expressed in relation to the number of pupils attending school.

H-19 State and Local Spending for Higher Education, FY 2000: This table relates spending data to population and personal income in each state. For source, see notes to Table H-13.

H-20 State and Local Spending for Higher Education as a Percentage of General Spending, FY 2000: This table, from the same source as Table H-13, shows the relative importance of higher education in state and local budgets. It is derived by comparing this spending with total "general" spending. General spending includes essentially all other spending excepting municipal electric and other utilities and trust funds, such as those for workers' compensation.

H-21 Public Higher Education Enrollment, 2000: This table shows the total number of students enrolled in public universities and colleges in fall 2000 and relates this number to the total population of each state. This percentage is an indicator of the relative costs of supporting public higher education in each state. The enrollment data are from the Department of Education's "Enrollment in Postsecondary Institutions, Fall 2000 and Financial Statistics, Fiscal Year 2000."

H-22 Per Pupil State Support of Higher Education, 2001-2002: There are a variety of different statistics seeking to measure state outlays for higher education on a per pupil basis. None are totally satisfactory for complex reasons, such as difficulty in classifying pupils as private or public in institutions that receive public support for some of their programs but are truly private in financing other programs. This table relates state government spending for fiscal year 2002 to the latest enrollment data available (see Table H-21). The amount of state support comes from a survey of FY 2002 state appropriations for higher education conducted by the Center for Higher Education at Illinois State University.

H-23 Average Tuition and Fees at Public Universities, 2000-2001: These data, from the National Center for Education Statistics (nces.ed.gov), reflect a composite of average in-state tuition and general fees charged by public four-year institutions of higher education in the 2000-2001 academic year.

H-24 Average Salary of Associate Professors at "Flagship" State Universities, 2001-2002: These statistics were developed for *State Fact Finder* based on detailed salary surveys by the American Association of University Professors as printed in its magazine *Academe* (March/April 2002).

To make the comparisons, the "flagship" university salary for an associate professor was used. Usually the "flagship" is the largest, oldest state university, but in some states several institutions can be considered flagships, such as the University of Michigan and Michigan State. In those cases, *State Fact Finder* generally selected the university originally constituted as the general land-grant institution (for example, the University of Michigan) rather than the one initially designated as an agricultural and mechanical school (for example, Michigan State).

H-25 State and Local Education Employees, 2001: This statistic comes from a Census Bureau survey of state and local government employment, available on the Internet (www.census.gov, "Public Employment"). It covers employees of public schools, from janitors to principals, but it does not include higher education employees.

H-26 Federal Research and Development Spending, FY 2000: The federal government is a major supplier of funds for research and development of new products and processes. This federally supported research provides an important source of income for state and private universities and a base from which state economies can develop in high technology industries. The table shows how federal R&D spending in fiscal 2000 was distributed among the states and relates that spending to the population of each state. The data were developed by the National Science Foundation in its *Survey of Federal Funds for Research and Development.*

H-27 Total Library Operating Expenditures, FY 2000: These data are from the same source as Table H-11.

Health

I-1	Immunization Rates, 2001	226
I-2	Infant Mortality Rates, 2000	227
I-3	State Health Rankings, 2002	228
I-4	Percentage of Non-Elderly Population Without Health Insurance, 2001	229
I-5	Abortions, 1998	230
I-6	Alcohol Consumption Per Capita, 1999	231
I-7	Percentage of Adult Smokers, 2001	232
I-8	Percentage of Population Obese, 2001	233
I-9	AIDS Cases, 2001	234
I-10	Physicians Per 100,000 Population, 2002	235
I-11	Hospital Beds Per 1,000 Population, 2000	236
I-12	Medicaid Recipients, FY 2000	237
I-13	Medicaid Recipients as a Percentage of Poverty Population, FY 2000	238
I-14	State and Local Spending for Health and Hospitals, FY 2000	239
I-15	State and Local Health and Hospital Spending as a Percentage of General Spending, FY 2000	240
I-16	Per Capita Medicaid Spending, FY 2000	241
I-17	Average Medicaid Spending Per Aged Recipient, FY 2000	242
I-18	Average Medicaid Spending Per Child, FY 2000	243
I-19	Medicare Payment Per Hospital Day, FY 2000	244
I-20	Hospital Expense Per Inpatient Day, 2000	245
I-21	Percentage of Population in Health Maintenance Organizations, 2002	246

The big news in healthcare is old news: Rapidly rising costs and the continuing struggle to pay. The elderly are dogged by escalating prescription drug costs, estimated to have increased 20 percent over the last three years. Employers are dealing with higher health insurance premiums, and employees are paying a higher percentage for less inclusive policies. Doctors testify that overhead for medical malpractice is squeezing some of their ranks into early retirement, while insurers claim that they are also losing: ninety-seven cents for every dollar collected in premiums, to be exact. America's uninsured population is growing, and state governments, already struggling with reduced revenues, are finding it more and more difficult to meet the fiscal demands of Medicaid—the joint federal and state program providing health insurance to some forty-three million low-income Americans.

What's worse: there is no solution on the horizon. Oregon took a stab at healthcare reform when it included a measure on the November ballot offering health insurance to all state residents. Voters rejected it. For the most part, action on healthcare in the fifty states has taken the form of stopgap measures to slow the rising costs of Medicaid. Florida, for instance, cut out non-emergency dental care for adults. Utah increased co-pay amounts. Some states are implementing a "preferred drug list." Typically, generics and other cost-effective drugs make the list; those that don't, won't be covered by Medicaid.

Other Medicaid cost-containment strategies include:

- Efforts to reduce fraud,
- Reductions or lids on provider rates,
- Raising cigarette taxes, and
- Dipping into tobacco settlement funds.

With health spending projected to grow 2.9 percent per year faster than gross domestic product it is no surprise that in fiscal years 2002 and 2003 forty-seven of the fifty states proposed some kind of cost-containment measure.

I-1 Immunization Rates, 2001

State	Vaccination coverage %	Rank
Alabama	84.5	8
Alaska	74.5	44
Arizona	73.8	47
Arkansas	74.1	45
California	76.5	35
Colorado	77.2	31
Connecticut	85.9	2
Delaware	81.0	21
Florida	79.4	27
Georgia	81.3	18
Hawaii	73.4	48
Idaho	75.0	41
Illinois	76.4	36
Indiana	75.5	38
Iowa	80.1	25
Kansas	76.7	33
Kentucky	80.2	24
Louisiana	69.9	50
Maine	83.3	12
Maryland	79.7	26
Massachusetts	81.9	15
Michigan	74.7	43
Minnesota	81.3	18
Mississippi	84.5	8
Missouri	79.0	28
Montana	83.0	13
Nebraska	81.5	17
Nevada	73.9	46
New Hampshire	84.9	4
New Jersey	77.9	30
New Mexico	72.7	49
New York	81.9	15
North Carolina	85.7	3
North Dakota	83.5	11
Ohio	76.3	37
Oklahoma	77.1	32
Oregon	75.3	39
Pennsylvania	84.6	6
Rhode Island	84.8	5
South Carolina	81.2	20
South Dakota	80.5	23
Tennessee	84.6	6
Texas	74.9	42
Utah	75.1	40
Vermont	89.2	1
Virginia	78.4	29
Washington	76.7	33
West Virginia	82.1	14
Wisconsin	83.8	10
Wyoming	80.9	22
50 States	n/a	
DC	75.5	
United States	78.6	

Rank in order by percentage

1	Vermont
2	Connecticut
3	North Carolina
4	New Hampshire
5	Rhode Island
6	Pennsylvania
6	Tennessee
8	Alabama
8	Mississippi
10	Wisconsin
11	North Dakota
12	Maine
13	Montana
14	West Virginia
15	Massachusetts
15	New York
17	Nebraska
18	Georgia
18	Minnesota
20	South Carolina
21	Delaware
22	Wyoming
23	South Dakota
24	Kentucky
25	Iowa
26	Maryland
27	Florida
28	Missouri
29	Virginia
30	New Jersey
31	Colorado
32	Oklahoma
33	Kansas
33	Washington
35	California
36	Illinois
37	Ohio
38	Indiana
39	Oregon
40	Utah
41	Idaho
42	Texas
43	Michigan
44	Alaska
45	Arkansas
46	Nevada
47	Arizona
48	Hawaii
49	New Mexico
50	Louisiana

Note: Ties in ranking reflect ties in actual values.

I-2 Infant Mortality Rates, 2000

State	Infant deaths per 1,000 live births	Rank
Alabama	9.4	2
Alaska	6.8	26
Arizona	6.7	28
Arkansas	8.4	11
California	5.4	46
Colorado	6.2	38
Connecticut	6.6	30
Delaware	9.2	3
Florida	7.0	24
Georgia	8.5	8
Hawaii	8.1	13
Idaho	7.5	19
Illinois	8.5	8
Indiana	7.8	15
Iowa	6.5	33
Kansas	6.8	26
Kentucky	7.2	21
Louisiana	9.0	5
Maine	4.9	49
Maryland	7.6	16
Massachusetts	4.6	50
Michigan	8.2	12
Minnesota	5.6	43
Mississippi	10.7	1
Missouri	7.2	21
Montana	6.1	39
Nebraska	7.3	20
Nevada	6.5	33
New Hampshire	5.7	41
New Jersey	6.3	36
New Mexico	6.6	30
New York	6.4	35
North Carolina	8.6	7
North Dakota	8.1	13
Ohio	7.6	16
Oklahoma	8.5	8
Oregon	5.6	43
Pennsylvania	7.1	23
Rhode Island	6.3	36
South Carolina	8.7	6
South Dakota	5.5	45
Tennessee	9.1	4
Texas	5.7	41
Utah	5.2	47
Vermont	6.0	40
Virginia	6.9	25
Washington	5.2	47
West Virginia	7.6	16
Wisconsin	6.6	30
Wyoming	6.7	28
50 States	n/a	
DC	12.0	
United States	6.9	

Rank in order by rate

1	Mississippi
2	Alabama
3	Delaware
4	Tennessee
5	Louisiana
6	South Carolina
7	North Carolina
8	Georgia
8	Illinois
8	Oklahoma
11	Arkansas
12	Michigan
13	Hawaii
13	North Dakota
15	Indiana
16	Maryland
16	Ohio
16	West Virginia
19	Idaho
20	Nebraska
21	Kentucky
21	Missouri
23	Pennsylvania
24	Florida
25	Virginia
26	Alaska
26	Kansas
28	Arizona
28	Wyoming
30	Connecticut
30	New Mexico
30	Wisconsin
33	Iowa
33	Nevada
35	New York
36	New Jersey
36	Rhode Island
38	Colorado
39	Montana
40	Vermont
41	New Hampshire
41	Texas
43	Minnesota
43	Oregon
45	South Dakota
46	California
47	Utah
47	Washington
49	Maine
50	Massachusetts

Note: Ties in ranking reflect ties in actual values.

I-3 State Health Rankings, 2002

State	State health rankings	Rank
Alabama	-12.8	45
Alaska	0.2	30
Arizona	-3.7	34
Arkansas	-14.9	47
California	3.7	24
Colorado	14.5	7
Connecticut	16.6	5
Delaware	-3.9	35
Florida	-12.2	43
Georgia	-8.8	40
Hawaii	11.6	14
Idaho	7.8	20
Illinois	-0.9	31
Indiana	4.3	22
Iowa	14.5	7
Kansas	6.7	21
Kentucky	-7.6	39
Louisiana	-23.9	50
Maine	13.8	10
Maryland	0.8	28
Massachusetts	18.5	3
Michigan	0.6	29
Minnesota	21.8	2
Mississippi	-22.2	49
Missouri	-2.6	32
Montana	3.7	24
Nebraska	10.5	15
Nevada	-5.8	38
New Hampshire	23.9	1
New Jersey	8.6	19
New Mexico	-10.1	42
New York	-2.6	32
North Carolina	-5.3	36
North Dakota	14.0	9
Ohio	1.7	27
Oklahoma	-13.3	46
Oregon	9.3	17
Pennsylvania	3.8	23
Rhode Island	11.8	13
South Carolina	-16.4	48
South Dakota	9.7	16
Tennessee	-12.3	44
Texas	-5.6	37
Utah	17.9	4
Vermont	15.8	6
Virginia	8.7	18
Washington	13.5	11
West Virginia	-8.9	41
Wisconsin	13.5	11
Wyoming	2.7	26
50 States	n/a	
DC	n/a	
United States	n/a	

Rank in order by ranking

1	New Hampshire
2	Minnesota
3	Massachusetts
4	Utah
5	Connecticut
6	Vermont
7	Colorado
7	Iowa
9	North Dakota
10	Maine
11	Washington
11	Wisconsin
13	Rhode Island
14	Hawaii
15	Nebraska
16	South Dakota
17	Oregon
18	Virginia
19	New Jersey
20	Idaho
21	Kansas
22	Indiana
23	Pennsylvania
24	California
24	Montana
26	Wyoming
27	Ohio
28	Maryland
29	Michigan
30	Alaska
31	Illinois
32	Missouri
32	New York
34	Arizona
35	Delaware
36	North Carolina
37	Texas
38	Nevada
39	Kentucky
40	Georgia
41	West Virginia
42	New Mexico
43	Florida
44	Tennessee
45	Alabama
46	Oklahoma
47	Arkansas
48	South Carolina
49	Mississippi
50	Louisiana

Note: Ties in ranking reflect ties in actual values.

I-4 Percentage of Non-Elderly Population Without Health Insurance, 2001

State	Percentage of non-elderly without health insurance	Rank
Alabama	14.9	23
Alaska	16.6	16
Arizona	20.0	7
Arkansas	18.8	8
California	21.3	4
Colorado	17.2	15
Connecticut	11.7	35
Delaware	10.5	45
Florida	20.6	6
Georgia	18.1	10
Hawaii	10.8	41
Idaho	17.9	12
Illinois	15.3	21
Indiana	13.6	29
Iowa	8.7	50
Kansas	13.5	30
Kentucky	14.1	26
Louisiana	21.7	3
Maine	12.3	33
Maryland	13.8	28
Massachusetts	9.3	46
Michigan	11.7	35
Minnesota	8.8	48
Mississippi	18.4	9
Missouri	11.6	37
Montana	15.9	19
Nebraska	10.8	41
Nevada	17.9	12
New Hampshire	11.0	39
New Jersey	15.1	22
New Mexico	23.9	2
New York	17.7	14
North Carolina	16.3	17
North Dakota	11.2	38
Ohio	12.8	31
Oklahoma	20.9	5
Oregon	14.2	25
Pennsylvania	10.6	44
Rhode Island	9.0	47
South Carolina	14.1	26
South Dakota	10.9	40
Tennessee	12.6	32
Texas	25.9	1
Utah	16.0	18
Vermont	10.8	41
Virginia	12.2	34
Washington	14.8	24
West Virginia	15.8	20
Wisconsin	8.8	48
Wyoming	18.1	10
50 States	n/a	
DC	14.2	
United States	16.5	

Rank in order by percentage

1. Texas
2. New Mexico
3. Louisiana
4. California
5. Oklahoma
6. Florida
7. Arizona
8. Arkansas
9. Mississippi
10. Georgia
10. Wyoming
12. Idaho
12. Nevada
14. New York
15. Colorado
16. Alaska
17. North Carolina
18. Utah
19. Montana
20. West Virginia
21. Illinois
22. New Jersey
23. Alabama
24. Washington
25. Oregon
26. Kentucky
26. South Carolina
28. Maryland
29. Indiana
30. Kansas
31. Ohio
32. Tennessee
33. Maine
34. Virginia
35. Connecticut
35. Michigan
37. Missouri
38. North Dakota
39. New Hampshire
40. South Dakota
41. Hawaii
41. Nebraska
41. Vermont
44. Pennsylvania
45. Delaware
46. Massachusetts
47. Rhode Island
48. Minnesota
48. Wisconsin
50. Iowa

Note: Ties in ranking reflect ties in actual values.

I-5 Abortions, 1998

State	Abortions #	Per 1,000 births	Rank per 1,000 births
Alabama	13,386	216	25
Alaska	n/a	n/a	n/a
Arizona	14,747	188	28
Arkansas	5,634	153	35
California	n/a	n/a	n/a
Colorado	7,493	126	39
Connecticut	12,939	295	11
Delaware	5,455	516	2
Florida	82,335	421	3
Georgia	32,349	264	15
Hawaii	4162	237	21
Idaho	888	46	45
Illinois	49,403	271	14
Indiana	12,443	146	36
Iowa	6,214	167	32
Kansas	11,495	299	9
Kentucky	6,706	123	40
Louisiana	11,351	170	31
Maine	2,408	175	29
Maryland	10,458	145	37
Massachusetts	27,714	340	5
Michigan	28,107	210	26
Minnesota	14,423	221	23
Mississippi	3,955	92	42
Missouri	9,089	121	41
Montana	2,573	238	20
Nebraska	5,140	218	24
Nevada	6,539	228	22
New Hampshire	n/a	n/a	n/a
New Jersey	35,686	312	8
New Mexico	5,395	197	27
New York	139,646	541	1
North Carolina	33,105	296	10
North Dakota	1,242	157	34
Ohio	37,479	245	16
Oklahoma	n/a	n/a	n/a
Oregon	14,344	317	7
Pennsylvania	35,617	244	17
Rhode Island	4,601	365	4
South Carolina	8,801	163	33
South Dakota	674	66	44
Tennessee	18,849	244	17
Texas	81,686	239	19
Utah	3,487	77	43
Vermont	1,870	284	12
Virginia	26,115	277	13
Washington	25,327	318	6
West Virginia	2,738	132	38
Wisconsin	11,681	173	30
Wyoming	188	30	46
50 States	875,937	n/a	
DC	8,336	n/a	
United States	884,273	264	

Rank in order per 1,000 births

1	New York
2	Delaware
3	Florida
4	Rhode Island
5	Massachusetts
6	Washington
7	Oregon
8	New Jersey
9	Kansas
10	North Carolina
11	Connecticut
12	Vermont
13	Virginia
14	Illinois
15	Georgia
16	Ohio
17	Pennsylvania
17	Tennessee
19	Texas
20	Montana
21	Hawaii
22	Nevada
23	Minnesota
24	Nebraska
25	Alabama
26	Michigan
27	New Mexico
28	Arizona
29	Maine
30	Wisconsin
31	Louisiana
32	Iowa
33	South Carolina
34	North Dakota
35	Arkansas
36	Indiana
37	Maryland
38	West Virginia
39	Colorado
40	Kentucky
41	Missouri
42	Mississippi
43	Utah
44	South Dakota
45	Idaho
46	Wyoming

Note: Ties in ranking reflect ties in actual values.

I-6 Alcohol Consumption Per Capita, 1999

State	Per capita consumption in gallons	Rank
Alabama	1.88	44
Alaska	2.88	4
Arizona	2.68	6
Arkansas	1.82	46
California	2.20	30
Colorado	2.57	8
Connecticut	2.26	26
Delaware	2.96	3
Florida	2.66	7
Georgia	2.27	25
Hawaii	2.31	23
Idaho	2.39	18
Illinois	2.32	20
Indiana	1.97	40
Iowa	1.98	39
Kansas	1.85	45
Kentucky	1.76	47
Louisiana	2.50	10
Maine	2.26	26
Maryland	2.11	34
Massachusetts	2.45	12
Michigan	2.11	34
Minnesota	2.41	15
Mississippi	2.19	32
Missouri	2.26	26
Montana	2.55	9
Nebraska	2.24	29
Nevada	4.06	2
New Hampshire	4.07	1
New Jersey	2.20	30
New Mexico	2.43	14
New York	1.92	41
North Carolina	2.00	37
North Dakota	2.45	12
Ohio	2.01	36
Oklahoma	1.72	48
Oregon	2.32	20
Pennsylvania	1.91	42
Rhode Island	2.41	15
South Carolina	2.41	15
South Dakota	2.32	20
Tennessee	1.91	42
Texas	2.29	24
Utah	1.33	50
Vermont	2.34	19
Virginia	1.99	38
Washington	2.16	33
West Virginia	1.66	49
Wisconsin	2.75	5
Wyoming	2.48	11
50 States	n/a	
DC	3.74	
United States	2.21	

Rank in order per capita	
1	New Hampshire
2	Nevada
3	Delaware
4	Alaska
5	Wisconsin
6	Arizona
7	Florida
8	Colorado
9	Montana
10	Louisiana
11	Wyoming
12	Massachusetts
12	North Dakota
14	New Mexico
15	Minnesota
15	Rhode Island
15	South Carolina
18	Idaho
19	Vermont
20	Illinois
20	Oregon
20	South Dakota
23	Hawaii
24	Texas
25	Georgia
26	Connecticut
26	Maine
26	Missouri
29	Nebraska
30	California
30	New Jersey
32	Mississippi
33	Washington
34	Maryland
34	Michigan
36	Ohio
37	North Carolina
38	Virginia
39	Iowa
40	Indiana
41	New York
42	Pennsylvania
42	Tennessee
44	Alabama
45	Kansas
46	Arkansas
47	Kentucky
48	Oklahoma
49	West Virginia
50	Utah

Note: Ties in ranking reflect ties in actual values.

I-7 Percentage of Adult Smokers, 2001

State	Percentage of adult smokers	Rank
Alabama	23.8	21
Alaska	26.2	7
Arizona	21.5	40
Arkansas	25.5	12
California	17.2	49
Colorado	22.3	32
Connecticut	20.6	43
Delaware	25.0	14
Florida	22.4	29
Georgia	23.7	23
Hawaii	20.5	44
Idaho	19.6	47
Illinois	23.7	23
Indiana	27.4	5
Iowa	22.1	37
Kansas	22.2	34
Kentucky	30.9	1
Louisiana	24.6	15
Maine	23.9	19
Maryland	21.1	41
Massachusetts	19.5	48
Michigan	25.6	11
Minnesota	22.2	34
Mississippi	25.3	13
Missouri	25.9	9
Montana	21.9	39
Nebraska	20.2	46
Nevada	26.9	6
New Hampshire	24.1	18
New Jersey	21.1	41
New Mexico	23.8	21
New York	23.2	26
North Carolina	25.7	10
North Dakota	22.1	37
Ohio	27.6	4
Oklahoma	28.7	2
Oregon	20.5	44
Pennsylvania	24.5	16
Rhode Island	23.9	19
South Carolina	26.0	8
South Dakota	22.3	32
Tennessee	24.4	17
Texas	22.4	29
Utah	13.2	50
Vermont	22.4	29
Virginia	22.5	27
Washington	22.5	27
West Virginia	28.2	3
Wisconsin	23.6	25
Wyoming	22.2	34
50 States	n/a	
DC	20.8	
United States	22.9	

Rank in order by percentage

1 Kentucky
2 Oklahoma
3 West Virginia
4 Ohio
5 Indiana
6 Nevada
7 Alaska
8 South Carolina
9 Missouri
10 North Carolina
11 Michigan
12 Arkansas
13 Mississippi
14 Delaware
15 Louisiana
16 Pennsylvania
17 Tennessee
18 New Hampshire
19 Maine
19 Rhode Island
21 Alabama
21 New Mexico
23 Georgia
23 Illinois
25 Wisconsin
26 New York
27 Virginia
27 Washington
29 Florida
29 Texas
29 Vermont
32 Colorado
32 South Dakota
34 Kansas
34 Minnesota
34 Wyoming
37 Iowa
37 North Dakota
39 Montana
40 Arizona
41 Maryland
41 New Jersey
43 Connecticut
44 Hawaii
44 Oregon
46 Nebraska
47 Idaho
48 Massachusetts
49 California
50 Utah

Note: Ties in ranking reflect ties in actual values.

I-8 Percentage of Population Obese, 2001

State	Percentage of population obese	Rank
Alabama	24.5	6
Alaska	22.1	19
Arizona	18.5	44
Arkansas	22.4	16
California	21.9	21
Colorado	14.9	50
Connecticut	17.9	45
Delaware	20.8	27
Florida	18.8	42
Georgia	22.7	12
Hawaii	17.9	45
Idaho	20.5	29
Illinois	21.0	25
Indiana	24.5	6
Iowa	22.5	14
Kansas	21.6	22
Kentucky	24.6	4
Louisiana	24.0	8
Maine	19.5	37
Maryland	20.5	29
Massachusetts	16.6	49
Michigan	25.0	3
Minnesota	19.9	33
Mississippi	26.5	1
Missouri	23.2	10
Montana	18.8	42
Nebraska	20.7	28
Nevada	19.5	37
New Hampshire	19.4	39
New Jersey	19.6	36
New Mexico	19.7	34
New York	20.3	32
North Carolina	22.9	11
North Dakota	20.4	31
Ohio	22.4	16
Oklahoma	22.6	13
Oregon	21.1	24
Pennsylvania	22.1	19
Rhode Island	17.7	47
South Carolina	22.5	14
South Dakota	21.2	23
Tennessee	23.4	9
Texas	24.6	4
Utah	19.1	41
Vermont	17.6	48
Virginia	20.9	26
Washington	19.3	40
West Virginia	25.1	2
Wisconsin	22.4	16
Wyoming	19.7	34
50 States	n/a	
DC	20.0	
United States	21.1	

Rank in order by percentage	
1	Mississippi
2	West Virginia
3	Michigan
4	Kentucky
4	Texas
6	Alabama
6	Indiana
8	Louisiana
9	Tennessee
10	Missouri
11	North Carolina
12	Georgia
13	Oklahoma
14	Iowa
14	South Carolina
16	Arkansas
16	Ohio
16	Wisconsin
19	Alaska
19	Pennsylvania
21	California
22	Kansas
23	South Dakota
24	Oregon
25	Illinois
26	Virginia
27	Delaware
28	Nebraska
29	Idaho
29	Maryland
31	North Dakota
32	New York
33	Minnesota
34	New Mexico
34	Wyoming
36	New Jersey
37	Maine
37	Nevada
39	New Hampshire
40	Washington
41	Utah
42	Florida
42	Montana
44	Arizona
45	Connecticut
45	Hawaii
47	Rhode Island
48	Vermont
49	Massachusetts
50	Colorado

Note: Ties in ranking reflect ties in actual values.

State	AIDS cases #	Rate per 100,000 residents	Rank by rate
Alabama	438	9.8	22
Alaska	18	2.8	46
Arizona	540	10.2	20
Arkansas	199	7.4	29
California	4,315	12.5	14
Colorado	288	6.5	31
Connecticut	584	17.1	9
Delaware	248	31.1	4
Florida	5,138	31.3	3
Georgia	1,745	20.8	5
Hawaii	124	10.1	21
Idaho	19	1.4	48
Illinois	1,323	10.6	18
Indiana	378	6.2	32
Iowa	90	3.1	45
Kansas	98	3.6	40
Kentucky	333	8.2	25
Louisiana	861	19.3	7
Maine	48	3.7	39
Maryland	1,860	34.6	2
Massachusetts	765	12.0	15
Michigan	548	5.5	33
Minnesota	157	3.2	43
Mississippi	418	14.6	11
Missouri	445	7.9	26
Montana	15	1.7	47
Nebraska	74	4.3	37
Nevada	252	12.0	15
New Hampshire	40	3.2	43
New Jersey	1,756	20.7	6
New Mexico	143	7.8	27
New York	7,476	39.3	1
North Carolina	942	11.5	17
North Dakota	3	0.5	50
Ohio	581	5.1	36
Oklahoma	243	7.0	30
Oregon	259	7.5	28
Pennsylvania	1,840	15.0	10
Rhode Island	103	9.7	23
South Carolina	729	17.9	8
South Dakota	25	3.3	42
Tennessee	602	10.5	19
Texas	2,892	13.6	12
Utah	124	5.5	33
Vermont	25	4.1	38
Virginia	951	13.2	13
Washington	532	8.9	24
West Virginia	100	5.5	33
Wisconsin	193	3.6	40
Wyoming	5	1.0	49
50 States	40,885	n/a	
DC	870	152.1	
United States	41,755	14.7	

Rank in order by rate

1	New York
2	Maryland
3	Florida
4	Delaware
5	Georgia
6	New Jersey
7	Louisiana
8	South Carolina
9	Connecticut
10	Pennsylvania
11	Mississippi
12	Texas
13	Virginia
14	California
15	Massachusetts
15	Nevada
17	North Carolina
18	Illinois
19	Tennessee
20	Arizona
21	Hawaii
22	Alabama
23	Rhode Island
24	Washington
25	Kentucky
26	Missouri
27	New Mexico
28	Oregon
29	Arkansas
30	Oklahoma
31	Colorado
32	Indiana
33	Michigan
33	Utah
33	West Virginia
36	Ohio
37	Nebraska
38	Vermont
39	Maine
40	Kansas
40	Wisconsin
42	South Dakota
43	Minnesota
43	New Hampshire
45	Iowa
46	Alaska
47	Montana
48	Idaho
49	Wyoming
50	North Dakota

Note: Ties in ranking reflect ties in actual values.

I-10 Physicians Per 100,000 Population, 2002

State	Physicians per 100,000 population	Rank
Alabama	206	41
Alaska	203	43
Arizona	210	36
Arkansas	195	46
California	246	21
Colorado	239	24
Connecticut	346	4
Delaware	256	16
Florida	245	22
Georgia	212	35
Hawaii	280	9
Idaho	159	50
Illinois	267	11
Indiana	206	40
Iowa	204	42
Kansas	229	30
Kentucky	216	34
Louisiana	256	15
Maine	263	13
Maryland	396	2
Massachusetts	404	1
Michigan	268	10
Minnesota	251	18
Mississippi	175	49
Missouri	254	17
Montana	207	39
Nebraska	230	28
Nevada	179	47
New Hampshire	241	23
New Jersey	319	8
New Mexico	219	32
New York	378	3
North Carolina	229	29
North Dakota	235	27
Ohio	265	12
Oklahoma	198	45
Oregon	227	31
Pennsylvania	324	7
Rhode Island	333	5
South Carolina	218	33
South Dakota	209	38
Tennessee	247	20
Texas	210	37
Utah	200	44
Vermont	325	6
Virginia	257	14
Washington	237	25
West Virginia	250	19
Wisconsin	236	26
Wyoming	178	48
50 States	260	
DC	694	
United States	267	

Rank in order per 100,000 population	
1	Massachusetts
2	Maryland
3	New York
4	Connecticut
5	Rhode Island
6	Vermont
7	Pennsylvania
8	New Jersey
9	Hawaii
10	Michigan
11	Illinois
12	Ohio
13	Maine
14	Virginia
15	Louisiana
16	Delaware
17	Missouri
18	Minnesota
19	West Virginia
20	Tennessee
21	California
22	Florida
23	New Hampshire
24	Colorado
25	Washington
26	Wisconsin
27	North Dakota
28	Nebraska
29	North Carolina
30	Kansas
31	Oregon
32	New Mexico
33	South Carolina
34	Kentucky
35	Georgia
36	Arizona
37	Texas
38	South Dakota
39	Montana
40	Indiana
41	Alabama
42	Iowa
43	Alaska
44	Utah
45	Oklahoma
46	Arkansas
47	Nevada
48	Wyoming
49	Mississippi
50	Idaho

Note: Numbers that appear to be identical are rounded and vary slightly in actual value. The rankings reflect the actual values before rounding. See the introduction for more details.

I-11 Hospital Beds Per 1,000 Population, 2000

State	Hospital beds per 1,000 population	Rank
Alabama	3.7	11
Alaska	2.3	41
Arizona	2.1	44
Arkansas	3.7	13
California	2.1	43
Colorado	2.2	42
Connecticut	2.3	40
Delaware	2.3	37
Florida	3.2	20
Georgia	2.9	25
Hawaii	2.5	35
Idaho	2.7	31
Illinois	3.0	23
Indiana	3.2	21
Iowa	4.0	7
Kansas	4.0	8
Kentucky	3.7	12
Louisiana	3.9	9
Maine	2.9	26
Maryland	2.1	45
Massachusetts	2.6	34
Michigan	2.6	33
Minnesota	3.4	18
Mississippi	4.8	3
Missouri	3.6	15
Montana	4.7	5
Nebraska	4.8	4
Nevada	1.9	49
New Hampshire	2.3	38
New Jersey	3.0	22
New Mexico	1.9	48
New York	3.5	16
North Carolina	2.9	28
North Dakota	6.0	1
Ohio	3.0	24
Oklahoma	3.2	19
Oregon	1.9	47
Pennsylvania	3.4	17
Rhode Island	2.3	39
South Carolina	2.9	27
South Dakota	5.7	2
Tennessee	3.6	14
Texas	2.7	32
Utah	1.9	46
Vermont	2.7	30
Virginia	2.4	36
Washington	1.9	50
West Virginia	4.4	6
Wisconsin	2.9	29
Wyoming	3.9	10
50 States	2.9	
DC	5.8	
United States	2.9	

Rank in order per 1,000 population

1	North Dakota
2	South Dakota
3	Mississippi
4	Nebraska
5	Montana
6	West Virginia
7	Iowa
8	Kansas
9	Louisiana
10	Wyoming
11	Alabama
12	Kentucky
13	Arkansas
14	Tennessee
15	Missouri
16	New York
17	Pennsylvania
18	Minnesota
19	Oklahoma
20	Florida
21	Indiana
22	New Jersey
23	Illinois
24	Ohio
25	Georgia
26	Maine
27	South Carolina
28	North Carolina
29	Wisconsin
30	Vermont
31	Idaho
32	Texas
33	Michigan
34	Massachusetts
35	Hawaii
36	Virginia
37	Delaware
38	New Hampshire
39	Rhode Island
40	Connecticut
41	Alaska
42	Colorado
43	California
44	Arizona
45	Maryland
46	Utah
47	Oregon
48	New Mexico
49	Nevada
50	Washington

Note: Numbers that appear to be identical are rounded and vary slightly in actual value. The rankings reflect the actual values before rounding. See the introduction for more details.

I-12 Medicaid Recipients, FY 2000

State	Medicaid recipients # (in thousands)	As a percentage of population	Rank by percentage
Alabama	619	13.9	24
Alaska	96	15.4	18
Arizona	681	13.3	28
Arkansas	489	18.3	8
California	7,915	23.4	2
Colorado	381	8.9	47
Connecticut	420	12.3	31
Delaware	115	14.7	23
Florida	2,360	14.8	22
Georgia	1,290	15.8	17
Hawaii	204	16.8	13
Idaho	131	10.1	40
Illinois	1,516	12.2	32
Indiana	705	11.6	34
Iowa	314	10.7	39
Kansas	263	9.8	43
Kentucky	771	19.1	6
Louisiana	761	17.0	12
Maine	192	15.0	20
Maryland	665	12.5	29
Massachusetts	1,047	16.5	14
Michigan	1,352	13.6	25
Minnesota	559	11.4	37
Mississippi	605	21.3	4
Missouri	890	15.9	15
Montana	104	11.5	35
Nebraska	229	13.4	27
Nevada	138	6.9	49
New Hampshire	97	7.8	48
New Jersey	822	9.8	42
New Mexico	376	20.6	5
New York	3,420	18.0	9
North Carolina	1,209	15.0	21
North Dakota	61	9.5	44
Ohio	1,305	11.5	36
Oklahoma	156	4.5	50
Oregon	542	15.9	16
Pennsylvania	1,492	12.2	33
Rhode Island	179	17.1	11
South Carolina	685	17.1	10
South Dakota	102	13.5	26
Tennessee	1,568	27.6	1
Texas	2,603	12.5	30
Utah	224	10.0	41
Vermont	139	22.8	3
Virginia	627	8.9	46
Washington	895	15.2	19
West Virginia	335	18.5	7
Wisconsin	577	10.8	38
Wyoming	46	9.4	45
50 States	42,274	15.1	
DC	139	24.2	
United States*	42,763	15.2	

*Due to rounding or data sources, the 50-state total plus D.C. may not equal the U.S. total. Please see introduction.

Rank in order by percentage	
1	Tennessee
2	California
3	Vermont
4	Mississippi
5	New Mexico
6	Kentucky
7	West Virginia
8	Arkansas
9	New York
10	South Carolina
11	Rhode Island
12	Louisiana
13	Hawaii
14	Massachusetts
15	Missouri
16	Oregon
17	Georgia
18	Alaska
19	Washington
20	Maine
21	North Carolina
22	Florida
23	Delaware
24	Alabama
25	Michigan
26	South Dakota
27	Nebraska
28	Arizona
29	Maryland
30	Texas
31	Connecticut
32	Illinois
33	Pennsylvania
34	Indiana
35	Montana
36	Ohio
37	Minnesota
38	Wisconsin
39	Iowa
40	Idaho
41	Utah
42	New Jersey
43	Kansas
44	North Dakota
45	Wyoming
46	Virginia
47	Colorado
48	New Hampshire
49	Nevada
50	Oklahoma

Note: Numbers that appear to be identical are rounded and vary slightly in actual value. The rankings reflect the actual values before rounding. See the introduction for more details.

I-13 Medicaid Recipients as a Percentage of Poverty Population, FY 2000

Rank in order by percentage

1 Rhode Island
2 Vermont
3 Connecticut
4 Missouri
5 Minnesota
6 Maine
7 Alaska
8 Tennessee
9 Hawaii
10 Maryland
11 New Hampshire
12 South Carolina
13 Delaware
14 California
15 Washington
16 Kentucky
17 Nebraska
18 Mississippi
19 Iowa
20 Massachusetts
21 South Dakota
22 Oregon
23 Indiana
24 Florida
25 Georgia
26 West Virginia
27 Pennsylvania
28 New York
29 Michigan
30 North Carolina
31 Wisconsin
32 Colorado
33 New Mexico
34 Virginia
35 New Jersey
36 Kansas
37 Arizona
38 Ohio
39 Utah
40 North Dakota
41 Illinois
42 Louisiana
43 Alabama
44 Arkansas
45 Nevada
46 Wyoming
47 Texas
48 Idaho
49 Montana
50 Oklahoma

State	Recipients as a percentage of poverty population	Rank
Alabama	101.1	43
Alaska	196.8	7
Arizona	111.5	37
Arkansas	100.7	44
California	173.6	14
Colorado	124.1	32
Connecticut	222.2	3
Delaware	177.3	13
Florida	143.2	24
Georgia	143.2	25
Hawaii	192.2	9
Idaho	78.0	48
Illinois	104.0	41
Indiana	153.5	23
Iowa	163.4	19
Kansas	112.7	36
Kentucky	168.6	16
Louisiana	101.1	42
Maine	197.6	6
Maryland	183.6	10
Massachusetts	161.4	20
Michigan	131.5	29
Minnesota	210.3	5
Mississippi	164.0	18
Missouri	219.3	4
Montana	73.1	49
Nebraska	164.8	17
Nevada	91.4	45
New Hampshire	182.9	11
New Jersey	119.7	35
New Mexico	122.7	33
New York	135.3	28
North Carolina	129.3	30
North Dakota	104.9	40
Ohio	107.9	38
Oklahoma	31.1	50
Oregon	158.6	22
Pennsylvania	136.0	27
Rhode Island	241.7	1
South Carolina	181.7	12
South Dakota	159.3	21
Tennessee	192.7	8
Texas	84.4	47
Utah	106.3	39
Vermont	231.4	2
Virginia	120.6	34
Washington	170.2	15
West Virginia	137.9	26
Wisconsin	125.6	31
Wyoming	89.3	46
50 States	136.1	
DC	190.0	
United States	137.3	

Note: Numbers that appear to be identical are rounded and vary slightly in actual value. The rankings reflect the actual values before rounding. See the introduction for more details.

I-14 State and Local Spending for Health and Hospitals, FY 2000

State	Total spending $ (in millions)	Per capita $	As a percentage of personal income	Rank per capita
Alabama	3,635	817	3.6	2
Alaska	236	376	1.3	26
Arizona	1,374	268	1.1	44
Arkansas	970	363	1.7	30
California	18,055	533	1.8	11
Colorado	1,341	312	1.0	38
Connecticut	1,596	469	1.2	14
Delaware	279	355	1.2	31
Florida	7,307	457	1.7	15
Georgia	3,554	434	1.7	18
Hawaii	601	495	1.8	12
Idaho	512	396	1.8	22
Illinois	4,381	353	1.2	33
Indiana	2,604	428	1.7	19
Iowa	1,678	574	2.3	8
Kansas	934	348	1.3	34
Kentucky	1,097	271	1.2	43
Louisiana	3,375	755	3.4	3
Maine	397	312	1.3	39
Maryland	1,295	244	0.8	46
Massachusetts	2,245	354	1.0	32
Michigan	4,179	421	1.5	21
Minnesota	1,826	371	1.2	28
Mississippi	2,114	743	3.7	5
Missouri	2,167	387	1.5	23
Montana	343	380	1.8	25
Nebraska	521	305	1.2	41
Nevada	737	369	1.3	29
New Hampshire	170	138	0.5	49
New Jersey	2,331	277	0.8	42
New Mexico	812	446	2.1	16
New York	11,568	610	1.9	7
North Carolina	5,536	688	2.8	6
North Dakota	91	141	0.6	48
Ohio	4,963	437	1.6	17
Oklahoma	1,324	384	1.7	24
Oregon	1,951	570	2.2	9
Pennsylvania	3,946	321	1.2	37
Rhode Island	278	265	1.0	45
South Carolina	3,016	752	3.3	4
South Dakota	150	199	0.8	47
Tennessee	2,739	481	2.0	13
Texas	8,854	425	1.6	20
Utah	741	332	1.5	36
Vermont	79	130	0.5	50
Virginia	2,634	372	1.3	27
Washington	3,317	563	1.9	10
West Virginia	552	305	1.5	40
Wisconsin	1,839	343	1.3	35
Wyoming	464	939	3.7	1
50 States	126,708	451	1.6	
DC	634	1,108	3.1	
United States	127,342	452	1.6	

Rank in order per capita	
1	Wyoming
2	Alabama
3	Louisiana
4	South Carolina
5	Mississippi
6	North Carolina
7	New York
8	Iowa
9	Oregon
10	Washington
11	California
12	Hawaii
13	Tennessee
14	Connecticut
15	Florida
16	New Mexico
17	Ohio
18	Georgia
19	Indiana
20	Texas
21	Michigan
22	Idaho
23	Missouri
24	Oklahoma
25	Montana
26	Alaska
27	Virginia
28	Minnesota
29	Nevada
30	Arkansas
31	Delaware
32	Massachusetts
33	Illinois
34	Kansas
35	Wisconsin
36	Utah
37	Pennsylvania
38	Colorado
39	Maine
40	West Virginia
41	Nebraska
42	New Jersey
43	Kentucky
44	Arizona
45	Rhode Island
46	Maryland
47	South Dakota
48	North Dakota
49	New Hampshire
50	Vermont

Note: Numbers that appear to be identical are rounded and vary slightly in actual value. The rankings reflect the actual values before rounding. See the introduction for more details.

I-15 State and Local Health and Hospital Spending as a Percentage of General Spending, FY 2000

State	Health and hospital spending as a percentage of general spending	Rank
Alabama	16.5	1
Alaska	3.1	47
Arizona	5.9	39
Arkansas	8.8	18
California	9.2	15
Colorado	6.0	36
Connecticut	7.5	28
Delaware	5.9	38
Florida	9.7	10
Georgia	9.3	13
Hawaii	8.2	22
Idaho	8.8	17
Illinois	6.8	30
Indiana	9.1	16
Iowa	10.8	8
Kansas	7.3	29
Kentucky	5.8	41
Louisiana	15.1	3
Maine	5.7	42
Maryland	4.7	45
Massachusetts	5.9	37
Michigan	7.6	24
Minnesota	5.9	40
Mississippi	15.2	2
Missouri	8.7	19
Montana	7.6	26
Nebraska	6.2	33
Nevada	7.6	27
New Hampshire	3.0	48
New Jersey	4.9	44
New Mexico	8.0	23
New York	8.3	21
North Carolina	13.7	6
North Dakota	2.5	49
Ohio	8.6	20
Oklahoma	9.6	12
Oregon	9.7	11
Pennsylvania	6.0	34
Rhode Island	5.0	43
South Carolina	14.9	4
South Dakota	4.4	46
Tennessee	10.8	7
Texas	9.2	14
Utah	6.7	31
Vermont	2.3	50
Virginia	7.6	25
Washington	9.9	9
West Virginia	6.3	32
Wisconsin	6.0	35
Wyoming	13.9	5
50 States	8.5	
DC	12.3	
United States	8.5	

Rank in order by percentage

1 Alabama
2 Mississippi
3 Louisiana
4 South Carolina
5 Wyoming
6 North Carolina
7 Tennessee
8 Iowa
9 Washington
10 Florida
11 Oregon
12 Oklahoma
13 Georgia
14 Texas
15 California
16 Indiana
17 Idaho
18 Arkansas
19 Missouri
20 Ohio
21 New York
22 Hawaii
23 New Mexico
24 Michigan
25 Virginia
26 Montana
27 Nevada
28 Connecticut
29 Kansas
30 Illinois
31 Utah
32 West Virginia
33 Nebraska
34 Pennsylvania
35 Wisconsin
36 Colorado
37 Massachusetts
38 Delaware
39 Arizona
40 Minnesota
41 Kentucky
42 Maine
43 Rhode Island
44 New Jersey
45 Maryland
46 South Dakota
47 Alaska
48 New Hampshire
49 North Dakota
50 Vermont

Note: Numbers that appear to be identical are rounded and vary slightly in actual value. The rankings reflect the actual values before rounding. See the introduction for more details.

I-16 Per Capita Medicaid Spending, FY 2000

State	Per capita Medicaid spending $	Rank
Alabama	538	27
Alaska	750	8
Arizona	412	48
Arkansas	565	22
California	504	32
Colorado	420	46
Connecticut	834	5
Delaware	674	12
Florida	460	38
Georgia	437	42
Hawaii	442	41
Idaho	459	39
Illinois	629	16
Indiana	489	35
Iowa	505	31
Kansas	456	40
Kentucky	721	9
Louisiana	589	20
Maine	1,025	2
Maryland	677	11
Massachusetts	850	4
Michigan	491	34
Minnesota	666	13
Mississippi	635	15
Missouri	584	21
Montana	480	36
Nebraska	560	23
Nevada	258	50
New Hampshire	526	29
New Jersey	559	24
New Mexico	686	10
New York	1,378	1
North Carolina	600	19
North Dakota	555	25
Ohio	625	17
Oklahoma	465	37
Oregon	497	33
Pennsylvania	518	30
Rhode Island	1,021	3
South Carolina	666	14
South Dakota	531	28
Tennessee	614	18
Texas	435	43
Utah	429	45
Vermont	787	6
Virginia	351	49
Washington	413	47
West Virginia	770	7
Wisconsin	542	26
Wyoming	433	44
50 States	596	
DC	1,385	
United States	598	

Rank in order per capita	
1	New York
2	Maine
3	Rhode Island
4	Massachusetts
5	Connecticut
6	Vermont
7	West Virginia
8	Alaska
9	Kentucky
10	New Mexico
11	Maryland
12	Delaware
13	Minnesota
14	South Carolina
15	Mississippi
16	Illinois
17	Ohio
18	Tennessee
19	North Carolina
20	Louisiana
21	Missouri
22	Arkansas
23	Nebraska
24	New Jersey
25	North Dakota
26	Wisconsin
27	Alabama
28	South Dakota
29	New Hampshire
30	Pennsylvania
31	Iowa
32	California
33	Oregon
34	Michigan
35	Indiana
36	Montana
37	Oklahoma
38	Florida
39	Idaho
40	Kansas
41	Hawaii
42	Georgia
43	Texas
44	Wyoming
45	Utah
46	Colorado
47	Washington
48	Arizona
49	Virginia
50	Nevada

Note: Numbers that appear to be identical are rounded and vary slightly in actual value. The rankings reflect the actual values before rounding. See the introduction for more details.

I-17 Average Medicaid Spending Per Aged Recipient, FY 2000

State	Average spending per aged recipient $	Rank
Alabama	9,793	34
Alaska	12,721	22
Arizona	10,402	29
Arkansas	8,089	46
California	6,314	49
Colorado	12,639	23
Connecticut	23,696	1
Delaware	15,455	9
Florida	9,218	37
Georgia	8,173	44
Hawaii	8,518	41
Idaho	14,314	15
Illinois	13,220	20
Indiana	15,053	12
Iowa	12,806	21
Kansas	13,955	16
Kentucky	9,964	32
Louisiana	8,192	43
Maine	12,404	24
Maryland	14,470	13
Massachusetts	15,762	8
Michigan	10,196	30
Minnesota	18,380	5
Mississippi	7,488	47
Missouri	11,996	25
Montana	13,296	19
Nebraska	13,791	17
Nevada	8,713	40
New Hampshire	19,512	3
New Jersey	15,452	10
New Mexico	9,274	36
New York	20,897	2
North Carolina	9,838	33
North Dakota	16,366	7
Ohio	18,951	4
Oklahoma	8,246	42
Oregon	10,068	31
Pennsylvania	13,494	18
Rhode Island	18,049	6
South Carolina	8,094	45
South Dakota	10,861	27
Tennessee	1,620	50
Texas	9,211	39
Utah	10,445	28
Vermont	7,411	48
Virginia	9,212	38
Washington	9,716	35
West Virginia	11,663	26
Wisconsin	15,306	11
Wyoming	14,420	14
50 States	11,367	
DC	16,628	
United States	11,394	

Rank in order by $	
1	Connecticut
2	New York
3	New Hampshire
4	Ohio
5	Minnesota
6	Rhode Island
7	North Dakota
8	Massachusetts
9	Delaware
10	New Jersey
11	Wisconsin
12	Indiana
13	Maryland
14	Wyoming
15	Idaho
16	Kansas
17	Nebraska
18	Pennsylvania
19	Montana
20	Illinois
21	Iowa
22	Alaska
23	Colorado
24	Maine
25	Missouri
26	West Virginia
27	South Dakota
28	Utah
29	Arizona
30	Michigan
31	Oregon
32	Kentucky
33	North Carolina
34	Alabama
35	Washington
36	New Mexico
37	Florida
38	Virginia
39	Texas
40	Nevada
41	Hawaii
42	Oklahoma
43	Louisiana
44	Georgia
45	South Carolina
46	Arkansas
47	Mississippi
48	Vermont
49	California
50	Tennessee

I-18 Average Medicaid Spending Per Child, FY 2000

State	Average spending per child $	Rank
Alabama	929	50
Alaska	3,177	2
Arizona	1,810	20
Arkansas	1,869	19
California	1,335	45
Colorado	2,199	10
Connecticut	1,705	30
Delaware	2,552	5
Florida	1,551	39
Georgia	1,292	47
Hawaii	1,678	33
Idaho	1,901	18
Illinois	1,720	28
Indiana	1,515	40
Iowa	2,067	12
Kansas	1,553	38
Kentucky	2,032	14
Louisiana	1,348	44
Maine	4,014	1
Maryland	2,603	4
Massachusetts	1,963	17
Michigan	1,114	49
Minnesota	2,385	8
Mississippi	1,298	46
Missouri	1,508	42
Montana	2,393	7
Nebraska	1,707	29
Nevada	2,002	15
New Hampshire	2,433	6
New Jersey	1,988	16
New Mexico	1,753	24
New York	3,025	3
North Carolina	1,686	31
North Dakota	1,805	21
Ohio	1,742	26
Oklahoma	1,383	43
Oregon	1,728	27
Pennsylvania	2,038	13
Rhode Island	2,151	11
South Carolina	1,645	34
South Dakota	1,685	32
Tennessee	1,512	41
Texas	1,634	35
Utah	1,804	22
Vermont	2,308	9
Virginia	1,562	37
Washington	1,255	48
West Virginia	1,580	36
Wisconsin	1,743	25
Wyoming	1,799	23
50 States	1,715	
DC	2,619	
United States	1,744	

Rank in order by $	
1	Maine
2	Alaska
3	New York
4	Maryland
5	Delaware
6	New Hampshire
7	Montana
8	Minnesota
9	Vermont
10	Colorado
11	Rhode Island
12	Iowa
13	Pennsylvania
14	Kentucky
15	Nevada
16	New Jersey
17	Massachusetts
18	Idaho
19	Arkansas
20	Arizona
21	North Dakota
22	Utah
23	Wyoming
24	New Mexico
25	Wisconsin
26	Ohio
27	Oregon
28	Illinois
29	Nebraska
30	Connecticut
31	North Carolina
32	South Dakota
33	Hawaii
34	South Carolina
35	Texas
36	West Virginia
37	Virginia
38	Kansas
39	Florida
40	Indiana
41	Tennessee
42	Missouri
43	Oklahoma
44	Louisiana
45	California
46	Mississippi
47	Georgia
48	Washington
49	Michigan
50	Alabama

I-19 Medicare Payment Per Hospital Day, FY 2000

State	Average payment per hospital day $	Rank
Alabama	2,842	12
Alaska	2,872	11
Arizona	3,793	3
Arkansas	2,144	40
California	4,605	1
Colorado	3,335	6
Connecticut	2,545	20
Delaware	1,913	47
Florida	3,371	5
Georgia	2,459	24
Hawaii	2,690	16
Idaho	2,414	26
Illinois	2,944	9
Indiana	2,223	37
Iowa	2,079	44
Kansas	2,518	22
Kentucky	2,208	38
Louisiana	2,656	17
Maine	2,267	36
Maryland	1,579	50
Massachusetts	2,376	29
Michigan	2,408	27
Minnesota	2,824	13
Mississippi	1,969	46
Missouri	2,730	15
Montana	2,198	39
Nebraska	2,922	10
Nevada	4,166	2
New Hampshire	2,388	28
New Jersey	3,673	4
New Mexico	2,478	23
New York	2,026	45
North Carolina	2,114	43
North Dakota	2,127	42
Ohio	2,307	33
Oklahoma	2,286	34
Oregon	2,650	18
Pennsylvania	2,946	8
Rhode Island	2,280	35
South Carolina	2,539	21
South Dakota	2,128	41
Tennessee	2,417	25
Texas	2,947	7
Utah	2,773	14
Vermont	1,884	48
Virginia	2,364	31
Washington	2,647	19
West Virginia	1,774	49
Wisconsin	2,366	30
Wyoming	2,325	32
50 States	2,716	
DC	3,263	
United States	2,694	

Rank in order by $	
1	California
2	Nevada
3	Arizona
4	New Jersey
5	Florida
6	Colorado
7	Texas
8	Pennsylvania
9	Illinois
10	Nebraska
11	Alaska
12	Alabama
13	Minnesota
14	Utah
15	Missouri
16	Hawaii
17	Louisiana
18	Oregon
19	Washington
20	Connecticut
21	South Carolina
22	Kansas
23	New Mexico
24	Georgia
25	Tennessee
26	Idaho
27	Michigan
28	New Hampshire
29	Massachusetts
30	Wisconsin
31	Virginia
32	Wyoming
33	Ohio
34	Oklahoma
35	Rhode Island
36	Maine
37	Indiana
38	Kentucky
39	Montana
40	Arkansas
41	South Dakota
42	North Dakota
43	North Carolina
44	Iowa
45	New York
46	Mississippi
47	Delaware
48	Vermont
49	West Virginia
50	Maryland

I-20 Hospital Expense Per Inpatient Day, 2000

State	Expense per inpatient day $	Rank
Alabama	1,666	49
Alaska	3,198	1
Arizona	2,069	29
Arkansas	1,702	47
California	2,247	23
Colorado	2,504	9
Connecticut	2,415	14
Delaware	2,478	10
Florida	1,793	45
Georgia	2,176	25
Hawaii	1,984	34
Idaho	2,317	18
Illinois	2,378	15
Indiana	2,331	17
Iowa	2,217	24
Kansas	2,022	33
Kentucky	1,808	43
Louisiana	1,770	46
Maine	2,296	20
Maryland	2,140	26
Massachusetts	2,779	3
Michigan	2,425	13
Minnesota	2,301	19
Mississippi	1,396	50
Missouri	2,253	22
Montana	2,573	6
Nebraska	2,032	31
Nevada	1,872	40
New Hampshire	2,662	5
New Jersey	1,827	41
New Mexico	2,365	16
New York	1,944	36
North Carolina	2,027	32
North Dakota	1,794	44
Ohio	2,277	21
Oklahoma	1,684	48
Oregon	2,767	4
Pennsylvania	1,938	37
Rhode Island	2,449	11
South Carolina	1,930	38
South Dakota	2,126	28
Tennessee	1,967	35
Texas	2,033	30
Utah	2,446	12
Vermont	2,138	27
Virginia	1,875	39
Washington	2,872	2
West Virginia	1,821	42
Wisconsin	2,539	8
Wyoming	2,544	7
50 States	2,099	
DC	2,271	
United States	2,100	

Rank in order by $

1. Alaska
2. Washington
3. Massachusetts
4. Oregon
5. New Hampshire
6. Montana
7. Wyoming
8. Wisconsin
9. Colorado
10. Delaware
11. Rhode Island
12. Utah
13. Michigan
14. Connecticut
15. Illinois
16. New Mexico
17. Indiana
18. Idaho
19. Minnesota
20. Maine
21. Ohio
22. Missouri
23. California
24. Iowa
25. Georgia
26. Maryland
27. Vermont
28. South Dakota
29. Arizona
30. Texas
31. Nebraska
32. North Carolina
33. Kansas
34. Hawaii
35. Tennessee
36. New York
37. Pennsylvania
38. South Carolina
39. Virginia
40. Nevada
41. New Jersey
42. West Virginia
43. Kentucky
44. North Dakota
45. Florida
46. Louisiana
47. Arkansas
48. Oklahoma
49. Alabama
50. Mississippi

I-21 Percentage of Population in Health Maintenance Organizations, 2002

State	Percentage of population in HMOs	Rank
Alabama	4.7	45
Alaska	0.0	50
Arizona	25.8	20
Arkansas	7.7	42
California	50.5	1
Colorado	32.9	7
Connecticut	38.3	3
Delaware	23.0	23
Florida	29.8	16
Georgia	15.2	30
Hawaii	32.8	8
Idaho	2.9	46
Illinois	18.0	27
Indiana	10.7	37
Iowa	5.1	44
Kansas	13.2	35
Kentucky	31.8	10
Louisiana	14.0	34
Maine	23.9	22
Maryland	34.7	5
Massachusetts	42.4	2
Michigan	25.5	21
Minnesota	26.9	19
Mississippi	1.4	48
Missouri	31.2	11
Montana	5.8	43
Nebraska	8.7	40
Nevada	22.4	24
New Hampshire	30.3	14
New Jersey	30.9	13
New Mexico	29.0	18
New York	33.6	6
North Carolina	14.8	32
North Dakota	0.4	49
Ohio	21.6	25
Oklahoma	14.8	32
Oregon	30.1	15
Pennsylvania	31.2	11
Rhode Island	34.8	4
South Carolina	8.0	41
South Dakota	11.5	36
Tennessee	18.6	26
Texas	14.9	31
Utah	32.0	9
Vermont	10.5	38
Virginia	15.9	29
Washington	17.4	28
West Virginia	10.0	39
Wisconsin	29.3	17
Wyoming	2.0	47
50 States	n/a	
DC	31.2	
United States	26.4	

Rank in order by percentage

1 California
2 Massachusetts
3 Connecticut
4 Rhode Island
5 Maryland
6 New York
7 Colorado
8 Hawaii
9 Utah
10 Kentucky
11 Missouri
11 Pennsylvania
13 New Jersey
14 New Hampshire
15 Oregon
16 Florida
17 Wisconsin
18 New Mexico
19 Minnesota
20 Arizona
21 Michigan
22 Maine
23 Delaware
24 Nevada
25 Ohio
26 Tennessee
27 Illinois
28 Washington
29 Virginia
30 Georgia
31 Texas
32 North Carolina
32 Oklahoma
34 Louisiana
35 Kansas
36 South Dakota
37 Indiana
38 Vermont
39 West Virginia
40 Nebraska
41 South Carolina
42 Arkansas
43 Montana
44 Iowa
45 Alabama
46 Idaho
47 Wyoming
48 Mississippi
49 North Dakota
50 Alaska

Note: Ties in ranking reflect ties in actual values.

Source Notes for Health (Section I)

I-1 Immunization Rates, 2001: Information on immunization is collected by the Centers for Disease Control and Prevention (CDC) as part of their National Immunization Survey and are available on the CDC website (www.cdc.gov).

I-2 Infant Mortality Rates, 2000: These data are collected by the Centers for Disease Control and Prevention and are available on the CDC website (www.cdc.gov). They cover deaths of all children under one year of age, expressed in relation to each one thousand live births. This statistic is considered one of the best indicators with which to compare health among states and local areas. Higher death rates are associated with poor health of the mother, absence of medical care during pregnancy, and lack of medical treatment for infants.

I-3 State Health Rankings, 2002: These scores and rankings are developed annually for UnitedHealth Group (Minneapolis, Minn.) by Arundel Street Consulting, Inc. (175 Arundel Street, St. Paul, MN 55102). The results are from *America's Health: UnitedHealth Foundation State Health Rankings 2002 Edition.* They reflect a composite of indicators, including unemployment, health practices (such as smoking), the availability of health services, and outcomes (such as death rates). Probably no two researchers would use identical lists to produce such rankings, but the state rankings would likely be similar. While decisions by states have some impact on health rankings, decisions on health practices by individual citizens have more of an impact.

I-4 Percentage of Non-Elderly Population Without Health Insurance, 2001: Most Americans get health insurance coverage through their employers. All Americans over age sixty-four are covered by Medicare. About 11 percent of the non-elderly, including all welfare recipients, get coverage paid for by state and federal governments through Medicaid. Non-elderly citizens who have no health insurance comprise 16.5 percent of the population. These data are part of a compilation titled "Table HI-6" from the Housing and Household Economic Statistics Division of the Census Bureau.

I-5 Abortions, 1998: This count comes from the Centers for Disease Control and Prevention (www.cdc.gov). The abortion rate compares the number of abortions with the number of live births.

I-6 Alcohol Consumption Per Capita, 1999: Some public health authorities consider high levels of alcoholic beverage consumption an indicator of poor health of a state's population. The data show the number of gallons of pure ethanol (typical liquor is about 43 percent ethanol or ethanol alcohol, wine 14 percent, and beer about 6 percent) consumed per resident age fourteen and over. The data are derived by dividing sales of alcoholic beverages by population. Those shown were developed by the Department of Health and Human Services (National Institute on Alcohol Abuse and Alcoholism) and are published on its website (www.niaaa.nih.gov). They are called "apparent" alcohol consumption because some alcoholic beverages are bought in one state for consumption by residents of another. This raises the apparent consumption of tourist-destination states, like Nevada, and states with low prices, like New Hampshire, which draw purchasers from other states.

I-7 Percentage of Adult Smokers, 2001: These estimates, results of sample surveys, are developed by the Behavioral Surveillance Branch of the Centers for Disease Control and Prevention (CDC) and are available on the CDC website (www.cdc.gov). They reflect the percentage of the population who have smoked 100 cigarettes in their lifetime and reported smoking every day or some days.

I-8 Percentage of Population Obese, 2001: These data are part of the Centers for Disease Control and Prevention's (CDC) behavioral risk factor surveillance system. Different definitions of how high a person's body mass index (BMI) can be without being considered a health risk would produce different percentages for every state, but not appreciably affect the rankings. These statistics were retrieved from the CDC website (www.cdc.gov). A person with a BMI of 30 or more is considered *obese*, while a BMI of 25 to 29.9 is considered *overweight.*

I-9 AIDS Cases, 2001: These data are developed by the Centers for Disease Control and Prevention (CDC) and reported in the *HIV/AIDS Surveillance Report* (Vol. 13, No. 2). They cover cases newly reported in calendar year 2001. The rate shown is cases per one hundred thousand residents. Because persons at most risk of contracting AIDS are predominantly found in larger metropolitan areas, states containing those areas typically show the highest rates.

I-10 Physicians Per 100,000 Population, 2002: This table shows the number of physicians in relation to population. Rural states will show below-average numbers in part because intensive medical care, such as that received from major hospitals, is often sought in nearby states with large metropolitan areas. The statistics are based on data from Medical Marketing Service, Inc. (www.mmslists.com).

I-11 Hospital Beds Per 1,000 Population, 2000: This table shows the number of community hospital beds in relation to population. The data come from *Hospital Statistics, 2002 Edition,* a publication of the American Hospital Association. As of 1998, the AHA state data no longer cover all hospitals. Thus, the data shown here reflect only community (non-federal, short-term, general and other special) hospitals.

I-12 Medicaid Recipients, FY 2000: Over 42 million people receive health care through the Medicaid program each year. The federal government sets minimum standards for this program and pays about 60 percent of the costs nationwide through a formula that provides 50 percent of the costs in the most affluent states and up to 76 percent in the poorest states. Within federal guidelines, states set the rules for eligibility, the health services covered, and the amount of reimbursements to the providers of care.

The primary recipients are families that receive cash assistance from states through Temporary Assistance for Needy Families or from the federal government through Supplemental Security Income. These data come from tabulations of the Department of Health and Human Services' Centers for Medicare and Medicaid Services (CMS) and are available on the internet (cms.hhs.gov).

I-13 Medicaid Recipients as a Percentage of Poverty Population, FY 2000: These data, from the same source as Table I-12, relate the number of Medicaid recipients to the number of persons in households with income below federally defined poverty levels (see Table A-11). The differences among states are a good indication of how inclusive are the eligibility criteria set by the individual states.

I-14 State and Local Spending for Health and Hospitals, FY 2000: This table relates spending data to population and personal income in each state. The data come from the Census Bureau's electronic publication "State and Local Government Finance Estimates, by State," available on the Census website (www.census.gov). See notes to Table F-1 for more extensive information on the source of the data.

The spending includes public health activities plus the gross outlays of hospitals and nursing homes run by state and local governments, including costs defrayed by the charges such as hospitals make to patients and their health insurance providers. The largest outlays appear in states that rely heavily on government-owned hospitals.

I-15 State and Local Health and Hospital Spending as a Percentage of General Spending, FY 2000: This table shows the relative importance of health and hospital outlays in state and local budgets. It is derived by comparing this spending (see Table I-14) with total "general" spending. General spending includes essentially all other spending except municipal electric and other utilities and trust funds, such as those for workers' compensation.

I-16 Per Capita Medicaid Spending, FY 2000: These data, from the same source as the number of recipients in Table I-12, reflect the major impact that Medicaid costs are having on government budgets. The amounts shown reflect primarily federal grants spent by states, about 60 percent of the total with differences among the states, and state

government matching funds. In a few states, particularly New York, some of the federally required state match is provided by local governments.

I-17 Average Medicaid Spending Per Aged Recipient, FY 2000: These data, from the same source as Table I-12, illustrate differences among the states in this component of Medicaid costs. They relate total spending on all Medicaid recipients age sixty-five and over to the number of recipients. Over half of the nursing home residents in the United States are having their bills paid by Medicaid. States differ in the extent and success of programs designed to encourage people to live at home and with relatives rather than enter nursing homes. Those programs typically provide visiting nurses and homemakers who assist frail elderly persons in their homes, thereby reducing the need for institutionalization.

I-18 Average Medicaid Spending Per Child, FY 2000: These data reflect the same concepts and come from the same source as those shown in Table I-17. Differences among states primarily reflect differences in how much doctors and other providers of health care are compensated for providing services.

I-19 Medicare Payment Per Hospital Day, FY 2000: These data are one way to measure healthcare cost differences among states. They reflect the cost of a day in short-stay hospitals as reimbursed by the federal Medicare program. The data come from the Centers for Medicare and Medicaid Services (CMS) and are available on the Internet (cms.hhs.gov). These data include both the basic rate for staying in the hospital (see Table I-20) and charges for specific services.

I-20 Hospital Expense Per Inpatient Day, 2000: These data result from a comparison of inpatient days and hospital unit total expenses at community hospitals as reported by the American Hospital Association. See source for Table I-11.

I-21 Percentage of Population in Health Maintenance Organizations, 2002: Most Americans receive their healthcare by purchasing it from individual doctors, hospitals, pharmacies, and others. However, a percentage are served by health maintenance organizations that provide complete packages of care for one monthly fee. Many people believe that this approach to buying care will reduce healthcare costs because the service providers cannot increase their incomes by providing additional services. The statistics, reflecting enrollment in January 2002 as a percentage of population, come from InterStudy (Saint Paul, Minn.) and are published in *InterStudy Competitive Edge 12.2 Part II: HMO Industry Report*.

Crime and Law Enforcement

J-1	Total Crime Rate, 2001	250
J-2	Violent Crime Rate, 2001	251
J-3	Murder and Rape Rates, 2001	252
J-4	Property Crime Rate, 2001	253
J-5	Motor Vehicle Theft Rate, 2001	254
J-6	Violent Crime Rate Change, 1996-2001	255
J-7	Prisoners, 2001	256
J-8	Change in Prisoners, 1995-2001	257
J-9	Incarceration Rate, 2001	258
J-10	Juvenile Violent Crime Index, 2000	259
J-11	State and Local Law Enforcement Employees, 2001	260
J-12	State and Local Corrections Employees, 2001	261
J-13	State Corrections Spending, FY 2001	262
J-14	Percentage Increase in State Corrections Spending, FY 1999-2001	263
J-15	State and Local Spending for Law Enforcement, FY 2000	264
J-16	State and Local Law Enforcement Spending as a Percentage of General Spending, FY 2000	265

After a decade of declines, the crime rate grew in 2001—although at 0.9 percent the increase was moderate. The 2001 rate—4,160 per 100,000 inhabitants—is still 30 percent under rates of just a decade ago. Though it's likely that a variety of factors contributed to the reduction in crime in the recent past, good economic times and fewer teenagers go far in explaining the trend. Likewise, it can be assumed that recent economic difficulties and a slight rise in the teenage population account in large part for the higher rate in 2001.

At 7 percent, corrections eats up a relatively small chunk of state spending, but its portion has swelled in recent years. Now, with crime rates still fairly low, prison populations growing at a record slow pace, and budgets feeling the crunch, states are looking for ways to tighten outlays on corrections. Twenty–seven states instituted cost-cutting measures in fiscal year 2002, including prison closings, hiring freezes, and the elimination of so-called "non-essential" programs for prisoners, such as educational and vocational training.

Some states are adding flexibility to the unforgiving "three strikes and you're out" policies of the mid-1990s. Twenty states have enacted or are considering sentencing policy changes. Connecticut, Indiana, Louisiana, and North Dakota repealed mandatory minimum sentences. California, Idaho, Oregon, and Washington allow drug treatment in place of jail for certain convictions. However, a similar drug treatment initiative on the 2002 Ohio ballot failed. Kentucky made national headlines when Governor Paul Patton ordered the early release of 567 non-violent criminals. The commutation is expected to save $3 million in a state facing a $500 million budget deficit.

In other news, in mid-2002 the federal government unveiled a new grant program to help states combat recidivism. The Reentry Initiative is designed to help offenders adapt to non-prison life. The program begins while offenders are inside correctional institutions and continues after they're released through short-and long-term monitoring and mentoring programs and services such as job skill development and substance abuse treatment.

J-1 Total Crime Rate, 2001

State	Crime rate (per 100,000 population)	Rank
Alabama	4,319	18
Alaska	4,236	21
Arizona	6,077	1
Arkansas	4,134	25
California	3,903	29
Colorado	4,219	22
Connecticut	3,118	40
Delaware	4,053	28
Florida	5,570	2
Georgia	4,646	14
Hawaii	5,386	3
Idaho	3,133	39
Illinois	4,098	26
Indiana	3,831	30
Iowa	3,301	36
Kansas	4,321	17
Kentucky	2,938	43
Louisiana	5,338	4
Maine	2,688	46
Maryland	4,867	11
Massachusetts	3,099	41
Michigan	4,082	27
Minnesota	3,584	33
Mississippi	4,185	23
Missouri	4,776	12
Montana	3,689	31
Nebraska	4,330	16
Nevada	4,266	19
New Hampshire	2,322	50
New Jersey	3,225	37
New Mexico	5,324	5
New York	2,925	44
North Carolina	4,938	10
North Dakota	2,418	48
Ohio	4,178	24
Oklahoma	4,607	15
Oregon	5,044	9
Pennsylvania	2,961	42
Rhode Island	3,685	32
South Carolina	4,753	13
South Dakota	2,332	49
Tennessee	5,153	6
Texas	5,153	7
Utah	4,243	20
Vermont	2,769	45
Virginia	3,178	38
Washington	5,152	8
West Virginia	2,560	47
Wisconsin	3,321	35
Wyoming	3,518	34
50 States	n/a	
DC	7,710	
United States	4,161	

Rank in order by rate	
1	Arizona
2	Florida
3	Hawaii
4	Louisiana
5	New Mexico
6	Tennessee
7	Texas
8	Washington
9	Oregon
10	North Carolina
11	Maryland
12	Missouri
13	South Carolina
14	Georgia
15	Oklahoma
16	Nebraska
17	Kansas
18	Alabama
19	Nevada
20	Utah
21	Alaska
22	Colorado
23	Mississippi
24	Ohio
25	Arkansas
26	Illinois
27	Michigan
28	Delaware
29	California
30	Indiana
31	Montana
32	Rhode Island
33	Minnesota
34	Wyoming
35	Wisconsin
36	Iowa
37	New Jersey
38	Virginia
39	Idaho
40	Connecticut
41	Massachusetts
42	Pennsylvania
43	Kentucky
44	New York
45	Vermont
46	Maine
47	West Virginia
48	North Dakota
49	South Dakota
50	New Hampshire

Note: Numbers that appear to be identical are rounded and vary slightly in actual value. The rankings reflect the actual values before rounding. See the introduction for more details.

J-2 Violent Crime Rate, 2001

State	Violent crime rate (per 100,000 population)	Rank
Alabama	439	22
Alaska	588	10
Arizona	540	15
Arkansas	453	21
California	617	8
Colorado	351	30
Connecticut	336	32
Delaware	611	9
Florida	797	1
Georgia	497	18
Hawaii	255	42
Idaho	243	43
Illinois	637	7
Indiana	372	26
Iowa	269	38
Kansas	405	24
Kentucky	257	41
Louisiana	687	6
Maine	112	48
Maryland	783	2
Massachusetts	480	20
Michigan	555	13
Minnesota	264	39
Mississippi	350	31
Missouri	541	14
Montana	352	28
Nebraska	304	35
Nevada	587	11
New Hampshire	170	46
New Jersey	390	25
New Mexico	781	3
New York	516	16
North Carolina	494	19
North Dakota	80	50
Ohio	352	29
Oklahoma	512	17
Oregon	307	34
Pennsylvania	410	23
Rhode Island	310	33
South Carolina	720	5
South Dakota	155	47
Tennessee	745	4
Texas	573	12
Utah	234	44
Vermont	105	49
Virginia	291	36
Washington	355	27
West Virginia	279	37
Wisconsin	231	45
Wyoming	257	40
50 States	n/a	
DC	1,737	
United States	504	

Rank in order by rate

1	Florida
2	Maryland
3	New Mexico
4	Tennessee
5	South Carolina
6	Louisiana
7	Illinois
8	California
9	Delaware
10	Alaska
11	Nevada
12	Texas
13	Michigan
14	Missouri
15	Arizona
16	New York
17	Oklahoma
18	Georgia
19	North Carolina
20	Massachusetts
21	Arkansas
22	Alabama
23	Pennsylvania
24	Kansas
25	New Jersey
26	Indiana
27	Washington
28	Montana
29	Ohio
30	Colorado
31	Mississippi
32	Connecticut
33	Rhode Island
34	Oregon
35	Nebraska
36	Virginia
37	West Virginia
38	Iowa
39	Minnesota
40	Wyoming
41	Kentucky
42	Hawaii
43	Idaho
44	Utah
45	Wisconsin
46	New Hampshire
47	South Dakota
48	Maine
49	Vermont
50	North Dakota

Note: Numbers that appear to be identical are rounded and vary slightly in actual value. The rankings reflect the actual values before rounding. See the introduction for more details.

J-3 Murder and Rape Rates, 2001

State	Murder rate (per 100,000 population)	Rape rate (per 100,000 population)	Rank by murder rate
Alabama	8.5	30.7	3
Alaska	6.1	78.9	17
Arizona	7.5	28.6	7
Arkansas	5.5	33.1	18
California	6.4	28.9	13
Colorado	3.6	43.7	30
Connecticut	3.1	18.7	33
Delaware	2.9	52.8	36
Florida	5.3	40.5	20
Georgia	7.1	26.0	9
Hawaii	2.6	33.4	37
Idaho	2.3	32.2	41
Illinois	7.9	31.5	6
Indiana	6.8	28.1	10
Iowa	1.7	22.2	45
Kansas	3.4	35.1	32
Kentucky	4.7	27.8	25
Louisiana	11.2	31.4	1
Maine	1.4	25.3	46
Maryland	8.3	27.0	5
Massachusetts	2.3	29.1	41
Michigan	6.7	52.7	11
Minnesota	2.4	45.0	39
Mississippi	9.9	40.1	2
Missouri	6.6	24.6	12
Montana	3.8	20.8	28
Nebraska	2.5	25.2	38
Nevada	8.5	41.9	3
New Hampshire	1.4	36.4	46
New Jersey	4.0	15.1	26
New Mexico	5.4	46.5	19
New York	5.0	18.7	24
North Carolina	6.2	25.4	15
North Dakota	1.1	25.8	48
Ohio	4.0	39.3	26
Oklahoma	5.3	42.9	20
Oregon	2.4	33.8	39
Pennsylvania	5.3	28.2	20
Rhode Island	3.7	39.3	29
South Carolina	6.3	34.0	14
South Dakota	0.9	46.4	50
Tennessee	7.4	38.3	8
Texas	6.2	38.3	15
Utah	3.0	39.5	34
Vermont	1.1	17.5	48
Virginia	5.1	24.6	23
Washington	3.0	43.4	34
West Virginia	2.2	17.8	43
Wisconsin	3.6	21.1	30
Wyoming	1.8	30.9	44
50 States	n/a	n/a	
DC	40.6	32.9	
United States	5.6	31.8	

Rank in order by murder rate

1	Louisiana
2	Mississippi
3	Alabama
3	Nevada
5	Maryland
6	Illinois
7	Arizona
8	Tennessee
9	Georgia
10	Indiana
11	Michigan
12	Missouri
13	California
14	South Carolina
15	North Carolina
15	Texas
17	Alaska
18	Arkansas
19	New Mexico
20	Florida
20	Oklahoma
20	Pennsylvania
23	Virginia
24	New York
25	Kentucky
26	New Jersey
26	Ohio
28	Montana
29	Rhode Island
30	Colorado
30	Wisconsin
32	Kansas
33	Connecticut
34	Utah
34	Washington
36	Delaware
37	Hawaii
38	Nebraska
39	Minnesota
39	Oregon
41	Idaho
41	Massachusetts
43	West Virginia
44	Wyoming
45	Iowa
46	Maine
46	New Hampshire
48	North Dakota
48	Vermont
50	South Dakota

Note: Ties in ranking reflect ties in actual values.

J-4 Property Crime Rate, 2001

State	Property crime rate (per 100,000 population)	Rank
Alabama	3,881	19
Alaska	3,648	25
Arizona	5,537	1
Arkansas	3,681	23
California	3,286	33
Colorado	3,868	20
Connecticut	2,782	40
Delaware	3,441	29
Florida	4,773	4
Georgia	4,149	12
Hawaii	5,132	2
Idaho	2,890	37
Illinois	3,461	27
Indiana	3,460	28
Iowa	3,032	36
Kansas	3,917	18
Kentucky	2,681	41
Louisiana	4,651	6
Maine	2,577	44
Maryland	4,084	14
Massachusetts	2,619	43
Michigan	3,527	26
Minnesota	3,319	32
Mississippi	3,835	21
Missouri	4,235	11
Montana	3,336	31
Nebraska	4,025	16
Nevada	3,679	24
New Hampshire	2,151	50
New Jersey	2,835	39
New Mexico	4,543	8
New York	2,409	46
North Carolina	4,444	9
North Dakota	2,338	47
Ohio	3,826	22
Oklahoma	4,095	13
Oregon	4,737	5
Pennsylvania	2,551	45
Rhode Island	3,375	30
South Carolina	4,032	15
South Dakota	2,177	49
Tennessee	4,408	10
Texas	4,580	7
Utah	4,009	17
Vermont	2,664	42
Virginia	2,887	38
Washington	4,797	3
West Virginia	2,280	48
Wisconsin	3,090	35
Wyoming	3,260	34
50 States	n/a	
DC	5,973	
United States	3,656	

Rank in order by rate	
1	Arizona
2	Hawaii
3	Washington
4	Florida
5	Oregon
6	Louisiana
7	Texas
8	New Mexico
9	North Carolina
10	Tennessee
11	Missouri
12	Georgia
13	Oklahoma
14	Maryland
15	South Carolina
16	Nebraska
17	Utah
18	Kansas
19	Alabama
20	Colorado
21	Mississippi
22	Ohio
23	Arkansas
24	Nevada
25	Alaska
26	Michigan
27	Illinois
28	Indiana
29	Delaware
30	Rhode Island
31	Montana
32	Minnesota
33	California
34	Wyoming
35	Wisconsin
36	Iowa
37	Idaho
38	Virginia
39	New Jersey
40	Connecticut
41	Kentucky
42	Vermont
43	Massachusetts
44	Maine
45	Pennsylvania
46	New York
47	North Dakota
48	West Virginia
49	South Dakota
50	New Hampshire

J-5 Motor Vehicle Theft Rate, 2001

State	Motor vehicle theft rate (per 100,000 population)	Rank
Alabama	283	35
Alaska	412	19
Arizona	984	1
Arkansas	272	37
California	591	5
Colorado	475	14
Connecticut	361	26
Delaware	349	28
Florida	548	7
Georgia	448	15
Hawaii	551	6
Idaho	181	43
Illinois	391	20
Indiana	352	27
Iowa	188	42
Kansas	296	32
Kentucky	230	40
Louisiana	486	11
Maine	130	48
Maryland	596	4
Massachusetts	436	17
Michigan	537	8
Minnesota	302	30
Mississippi	332	29
Missouri	498	9
Montana	201	41
Nebraska	379	22
Nevada	698	2
New Hampshire	170	46
New Jersey	444	16
New Mexico	390	21
New York	254	39
North Carolina	301	31
North Dakota	171	45
Ohio	371	23
Oklahoma	363	24
Oregon	427	18
Pennsylvania	291	33
Rhode Island	476	13
South Carolina	363	24
South Dakota	108	50
Tennessee	493	10
Texas	481	12
Utah	287	34
Vermont	124	49
Virginia	262	38
Washington	653	3
West Virginia	179	44
Wisconsin	273	36
Wyoming	141	47
50 States	n/a	
DC	1,341	
United States	431	

Rank in order by rate

1	Arizona
2	Nevada
3	Washington
4	Maryland
5	California
6	Hawaii
7	Florida
8	Michigan
9	Missouri
10	Tennessee
11	Louisiana
12	Texas
13	Rhode Island
14	Colorado
15	Georgia
16	New Jersey
17	Massachusetts
18	Oregon
19	Alaska
20	Illinois
21	New Mexico
22	Nebraska
23	Ohio
24	Oklahoma
24	South Carolina
26	Connecticut
27	Indiana
28	Delaware
29	Mississippi
30	Minnesota
31	North Carolina
32	Kansas
33	Pennsylvania
34	Utah
35	Alabama
36	Wisconsin
37	Arkansas
38	Virginia
39	New York
40	Kentucky
41	Montana
42	Iowa
43	Idaho
44	West Virginia
45	North Dakota
46	New Hampshire
47	Wyoming
48	Maine
49	Vermont
50	South Dakota

Note: Ties in ranking reflect ties in actual values.

J-6 Violent Crime Rate Change, 1996-2001

State	1996 violent crime rate (per 100,000 population)	Percentage increase in violent crime 1996-2001	Rank by percentage increase
Alabama	565	-22.4	33
Alaska	728	-19.2	29
Arizona	632	-14.4	22
Arkansas	524	-13.6	20
California	863	-28.5	42
Colorado	405	-13.3	18
Connecticut	412	-18.6	28
Delaware	668	-8.5	9
Florida	1,051	-24.1	34
Georgia	639	-22.2	32
Hawaii	281	-9.3	12
Idaho	267	-9.0	11
Illinois	886	-28.1	40
Indiana	537	-30.8	46
Iowa	273	-1.2	2
Kansas	414	-2.2	3
Kentucky	321	-19.8	30
Louisiana	929	-26.1	36
Maine	125	-10.7	13
Maryland	931	-15.9	24
Massachusetts	642	-25.3	35
Michigan	635	-12.7	17
Minnesota	339	-22.0	31
Mississippi	488	-28.3	41
Missouri	591	-8.4	8
Montana	161	n/a	n/a
Nebraska	435	-30.0	45
Nevada	811	-27.7	38
New Hampshire	118	n/a	n/a
New Jersey	532	-26.6	37
New Mexico	841	-7.1	7
New York	727	-29.0	43
North Carolina	588	-15.9	25
North Dakota	84	-5.2	6
Ohio	429	-17.9	27
Oklahoma	597	-14.2	21
Oregon	463	-33.8	47
Pennsylvania	433	-5.1	5
Rhode Island	347	-10.8	14
South Carolina	997	-27.7	39
South Dakota	177	-12.6	16
Tennessee	774	-3.7	4
Texas	644	-11.1	15
Utah	332	-29.5	44
Vermont	121	-13.4	19
Virginia	341	-14.6	23
Washington	431	-17.7	26
West Virginia	210	n/a	n/a
Wisconsin	253	-8.5	10
Wyoming	250	3.0	1
50 States	n/a	n/a	
DC	2,470	-29.7	
United States	634	-20.4	

Rank in order by percentage increase

1 Wyoming
2 Iowa
3 Kansas
4 Tennessee
5 Pennsylvania
6 North Dakota
7 New Mexico
8 Missouri
9 Delaware
10 Wisconsin
11 Idaho
12 Hawaii
13 Maine
14 Rhode Island
15 Texas
16 South Dakota
17 Michigan
18 Colorado
19 Vermont
20 Arkansas
21 Oklahoma
22 Arizona
23 Virginia
24 Maryland
25 North Carolina
26 Washington
27 Ohio
28 Connecticut
29 Alaska
30 Kentucky
31 Minnesota
32 Georgia
33 Alabama
34 Florida
35 Massachusetts
36 Louisiana
37 New Jersey
38 Nevada
39 South Carolina
40 Illinois
41 Mississippi
42 California
43 New York
44 Utah
45 Nebraska
46 Indiana
47 Oregon

Note: Numbers that appear to be identical are rounded and vary slightly in actual value. The rankings reflect the actual values before rounding. See the introduction for more details.

J-7 Prisoners, 2001

	Rank in order by #
1	Texas
2	California
3	Florida
4	New York
5	Michigan
6	Georgia
7	Ohio
8	Illinois
9	Pennsylvania
10	Louisiana
11	North Carolina
12	Virginia
13	Missouri
14	New Jersey
15	Arizona
16	Alabama
17	Maryland
18	Tennessee
19	Oklahoma
20	South Carolina
21	Wisconsin
22	Mississippi
23	Indiana
24	Connecticut
25	Colorado
26	Kentucky
27	Washington
28	Arkansas
29	Oregon
30	Massachusetts
31	Nevada
32	Kansas
33	Iowa
34	Delaware
35	Minnesota
36	Idaho
37	New Mexico
38	Hawaii
39	Utah
40	Alaska
41	West Virginia
42	Nebraska
43	Montana
44	Rhode Island
45	South Dakota
46	New Hampshire
47	Vermont
48	Maine
49	Wyoming
50	North Dakota

State	Prisoners #	Rank
Alabama	26,741	16
Alaska	4,546	40
Arizona	27,710	15
Arkansas	12,159	28
California	159,444	2
Colorado	17,448	25
Connecticut	19,196	24
Delaware	7,006	34
Florida	72,406	3
Georgia	45,937	6
Hawaii	5,454	38
Idaho	6,006	36
Illinois	44,348	8
Indiana	20,966	23
Iowa	7,962	33
Kansas	8,577	32
Kentucky	15,424	26
Louisiana	35,710	10
Maine	1,704	48
Maryland	23,752	17
Massachusetts	10,602	30
Michigan	48,849	5
Minnesota	6,606	35
Mississippi	21,460	22
Missouri	28,757	13
Montana	3,328	43
Nebraska	3,937	42
Nevada	10,201	31
New Hampshire	2,392	46
New Jersey	28,142	14
New Mexico	5,668	37
New York	67,534	4
North Carolina	31,979	11
North Dakota	1,111	50
Ohio	45,281	7
Oklahoma	22,780	19
Oregon	11,455	29
Pennsylvania	38,062	9
Rhode Island	3,241	44
South Carolina	22,576	20
South Dakota	2,812	45
Tennessee	23,671	18
Texas	162,070	1
Utah	5,343	39
Vermont	1,741	47
Virginia	31,603	12
Washington	15,159	27
West Virginia	4,215	41
Wisconsin	21,533	21
Wyoming	1,684	49
50 States	**1,246,288**	
DC	**2,750**	
United States	**1,249,038**	

J-8 Change in Prisoners, 1995-2001

State	Percentage change in prisoners	Rank
Alabama	29.8	23
Alaska	-6.0	48
Arizona	30.4	21
Arkansas	41.7	12
California	19.4	34
Colorado	57.7	7
Connecticut	27.4	26
Delaware	33.8	19
Florida	13.4	41
Georgia	34.3	18
Hawaii	41.7	14
Idaho	80.5	2
Illinois	17.8	37
Indiana	30.1	22
Iowa	34.8	17
Kansas	21.6	31
Kentucky	25.2	29
Louisiana	41.7	13
Maine	23.8	30
Maryland	11.7	42
Massachusetts	-10.3	49
Michigan	18.8	35
Minnesota	36.3	16
Mississippi	67.1	5
Missouri	50.2	10
Montana	66.5	6
Nebraska	28.6	25
Nevada	32.3	20
New Hampshire	18.7	36
New Jersey	4.0	44
New Mexico	37.8	15
New York	-1.4	47
North Carolina	-1.0	46
North Dakota	86.9	1
Ohio	1.4	45
Oklahoma	25.5	27
Oregon	75.2	3
Pennsylvania	17.4	38
Rhode Island	5.1	43
South Carolina	13.6	40
South Dakota	49.8	11
Tennessee	55.7	8
Texas	19.8	33
Utah	52.3	9
Vermont	25.3	28
Virginia	14.4	39
Washington	29.4	24
West Virginia	67.7	4
Wisconsin	n/a	n/a
Wyoming	20.7	32
50 States	n/a	
DC	n/a	
United States	20.6	

Rank in order
by percentage

1	North Dakota
2	Idaho
3	Oregon
4	West Virginia
5	Mississippi
6	Montana
7	Colorado
8	Tennessee
9	Utah
10	Missouri
11	South Dakota
12	Arkansas
13	Louisiana
14	Hawaii
15	New Mexico
16	Minnesota
17	Iowa
18	Georgia
19	Delaware
20	Nevada
21	Arizona
22	Indiana
23	Alabama
24	Washington
25	Nebraska
26	Connecticut
27	Oklahoma
28	Vermont
29	Kentucky
30	Maine
31	Kansas
32	Wyoming
33	Texas
34	California
35	Michigan
36	New Hampshire
37	Illinois
38	Pennsylvania
39	Virginia
40	South Carolina
41	Florida
42	Maryland
43	Rhode Island
44	New Jersey
45	Ohio
46	North Carolina
47	New York
48	Alaska
49	Massachusetts

Note: Numbers that appear to be identical are rounded and vary slightly in actual value. The rankings reflect the actual values before rounding. See the introduction for more details.

J-9 Incarceration Rate, 2001

State	Incarceration rate (per 100,000 population)	Rank
Alabama	584	5
Alaska	300	36
Arizona	492	10
Arkansas	447	15
California	453	13
Colorado	391	21
Connecticut	387	22
Delaware	504	9
Florida	437	16
Georgia	542	6
Hawaii	298	37
Idaho	451	14
Illinois	355	28
Indiana	341	29
Iowa	272	39
Kansas	318	34
Kentucky	371	24
Louisiana	800	1
Maine	127	50
Maryland	422	18
Massachusetts	243	41
Michigan	488	11
Minnesota	132	49
Mississippi	715	2
Missouri	509	8
Montana	368	26
Nebraska	225	44
Nevada	474	12
New Hampshire	188	46
New Jersey	331	32
New Mexico	295	38
New York	355	27
North Carolina	335	31
North Dakota	161	48
Ohio	398	20
Oklahoma	658	4
Oregon	327	33
Pennsylvania	310	35
Rhode Island	181	47
South Carolina	529	7
South Dakota	370	25
Tennessee	411	19
Texas	711	3
Utah	230	43
Vermont	213	45
Virginia	431	17
Washington	249	40
West Virginia	231	42
Wisconsin	383	23
Wyoming	340	30
50 States	n/a	
DC	n/a	
United States	422	

Rank in order by rate	
1	Louisiana
2	Mississippi
3	Texas
4	Oklahoma
5	Alabama
6	Georgia
7	South Carolina
8	Missouri
9	Delaware
10	Arizona
11	Michigan
12	Nevada
13	California
14	Idaho
15	Arkansas
16	Florida
17	Virginia
18	Maryland
19	Tennessee
20	Ohio
21	Colorado
22	Connecticut
23	Wisconsin
24	Kentucky
25	South Dakota
26	Montana
27	New York
28	Illinois
29	Indiana
30	Wyoming
31	North Carolina
32	New Jersey
33	Oregon
34	Kansas
35	Pennsylvania
36	Alaska
37	Hawaii
38	New Mexico
39	Iowa
40	Washington
41	Massachusetts
42	West Virginia
43	Utah
44	Nebraska
45	Vermont
46	New Hampshire
47	Rhode Island
48	North Dakota
49	Minnesota
50	Maine

J-10 Juvenile Violent Crime Index, 2000

State	Juvenile crime rate (per 100,000 youths)	Rank
Alabama	149	39
Alaska	243	27
Arizona	294	17
Arkansas	183	34
California	405	8
Colorado	238	28
Connecticut	279	20
Delaware	1,053	1
Florida	612	3
Georgia	272	22
Hawaii	247	25
Idaho	176	35
Illinois	939	2
Indiana	350	11
Iowa	244	26
Kansas	n/a	n/a
Kentucky	206	32
Louisiana	408	7
Maine	121	43
Maryland	528	4
Massachusetts	449	6
Michigan	149	39
Minnesota	283	18
Mississippi	147	41
Missouri	329	12
Montana	379	9
Nebraska	118	44
Nevada	254	23
New Hampshire	96	45
New Jersey	360	10
New Mexico	281	19
New York	315	16
North Carolina	317	15
North Dakota	32	48
Ohio	218	29
Oklahoma	248	24
Oregon	201	33
Pennsylvania	462	5
Rhode Island	274	21
South Carolina	322	14
South Dakota	138	42
Tennessee	176	35
Texas	215	30
Utah	213	31
Vermont	57	47
Virginia	158	38
Washington	328	13
West Virginia	85	46
Wisconsin	n/a	n/a
Wyoming	159	37
50 States	n/a	
DC	n/a	
United States	330	

Rank in order by rate	
1	Delaware
2	Illinois
3	Florida
4	Maryland
5	Pennsylvania
6	Massachusetts
7	Louisiana
8	California
9	Montana
10	New Jersey
11	Indiana
12	Missouri
13	Washington
14	South Carolina
15	North Carolina
16	New York
17	Arizona
18	Minnesota
19	New Mexico
20	Connecticut
21	Rhode Island
22	Georgia
23	Nevada
24	Oklahoma
25	Hawaii
26	Iowa
27	Alaska
28	Colorado
29	Ohio
30	Texas
31	Utah
32	Kentucky
33	Oregon
34	Arkansas
35	Idaho
35	Tennessee
37	Wyoming
38	Virginia
39	Alabama
39	Michigan
41	Mississippi
42	South Dakota
43	Maine
44	Nebraska
45	New Hampshire
46	West Virginia
47	Vermont
48	North Dakota

Note: Ties in ranking reflect ties in actual values.

J-11 State and Local Law Enforcement Employees, 2001

State	Law enforcement employees #	Per 10,000 population #	Rank per 10,000 population
Alabama	12,861	28.8	29
Alaska	1,640	25.8	39
Arizona	16,606	31.3	15
Arkansas	7,900	29.3	25
California	100,079	29.0	28
Colorado	12,401	28.1	31
Connecticut	10,704	31.3	16
Delaware	2,431	30.5	21
Florida	57,580	35.1	6
Georgia	25,420	30.3	22
Hawaii	3,631	29.7	24
Idaho	3,834	29.0	27
Illinois	44,229	35.4	5
Indiana	16,687	27.3	33
Iowa	7,224	24.7	43
Kansas	8,820	32.7	10
Kentucky	10,233	25.2	40
Louisiana	16,253	36.4	4
Maine	3,377	26.2	36
Maryland	16,892	31.4	14
Massachusetts	24,467	38.4	3
Michigan	26,140	26.2	37
Minnesota	11,164	22.5	48
Mississippi	8,771	30.7	20
Missouri	17,371	30.9	17
Montana	2,265	25.0	42
Nebraska	4,595	26.8	34
Nevada	6,632	31.5	13
New Hampshire	3,871	30.7	19
New Jersey	34,972	41.2	2
New Mexico	5,642	30.8	18
New York	86,453	45.5	1
North Carolina	23,397	28.6	30
North Dakota	1,500	23.6	46
Ohio	34,103	30.0	23
Oklahoma	11,037	31.9	12
Oregon	8,704	25.1	41
Pennsylvania	31,939	26.0	38
Rhode Island	3,488	32.9	9
South Carolina	13,737	33.8	7
South Dakota	1,703	22.5	47
Tennessee	18,711	32.6	11
Texas	59,604	28.0	32
Utah	5,541	24.4	44
Vermont	1,258	20.5	50
Virginia	19,202	26.7	35
Washington	14,162	23.7	45
West Virginia	3,720	20.6	49
Wisconsin	15,732	29.1	26
Wyoming	1,639	33.1	8
50 States	880,322	31.0	
DC	4,349	76.1	
United States	884,671	31.1	

Rank in order per 10,000 population	
1	New York
2	New Jersey
3	Massachusetts
4	Louisiana
5	Illinois
6	Florida
7	South Carolina
8	Wyoming
9	Rhode Island
10	Kansas
11	Tennessee
12	Oklahoma
13	Nevada
14	Maryland
15	Arizona
16	Connecticut
17	Missouri
18	New Mexico
19	New Hampshire
20	Mississippi
21	Delaware
22	Georgia
23	Ohio
24	Hawaii
25	Arkansas
26	Wisconsin
27	Idaho
28	California
29	Alabama
30	North Carolina
31	Colorado
32	Texas
33	Indiana
34	Nebraska
35	Virginia
36	Maine
37	Michigan
38	Pennsylvania
39	Alaska
40	Kentucky
41	Oregon
42	Montana
43	Iowa
44	Utah
45	Washington
46	North Dakota
47	South Dakota
48	Minnesota
49	West Virginia
50	Vermont

Note: Numbers that appear to be identical are rounded and vary slightly in actual value. The rankings reflect the actual values before rounding. See the introduction for more details.

J-12 State and Local Corrections Employees, 2001

State	Correction employees #	Per 10,000 population #	Rank per 10,000 population
Alabama	7,360	16.5	42
Alaska	1,783	28.1	9
Arizona	13,646	25.7	13
Arkansas	5,846	21.7	27
California	80,335	23.3	22
Colorado	9,698	22.0	26
Connecticut	8,702	25.4	15
Delaware	2,454	30.8	6
Florida	43,541	26.6	12
Georgia	26,911	32.1	3
Hawaii	2,463	20.1	32
Idaho	2,816	21.3	29
Illinois	25,437	20.4	31
Indiana	13,432	22.0	25
Iowa	4,559	15.6	45
Kansas	5,842	21.7	28
Kentucky	6,831	16.8	41
Louisiana	13,942	31.2	5
Maine	1,854	14.4	48
Maryland	14,624	27.2	11
Massachusetts	9,900	15.5	46
Michigan	24,442	24.5	19
Minnesota	8,056	16.2	44
Mississippi	6,409	22.4	24
Missouri	13,736	24.4	20
Montana	1,664	18.4	37
Nebraska	3,060	17.9	38
Nevada	5,315	25.2	16
New Hampshire	1,817	14.4	47
New Jersey	16,287	19.2	36
New Mexico	5,436	29.7	7
New York	62,429	32.8	1
North Carolina	24,303	29.7	8
North Dakota	818	12.9	49
Ohio	27,327	24.0	21
Oklahoma	6,958	20.1	33
Oregon	8,564	24.7	18
Pennsylvania	28,143	22.9	23
Rhode Island	1,852	17.5	40
South Carolina	11,254	27.7	10
South Dakota	1,330	17.6	39
Tennessee	11,246	19.6	35
Texas	69,833	32.7	2
Utah	4,626	20.4	30
Vermont	998	16.3	43
Virginia	22,582	31.4	4
Washington	11,907	19.9	34
West Virginia	1,630	9.0	50
Wisconsin	13,448	24.9	17
Wyoming	1,262	25.5	14
50 States	698,708	24.6	
DC	2,026	35.4	
United States	700,734	24.6	

Rank in order per 10,000 population

1 New York
2 Texas
3 Georgia
4 Virginia
5 Louisiana
6 Delaware
7 New Mexico
8 North Carolina
9 Alaska
10 South Carolina
11 Maryland
12 Florida
13 Arizona
14 Wyoming
15 Connecticut
16 Nevada
17 Wisconsin
18 Oregon
19 Michigan
20 Missouri
21 Ohio
22 California
23 Pennsylvania
24 Mississippi
25 Indiana
26 Colorado
27 Arkansas
28 Kansas
29 Idaho
30 Utah
31 Illinois
32 Hawaii
33 Oklahoma
34 Washington
35 Tennessee
36 New Jersey
37 Montana
38 Nebraska
39 South Dakota
40 Rhode Island
41 Kentucky
42 Alabama
43 Vermont
44 Minnesota
45 Iowa
46 Massachusetts
47 New Hampshire
48 Maine
49 North Dakota
50 West Virginia

Note: Numbers that appear to be identical are rounded and vary slightly in actual value. The rankings reflect the actual values before rounding. See the introduction for more details.

J-13 State Corrections Spending, FY 2001

State	Corrections spending $ (in millions)	Corrections spending per prisoner $	Rank per prisoner
Alabama	266	9,947	49
Alaska	n/a	n/a	n/a
Arizona	645	23,277	34
Arkansas	165	13,570	47
California	5,672	35,574	12
Colorado	440	25,218	32
Connecticut	524	27,297	27
Delaware	189	26,977	28
Florida	1,564	21,600	37
Georgia	1,171	25,491	31
Hawaii	133	24,386	33
Idaho	125	20,813	38
Illinois	1,178	26,563	30
Indiana	560	26,710	29
Iowa	253	31,776	18
Kansas	267	31,130	19
Kentucky	357	23,146	35
Louisiana	552	15,458	45
Maine	95	55,751	3
Maryland	739	31,113	20
Massachusetts	921	86,870	1
Michigan	1,758	35,988	11
Minnesota	390	59,037	2
Mississippi	231	10,764	48
Missouri	429	14,918	46
Montana	95	28,546	24
Nebraska	137	34,798	14
Nevada	160	15,685	44
New Hampshire	67	28,010	26
New Jersey	1,146	40,722	7
New Mexico	172	30,346	22
New York	2,275	33,687	17
North Carolina	900	28,143	25
North Dakota	33	29,703	23
Ohio	1,574	34,761	15
Oklahoma	370	16,242	43
Oregon	505	44,086	6
Pennsylvania	1,354	35,574	13
Rhode Island	149	45,973	5
South Carolina	445	19,711	39
South Dakota	48	17,070	42
Tennessee	406	17,152	41
Texas	3,069	18,936	40
Utah	247	46,229	4
Vermont	70	40,207	8
Virginia	974	30,820	21
Washington	576	37,997	9
West Virginia	95	22,539	36
Wisconsin	804	37,338	10
Wyoming	58	34,442	16
50 States	34,353	27,564	
DC	n/a	n/a	
United States	34,353	27,504	

Rank in order per prisoner

1 Massachusetts
2 Minnesota
3 Maine
4 Utah
5 Rhode Island
6 Oregon
7 New Jersey
8 Vermont
9 Washington
10 Wisconsin
11 Michigan
12 California
13 Pennsylvania
14 Nebraska
15 Ohio
16 Wyoming
17 New York
18 Iowa
19 Kansas
20 Maryland
21 Virginia
22 New Mexico
23 North Dakota
24 Montana
25 North Carolina
26 New Hampshire
27 Connecticut
28 Delaware
29 Indiana
30 Illinois
31 Georgia
32 Colorado
33 Hawaii
34 Arizona
35 Kentucky
36 West Virginia
37 Florida
38 Idaho
39 South Carolina
40 Texas
41 Tennessee
42 South Dakota
43 Oklahoma
44 Nevada
45 Louisiana
46 Missouri
47 Arkansas
48 Mississippi
49 Alabama

Note: Numbers that appear to be identical are rounded and vary slightly in actual value. The rankings reflect the actual values before rounding. See the introduction for more details.

J-14 Percentage Increase in State Corrections Spending, FY 1999-2001

State	Percentage increase in state corrections spending	Rank
Alabama	6.8	41
Alaska	n/a	n/a
Arizona	10.1	37
Arkansas	10.7	35
California	24.7	13
Colorado	29.8	6
Connecticut	26.3	11
Delaware	33.1	4
Florida	0.6	44
Georgia	16.9	20
Hawaii	-8.3	48
Idaho	15.7	24
Illinois	13.5	30
Indiana	26.4	10
Iowa	15.5	25
Kansas	7.7	39
Kentucky	16.3	21
Louisiana	20.3	16
Maine	18.8	17
Maryland	14.0	29
Massachusetts	29.4	9
Michigan	24.9	12
Minnesota	13.0	31
Mississippi	6.9	40
Missouri	0.0	45
Montana	15.9	23
Nebraska	34.3	3
Nevada	-0.6	46
New Hampshire	36.7	2
New Jersey	20.9	15
New Mexico	16.2	22
New York	-5.2	47
North Carolina	1.4	42
North Dakota	37.5	1
Ohio	14.3	28
Oklahoma	14.9	26
Oregon	29.5	8
Pennsylvania	10.4	36
Rhode Island	0.7	43
South Carolina	11.5	34
South Dakota	17.1	19
Tennessee	8.3	38
Texas	29.8	5
Utah	12.8	32
Vermont	18.6	18
Virginia	14.6	27
Washington	12.3	33
West Virginia	23.4	14
Wisconsin	29.7	7
Wyoming	n/a	n/a
50 States	15.5	
DC	n/a	
United States	15.5	

Rank in order by percentage	
1	North Dakota
2	New Hampshire
3	Nebraska
4	Delaware
5	Texas
6	Colorado
7	Wisconsin
8	Oregon
9	Massachusetts
10	Indiana
11	Connecticut
12	Michigan
13	California
14	West Virginia
15	New Jersey
16	Louisiana
17	Maine
18	Vermont
19	South Dakota
20	Georgia
21	Kentucky
22	New Mexico
23	Montana
24	Idaho
25	Iowa
26	Oklahoma
27	Virginia
28	Ohio
29	Maryland
30	Illinois
31	Minnesota
32	Utah
33	Washington
34	South Carolina
35	Arkansas
36	Pennsylvania
37	Arizona
38	Tennessee
39	Kansas
40	Mississippi
41	Alabama
42	North Carolina
43	Rhode Island
44	Florida
45	Missouri
46	Nevada
47	New York
48	Hawaii

Note: Numbers that appear to be identical are rounded and vary slightly in actual value. The rankings reflect the actual values before rounding. See the introduction for more details.

J-15 State and Local Spending for Law Enforcement, FY 2000

State	Law enforcement spending $ (in millions)	Law enforcement spending per capita $	Rank per capita
Alabama	1,060	238	45
Alaska	352	561	1
Arizona	2,051	400	11
Arkansas	680	254	41
California	15,874	469	5
Colorado	1,650	384	14
Connecticut	1,236	363	17
Delaware	394	503	4
Florida	7,011	439	7
Georgia	2,655	324	27
Hawaii	377	311	29
Idaho	398	308	30
Illinois	4,816	388	13
Indiana	1,570	258	40
Iowa	724	248	42
Kansas	779	290	34
Kentucky	1,099	272	38
Louisiana	1,609	360	19
Maine	287	225	47
Maryland	2,224	420	9
Massachusetts	2,273	358	20
Michigan	3,645	367	16
Minnesota	1,465	298	33
Mississippi	696	245	43
Missouri	1,558	278	36
Montana	261	289	35
Nebraska	467	273	37
Nevada	1,011	506	3
New Hampshire	302	245	44
New Jersey	3,712	441	6
New Mexico	698	384	15
New York	10,109	533	2
North Carolina	2,540	316	28
North Dakota	109	169	50
Ohio	4,062	358	21
Oklahoma	1,030	298	32
Oregon	1,443	422	8
Pennsylvania	4,443	362	18
Rhode Island	350	334	24
South Carolina	1,212	302	31
South Dakota	169	224	48
Tennessee	1,544	271	39
Texas	6,960	334	25
Utah	732	328	26
Vermont	144	237	46
Virginia	2,422	342	23
Washington	2,061	350	22
West Virginia	355	197	49
Wisconsin	2,154	402	10
Wyoming	197	399	12
50 States	104,970	374	
DC	634	1,108	
United States	105,604	375	

Rank in order per capita	
1	Alaska
2	New York
3	Nevada
4	Delaware
5	California
6	New Jersey
7	Florida
8	Oregon
9	Maryland
10	Wisconsin
11	Arizona
12	Wyoming
13	Illinois
14	Colorado
15	New Mexico
16	Michigan
17	Connecticut
18	Pennsylvania
19	Louisiana
20	Massachusetts
21	Ohio
22	Washington
23	Virginia
24	Rhode Island
25	Texas
26	Utah
27	Georgia
28	North Carolina
29	Hawaii
30	Idaho
31	South Carolina
32	Oklahoma
33	Minnesota
34	Kansas
35	Montana
36	Missouri
37	Nebraska
38	Kentucky
39	Tennessee
40	Indiana
41	Arkansas
42	Iowa
43	Mississippi
44	New Hampshire
45	Alabama
46	Vermont
47	Maine
48	South Dakota
49	West Virginia
50	North Dakota

Note: Numbers that appear to be identical are rounded and vary slightly in actual value. The rankings reflect the actual values before rounding. See the introduction for more details.

J-16 State and Local Law Enforcement Spending as a Percentage of General Spending, FY 2000

State	Law enforcement spending as a percentage of general spending	Rank
Alabama	4.81	43
Alaska	4.63	46
Arizona	8.82	3
Arkansas	6.15	28
California	8.11	5
Colorado	7.33	10
Connecticut	5.77	35
Delaware	8.41	4
Florida	9.31	2
Georgia	6.97	18
Hawaii	5.16	40
Idaho	6.84	20
Illinois	7.48	9
Indiana	5.46	38
Iowa	4.65	45
Kansas	6.05	30
Kentucky	5.78	34
Louisiana	7.22	12
Maine	4.13	48
Maryland	8.10	6
Massachusetts	6.02	31
Michigan	6.66	22
Minnesota	4.70	44
Mississippi	4.99	41
Missouri	6.28	26
Montana	5.76	36
Nebraska	5.55	37
Nevada	10.36	1
New Hampshire	5.34	39
New Jersey	7.86	7
New Mexico	6.91	19
New York	7.22	13
North Carolina	6.28	25
North Dakota	2.96	50
Ohio	7.05	15
Oklahoma	7.48	8
Oregon	7.16	14
Pennsylvania	6.74	21
Rhode Island	6.30	24
South Carolina	5.98	32
South Dakota	4.91	42
Tennessee	6.11	29
Texas	7.27	11
Utah	6.65	23
Vermont	4.18	47
Virginia	6.97	17
Washington	6.16	27
West Virginia	4.08	49
Wisconsin	7.00	16
Wyoming	5.93	33
50 States	7.01	
DC	12.31	
United States	7.03	

Rank in order by percentage	
1	Nevada
2	Florida
3	Arizona
4	Delaware
5	California
6	Maryland
7	New Jersey
8	Oklahoma
9	Illinois
10	Colorado
11	Texas
12	Louisiana
13	New York
14	Oregon
15	Ohio
16	Wisconsin
17	Virginia
18	Georgia
19	New Mexico
20	Idaho
21	Pennsylvania
22	Michigan
23	Utah
24	Rhode Island
25	North Carolina
26	Missouri
27	Washington
28	Arkansas
29	Tennessee
30	Kansas
31	Massachusetts
32	South Carolina
33	Wyoming
34	Kentucky
35	Connecticut
36	Montana
37	Nebraska
38	Indiana
39	New Hampshire
40	Hawaii
41	Mississippi
42	South Dakota
43	Alabama
44	Minnesota
45	Iowa
46	Alaska
47	Vermont
48	Maine
49	West Virginia
50	North Dakota

Note: Numbers that appear to be identical are rounded and vary slightly in actual value. The rankings reflect the actual values before rounding. See the introduction for more details.

Source Notes for Crime and Law Enforcement (Section J)

J-1 Total Crime Rate, 2001: This table reflects the total crime rate as defined by the uniform crime reporting system of the U.S. Department of Justice (Federal Bureau of Investigation). The reports are compiled by individual law enforcement agencies throughout the nation and summarized in the Justice Department publication *Crime in the United States, 2001.*

These statistics inherently cover only crime known to law enforcement agencies, so they are often cited as "crime reported to the police." Certain crimes, such as murder and thefts for which victims seek insurance reimbursement, are almost always reported to police. Victims often fail to report other categories of crime, ranging from rape to thefts of small items. To capture information on crimes actually committed, the Justice Department does a survey (known as the "victimization survey") of U.S. households. Because that survey is based on nationwide samples, data from it are not available on a state-by-state basis.

The FBI has worked for years to make the statistics reported from different states and cities more comparable. However, some significant differences remain. Some reflect differences among states in their criminal laws and crime reporting systems. Some reflect inherent differences among citizens in reporting crime that are in turn related to differences in perceptions of whether law enforcement authorities will be able to solve the crimes. Small thefts, for example, are often not reported in large cities but are commonly reported in some smaller communities.

J-2 Violent Crime Rate, 2001: Crimes fall into two major classes. Some, such as murder and assault, involve violence or the threat of violence. Others, such as auto theft and burglary, do not. This table, from the same source as Table J-1, shows the rates for all violent crimes combined.

J-3 Murder and Rape Rates, 2001: This table, from the same source as Table J-1, shows the rates for two specific crimes.

J-4 Property Crime Rate, 2001: This table, from the same source as Table J-1, shows the rates for crimes against property, such as burglary and auto theft.

J-5 Motor Vehicle Theft Rate, 2001: This table combines auto theft with theft of other vehicles, such as pickup trucks, using the same source as Table J-1.

J-6 Violent Crime Rate Change, 1996-2001: In the five-year period from 1996 to 2001 there was a nationwide decrease in the crime rate (crimes per one hundred thousand people) of 20.4 percent. The data come from the 1996 and 2001 editions of the Justice Department's *Crime in the United States.* Because of changes in reporting procedures, 1996 rates in New Hampshire, Montana, and West Virginia are not comparable to current rates.

J-7 Prisoners, 2001: This table shows the total number of prisoners held in state penal institutions at the end of 2001. These data are developed by the Department of Justice from statistical reports of state and federal corrections agencies. The data shown come from the Department's website (www.ojp.usdoj.gov). They reflect state prisoners only. Federal prisoners constitute about 11 percent of all prisoners. The count of total state prisoners covers only those sentenced for more than a year and thus excludes persons who are being held for short periods in local jails.

J-8 Change in Prisoners, 1995-2001: This table, from the same source as Table J-7, shows the percentage change in the number of prisoners, reflecting a net increase of 20.6 percent over this six-year period. Wisconsin, shown as not having data available, did know how many prisoners they had, but the Department of Justice concluded that changes in methods of counting between 1995 and 2001 made comparisons inappropriate.

J-9 Incarceration Rate, 2001: This table measures the relationship between state prison populations (see Table J-7) and total population. While the national rate is equivalent to having 0.4 percent of the population in prison, the percentages are much higher for certain age and ethnic groups and for males.

J-10 Juvenile Violent Crime Index, 2000: This table is from the website of the Office of Juvenile Justice and Delinquency Prevention of the U.S. Department of Justice (www.ojjdp.ncjrs.org). It reflects the number of violent crime arrests during 2000 of youths between the ages of ten and seventeen per one hundred thousand youths in the population of each state.

J-11 State and Local Law Enforcement Employees, 2001: These statistics come from a Census Bureau survey of state and local government employment, *Public Employment in 2001.* The survey is available only on the Census Bureau website (www.census.gov).

J-12 State and Local Corrections Employees, 2001: This statistic comes from the same source as Table J-12.

J-13 State Corrections Spending, FY 2001: These data provide one way to look at the costs of maintaining prison systems in each state. The total spending shown is the general fund spending reported by state budget offices in the National Association of State Budget Officers' *2001 State Expenditure Report.* These general fund data showing about $34.4 billion for the fifty states exclude about $3.8 billion financed outside state general funds, primarily by bond funds used to finance prison construction. The per-inmate spending is the result of dividing the spending in FY 2001 by the number of inmates in prison at the end of 2001.

The resulting calculation is somewhat arbitrary as it does not separately account for the supervision of inmates on parole, which is another major function of corrections agencies not associated directly with inmates in prison.

J-14 Percentage Increase in State Corrections Spending, FY 1999-2001: These data, from the same source as Table J-14, reflect the major impact that growing prison populations are having on state government budgets. Large deviations from one year to the next are often associated with large one-time expenditures for capital outlays in one of the years being compared. *State Fact Finder* has accounted for this by comparing spending over a two-year interval.

J-15 State and Local Spending for Law Enforcement, FY 2000: This table relates spending on police and corrections to population in each state. The data come from the Census Bureau's electronic publication "State and Local Government Finance Estimates, by State," available on the Census website (www.census.gov). Population numbers, also from the census, are as of July 1, 2000, and personal income numbers are from the Department of Commerce. Based on census historical practices, *State Fact Finder* used calendar year 1999 numbers. See notes to Table F-1 for more extensive information on the source of the data.

J-16 State and Local Law Enforcement Spending as a Percentage of General Spending, FY 2000: This table shows the relative importance of law enforcement outlays in state and local budgets. It is derived by comparing this spending (see Table J-16) with total "general" spending. General spending includes essentially all other spending except municipal electric and other utilities and trust funds, such as those for workers' compensation.

Transportation

K-1	Travel on Interstate Highways, 2001	270
K-2	Percentage of Interstate Mileage in "Unacceptable" Condition, 2001	271
K-3	Deficient Bridges, 2001	272
K-4	Traffic Deaths Per 100 Million Vehicle-miles, 2001	273
K-5	Percentage of Drivers Using Seat Belts, 2001	274
K-6	Vehicle-miles Traveled Per Capita, 2001	275
K-7	Percentage of Workers Using Public Transportation, 2000	276
K-8	Road and Street Miles, 2001	277
K-9	State and Local Highway Employees, 2001	278
K-10	State and Local Public Transit Employees, 2001	279
K-11	State and Local Spending for Highways, FY 2000	280
K-12	State and Local Highway Spending as a Percentage of General Spending, FY 2000	281

"Americans are becoming so disturbed by grueling commutes and traffic tie-ups that transportation—a perennial also-ran in elections—is on a fast rise." So wrote columnist Neil Pierce of the Washington Writers Group for Stateline.org.

A quick look at 2002 ballot measures confirms the trend. Voters were presented with thirty transportation measures in nineteen states in November. When added to the eleven measures from earlier in the year, voters considered more than forty transportation issues in 2002. A year earlier there were eleven, and in 2000 a total of twenty-three.

Though some asked for voter approval of new bonds, most measures called for tax increases. A Louisiana parish and an Ohio county tried and failed to increase property taxes for improvements to bus services. Some eighteen other measures looked to tap the sales tax. Increases are not an easy sell at any time but are especially difficult during a recession. In Washington, voters declined to finance improvements with an increase in fuel taxes and an additional vehicle sales tax, while passing a measure to cut license fees. In Seattle, where traffic delays are purported to be the fourth worst in the country, officials have started talking about congestion pricing, a policy enabling drivers of single occupant vehicles to pay their way onto faster moving traffic lanes, often dubbed "Lexus lanes" by critics and "value-priced" lanes by proponents.

Voters were a little more likely to commit additional monies to transportation at the local level. Twelve transportation measures on the fall ballot were approved, slightly increasing the sales tax in regions of California, Florida, Georgia, Kansas, Nevada, South Carolina and Texas. Eleven measures failed.

In other issues: Due to national security concerns and the problem of identity theft, states are reexamining driver's licensing requirements. According to the National Conference of State Legislatures, forty states considered legislation to strengthen security of licenses and ID cards in 2001 and 2002. In light of September 11, 2001, states also are expanding the role of ITS (Intelligent Transportation Systems). The communication technologies—everything from traffic cameras to highway message signs—were originally put in place to curb congestion and improve traffic safety.

K-1 Travel on Interstate Highways, 2001

State	Annual interstate vehicle-miles (in millions)	Percentage of travel on interstates	Rank by percentage
Alabama	12,159	21.4	38
Alaska	1,439	30.5	4
Arizona	13,222	26.0	20
Arkansas	7,476	25.4	23
California	80,862	26.0	18
Colorado	9,927	23.1	29
Connecticut	10,005	32.4	2
Delaware	1,383	16.1	50
Florida	30,708	19.7	43
Georgia	28,156	26.1	17
Hawaii	1,811	20.8	39
Idaho	3,201	22.7	31
Illinois	29,317	28.5	9
Indiana	16,962	23.7	26
Iowa	6,681	22.3	35
Kansas	6,577	23.4	27
Kentucky	11,951	25.8	21
Louisiana	10,622	25.8	22
Maine	2,974	20.6	42
Maryland	15,633	30.1	5
Massachusetts	15,699	29.6	6
Michigan	21,577	21.8	36
Minnesota	12,337	23.1	28
Mississippi	6,581	18.3	47
Missouri	17,764	26.3	16
Montana	2,479	24.8	24
Nebraska	3,770	20.8	40
Nevada	4,198	22.9	30
New Hampshire	2,762	22.4	33
New Jersey	13,198	19.2	46
New Mexico	6,390	27.5	14
New York	25,126	19.2	45
North Carolina	17,824	19.5	44
North Dakota	1,552	21.5	37
Ohio	30,576	28.7	8
Oklahoma	9,011	20.7	41
Oregon	8,485	24.7	25
Pennsylvania	23,009	22.3	34
Rhode Island	2,261	28.3	10
South Carolina	12,116	26.0	19
South Dakota	2,334	27.3	15
Tennessee	18,645	27.6	13
Texas	49,145	22.7	32
Utah	8,379	35.7	1
Vermont	1,621	16.9	49
Virginia	21,778	29.5	7
Washington	15,166	28.3	11
West Virginia	5,484	27.8	12
Wisconsin	10,183	17.8	48
Wyoming	2,768	32.1	3
50 States	673,284	24.2	
DC	630	16.8	
United States	673,914	24.2	

Rank in order by percentage

1	Utah
2	Connecticut
3	Wyoming
4	Alaska
5	Maryland
6	Massachusetts
7	Virginia
8	Ohio
9	Illinois
10	Rhode Island
11	Washington
12	West Virginia
13	Tennessee
14	New Mexico
15	South Dakota
16	Missouri
17	Georgia
18	California
19	South Carolina
20	Arizona
21	Kentucky
22	Louisiana
23	Arkansas
24	Montana
25	Oregon
26	Indiana
27	Kansas
28	Minnesota
29	Colorado
30	Nevada
31	Idaho
32	Texas
33	New Hampshire
34	Pennsylvania
35	Iowa
36	Michigan
37	North Dakota
38	Alabama
39	Hawaii
40	Nebraska
41	Oklahoma
42	Maine
43	Florida
44	North Carolina
45	New York
46	New Jersey
47	Mississippi
48	Wisconsin
49	Vermont
50	Delaware

Note: Numbers that appear to be identical are rounded and vary slightly in actual value. The rankings reflect the actual values before rounding. See the introduction for more details.

K-2 Percentage of Interstate Mileage in "Unacceptable" Condition, 2001

State	Percentage of interstate mileage in "unacceptable" condition	Rank
Alabama	0.3	37
Alaska	3.0	16
Arizona	0.0	44
Arkansas	27.7	3
California	14.2	5
Colorado	0.1	41
Connecticut	4.6	12
Delaware	28.2	2
Florida	0.0	44
Georgia	0.0	44
Hawaii	34.5	1
Idaho	2.0	22
Illinois	2.3	20
Indiana	0.4	34
Iowa	2.2	21
Kansas	0.2	39
Kentucky	1.1	29
Louisiana	5.9	8
Maine	0.0	44
Maryland	4.5	13
Massachusetts	1.9	24
Michigan	13.4	6
Minnesota	0.2	39
Mississippi	3.7	15
Missouri	5.6	10
Montana	1.6	25
Nebraska	2.9	17
Nevada	0.4	34
New Hampshire	0.0	44
New Jersey	16.7	4
New Mexico	0.7	31
New York	10.3	7
North Carolina	3.9	14
North Dakota	0.0	44
Ohio	0.6	33
Oklahoma	5.9	8
Oregon	0.1	41
Pennsylvania	2.6	18
Rhode Island	1.4	27
South Carolina	0.1	41
South Dakota	0.3	37
Tennessee	0.7	31
Texas	1.3	28
Utah	4.9	11
Vermont	1.6	25
Virginia	1.0	30
Washington	2.0	22
West Virginia	2.4	19
Wisconsin	0.0	44
Wyoming	0.4	34
50 States	3.5	
DC	0.0	
United States	3.5	

Rank in order by percentage

1	Hawaii
2	Delaware
3	Arkansas
4	New Jersey
5	California
6	Michigan
7	New York
8	Louisiana
8	Oklahoma
10	Missouri
11	Utah
12	Connecticut
13	Maryland
14	North Carolina
15	Mississippi
16	Alaska
17	Nebraska
18	Pennsylvania
19	West Virginia
20	Illinois
21	Iowa
22	Washington
22	Idaho
24	Massachusetts
25	Montana
25	Vermont
27	Rhode Island
28	Texas
29	Kentucky
30	Virginia
31	New Mexico
31	Tennessee
33	Ohio
34	Wyoming
34	Indiana
34	Nevada
37	Alabama
37	South Dakota
39	Kansas
39	Minnesota
41	Oregon
41	South Carolina
41	Colorado
44	Arizona
44	Florida
44	Georgia
44	Maine
44	New Hampshire
44	North Dakota
44	Wisconsin

Note: Ties in ranking reflect ties in actual values.

K-3 Deficient Bridges, 2001

State	Total deficient bridges #	Percentage of bridges deficient	Rank by percentage
Alabama	4,922	31.5	15
Alaska	412	28.8	23
Arizona	735	10.6	50
Arkansas	3,475	27.9	26
California	6,840	28.8	22
Colorado	1,443	17.9	46
Connecticut	1,305	31.3	16
Delaware	129	15.6	47
Florida	2,114	18.7	43
Georgia	3,502	24.3	33
Hawaii	537	50.1	2
Idaho	756	18.6	44
Illinois	4,824	18.9	42
Indiana	4,418	24.5	32
Iowa	7,096	28.3	24
Kansas	6,424	25.1	31
Kentucky	4,053	30.2	18
Louisiana	4,591	34.2	12
Maine	866	36.6	10
Maryland	1,446	29.2	20
Massachusetts	2,488	49.9	3
Michigan	3,366	31.7	14
Minnesota	1,784	13.9	49
Mississippi	5,002	29.7	19
Missouri	8,830	37.4	8
Montana	1,130	22.6	38
Nebraska	4,337	28.0	25
Nevada	221	14.6	48
New Hampshire	802	34.1	13
New Jersey	2,350	36.9	9
New Mexico	703	18.5	45
New York	6,588	37.9	7
North Carolina	5,307	31.2	17
North Dakota	1,137	25.2	30
Ohio	7,166	25.6	29
Oklahoma	9,123	40.2	5
Oregon	1,653	22.6	37
Pennsylvania	9,440	42.7	4
Rhode Island	379	50.6	1
South Carolina	2,056	22.7	36
South Dakota	1,744	29.1	21
Tennessee	4,701	24.3	34
Texas	10,555	22.0	39
Utah	634	23.1	35
Vermont	955	35.2	11
Virginia	3,465	27.1	27
Washington	2,142	27.0	28
West Virginia	2,667	39.4	6
Wisconsin	2,657	19.7	41
Wyoming	642	20.9	40
50 States	163,912	27.9	
DC	161	66.3	
United States*	165,099	28.0	

Rank in order by percentage

1 Rhode Island
2 Hawaii
3 Massachusetts
4 Pennsylvania
5 Oklahoma
6 West Virginia
7 New York
8 Missouri
9 New Jersey
10 Maine
11 Vermont
12 Louisiana
13 New Hampshire
14 Michigan
15 Alabama
16 Connecticut
17 North Carolina
18 Kentucky
19 Mississippi
20 Maryland
21 South Dakota
22 California
23 Alaska
24 Iowa
25 Nebraska
26 Arkansas
27 Virginia
28 Washington
29 Ohio
30 North Dakota
31 Kansas
32 Indiana
33 Georgia
34 Tennessee
35 Utah
36 South Carolina
37 Oregon
38 Montana
39 Texas
40 Wyoming
41 Wisconsin
42 Illinois
43 Florida
44 Idaho
45 New Mexico
46 Colorado
47 Delaware
48 Nevada
49 Minnesota
50 Arizona

Note: Numbers that appear to be identical are rounded and vary slightly in actual value. The rankings reflect the actual values before rounding. See the introduction for more details.

*Due to rounding or data sources, the 50-state total plus D.C. may not equal the U.S. total. Please see introduction.

K-4 Traffic Deaths Per 100 Million Vehicle-miles, 2001

State	Traffic deaths per 100 million vehicle-miles	Rank
Alabama	1.75	17
Alaska	1.80	15
Arizona	2.06	7
Arkansas	2.08	6
California	1.27	37
Colorado	1.71	19
Connecticut	1.01	48
Delaware	1.58	24
Florida	1.93	10
Georgia	1.50	26
Hawaii	1.61	23
Idaho	1.84	13
Illinois	1.37	31
Indiana	1.27	39
Iowa	1.49	27
Kansas	1.75	16
Kentucky	1.83	14
Louisiana	2.32	1
Maine	1.33	35
Maryland	1.27	38
Massachusetts	0.90	50
Michigan	1.34	33
Minnesota	1.06	46
Mississippi	2.18	4
Missouri	1.62	22
Montana	2.30	2
Nebraska	1.36	32
Nevada	1.71	20
New Hampshire	1.15	44
New Jersey	1.09	45
New Mexico	1.99	9
New York	1.18	43
North Carolina	1.67	21
North Dakota	1.45	29
Ohio	1.29	36
Oklahoma	1.55	25
Oregon	1.42	30
Pennsylvania	1.49	28
Rhode Island	1.01	47
South Carolina	2.27	3
South Dakota	2.00	8
Tennessee	1.85	12
Texas	1.72	18
Utah	1.25	41
Vermont	0.96	49
Virginia	1.27	40
Washington	1.21	42
West Virginia	1.91	11
Wisconsin	1.33	34
Wyoming	2.16	5
50 States	1.51	
DC	1.81	
United States	1.51	

Rank in order by rate

1. Louisiana
2. Montana
3. South Carolina
4. Mississippi
5. Wyoming
6. Arkansas
7. Arizona
8. South Dakota
9. New Mexico
10. Florida
11. West Virginia
12. Tennessee
13. Idaho
14. Kentucky
15. Alaska
16. Kansas
17. Alabama
18. Texas
19. Colorado
20. Nevada
21. North Carolina
22. Missouri
23. Hawaii
24. Delaware
25. Oklahoma
26. Georgia
27. Iowa
28. Pennsylvania
29. North Dakota
30. Oregon
31. Illinois
32. Nebraska
33. Michigan
34. Wisconsin
35. Maine
36. Ohio
37. California
38. Maryland
39. Indiana
40. Virginia
41. Utah
42. Washington
43. New York
44. New Hampshire
45. New Jersey
46. Minnesota
47. Rhode Island
48. Connecticut
49. Vermont
50. Massachusetts

Note: Numbers that appear to be identical are rounded and vary slightly in actual value. The rankings reflect the actual values before rounding. See the introduction for more details.

K-5 Percentage of Drivers Using Seat Belts, 2001

State	Percentage of drivers using seat belts	Rank
Alabama	79.4	11
Alaska	62.6	39
Arizona	74.4	19
Arkansas	54.5	46
California	91.1	1
Colorado	72.1	22
Connecticut	78.0	13
Delaware	67.3	35
Florida	69.5	27
Georgia	79.0	12
Hawaii	82.5	7
Idaho	60.4	43
Illinois	71.4	23
Indiana	67.4	33
Iowa	80.9	9
Kansas	60.8	42
Kentucky	61.9	40
Louisiana	68.1	30
Maine	n/a	n/a
Maryland	82.9	4
Massachusetts	56.0	45
Michigan	82.3	8
Minnesota	73.9	20
Mississippi	61.6	41
Missouri	67.9	31
Montana	76.3	16
Nebraska	70.2	25
Nevada	74.5	18
New Hampshire	n/a	n/a
New Jersey	77.6	15
New Mexico	87.8	2
New York	80.3	10
North Carolina	82.7	5
North Dakota	57.9	44
Ohio	66.9	36
Oklahoma	67.9	31
Oregon	87.5	3
Pennsylvania	70.5	24
Rhode Island	63.2	38
South Carolina	69.6	26
South Dakota	63.3	37
Tennessee	68.3	29
Texas	76.1	17
Utah	77.8	14
Vermont	67.4	33
Virginia	72.3	21
Washington	82.6	6
West Virginia	52.3	47
Wisconsin	68.7	28
Wyoming	n/a	n/a
50 States	n/a	
DC	83.6	
United States	75.0	

Rank in order by percentage

1	California
2	New Mexico
3	Oregon
4	Maryland
5	North Carolina
6	Washington
7	Hawaii
8	Michigan
9	Iowa
10	New York
11	Alabama
12	Georgia
13	Connecticut
14	Utah
15	New Jersey
16	Montana
17	Texas
18	Nevada
19	Arizona
20	Minnesota
21	Virginia
22	Colorado
23	Illinois
24	Pennsylvania
25	Nebraska
26	South Carolina
27	Florida
28	Wisconsin
29	Tennessee
30	Louisiana
31	Missouri
31	Oklahoma
33	Indiana
33	Vermont
35	Delaware
36	Ohio
37	South Dakota
38	Rhode Island
39	Alaska
40	Kentucky
41	Mississippi
42	Kansas
43	Idaho
44	North Dakota
45	Massachusetts
46	Arkansas
47	West Virginia

Note: Ties in ranking reflect ties in actual values.

K-6 Vehicle-miles Traveled Per Capita, 2001

State	Vehicle-miles traveled (in millions)	Vehicle-miles traveled per capita	Rank per capita
Alabama	56,769	12,716	4
Alaska	4,721	7,436	48
Arizona	50,860	9,583	35
Arkansas	29,433	10,933	19
California	310,703	9,006	39
Colorado	42,955	9,723	33
Connecticut	30,844	9,005	40
Delaware	8,615	10,821	20
Florida	155,664	9,494	36
Georgia	107,897	12,870	3
Hawaii	8,694	7,101	49
Idaho	14,078	10,657	22
Illinois	103,038	8,255	45
Indiana	71,624	11,713	10
Iowa	30,016	10,268	27
Kansas	28,155	10,449	25
Kentucky	46,258	11,378	13
Louisiana	41,177	9,221	38
Maine	14,433	11,217	15
Maryland	51,996	9,673	34
Massachusetts	53,015	8,310	44
Michigan	98,987	9,908	30
Minnesota	53,341	10,728	21
Mississippi	35,988	12,592	6
Missouri	67,632	12,013	8
Montana	10,011	11,069	17
Nebraska	18,102	10,566	24
Nevada	18,309	8,693	42
New Hampshire	12,315	9,780	32
New Jersey	68,725	8,100	46
New Mexico	23,232	12,701	5
New York	130,722	6,876	50
North Carolina	91,580	11,187	16
North Dakota	7,235	11,404	12
Ohio	106,589	9,372	37
Oklahoma	43,527	12,580	7
Oregon	34,398	9,905	31
Pennsylvania	103,004	8,383	43
Rhode Island	7,991	7,546	47
South Carolina	46,601	11,470	11
South Dakota	8,542	11,290	14
Tennessee	67,632	11,783	9
Texas	216,217	10,139	29
Utah	23,452	10,332	26
Vermont	9,617	15,686	2
Virginia	73,745	10,260	28
Washington	53,665	8,962	41
West Virginia	19,714	10,941	18
Wisconsin	57,269	10,602	23
Wyoming	8,625	17,445	1
50 States	2,777,712	9,773	
DC	3,750	6,558	
United States	2,781,462	9,766	

Rank in order per capita	
1	Wyoming
2	Vermont
3	Georgia
4	Alabama
5	New Mexico
6	Mississippi
7	Oklahoma
8	Missouri
9	Tennessee
10	Indiana
11	South Carolina
12	North Dakota
13	Kentucky
14	South Dakota
15	Maine
16	North Carolina
17	Montana
18	West Virginia
19	Arkansas
20	Delaware
21	Minnesota
22	Idaho
23	Wisconsin
24	Nebraska
25	Kansas
26	Utah
27	Iowa
28	Virginia
29	Texas
30	Michigan
31	Oregon
32	New Hampshire
33	Colorado
34	Maryland
35	Arizona
36	Florida
37	Ohio
38	Louisiana
39	California
40	Connecticut
41	Washington
42	Nevada
43	Pennsylvania
44	Massachusetts
45	Illinois
46	New Jersey
47	Rhode Island
48	Alaska
49	Hawaii
50	New York

K-7 Percentage of Workers Using Public Transportation, 2000

State	Percentage of workers using public transportation	Rank
Alabama	0.4	48
Alaska	2.8	17
Arizona	2.2	22
Arkansas	0.4	49
California	5.4	8
Colorado	3.4	14
Connecticut	4.4	10
Delaware	3.0	16
Florida	2.1	23
Georgia	2.7	18
Hawaii	6.5	6
Idaho	1.2	29
Illinois	9.3	4
Indiana	1.1	33
Iowa	0.8	40
Kansas	0.4	50
Kentucky	1.4	27
Louisiana	2.6	19
Maine	0.8	39
Maryland	8.4	5
Massachusetts	10.0	3
Michigan	1.1	32
Minnesota	3.2	15
Mississippi	0.6	42
Missouri	1.2	28
Montana	0.4	47
Nebraska	1.0	35
Nevada	3.8	13
New Hampshire	0.6	43
New Jersey	11.4	2
New Mexico	1.2	30
New York	26.9	1
North Carolina	0.7	41
North Dakota	0.5	45
Ohio	2.4	21
Oklahoma	0.5	44
Oregon	3.8	12
Pennsylvania	5.8	7
Rhode Island	2.1	24
South Carolina	1.0	34
South Dakota	0.4	46
Tennessee	0.9	36
Texas	1.9	25
Utah	2.4	20
Vermont	0.8	38
Virginia	4.2	11
Washington	5.0	9
West Virginia	0.9	37
Wisconsin	1.7	26
Wyoming	1.1	31
50 States	5.1	
DC	34.7	
United States	5.2	

Rank in order by percentage

1 New York
2 New Jersey
3 Massachusetts
4 Illinois
5 Maryland
6 Hawaii
7 Pennsylvania
8 California
9 Washington
10 Connecticut
11 Virginia
12 Oregon
13 Nevada
14 Colorado
15 Minnesota
16 Delaware
17 Alaska
18 Georgia
19 Louisiana
20 Utah
21 Ohio
22 Arizona
23 Florida
24 Rhode Island
25 Texas
26 Wisconsin
27 Kentucky
28 Missouri
29 Idaho
30 New Mexico
31 Wyoming
32 Michigan
33 Indiana
34 South Carolina
35 Nebraska
36 Tennessee
37 West Virginia
38 Vermont
39 Maine
40 Iowa
41 North Carolina
42 Mississippi
43 New Hampshire
44 Oklahoma
45 North Dakota
46 South Dakota
47 Montana
48 Alabama
49 Arkansas
50 Kansas

Note: Numbers that appear to be identical are rounded and vary slightly in actual value. The rankings reflect the actual values before rounding. See the introduction for more details.

K-8 Road and Street Miles, 2001

State	Total road and street miles #	Total miles under state control #	Percentage under state control	Rank by percentage
Alabama	94,441	10,900	11.5	32
Alaska	13,628	5,677	41.7	6
Arizona	55,246	6,651	12.0	29
Arkansas	98,132	16,369	16.7	21
California	168,770	15,201	9.0	43
Colorado	85,852	9,092	10.6	38
Connecticut	20,909	3,717	17.8	19
Delaware	5,814	5,122	88.1	2
Florida	117,300	12,052	10.3	40
Georgia	115,534	17,882	15.5	24
Hawaii	4,278	945	22.1	15
Idaho	46,309	4,955	10.7	37
Illinois	138,357	16,247	11.7	31
Indiana	94,038	11,193	11.9	30
Iowa	113,435	9,727	8.6	45
Kansas	134,725	10,380	7.7	49
Kentucky	78,913	27,480	34.8	8
Louisiana	60,829	16,704	27.5	10
Maine	22,671	8,403	37.1	7
Maryland	30,622	5,131	16.8	20
Massachusetts	35,408	2,843	8.0	47
Michigan	121,789	9,725	8.0	48
Minnesota	132,280	11,958	9.0	42
Mississippi	73,701	10,663	14.5	25
Missouri	124,324	32,425	26.1	12
Montana	69,504	7,858	11.3	34
Nebraska	92,766	9,993	10.8	36
Nevada	38,656	5,447	14.1	26
New Hampshire	15,509	4,000	25.8	13
New Jersey	36,176	2,311	6.4	50
New Mexico	59,883	11,414	19.1	16
New York	112,961	15,038	13.3	28
North Carolina	101,195	78,376	77.5	4
North Dakota	86,591	7,378	8.5	46
Ohio	117,268	19,294	16.5	22
Oklahoma	112,693	12,267	10.9	35
Oregon	66,784	7,590	11.4	33
Pennsylvania	119,986	39,935	33.3	9
Rhode Island	6,052	1,114	18.4	17
South Carolina	66,169	41,477	62.7	5
South Dakota	83,560	7,840	9.4	41
Tennessee	87,823	13,791	15.7	23
Texas	300,766	79,346	26.4	11
Utah	42,209	5,823	13.8	27
Vermont	14,290	2,629	18.4	18
Virginia	70,719	56,942	80.5	3
Washington	80,985	7,048	8.7	44
West Virginia	36,996	33,975	91.8	1
Wisconsin	112,664	11,753	10.4	39
Wyoming	27,292	6,760	24.8	14
50 States	3,946,802	770,841	19.5	
DC	1,533	1,429	93.2	
United States	3,948,335	772,270	19.6	

Rank in order by percentage	
1	West Virginia
2	Delaware
3	Virginia
4	North Carolina
5	South Carolina
6	Alaska
7	Maine
8	Kentucky
9	Pennsylvania
10	Louisiana
11	Texas
12	Missouri
13	New Hampshire
14	Wyoming
15	Hawaii
16	New Mexico
17	Rhode Island
18	Vermont
19	Connecticut
20	Maryland
21	Arkansas
22	Ohio
23	Tennessee
24	Georgia
25	Mississippi
26	Nevada
27	Utah
28	New York
29	Arizona
30	Indiana
31	Illinois
32	Alabama
33	Oregon
34	Montana
35	Oklahoma
36	Nebraska
37	Idaho
38	Colorado
39	Wisconsin
40	Florida
41	South Dakota
42	Minnesota
43	California
44	Washington
45	Iowa
46	North Dakota
47	Massachusetts
48	Michigan
49	Kansas
50	New Jersey

Note: Numbers that appear to be identical are rounded and vary slightly in actual value. The rankings reflect the actual values before rounding. See the introduction for more details.

K-9 State and Local Highway Employees, 2001

State	Highway employees #	Per 10,000 population	Rank per 10,000 population
Alabama	10,938	24.5	19
Alaska	3,558	56.0	1
Arizona	7,442	14.0	47
Arkansas	7,098	26.4	17
California	45,780	13.3	50
Colorado	8,703	19.7	34
Connecticut	7,728	22.6	23
Delaware	2,212	27.8	14
Florida	23,583	14.4	46
Georgia	13,788	16.4	43
Hawaii	1,685	13.8	48
Idaho	3,612	27.3	15
Illinois	21,239	17.0	40
Indiana	11,128	18.2	36
Iowa	8,380	28.7	13
Kansas	8,837	32.8	8
Kentucky	8,971	22.1	26
Louisiana	10,473	23.5	20
Maine	4,751	36.9	4
Maryland	9,648	17.9	38
Massachusetts	11,234	17.6	39
Michigan	13,504	13.5	49
Minnesota	12,807	25.8	18
Mississippi	8,607	30.1	12
Missouri	13,020	23.1	22
Montana	3,352	37.1	3
Nebraska	5,244	30.6	11
Nevada	3,220	15.3	44
New Hampshire	4,045	32.1	9
New Jersey	18,271	21.5	27
New Mexico	4,278	23.4	21
New York	40,064	21.1	29
North Carolina	16,317	19.9	32
North Dakota	1,983	31.3	10
Ohio	21,579	19.0	35
Oklahoma	9,248	26.7	16
Oregon	7,720	22.2	25
Pennsylvania	24,428	19.9	33
Rhode Island	1,771	16.7	41
South Carolina	7,335	18.1	37
South Dakota	2,598	34.3	7
Tennessee	11,691	20.4	31
Texas	35,467	16.6	42
Utah	3,407	15.0	45
Vermont	2,199	35.9	5
Virginia	14,719	20.5	30
Washington	13,493	22.5	24
West Virginia	6,274	34.8	6
Wisconsin	11,480	21.3	28
Wyoming	2,427	49.1	2
50 States	551,336	19.4	
DC	370	6.5	
United States	551,706	19.4	

Rank in order per 10,000 population

1 Alaska
2 Wyoming
3 Montana
4 Maine
5 Vermont
6 West Virginia
7 South Dakota
8 Kansas
9 New Hampshire
10 North Dakota
11 Nebraska
12 Mississippi
13 Iowa
14 Delaware
15 Idaho
16 Oklahoma
17 Arkansas
18 Minnesota
19 Alabama
20 Louisiana
21 New Mexico
22 Missouri
23 Connecticut
24 Washington
25 Oregon
26 Kentucky
27 New Jersey
28 Wisconsin
29 New York
30 Virginia
31 Tennessee
32 North Carolina
33 Pennsylvania
34 Colorado
35 Ohio
36 Indiana
37 South Carolina
38 Maryland
39 Massachusetts
40 Illinois
41 Rhode Island
42 Texas
43 Georgia
44 Nevada
45 Utah
46 Florida
47 Arizona
48 Hawaii
49 Michigan
50 California

Note: Numbers that appear to be identical are rounded and vary slightly in actual value. The rankings reflect the actual values before rounding. See the introduction for more details.

K-10 State and Local Public Transit Employees, 2001

State	Transit employees #	Per 10,000 population	Rank per 10,000 population
Alabama	221	0.5	46
Alaska	215	3.4	23
Arizona	169	0.3	48
Arkansas	238	0.9	38
California	32,802	9.5	6
Colorado	2,976	6.7	11
Connecticut	480	1.4	34
Delaware	575	7.2	9
Florida	6,800	4.1	21
Georgia	5,615	6.7	12
Hawaii	44	0.4	47
Idaho	31	0.2	50
Illinois	15,988	12.8	2
Indiana	1,561	2.6	26
Iowa	822	2.8	25
Kansas	329	1.2	35
Kentucky	955	2.3	28
Louisiana	1,389	3.1	24
Maine	96	0.7	41
Maryland	3,111	5.8	14
Massachusetts	6,027	9.4	7
Michigan	4,864	4.9	19
Minnesota	2,848	5.7	16
Mississippi	150	0.5	45
Missouri	2,991	5.3	17
Montana	172	1.9	31
Nebraska	407	2.4	27
Nevada	238	1.1	36
New Hampshire	87	0.7	43
New Jersey	10,456	12.3	3
New Mexico	742	4.1	22
New York	56,277	29.6	1
North Carolina	715	0.9	40
North Dakota	40	0.6	44
Ohio	6,527	5.7	15
Oklahoma	240	0.7	42
Oregon	3,087	8.9	8
Pennsylvania	13,483	11.0	5
Rhode Island	701	6.6	13
South Carolina	356	0.9	39
South Dakota	18	0.2	49
Tennessee	899	1.6	33
Texas	10,709	5.0	18
Utah	1,613	7.1	10
Vermont	131	2.1	30
Virginia	1,354	1.9	32
Washington	6,660	11.1	4
West Virginia	399	2.2	29
Wisconsin	2,342	4.3	20
Wyoming	55	1.1	37
50 States	209,005	7.4	
DC	8,680	151.8	
United States	217,685	7.6	

Rank in order per 10,000 population	
1	New York
2	Illinois
3	New Jersey
4	Washington
5	Pennsylvania
6	California
7	Massachusetts
8	Oregon
9	Delaware
10	Utah
11	Colorado
12	Georgia
13	Rhode Island
14	Maryland
15	Ohio
16	Minnesota
17	Missouri
18	Texas
19	Michigan
20	Wisconsin
21	Florida
22	New Mexico
23	Alaska
24	Louisiana
25	Iowa
26	Indiana
27	Nebraska
28	Kentucky
29	West Virginia
30	Vermont
31	Montana
32	Virginia
33	Tennessee
34	Connecticut
35	Kansas
36	Nevada
37	Wyoming
38	Arkansas
39	South Carolina
40	North Carolina
41	Maine
42	Oklahoma
43	New Hampshire
44	North Dakota
45	Mississippi
46	Alabama
47	Hawaii
48	Arizona
49	South Dakota
50	Idaho

Note: Numbers that appear to be identical are rounded and vary slightly in actual value. The rankings reflect the actual values before rounding. See the introduction for more details.

K-11 State and Local Spending for Highways, FY 2000

State	Highway spending $ (in millions)	Highway spending per capita $	Highway spending as a percentage of personal income	Rank per capita
Alabama	1,492	336	1.49	36
Alaska	827	1,319	4.67	1
Arizona	1,959	382	1.63	25
Arkansas	870	325	1.53	40
California	8,604	254	0.87	50
Colorado	1,743	405	1.36	23
Connecticut	1,187	349	0.92	32
Delaware	427	544	1.84	10
Florida	5,175	324	1.23	41
Georgia	2,496	305	1.17	45
Hawaii	353	291	1.08	46
Idaho	561	433	1.96	20
Illinois	4,077	328	1.08	38
Indiana	1,965	323	1.26	42
Iowa	1,836	627	2.50	6
Kansas	1,714	638	2.41	5
Kentucky	1,754	434	1.91	19
Louisiana	1,652	370	1.65	29
Maine	572	449	1.86	18
Maryland	1,487	281	0.89	47
Massachusetts	3,235	510	1.47	13
Michigan	3,085	310	1.11	44
Minnesota	2,388	486	1.62	16
Mississippi	1,231	433	2.15	21
Missouri	2,147	384	1.49	24
Montana	518	575	2.67	8
Nebraska	880	514	1.95	12
Nevada	1,127	564	2.01	9
New Hampshire	469	379	1.25	26
New Jersey	2,341	278	0.81	48
New Mexico	1,064	585	2.80	7
New York	6,835	360	1.11	31
North Carolina	2,637	328	1.33	39
North Dakota	450	701	3.05	4
Ohio	3,951	348	1.29	33
Oklahoma	1,404	407	1.82	22
Oregon	1,246	364	1.39	30
Pennsylvania	4,123	336	1.20	35
Rhode Island	286	273	0.98	49
South Carolina	1,328	331	1.45	37
South Dakota	540	715	2.94	3
Tennessee	1,839	323	1.31	43
Texas	7,201	345	1.34	34
Utah	1,033	462	2.08	17
Vermont	327	538	2.13	11
Virginia	2,627	371	1.28	28
Washington	2,212	375	1.26	27
West Virginia	888	491	2.34	15
Wisconsin	2,711	505	1.90	14
Wyoming	426	862	3.36	2
50 States	101,298	361	1.31	
DC	38	67	0.18	
United States	101,336	360	1.30	

Rank in order per capita	
1	Alaska
2	Wyoming
3	South Dakota
4	North Dakota
5	Kansas
6	Iowa
7	New Mexico
8	Montana
9	Nevada
10	Delaware
11	Vermont
12	Nebraska
13	Massachusetts
14	Wisconsin
15	West Virginia
16	Minnesota
17	Utah
18	Maine
19	Kentucky
20	Idaho
21	Mississippi
22	Oklahoma
23	Colorado
24	Missouri
25	Arizona
26	New Hampshire
27	Washington
28	Virginia
29	Louisiana
30	Oregon
31	New York
32	Connecticut
33	Ohio
34	Texas
35	Pennsylvania
36	Alabama
37	South Carolina
38	Illinois
39	North Carolina
40	Arkansas
41	Florida
42	Indiana
43	Tennessee
44	Michigan
45	Georgia
46	Hawaii
47	Maryland
48	New Jersey
49	Rhode Island
50	California

Note: Numbers that appear to be identical are rounded and vary slightly in actual value. The rankings reflect the actual values before rounding. See the introduction for more details.

K-12 State and Local Highway Spending as a Percentage of General Spending, FY 2000

State	Highway spending as a percentage of general spending	Rank
Alabama	6.76	35
Alaska	10.88	8
Arizona	8.42	22
Arkansas	7.87	25
California	4.39	50
Colorado	7.74	26
Connecticut	5.54	44
Delaware	9.09	17
Florida	6.87	32
Georgia	6.55	37
Hawaii	4.84	49
Idaho	9.62	13
Illinois	6.33	40
Indiana	6.84	34
Iowa	11.80	5
Kansas	13.31	2
Kentucky	9.22	16
Louisiana	7.42	30
Maine	8.23	24
Maryland	5.42	45
Massachusetts	8.56	21
Michigan	5.63	43
Minnesota	7.66	27
Mississippi	8.83	18
Missouri	8.65	20
Montana	11.46	7
Nebraska	10.46	10
Nevada	11.55	6
New Hampshire	8.28	23
New Jersey	4.96	47
New Mexico	10.54	9
New York	4.88	48
North Carolina	6.52	39
North Dakota	12.25	4
Ohio	6.85	33
Oklahoma	10.20	11
Oregon	6.18	42
Pennsylvania	6.26	41
Rhode Island	5.14	46
South Carolina	6.55	38
South Dakota	15.68	1
Tennessee	7.27	31
Texas	7.52	29
Utah	9.38	15
Vermont	9.50	14
Virginia	7.57	28
Washington	6.61	36
West Virginia	10.20	12
Wisconsin	8.81	19
Wyoming	12.79	3
50 States	6.76	
DC	0.74	
United States	6.74	

Rank in order by percentage

1. South Dakota
2. Kansas
3. Wyoming
4. North Dakota
5. Iowa
6. Nevada
7. Montana
8. Alaska
9. New Mexico
10. Nebraska
11. Oklahoma
12. West Virginia
13. Idaho
14. Vermont
15. Utah
16. Kentucky
17. Delaware
18. Mississippi
19. Wisconsin
20. Missouri
21. Massachusetts
22. Arizona
23. New Hampshire
24. Maine
25. Arkansas
26. Colorado
27. Minnesota
28. Virginia
29. Texas
30. Louisiana
31. Tennessee
32. Florida
33. Ohio
34. Indiana
35. Alabama
36. Washington
37. Georgia
38. South Carolina
39. North Carolina
40. Illinois
41. Pennsylvania
42. Oregon
43. Michigan
44. Connecticut
45. Maryland
46. Rhode Island
47. New Jersey
48. New York
49. Hawaii
50. California

Note: Numbers that appear to be identical are rounded and vary slightly in actual value. The rankings reflect the actual values before rounding. See the introduction for more details.

Source Notes for Transportation (Section K)

K-1 Travel on Interstate Highways, 2001: Use of highways is measured by vehicle-miles (travel by one vehicle for one mile). By this measure, interstate highways account for nearly one-fourth of the nation's highway travel, according to calculations based on the U.S. Department of Transportation's *2001 Highway Statistics*. The federal government provides 90 percent of the money used to build interstates, but lower percentages for other highways. Having a large percentage of travel on interstates is good fiscal news as well as an indication of highway quality.

K-2 Percentage of Interstate Mileage in "Unacceptable" Condition, 2001: This table provides one measurement of pavement conditions. It is based on the International Roughness Index (IRI) which is an objective, equipment-based (as opposed to human observation) rating of the smoothness/bumpiness of interstate pavement. The IRI does not measure deterioration of other types. This table shows the percentage of interstate mileage given an IRI rating of 170 or above, the level identified as "unacceptable" in the Federal Highway Administration's *Conditions and Performance Report 1999*. The IRI data come from FHA's *2001 Highway Statistics*.

K-3 Deficient Bridges, 2001: This table shows the total number of deficient bridges on major highways in each state. Details appear in the complete inventory, *The Status of the Nation's Highway Bridges* to be published by the Department of Transportation (DOT) and updated biannually. The statistics are also posted on the DOT website (wwwcf.fhwa.dot.gov). Bridges can be classified as deficient as a result of deterioration, poor maintenance, or by original design (for example, too narrow for modern traffic).

K-4 Traffic Deaths Per 100 Million Vehicle-miles, 2001: Relating deaths to total miles traveled is a common way of measuring the safety of highways. Many factors could affect the totals, including weather conditions, highway designs, congestion, and traffic law enforcement by the states. The figures come from the Department of Transportation (see notes to Table K-1).

K-5 Percentage of Drivers Using Seat Belts, 2001: These data come from periodic checks of safety belt usage, as reported by the Department of Transportation, National Highway Traffic Safety Administration in "Research Note DOT HS 809 501."

K-6 Vehicle-miles Traveled Per Capita, 2001: Vehicle-miles of travel, as reported by the Department of Transportation in *2001 Highway Statistics*, show the intensity of use of state highway systems. Vehicle-miles per capita show that the average American travels 9,766 miles a year. Short distances between homes, stores, and offices plus mass transit make usage lowest in northern urban areas.

K-7 Percentage of Workers Using Public Transportation, 2000: This table shows the percentage of workers who used public transportation systems for their journeys to work in 2000. The estimates come from questions about transportation usage from the Census 2000 Supplementary Survey.

K-8 Road and Street Miles, 2001: These data, from the same source as Table K-1, reflect total road and street (as distinct from highway) miles. They show the percentage of these miles that are controlled and maintained by state governments. Some states, such as Delaware and Virginia, maintain many local service roads that are controlled and maintained by counties and municipalities in other states.

K-9 State and Local Highway Employees, 2001: This statistic comes from a Census Bureau survey of state and local government employment, *Public Employment in 2001*. It is available on the Internet at the Census Bureau website (www.census.gov). The data show the higher levels of employees, and thus costs, associated with maintaining highways in rural states.

K-10 State and Local Public Transit Employees, 2001: This statistic, from the same source as Table K-9, shows the higher levels of employees, and thus costs, associated with transit in urbanized states.

K-11 State and Local Spending for Highways, FY 2000: This table relates spending data to population and personal income in each state. The spending data, which cover local streets as well as state highways, come from the Census Bureau's electronic publication "State and Local Government Finance Estimates, by State," available on the Census Bureau's website (www.census.gov). Population numbers, also from the census, are as of July 1, 2000, and personal income numbers are from the Department of Commerce. Based on census historical practices, *State Fact Finder* used calendar year 1999 numbers. See notes to Table F-1 for more extensive information on the source of the data.

K-12 State and Local Highway Spending as a Percentage of General Spending, FY 2000: This table shows the relative importance of highway outlays in state and local budgets. It is derived by comparing highway spending with total "general" spending (see notes to Table K-11). General spending includes essentially all other spending excepting municipal electric and other utilities and trust funds, such as those for workers' compensation.

Welfare

L-1	Percentage of Births to Unwed Mothers, 2001	284
L-2	Temporary Assistance for Needy Families (TANF) Recipients, Total and as a Percentage of Population, 2001	285
L-3	Food Stamp Recipients, Total and as a Percentage of Population, FY 2001	286
L-4	Supplemental Security Income (SSI) Recipients, Total and as a Percentage of Population, 2001	287
L-5	Change in TANF/AFDC Recipients, FY 1996-2001	288
L-6	Condition of Children Index, 2002	289
L-7	Percentage of Families with Children Headed by a Single Parent, 1998-2000 (three-year average)	290
L-8	Average Monthly TANF Cash Assistance Per Family, FY 2000	291
L-9	Welfare Assistance and Earnings of Three-person TANF Family as a Percentage of Poverty-level Income, 2000	292
L-10	Supplemental Security Income (SSI) State Supplements, 2001	293
L-11	State Income Tax Liability of Typical Family in Poverty, 2001	294
L-12	Child Support Collections, FY 2001	295
L-13	Child Support Collections Per Dollar of Administrative Costs, FY 2001	296
L-14	Children in Foster Care, FY 2000	297
L-15	State and Local Welfare Spending, FY 2000	298
L-16	State and Local Welfare Spending as a Percentage of General Spending, FY 2000	299
L-17	Average Monthly Administrative Costs Per TANF Case, FY 2000	300

After six years of sweeping changes, 2002 was to be the year to debate, re-evaluate, and fine-tune the country's work-oriented welfare program—Temporary Assistance to Needy Families (TANF). But, reauthorization has had to wait, however, pushed off the docket by anti-terrorism, accounting scandals, and foreign policy issues. Instead, Congress temporarily extended the program (which was slated to expire in October 2002). It is unclear whether the 108th Congress, which convenes in January, will draft a new five-year reauthorization bill or extend the extension, perhaps with minor changes.

New research and changed economic times offer plenty of fodder for welfare debates, should they ever happen. Caseload reduction, for instance, is a major success of welfare reform. There have always been questions, though, about how much of the reduction should be credited to the boom of the 1990s. For instance, a study by Manpower Demonstration Research found that caseloads in the Ohio county of Cuyahoga fell before reform was enacted and continued to fall at a constant rate after reform. More studies and caseload figures from less prosperous years should provide a broader picture.

TANF can also be evaluated by considering what happens to clients after they leave the welfare rolls. It can be argued that TANF's work requirement has helped people out of a long-term cycle of joblessness. Yet when hourly pay for some jobs is little more than minimum wage, past welfare recipients may find themselves part of a new sector of society—the working poor. As states find they have populations off the dole but still in need of services, TANF priorities may shift and expand.

L-1 Percentage of Births to Unwed Mothers, 2001

State	Percentage of births to unwed others	Rank
Alabama	34.4	17
Alaska	32.7	26
Arizona	39.5	6
Arkansas	36.1	10
California	32.7	26
Colorado	25.0	47
Connecticut	28.9	40
Delaware	39.9	4
Florida	39.0	7
Georgia	37.3	8
Hawaii	33.0	25
Idaho	22.0	49
Illinois	34.1	21
Indiana	35.5	13
Iowa	28.8	41
Kansas	29.9	36
Kentucky	31.6	30
Louisiana	46.2	2
Maine	31.8	29
Maryland	34.4	17
Massachusetts	26.7	45
Michigan	34.2	20
Minnesota	26.3	46
Mississippi	46.3	1
Missouri	34.6	16
Montana	31.4	31
Nebraska	27.7	44
Nevada	37.1	9
New Hampshire	24.2	48
New Jersey	29.0	39
New Mexico	46.2	2
New York	35.6	12
North Carolina	34.3	19
North Dakota	27.9	43
Ohio	35.1	14
Oklahoma	34.7	15
Oregon	30.4	34
Pennsylvania	33.7	23
Rhode Island	33.8	22
South Carolina	39.9	4
South Dakota	33.6	24
Tennessee	35.7	11
Texas	30.6	33
Utah	17.4	50
Vermont	31.0	32
Virginia	30.3	35
Washington	28.7	42
West Virginia	32.6	28
Wisconsin	29.9	36
Wyoming	29.6	38
50 States	n/a	
DC	57.1	
United States	33.4	

Rank in order by percentage

1	Mississippi
2	Louisiana
2	New Mexico
4	Delaware
4	South Carolina
6	Arizona
7	Florida
8	Georgia
9	Nevada
10	Arkansas
11	Tennessee
12	New York
13	Indiana
14	Ohio
15	Oklahoma
16	Missouri
17	Alabama
17	Maryland
19	North Carolina
20	Michigan
21	Illinois
22	Rhode Island
23	Pennsylvania
24	South Dakota
25	Hawaii
26	Alaska
26	California
28	West Virginia
29	Maine
30	Kentucky
31	Montana
32	Vermont
33	Texas
34	Oregon
35	Virginia
36	Kansas
36	Wisconsin
38	Wyoming
39	New Jersey
40	Connecticut
41	Iowa
42	Washington
43	North Dakota
44	Nebraska
45	Massachusetts
46	Minnesota
47	Colorado
48	New Hampshire
49	Idaho
50	Utah

Note: Ties in ranking reflect ties in actual values.

L-2 Temporary Assistance for Needy Families (TANF) Recipients, 2001

State	Average monthly number of recipients	Recipients as a percentage of population	Rank by percentage
Alabama	44,372	1.0	42
Alaska	17,343	2.7	4
Arizona	106,592	2.0	14
Arkansas	28,415	1.1	40
California	1,179,133	3.4	2
Colorado	30,288	0.7	48
Connecticut	56,390	1.6	23
Delaware	12,430	1.6	25
Florida	129,448	0.8	47
Georgia	129,935	1.5	26
Hawaii	32,932	2.7	6
Idaho	2,360	0.2	49
Illinois	153,898	1.2	34
Indiana	134,229	2.2	11
Iowa	54,680	1.9	18
Kansas	34,859	1.3	32
Kentucky	78,590	1.9	16
Louisiana	64,585	1.4	28
Maine	25,629	2.0	15
Maryland	69,852	1.3	31
Massachusetts	105,815	1.7	22
Michigan	210,282	2.1	13
Minnesota	93,304	1.9	17
Mississippi	41,054	1.4	29
Missouri	122,835	2.2	12
Montana	16,003	1.8	19
Nebraska	24,972	1.5	27
Nevada	25,589	1.2	35
New Hampshire	14,217	1.1	39
New Jersey	105,687	1.2	33
New Mexico	49,604	2.7	5
New York	443,344	2.3	9
North Carolina	95,355	1.2	38
North Dakota	8,340	1.3	30
Ohio	192,973	1.7	21
Oklahoma	35,981	1.0	41
Oregon	40,632	1.2	37
Pennsylvania	216,900	1.8	20
Rhode Island	40,057	3.8	1
South Carolina	49,227	1.2	36
South Dakota	6,738	0.9	44
Tennessee	162,102	2.8	3
Texas	337,258	1.6	24
Utah	20,003	0.9	45
Vermont	13,661	2.2	10
Virginia	67,156	0.9	43
Washington	143,649	2.4	7
West Virginia	42,927	2.4	8
Wisconsin	43,600	0.8	46
Wyoming	856	0.2	50
50 States	5,156,081	1.8	
DC	43,514	7.6	
United States*	5,284,711	1.9	

	Rank in order by percentage
1	Rhode Island
2	California
3	Tennessee
4	Alaska
5	New Mexico
6	Hawaii
7	Washington
8	West Virginia
9	New York
10	Vermont
11	Indiana
12	Missouri
13	Michigan
14	Arizona
15	Maine
16	Kentucky
17	Minnesota
18	Iowa
19	Montana
20	Pennsylvania
21	Ohio
22	Massachusetts
23	Connecticut
24	Texas
25	Delaware
26	Georgia
27	Nebraska
28	Louisiana
29	Mississippi
30	North Dakota
31	Maryland
32	Kansas
33	New Jersey
34	Illinois
35	Nevada
36	South Carolina
37	Oregon
38	North Carolina
39	New Hampshire
40	Arkansas
41	Oklahoma
42	Alabama
43	Virginia
44	South Dakota
45	Utah
46	Wisconsin
47	Florida
48	Colorado
49	Idaho
50	Wyoming

Note: Numbers that appear to be identical are rounded and vary slightly in actual value. The rankings reflect the actual values before rounding. See the introduction for more details.

Due to rounding or data sources, the 50-state total plus D.C. may not equal the TANF U.S. total. Please see introduction.

L-3 Food Stamp Recipients, FY 2001

State	Food stamp recipients # (in thousands)	Recipients as a percentage of population	Rank by percentage
Alabama	411	9.2	6
Alaska	38	6.0	25
Arizona	291	5.5	30
Arkansas	256	9.5	5
California	1,668	4.8	33
Colorado	154	3.5	47
Connecticut	157	4.6	37
Delaware	32	4.0	41
Florida	887	5.4	31
Georgia	574	6.8	17
Hawaii	108	8.8	9
Idaho	60	4.5	39
Illinois	825	6.6	19
Indiana	347	5.7	28
Iowa	126	4.3	40
Kansas	124	4.6	36
Kentucky	413	10.2	4
Louisiana	518	11.6	2
Maine	104	8.1	11
Maryland	208	3.9	44
Massachusetts	219	3.4	48
Michigan	641	6.4	20
Minnesota	198	4.0	43
Mississippi	298	10.4	3
Missouri	454	8.1	12
Montana	62	6.9	16
Nebraska	81	4.7	34
Nevada	69	3.3	49
New Hampshire	36	2.8	50
New Jersey	318	3.7	45
New Mexico	163	8.9	8
New York	1,354	7.1	15
North Carolina	494	6.0	24
North Dakota	38	6.0	26
Ohio	641	5.6	29
Oklahoma	271	7.8	13
Oregon	284	8.2	10
Pennsylvania	748	6.1	23
Rhode Island	71	6.7	18
South Carolina	316	7.8	14
South Dakota	45	5.9	27
Tennessee	522	9.1	7
Texas	1,361	6.4	21
Utah	80	3.5	46
Vermont	39	6.3	22
Virginia	332	4.6	35
Washington	309	5.2	32
West Virginia	221	12.3	1
Wisconsin	216	4.0	42
Wyoming	23	4.6	38
50 States	17,203	6.1	
DC	73	12.9	
United States*	17,313	6.1	

Due to rounding or data sources, the 50-state total plus D.C. may not equal the U.S. total. Please see introduction.

Rank in order by percentage

1 West Virginia
2 Louisiana
3 Mississippi
4 Kentucky
5 Arkansas
6 Alabama
7 Tennessee
8 New Mexico
9 Hawaii
10 Oregon
11 Maine
12 Missouri
13 Oklahoma
14 South Carolina
15 New York
16 Montana
17 Georgia
18 Rhode Island
19 Illinois
20 Michigan
21 Texas
22 Vermont
23 Pennsylvania
24 North Carolina
25 Alaska
26 North Dakota
27 South Dakota
28 Indiana
29 Ohio
30 Arizona
31 Florida
32 Washington
33 California
34 Nebraska
35 Virginia
36 Kansas
37 Connecticut
38 Wyoming
39 Idaho
40 Iowa
41 Delaware
42 Wisconsin
43 Minnesota
44 Maryland
45 New Jersey
46 Utah
47 Colorado
48 Massachusetts
49 Nevada
50 New Hampshire

Note: Numbers that appear to be identical are rounded and vary slightly in actual value. The rankings reflect the actual values before rounding. See the introduction for more details.

L-4 Supplemental Security Income (SSI) Recipients, 2001

State	SSI recipients #	Recipients as a percentage of population	Rank by percentage
Alabama	161,584	3.6	5
Alaska	9,153	1.4	39
Arizona	84,977	1.6	32
Arkansas	85,203	3.2	8
California	1,105,019	3.2	7
Colorado	53,538	1.2	47
Connecticut	49,650	1.4	38
Delaware	12,218	1.5	36
Florida	386,931	2.4	16
Georgia	198,229	2.4	15
Hawaii	21,301	1.7	28
Idaho	18,883	1.4	40
Illinois	248,883	2.0	24
Indiana	89,138	1.5	37
Iowa	40,729	1.4	41
Kansas	36,599	1.4	42
Kentucky	175,958	4.3	2
Louisiana	166,228	3.7	4
Maine	30,174	2.3	17
Maryland	89,276	1.7	31
Massachusetts	166,617	2.6	12
Michigan	210,442	2.1	20
Minnesota	65,518	1.3	43
Mississippi	128,568	4.5	1
Missouri	113,274	2.0	23
Montana	14,212	1.6	34
Nebraska	21,491	1.3	46
Nevada	27,293	1.3	44
New Hampshire	11,971	1.0	49
New Jersey	147,493	1.7	29
New Mexico	47,664	2.6	13
New York	621,937	3.3	6
North Carolina	191,792	2.3	18
North Dakota	8,137	1.3	45
Ohio	241,837	2.1	19
Oklahoma	72,821	2.1	21
Oregon	54,265	1.6	35
Pennsylvania	294,300	2.4	14
Rhode Island	28,601	2.7	10
South Carolina	107,022	2.6	11
South Dakota	12,712	1.7	30
Tennessee	162,993	2.8	9
Texas	418,594	2.0	25
Utah	20,566	0.9	50
Vermont	12,531	2.0	22
Virginia	132,923	1.8	26
Washington	104,524	1.7	27
West Virginia	72,954	4.0	3
Wisconsin	85,349	1.6	33
Wyoming	5,783	1.2	48
50 States	6,667,855	2.3	
DC	19,938	3.5	
United States*	6,688,489	2.3	

Rank in order by percentage	
1	Mississippi
2	Kentucky
3	West Virginia
4	Louisiana
5	Alabama
6	New York
7	California
8	Arkansas
9	Tennessee
10	Rhode Island
11	South Carolina
12	Massachusetts
13	New Mexico
14	Pennsylvania
15	Georgia
16	Florida
17	Maine
18	North Carolina
19	Ohio
20	Michigan
21	Oklahoma
22	Vermont
23	Missouri
24	Illinois
25	Texas
26	Virginia
27	Washington
28	Hawaii
29	New Jersey
30	South Dakota
31	Maryland
32	Arizona
33	Wisconsin
34	Montana
35	Oregon
36	Delaware
37	Indiana
38	Connecticut
39	Alaska
40	Idaho
41	Iowa
42	Kansas
43	Minnesota
44	Nevada
45	North Dakota
46	Nebraska
47	Colorado
48	Wyoming
49	New Hampshire
50	Utah

Note: Numbers that appear to be identical are rounded and vary slightly in actual value. The rankings reflect the actual values before rounding. See the introduction for more details.

Due to rounding or data sources, the 50-state total plus D.C. may not equal the U.S. total. Please see introduction.

L-5 Change in TANF/AFDC Recipients, FY 1996-2001

State	Average monthly AFDC recipients FY 1996	Percentage decrease FY 1996-2001	Rank by percentage decrease
Alabama	100,662	-57.1	21
Alaska	35,544	-54.1	24
Arizona	169,442	-46.1	36
Arkansas	56,343	-50.8	29
California	2,581,948	-54.9	23
Colorado	95,788	-71.0	7
Connecticut	159,246	-62.6	14
Delaware	23,654	-47.4	34
Florida	533,801	-76.5	3
Georgia	330,302	-63.0	13
Hawaii	66,482	-48.7	33
Idaho	21,780	-89.8	2
Illinois	642,644	-74.9	4
Indiana	142,604	-11.0	50
Iowa	86,146	-35.0	45
Kansas	63,783	-45.5	38
Kentucky	172,193	-53.5	25
Louisiana	228,115	-72.7	5
Maine	53,873	-52.8	27
Maryland	194,127	-65.7	9
Massachusetts	226,030	-56.1	22
Michigan	502,354	-59.8	19
Minnesota	169,744	-31.5	47
Mississippi	123,828	-68.7	8
Missouri	222,820	-46.2	35
Montana	29,130	-49.4	31
Nebraska	39,228	-37.9	42
Nevada	34,261	-32.3	46
New Hampshire	22,937	-39.9	41
New Jersey	275,637	-60.8	16
New Mexico	99,661	-50.0	30
New York	1,143,962	-51.5	28
North Carolina	267,326	-65.7	9
North Dakota	13,146	-29.4	48
Ohio	549,312	-65.3	11
Oklahoma	96,201	-64.3	12
Oregon	78,419	-41.7	40
Pennsylvania	531,059	-60.1	17
Rhode Island	56,560	-28.8	49
South Carolina	114,273	-61.3	15
South Dakota	15,896	-59.9	18
Tennessee	254,818	-36.9	44
Texas	649,018	-45.9	37
Utah	39,073	-43.9	39
Vermont	24,331	-37.1	43
Virginia	152,845	-57.4	20
Washington	268,927	-48.9	32
West Virginia	89,039	-52.9	26
Wisconsin	148,888	-71.1	6
Wyoming	11,398	-92.3	1
50 States	12,008,598	-56.6	
DC	69,292	-37.9	
United States*	12,242,125	-56.4	

Rank in order by percentage decrease

1 Wyoming
2 Idaho
3 Florida
4 Illinois
5 Louisiana
6 Wisconsin
7 Colorado
8 Mississippi
9 Maryland
9 North Carolina
11 Ohio
12 Oklahoma
13 Georgia
14 Connecticut
15 South Carolina
16 New Jersey
17 Pennsylvania
18 South Dakota
19 Michigan
20 Virginia
21 Alabama
22 Massachusetts
23 California
24 Alaska
25 Kentucky
26 West Virginia
27 Maine
28 New York
29 Arkansas
30 New Mexico
31 Montana
32 Washington
33 Hawaii
34 Delaware
35 Missouri
36 Arizona
37 Texas
38 Kansas
39 Utah
40 Oregon
41 New Hampshire
42 Nebraska
43 Vermont
44 Tennessee
45 Iowa
46 Nevada
47 Minnesota
48 North Dakota
49 Rhode Island
50 Indiana

Note: Ties in ranking reflect ties in actual values.

Due to rounding or data sources, the 50-state total plus D.C. may not equal the U.S. total. Please see introduction.

L-6 Condition of Children Index, 2002

State	Condition of Children Index "child well-being" ranked from 1 (highest) to 50 (lowest)
Alabama	48
Alaska	27
Arizona	43
Arkansas	47
California	22
Colorado	24
Connecticut	8
Delaware	33
Florida	36
Georgia	44
Hawaii	15
Idaho	28
Illinois	30
Indiana	19
Iowa	4
Kansas	18
Kentucky	37
Louisiana	49
Maine	12
Maryland	21
Massachusetts	6
Michigan	29
Minnesota	1
Mississippi	50
Missouri	26
Montana	34
Nebraska	10
Nevada	35
New Hampshire	2
New Jersey	5
New Mexico	46
New York	31
North Carolina	39
North Dakota	7
Ohio	25
Oklahoma	40
Oregon	23
Pennsylvania	17
Rhode Island	16
South Carolina	45
South Dakota	20
Tennessee	42
Texas	38
Utah	3
Vermont	9
Virginia	14
Washington	13
West Virginia	41
Wisconsin	11
Wyoming	32
50 States	n/a
DC	n/a
United States	n/a

Rank in order
by Index ranked highest (1)
to lowest (50)

1	Minnesota
2	New Hampshire
3	Utah
4	Iowa
5	New Jersey
6	Massachusetts
7	North Dakota
8	Connecticut
9	Vermont
10	Nebraska
11	Wisconsin
12	Maine
13	Washington
14	Virginia
15	Hawaii
16	Rhode Island
17	Pennsylvania
18	Kansas
19	Indiana
20	South Dakota
21	Maryland
22	California
23	Oregon
24	Colorado
25	Ohio
26	Missouri
27	Alaska
28	Idaho
29	Michigan
30	Illinois
31	New York
32	Wyoming
33	Delaware
34	Montana
35	Nevada
36	Florida
37	Kentucky
38	Texas
39	North Carolina
40	Oklahoma
41	West Virginia
42	Tennessee
43	Arizona
44	Georgia
45	South Carolina
46	New Mexico
47	Arkansas
48	Alabama
49	Louisiana
50	Mississippi

L-7 Percentage of Families with Children Headed by a Single Parent, 1998-2000 (three-year average)

State	Percentage of families headed by single parent	Rank
Alabama	29	7
Alaska	28	13
Arizona	29	7
Arkansas	28	13
California	26	34
Colorado	23	45
Connecticut	27	27
Delaware	33	3
Florida	29	7
Georgia	31	4
Hawaii	27	27
Idaho	21	48
Illinois	28	13
Indiana	22	47
Iowa	24	40
Kansas	27	27
Kentucky	27	27
Louisiana	36	1
Maine	28	13
Maryland	28	13
Massachusetts	28	13
Michigan	28	13
Minnesota	21	48
Mississippi	35	2
Missouri	27	27
Montana	28	13
Nebraska	24	40
Nevada	28	13
New Hampshire	25	38
New Jersey	23	45
New Mexico	31	4
New York	31	4
North Carolina	28	13
North Dakota	24	40
Ohio	29	7
Oklahoma	26	34
Oregon	28	13
Pennsylvania	25	38
Rhode Island	29	7
South Carolina	28	13
South Dakota	24	40
Tennessee	29	7
Texas	27	27
Utah	17	50
Vermont	27	27
Virginia	26	34
Washington	28	13
West Virginia	28	13
Wisconsin	26	34
Wyoming	24	40
50 States	n/a	
DC	59	
United States	27	

Rank in order by percentage

1	Louisiana
2	Mississippi
3	Delaware
4	Georgia
4	New Mexico
4	New York
7	Alabama
7	Arizona
7	Florida
7	Ohio
7	Rhode Island
7	Tennessee
13	Alaska
13	Arkansas
13	Illinois
13	Maine
13	Maryland
13	Massachusetts
13	Michigan
13	Montana
13	Nevada
13	North Carolina
13	Oregon
13	South Carolina
13	Washington
13	West Virginia
27	Connecticut
27	Hawaii
27	Kansas
27	Kentucky
27	Missouri
27	Texas
27	Vermont
34	California
34	Oklahoma
34	Virginia
34	Wisconsin
38	New Hampshire
38	Pennsylvania
40	Iowa
40	Nebraska
40	North Dakota
40	South Dakota
40	Wyoming
45	Colorado
45	New Jersey
47	Indiana
48	Idaho
48	Minnesota
50	Utah

Note: Ties in ranking reflect ties in actual values.

L-8 Average Monthly TANF Cash Assistance Per Family, FY 2000

State	Average monthly TANF payment $	Rank
Alabama	166	48
Alaska	746	1
Arizona	282	32
Arkansas	216	42
California	623	3
Colorado	372	21
Connecticut	513	9
Delaware	277	35
Florida	317	28
Georgia	224	41
Hawaii	584	4
Idaho	213	43
Illinois	336	25
Indiana	172	46
Iowa	324	27
Kansas	276	37
Kentucky	239	38
Louisiana	234	40
Maine	521	7
Maryland	416	16
Massachusetts	468	14
Michigan	385	20
Minnesota	420	15
Mississippi	113	50
Missouri	237	39
Montana	350	24
Nebraska	292	30
Nevada	202	44
New Hampshire	478	11
New Jersey	391	19
New Mexico	498	10
New York	671	2
North Carolina	277	34
North Dakota	328	26
Ohio	364	23
Oklahoma	392	18
Oregon	372	22
Pennsylvania	519	8
Rhode Island	474	12
South Carolina	135	49
South Dakota	311	29
Tennessee	189	45
Texas	170	47
Utah	397	17
Vermont	537	5
Virginia	279	33
Washington	471	13
West Virginia	276	36
Wisconsin	292	31
Wyoming	532	6
50 States	433	
DC	368	
United States	426	

Rank in order by $	
1	Alaska
2	New York
3	California
4	Hawaii
5	Vermont
6	Wyoming
7	Maine
8	Pennsylvania
9	Connecticut
10	New Mexico
11	New Hampshire
12	Rhode Island
13	Washington
14	Massachusetts
15	Minnesota
16	Maryland
17	Utah
18	Oklahoma
19	New Jersey
20	Michigan
21	Colorado
22	Oregon
23	Ohio
24	Montana
25	Illinois
26	North Dakota
27	Iowa
28	Florida
29	South Dakota
30	Nebraska
31	Wisconsin
32	Arizona
33	Virginia
34	North Carolina
35	Delaware
36	West Virginia
37	Kansas
38	Kentucky
39	Missouri
40	Louisiana
41	Georgia
42	Arkansas
43	Idaho
44	Nevada
45	Tennessee
46	Indiana
47	Texas
48	Alabama
49	South Carolina
50	Mississippi

Note: Numbers that appear to be identical are rounded and vary slightly in actual value. The rankings reflect the actual values before rounding. See the introduction for more details.

L-9 Welfare Assistance and Earnings of Three-person TANF Family as a Percentage of Poverty-level Income, 2000

State	Welfare and estimated part-time minimum wage earnings as a percentage of poverty-level income	Rank
Alabama	76.8	41
Alaska	140.5	1
Arizona	82.8	36
Arkansas	91.9	22
California	112.4	4
Colorado	80.1	40
Connecticut	136.4	2
Delaware	95.5	14
Florida	88.0	29
Georgia	80.9	39
Hawaii	123.5	3
Idaho	83.8	35
Illinois	91.0	24
Indiana	76.8	41
Iowa	92.2	21
Kansas	90.2	25
Kentucky	76.8	41
Louisiana	76.8	41
Maine	103.5	8
Maryland	84.7	34
Massachusetts	92.3	20
Michigan	93.1	19
Minnesota	105.7	5
Mississippi	76.8	41
Missouri	76.8	41
Montana	94.5	16
Nebraska	76.8	41
Nevada	76.8	41
New Hampshire	98.7	13
New Jersey	89.3	26
New Mexico	95.3	15
New York	100.8	9
North Carolina	76.8	41
North Dakota	84.9	32
Ohio	93.9	18
Oklahoma	84.8	33
Oregon	99.2	11
Pennsylvania	89.1	27
Rhode Island	105.6	6
South Carolina	81.8	38
South Dakota	85.8	31
Tennessee	88.3	28
Texas	76.8	41
Utah	94.1	17
Vermont	100.5	10
Virginia	98.9	12
Washington	104.6	7
West Virginia	86.1	30
Wisconsin	91.2	23
Wyoming	82.5	37
50 States	n/a	
DC	95.3	
United States	n/a	

Rank in order by percentage

1	Alaska
2	Connecticut
3	Hawaii
4	California
5	Minnesota
6	Rhode Island
7	Washington
8	Maine
9	New York
10	Vermont
11	Oregon
12	Virginia
13	New Hampshire
14	Delaware
15	New Mexico
16	Montana
17	Utah
18	Ohio
19	Michigan
20	Massachusetts
21	Iowa
22	Arkansas
23	Wisconsin
24	Illinois
25	Kansas
26	New Jersey
27	Pennsylvania
28	Tennessee
29	Florida
30	West Virginia
31	South Dakota
32	North Dakota
33	Oklahoma
34	Maryland
35	Idaho
36	Arizona
37	Wyoming
38	South Carolina
39	Georgia
40	Colorado
41	Alabama
41	Indiana
41	Kentucky
41	Louisiana
41	Mississippi
41	Missouri
41	Nebraska
41	Nevada
41	North Carolina
41	Texas

Note: Ties in ranking reflect ties in actual values.

L-10 Supplemental Security Income (SSI) State Supplements, 2001

State	Average monthly SSI state supplements per recipient $	Rank
Alabama	55	32
Alaska	308	5
Arizona	50	35
Arkansas	111	16
California	189	13
Colorado	207	12
Connecticut	326	3
Delaware	132	15
Florida	61	29
Georgia	59	30
Hawaii	53	33
Idaho	67	27
Illinois	71	26
Indiana	261	8
Iowa	280	7
Kansas	0	n/a
Kentucky	309	4
Louisiana	8	46
Maine	16	45
Maryland	221	11
Massachusetts	87	22
Michigan	47	39
Minnesota	179	14
Mississippi	48	38
Missouri	241	9
Montana	82	23
Nebraska	93	21
Nevada	57	31
New Hampshire	52	34
New Jersey	48	37
New Mexico	102	17
New York	79	24
North Carolina	493	1
North Dakota	451	2
Ohio	40	42
Oklahoma	44	40
Oregon	99	20
Pennsylvania	43	41
Rhode Island	76	25
South Carolina	284	6
South Dakota	49	36
Tennessee	100	18
Texas	0	n/a
Utah	3	47
Vermont	64	28
Virginia	237	10
Washington	35	43
West Virginia	0	n/a
Wisconsin	99	19
Wyoming	20	44
50 States	118	
DC	176	
United States	118	

Rank in order by $	
1	North Carolina
2	North Dakota
3	Connecticut
4	Kentucky
5	Alaska
6	South Carolina
7	Iowa
8	Indiana
9	Missouri
10	Virginia
11	Maryland
12	Colorado
13	California
14	Minnesota
15	Delaware
16	Arkansas
17	New Mexico
18	Tennessee
19	Wisconsin
20	Oregon
21	Nebraska
22	Massachusetts
23	Montana
24	New York
25	Rhode Island
26	Illinois
27	Idaho
28	Vermont
29	Florida
30	Georgia
31	Nevada
32	Alabama
33	Hawaii
34	New Hampshire
35	Arizona
36	South Dakota
37	New Jersey
38	Mississippi
39	Michigan
40	Oklahoma
41	Pennsylvania
42	Ohio
43	Washington
44	Wyoming
45	Maine
46	Louisiana
47	Utah

Note: Numbers that appear to be identical are rounded and vary slightly in actual value. The rankings reflect the actual values before rounding. See the introduction for more details.

L-11 State Income Tax Liability of Typical Family in Poverty, 2001

State	Income tax liability $	Rank
Alabama	388	1
Alaska	n/a	n/a
Arizona	0	18
Arkansas	20	16
California	0	18
Colorado	-679	38
Connecticut	0	18
Delaware	0	18
Florida	n/a	n/a
Georgia	48	13
Hawaii	294	3
Idaho	0	18
Illinois	54	12
Indiana	276	4
Iowa	0	18
Kansas	-357	33
Kentucky	361	2
Louisiana	125	9
Maine	0	18
Maryland	-428	35
Massachusetts	-569	37
Michigan	178	7
Minnesota	-1,002	40
Mississippi	0	18
Missouri	26	14
Montana	179	6
Nebraska	0	18
Nevada	n/a	n/a
New Hampshire	n/a	n/a
New Jersey	-568	36
New Mexico	-75	32
New York	-882	39
North Carolina	14	17
North Dakota	0	18
Ohio	72	11
Oklahoma	139	8
Oregon	86	10
Pennsylvania	0	18
Rhode Island	0	18
South Carolina	0	18
South Dakota	n/a	n/a
Tennessee	n/a	n/a
Texas	n/a	n/a
Utah	22	15
Vermont	-1,213	41
Virginia	0	18
Washington	n/a	n/a
West Virginia	245	5
Wisconsin	-381	34
Wyoming	n/a	n/a
50 States	n/a	
DC	-616	
United States	n/a	

Rank in order by $	
1	Alabama
2	Kentucky
3	Hawaii
4	Indiana
5	West Virginia
6	Montana
7	Michigan
8	Oklahoma
9	Louisiana
10	Oregon
11	Ohio
12	Illinois
13	Georgia
14	Missouri
15	Utah
16	Arkansas
17	North Carolina
18	Arizona
18	California
18	Connecticut
18	Delaware
18	Idaho
18	Iowa
18	Maine
18	Mississippi
18	Nebraska
18	North Dakota
18	Pennsylvania
18	Rhode Island
18	South Carolina
18	Virginia
32	New Mexico
33	Kansas
34	Wisconsin
35	Maryland
36	New Jersey
37	Massachusetts
38	Colorado
39	New York
40	Minnesota
41	Vermont

Note: Ties in ranking reflect ties in actual values.

L-12 Child Support Collections, FY 2001

State	Total collections $ (in thousands)	Per capita collections $	Rank per capita
Alabama	200,240	44.85	43
Alaska	77,905	122.71	3
Arizona	212,384	40.02	46
Arkansas	122,150	45.37	41
California	1,987,762	57.61	27
Colorado	189,730	42.95	44
Connecticut	202,950	59.25	25
Delaware	53,406	67.08	17
Florida	700,413	42.72	45
Georgia	383,496	45.74	40
Hawaii	69,349	56.64	29
Idaho	87,411	66.17	20
Illinois	424,100	33.98	48
Indiana	366,782	59.98	24
Iowa	236,937	81.05	11
Kansas	127,176	47.20	38
Kentucky	248,957	61.24	22
Louisiana	233,492	52.29	35
Maine	95,101	73.91	15
Maryland	379,403	70.58	16
Massachusetts	363,060	56.91	28
Michigan	1,385,226	138.65	1
Minnesota	477,368	96.01	6
Mississippi	158,092	55.31	32
Missouri	372,655	66.19	19
Montana	41,027	45.36	42
Nebraska	159,887	93.32	8
Nevada	84,050	39.91	47
New Hampshire	73,226	58.15	26
New Jersey	724,683	85.41	10
New Mexico	43,595	23.83	50
New York	1,148,801	60.43	23
North Carolina	430,346	52.57	34
North Dakota	47,629	75.07	14
Ohio	1,461,377	128.49	2
Oklahoma	116,246	33.60	49
Oregon	271,049	78.05	12
Pennsylvania	1,252,202	101.91	5
Rhode Island	48,928	46.21	39
South Carolina	208,156	51.23	36
South Dakota	47,463	62.73	21
Tennessee	276,337	48.14	37
Texas	1,174,225	55.06	33
Utah	127,371	56.12	30
Vermont	40,697	66.38	18
Virginia	403,165	56.09	31
Washington	572,903	95.68	7
West Virginia	137,233	76.16	13
Wisconsin	583,722	108.06	4
Wyoming	44,714	90.44	9
50 States	18,674,577	65.70	
DC	37,760	66.03	
United States*	18,957,597	66.57	

Rank in order per capita

1	Michigan
2	Ohio
3	Alaska
4	Wisconsin
5	Pennsylvania
6	Minnesota
7	Washington
8	Nebraska
9	Wyoming
10	New Jersey
11	Iowa
12	Oregon
13	West Virginia
14	North Dakota
15	Maine
16	Maryland
17	Delaware
18	Vermont
19	Missouri
20	Idaho
21	South Dakota
22	Kentucky
23	New York
24	Indiana
25	Connecticut
26	New Hampshire
27	California
28	Massachusetts
29	Hawaii
30	Utah
31	Virginia
32	Mississippi
33	Texas
34	North Carolina
35	Louisiana
36	South Carolina
37	Tennessee
38	Kansas
39	Rhode Island
40	Georgia
41	Arkansas
42	Montana
43	Alabama
44	Colorado
45	Florida
46	Arizona
47	Nevada
48	Illinois
49	Oklahoma
50	New Mexico

Due to rounding or data sources, the 50-state total plus D.C. may not equal the U.S. total. Please see introduction.

L-13 Child Support Collections Per Dollar of Administrative Costs, FY 2001

State	Collections per dollar of costs $	Rank
Alabama	4.01	33
Alaska	4.14	27
Arizona	4.12	28
Arkansas	2.83	46
California	2.61	47
Colorado	3.58	41
Connecticut	3.86	37
Delaware	2.93	44
Florida	3.60	40
Georgia	3.96	34
Hawaii	6.16	5
Idaho	4.62	19
Illinois	2.50	49
Indiana	6.34	4
Iowa	5.27	11
Kansas	2.51	48
Kentucky	4.08	31
Louisiana	4.38	22
Maine	6.01	8
Maryland	4.22	25
Massachusetts	5.14	14
Michigan	4.82	17
Minnesota	4.11	29
Mississippi	5.96	9
Missouri	3.81	38
Montana	3.91	35
Nebraska	3.35	42
Nevada	3.24	43
New Hampshire	5.40	10
New Jersey	5.27	11
New Mexico	1.07	50
New York	5.07	15
North Carolina	4.04	32
North Dakota	4.19	26
Ohio	4.23	23
Oklahoma	2.90	45
Oregon	6.63	3
Pennsylvania	6.98	2
Rhode Island	4.23	23
South Carolina	4.60	20
South Dakota	7.72	1
Tennessee	4.99	16
Texas	5.23	13
Utah	3.69	39
Vermont	3.90	36
Virginia	6.12	6
Washington	4.55	21
West Virginia	4.64	18
Wisconsin	6.06	7
Wyoming	4.09	30
50 States	n/a	
DC	2.26	
United States	4.18	

Rank in order by $

1	South Dakota
2	Pennsylvania
3	Oregon
4	Indiana
5	Hawaii
6	Virginia
7	Wisconsin
8	Maine
9	Mississippi
10	New Hampshire
11	Iowa
11	New Jersey
13	Texas
14	Massachusetts
15	New York
16	Tennessee
17	Michigan
18	West Virginia
19	Idaho
20	South Carolina
21	Washington
22	Louisiana
23	Ohio
23	Rhode Island
25	Maryland
26	North Dakota
27	Alaska
28	Arizona
29	Minnesota
30	Wyoming
31	Kentucky
32	North Carolina
33	Alabama
34	Georgia
35	Montana
36	Vermont
37	Connecticut
38	Missouri
39	Utah
40	Florida
41	Colorado
42	Nebraska
43	Nevada
44	Delaware
45	Oklahoma
46	Arkansas
47	California
48	Kansas
49	Illinois
50	New Mexico

Note: Ties in ranking reflect ties in actual values.

L-14 Children in Foster Care, FY 2000

State	Children in foster care #	Children in foster care per 10,000 children #	Rank per 10,000 children
Alabama	5,621	50	36
Alaska	2,193	115	3
Arizona	6,475	47	38
Arkansas	3,045	45	40
California	112,807	122	2
Colorado	7,533	68	27
Connecticut	6,996	83	17
Delaware	1,098	56	33
Florida	35,656	98	7
Georgia	11,204	52	35
Hawaii	2,379	80	18
Idaho	1,034	28	49
Illinois	33,125	102	5
Indiana	7,482	48	37
Iowa	5,068	69	26
Kansas	6,569	92	13
Kentucky	6,152	62	30
Louisiana	5,406	44	42
Maine	3,191	106	4
Maryland	13,113	97	8
Massachusetts	11,619	77	19
Michigan	20,034	77	20
Minnesota	8,530	66	28
Mississippi	3,292	42	45
Missouri	13,181	92	12
Montana	2,180	95	9
Nebraska	5,674	126	1
Nevada	1,615	32	47
New Hampshire	1,342	43	43
New Jersey	9,258	44	41
New Mexico	1,912	38	46
New York	47,208	101	6
North Carolina	10,847	55	34
North Dakota	1,129	70	25
Ohio	20,365	71	24
Oklahoma	8,406	94	10
Oregon	7,400	87	15
Pennsylvania	21,631	74	22
Rhode Island	2,302	93	11
South Carolina	4,566	45	39
South Dakota	1,215	60	31
Tennessee	10,144	73	23
Texas	18,236	31	48
Utah	1,805	25	50
Vermont	1,318	89	14
Virginia	7,391	43	44
Washington	8,945	59	32
West Virginia	3,388	84	16
Wisconsin	10,148	74	21
Wyoming	815	63	29
50 States	542,043	75	
DC	3,054	266	
United States	545,097	75	

Rank in order per 10,000 children

1 Nebraska
2 California
3 Alaska
4 Maine
5 Illinois
6 New York
7 Florida
8 Maryland
9 Montana
10 Oklahoma
11 Rhode Island
12 Missouri
13 Kansas
14 Vermont
15 Oregon
16 West Virginia
17 Connecticut
18 Hawaii
19 Massachusetts
20 Michigan
21 Wisconsin
22 Pennsylvania
23 Tennessee
24 Ohio
25 North Dakota
26 Iowa
27 Colorado
28 Minnesota
29 Wyoming
30 Kentucky
31 South Dakota
32 Washington
33 Delaware
34 North Carolina
35 Georgia
36 Alabama
37 Indiana
38 Arizona
39 South Carolina
40 Arkansas
41 New Jersey
42 Louisiana
43 New Hampshire
44 Virginia
45 Mississippi
46 New Mexico
47 Nevada
48 Texas
49 Idaho
50 Utah

Note: Numbers that appear to be identical are rounded and vary slightly in actual value. The rankings reflect the actual values before rounding. See the introduction for more details.

L-15 State and Local Welfare Spending, FY 2000

State	Welfare spending $ (in millions)	Per capita $	As a percentage of personal income	Rank per capita
Alabama	3,525	793	3.5	26
Alaska	810	1,292	4.6	2
Arizona	2,945	574	2.4	46
Arkansas	1,999	748	3.5	30
California	29,214	862	2.9	16
Colorado	2,731	635	2.1	40
Connecticut	3,116	915	2.4	11
Delaware	548	699	2.4	34
Florida	9,506	595	2.3	44
Georgia	5,568	680	2.6	37
Hawaii	1,040	858	3.2	18
Idaho	790	611	2.8	43
Illinois	8,853	713	2.3	32
Indiana	4,264	701	2.7	33
Iowa	2,259	772	3.1	28
Kansas	1,354	504	1.9	48
Kentucky	4,096	1,013	4.5	8
Louisiana	3,071	687	3.1	36
Maine	1,586	1,244	5.1	3
Maryland	4,009	757	2.4	29
Massachusetts	6,309	994	2.9	9
Michigan	8,242	829	3.0	24
Minnesota	5,970	1,214	4.1	4
Mississippi	2,320	816	4.1	25
Missouri	4,041	722	2.8	31
Montana	555	616	2.9	42
Nebraska	1,425	833	3.2	22
Nevada	886	443	1.6	49
New Hampshire	1,113	900	3.0	13
New Jersey	5,823	692	2.0	35
New Mexico	1,515	833	4.0	23
New York	29,185	1,538	4.7	1
North Carolina	6,299	783	3.2	27
North Dakota	580	903	3.9	12
Ohio	9,567	843	3.1	20
Oklahoma	885	257	1.1	50
Oregon	3,070	898	3.4	14
Pennsylvania	13,318	1,084	3.9	7
Rhode Island	1,144	1,092	3.9	6
South Carolina	3,458	862	3.8	17
South Dakota	488	646	2.7	39
Tennessee	4,872	856	3.5	19
Texas	11,460	550	2.1	47
Utah	1,473	659	3.0	38
Vermont	701	1,151	4.6	5
Virginia	4,487	634	2.2	41
Washington	5,100	865	2.9	15
West Virginia	1,763	975	4.7	10
Wisconsin	4,470	833	3.1	21
Wyoming	291	590	2.3	45
50 States	232,096	826	3.0	
DC	1,254	2,193	6.1	
United States	233,350	829	3.0	

Rank in order per capita

1 New York
2 Alaska
3 Maine
4 Minnesota
5 Vermont
6 Rhode Island
7 Pennsylvania
8 Kentucky
9 Massachusetts
10 West Virginia
11 Connecticut
12 North Dakota
13 New Hampshire
14 Oregon
15 Washington
16 California
17 South Carolina
18 Hawaii
19 Tennessee
20 Ohio
21 Wisconsin
22 Nebraska
23 New Mexico
24 Michigan
25 Mississippi
26 Alabama
27 North Carolina
28 Iowa
29 Maryland
30 Arkansas
31 Missouri
32 Illinois
33 Indiana
34 Delaware
35 New Jersey
36 Louisiana
37 Georgia
38 Utah
39 South Dakota
40 Colorado
41 Virginia
42 Montana
43 Idaho
44 Florida
45 Wyoming
46 Arizona
47 Texas
48 Kansas
49 Nevada
50 Oklahoma

Note: Numbers that appear to be identical are rounded and vary slightly in actual value. The rankings reflect the actual values before rounding. See the introduction for more details.

L-16 State and Local Welfare Spending as a Percentage of General Spending, FY 2000

State	Welfare spending as a percentage of general spending	Rank by percentage
Alabama	16.0	18
Alaska	10.7	46
Arizona	12.7	39
Arkansas	18.1	11
California	14.9	25
Colorado	12.1	43
Connecticut	14.5	29
Delaware	11.7	45
Florida	12.6	40
Georgia	14.6	27
Hawaii	14.3	32
Idaho	13.6	36
Illinois	13.7	35
Indiana	14.8	26
Iowa	14.5	31
Kansas	10.5	47
Kentucky	21.5	2
Louisiana	13.8	34
Maine	22.8	1
Maryland	14.6	28
Massachusetts	16.7	14
Michigan	15.1	23
Minnesota	19.2	10
Mississippi	16.7	15
Missouri	16.3	17
Montana	12.3	42
Nebraska	17.0	13
Nevada	9.1	48
New Hampshire	19.6	8
New Jersey	12.3	41
New Mexico	15.0	24
New York	20.8	3
North Carolina	15.6	20
North Dakota	15.8	19
Ohio	16.6	16
Oklahoma	6.4	50
Oregon	15.2	22
Pennsylvania	20.2	7
Rhode Island	20.6	4
South Carolina	17.1	12
South Dakota	14.2	33
Tennessee	19.3	9
Texas	12.0	44
Utah	13.4	37
Vermont	20.3	5
Virginia	12.9	38
Washington	15.2	21
West Virginia	20.2	6
Wisconsin	14.5	30
Wyoming	8.8	49
50 States	15.5	
DC	24.3	
United States	15.5	

Rank in order by percentage

1 Maine
2 Kentucky
3 New York
4 Rhode Island
5 Vermont
6 West Virginia
7 Pennsylvania
8 New Hampshire
9 Tennessee
10 Minnesota
11 Arkansas
12 South Carolina
13 Nebraska
14 Massachusetts
15 Mississippi
16 Ohio
17 Missouri
18 Alabama
19 North Dakota
20 North Carolina
21 Washington
22 Oregon
23 Michigan
24 New Mexico
25 California
26 Indiana
27 Georgia
28 Maryland
29 Connecticut
30 Wisconsin
31 Iowa
32 Hawaii
33 South Dakota
34 Louisiana
35 Illinois
36 Idaho
37 Utah
38 Virginia
39 Arizona
40 Florida
41 New Jersey
42 Montana
43 Colorado
44 Texas
45 Delaware
46 Alaska
47 Kansas
48 Nevada
49 Wyoming
50 Oklahoma

Note: Numbers that appear to be identical are rounded and vary slightly in actual value. The rankings reflect the actual values before rounding. See the introduction for more details.

L-17 Average Monthly Administrative Costs Per TANF Case, FY 2000

State	Costs per case $	Rank
Alabama	62.34	42
Alaska	131.20	17
Arizona	119.21	21
Arkansas	118.61	22
California	75.66	36
Colorado	139.42	12
Connecticut	127.85	18
Delaware	123.67	19
Florida	140.56	11
Georgia	1.67	50
Hawaii	74.34	37
Idaho	195.28	3
Illinois	132.62	15
Indiana	81.41	34
Iowa	98.15	28
Kansas	297.95	1
Kentucky	56.67	45
Louisiana	60.29	43
Maine	48.25	46
Maryland	82.62	32
Massachusetts	92.47	30
Michigan	119.60	20
Minnesota	93.64	29
Mississippi	41.42	49
Missouri	41.88	47
Montana	147.60	10
Nebraska	109.68	23
Nevada	182.08	4
New Hampshire	230.39	2
New Jersey	70.90	38
New Mexico	41.52	48
New York	136.10	13
North Carolina	77.75	35
North Dakota	158.82	7
Ohio	156.50	8
Oklahoma	151.48	9
Oregon	99.75	27
Pennsylvania	102.38	26
Rhode Island	65.94	40
South Carolina	131.23	16
South Dakota	82.43	33
Tennessee	56.86	44
Texas	64.64	41
Utah	181.77	5
Vermont	104.94	25
Virginia	88.35	31
Washington	70.54	39
West Virginia	105.88	24
Wisconsin	163.84	6
Wyoming	134.60	14
50 States	95.10	
DC	94.25	
United States	93.77	

Rank in order by $	
1	Kansas
2	New Hampshire
3	Idaho
4	Nevada
5	Utah
6	Wisconsin
7	North Dakota
8	Ohio
9	Oklahoma
10	Montana
11	Florida
12	Colorado
13	New York
14	Wyoming
15	Illinois
16	South Carolina
17	Alaska
18	Connecticut
19	Delaware
20	Michigan
21	Arizona
22	Arkansas
23	Nebraska
24	West Virginia
25	Vermont
26	Pennsylvania
27	Oregon
28	Iowa
29	Minnesota
30	Massachusetts
31	Virginia
32	Maryland
33	South Dakota
34	Indiana
35	North Carolina
36	California
37	Hawaii
38	New Jersey
39	Washington
40	Rhode Island
41	Texas
42	Alabama
43	Louisiana
44	Tennessee
45	Kentucky
46	Maine
47	Missouri
48	New Mexico
49	Mississippi
50	Georgia

Source Notes for Welfare (Section L)

L-1 Percentage of Births to Unwed Mothers, 2001: These data come from state reports summarized by the National Center for Health Statistics in its *National Vital Statistics Report* (Vol. 50, no. 10, June 6, 2002). The birth data, which come from hospitals, are highly reliable, but some states report the marital status of mothers somewhat differently.

L-2 TANF Recipients, Total and as a Percentage of Population, 2001: The primary federal welfare program has been Aid to Families with Dependent Children (AFDC) for households with children and income below stipulated levels. During 1997 and 1998 states made the transition to new programs under federal welfare reform legislation passed in 1996.

The table, from the U.S. Department of Health and Human Services website (www.acf.dhhs.gov), expresses the total number of people in households receiving Temporary Assistance to Needy Families (TANF) as of December 2001 as a percentage of population. Because states set their own eligibility standards, states with high percentages of persons in poverty do not necessarily have a larger-than-average percentage.

L-3 Food Stamp Recipients, Total and as a Percentage of Population, FY 2001: Unlike those for Temporary Assistance for Needy Families, food stamp standards of eligibility are uniform nationwide, so participation in this program tends to resemble closely the percentage of state population in poverty. The data are compiled by the U.S. Department of Agriculture, Food and Nutrition Service and are available on their website (www.fns.usda.gov).

L-4 SSI Recipients, Total and as a Percentage of Population, 2001: The Supplemental Security Income (SSI) program provides federal cash payments to persons eligible by reason of a combination of low incomes and disability, blindness, or age over sixty-five. The eligibility standards are uniform nationwide, as are the cash payments, except in about half the states that supplement the federal payments with state money (see Table L-10).

The data, reflecting recipients at year-end 2001, were calculated from information posted on the Social Security Administration's website (www.ssa.gov).

L-5 Change in TANF/AFDC Recipients, FY 1996-2001: This table compares the 1996 average monthly number of recipients in each state with the 2001 average to show changes in welfare participation over the past five years. The data come from the same source as Table L-2. Welfare reform and a strong economy are typically credited for the dramatic reduction in welfare caseloads after 1996.

L-6 Condition of Children Index, 2002: This is a ranking of states and the District of Columbia (1 highest, 50 lowest) prepared by the Annie E. Casey Foundation based on ten indicators of health, income, education, and other factors.

The details behind the rankings are found in *Kids Count Data Book* for 2002, the foundation's annual comprehensive publication.

L-7 Percentage of Families with Children Headed by a Single Parent, 1998-2000 (three-year average): A large and growing number of American children do not live in households with two parents. These statistics (from *Kids Count*; see notes to Table L-6) are averaged over three years and include only children in households with a single parent present.

L-8 Average Monthly TANF Cash Assistance Per Family, FY 2000: These data (reflecting the situation over the year ending in September 2000) show what a welfare family would receive to cover basic needs in a month. Assistance comes largely in the form of cash payments but can also include vouchers. Each state sets its own level of benefits. In addition to these cash payments, a typical welfare household would receive food stamps, assistance in paying heating and cooling bills, and free medical care under the Medicaid program. Some households would also receive additional cash as "emergency assistance" and reduced rents under various federal housing subsidy programs. For the source see Table L-2.

L-9 Welfare Assistance and Earnings of Three-person TANF Family as a Percentage of Poverty-level Income, 2000: These data are from a special compilation of the Congressional Research Service (CRS) and are included in the 2000 "Green Book" of the Ways and Means Committee of the U.S. House of Representatives available on the internet (www.access.gpo.gov). Because of TANF's work trigger (after 2 years of benefits) this table differs from previous years. Assumed earnings from part-time minimum wage employment (approximately $5,000 annually in most states) and an assumed earned income credit are combined with TANF cash payments and food stamps. The total is compared with poverty level income, which, in 2000, was $13,738 for a family of three.

The TANF cash payments are set by the states (see notes to Table L-8). Federally determined food stamp values differ from state to state, as greater amounts are provided in states with low cash welfare payments. The poverty level is uniform nationwide. CRS provides two numbers for the states of Michigan, New York, and California. *State Fact Finder* included the data for Wayne County, Michigan, rather than Washtenaw County (95%), New York City rather than Suffolk County (108.6%) and those for Region 1 in California rather than Region 2 (110.5%).

L-10 SSI State Supplements, 2001: These data compare the extent to which states supplement benefits under the federal Supplemental Security Income (SSI) program. For a description of the program see the notes to Table L-4. The complex rules for determining who receives supplements and how large they are mean that the averages shown are not necessarily indicative of the average supplement received. Some states provide relatively large supplements to some beneficiaries and none to the rest. However, the extreme differences among states show marked differences in their willingness to add to federally funded benefits using their own funds. The data were calculated from information from the Social Security Administration available on their website (www.ssa.gov).

L-11 State Income Tax Liability of Typical Family in Poverty, 2001: States have quite different approaches toward taxes on poor working families. The table illustrates these by showing how much state income tax a family of three making the poverty-level income ($14,129) would have to pay in tax on their 2001 income. A few states, like the federal government, supplement the income of poverty-level families with a refundable credit indicated by the minus amounts shown in the table. Some states do not have income taxes (n/a on the table) or have a tax but do not make such families pay it (shown as zeros on the table). The others charge the taxes shown. The calculations were performed by the Center on Budget and Policy Priorities and are available on their website (www.cbpp.org).

L-12 Child Support Collections, FY 2001: Because large numbers of families on welfare consist of mothers and children who receive little or no child support from fathers, state and federal officials are intensifying efforts to ensure that fathers pay the support amounts they owe. The table provides an indication of the relative significance of the resulting child support payments in each state.

Collections are reported by the Department of Health and Human Services Office of Child Support Enforcement (www.acf.dhhs.gov). The per capita amounts are those collections divided by each state's population on July 1, 2001. While most differences among states are real, some reflect the different degrees to which individual states enforce child support requirements through centralized systems.

L-13 Child Support Collections Per Dollar of Administrative Costs, FY 2001: Nationwide, it costs about twenty-four cents to collect every dollar of child support. These data, from the same source as Table L-12, indicate that the effectiveness of collections efforts varies considerably among the states.

L-14 Children in Foster Care, FY 2000: On the last day of FY 2000 545,097 were in foster care. Most commonly, these are children who have been removed from their natural parent(s) because of suspected abuse or neglect. The count is from the U.S. Department of Health and Human Services' Administration for Children and Families (www.acf.hhs.gov). High rankings are not necessarily good or bad. Having large numbers of children in foster care for long periods is generally viewed as undesirable because the alternatives (adoption, return to natural parents) provide more stability for the child than do temporary homes with strangers. However, having small numbers may indicate that child welfare authorities are leaving abused and neglected children in homes where they should not be left.

L-15 State and Local Welfare Spending, FY 2000: This table relates spending data to population and personal income in each state. The data come from the Census Bureau's electronic publication "State and Local Government Finance Estimates, by State," available on the Census website (www.census.gov). Population numbers, also from the census, are as of July 1, 2000, and personal income numbers are from the Department of Commerce. Based on census historical practices, *State Fact Finder* used calendar year 1999 numbers. See notes to Table F-1 for more extensive information on the source of the data. In addition to cash payments, the Bureau's definition of welfare spending includes Medicaid and other payments to vendors, administrative costs, and welfare-related social services.

L-16 State and Local Welfare Spending as a Percentage of General Spending, FY 2000: These data (see notes to Table L-15) show the importance of welfare spending relative to total spending of state and local governments for "general" activities, a category that excludes spending for certain trust funds such as unemployment compensation and municipal utilities.

L-17 Average Monthly Administrative Costs Per TANF Case, FY 2000: In FY 2000 the average monthly costs of administering welfare run about $94 per case, with substantial variation among the states. The information comes from unpublished tabulations by the Department of Health and Human Services (see notes to Table L-2).

Technology

M-1	Percentage of Households with Computers, 2001	304
M-2	Percentage of Households with Internet Access, 2001	305
M-3	Percentage of Zip Codes with Broadband Telecommunications Service, 2001	306
M-4	High-tech Jobs, 2001	307
M-5	Dot.com Domain Names, 2001	308
M-6	State Government Web site Ratings, 2002	309
M-7	Students Per Computer, 2001	310

E-government can be good for citizens and good for governments. For taxpayers maneuvering through the bureaucracies of government, electronic access to services and agencies can add convenience and efficiency. Although it comes with hefty up-front costs, e-government can eventually reduce expenditures on personnel and paperwork. But just as importantly, e-government has the potential to encourage the democratic process by serving as a gateway to government activity and a portal of communication between citizens and officials.

Virginia made news in late 2002 when Governor Mark R. Warner proposed legislation to consolidate a dozen of the state's information and technology agencies. The proposal would reduce duplicated technologies, enable the state to create a unified information-security system, and improve contracts with vendors by sweeping multiple agreements into one big contract. Including the initial costs, Warner expects the proposed consolidation to save the state $23 million in fiscal year 2004.

The Internet Tax Freedom Act (ITFA) is set to expire in November of 2003. Essentially, the act prohibits (with minor exceptions) state and local governments from taxing Internet services (if there is no physical presence in that state). Taxation of e-commerce is thorny terrain with vigorous advocates on both sides. The pending expiration of the ITFA, and the on-going Streamlined Sales Tax Project (See pg. 165), should generate more discussion on the issue.

Meanwhile, officials are still tackling the virtual nuts and bolts of e-government. States, localities, departments and divisions have much to sort out. One issue is who should run, maintain, and program these portals. Another is the best way to balance services contracted to private companies with activities kept within government agencies. Governments are figuring out how to pay for e-government services and how to convince elected officials that it is a worthy investment. In addition, the expansion of e-government has been complicated by concerns about individual privacy as well as national security in the wake of the September 11, 2001 terrorist attacks.

M-1 Percentage of Households with Computers, 2001

State	Percentage with computers	Rank
Alabama	43.7	49
Alaska	68.7	1
Arizona	59.4	15
Arkansas	46.8	47
California	61.5	12
Colorado	64.7	6
Connecticut	58.7	19
Delaware	58.4	21
Florida	55.9	29
Georgia	52.4	39
Hawaii	63.1	9
Idaho	62.8	10
Illinois	53.0	37
Indiana	53.2	36
Iowa	59.4	15
Kansas	57.5	26
Kentucky	49.8	45
Louisiana	45.7	48
Maine	62.8	10
Maryland	64.1	8
Massachusetts	59.1	17
Michigan	58.3	22
Minnesota	64.6	7
Mississippi	41.9	50
Missouri	55.3	31
Montana	56.0	28
Nebraska	55.6	30
Nevada	58.2	23
New Hampshire	67.7	2
New Jersey	61.2	13
New Mexico	50.6	42
New York	55.0	33
North Carolina	50.1	43
North Dakota	53.0	37
Ohio	57.6	25
Oklahoma	49.9	44
Oregon	65.8	5
Pennsylvania	53.5	35
Rhode Island	58.6	20
South Carolina	52.2	40
South Dakota	55.3	31
Tennessee	51.3	41
Texas	53.7	34
Utah	67.7	2
Vermont	60.4	14
Virginia	58.8	18
Washington	66.5	4
West Virginia	48.0	46
Wisconsin	56.4	27
Wyoming	58.1	24
50 States	n/a	
DC	49.3	
United States	56.5	

Rank in order by percentage

1	Alaska
2	New Hampshire
2	Utah
4	Washington
5	Oregon
6	Colorado
7	Minnesota
8	Maryland
9	Hawaii
10	Idaho
10	Maine
12	California
13	New Jersey
14	Vermont
15	Arizona
15	Iowa
17	Massachusetts
18	Virginia
19	Connecticut
20	Rhode Island
21	Delaware
22	Michigan
23	Nevada
24	Wyoming
25	Ohio
26	Kansas
27	Wisconsin
28	Montana
29	Florida
30	Nebraska
31	Missouri
31	South Dakota
33	New York
34	Texas
35	Pennsylvania
36	Indiana
37	Illinois
37	North Dakota
39	Georgia
40	South Carolina
41	Tennessee
42	New Mexico
43	North Carolina
44	Oklahoma
45	Kentucky
46	West Virginia
47	Arkansas
48	Louisiana
49	Alabama
50	Mississippi

Note: Ties in ranking reflect ties in actual values.

M-2 Percentage of Households with Internet Access, 2001

State	Percentage with Internet access	Rank
Alabama	37.6	48
Alaska	64.1	1
Arizona	51.9	22
Arkansas	36.9	49
California	55.3	9
Colorado	58.5	4
Connecticut	55.0	11
Delaware	52.5	20
Florida	52.8	18
Georgia	46.7	37
Hawaii	55.2	10
Idaho	52.7	19
Illinois	46.9	36
Indiana	47.3	35
Iowa	51.0	24
Kansas	50.9	26
Kentucky	44.2	43
Louisiana	40.2	47
Maine	53.3	16
Maryland	57.8	6
Massachusetts	54.7	13
Michigan	51.2	23
Minnesota	55.6	8
Mississippi	36.1	50
Missouri	49.9	30
Montana	47.5	34
Nebraska	45.5	39
Nevada	52.5	20
New Hampshire	61.6	2
New Jersey	57.2	7
New Mexico	43.1	45
New York	50.2	28
North Carolina	44.5	42
North Dakota	46.5	38
Ohio	50.9	26
Oklahoma	43.8	44
Oregon	58.2	5
Pennsylvania	48.7	31
Rhode Island	53.1	17
South Carolina	45.0	40
South Dakota	47.6	33
Tennessee	44.8	41
Texas	47.7	32
Utah	54.1	14
Vermont	53.4	15
Virginia	54.9	12
Washington	60.4	3
West Virginia	40.7	46
Wisconsin	50.2	28
Wyoming	51.0	24
50 States	n/a	
DC	41.4	
United States	50.5	

Rank in order by percentage

1. Alaska
2. New Hampshire
3. Washington
4. Colorado
5. Oregon
6. Maryland
7. New Jersey
8. Minnesota
9. California
10. Hawaii
11. Connecticut
12. Virginia
13. Massachusetts
14. Utah
15. Vermont
16. Maine
17. Rhode Island
18. Florida
19. Idaho
20. Delaware
20. Nevada
22. Arizona
23. Michigan
24. Iowa
24. Wyoming
26. Kansas
26. Ohio
28. New York
28. Wisconsin
30. Missouri
31. Pennsylvania
32. Texas
33. South Dakota
34. Montana
35. Indiana
36. Illinois
37. Georgia
38. North Dakota
39. Nebraska
40. South Carolina
41. Tennessee
42. North Carolina
43. Kentucky
44. Oklahoma
45. New Mexico
46. West Virginia
47. Louisiana
48. Alabama
49. Arkansas
50. Mississippi

Note: Ties in ranking reflect ties in actual values.

M-3 Percentage of Zip Codes with Broadband Telecommunications Service, 2001

State	Percentage of zip codes with at least one subscriber	Number of broadband providers	Rank by percentage
Alabama	81	16	25
Alaska	21	7	50
Arizona	93	11	7
Arkansas	61	7	41
California	93	28	7
Colorado	85	14	17
Connecticut	97	13	5
Delaware	100	5	1
Florida	98	27	3
Georgia	83	24	20
Hawaii	80	1-3	27
Idaho	66	7	36
Illinois	82	23	23
Indiana	81	17	25
Iowa	50	15	46
Kansas	65	14	37
Kentucky	60	14	42
Louisiana	79	12	28
Maine	65	8	37
Maryland	87	17	16
Massachusetts	99	16	2
Michigan	90	20	12
Minnesota	65	22	37
Mississippi	73	8	33
Missouri	65	17	37
Montana	51	7	45
Nebraska	56	11	43
Nevada	79	11	28
New Hampshire	92	9	9
New Jersey	98	16	3
New Mexico	67	10	35
New York	90	26	12
North Carolina	88	21	15
North Dakota	28	5	49
Ohio	91	23	10
Oklahoma	71	14	34
Oregon	91	11	10
Pennsylvania	78	25	30
Rhode Island	94	4	6
South Carolina	84	15	18
South Dakota	38	7	48
Tennessee	83	16	20
Texas	83	33	20
Utah	75	11	31
Vermont	75	6	31
Virginia	82	23	23
Washington	89	17	14
West Virginia	41	6	47
Wisconsin	84	16	18
Wyoming	53	1-3	44
50 States	n/a	n/a	
DC	93	11	
United States	78	160	

Rank in order by percentage

1	Delaware
2	Massachusetts
3	Florida
3	New Jersey
5	Connecticut
6	Rhode Island
7	Arizona
7	California
9	New Hampshire
10	Ohio
10	Oregon
12	Michigan
12	New York
14	Washington
15	North Carolina
16	Maryland
17	Colorado
18	South Carolina
18	Wisconsin
20	Georgia
20	Tennessee
20	Texas
23	Illinois
23	Virginia
25	Alabama
25	Indiana
27	Hawaii
28	Louisiana
28	Nevada
30	Pennsylvania
31	Utah
31	Vermont
33	Mississippi
34	Oklahoma
35	New Mexico
36	Idaho
37	Kansas
37	Maine
37	Minnesota
37	Missouri
41	Arkansas
42	Kentucky
43	Nebraska
44	Wyoming
45	Montana
46	Iowa
47	West Virginia
48	South Dakota
49	North Dakota
50	Alaska

Note: Ties in ranking reflect ties in actual values.

M-4 High-tech Jobs, 2001

State	Employment in the high-tech industry	High-tech employment per 1,000 private sector workers	Rank per 1,000 workers
Alabama	53,530	35	29
Alaska	5,607	27	38
Arizona	108,420	57	15
Arkansas	22,867	24	43
California	997,951	78	5
Colorado	183,559	98	1
Connecticut	80,668	56	16
Delaware	9,388	26	41
Florida	238,747	39	27
Georgia	174,216	53	17
Hawaii	8,629	19	46
Idaho	28,544	61	9
Illinois	226,348	44	22
Indiana	66,066	27	40
Iowa	34,892	29	34
Kansas	52,557	48	19
Kentucky	39,398	27	37
Louisiana	28,738	19	48
Maine	14,773	30	33
Maryland	119,089	60	11
Massachusetts	252,421	88	2
Michigan	110,050	28	36
Minnesota	136,437	60	10
Mississippi	16,802	19	49
Missouri	90,096	40	25
Montana	7,372	24	44
Nebraska	35,470	48	20
Nevada	19,188	21	45
New Hampshire	46,106	86	3
New Jersey	197,749	59	12
New Mexico	26,786	47	21
New York	364,887	52	18
North Carolina	141,477	44	23
North Dakota	7,685	30	32
Ohio	151,283	32	31
Oklahoma	39,723	34	30
Oregon	89,443	66	6
Pennsylvania	193,985	40	26
Rhode Island	14,934	37	28
South Carolina	39,528	27	39
South Dakota	12,299	40	24
Tennessee	56,226	25	42
Texas	459,638	59	13
Utah	51,078	59	14
Vermont	16,036	64	7
Virginia	228,882	81	4
Washington	135,763	61	8
West Virginia	10,653	19	47
Wisconsin	67,760	29	35
Wyoming	2,422	13	50
50 States	5,516,166	n/a	
DC	17,889	43	
United States*	5,607,091	51	

Rank in order per 1,000 workers

1 Colorado
2 Massachusetts
3 New Hampshire
4 Virginia
5 California
6 Oregon
7 Vermont
8 Washington
9 Idaho
10 Minnesota
11 Maryland
12 New Jersey
13 Texas
14 Utah
15 Arizona
16 Connecticut
17 Georgia
18 New York
19 Kansas
20 Nebraska
21 New Mexico
22 Illinois
23 North Carolina
24 South Dakota
25 Missouri
26 Pennsylvania
27 Florida
28 Rhode Island
29 Alabama
30 Oklahoma
31 Ohio
32 North Dakota
33 Maine
34 Iowa
35 Wisconsin
36 Michigan
37 Kentucky
38 Alaska
39 South Carolina
40 Indiana
41 Delaware
42 Tennessee
43 Arkansas
44 Montana
45 Nevada
46 Hawaii
47 West Virginia
48 Louisiana
49 Mississippi
50 Wyoming

Note: Numbers that appear to be identical are rounded and vary slightly in actual value. The rankings reflect the actual values before rounding. See the introduction for more details.

*Due to rounding or data sources, the 50-state total plus D.C. may not equal the U.S. total. Please see introduction.

M-5 Dot.com Domain Names, 2001

State	Number of domain names	Domain names per 1,000 population	Domain names per business firm	Rank per business firm
Alabama	108,225	24.3	1.3	40
Alaska	36,000	57.4	2.3	20
Arizona	308,325	60.1	3.4	4
Arkansas	53,850	20.1	1.0	47
California	3,179,025	93.9	5.0	1
Colorado	325,875	75.8	2.9	12
Connecticut	226,200	66.4	2.9	13
Delaware	47,775	61.0	2.5	19
Florida	1,046,025	65.4	3.0	9
Georgia	408,975	50.0	2.6	15
Hawaii	75,600	62.4	3.2	6
Idaho	49,725	38.4	1.6	32
Illinois	577,725	46.5	2.3	21
Indiana	164,400	27.0	1.4	35
Iowa	67,575	23.1	1.0	48
Kansas	93,750	34.9	1.5	34
Kentucky	88,125	21.8	1.2	43
Louisiana	110,400	24.7	1.3	38
Maine	55,875	43.8	1.7	31
Maryland	316,800	59.8	3.0	8
Massachusetts	500,925	78.9	3.6	3
Michigan	327,675	33.0	1.7	30
Minnesota	237,000	48.2	2.1	22
Mississippi	40,500	14.2	0.8	49
Missouri	186,300	33.3	1.6	33
Montana	31,650	35.1	1.2	44
Nebraska	53,250	31.1	1.3	42
Nevada	168,525	84.3	4.5	2
New Hampshire	83,025	67.2	2.6	16
New Jersey	526,875	62.6	2.6	14
New Mexico	65,250	35.9	1.8	26
New York	1,248,975	65.8	3.0	10
North Carolina	287,475	35.7	1.8	27
North Dakota	23,475	36.6	1.3	36
Ohio	376,275	33.1	1.8	28
Oklahoma	94,575	27.4	1.3	39
Oregon	212,175	62.0	2.5	18
Pennsylvania	453,525	36.9	1.9	23
Rhode Island	44,325	42.3	1.7	29
South Carolina	101,100	25.2	1.3	41
South Dakota	21,375	28.3	1.0	45
Tennessee	197,925	34.8	1.9	24
Texas	950,325	45.6	2.6	17
Utah	137,625	61.6	3.1	7
Vermont	35,325	58.0	1.9	25
Virginia	410,175	57.9	3.0	11
Washington	434,325	73.7	3.2	5
West Virginia	27,225	15.1	0.8	50
Wisconsin	155,325	29.0	1.3	37
Wyoming	16,500	33.4	1.0	46
50 States	14,789,250	52.7	2.6	
DC	136,275	238.2	8.3	
United States*	19,003,575	67.5	3.4	

Rank in order per business firm	
1	California
2	Nevada
3	Massachusetts
4	Arizona
5	Washington
6	Hawaii
7	Utah
8	Maryland
9	Florida
10	New York
11	Virginia
12	Colorado
13	Connecticut
14	New Jersey
15	Georgia
16	New Hampshire
17	Texas
18	Oregon
19	Delaware
20	Alaska
21	Illinois
22	Minnesota
23	Pennsylvania
24	Tennessee
25	Vermont
26	New Mexico
27	North Carolina
28	Ohio
29	Rhode Island
30	Michigan
31	Maine
32	Idaho
33	Missouri
34	Kansas
35	Indiana
36	North Dakota
37	Wisconsin
38	Louisiana
39	Oklahoma
40	Alabama
41	South Carolina
42	Nebraska
43	Kentucky
44	Montana
45	South Dakota
46	Wyoming
47	Arkansas
48	Iowa
49	Mississippi
50	West Virginia

Note: Numbers that appear to be identical are rounded and vary slightly in actual value. The rankings reflect the actual values before rounding. See the introduction for more details.

*Due to rounding or data sources, the 50-state total plus D.C. may not equal the U.S. total. Please see introduction.

M-6 State Government Web site Ratings, 2002

State	Web site rating	Rank
Alabama	35.8	49
Alaska	44.1	33
Arizona	44.2	31
Arkansas	44.5	30
California	54.8	3
Colorado	40.0	47
Connecticut	53.3	4
Delaware	42.4	41
Florida	51.5	12
Georgia	43.1	38
Hawaii	41.9	45
Idaho	42.8	39
Illinois	49.3	16
Indiana	51.5	12
Iowa	44.9	27
Kansas	45.6	23
Kentucky	42.0	44
Louisiana	42.3	43
Maine	43.7	34
Maryland	44.9	27
Massachusetts	45.6	23
Michigan	48.2	19
Minnesota	43.3	37
Mississippi	37.4	48
Missouri	46.3	22
Montana	45.5	25
Nebraska	42.6	40
Nevada	51.9	8
New Hampshire	51.1	14
New Jersey	55.0	2
New Mexico	44.2	31
New York	51.6	11
North Carolina	48.6	17
North Dakota	46.9	20
Ohio	46.4	21
Oklahoma	44.9	27
Oregon	48.5	18
Pennsylvania	52.9	5
Rhode Island	43.5	35
South Carolina	45.4	26
South Dakota	51.9	8
Tennessee	56.0	1
Texas	52.8	6
Utah	51.7	10
Vermont	42.4	41
Virginia	49.6	15
Washington	52.4	7
West Virginia	43.5	35
Wisconsin	40.4	46
Wyoming	34.8	50
50 States	n/a	
DC	n/a	
United States	n/a	

Rank in order by rating

1	Tennessee
2	New Jersey
3	California
4	Connecticut
5	Pennsylvania
6	Texas
7	Washington
8	Nevada
8	South Dakota
10	Utah
11	New York
12	Florida
12	Indiana
14	New Hampshire
15	Virginia
16	Illinois
17	North Carolina
18	Oregon
19	Michigan
20	North Dakota
21	Ohio
22	Missouri
23	Kansas
23	Massachusetts
25	Montana
26	South Carolina
27	Iowa
27	Maryland
27	Oklahoma
30	Arkansas
31	Arizona
31	New Mexico
33	Alaska
34	Maine
35	Rhode Island
35	West Virginia
37	Minnesota
38	Georgia
39	Idaho
40	Nebraska
41	Delaware
41	Vermont
43	Louisiana
44	Kentucky
45	Hawaii
46	Wisconsin
47	Colorado
48	Mississippi
49	Alabama
50	Wyoming

Note: Ties in ranking reflect ties in actual values.

State	Students per instructional computer	Students per Internet connected instructional computer	Rank per instructional computer only
Alabama	5.6	8.6	4
Alaska	3.0	5.2	46
Arizona	4.1	7.1	23
Arkansas	4.3	6.4	19
California	6.0	10.1	3
Colorado	4.0	6.7	27
Connecticut	4.7	8.7	12
Delaware	4.3	5.2	19
Florida	3.6	7.1	38
Georgia	4.3	7.5	19
Hawaii	5.5	8.4	5
Idaho	3.8	5.1	36
Illinois	4.4	6.9	15
Indiana	3.4	5.6	40
Iowa	3.3	5.3	41
Kansas	2.8	5.1	47
Kentucky	4.1	6.0	23
Louisiana	6.2	9.3	1
Maine	4.0	5.8	27
Maryland	5.2	8.5	7
Massachusetts	4.6	7.3	14
Michigan	4.4	6.5	15
Minnesota	3.2	5.3	42
Mississippi	6.1	7.9	2
Missouri	3.9	5.8	33
Montana	3.2	5.9	42
Nebraska	3.1	4.6	44
Nevada	5.5	8.8	5
New Hampshire	4.7	6.7	12
New Jersey	4.1	6.8	23
New Mexico	3.6	6.2	38
New York	4.4	8.1	15
North Carolina	4.8	8.8	10
North Dakota	2.8	4.9	47
Ohio	3.9	5.7	33
Oklahoma	4.0	5.6	27
Oregon	4.3	6.8	19
Pennsylvania	4.0	7.2	27
Rhode Island	5.2	8.3	7
South Carolina	4.4	5.8	15
South Dakota	2.4	3.4	50
Tennessee	4.8	7.6	10
Texas	3.7	5.9	37
Utah	5.0	6.7	9
Vermont	4.1	6.8	23
Virginia	4.0	6.3	27
Washington	3.9	6.5	33
West Virginia	4.0	5.6	27
Wisconsin	3.1	5.6	44
Wyoming	2.6	3.8	49
50 States	n/a	n/a	
DC	3.5	8.6	
United States	4.2	6.8	

Rank in order per instructional computer

1	Louisiana
2	Mississippi
3	California
4	Alabama
5	Hawaii
5	Nevada
7	Maryland
7	Rhode Island
9	Utah
10	North Carolina
10	Tennessee
12	Connecticut
12	New Hampshire
14	Massachusetts
15	Illinois
15	Michigan
15	New York
15	South Carolina
19	Arkansas
19	Delaware
19	Georgia
19	Oregon
23	Arizona
23	Kentucky
23	New Jersey
23	Vermont
27	Colorado
27	Maine
27	Oklahoma
27	Pennsylvania
27	Virginia
27	West Virginia
33	Missouri
33	Ohio
33	Washington
36	Idaho
37	Texas
38	Florida
38	New Mexico
40	Indiana
41	Iowa
42	Minnesota
42	Montana
44	Nebraska
44	Wisconsin
46	Alaska
47	Kansas
47	North Dakota
49	Wyoming
50	South Dakota

Note: Ties in ranking reflect ties in actual values.

Source Notes for Technology (Section M)

M-1 Percentage of Households with Computers, 2001: In 1995, the National Telecommunication and Information Administration (NTIA), an agency of the Department of Commerce, began publishing a series of reports on access to technology in the United States. The statistics on computer ownership are from the fifth and most recent report, *A Nation Online: How Americans Are Expanding Their Use of the Internet* available on the NTIA website (www.ntia.doc.gov). The data come from Census Bureau interviews with approximately 57,000 sample households. Besides geographical data the report contains information on computer ownership by race and ethnicity, income, and education. The report finds that since 1997 computer use has grown at a rate of 5.3 percent on an annualized basis.

M-2 Percentage of Households with Internet Access, 2001: 50.5 percent of American households were connected to the Internet in 2001, 20 percent of these were connected by a high-speed broadband service. This table is from the same NTIA report cited in the notes to Table M-1. According to the report, the most common use of the Internet, whether connected at or away from home, is e-mail (84%). Over two-thirds of those "connected" use the Internet on a regular basis to search for information (67.3%). Game playing accounted for 42.1 percent of online activity. Shopping accounted for 39.1 percent. Less than a third of users used the Internet to search for government services (30.9%).

M-3 Percentage of Zip Codes with Broadband Telecommunications Service, 2001: High-speed, high-capacity, "always on" broadband telecommunications services allow large amounts of information to be transmitted quickly, providing at least the promise of increased productivity. The majority of these services are supplied by cable lines and digital subscriber lines (DSL), a small percentage come from satellite, wireless, and other technologies. As many who live in rural areas know, broadband service is not yet universally available.

The Federal Communications Commission (FCC) began tracking access to broadband services in 1998. While it does not count individual subscribers, the FCC does keep statistics on the number of broadband providers in each zip code. This information for 2001 is provided in the table. The first column shows the percentage of zip codes in each state that have one or more subscribers to one or more broadband services. According to the FCC report from which the data is culled ("High-Speed Services for Internet Access: Subscribership as of June 30, 2001"), 97 percent of the U.S. population resides in those zip codes. Because access can vary greatly within a zip code—cable lines tend to be laid in residential rather than business and industrial areas, and one neighbor can be offered DSL while another is not—presumptions about access should be made with caution. The second column of the table shows the number of companies that supply broadband service within each state, providing some indication of competition in the broadband market.

M-4 High-tech Jobs, 2001: The recognized authority on employment statistics—the Bureau of Labor Statistics (BLS)—does not currently release "high-tech" industry data for states, but BLS does assign every category of job an employment code (Standard Industrial Classification, or SIC code). In order to create this table, the American Electronics Association (AeA) sifted through these SIC codes to create its own definition of the high-tech industry. In *Cyberstates 2002,* the source of the data in this table, AeA calls their definition "a solid, yet conservative, representation of the core components of today's high-tech industry." It includes high-tech manufacturing, communications services, and software and computer-related services. It does not include wholesale and retail trade of high-tech goods, nor does it include the biotechnology industry (due to the difficulty of separating "tech" from "bio" activities), temporary employees, consultants, or freelance workers. AeA's definition tends to overlook industries that utilize high-tech processes, such as drug, chemical, or architectural services, even if their product is not considered "high-tech." High-technology is not an easy industry to isolate. Other groups are bound to develop differing definitions.

M-5 Dot.com Domain Names, 2001: This table presents a count of commercial domain names (".coms") registered in each state. Anyone who pays a modest fee ($20-$50 a year) can register a domain name and use their website for virtually any purpose, such as sharing vacation photos, idolizing popstars, or espousing the latest conspiracy theory. Presumably, though, a large number of these domain names are used for commercial enterprises. Thus, domain names per business is included in this table as a subject of possible interest. The statistics are compiled by Matthew Zook at UC Berkeley using a sampling method. Large collections of domain names owned by a single entity were removed to reduce geographical bias. These and other domain name statistics are available at www.zooknic.com.

M-6 State Government Web site Ratings, 2002: Citing the Internet as an important means for governments to deliver information and services to citizens, Daniel M. West, Director of the Taubman Center for Public Policy at Brown University, has taken on the task of rating "e-government." West's report, "State and Federal E-Government in the United States, 2002," published on www.InsidePolitics.org, analyzes 1,265 government websites from a "citizen's perspective." Thirty-two measures were used to evaluate websites. These include the presence of on-line services, publications and databases, security and privacy measures, handicap accessibility, and other services such as foreign language translation, digital signatures, credit card payments, and comment forms. Each state was given a score out of a possible 100. Tennessee topped the scale with a score of 56.

M-7 Students Per Computer, 2001: This table is one measure of student access to technology in public schools. The data come from *Education Week's* "Technology Counts 2002" (www.edweek.org), which includes additional information on how computers and the Internet are used in the classroom. For more information on the capacity to use technology see also, the National Center for Education Statistics' report, "Teachers' Tools for the 21st Century: A Report on Teachers' Use of Technology."

State Rankings

Alabama

Population · Section A

Population 2001	23
Population Change 2000-2001	37
Population Change 1990-2001	25
Population 2015	14
Population 2025	22
Percentage 65 and Over	20
Percentage 17 and Under	29
Median Age	26
Percentage African American	6
Percentage Hispanic	42
Percentage in Poverty	6
Child Poverty Rate	3
Percentage Female	4
Birth Rates	31
Death Rates	4
Population Density	26
New Legal Immigrants 2000	39

Economies · Section B

Personal Income 2001	24
Gross State Product	45
Per Capita Personal Income	43
Personal Income from Wages and Salaries	35
Average Annual Pay	33
Average Hourly Earnings	42
Value Added in Manufacturing	29
Cost of Living	40
Average Annual Pay in Manufacturing	41
Average Annual Pay in Retailing	35
Labor Force	41
Unemployment Rate	14
Employment Rate	37
Government Employment	15
Manufacturing Employment	8
Fortune 500 Companies	25
Forbes 500 Companies	24
Tourism Spending Per Capita	47
Exports Per Capita	27
Housing Permits	36
Percentage Change in Home Prices	41
Net Farm Income	8
Financial Institution Assets	8
Bankruptcy Filings	4
Patents Issued	45
WC Disability Payment	29
UC Average Weekly Benefit	49
Economic Momentum	39
One-year Employment Change	38
Manufacturing Employment Change	23
Home Ownership	12
Gambling	41

Electricity Use Per Residential Customer	5
Cost Per Kwh	12
New Companies	38

Geography · Section C

Total Land Area	28
Federally Owned Land	29
State Park Acreage	41
State Park Visitors	45
Population Not Active	9
Hunters with Firearms	9
Registered Boats	17
State Spending for the Arts	18
Energy Consumption Per Capita	9
Toxic Chemical Release Per Capita	12
Hazardous Waste Sites	25
Polluted Rivers and Streams	5
Expired Surface Water Pollution Permits	44
Air Pollution Emissions	12

Government · Section D

Members of United States House	22
State Legislators	27
Legislators Per Million Population	28
Units of Government	32
Legislators Compensation	48
Female Legislators	50
Turnover in Legislatures	28
Term Limits	n/a
Legislative Session Length	24
Republicans in State Legislatures	41
Governor's Power Rating	47
Number of Statewide Elected Officials	4
State and Local Government Employees	12
State and Local Average Salaries	36
Local Employment	31
Local Spending Accountability	38
Registered Voters	38
Percentage of Population Voting	24
Statewide Initiatives	n/a
Campaign Costs Per Vote	4

Federal Impacts · Section E

Per Capita Federal Spending	10
Increase in Federal Spending	14
Per Capita Federal Grant Spending	26
Per Capita Federal Spending on Procurement	8

Per Capita Federal Spending on Payments to Individuals	11
Per Capita Federal Spending on Social Security and Medicare	7
Social Security Benefits	43
Federal Spending on Employee Wages and Salaries	19
Federal Grant Spending Per Dollar of State Tax Revenue	8
General Revenue from Federal Government	11
Federal Tax Burden Per Capita	42
Federal Spending Per Dollar of Taxes Paid	8
Highway Charges Returned to States	14
Terms of Trade	15
Federal Personal Income Taxes	43
Federal Share of Medicaid	9

Taxes · Section F

Tax Revenue	48
Per Capita Tax Revenue	50
Tax Effort	43
Tax Capacity	47
Percentage Change in Taxes	31
Property Taxes as a Percentage of Income	50
Property Taxes Per Capita	50
Property Tax Revenue as a Percentage of 3-tax Revenues	48
Sales Taxes as a Percentage of Income	17
Sales Taxes Per Capita	25
Sales Tax Revenue as a Percentage of 3-tax Revenues	9
Sales Tax Rate	37
Income Taxes as a Percentage of Income	36
Income Taxes Per Capita	36
Income Tax Revenue as a Percentage of 3-tax Revenues	29
Highest Personal Income Rate	39
Corporate Income Taxes	44
Motor Fuel Taxes	35
Tobacco Taxes	44
Taxes on High Income Families	37
Taxes in the Largest City in Each State	25
Progressivity of Taxes	42

Revenues and Finances · Section G

Per Capita Total Revenue	42
Per Capita General Revenue	41
Own-source General Revenue	46
Per Capita Non-tax Revenue	14

Per Capita Total Spending	30
General Spending as a Percentage of Income	16
Per Capita General Spending	30
Change in General Expenditures	9
State Government General Revenue	37
State Government General Spending	32
State Government General Fund Spending	17
State and Local Debt	39
Debt as a Percentage of Revenue	32
Per Capita Full Faith and Credit Debt	29
Bond Ratings	4
State Solvency Index	33
Pension Plan Assets	38
State Reserves	14
Capital Outlays and Interest	34
State Budget Process Quality	40
Relative State Spending "Needs"	41
Structural Deficits	31

Education - Section H

Math Proficiency, Eighth Grade	34
Science Proficiency, Eighth Grade	33
AFQT Ranks	44
SAT Scores	n/a
ACT Scores	19
Over-25 Population with a High School Diploma	49
Students in Private Schools	26
High School Completion Rates	46
Pupil-Teacher Ratio	25
Public School Enrollment	32
Library Holdings Per Capita	41
Children with Disabilities	24
Education Spending Per Capita	36
Education Spending as a Percentage of Total Spending	27
Spending Per Pupil	47
Average Teacher Salary	27
Sources of School Funds	43
State Aid Per Pupil	30
Higher Education Spending Per Capita	21
Higher Education Spending as a Percentage of Total Spending	17
Public Higher Education Enrollment	11
Per Pupil Support of Higher Education	27
Tuition and Fees	28
Average Professor Salary	44
Education Employees	32
R and D Spending	7
Library Operating Spending	44

Health - Section I

Immunization Rates	8
Infant Mortality Rates	2
State Health Rankings	45
Population Without Health Insurance	23
Abortions	25
Alcohol Consumption	44
Percentage of Adult Smokers	21
Percentage Obese	6
AIDS Cases	22
Physicians Per 100,000 Population	41
Hospital Beds Per 1,000 Population	11
Medicaid Recipients	24
Medicaid Recipients as a Percentage of Poverty Population	43
Health and Hospital Spending	2
Health and Hospital Spending as a Percentage of Total Spending	1
Per Capita Medicaid Spending	27
Medicaid Spending Per Aged Recipient	34
Medicaid Spending Per Child	50
Medicare Payment Per Hospital Day	12
Hospital Expense Per Inpatient Day	49
Population in HMOs	45

Crime - Section J

Crime Rate	18
Violent Crime Rate	22
Murder Rate	3
Property Crime Rate	19
Motor Vehicle Theft Rate	35
Violent Crime Rate Change	33
Prisoners	16
Change in Prisoners	23
Incarceration Rate	5
Juvenile Violent Crime Rate	39
Law Enforcement Employees	29
Corrections Employees	42
State Corrections Spending	49
Increase in State Corrections Spending	41
Law Enforcement Spending	45
Law Enforcement Spending as a Percentage of Total Spending	43

Transportation - Section K

Travel on Interstates	38
Interstate Mileage in Unacceptable Condition	37
Deficient Bridges	15

Traffic Deaths	17
Seat Belt Use	11
Vehicle-miles Traveled Per Capita	4
Workers Using Public Transportation	48
Road and Street Miles	32
Highway Employees	19
Public Transit Employees	46
Highway Spending Per Capita	36
Highway Spending as a Percentage of Total Spending	35

Welfare - Section L

Percentage of Births to Unwed Mothers	17
TANF Recipients as a Percentage of Population	42
Food Stamp Recipients as a Percentage of Population	6
SSI Recipients as a Percentage of Population	5
Change in TANF/AFDC Recipients	21
Condition of Children Index	48
Percentage of Families with Single Parent	7
Average Monthly TANF Payments	48
Welfare as a Percentage of Poverty-level Income	41
State Supplements of SSI	32
State Income Tax Liability of Typical Family in Poverty	1
Child Support Collections	43
Child Support Collections Per Dollar of Administrative Costs	33
Children in Foster Care	36
Welfare Spending Per Capita	26
Welfare Spending as a Percentage of Total Spending	18
Administrative Costs Per TANF Case	42

Technology - Section M

Percentage of Households with Computers	49
Percentage of Households with Internet Access	48
Zip codes with Broadband Service	25
High-tech Jobs	29
Dot-com Domain Names	40
State Government Website Ratings	49
Students per Computer	4

Alaska

Population - Section A

Population 2001	47
Population Change 2000-2001	18
Population Change 1990-2001	18
Population 2015	4
Population 2025	45
Percentage 65 and Over	50
Percentage 17 and Under	2
Median Age	48
Percentage African American	33
Percentage Hispanic	28
Percentage in Poverty	38
Child Poverty Rate	31
Percentage Female	50
Birth Rates	6
Death Rates	24
Population Density	50
New Legal Immigrants 2000	42

Economies - Section B

Personal Income 2001	47
Gross State Product	4
Per Capita Personal Income	14
Personal Income from Wages and Salaries	14
Average Annual Pay	14
Average Hourly Earnings	2
Value Added in Manufacturing	49
Cost of Living	5
Average Annual Pay in Manufacturing	46
Average Annual Pay in Retailing	11
Labor Force	15
Unemployment Rate	1
Employment Rate	50
Government Employment	1
Manufacturing Employment	47
Fortune 500 Companies	n/a
Forbes 500 Companies	n/a
Tourism Spending Per Capita	6
Exports Per Capita	4
Housing Permits	27
Percentage Change in Home Prices	36
Net Farm Income	49
Financial Institution Assets	43
Bankruptcy Filings	50
Patents Issued	47
WC Disability Payment	9
UC Average Weekly Benefit	45
Economic Momentum	2
One-year Employment Change	7
Manufacturing Employment Change	29
Home Ownership	39
Gambling	42

Electricity Use Per Residential Customer	38
Cost Per Kwh	36
New Companies	11

Geography - Section C

Total Land Area	1
Federally Owned Land	1
State Park Acreage	1
State Park Visitors	7
Population Not Active	40
Hunters with Firearms	n/a
Registered Boats	46
State Spending for the Arts	33
Energy Consumption Per Capita	3
Toxic Chemical Release Per Capita	1
Hazardous Waste Sites	44
Polluted Rivers and Streams	30
Expired Surface Water Pollution Permits	40
Air Pollution Emissions	24

Government - Section D

Members of United States House	44
State Legislators	49
Legislators Per Million Population	9
Units of Government	30
Legislators Compensation	20
Female Legislators	32
Turnover in Legislatures	8
Term Limits	n/a
Legislative Session Length	16
Republicans in State Legislatures	10
Governor's Power Rating	2
Number of Statewide Elected Officials	45
State and Local Government Employees	2
State and Local Average Salaries	5
Local Employment	48
Local Spending Accountability	39
Registered Voters	1
Percentage of Population Voting	3
Statewide Initiatives	9
Campaign Costs Per Vote	10

Federal Impacts - Section E

Per Capita Federal Spending	1
Increase in Federal Spending	3
Per Capita Federal Grant Spending	1
Per Capita Federal Spending on Procurement	4

Per Capita Federal Spending on Payments to Individuals	49
Per Capita Federal Spending on Social Security and Medicare	50
Social Security Benefits	41
Federal Spending on Employee Wages and Salaries	1
Federal Grant Spending Per Dollar of State Tax Revenue	3
General Revenue from Federal Government	45
Federal Tax Burden Per Capita	20
Federal Spending Per Dollar of Taxes Paid	6
Highway Charges Returned to States	1
Terms of Trade	1
Federal Personal Income Taxes	17
Federal Share of Medicaid	33

Taxes - Section F

Tax Revenue	3
Per Capita Tax Revenue	6
Tax Effort	4
Tax Capacity	3
Percentage Change in Taxes	50
Property Taxes as a Percentage of Income	7
Property Taxes Per Capita	8
Property Tax Revenue as a Percentage of 3-tax Revenues	2
Sales Taxes as a Percentage of Income	47
Sales Taxes Per Capita	46
Sales Tax Revenue as a Percentage of 3-tax Revenues	45
Sales Tax Rate	n/a
Income Taxes as a Percentage of Income	n/a
Income Taxes Per Capita	n/a
Income Tax Revenue as a Percentage of 3-tax Revenues	n/a
Highest Personal Income Rate	n/a
Corporate Income Taxes	1
Motor Fuel Taxes	49
Tobacco Taxes	10
Taxes on High Income Families	49
Taxes in the Largest City in Each State	49
Progressivity of Taxes	50

Revenues and Finances - Section G

Per Capita Total Revenue	1
Per Capita General Revenue	1
Own-source General Revenue	1
Per Capita Non-tax Revenue	1

Per Capita Total Spending	1
General Spending as a Percentage of Income	1
Per Capita General Spending	1
Change in General Expenditures	45
State Government General Revenue	1
State Government General Spending	1
State Government General Fund Spending	n/a
State and Local Debt	1
Debt as a Percentage of Revenue	25
Per Capita Full Faith and Credit Debt	5
Bond Ratings	3
State Solvency Index	1
Pension Plan Assets	5
State Reserves	1
Capital Outlays and Interest	1
State Budget Process Quality	45
Relative State Spending "Needs"	38
Structural Deficits	49

Education - Section H

Math Proficiency, Eighth Grade	n/a
Science Proficiency, Eighth Grade	n/a
AFQT Ranks	9
SAT Scores	5
ACT Scores	n/a
Over-25 Population with a High School Diploma	5
Students in Private Schools	46
High School Completion Rates	3
Pupil-Teacher Ratio	12
Public School Enrollment	1
Library Holdings Per Capita	19
Children with Disabilities	32
Education Spending Per Capita	1
Education Spending as a Percentage of Total Spending	50
Spending Per Pupil	6
Average Teacher Salary	9
Sources of School Funds	45
State Aid Per Pupil	4
Higher Education Spending Per Capita	12
Higher Education Spending as a Percentage of Total Spending	49
Public Higher Education Enrollment	25
Per Pupil Support of Higher Education	2
Tuition and Fees	34
Average Professor Salary	45
Education Employees	2
R and D Spending	12
Library Operating Spending	4

Health - Section I

Immunization Rates	44
Infant Mortality Rates	26
State Health Rankings	30
Population Without Health Insurance	16
Abortions	n/a
Alcohol Consumption	4
Percentage of Adult Smokers	7
Percentage Obese	19
AIDS Cases	46
Physicians Per 100,000 Population	43
Hospital Beds Per 1,000 Population	41
Medicaid Recipients	18
Medicaid Recipients as a Percentage of Poverty Population	7
Health and Hospital Spending	26
Health and Hospital Spending as a Percentage of Total Spending	47
Per Capita Medicaid Spending	8
Medicaid Spending Per Aged Recipient	22
Medicaid Spending Per Child	2
Medicare Payment Per Hospital Day	11
Hospital Expense Per Inpatient Day	1
Population in HMOs	50

Crime - Section J

Crime Rate	21
Violent Crime Rate	10
Murder Rate	17
Property Crime Rate	25
Motor Vehicle Theft Rate	19
Violent Crime Rate Change	29
Prisoners	40
Change in Prisoners	48
Incarceration Rate	36
Juvenile Violent Crime Rate	27
Law Enforcement Employees	39
Corrections Employees	9
State Corrections Spending	n/a
Increase in State Corrections Spending	n/a
Law Enforcement Spending	1
Law Enforcement Spending as a Percentage of Total Spending	46

Transportation - Section K

Travel on Interstates	4
Interstate Mileage in Unacceptable Condition	16
Deficient Bridges	23

Traffic Deaths	15
Seat Belt Use	39
Vehicle-miles Traveled Per Capita	48
Workers Using Public Transportation	17
Road and Street Miles	6
Highway Employees	1
Public Transit Employees	23
Highway Spending Per Capita	1
Highway Spending as a Percentage of Total Spending	8

Welfare - Section L

Percentage of Births to Unwed Mothers	26
TANF Recipients as a Percentage of Population	4
Food Stamp Recipients as a Percentage of Population	25
SSI Recipients as a Percentage of Population	39
Change in TANF/AFDC Recipients	24
Condition of Children Index	27
Percentage of Families with Single Parent	13
Average Monthly TANF Payments	1
Welfare as a Percentage of Poverty-level Income	1
State Supplements of SSI	5
State Income Tax Liability of Typical Family in Poverty	n/a
Child Support Collections	3
Child Support Collections Per Dollar of Administrative Costs	27
Children in Foster Care	3
Welfare Spending Per Capita	2
Welfare Spending as a Percentage of Total Spending	46
Administrative Costs Per TANF Case	17

Technology - Section M

Percentage of Households with Computers	1
Percentage of Households with Internet Access	1
Zip codes with Broadband Service	50
High-tech Jobs	38
Dot-com Domain Names	20
State Government Website Ratings	33
Students per Computer	46

Arizona

Population - Section A

Population 2001	20
Population Change 2000-2001	2
Population Change 1990-2001	2
Population 2015	20
Population 2025	17
Percentage 65 and Over	22
Percentage 17 and Under	10
Median Age	42
Percentage African American	36
Percentage Hispanic	4
Percentage in Poverty	10
Child Poverty Rate	7
Percentage Female	43
Birth Rates	3
Death Rates	29
Population Density	36
New Legal Immigrants 2000	14

Economies - Section B

Personal Income 2001	23
Gross State Product	36
Per Capita Personal Income	38
Personal Income from Wages and Salaries	18
Average Annual Pay	20
Average Hourly Earnings	36
Value Added in Manufacturing	37
Cost of Living	25
Average Annual Pay in Manufacturing	6
Average Annual Pay in Retailing	7
Labor Force	46
Unemployment Rate	13
Employment Rate	38
Government Employment	28
Manufacturing Employment	40.0
Fortune 500 Companies	32
Forbes 500 Companies	37
Tourism Spending Per Capita	14
Exports Per Capita	15
Housing Permits	3
Percentage Change in Home Prices	19
Net Farm Income	16
Financial Institution Assets	47
Bankruptcy Filings	24
Patents Issued	19
WC Disability Payment	49
UC Average Weekly Benefit	47
Economic Momentum	6
One-year Employment Change	40
Manufacturing Employment Change	49
Home Ownership	40
Gambling	33

Electricity Use Per Residential Customer	11
Cost Per Kwh	35
New Companies	22

Geography - Section C

Total Land Area	6.0
Federally Owned Land	6
State Park Acreage	39
State Park Visitors	49
Population Not Active	37
Hunters with Firearms	23
Registered Boats	30
State Spending for the Arts	28
Energy Consumption Per Capita	35
Toxic Chemical Release Per Capita	4
Hazardous Waste Sites	40
Polluted Rivers and Streams	39
Expired Surface Water Pollution Permits	43
Air Pollution Emissions	21

Government - Section D

Members of United States House	18
State Legislators	43
Legislators Per Million Population	42
Units of Government	42
Legislators Compensation	21
Female Legislators	2
Turnover in Legislatures	2
Term Limits	6
Legislative Session Length	26
Republicans in State Legislatures	12
Governor's Power Rating	34
Number of Statewide Elected Officials	21
State and Local Government Employees	48
State and Local Average Salaries	22
Local Employment	9
Local Spending Accountability	35
Registered Voters	43
Percentage of Population Voting	47
Statewide Initiatives	4
Campaign Costs Per Vote	43

Federal Impacts - Section E

Per Capita Federal Spending	32
Increase in Federal Spending	8
Per Capita Federal Grant Spending	43
Per Capita Federal Spending on Procurement	12

Per Capita Federal Spending on Payments to Individuals	39
Per Capita Federal Spending on Social Security and Medicare	35
Social Security Benefits	16
Federal Spending on Employee Wages and Salaries	28
Federal Grant Spending Per Dollar of State Tax Revenue	26
General Revenue from Federal Government	22
Federal Tax Burden Per Capita	33
Federal Spending Per Dollar of Taxes Paid	25
Highway Charges Returned to States	40
Terms of Trade	30
Federal Personal Income Taxes	28
Federal Share of Medicaid	14

Taxes - Section F

Tax Revenue	21
Per Capita Tax Revenue	36
Tax Effort	28
Tax Capacity	34
Percentage Change in Taxes	8
Property Taxes as a Percentage of Income	22
Property Taxes Per Capita	32
Property Tax Revenue as a Percentage of 3-tax Revenues	26
Sales Taxes as a Percentage of Income	10
Sales Taxes Per Capita	12
Sales Tax Revenue as a Percentage of 3-tax Revenues	16
Sales Tax Rate	17
Income Taxes as a Percentage of Income	38
Income Taxes Per Capita	38
Income Tax Revenue as a Percentage of 3-tax Revenues	38
Highest Personal Income Rate	31
Corporate Income Taxes	22
Motor Fuel Taxes	35
Tobacco Taxes	21
Taxes on High Income Families	33
Taxes in the Largest City in Each State	33
Progressivity of Taxes	20

Revenues and Finances - Section G

Per Capita Total Revenue	48
Per Capita General Revenue	48
Own-source General Revenue	45
Per Capita Non-tax Revenue	50

Per Capita Total Spending — 39
General Spending as a Percentage of
  Income — 27
Per Capita General Spending — 45
Change in General Expenditures — 3
State Government General Revenue — 45
State Government General Spending — 40
State Government General Fund
  Spending — 25
State and Local Debt — 26
Debt as a Percentage of Revenue — 10
Per Capita Full Faith and Credit Debt — 20
Bond Ratings — n/a
State Solvency Index — 13
Pension Plan Assets — 33
State Reserves — 38
Capital Outlays and Interest — 14
State Budget Process Quality — 46
Relative State Spending "Needs" — 45
Structural Deficits — 44

Education - Section H

Math Proficiency, Eighth Grade — 27
Science Proficiency, Eighth Grade — 26
AFQT Ranks — 23
SAT Scores — 3
ACT Scores — n/a
Over-25 Population with a High
  School Diploma — 31
Students in Private Schools — 44
High School Completion Rates — 50
Pupil-Teacher Ratio — 1
Public School Enrollment — 13
Library Holdings Per Capita — 48
Children with Disabilities — 49
Education Spending Per Capita — 46
Education Spending as a Percentage
  of Total Spending — 34
Spending Per Pupil — 48
Average Teacher Salary — 25
Sources of School Funds — 29
State Aid Per Pupil — 40
Higher Education Spending Per
  Capita — 30
Higher Education Spending as a
  Percentage of Total Spending — 19
Public Higher Education Enrollment — 6
Per Pupil Support of Higher
  Education — 49
Tuition and Fees — 47
Average Professor Salary — 25
Education Employees — 45
R and D Spending — 15
Library Operating Spending — 26

Health - Section I

Immunization Rates — 47
Infant Mortality Rates — 28
State Health Rankings — 34
Population Without Health
  Insurance — 7
Abortions — 28
Alcohol Consumption — 6
Percentage of Adult Smokers — 40
Percentage Obese — 44
AIDS Cases — 20
Physicians Per 100,000 Population — 36
Hospital Beds Per 1,000 Population — 44
Medicaid Recipients — 28
Medicaid Recipients as a Percentage
  of Poverty Population — 37
Health and Hospital Spending — 44
Health and Hospital Spending as a
  Percentage of Total Spending — 39
Per Capita Medicaid Spending — 48
Medicaid Spending Per Aged
  Recipient — 29
Medicaid Spending Per Child — 20
Medicare Payment Per Hospital Day — 3
Hospital Expense Per Inpatient Day — 29
Population in HMOs — 20

Crime - Section J

Crime Rate — 1
Violent Crime Rate — 15
Murder Rate — 7
Property Crime Rate — 1
Motor Vehicle Theft Rate — 1
Violent Crime Rate Change — 22
Prisoners — 15
Change in Prisoners — 21
Incarceration Rate — 10
Juvenile Violent Crime Rate — 17
Law Enforcement Employees — 15
Corrections Employees — 13
State Corrections Spending — 34
Increase in State Corrections
  Spending — 37
Law Enforcement Spending — 11
Law Enforcement Spending as a
  Percentage of Total Spending — 3

Transportation - Section K

Travel on Interstates — 20
Interstate Mileage in Unacceptable
  Condition — 44
Deficient Bridges — 50

Traffic Deaths — 7
Seat Belt Use — 19
Vehicle-miles Traveled Per Capita — 35
Workers Using Public
  Transportation — 22
Road and Street Miles — 29
Highway Employees — 47
Public Transit Employees — 48
Highway Spending Per Capita — 25
Highway Spending as a Percentage
  of Total Spending — 22

Welfare - Section L

Percentage of Births to Unwed
  Mothers — 6
TANF Recipients as a Percentage
  of Population — 14
Food Stamp Recipients as a
  Percentage of Population — 30
SSI Recipients as a Percentage of
  Population — 32
Change in TANF/AFDC Recipients — 36
Condition of Children Index — 43
Percentage of Families with Single
  Parent — 7
Average Monthly TANF
  Payments — 32
Welfare as a Percentage of Poverty-
  level Income — 36
State Supplements of SSI — 35
State Income Tax Liability of Typical
  Family in Poverty — 18
Child Support Collections — 46
Child Support Collections Per Dollar
  of Administrative Costs — 28
Children in Foster Care — 38
Welfare Spending Per Capita — 46
Welfare Spending as a Percentage of
  Total Spending — 39
Administrative Costs Per TANF Case — 21

Technology - Section M

Percentage of Households with
  Computers — 15
Percentage of Households with
  Internet Access — 22
Zip codes with Broadband
  Service — 7
High-tech Jobs — 15
Dot-com Domain Names — 4
State Government Website
  Ratings — 31
Students per Computer — 23

Arkansas

Population - Section A

Population 2001	33
Population Change 2000-2001	27
Population Change 1990-2001	19
Population 2015	25
Population 2025	32
Percentage 65 and Over	9
Percentage 17 and Under	27
Median Age	19
Percentage African American	12
Percentage Hispanic	32
Percentage in Poverty	3
Child Poverty Rate	1
Percentage Female	19
Birth Rates	20
Death Rates	8
Population Density	34
New Legal Immigrants 2000	40

Economies - Section B

Personal Income 2001	34
Gross State Product	47
Per Capita Personal Income	48
Personal Income from Wages and Salaries	38
Average Annual Pay	46
Average Hourly Earnings	44
Value Added in Manufacturing	16
Cost of Living	45
Average Annual Pay in Manufacturing	48
Average Annual Pay in Retailing	50
Labor Force	43
Unemployment Rate	29
Employment Rate	22
Government Employment	27
Manufacturing Employment	4
Fortune 500 Companies	19
Forbes 500 Companies	30
Tourism Spending Per Capita	40
Exports Per Capita	42
Housing Permits	38
Percentage Change in Home Prices	46
Net Farm Income	10
Financial Institution Assets	38
Bankruptcy Filings	7
Patents Issued	46
WC Disability Payment	44
UC Average Weekly Benefit	33
Economic Momentum	13
One-year Employment Change	20
Manufacturing Employment Change	37
Home Ownership	35
Gambling	43

Electricity Use Per Residential Customer	14
Cost Per Kwh	19
New Companies	50

Geography - Section C

Total Land Area	27
Federally Owned Land	17
State Park Acreage	40
State Park Visitors	22
Population Not Active	7
Hunters with Firearms	3
Registered Boats	25
State Spending for the Arts	45
Energy Consumption Per Capita	15
Toxic Chemical Release Per Capita	22
Hazardous Waste Sites	34
Polluted Rivers and Streams	47
Expired Surface Water Pollution Permits	32
Air Pollution Emissions	32

Government - Section D

Members of United States House	31
State Legislators	30
Legislators Per Million Population	19
Units of Government	13
Legislators Compensation	32
Female Legislators	45
Turnover in Legislatures	7
Term Limits	15
Legislative Session Length	36
Republicans in State Legislatures	46
Governor's Power Rating	41
Number of Statewide Elected Officials	21
State and Local Government Employees	23
State and Local Average Salaries	49
Local Employment	37
Local Spending Accountability	46
Registered Voters	26
Percentage of Population Voting	26
Statewide Initiatives	9
Campaign Costs Per Vote	34

Federal Impacts - Section E

Per Capita Federal Spending	25
Increase in Federal Spending	10
Per Capita Federal Grant Spending	16
Per Capita Federal Spending on Procurement	49

Per Capita Federal Spending on Payments to Individuals	10
Per Capita Federal Spending on Social Security and Medicare	9
Social Security Benefits	48
Federal Spending on Employee Wages and Salaries	41
Federal Grant Spending Per Dollar of State Tax Revenue	21
General Revenue from Federal Government	10
Federal Tax Burden Per Capita	48
Federal Spending Per Dollar of Taxes Paid	11
Highway Charges Returned to States	13
Terms of Trade	11
Federal Personal Income Taxes	47
Federal Share of Medicaid	4

Taxes - Section F

Tax Revenue	38
Per Capita Tax Revenue	47
Tax Effort	29
Tax Capacity	48
Percentage Change in Taxes	11
Property Taxes as a Percentage of Income	46
Property Taxes Per Capita	48
Property Tax Revenue as a Percentage of 3-tax Revenues	47
Sales Taxes as a Percentage of Income	9
Sales Taxes Per Capita	20
Sales Tax Revenue as a Percentage of 3-tax Revenues	12
Sales Tax Rate	18
Income Taxes as a Percentage of Income	32
Income Taxes Per Capita	34
Income Tax Revenue as a Percentage of 3-tax Revenues	27
Highest Personal Income Rate	12
Corporate Income Taxes	25
Motor Fuel Taxes	21
Tobacco Taxes	33
Taxes on High Income Families	24
Taxes in the Largest City in Each State	28
Progressivity of Taxes	26

Revenues and Finances - Section G

Per Capita Total Revenue	50
Per Capita General Revenue	50
Own-source General Revenue	49
Per Capita Non-tax Revenue	49

Per Capita Total Spending	50
General Spending as a Percentage of Income	26
Per Capita General Spending	49
Change in General Expenditures	14
State Government General Revenue	25
State Government General Spending	28
State Government General Fund Spending	4
State and Local Debt	48
Debt as a Percentage of Revenue	43
Per Capita Full Faith and Credit Debt	43
Bond Ratings	3
State Solvency Index	25
Pension Plan Assets	23
State Reserves	48
Capital Outlays and Interest	50
State Budget Process Quality	42
Relative State Spending "Needs"	30
Structural Deficits	21

Education · Section H

Math Proficiency, Eighth Grade	36
Science Proficiency, Eighth Grade	30
AFQT Ranks	45
SAT Scores	n/a
ACT Scores	18
Over-25 Population with a High School Diploma	40
Students in Private Schools	40
High School Completion Rates	39
Pupil-Teacher Ratio	32
Public School Enrollment	26
Library Holdings Per Capita	36
Children with Disabilities	18
Education Spending Per Capita	45
Education Spending as a Percentage of Total Spending	11
Spending Per Pupil	46
Average Teacher Salary	40
Sources of School Funds	38
State Aid Per Pupil	33
Higher Education Spending Per Capita	32
Higher Education Spending as a Percentage of Total Spending	11
Public Higher Education Enrollment	34
Per Pupil Support of Higher Education	8
Tuition and Fees	27
Average Professor Salary	35
Education Employees	9
R and D Spending	50
Library Operating Spending	49

Health · Section I

Immunization Rates	45
Infant Mortality Rates	11
State Health Rankings	47
Population Without Health Insurance	8
Abortions	35
Alcohol Consumption	46
Percentage of Adult Smokers	12
Percentage Obese	16
AIDS Cases	29
Physicians Per 100,000 Population	46
Hospital Beds Per 1,000 Population	13
Medicaid Recipients	8
Medicaid Recipients as a Percentage of Poverty Population	44
Health and Hospital Spending	30
Health and Hospital Spending as a Percentage of Total Spending	18
Per Capita Medicaid Spending	22
Medicaid Spending Per Aged Recipient	46
Medicaid Spending Per Child	19
Medicare Payment Per Hospital Day	40
Hospital Expense Per Inpatient Day	47
Population in HMOs	42

Crime · Section J

Crime Rate	25
Violent Crime Rate	21
Murder Rate	18
Property Crime Rate	23
Motor Vehicle Theft Rate	37
Violent Crime Rate Change	20
Prisoners	28
Change in Prisoners	12
Incarceration Rate	15
Juvenile Violent Crime Rate	34
Law Enforcement Employees	25
Corrections Employees	27
State Corrections Spending	47
Increase in State Corrections Spending	35
Law Enforcement Spending	41
Law Enforcement Spending as a Percentage of Total Spending	28

Transportation · Section K

Travel on Interstates	23
Interstate Mileage in Unacceptable Condition	3
Deficient Bridges	26

Traffic Deaths	6
Seat Belt Use	46
Vehicle-miles Traveled Per Capita	19
Workers Using Public Transportation	49
Road and Street Miles	21
Highway Employees	17
Public Transit Employees	38
Highway Spending Per Capita	40
Highway Spending as a Percentage of Total Spending	25

Welfare · Section L

Percentage of Births to Unwed Mothers	10
TANF Recipients as a Percentage of Population	40
Food Stamp Recipients as a Percentage of Population	5
SSI Recipients as a Percentage of Population	8
Change in TANF/AFDC Recipients	29
Condition of Children Index	47
Percentage of Families with Single Parent	13
Average Monthly TANF Payments	42
Welfare as a Percentage of Poverty-level Income	22
State Supplements of SSI	16
State Income Tax Liability of Typical Family in Poverty	16
Child Support Collections	41
Child Support Collections Per Dollar of Administrative Costs	46
Children in Foster Care	40
Welfare Spending Per Capita	30
Welfare Spending as a Percentage of Total Spending	11
Administrative Costs Per TANF Case	22

Technology · Section M

Percentage of Households with Computers	47
Percentage of Households with Internet Access	49
Zip codes with Broadband Service	41
High-tech Jobs	43
Dot-com Domain Names	47
State Government Website Ratings	30
Students per Computer	19

California

Population - Section A

Population 2001	1
Population Change 2000-2001	9
Population Change 1990-2001	17
Population 2015	6
Population 2025	1
Percentage 65 and Over	45
Percentage 17 and Under	6
Median Age	46
Percentage African American	26
Percentage Hispanic	2
Percentage in Poverty	17
Child Poverty Rate	17
Percentage Female	40
Birth Rates	9
Death Rates	49
Population Density	12
New Legal Immigrants 2000	1

Economies - Section B

Personal Income 2001	1
Gross State Product	7
Per Capita Personal Income	10
Personal Income from Wages and Salaries	17
Average Annual Pay	5
Average Hourly Earnings	25
Value Added in Manufacturing	26
Cost of Living	6
Average Annual Pay in Manufacturing	4
Average Annual Pay in Retailing	1
Labor Force	26
Unemployment Rate	5
Employment Rate	46
Government Employment	30
Manufacturing Employment	27
Fortune 500 Companies	24
Forbes 500 Companies	15
Tourism Spending Per Capita	8
Exports Per Capita	7
Housing Permits	34
Percentage Change in Home Prices	3
Net Farm Income	2
Financial Institution Assets	16
Bankruptcy Filings	30
Patents Issued	5
WC Disability Payment	37
UC Average Weekly Benefit	48
Economic Momentum	29
One-year Employment Change	21
Manufacturing Employment Change	33
Home Ownership	48
Gambling	6

(Section B continued)

Electricity Use Per Residential Customer	49
Cost Per Kwh	38
New Companies	13

Geography - Section C

Total Land Area	3
Federally Owned Land	3
State Park Acreage	2
State Park Visitors	27
Population Not Active	16
Hunters with Firearms	42
Registered Boats	2
State Spending for the Arts	19
Energy Consumption Per Capita	48
Toxic Chemical Release Per Capita	46
Hazardous Waste Sites	2
Polluted Rivers and Streams	2
Expired Surface Water Pollution Permits	20
Air Pollution Emissions	2

Government - Section D

Members of United States House	1
State Legislators	35
Legislators Per Million Population	50
Units of Government	40
Legislators Compensation	1
Female Legislators	13
Turnover in Legislatures	11
Term Limits	15
Legislative Session Length	1
Republicans in State Legislatures	40
Governor's Power Rating	24
Number of Statewide Elected Officials	9
State and Local Government Employees	44
State and Local Average Salaries	1
Local Employment	3
Local Spending Accountability	41
Registered Voters	40
Percentage of Population Voting	42
Statewide Initiatives	4
Campaign Costs Per Vote	8

Federal Impacts - Section E

Per Capita Federal Spending	36
Increase in Federal Spending	47
Per Capita Federal Grant Spending	28
Per Capita Federal Spending on Procurement	17

(Section E continued)

Per Capita Federal Spending on Payments to Individuals	46
Per Capita Federal Spending on Social Security and Medicare	38
Social Security Benefits	20
Federal Spending on Employee Wages and Salaries	31
Federal Grant Spending Per Dollar of State Tax Revenue	40
General Revenue from Federal Government	31
Federal Tax Burden Per Capita	10
Federal Spending Per Dollar of Taxes Paid	44
Highway Charges Returned to States	32
Terms of Trade	40
Federal Personal Income Taxes	5
Federal Share of Medicaid	39

Taxes - Section F

Tax Revenue	10
Per Capita Tax Revenue	7
Tax Effort	15
Tax Capacity	16
Percentage Change in Taxes	3
Property Taxes as a Percentage of Income	35
Property Taxes Per Capita	31
Property Tax Revenue as a Percentage of 3-tax Revenues	40
Sales Taxes as a Percentage of Income	24
Sales Taxes Per Capita	14
Sales Tax Revenue as a Percentage of 3-tax Revenues	28
Sales Tax Rate	9
Income Taxes as a Percentage of Income	6
Income Taxes Per Capita	5
Income Tax Revenue as a Percentage of 3-tax Revenues	8
Highest Personal Income Rate	3
Corporate Income Taxes	7
Motor Fuel Taxes	35
Tobacco Taxes	16
Taxes on High Income Families	7
Taxes in the Largest City in Each State	23
Progressivity of Taxes	14

Revenues and Finances - Section G

Per Capita Total Revenue	6
Per Capita General Revenue	7
Own-source General Revenue	9
Per Capita Non-tax Revenue	11

Per Capita Total Spending	9
General Spending as a Percentage of Income	24
Per Capita General Spending	10
Change in General Expenditures	18
State Government General Revenue	14
State Government General Spending	12
State Government General Fund Spending	28
State and Local Debt	18
Debt as a Percentage of Revenue	31
Per Capita Full Faith and Credit Debt	33
Bond Ratings	5
State Solvency Index	10
Pension Plan Assets	1
State Reserves	47
Capital Outlays and Interest	26
State Budget Process Quality	35
Relative State Spending "Needs"	48
Structural Deficits	23

Education - Section H

Math Proficiency, Eighth Grade	34
Science Proficiency, Eighth Grade	37
AFQT Ranks	38
SAT Scores	11
ACT Scores	n/a
Over-25 Population with a High School Diploma	42
Students in Private Schools	23
High School Completion Rates	42
Pupil-Teacher Ratio	3
Public School Enrollment	6
Library Holdings Per Capita	45
Children with Disabilities	50
Education Spending Per Capita	22
Education Spending as a Percentage of Total Spending	40
Spending Per Pupil	28
Average Teacher Salary	1
Sources of School Funds	39
State Aid Per Pupil	17
Higher Education Spending Per Capita	22
Higher Education Spending as a Percentage of Total Spending	32
Public Higher Education Enrollment	3
Per Pupil Support of Higher Education	38
Tuition and Fees	43
Average Professor Salary	5
Education Employees	44
R and D Spending	5
Library Operating Spending	24

Health - Section I

Immunization Rates	35
Infant Mortality Rates	46
State Health Rankings	24
Population Without Health Insurance	4
Abortions	n/a
Alcohol Consumption	30
Percentage of Adult Smokers	49
Percentage Obese	21
AIDS Cases	14
Physicians Per 100,000 Population	21
Hospital Beds Per 1,000 Population	43
Medicaid Recipients	2
Medicaid Recipients as a Percentage of Poverty Population	14
Health and Hospital Spending	11
Health and Hospital Spending as a Percentage of Total Spending	15
Per Capita Medicaid Spending	32
Medicaid Spending Per Aged Recipient	49
Medicaid Spending Per Child	45
Medicare Payment Per Hospital Day	1
Hospital Expense Per Inpatient Day	23
Population in HMOs	1

Crime - Section J

Crime Rate	29
Violent Crime Rate	8
Murder Rate	13
Property Crime Rate	33
Motor Vehicle Theft Rate	5
Violent Crime Rate Change	42
Prisoners	2
Change in Prisoners	34
Incarceration Rate	13
Juvenile Violent Crime Rate	8
Law Enforcement Employees	28
Corrections Employees	22
State Corrections Spending	12
Increase in State Corrections Spending	13
Law Enforcement Spending	5
Law Enforcement Spending as a Percentage of Total Spending	5

Transportation - Section K

Travel on Interstates	18
Interstate Mileage in Unacceptable Condition	5
Deficient Bridges	22

Traffic Deaths	37
Seat Belt Use	1
Vehicle-miles Traveled Per Capita	39
Workers Using Public Transportation	8
Road and Street Miles	43
Highway Employees	50
Public Transit Employees	6
Highway Spending Per Capita	50
Highway Spending as a Percentage of Total Spending	50

Welfare - Section L

Percentage of Births to Unwed Mothers	26
TANF Recipients as a Percentage of Population	2
Food Stamp Recipients as a Percentage of Population	33
SSI Recipients as a Percentage of Population	7
Change in TANF/AFDC Recipients	23
Condition of Children Index	22
Percentage of Families with Single Parent	34
Average Monthly TANF Payments	3
Welfare as a Percentage of Poverty-level Income	4
State Supplements of SSI	13
State Income Tax Liability of Typical Family in Poverty	18
Child Support Collections	27
Child Support Collections Per Dollar of Administrative Costs	47
Children in Foster Care	2
Welfare Spending Per Capita	16
Welfare Spending as a Percentage of Total Spending	25
Administrative Costs Per TANF Case	36

Technology - Section M

Percentage of Households with Computers	12
Percentage of Households with Internet Access	9
Zip codes with Broadband Service	7
High-tech Jobs	5
Dot-com Domain Names	1
State Government Website Ratings	3
Students per Computer	3

Colorado

Population - Section A

Population 2001	24
Population Change 2000-2001	3
Population Change 1990-2001	3
Population 2015	21
Population 2025	23
Percentage 65 and Over	47
Percentage 17 and Under	23
Median Age	41
Percentage African American	31
Percentage Hispanic	6
Percentage in Poverty	36
Child Poverty Rate	40
Percentage Female	48
Birth Rates	8
Death Rates	45
Population Density	37
New Legal Immigrants 2000	20

Economies - Section B

Personal Income 2001	21
Gross State Product	9
Per Capita Personal Income	7
Personal Income from Wages and Salaries	7
Average Annual Pay	9
Average Hourly Earnings	15
Value Added in Manufacturing	41
Cost of Living	15
Average Annual Pay in Manufacturing	8
Average Annual Pay in Retailing	10
Labor Force	11
Unemployment Rate	24
Employment Rate	27
Government Employment	32
Manufacturing Employment	41
Fortune 500 Companies	26
Forbes 500 Companies	13
Tourism Spending Per Capita	7
Exports Per Capita	36
Housing Permits	2
Percentage Change in Home Prices	5
Net Farm Income	17
Financial Institution Assets	39
Bankruptcy Filings	32
Patents Issued	10
WC Disability Payment	16
UC Average Weekly Benefit	6
Economic Momentum	42
One-year Employment Change	50
Manufacturing Employment Change	48
Home Ownership	38
Gambling	18

Electricity Use Per Residential Customer	39
Cost Per Kwh	21
New Companies	2

Geography - Section C

Total Land Area	8
Federally Owned Land	11
State Park Acreage	6
State Park Visitors	26
Population Not Active	46
Hunters with Firearms	20
Registered Boats	33
State Spending for the Arts	46
Energy Consumption Per Capita	39
Toxic Chemical Release Per Capita	39
Hazardous Waste Sites	22
Polluted Rivers and Streams	49
Expired Surface Water Pollution Permits	10
Air Pollution Emissions	29

Government - Section D

Members of United States House	22
State Legislators	42
Legislators Per Million Population	38
Units of Government	20
Legislators Compensation	17
Female Legislators	5
Turnover in Legislatures	25
Term Limits	6
Legislative Session Length	17
Republicans in State Legislatures	22
Governor's Power Rating	5
Number of Statewide Elected Officials	35
State and Local Government Employees	38
State and Local Average Salaries	15
Local Employment	20
Local Spending Accountability	3
Registered Voters	9
Percentage of Population Voting	20
Statewide Initiatives	2
Campaign Costs Per Vote	46

Federal Impacts - Section E

Per Capita Federal Spending	35
Increase in Federal Spending	45
Per Capita Federal Grant Spending	47
Per Capita Federal Spending on Procurement	11

Per Capita Federal Spending on Payments to Individuals	48
Per Capita Federal Spending on Social Security and Medicare	48
Social Security Benefits	30
Federal Spending on Employee Wages and Salaries	9
Federal Grant Spending Per Dollar of State Tax Revenue	34
General Revenue from Federal Government	44
Federal Tax Burden Per Capita	9
Federal Spending Per Dollar of Taxes Paid	43
Highway Charges Returned to States	44
Terms of Trade	46
Federal Personal Income Taxes	8
Federal Share of Medicaid	39

Taxes - Section F

Tax Revenue	42
Per Capita Tax Revenue	18
Tax Effort	44
Tax Capacity	10
Percentage Change in Taxes	1
Property Taxes as a Percentage of Income	32
Property Taxes Per Capita	23
Property Tax Revenue as a Percentage of 3-tax Revenues	30
Sales Taxes as a Percentage of Income	28
Sales Taxes Per Capita	17
Sales Tax Revenue as a Percentage of 3-tax Revenues	24
Sales Tax Rate	45
Income Taxes as a Percentage of Income	20
Income Taxes Per Capita	16
Income Tax Revenue as a Percentage of 3-tax Revenues	17
Highest Personal Income Rate	34
Corporate Income Taxes	32
Motor Fuel Taxes	17
Tobacco Taxes	38
Taxes on High Income Families	42
Taxes in the Largest City in Each State	45
Progressivity of Taxes	8

Revenues and Finances - Section G

Per Capita Total Revenue	19
Per Capita General Revenue	21
Own-source General Revenue	16
Per Capita Non-tax Revenue	9

Per Capita Total Spending	21
General Spending as a Percentage of Income	41
Per Capita General Spending	22
Change in General Expenditures	6
State Government General Revenue	43
State Government General Spending	43
State Government General Fund Spending	46
State and Local Debt	17
Debt as a Percentage of Revenue	18
Per Capita Full Faith and Credit Debt	16
Bond Ratings	n/a
State Solvency Index	14
Pension Plan Assets	37
State Reserves	29
Capital Outlays and Interest	11
State Budget Process Quality	14
Relative State Spending "Needs"	8
Structural Deficits	38

Education · Section H

Math Proficiency, Eighth Grade	n/a
Science Proficiency, Eighth Grade	n/a
AFQT Ranks	12
SAT Scores	n/a
ACT Scores	19
Over-25 Population with a High School Diploma	9
Students in Private Schools	36
High School Completion Rates	46
Pupil-Teacher Ratio	11
Public School Enrollment	20
Library Holdings Per Capita	32
Children with Disabilities	48
Education Spending Per Capita	24
Education Spending as a Percentage of Total Spending	29
Spending Per Pupil	34
Average Teacher Salary	24
Sources of School Funds	9
State Aid Per Pupil	42
Higher Education Spending Per Capita	15
Higher Education Spending as a Percentage of Total Spending	13
Public Higher Education Enrollment	9
Per Pupil Support of Higher Education	48
Tuition and Fees	29
Average Professor Salary	16
Education Employees	43
R and D Spending	9
Library Operating Spending	9

Health · Section I

Immunization Rates	31
Infant Mortality Rates	38
State Health Rankings	7
Population Without Health Insurance	15
Abortions	39
Alcohol Consumption	8
Percentage of Adult Smokers	32
Percentage Obese	50
AIDS Cases	31
Physicians Per 100,000 Population	24
Hospital Beds Per 1,000 Population	42
Medicaid Recipients	47
Medicaid Recipients as a Percentage of Poverty Population	32
Health and Hospital Spending	38
Health and Hospital Spending as a Percentage of Total Spending	36
Per Capita Medicaid Spending	46
Medicaid Spending Per Aged Recipient	23
Medicaid Spending Per Child	10
Medicare Payment Per Hospital Day	6
Hospital Expense Per Inpatient Day	9
Population in HMOs	7

Crime · Section J

Crime Rate	22
Violent Crime Rate	30
Murder Rate	30
Property Crime Rate	20
Motor Vehicle Theft Rate	14
Violent Crime Rate Change	18
Prisoners	25
Change in Prisoners	7
Incarceration Rate	21
Juvenile Violent Crime Rate	28
Law Enforcement Employees	31
Corrections Employees	26
State Corrections Spending	32
Increase in State Corrections Spending	6
Law Enforcement Spending	14
Law Enforcement Spending as a Percentage of Total Spending	10

Transportation · Section K

Travel on Interstates	29
Interstate Mileage in Unacceptable Condition	41
Deficient Bridges	46

Traffic Deaths	19
Seat Belt Use	22
Vehicle-miles Traveled Per Capita	33
Workers Using Public Transportation	14
Road and Street Miles	38
Highway Employees	34
Public Transit Employees	11
Highway Spending Per Capita	23
Highway Spending as a Percentage of Total Spending	26

Welfare · Section L

Percentage of Births to Unwed Mothers	47
TANF Recipients as a Percentage of Population	48
Food Stamp Recipients as a Percentage of Population	47
SSI Recipients as a Percentage of Population	47
Change in TANF/AFDC Recipients	7
Condition of Children Index	24
Percentage of Families with Single Parent	45
Average Monthly TANF Payments	21
Welfare as a Percentage of Poverty-level Income	40
State Supplements of SSI	12
State Income Tax Liability of Typical Family in Poverty	38
Child Support Collections	44
Child Support Collections Per Dollar of Administrative Costs	41
Children in Foster Care	27
Welfare Spending Per Capita	40
Welfare Spending as a Percentage of Total Spending	43
Administrative Costs Per TANF Case	12

Technology · Section M

Percentage of Households with Computers	6
Percentage of Households with Internet Access	4
Zip codes with Broadband Service	17
High-tech Jobs	1
Dot-com Domain Names	12
State Government Website Ratings	47
Students per Computer	27

Connecticut

Population - Section A

Population 2001	29
Population Change 2000-2001	30
Population Change 1990-2001	47
Population 2015	45
Population 2025	29
Percentage 65 and Over	10
Percentage 17 and Under	38
Median Age	7
Percentage African American	21
Percentage Hispanic	11
Percentage in Poverty	46
Child Poverty Rate	42
Percentage Female	9
Birth Rates	41
Death Rates	44
Population Density	4
New Legal Immigrants 2000	15

Economies - Section B

Personal Income 2001	22
Gross State Product	1
Per Capita Personal Income	1
Personal Income from Wages and Salaries	25
Average Annual Pay	1
Average Hourly Earnings	10
Value Added in Manufacturing	15
Cost of Living	4
Average Annual Pay in Manufacturing	1
Average Annual Pay in Retailing	2
Labor Force	29
Unemployment Rate	38
Employment Rate	13
Government Employment	38
Manufacturing Employment	20
Fortune 500 Companies	1
Forbes 500 Companies	1
Tourism Spending Per Capita	15
Exports Per Capita	10
Housing Permits	46
Percentage Change in Home Prices	11
Net Farm Income	41
Financial Institution Assets	29
Bankruptcy Filings	46
Patents Issued	4
WC Disability Payment	5
UC Average Weekly Benefit	9
Economic Momentum	47
One-year Employment Change	24
Manufacturing Employment Change	32
Home Ownership	26
Gambling	28

Electricity Use Per Residential Customer	37
Cost Per Kwh	43
New Companies	31

Geography - Section C

Total Land Area	48
Federally Owned Land	49
State Park Acreage	17
State Park Visitors	29
Population Not Active	30
Hunters with Firearms	36
Registered Boats	32
State Spending for the Arts	2
Energy Consumption Per Capita	45
Toxic Chemical Release Per Capita	45
Hazardous Waste Sites	23
Polluted Rivers and Streams	32
Expired Surface Water Pollution Permits	30
Air Pollution Emissions	41

Government - Section D

Members of United States House	27
State Legislators	9
Legislators Per Million Population	17
Units of Government	37
Legislators Compensation	18
Female Legislators	8
Turnover in Legislatures	34
Term Limits	n/a
Legislative Session Length	9
Republicans in State Legislatures	39
Governor's Power Rating	18
Number of Statewide Elected Officials	21
State and Local Government Employees	35
State and Local Average Salaries	4
Local Employment	41
Local Spending Accountability	15
Registered Voters	19
Percentage of Population Voting	22
Statewide Initiatives	n/a
Campaign Costs Per Vote	29

Federal Impacts - Section E

Per Capita Federal Spending	15
Increase in Federal Spending	35
Per Capita Federal Grant Spending	17
Per Capita Federal Spending on Procurement	5

Per Capita Federal Spending on Payments to Individuals	24
Per Capita Federal Spending on Social Security and Medicare	6
Social Security Benefits	2
Federal Spending on Employee Wages and Salaries	45
Federal Grant Spending Per Dollar of State Tax Revenue	48
General Revenue from Federal Government	42
Federal Tax Burden Per Capita	1
Federal Spending Per Dollar of Taxes Paid	49
Highway Charges Returned to States	12
Terms of Trade	47
Federal Personal Income Taxes	1
Federal Share of Medicaid	39

Taxes - Section F

Tax Revenue	9
Per Capita Tax Revenue	1
Tax Effort	5
Tax Capacity	2
Percentage Change in Taxes	29
Property Taxes as a Percentage of Income	8
Property Taxes Per Capita	3
Property Tax Revenue as a Percentage of 3-tax Revenues	13
Sales Taxes as a Percentage of Income	25
Sales Taxes Per Capita	4
Sales Tax Revenue as a Percentage of 3-tax Revenues	34
Sales Tax Rate	9
Income Taxes as a Percentage of Income	17
Income Taxes Per Capita	6
Income Tax Revenue as a Percentage of 3-tax Revenues	26
Highest Personal Income Rate	35
Corporate Income Taxes	14
Motor Fuel Taxes	8
Tobacco Taxes	9
Taxes on High Income Families	1
Taxes in the Largest City in Each State	1
Progressivity of Taxes	39

Revenues and Finances - Section G

Per Capita Total Revenue	10
Per Capita General Revenue	4
Own-source General Revenue	3
Per Capita Non-tax Revenue	44

Per Capita Total Spending	6
General Spending as a Percentage of Income	47
Per Capita General Spending	5
Change in General Expenditures	40
State Government General Revenue	5
State Government General Spending	7
State Government General Fund Spending	20
State and Local Debt	4
Debt as a Percentage of Revenue	9
Per Capita Full Faith and Credit Debt	2
Bond Ratings	3
State Solvency Index	50
Pension Plan Assets	14
State Reserves	48
Capital Outlays and Interest	16
State Budget Process Quality	15
Relative State Spending "Needs"	38
Structural Deficits	6

Education - Section H

Math Proficiency, Eighth Grade	10
Science Proficiency, Eighth Grade	15
AFQT Ranks	28
SAT Scores	9
ACT Scores	n/a
Over-25 Population with a High School Diploma	13
Students in Private Schools	15
High School Completion Rates	8
Pupil-Teacher Ratio	39
Public School Enrollment	21
Library Holdings Per Capita	9
Children with Disabilities	27
Education Spending Per Capita	12
Education Spending as a Percentage of Total Spending	44
Spending Per Pupil	3
Average Teacher Salary	2
Sources of School Funds	10
State Aid Per Pupil	19
Higher Education Spending Per Capita	46
Higher Education Spending as a Percentage of Total Spending	47
Public Higher Education Enrollment	47
Per Pupil Support of Higher Education	3
Tuition and Fees	10
Average Professor Salary	2
Education Employees	16
R and D Spending	11
Library Operating Spending	3

Health - Section I

Immunization Rates	2
Infant Mortality Rates	30
State Health Rankings	5
Population Without Health Insurance	35
Abortions	11
Alcohol Consumption	26
Percentage of Adult Smokers	43
Percentage Obese	45
AIDS Cases	9
Physicians Per 100,000 Population	4
Hospital Beds Per 1,000 Population	40
Medicaid Recipients	31
Medicaid Recipients as a Percentage of Poverty Population	3
Health and Hospital Spending	14
Health and Hospital Spending as a Percentage of Total Spending	28
Per Capita Medicaid Spending	5
Medicaid Spending Per Aged Recipient	1
Medicaid Spending Per Child	30
Medicare Payment Per Hospital Day	20
Hospital Expense Per Inpatient Day	14
Population in HMOs	3

Crime - Section J

Crime Rate	40
Violent Crime Rate	32
Murder Rate	33
Property Crime Rate	40
Motor Vehicle Theft Rate	26
Violent Crime Rate Change	28
Prisoners	24
Change in Prisoners	26
Incarceration Rate	22
Juvenile Violent Crime Rate	20
Law Enforcement Employees	16
Corrections Employees	15
State Corrections Spending	27
Increase in State Corrections Spending	11
Law Enforcement Spending	17
Law Enforcement Spending as a Percentage of Total Spending	35

Transportation - Section K

Travel on Interstates	2
Interstate Mileage in Unacceptable Condition	12
Deficient Bridges	16

Traffic Deaths	48
Seat Belt Use	13
Vehicle-miles Traveled Per Capita	40
Workers Using Public Transportation	10
Road and Street Miles	19
Highway Employees	23
Public Transit Employees	34
Highway Spending Per Capita	32
Highway Spending as a Percentage of Total Spending	44

Welfare - Section L

Percentage of Births to Unwed Mothers	40
TANF Recipients as a Percentage of Population	23
Food Stamp Recipients as a Percentage of Population	37
SSI Recipients as a Percentage of Population	38
Change in TANF/AFDC Recipients	14
Condition of Children Index	8
Percentage of Families with Single Parent	27
Average Monthly TANF Payments	9
Welfare as a Percentage of Poverty-level Income	2
State Supplements of SSI	3
State Income Tax Liability of Typical Family in Poverty	18
Child Support Collections	25
Child Support Collections Per Dollar of Administrative Costs	37
Children in Foster Care	17
Welfare Spending Per Capita	11
Welfare Spending as a Percentage of Total Spending	29
Administrative Costs Per TANF Case	18

Technology - Section M

Percentage of Households with Computers	19
Percentage of Households with Internet Access	11
Zip codes with Broadband Service	5
High-tech Jobs	16
Dot-com Domain Names	13
State Government Website Ratings	4
Students per Computer	12

Delaware

Population · Section A

Population 2001	45
Population Change 2000-2001	12
Population Change 1990-2001	13
Population 2015	38
Population 2025	47
Percentage 65 and Over	21
Percentage 17 and Under	34
Median Age	19
Percentage African American	9
Percentage Hispanic	24
Percentage in Poverty	49
Child Poverty Rate	42
Percentage Female	12
Birth Rates	29
Death Rates	16
Population Density	6
New Legal Immigrants 2000	41

Economies · Section B

Personal Income 2001	44
Gross State Product	2
Per Capita Personal Income	11
Personal Income from Wages and Salaries	1
Average Annual Pay	7
Average Hourly Earnings	5
Value Added in Manufacturing	19
Cost of Living	13
Average Annual Pay in Manufacturing	15
Average Annual Pay in Retailing	21
Labor Force	21
Unemployment Rate	39
Employment Rate	12
Government Employment	47
Manufacturing Employment	24
Fortune 500 Companies	2
Forbes 500 Companies	2
Tourism Spending Per Capita	39
Exports Per Capita	11
Housing Permits	17
Percentage Change in Home Prices	16
Net Farm Income	37
Financial Institution Assets	1
Bankruptcy Filings	23
Patents Issued	8
WC Disability Payment	41
UC Average Weekly Benefit	32
Economic Momentum	12
One-year Employment Change	26
Manufacturing Employment Change	9
Home Ownership	14
Gambling	22

Electricity Use Per Residential Customer	25
Cost Per Kwh	2
New Companies	8

Geography · Section C

Total Land Area	49
Federally Owned Land	48
State Park Acreage	48
State Park Visitors	15
Population Not Active	25
Hunters with Firearms	n/a
Registered Boats	44
State Spending for the Arts	10
Energy Consumption Per Capita	30
Toxic Chemical Release Per Capita	25
Hazardous Waste Sites	23
Polluted Rivers and Streams	7
Expired Surface Water Pollution Permits	18
Air Pollution Emissions	48

Government · Section D

Members of United States House	44
State Legislators	48
Legislators Per Million Population	11
Units of Government	22
Legislators Compensation	11
Female Legislators	17
Turnover in Legislatures	37
Term Limits	n/a
Legislative Session Length	4
Republicans in State Legislatures	13
Governor's Power Rating	24
Number of Statewide Elected Officials	21
State and Local Government Employees	18
State and Local Average Salaries	18
Local Employment	49
Local Spending Accountability	45
Registered Voters	11
Percentage of Population Voting	29
Statewide Initiatives	n/a
Campaign Costs Per Vote	16

Federal Impacts · Section E

Per Capita Federal Spending	40
Increase in Federal Spending	38
Per Capita Federal Grant Spending	31
Per Capita Federal Spending on Procurement	50

Per Capita Federal Spending on Payments to Individuals	29
Per Capita Federal Spending on Social Security and Medicare	21
Social Security Benefits	6
Federal Spending on Employee Wages and Salaries	29
Federal Grant Spending Per Dollar of State Tax Revenue	43
General Revenue from Federal Government	41
Federal Tax Burden Per Capita	14
Federal Spending Per Dollar of Taxes Paid	39
Highway Charges Returned to States	9
Terms of Trade	38
Federal Personal Income Taxes	15
Federal Share of Medicaid	39

Taxes · Section F

Tax Revenue	19
Per Capita Tax Revenue	12
Tax Effort	32
Tax Capacity	5
Percentage Change in Taxes	13
Property Taxes as a Percentage of Income	48
Property Taxes Per Capita	43
Property Tax Revenue as a Percentage of 3-tax Revenues	37
Sales Taxes as a Percentage of Income	49
Sales Taxes Per Capita	49
Sales Tax Revenue as a Percentage of 3-tax Revenues	48
Sales Tax Rate	n/a
Income Taxes as a Percentage of Income	13
Income Taxes Per Capita	10
Income Tax Revenue as a Percentage of 3-tax Revenues	1
Highest Personal Income Rate	25
Corporate Income Taxes	3
Motor Fuel Taxes	14
Tobacco Taxes	35
Taxes on High Income Families	38
Taxes in the Largest City in Each State	40
Progressivity of Taxes	23

Revenues and Finances · Section G

Per Capita Total Revenue	7
Per Capita General Revenue	5
Own-source General Revenue	4
Per Capita Non-tax Revenue	3

Per Capita Total Spending	11
General Spending as a Percentage of Income	23
Per Capita General Spending	7
Change in General Expenditures	20
State Government General Revenue	2
State Government General Spending	3
State Government General Fund Spending	2
State and Local Debt	11
Debt as a Percentage of Revenue	20
Per Capita Full Faith and Credit Debt	18
Bond Ratings	1
State Solvency Index	5
Pension Plan Assets	11
State Reserves	2
Capital Outlays and Interest	13
State Budget Process Quality	21
Relative State Spending "Needs"	4
Structural Deficits	25

Education · Section H

Math Proficiency, Eighth Grade	n/a
Science Proficiency, Eighth Grade	n/a
AFQT Ranks	36
SAT Scores	16
ACT Scores	n/a
Over-25 Population with a High School Diploma	25
Students in Private Schools	1
High School Completion Rates	11
Pupil-Teacher Ratio	23
Public School Enrollment	50
Library Holdings Per Capita	36
Children with Disabilities	16
Education Spending Per Capita	5
Education Spending as a Percentage of Total Spending	19
Spending Per Pupil	5
Average Teacher Salary	11
Sources of School Funds	44
State Aid Per Pupil	3
Higher Education Spending Per Capita	4
Higher Education Spending as a Percentage of Total Spending	10
Public Higher Education Enrollment	21
Per Pupil Support of Higher Education	23
Tuition and Fees	5
Average Professor Salary	10
Education Employees	42
R and D Spending	39
Library Operating Spending	37

Health · Section I

Immunization Rates	21
Infant Mortality Rates	3
State Health Rankings	35
Population Without Health Insurance	45
Abortions	2
Alcohol Consumption	3
Percentage of Adult Smokers	14
Percentage Obese	27
AIDS Cases	4
Physicians Per 100,000 Population	16
Hospital Beds Per 1,000 Population	37
Medicaid Recipients	23
Medicaid Recipients as a Percentage of Poverty Population	13
Health and Hospital Spending	31
Health and Hospital Spending as a Percentage of Total Spending	38
Per Capita Medicaid Spending	12
Medicaid Spending Per Aged Recipient	9
Medicaid Spending Per Child	5
Medicare Payment Per Hospital Day	47
Hospital Expense Per Inpatient Day	10
Population in HMOs	23

Crime · Section J

Crime Rate	28
Violent Crime Rate	9
Murder Rate	36
Property Crime Rate	29
Motor Vehicle Theft Rate	28
Violent Crime Rate Change	9
Prisoners	34
Change in Prisoners	19
Incarceration Rate	9
Juvenile Violent Crime Rate	1
Law Enforcement Employees	21
Corrections Employees	6
State Corrections Spending	28
Increase in State Corrections Spending	4
Law Enforcement Spending	4
Law Enforcement Spending as a Percentage of Total Spending	4

Transportation · Section K

Travel on Interstates	50
Interstate Mileage in Unacceptable Condition	2
Deficient Bridges	47

Traffic Deaths	24
Seat Belt Use	35
Vehicle-miles Traveled Per Capita	20
Workers Using Public Transportation	16
Road and Street Miles	2
Highway Employees	14
Public Transit Employees	9
Highway Spending Per Capita	10
Highway Spending as a Percentage of Total Spending	17

Welfare · Section L

Percentage of Births to Unwed Mothers	4
TANF Recipients as a Percentage of Population	25
Food Stamp Recipients as a Percentage of Population	41
SSI Recipients as a Percentage of Population	36
Change in TANF/AFDC Recipients	34
Condition of Children Index	33
Percentage of Families with Single Parent	3
Average Monthly TANF Payments	35
Welfare as a Percentage of Poverty-level Income	14
State Supplements of SSI	15
State Income Tax Liability of Typical Family in Poverty	18
Child Support Collections	17
Child Support Collections Per Dollar of Administrative Costs	44
Children in Foster Care	33
Welfare Spending Per Capita	34
Welfare Spending as a Percentage of Total Spending	45
Administrative Costs Per TANF Case	19

Technology · Section M

Percentage of Households with Computers	21
Percentage of Households with Internet Access	20
Zip codes with Broadband Service	1
High-tech Jobs	41
Dot-com Domain Names	19
State Government Website Ratings	41
Students per Computer	19

Florida

Population · Section A

Population 2001	4
Population Change 2000-2001	4
Population Change 1990-2001	7
Population 2015	12
Population 2025	3
Percentage 65 and Over	1
Percentage 17 and Under	49
Median Age	2
Percentage African American	14
Percentage Hispanic	7
Percentage in Poverty	16
Child Poverty Rate	15
Percentage Female	18
Birth Rates	37
Death Rates	34
Population Density	8
New Legal Immigrants 2000	3

Economies · Section B

Personal Income 2001	4
Gross State Product	39
Per Capita Personal Income	22
Personal Income from Wages and Salaries	44
Average Annual Pay	28
Average Hourly Earnings	41
Value Added in Manufacturing	46
Cost of Living	21
Average Annual Pay in Manufacturing	30
Average Annual Pay in Retailing	15
Labor Force	44
Unemployment Rate	25
Employment Rate	26
Government Employment	41
Manufacturing Employment	44
Fortune 500 Companies	35
Forbes 500 Companies	41
Tourism Spending Per Capita	3
Exports Per Capita	28
Housing Permits	5
Percentage Change in Home Prices	10
Net Farm Income	5
Financial Institution Assets	49
Bankruptcy Filings	21
Patents Issued	28
WC Disability Payment	22
UC Average Weekly Benefit	31
Economic Momentum	5
One-year Employment Change	10
Manufacturing Employment Change	36
Home Ownership	36
Gambling	10

Electricity Use Per Residential Customer	7
Cost Per Kwh	34
New Companies	9

Geography · Section C

Total Land Area	26
Federally Owned Land	14
State Park Acreage	5
State Park Visitors	46
Population Not Active	11
Hunters with Firearms	41
Registered Boats	3
State Spending for the Arts	11
Energy Consumption Per Capita	44
Toxic Chemical Release Per Capita	36
Hazardous Waste Sites	6
Polluted Rivers and Streams	34
Expired Surface Water Pollution Permits	28
Air Pollution Emissions	3

Government · Section D

Members of United States House	4
State Legislators	18
Legislators Per Million Population	48
Units of Government	48
Legislators Compensation	19
Female Legislators	21
Turnover in Legislatures	20
Term Limits	6
Legislative Session Length	36
Republicans in State Legislatures	7
Governor's Power Rating	18
Number of Statewide Elected Officials	2
State and Local Government Employees	47
State and Local Average Salaries	23
Local Employment	6
Local Spending Accountability	7
Registered Voters	25
Percentage of Population Voting	18
Statewide Initiatives	2
Campaign Costs Per Vote	45

Federal Impacts · Section E

Per Capita Federal Spending	28
Increase in Federal Spending	34
Per Capita Federal Grant Spending	48
Per Capita Federal Spending on Procurement	27

Per Capita Federal Spending on Payments to Individuals	9
Per Capita Federal Spending on Social Security and Medicare	3
Social Security Benefits	21
Federal Spending on Employee Wages and Salaries	33
Federal Grant Spending Per Dollar of State Tax Revenue	41
General Revenue from Federal Government	46
Federal Tax Burden Per Capita	17
Federal Spending Per Dollar of Taxes Paid	31
Highway Charges Returned to States	46
Terms of Trade	44
Federal Personal Income Taxes	16
Federal Share of Medicaid	29

Taxes · Section F

Tax Revenue	44
Per Capita Tax Revenue	35
Tax Effort	32
Tax Capacity	19
Percentage Change in Taxes	24
Property Taxes as a Percentage of Income	21
Property Taxes Per Capita	22
Property Tax Revenue as a Percentage of 3-tax Revenues	12
Sales Taxes as a Percentage of Income	7
Sales Taxes Per Capita	6
Sales Tax Revenue as a Percentage of 3-tax Revenues	6
Sales Tax Rate	9
Income Taxes as a Percentage of Income	n/a
Income Taxes Per Capita	n/a
Income Tax Revenue as a Percentage of 3-tax Revenues	n/a
Highest Personal Income Rate	n/a
Corporate Income Taxes	35
Motor Fuel Taxes	48
Tobacco Taxes	31
Taxes on High Income Families	47
Taxes in the Largest City in Each State	48
Progressivity of Taxes	34

Revenues and Finances · Section G

Per Capita Total Revenue	43
Per Capita General Revenue	40
Own-source General Revenue	32
Per Capita Non-tax Revenue	20

Per Capita Total Spending	42
General Spending as a Percentage of Income	37
Per Capita General Spending	39
Change in General Expenditures	31
State Government General Revenue	50
State Government General Spending	48
State Government General Fund Spending	36
State and Local Debt	19
Debt as a Percentage of Revenue	11
Per Capita Full Faith and Credit Debt	40
Bond Ratings	3
State Solvency Index	12
Pension Plan Assets	20
State Reserves	n/a
Capital Outlays and Interest	15
State Budget Process Quality	13
Relative State Spending "Needs"	24
Structural Deficits	42

Education - Section H

Math Proficiency, Eighth Grade	n/a
Science Proficiency, Eighth Grade	n/a
AFQT Ranks	30
SAT Scores	21
ACT Scores	n/a
Over-25 Population with a High School Diploma	34
Students in Private Schools	16
High School Completion Rates	38
Pupil-Teacher Ratio	7
Public School Enrollment	45
Library Holdings Per Capita	48
Children with Disabilities	11
Education Spending Per Capita	50
Education Spending as a Percentage of Total Spending	46
Spending Per Pupil	40
Average Teacher Salary	26
Sources of School Funds	24
State Aid Per Pupil	39
Higher Education Spending Per Capita	50
Higher Education Spending as a Percentage of Total Spending	44
Public Higher Education Enrollment	41
Per Pupil Support of Higher Education	35
Tuition and Fees	45
Average Professor Salary	27
Education Employees	46
R and D Spending	25
Library Operating Spending	28

Health - Section I

Immunization Rates	27
Infant Mortality Rates	24
State Health Rankings	43
Population Without Health Insurance	6
Abortions	3
Alcohol Consumption	7
Percentage of Adult Smokers	29
Percentage Obese	42
AIDS Cases	3
Physicians Per 100,000 Population	22
Hospital Beds Per 1,000 Population	20
Medicaid Recipients	22
Medicaid Recipients as a Percentage of Poverty Population	24
Health and Hospital Spending	15
Health and Hospital Spending as a Percentage of Total Spending	10
Per Capita Medicaid Spending	38
Medicaid Spending Per Aged Recipient	37
Medicaid Spending Per Child	39
Medicare Payment Per Hospital Day	5
Hospital Expense Per Inpatient Day	45
Population in HMOs	16

Crime - Section J

Crime Rate	2
Violent Crime Rate	1
Murder Rate	20
Property Crime Rate	4
Motor Vehicle Theft Rate	7
Violent Crime Rate Change	34
Prisoners	3
Change in Prisoners	41
Incarceration Rate	16
Juvenile Violent Crime Rate	3
Law Enforcement Employees	6
Corrections Employees	12
State Corrections Spending	37
Increase in State Corrections Spending	44
Law Enforcement Spending	7
Law Enforcement Spending as a Percentage of Total Spending	2

Transportation - Section K

Travel on Interstates	43
Interstate Mileage in Unacceptable Condition	44
Deficient Bridges	43

Traffic Deaths	10
Seat Belt Use	27
Vehicle-miles Traveled Per Capita	36
Workers Using Public Transportation	23
Road and Street Miles	40
Highway Employees	46
Public Transit Employees	21
Highway Spending Per Capita	41
Highway Spending as a Percentage of Total Spending	32

Welfare - Section L

Percentage of Births to Unwed Mothers	7
TANF Recipients as a Percentage of Population	47
Food Stamp Recipients as a Percentage of Population	31
SSI Recipients as a Percentage of Population	16
Change in TANF/AFDC Recipients	3
Condition of Children Index	36
Percentage of Families with Single Parent	7
Average Monthly TANF Payments	28
Welfare as a Percentage of Poverty-level Income	29
State Supplements of SSI	29
State Income Tax Liability of Typical Family in Poverty	n/a
Child Support Collections	45
Child Support Collections Per Dollar of Administrative Costs	40
Children in Foster Care	7
Welfare Spending Per Capita	44
Welfare Spending as a Percentage of Total Spending	40
Administrative Costs Per TANF Case	11

Technology - Section M

Percentage of Households with Computers	29
Percentage of Households with Internet Access	18
Zip codes with Broadband Service	3
High-tech Jobs	27
Dot-com Domain Names	9
State Government Website Ratings	12
Students per Computer	38

Georgia

Population · Section A

Population 2001	10
Population Change 2000-2001	5
Population Change 1990-2001	6
Population 2015	18
Population 2025	9
Percentage 65 and Over	48
Percentage 17 and Under	12
Median Age	45
Percentage African American	4
Percentage Hispanic	22
Percentage in Poverty	15
Child Poverty Rate	13
Percentage Female	31
Birth Rates	4
Death Rates	7
Population Density	18
New Legal Immigrants 2000	13

Economies · Section B

Personal Income 2001	11
Gross State Product	16
Per Capita Personal Income	25
Personal Income from Wages and Salaries	6
Average Annual Pay	17
Average Hourly Earnings	43
Value Added in Manufacturing	23
Cost of Living	42
Average Annual Pay in Manufacturing	34
Average Annual Pay in Retailing	16
Labor Force	27
Unemployment Rate	33
Employment Rate	18
Government Employment	34
Manufacturing Employment	21
Fortune 500 Companies	23
Forbes 500 Companies	27
Tourism Spending Per Capita	20
Exports Per Capita	26
Housing Permits	4
Percentage Change in Home Prices	15
Net Farm Income	4
Financial Institution Assets	18
Bankruptcy Filings	5
Patents Issued	29
WC Disability Payment	46
UC Average Weekly Benefit	28
Economic Momentum	24
One-year Employment Change	49
Manufacturing Employment Change	11
Home Ownership	22
Gambling	16

Electricity Use Per Residential Customer	12
Cost Per Kwh	14
New Companies	28

Geography · Section C

Total Land Area	21
Federally Owned Land	23
State Park Acreage	32
State Park Visitors	34
Population Not Active	13
Hunters with Firearms	37
Registered Boats	14
State Spending for the Arts	38
Energy Consumption Per Capita	27
Toxic Chemical Release Per Capita	26
Hazardous Waste Sites	25
Polluted Rivers and Streams	14
Expired Surface Water Pollution Permits	48
Air Pollution Emissions	5

Government · Section D

Members of United States House	9
State Legislators	3
Legislators Per Million Population	32
Units of Government	36
Legislators Compensation	26
Female Legislators	30
Turnover in Legislatures	19
Term Limits	n/a
Legislative Session Length	35
Republicans in State Legislatures	35
Governor's Power Rating	43
Number of Statewide Elected Officials	4
State and Local Government Employees	27
State and Local Average Salaries	33
Local Employment	10
Local Spending Accountability	6
Registered Voters	42
Percentage of Population Voting	45
Statewide Initiatives	n/a
Campaign Costs Per Vote	2

Federal Impacts · Section E

Per Capita Federal Spending	34
Increase in Federal Spending	12
Per Capita Federal Grant Spending	46
Per Capita Federal Spending on Procurement	16

Per Capita Federal Spending on Payments to Individuals	44
Per Capita Federal Spending on Social Security and Medicare	44
Social Security Benefits	39
Federal Spending on Employee Wages and Salaries	10
Federal Grant Spending Per Dollar of State Tax Revenue	30
General Revenue from Federal Government	35
Federal Tax Burden Per Capita	23
Federal Spending Per Dollar of Taxes Paid	33
Highway Charges Returned to States	49
Terms of Trade	39
Federal Personal Income Taxes	22
Federal Share of Medicaid	27

Taxes · Section F

Tax Revenue	28
Per Capita Tax Revenue	25
Tax Effort	26
Tax Capacity	29
Percentage Change in Taxes	5
Property Taxes as a Percentage of Income	34
Property Taxes Per Capita	33
Property Tax Revenue as a Percentage of 3-tax Revenues	36
Sales Taxes as a Percentage of Income	18
Sales Taxes Per Capita	16
Sales Tax Revenue as a Percentage of 3-tax Revenues	20
Sales Tax Rate	37
Income Taxes as a Percentage of Income	18
Income Taxes Per Capita	20
Income Tax Revenue as a Percentage of 3-tax Revenues	18
Highest Personal Income Rate	22
Corporate Income Taxes	27
Motor Fuel Taxes	50
Tobacco Taxes	45
Taxes on High Income Families	11
Taxes in the Largest City in Each State	14
Progressivity of Taxes	14

Revenues and Finances · Section G

Per Capita Total Revenue	33
Per Capita General Revenue	36
Own-source General Revenue	34
Per Capita Non-tax Revenue	42

Per Capita Total Spending	40
General Spending as a Percentage of Income	38
Per Capita General Spending	41
Change in General Expenditures	29
State Government General Revenue	46
State Government General Spending	45
State Government General Fund Spending	43
State and Local Debt	41
Debt as a Percentage of Revenue	37
Per Capita Full Faith and Credit Debt	34
Bond Ratings	1
State Solvency Index	17
Pension Plan Assets	42
State Reserves	8
Capital Outlays and Interest	20
State Budget Process Quality	1
Relative State Spending "Needs"	41
Structural Deficits	35

Education - Section H

Math Proficiency, Eighth Grade	30
Science Proficiency, Eighth Grade	28
AFQT Ranks	46
SAT Scores	24
ACT Scores	n/a
Over-25 Population with a High School Diploma	37
Students in Private Schools	33
High School Completion Rates	40
Pupil-Teacher Ratio	18
Public School Enrollment	8
Library Holdings Per Capita	45
Children with Disabilities	46
Education Spending Per Capita	29
Education Spending as a Percentage of Total Spending	7
Spending Per Pupil	19
Average Teacher Salary	16
Sources of School Funds	19
State Aid Per Pupil	23
Higher Education Spending Per Capita	39
Higher Education Spending as a Percentage of Total Spending	35
Public Higher Education Enrollment	42
Per Pupil Support of Higher Education	10
Tuition and Fees	38
Average Professor Salary	24
Education Employees	10
R and D Spending	8
Library Operating Spending	38

Health - Section I

Immunization Rates	18
Infant Mortality Rates	8
State Health Rankings	40
Population Without Health Insurance	10
Abortions	15
Alcohol Consumption	25
Percentage of Adult Smokers	23
Percentage Obese	12
AIDS Cases	5
Physicians Per 100,000 Population	35
Hospital Beds Per 1,000 Population	25
Medicaid Recipients	17
Medicaid Recipients as a Percentage of Poverty Population	25
Health and Hospital Spending	18
Health and Hospital Spending as a Percentage of Total Spending	13
Per Capita Medicaid Spending	42
Medicaid Spending Per Aged Recipient	44
Medicaid Spending Per Child	47
Medicare Payment Per Hospital Day	24
Hospital Expense Per Inpatient Day	25
Population in HMOs	30

Crime - Section J

Crime Rate	14
Violent Crime Rate	18
Murder Rate	9
Property Crime Rate	12
Motor Vehicle Theft Rate	15
Violent Crime Rate Change	32
Prisoners	6
Change in Prisoners	18
Incarceration Rate	6
Juvenile Violent Crime Rate	22
Law Enforcement Employees	22
Corrections Employees	3
State Corrections Spending	31
Increase in State Corrections Spending	20
Law Enforcement Spending	27
Law Enforcement Spending as a Percentage of Total Spending	18

Transportation - Section K

Travel on Interstates	17
Interstate Mileage in Unacceptable Condition	44
Deficient Bridges	33

Traffic Deaths	26
Seat Belt Use	12
Vehicle-miles Traveled Per Capita	3
Workers Using Public Transportation	18
Road and Street Miles	24
Highway Employees	43
Public Transit Employees	12
Highway Spending Per Capita	45
Highway Spending as a Percentage of Total Spending	37

Welfare - Section L

Percentage of Births to Unwed Mothers	8
TANF Recipients as a Percentage of Population	26
Food Stamp Recipients as a Percentage of Population	17
SSI Recipients as a Percentage of Population	15
Change in TANF/AFDC Recipients	13
Condition of Children Index	44
Percentage of Families with Single Parent	4
Average Monthly TANF Payments	41
Welfare as a Percentage of Poverty-level Income	39
State Supplements of SSI	30
State Income Tax Liability of Typical Family in Poverty	13
Child Support Collections	40
Child Support Collections Per Dollar of Administrative Costs	34
Children in Foster Care	35
Welfare Spending Per Capita	37
Welfare Spending as a Percentage of Total Spending	27
Administrative Costs Per TANF Case	50

Technology - Section M

Percentage of Households with Computers	39
Percentage of Households with Internet Access	37
Zip codes with Broadband Service	20
High-tech Jobs	17
Dot-com Domain Names	15
State Government Website Ratings	38
Students per Computer	19

Hawaii

Population - Section A

Population 2001	42
Population Change 2000-2001	20
Population Change 1990-2001	26
Population 2015	2
Population 2025	39
Percentage 65 and Over	15
Percentage 17 and Under	42
Median Age	14
Percentage African American	38
Percentage Hispanic	17
Percentage in Poverty	22
Child Poverty Rate	21
Percentage Female	46
Birth Rates	17
Death Rates	50
Population Density	13
New Legal Immigrants 2000	22

Economies - Section B

Personal Income 2001	40
Gross State Product	20
Per Capita Personal Income	21
Personal Income from Wages and Salaries	23
Average Annual Pay	30
Average Hourly Earnings	34
Value Added in Manufacturing	50
Cost of Living	2
Average Annual Pay in Manufacturing	47
Average Annual Pay in Retailing	19
Labor Force	39
Unemployment Rate	36
Employment Rate	15
Government Employment	6
Manufacturing Employment	50
Fortune 500 Companies	n/a
Forbes 500 Companies	35
Tourism Spending Per Capita	1
Exports Per Capita	50
Housing Permits	37
Percentage Change in Home Prices	48
Net Farm Income	44
Financial Institution Assets	14
Bankruptcy Filings	37
Patents Issued	49
WC Disability Payment	25
UC Average Weekly Benefit	5
Economic Momentum	18
One-year Employment Change	37
Manufacturing Employment Change	4
Home Ownership	49
Gambling	n/a

Electricity Use Per Residential Customer	42
Cost Per Kwh	44
New Companies	21

Geography - Section C

Total Land Area	47
Federally Owned Land	37
State Park Acreage	46
State Park Visitors	1
Population Not Active	47
Hunters with Firearms	n/a
Registered Boats	50
State Spending for the Arts	1
Energy Consumption Per Capita	46
Toxic Chemical Release Per Capita	49
Hazardous Waste Sites	46
Polluted Rivers and Streams	9
Expired Surface Water Pollution Permits	24
Air Pollution Emissions	47

Government - Section D

Members of United States House	39
State Legislators	46
Legislators Per Million Population	13
Units of Government	50
Legislators Compensation	13
Female Legislators	19
Turnover in Legislatures	23
Term Limits	n/a
Legislative Session Length	21
Republicans in State Legislatures	47
Governor's Power Rating	18
Number of Statewide Elected Officials	45
State and Local Government Employees	21
State and Local Average Salaries	20
Local Employment	50
Local Spending Accountability	1
Registered Voters	24
Percentage of Population Voting	13
Statewide Initiatives	n/a
Campaign Costs Per Vote	3

Federal Impacts - Section E

Per Capita Federal Spending	6
Increase in Federal Spending	44
Per Capita Federal Grant Spending	20
Per Capita Federal Spending on Procurement	6

Per Capita Federal Spending on Payments to Individuals	30
Per Capita Federal Spending on Social Security and Medicare	39
Social Security Benefits	24
Federal Spending on Employee Wages and Salaries	2
Federal Grant Spending Per Dollar of State Tax Revenue	46
General Revenue from Federal Government	34
Federal Tax Burden Per Capita	36
Federal Spending Per Dollar of Taxes Paid	7
Highway Charges Returned to States	2
Terms of Trade	19
Federal Personal Income Taxes	34
Federal Share of Medicaid	31

Taxes - Section F

Tax Revenue	6
Per Capita Tax Revenue	10
Tax Effort	9
Tax Capacity	6
Percentage Change in Taxes	49
Property Taxes as a Percentage of Income	44
Property Taxes Per Capita	42
Property Tax Revenue as a Percentage of 3-tax Revenues	49
Sales Taxes as a Percentage of Income	2
Sales Taxes Per Capita	3
Sales Tax Revenue as a Percentage of 3-tax Revenues	11
Sales Tax Rate	37
Income Taxes as a Percentage of Income	16
Income Taxes Per Capita	13
Income Tax Revenue as a Percentage of 3-tax Revenues	24
Highest Personal Income Rate	6
Corporate Income Taxes	39
Motor Fuel Taxes	43
Tobacco Taxes	8
Taxes on High Income Families	25
Taxes in the Largest City in Each State	27
Progressivity of Taxes	22

Revenues and Finances - Section G

Per Capita Total Revenue	17
Per Capita General Revenue	12
Own-source General Revenue	10
Per Capita Non-tax Revenue	19

Per Capita Total Spending — 10
General Spending as a Percentage of Income — 12
Per Capita General Spending — 6
Change in General Expenditures — 50
State Government General Revenue — 6
State Government General Spending — 4
State Government General Fund Spending — 3
State and Local Debt — 8
Debt as a Percentage of Revenue — 5
Per Capita Full Faith and Credit Debt — 1
Bond Ratings — 4
State Solvency Index — 48
Pension Plan Assets — 49
State Reserves — 16
Capital Outlays and Interest — 7
State Budget Process Quality — 12
Relative State Spending "Needs" — 8
Structural Deficits — 48

Education - Section H

Math Proficiency, Eighth Grade — 32
Science Proficiency, Eighth Grade — 37
AFQT Ranks — 48
SAT Scores — 13
ACT Scores — n/a
Over-25 Population with a High School Diploma — 17
Students in Private Schools — 4
High School Completion Rates — 7
Pupil-Teacher Ratio — 14
Public School Enrollment — 46
Library Holdings Per Capita — 27
Children with Disabilities — 39
Education Spending Per Capita — 47
Education Spending as a Percentage of Total Spending — 49
Spending Per Pupil — 33
Average Teacher Salary — 20
Sources of School Funds — 50
State Aid Per Pupil — 1
Higher Education Spending Per Capita — 16
Higher Education Spending as a Percentage of Total Spending — 29
Public Higher Education Enrollment — 36
Per Pupil Support of Higher Education — 1
Tuition and Fees — 30
Average Professor Salary — 31
Education Employees — 38
R and D Spending — 18
Library Operating Spending — 33

Health - Section I

Immunization Rates — 48
Infant Mortality Rates — 13
State Health Rankings — 14
Population Without Health Insurance — 41
Abortions — 21
Alcohol Consumption — 23
Percentage of Adult Smokers — 44
Percentage Obese — 45
AIDS Cases — 21
Physicians Per 100,000 Population — 9
Hospital Beds Per 1,000 Population — 35
Medicaid Recipients — 13
Medicaid Recipients as a Percentage of Poverty Population — 9
Health and Hospital Spending — 12
Health and Hospital Spending as a Percentage of Total Spending — 22
Per Capita Medicaid Spending — 41
Medicaid Spending Per Aged Recipient — 41
Medicaid Spending Per Child — 33
Medicare Payment Per Hospital Day — 16
Hospital Expense Per Inpatient Day — 34
Population in HMOs — 8

Crime - Section J

Crime Rate — 3
Violent Crime Rate — 42
Murder Rate — 37
Property Crime Rate — 2
Motor Vehicle Theft Rate — 6
Violent Crime Rate Change — 12
Prisoners — 38
Change in Prisoners — 14
Incarceration Rate — 37
Juvenile Violent Crime Rate — 25
Law Enforcement Employees — 24
Corrections Employees — 32
State Corrections Spending — 33
Increase in State Corrections Spending — 48
Law Enforcement Spending — 29
Law Enforcement Spending as a Percentage of Total Spending — 40

Transportation - Section K

Travel on Interstates — 39
Interstate Mileage in Unacceptable Condition — 1
Deficient Bridges — 2

Traffic Deaths — 23
Seat Belt Use — 7
Vehicle-miles Traveled Per Capita — 49
Workers Using Public Transportation — 6
Road and Street Miles — 15
Highway Employees — 48
Public Transit Employees — 47
Highway Spending Per Capita — 46
Highway Spending as a Percentage of Total Spending — 49

Welfare - Section L

Percentage of Births to Unwed Mothers — 25
TANF Recipients as a Percentage of Population — 6
Food Stamp Recipients as a Percentage of Population — 9
SSI Recipients as a Percentage of Population — 28
Change in TANF/AFDC Recipients — 33
Condition of Children Index — 15
Percentage of Families with Single Parent — 27
Average Monthly TANF Payments — 4
Welfare as a Percentage of Poverty-level Income — 3
State Supplements of SSI — 33
State Income Tax Liability of Typical Family in Poverty — 3
Child Support Collections — 29
Child Support Collections Per Dollar of Administrative Costs — 5
Children in Foster Care — 18
Welfare Spending Per Capita — 18
Welfare Spending as a Percentage of Total Spending — 32
Administrative Costs Per TANF Case — 37

Technology - Section M

Percentage of Households with Computers — 9
Percentage of Households with Internet Access — 10
Zip codes with Broadband Service — 27
High-tech Jobs — 46
Dot-com Domain Names — 6
State Government Website Ratings — 45
Students per Computer — 5

Idaho

Population - Section A

Population 2001	39
Population Change 2000-2001	7
Population Change 1990-2001	5
Population 2015	5
Population 2025	40
Percentage 65 and Over	41
Percentage 17 and Under	3
Median Age	47
Percentage African American	49
Percentage Hispanic	15
Percentage in Poverty	21
Child Poverty Rate	21
Percentage Female	45
Birth Rates	6
Death Rates	39
Population Density	44
New Legal Immigrants 2000	38

Economies - Section B

Personal Income 2001	42
Gross State Product	41
Per Capita Personal Income	42
Personal Income from Wages and Salaries	43
Average Annual Pay	45
Average Hourly Earnings	16
Value Added in Manufacturing	4
Cost of Living	27
Average Annual Pay in Manufacturing	31
Average Annual Pay in Retailing	32
Labor Force	18
Unemployment Rate	17
Employment Rate	34
Government Employment	8
Manufacturing Employment	25
Fortune 500 Companies	4
Forbes 500 Companies	17
Tourism Spending Per Capita	26
Exports Per Capita	30
Housing Permits	7
Percentage Change in Home Prices	47
Net Farm Income	13
Financial Institution Assets	50
Bankruptcy Filings	14
Patents Issued	1
WC Disability Payment	38
UC Average Weekly Benefit	30
Economic Momentum	16
One-year Employment Change	32
Manufacturing Employment Change	47
Home Ownership	17
Gambling	44

Electricity Use Per Residential Customer	13
Cost Per Kwh	23
New Companies	7

Geography - Section C

Total Land Area	11
Federally Owned Land	5
State Park Acreage	43
State Park Visitors	33
Population Not Active	41
Hunters with Firearms	4
Registered Boats	36
State Spending for the Arts	30
Energy Consumption Per Capita	34
Toxic Chemical Release Per Capita	7
Hazardous Waste Sites	40
Polluted Rivers and Streams	23
Expired Surface Water Pollution Permits	37
Air Pollution Emissions	36

Government - Section D

Members of United States House	39
State Legislators	39
Legislators Per Million Population	10
Units of Government	8
Legislators Compensation	28
Female Legislators	15
Turnover in Legislatures	10
Term Limits	n/a
Legislative Session Length	33
Republicans in State Legislatures	1
Governor's Power Rating	24
Number of Statewide Elected Officials	16
State and Local Government Employees	17
State and Local Average Salaries	42
Local Employment	28
Local Spending Accountability	33
Registered Voters	37
Percentage of Population Voting	21
Statewide Initiatives	9
Campaign Costs Per Vote	36

Federal Impacts - Section E

Per Capita Federal Spending	33
Increase in Federal Spending	9
Per Capita Federal Grant Spending	29
Per Capita Federal Spending on Procurement	15

Per Capita Federal Spending on Payments to Individuals	42
Per Capita Federal Spending on Social Security and Medicare	45
Social Security Benefits	31
Federal Spending on Employee Wages and Salaries	25
Federal Grant Spending Per Dollar of State Tax Revenue	35
General Revenue from Federal Government	28
Federal Tax Burden Per Capita	43
Federal Spending Per Dollar of Taxes Paid	19
Highway Charges Returned to States	10
Terms of Trade	18
Federal Personal Income Taxes	38
Federal Share of Medicaid	8

Taxes - Section F

Tax Revenue	15
Per Capita Tax Revenue	38
Tax Effort	29
Tax Capacity	40
Percentage Change in Taxes	9
Property Taxes as a Percentage of Income	28
Property Taxes Per Capita	35
Property Tax Revenue as a Percentage of 3-tax Revenues	31
Sales Taxes as a Percentage of Income	30
Sales Taxes Per Capita	43
Sales Tax Revenue as a Percentage of 3-tax Revenues	31
Sales Tax Rate	19
Income Taxes as a Percentage of Income	12
Income Taxes Per Capita	22
Income Tax Revenue as a Percentage of 3-tax Revenues	13
Highest Personal Income Rate	10
Corporate Income Taxes	24
Motor Fuel Taxes	5
Tobacco Taxes	34
Taxes on High Income Families	21
Taxes in the Largest City in Each State	36
Progressivity of Taxes	1

Revenues and Finances - Section G

Per Capita Total Revenue	38
Per Capita General Revenue	42
Own-source General Revenue	38
Per Capita Non-tax Revenue	30

Per Capita Total Spending	48
General Spending as a Percentage of Income	21
Per Capita General Spending	46
Change in General Expenditures	19
State Government General Revenue	33
State Government General Spending	38
State Government General Fund Spending	26
State and Local Debt	49
Debt as a Percentage of Revenue	48
Per Capita Full Faith and Credit Debt	45
Bond Ratings	n/a
State Solvency Index	20
Pension Plan Assets	19
State Reserves	27
Capital Outlays and Interest	46
State Budget Process Quality	47
Relative State Spending "Needs"	30
Structural Deficits	47

Education - Section H

Math Proficiency, Eighth Grade	14
Science Proficiency, Eighth Grade	8
AFQT Ranks	13
SAT Scores	n/a
ACT Scores	14
Over-25 Population with a High School Diploma	23
Students in Private Schools	48
High School Completion Rates	31
Pupil-Teacher Ratio	9
Public School Enrollment	4
Library Holdings Per Capita	21
Children with Disabilities	43
Education Spending Per Capita	41
Education Spending as a Percentage of Total Spending	18
Spending Per Pupil	42
Average Teacher Salary	37
Sources of School Funds	34
State Aid Per Pupil	25
Higher Education Spending Per Capita	28
Higher Education Spending as a Percentage of Total Spending	15
Public Higher Education Enrollment	29
Per Pupil Support of Higher Education	11
Tuition and Fees	40
Average Professor Salary	42
Education Employees	28
R and D Spending	19
Library Operating Spending	35

Health - Section I

Immunization Rates	41
Infant Mortality Rates	19
State Health Rankings	20
Population Without Health Insurance	12
Abortions	45
Alcohol Consumption	18
Percentage of Adult Smokers	47
Percentage Obese	29
AIDS Cases	48
Physicians Per 100,000 Population	50
Hospital Beds Per 1,000 Population	31
Medicaid Recipients	40
Medicaid Recipients as a Percentage of Poverty Population	48
Health and Hospital Spending	22
Health and Hospital Spending as a Percentage of Total Spending	17
Per Capita Medicaid Spending	39
Medicaid Spending Per Aged Recipient	15
Medicaid Spending Per Child	18
Medicare Payment Per Hospital Day	26
Hospital Expense Per Inpatient Day	18
Population in HMOs	46

Crime - Section J

Crime Rate	39
Violent Crime Rate	43
Murder Rate	41
Property Crime Rate	37
Motor Vehicle Theft Rate	43
Violent Crime Rate Change	11
Prisoners	36
Change in Prisoners	2
Incarceration Rate	14
Juvenile Violent Crime Rate	35
Law Enforcement Employees	27
Corrections Employees	29
State Corrections Spending	38
Increase in State Corrections Spending	24
Law Enforcement Spending	30
Law Enforcement Spending as a Percentage of Total Spending	20

Transportation - Section K

Travel on Interstates	31
Interstate Mileage in Unacceptable Condition	22
Deficient Bridges	44

Traffic Deaths	13
Seat Belt Use	43
Vehicle-miles Traveled Per Capita	22
Workers Using Public Transportation	29
Road and Street Miles	37
Highway Employees	15
Public Transit Employees	50
Highway Spending Per Capita	20
Highway Spending as a Percentage of Total Spending	13

Welfare - Section L

Percentage of Births to Unwed Mothers	49
TANF Recipients as a Percentage of Population	49
Food Stamp Recipients as a Percentage of Population	39
SSI Recipients as a Percentage of Population	40
Change in TANF/AFDC Recipients	2
Condition of Children Index	28
Percentage of Families with Single Parent	48
Average Monthly TANF Payments	43
Welfare as a Percentage of Poverty-level Income	35
State Supplements of SSI	27
State Income Tax Liability of Typical Family in Poverty	18
Child Support Collections	20
Child Support Collections Per Dollar of Administrative Costs	19
Children in Foster Care	49
Welfare Spending Per Capita	43
Welfare Spending as a Percentage of Total Spending	36
Administrative Costs Per TANF Case	3

Technology - Section M

Percentage of Households with Computers	10
Percentage of Households with Internet Access	19
Zip codes with Broadband Service	36
High-tech Jobs	9
Dot-com Domain Names	32
State Government Website Ratings	39
Students per Computer	36

Illinois

Population - Section A

Population 2001	5
Population Change 2000-2001	34
Population Change 1990-2001	33
Population 2015	43
Population 2025	5
Percentage 65 and Over	35
Percentage 17 and Under	15
Median Age	39
Percentage African American	13
Percentage Hispanic	10
Percentage in Poverty	27
Child Poverty Rate	23
Percentage Female	21
Birth Rates	14
Death Rates	23
Population Density	11
New Legal Immigrants 2000	6

Economies - Section B

Personal Income 2001	5
Gross State Product	11
Per Capita Personal Income	9
Personal Income from Wages and Salaries	10
Average Annual Pay	6
Average Hourly Earnings	29
Value Added in Manufacturing	13
Cost of Living	10
Average Annual Pay in Manufacturing	14
Average Annual Pay in Retailing	14
Labor Force	33
Unemployment Rate	4
Employment Rate	47
Government Employment	44
Manufacturing Employment	16
Fortune 500 Companies	6
Forbes 500 Companies	6
Tourism Spending Per Capita	19
Exports Per Capita	13
Housing Permits	31
Percentage Change in Home Prices	25
Net Farm Income	9
Financial Institution Assets	9
Bankruptcy Filings	16
Patents Issued	16
WC Disability Payment	3
UC Average Weekly Benefit	11
Economic Momentum	49
One-year Employment Change	44
Manufacturing Employment Change	16
Home Ownership	33
Gambling	5

Electricity Use Per Residential Customer	34
Cost Per Kwh	3
New Companies	40

Geography - Section C

Total Land Area	24
Federally Owned Land	38
State Park Acreage	11
State Park Visitors	16
Population Not Active	18
Hunters with Firearms	39
Registered Boats	9
State Spending for the Arts	13
Energy Consumption Per Capita	25
Toxic Chemical Release Per Capita	32
Hazardous Waste Sites	8
Polluted Rivers and Streams	18
Expired Surface Water Pollution Permits	26
Air Pollution Emissions	6

Government - Section D

Members of United States House	5
State Legislators	13
Legislators Per Million Population	44
Units of Government	15
Legislators Compensation	5
Female Legislators	16
Turnover in Legislatures	24
Term Limits	n/a
Legislative Session Length	n/a
Republicans in State Legislatures	34
Governor's Power Rating	10
Number of Statewide Elected Officials	4
State and Local Government Employees	46
State and Local Average Salaries	13
Local Employment	1
Local Spending Accountability	24
Registered Voters	28
Percentage of Population Voting	28
Statewide Initiatives	n/a
Campaign Costs Per Vote	26

Federal Impacts - Section E

Per Capita Federal Spending	44
Increase in Federal Spending	33
Per Capita Federal Grant Spending	45
Per Capita Federal Spending on Procurement	43

Per Capita Federal Spending on Payments to Individuals	31
Per Capita Federal Spending on Social Security and Medicare	24
Social Security Benefits	5
Federal Spending on Employee Wages and Salaries	36
Federal Grant Spending Per Dollar of State Tax Revenue	36
General Revenue from Federal Government	39
Federal Tax Burden Per Capita	7
Federal Spending Per Dollar of Taxes Paid	46
Highway Charges Returned to States	42
Terms of Trade	45
Federal Personal Income Taxes	9
Federal Share of Medicaid	39

Taxes - Section F

Tax Revenue	36
Per Capita Tax Revenue	14
Tax Effort	25
Tax Capacity	11
Percentage Change in Taxes	26
Property Taxes as a Percentage of Income	12
Property Taxes Per Capita	10
Property Tax Revenue as a Percentage of 3-tax Revenues	11
Sales Taxes as a Percentage of Income	36
Sales Taxes Per Capita	22
Sales Tax Revenue as a Percentage of 3-tax Revenues	27
Sales Tax Rate	7
Income Taxes as a Percentage of Income	37
Income Taxes Per Capita	31
Income Tax Revenue as a Percentage of 3-tax Revenues	37
Highest Personal Income Rate	40
Corporate Income Taxes	8
Motor Fuel Taxes	31
Tobacco Taxes	14
Taxes on High Income Families	23
Taxes in the Largest City in Each State	15
Progressivity of Taxes	37

Revenues and Finances - Section G

Per Capita Total Revenue	25
Per Capita General Revenue	26
Own-source General Revenue	20
Per Capita Non-tax Revenue	46

Per Capita Total Spending — 23

General Spending as a Percentage of Income — 45

Per Capita General Spending — 23

Change in General Expenditures — 25

State Government General Revenue — 40

State Government General Spending — 41

State Government General Fund Spending — 45

State and Local Debt — 16

Debt as a Percentage of Revenue — 12

Per Capita Full Faith and Credit Debt — 9

Bond Ratings — 3

State Solvency Index — 45

Pension Plan Assets — 31

State Reserves — 32

Capital Outlays and Interest — 19

State Budget Process Quality — 3

Relative State Spending "Needs" — 33

Structural Deficits — 13

Education - Section H

Math Proficiency, Eighth Grade — 16

Science Proficiency, Eighth Grade — 19

AFQT Ranks — 30

SAT Scores — n/a

ACT Scores — 19

Over-25 Population with a High School Diploma — 29

Students in Private Schools — 10

High School Completion Rates — 29

Pupil-Teacher Ratio — 17

Public School Enrollment — 24

Library Holdings Per Capita — 17

Children with Disabilities — 17

Education Spending Per Capita — 25

Education Spending as a Percentage of Total Spending — 26

Spending Per Pupil — 10

Average Teacher Salary — 7

Sources of School Funds — 2

State Aid Per Pupil — 44

Higher Education Spending Per Capita — 41

Higher Education Spending as a Percentage of Total Spending — 40

Public Higher Education Enrollment — 23

Per Pupil Support of Higher Education — 26

Tuition and Fees — 13

Average Professor Salary — 11

Education Employees — 40

R and D Spending — 34

Library Operating Spending — 8

Health - Section I

Immunization Rates — 36

Infant Mortality Rates — 8

State Health Rankings — 31

Population Without Health Insurance — 21

Abortions — 14

Alcohol Consumption — 20

Percentage of Adult Smokers — 23

Percentage Obese — 25

AIDS Cases — 18

Physicians Per 100,000 Population — 11

Hospital Beds Per 1,000 Population — 23

Medicaid Recipients — 32

Medicaid Recipients as a Percentage of Poverty Population — 41

Health and Hospital Spending — 33

Health and Hospital Spending as a Percentage of Total Spending — 30

Per Capita Medicaid Spending — 16

Medicaid Spending Per Aged Recipient — 20

Medicaid Spending Per Child — 28

Medicare Payment Per Hospital Day — 9

Hospital Expense Per Inpatient Day — 15

Population in HMOs — 27

Crime - Section J

Crime Rate — 26

Violent Crime Rate — 7

Murder Rate — 6

Property Crime Rate — 27

Motor Vehicle Theft Rate — 20

Violent Crime Rate Change — 40

Prisoners — 8

Change in Prisoners — 37

Incarceration Rate — 28

Juvenile Violent Crime Rate — 2

Law Enforcement Employees — 5

Corrections Employees — 31

State Corrections Spending — 30

Increase in State Corrections Spending — 30

Law Enforcement Spending — 13

Law Enforcement Spending as a Percentage of Total Spending — 9

Transportation - Section K

Travel on Interstates — 9

Interstate Mileage in Unacceptable Condition — 20

Deficient Bridges — 42

Traffic Deaths — 31

Seat Belt Use — 23

Vehicle-miles Traveled Per Capita — 45

Workers Using Public Transportation — 4

Road and Street Miles — 31

Highway Employees — 40

Public Transit Employees — 2

Highway Spending Per Capita — 38

Highway Spending as a Percentage of Total Spending — 40

Welfare - Section L

Percentage of Births to Unwed Mothers — 21

TANF Recipients as a Percentage of Population — 34

Food Stamp Recipients as a Percentage of Population — 19

SSI Recipients as a Percentage of Population — 24

Change in TANF/AFDC Recipients — 4

Condition of Children Index — 30

Percentage of Families with Single Parent — 13

Average Monthly TANF Payments — 25

Welfare as a Percentage of Poverty-level Income — 24

State Supplements of SSI — 26

State Income Tax Liability of Typical Family in Poverty — 12

Child Support Collections — 48

Child Support Collections Per Dollar of Administrative Costs — 49

Children in Foster Care — 5

Welfare Spending Per Capita — 32

Welfare Spending as a Percentage of Total Spending — 35

Administrative Costs Per TANF Case — 15

Technology - Section M

Percentage of Households with Computers — 37

Percentage of Households with Internet Access — 36

Zip codes with Broadband Service — 23

High-tech Jobs — 22

Dot-com Domain Names — 21

State Government Website Ratings — 16

Students per Computer — 15

Indiana

Population - Section A

Population 2001	14
Population Change 2000-2001	31
Population Change 1990-2001	29
Population 2015	37
Population 2025	16
Percentage 65 and Over	29
Percentage 17 and Under	18
Median Age	36
Percentage African American	22
Percentage Hispanic	30
Percentage in Poverty	38
Child Poverty Rate	37
Percentage Female	26
Birth Rates	19
Death Rates	13
Population Density	16
New Legal Immigrants 2000	28

Economies - Section B

Personal Income 2001	16
Gross State Product	30
Per Capita Personal Income	31
Personal Income from Wages and Salaries	22
Average Annual Pay	26
Average Hourly Earnings	6
Value Added in Manufacturing	1
Cost of Living	32
Average Annual Pay in Manufacturing	18
Average Annual Pay in Retailing	37
Labor Force	23
Unemployment Rate	28
Employment Rate	23
Government Employment	43
Manufacturing Employment	1
Fortune 500 Companies	31
Forbes 500 Companies	28
Tourism Spending Per Capita	49
Exports Per Capita	16
Housing Permits	15
Percentage Change in Home Prices	43
Net Farm Income	19
Financial Institution Assets	19
Bankruptcy Filings	6
Patents Issued	26
WC Disability Payment	35
UC Average Weekly Benefit	19
Economic Momentum	44
One-year Employment Change	41
Manufacturing Employment Change	21
Home Ownership	10
Gambling	8

Electricity Use Per Residential Customer	24
Cost Per Kwh	13
New Companies	44

Geography - Section C

Total Land Area	38
Federally Owned Land	39
State Park Acreage	18
State Park Visitors	21
Population Not Active	21
Hunters with Firearms	22
Registered Boats	22
State Spending for the Arts	40
Energy Consumption Per Capita	8
Toxic Chemical Release Per Capita	13
Hazardous Waste Sites	14
Polluted Rivers and Streams	40
Expired Surface Water Pollution Permits	6
Air Pollution Emissions	10

Government - Section D

Members of United States House	14
State Legislators	19
Legislators Per Million Population	35
Units of Government	16
Legislators Compensation	34
Female Legislators	36
Turnover in Legislatures	41
Term Limits	n/a
Legislative Session Length	22
Republicans in State Legislatures	25
Governor's Power Rating	46
Number of Statewide Elected Officials	9
State and Local Government Employees	37
State and Local Average Salaries	28
Local Employment	12
Local Spending Accountability	16
Registered Voters	5
Percentage of Population Voting	43
Statewide Initiatives	n/a
Campaign Costs Per Vote	21

Federal Impacts - Section E

Per Capita Federal Spending	43
Increase in Federal Spending	22
Per Capita Federal Grant Spending	44
Per Capita Federal Spending on Procurement	34

Per Capita Federal Spending on Payments to Individuals	28
Per Capita Federal Spending on Social Security and Medicare	22
Social Security Benefits	7
Federal Spending on Employee Wages and Salaries	48
Federal Grant Spending Per Dollar of State Tax Revenue	31
General Revenue from Federal Government	37
Federal Tax Burden Per Capita	29
Federal Spending Per Dollar of Taxes Paid	35
Highway Charges Returned to States	39
Terms of Trade	37
Federal Personal Income Taxes	30
Federal Share of Medicaid	21

Taxes - Section F

Tax Revenue	37
Per Capita Tax Revenue	30
Tax Effort	39
Tax Capacity	24
Percentage Change in Taxes	32
Property Taxes as a Percentage of Income	14
Property Taxes Per Capita	18
Property Tax Revenue as a Percentage of 3-tax Revenues	14
Sales Taxes as a Percentage of Income	39
Sales Taxes Per Capita	42
Sales Tax Revenue as a Percentage of 3-tax Revenues	35
Sales Tax Rate	19
Income Taxes as a Percentage of Income	24
Income Taxes Per Capita	25
Income Tax Revenue as a Percentage of 3-tax Revenues	21
Highest Personal Income Rate	38
Corporate Income Taxes	11
Motor Fuel Taxes	45
Tobacco Taxes	22
Taxes on High Income Families	39
Taxes in the Largest City in Each State	34
Progressivity of Taxes	40

Revenues and Finances - Section G

Per Capita Total Revenue	49
Per Capita General Revenue	35
Own-source General Revenue	31
Per Capita Non-tax Revenue	22

Per Capita Total Spending	44
General Spending as a Percentage of Income	34
Per Capita General Spending	38
Change in General Expenditures	17
State Government General Revenue	41
State Government General Spending	36
State Government General Fund Spending	41
State and Local Debt	45
Debt as a Percentage of Revenue	38
Per Capita Full Faith and Credit Debt	49
Bond Ratings	n/a
State Solvency Index	29
Pension Plan Assets	48
State Reserves	26
Capital Outlays and Interest	42
State Budget Process Quality	49
Relative State Spending "Needs"	12
Structural Deficits	33

Education - Section H

Math Proficiency, Eighth Grade	5
Science Proficiency, Eighth Grade	11
AFQT Ranks	16
SAT Scores	17
ACT Scores	n/a
Over-25 Population with a High School Diploma	33
Students in Private Schools	21
High School Completion Rates	20
Pupil-Teacher Ratio	13
Public School Enrollment	30
Library Holdings Per Capita	11
Children with Disabilities	8
Education Spending Per Capita	20
Education Spending as a Percentage of Total Spending	4
Spending Per Pupil	16
Average Teacher Salary	15
Sources of School Funds	24
State Aid Per Pupil	15
Higher Education Spending Per Capita	14
Higher Education Spending as a Percentage of Total Spending	7
Public Higher Education Enrollment	32
Per Pupil Support of Higher Education	25
Tuition and Fees	18
Average Professor Salary	18
Education Employees	33
R and D Spending	40
Library Operating Spending	5

Health - Section I

Immunization Rates	38
Infant Mortality Rates	15
State Health Rankings	22
Population Without Health Insurance	29
Abortions	36
Alcohol Consumption	40
Percentage of Adult Smokers	5
Percentage Obese	6
AIDS Cases	32
Physicians Per 100,000 Population	40
Hospital Beds Per 1,000 Population	21
Medicaid Recipients	34
Medicaid Recipients as a Percentage of Poverty Population	23
Health and Hospital Spending	19
Health and Hospital Spending as a Percentage of Total Spending	16
Per Capita Medicaid Spending	35
Medicaid Spending Per Aged Recipient	12
Medicaid Spending Per Child	40
Medicare Payment Per Hospital Day	37
Hospital Expense Per Inpatient Day	17
Population in HMOs	37

Crime - Section J

Crime Rate	30
Violent Crime Rate	26
Murder Rate	10
Property Crime Rate	28
Motor Vehicle Theft Rate	27
Violent Crime Rate Change	46
Prisoners	23
Change in Prisoners	22
Incarceration Rate	29
Juvenile Violent Crime Rate	11
Law Enforcement Employees	33
Corrections Employees	25
State Corrections Spending	29
Increase in State Corrections Spending	10
Law Enforcement Spending	40
Law Enforcement Spending as a Percentage of Total Spending	38

Transportation - Section K

Travel on Interstates	26
Interstate Mileage in Unacceptable Condition	34
Deficient Bridges	32
Traffic Deaths	39
Seat Belt Use	33
Vehicle-miles Traveled Per Capita	10
Workers Using Public Transportation	33
Road and Street Miles	30
Highway Employees	36
Public Transit Employees	26
Highway Spending Per Capita	42
Highway Spending as a Percentage of Total Spending	34

Welfare - Section L

Percentage of Births to Unwed Mothers	13
TANF Recipients as a Percentage of Population	11
Food Stamp Recipients as a Percentage of Population	28
SSI Recipients as a Percentage of Population	37
Change in TANF/AFDC Recipients	50
Condition of Children Index	19
Percentage of Families with Single Parent	47
Average Monthly TANF Payments	46
Welfare as a Percentage of Poverty-level Income	41
State Supplements of SSI	8
State Income Tax Liability of Typical Family in Poverty	4
Child Support Collections	24
Child Support Collections Per Dollar of Administrative Costs	4
Children in Foster Care	37
Welfare Spending Per Capita	33
Welfare Spending as a Percentage of Total Spending	26
Administrative Costs Per TANF Case	34

Technology - Section M

Percentage of Households with Computers	36
Percentage of Households with Internet Access	35
Zip codes with Broadband Service	25
High-tech Jobs	40
Dot-com Domain Names	35
State Government Website Ratings	12
Students per Computer	40

Iowa

Population - Section A

Population 2001	30
Population Change 2000-2001	48
Population Change 1990-2001	44
Population 2015	44
Population 2025	33
Percentage 65 and Over	4
Percentage 17 and Under	31
Median Age	11
Percentage African American	39
Percentage Hispanic	35
Percentage in Poverty	44
Child Poverty Rate	49
Percentage Female	27
Birth Rates	38
Death Rates	42
Population Density	33
New Legal Immigrants 2000	31

Economies - Section B

Personal Income 2001	30
Gross State Product	35
Per Capita Personal Income	33
Personal Income from Wages and Salaries	32
Average Annual Pay	38
Average Hourly Earnings	23
Value Added in Manufacturing	5
Cost of Living	30
Average Annual Pay in Manufacturing	32
Average Annual Pay in Retailing	41
Labor Force	5
Unemployment Rate	46
Employment Rate	5
Government Employment	29
Manufacturing Employment	11
Fortune 500 Companies	34
Forbes 500 Companies	33
Tourism Spending Per Capita	36
Exports Per Capita	31
Housing Permits	29
Percentage Change in Home Prices	29
Net Farm Income	6
Financial Institution Assets	23
Bankruptcy Filings	38
Patents Issued	24
WC Disability Payment	1
UC Average Weekly Benefit	16
Economic Momentum	41
One-year Employment Change	22
Manufacturing Employment Change	13
Home Ownership	9
Gambling	17

Electricity Use Per Residential Customer	29
Cost Per Kwh	4
New Companies	49

Geography - Section C

Total Land Area	23
Federally Owned Land	42
State Park Acreage	37
State Park Visitors	10
Population Not Active	23
Hunters with Firearms	17
Registered Boats	23
State Spending for the Arts	41
Energy Consumption Per Capita	16
Toxic Chemical Release Per Capita	27
Hazardous Waste Sites	29
Polluted Rivers and Streams	36
Expired Surface Water Pollution Permits	29
Air Pollution Emissions	30

Government - Section D

Members of United States House	27
State Legislators	19
Legislators Per Million Population	18
Units of Government	11
Legislators Compensation	22
Female Legislators	28
Turnover in Legislatures	5
Term Limits	n/a
Legislative Session Length	26
Republicans in State Legislatures	21
Governor's Power Rating	24
Number of Statewide Elected Officials	16
State and Local Government Employees	10
State and Local Average Salaries	24
Local Employment	29
Local Spending Accountability	28
Registered Voters	8
Percentage of Population Voting	12
Statewide Initiatives	n/a
Campaign Costs Per Vote	19

Federal Impacts - Section E

Per Capita Federal Spending	31
Increase in Federal Spending	28
Per Capita Federal Grant Spending	36
Per Capita Federal Spending on Procurement	45

Per Capita Federal Spending on Payments to Individuals	6
Per Capita Federal Spending on Social Security and Medicare	19
Social Security Benefits	22
Federal Spending on Employee Wages and Salaries	47
Federal Grant Spending Per Dollar of State Tax Revenue	25
General Revenue from Federal Government	26
Federal Tax Burden Per Capita	34
Federal Spending Per Dollar of Taxes Paid	21
Highway Charges Returned to States	24
Terms of Trade	27
Federal Personal Income Taxes	37
Federal Share of Medicaid	18

Taxes - Section F

Tax Revenue	24
Per Capita Tax Revenue	27
Tax Effort	24
Tax Capacity	24
Percentage Change in Taxes	48
Property Taxes as a Percentage of Income	16
Property Taxes Per Capita	21
Property Tax Revenue as a Percentage of 3-tax Revenues	16
Sales Taxes as a Percentage of Income	32
Sales Taxes Per Capita	34
Sales Tax Revenue as a Percentage of 3-tax Revenues	29
Sales Tax Rate	19
Income Taxes as a Percentage of Income	29
Income Taxes Per Capita	29
Income Tax Revenue as a Percentage of 3-tax Revenues	30
Highest Personal Income Rate	30
Corporate Income Taxes	36
Motor Fuel Taxes	26
Tobacco Taxes	28
Taxes on High Income Families	4
Taxes in the Largest City in Each State	5
Progressivity of Taxes	28

Revenues and Finances - Section G

Per Capita Total Revenue	37
Per Capita General Revenue	27
Own-source General Revenue	27
Per Capita Non-tax Revenue	17

Per Capita Total Spending	25	**Health - Section I**	
General Spending as a Percentage of Income	19	Immunization Rates	25
Per Capita General Spending	20	Infant Mortality Rates	33
Change in General Expenditures	32	State Health Rankings	7
State Government General Revenue	29	Population Without Health Insurance	50
State Government General Spending	20	Abortions	32
State Government General Fund Spending	10	Alcohol Consumption	39
State and Local Debt	50	Percentage of Adult Smokers	37
Debt as a Percentage of Revenue	49	Percentage Obese	14
Per Capita Full Faith and Credit Debt	38	AIDS Cases	45
Bond Ratings	n/a	Physicians Per 100,000 Population	42
State Solvency Index	22	Hospital Beds Per 1,000 Population	7
Pension Plan Assets	41	Medicaid Recipients	39

Health - Section I

Immunization Rates	25
Infant Mortality Rates	33
State Health Rankings	7
Population Without Health Insurance	50
Abortions	32
Alcohol Consumption	39
Percentage of Adult Smokers	37
Percentage Obese	14
AIDS Cases	45
Physicians Per 100,000 Population	42
Hospital Beds Per 1,000 Population	7
Medicaid Recipients	39
Medicaid Recipients as a Percentage of Poverty Population	19
Health and Hospital Spending	8
Health and Hospital Spending as a Percentage of Total Spending	8
Per Capita Medicaid Spending	31
Medicaid Spending Per Aged Recipient	21
Medicaid Spending Per Child	12
Medicare Payment Per Hospital Day	44
Hospital Expense Per Inpatient Day	24
Population in HMOs	44

Per Capita Total Spending — 25
General Spending as a Percentage of Income — 19
Per Capita General Spending — 20
Change in General Expenditures — 32
State Government General Revenue — 29
State Government General Spending — 20
State Government General Fund Spending — 10
State and Local Debt — 50
Debt as a Percentage of Revenue — 49
Per Capita Full Faith and Credit Debt — 38
Bond Ratings — n/a
State Solvency Index — 22
Pension Plan Assets — 41
State Reserves — 16
Capital Outlays and Interest — 29
State Budget Process Quality — 16
Relative State Spending "Needs" — 4
Structural Deficits — 1

Education - Section H

Math Proficiency, Eighth Grade — n/a
Science Proficiency, Eighth Grade — n/a
AFQT Ranks — 5
SAT Scores — n/a
ACT Scores — 3
Over-25 Population with a High School Diploma — 9
Students in Private Schools — 27
High School Completion Rates — 13
Pupil-Teacher Ratio — 38
Public School Enrollment — 22
Library Holdings Per Capita — 14
Children with Disabilities — 14
Education Spending Per Capita — 10
Education Spending as a Percentage of Total Spending — 10
Spending Per Pupil — 32
Average Teacher Salary — 33
Sources of School Funds — 26
State Aid Per Pupil — 28
Higher Education Spending Per Capita — 5
Higher Education Spending as a Percentage of Total Spending — 3
Public Higher Education Enrollment — 15
Per Pupil Support of Higher Education — 12
Tuition and Fees — 24
Average Professor Salary — 20
Education Employees — 22
R and D Spending — 38
Library Operating Spending — 23

Crime - Section J

Crime Rate — 36
Violent Crime Rate — 38
Murder Rate — 45
Property Crime Rate — 36
Motor Vehicle Theft Rate — 42
Violent Crime Rate Change — 2
Prisoners — 33
Change in Prisoners — 17
Incarceration Rate — 39
Juvenile Violent Crime Rate — 26
Law Enforcement Employees — 43
Corrections Employees — 45
State Corrections Spending — 18
Increase in State Corrections Spending — 25
Law Enforcement Spending — 42
Law Enforcement Spending as a Percentage of Total Spending — 45

Transportation - Section K

Travel on Interstates — 35
Interstate Mileage in Unacceptable Condition — 21
Deficient Bridges — 24

Traffic Deaths — 27
Seat Belt Use — 9
Vehicle-miles Traveled Per Capita — 27
Workers Using Public Transportation — 40
Road and Street Miles — 45
Highway Employees — 13
Public Transit Employees — 25
Highway Spending Per Capita — 6
Highway Spending as a Percentage of Total Spending — 5

Welfare - Section L

Percentage of Births to Unwed Mothers — 41
TANF Recipients as a Percentage of Population — 18
Food Stamp Recipients as a Percentage of Population — 40
SSI Recipients as a Percentage of Population — 41
Change in TANF/AFDC Recipients — 45
Condition of Children Index — 4
Percentage of Families with Single Parent — 40
Average Monthly TANF Payments — 27
Welfare as a Percentage of Poverty-level Income — 21
State Supplements of SSI — 7
State Income Tax Liability of Typical Family in Poverty — 18
Child Support Collections — 11
Child Support Collections Per Dollar of Administrative Costs — 11
Children in Foster Care — 26
Welfare Spending Per Capita — 28
Welfare Spending as a Percentage of Total Spending — 31
Administrative Costs Per TANF Case — 28

Technology - Section M

Percentage of Households with Computers — 15
Percentage of Households with Internet Access — 24
Zip codes with Broadband Service — 46
High-tech Jobs — 34
Dot-com Domain Names — 48
State Government Website Ratings — 27
Students per Computer — 41

Kansas

Population - Section A

Population 2001	32
Population Change 2000-2001	41
Population Change 1990-2001	36
Population 2015	22
Population 2025	31
Percentage 65 and Over	18
Percentage 17 and Under	11
Median Age	36
Percentage African American	27
Percentage Hispanic	18
Percentage in Poverty	27
Child Poverty Rate	25
Percentage Female	34
Birth Rates	17
Death Rates	28
Population Density	40
New Legal Immigrants 2000	27

Economies - Section B

Personal Income 2001	31
Gross State Product	29
Per Capita Personal Income	28
Personal Income from Wages and Salaries	26
Average Annual Pay	32
Average Hourly Earnings	13
Value Added in Manufacturing	18
Cost of Living	31
Average Annual Pay in Manufacturing	23
Average Annual Pay in Retailing	38
Labor Force	9
Unemployment Rate	34
Employment Rate	17
Government Employment	16
Manufacturing Employment	18
Fortune 500 Companies	33
Forbes 500 Companies	31
Tourism Spending Per Capita	41
Exports Per Capita	25
Housing Permits	22
Percentage Change in Home Prices	20
Net Farm Income	20
Financial Institution Assets	22
Bankruptcy Filings	22
Patents Issued	39
WC Disability Payment	45
UC Average Weekly Benefit	12
Economic Momentum	33
One-year Employment Change	9
Manufacturing Employment Change	27
Home Ownership	34
Gambling	36

Electricity Use Per Residential Customer	27
Cost Per Kwh	28
New Companies	33

Geography - Section C

Total Land Area	13
Federally Owned Land	35
State Park Acreage	45
State Park Visitors	23
Population Not Active	15
Hunters with Firearms	34
Registered Boats	34
State Spending for the Arts	39
Energy Consumption Per Capita	11
Toxic Chemical Release Per Capita	29
Hazardous Waste Sites	34
Polluted Rivers and Streams	3
Expired Surface Water Pollution Permits	47
Air Pollution Emissions	28

Government - Section D

Members of United States House	31
State Legislators	17
Legislators Per Million Population	14
Units of Government	4
Legislators Compensation	43
Female Legislators	6
Turnover in Legislatures	33
Term Limits	n/a
Legislative Session Length	26
Republicans in State Legislatures	8
Governor's Power Rating	30
Number of Statewide Elected Officials	16
State and Local Government Employees	6
State and Local Average Salaries	34
Local Employment	8
Local Spending Accountability	18
Registered Voters	23
Percentage of Population Voting	23
Statewide Initiatives	n/a
Campaign Costs Per Vote	42

Federal Impacts - Section E

Per Capita Federal Spending	24
Increase in Federal Spending	13
Per Capita Federal Grant Spending	40
Per Capita Federal Spending on Procurement	30

Per Capita Federal Spending on Payments to Individuals	13
Per Capita Federal Spending on Social Security and Medicare	23
Social Security Benefits	13
Federal Spending on Employee Wages and Salaries	16
Federal Grant Spending Per Dollar of State Tax Revenue	29
General Revenue from Federal Government	29
Federal Tax Burden Per Capita	26
Federal Spending Per Dollar of Taxes Paid	24
Highway Charges Returned to States	25
Terms of Trade	33
Federal Personal Income Taxes	26
Federal Share of Medicaid	25

Taxes - Section F

Tax Revenue	34
Per Capita Tax Revenue	26
Tax Effort	20
Tax Capacity	29
Percentage Change in Taxes	41
Property Taxes as a Percentage of Income	27
Property Taxes Per Capita	30
Property Tax Revenue as a Percentage of 3-tax Revenues	27
Sales Taxes as a Percentage of Income	20
Sales Taxes Per Capita	23
Sales Tax Revenue as a Percentage of 3-tax Revenues	21
Sales Tax Rate	32
Income Taxes as a Percentage of Income	30
Income Taxes Per Capita	26
Income Tax Revenue as a Percentage of 3-tax Revenues	28
Highest Personal Income Rate	20
Corporate Income Taxes	23
Motor Fuel Taxes	23
Tobacco Taxes	18
Taxes on High Income Families	34
Taxes in the Largest City in Each State	41
Progressivity of Taxes	5

Revenues and Finances - Section G

Per Capita Total Revenue	32
Per Capita General Revenue	33
Own-source General Revenue	29
Per Capita Non-tax Revenue	33

Per Capita Total Spending	38
General Spending as a Percentage of Income	35
Per Capita General Spending	37
Change in General Expenditures	39
State Government General Revenue	36
State Government General Spending	39
State Government General Fund Spending	34
State and Local Debt	38
Debt as a Percentage of Revenue	33
Per Capita Full Faith and Credit Debt	25
Bond Ratings	n/a
State Solvency Index	34
Pension Plan Assets	45
State Reserves	43
Capital Outlays and Interest	41
State Budget Process Quality	39
Relative State Spending "Needs"	18
Structural Deficits	18

Education · Section H

Math Proficiency, Eighth Grade	3
Science Proficiency, Eighth Grade	n/a
AFQT Ranks	19
SAT Scores	n/a
ACT Scores	6
Over-25 Population with a High School Diploma	14
Students in Private Schools	28
High School Completion Rates	15
Pupil-Teacher Ratio	36
Public School Enrollment	11
Library Holdings Per Capita	6
Children with Disabilities	33
Education Spending Per Capita	27
Education Spending as a Percentage of Total Spending	12
Spending Per Pupil	29
Average Teacher Salary	42
Sources of School Funds	35
State Aid Per Pupil	11
Higher Education Spending Per Capita	9
Higher Education Spending as a Percentage of Total Spending	5
Public Higher Education Enrollment	1
Per Pupil Support of Higher Education	43
Tuition and Fees	39
Average Professor Salary	33
Education Employees	7
R and D Spending	41
Library Operating Spending	18

Health · Section I

Immunization Rates	33
Infant Mortality Rates	26
State Health Rankings	21
Population Without Health Insurance	30
Abortions	9
Alcohol Consumption	45
Percentage of Adult Smokers	34
Percentage Obese	22
AIDS Cases	40
Physicians Per 100,000 Population	30
Hospital Beds Per 1,000 Population	8
Medicaid Recipients	43
Medicaid Recipients as a Percentage of Poverty Population	36
Health and Hospital Spending	34
Health and Hospital Spending as a Percentage of Total Spending	29
Per Capita Medicaid Spending	40
Medicaid Spending Per Aged Recipient	16
Medicaid Spending Per Child	38
Medicare Payment Per Hospital Day	22
Hospital Expense Per Inpatient Day	33
Population in HMOs	35

Crime · Section J

Crime Rate	17
Violent Crime Rate	24
Murder Rate	32
Property Crime Rate	18
Motor Vehicle Theft Rate	32
Violent Crime Rate Change	3
Prisoners	32
Change in Prisoners	31
Incarceration Rate	34
Juvenile Violent Crime Rate	n/a
Law Enforcement Employees	10
Corrections Employees	28
State Corrections Spending	19
Increase in State Corrections Spending	39
Law Enforcement Spending	34
Law Enforcement Spending as a Percentage of Total Spending	30

Transportation · Section K

Travel on Interstates	27
Interstate Mileage in Unacceptable Condition	39
Deficient Bridges	31
Traffic Deaths	16
Seat Belt Use	42
Vehicle-miles Traveled Per Capita	25
Workers Using Public Transportation	50
Road and Street Miles	49
Highway Employees	8
Public Transit Employees	35
Highway Spending Per Capita	5
Highway Spending as a Percentage of Total Spending	2

Welfare · Section L

Percentage of Births to Unwed Mothers	36
TANF Recipients as a Percentage of Population	32
Food Stamp Recipients as a Percentage of Population	36
SSI Recipients as a Percentage of Population	42
Change in TANF/AFDC Recipients	38
Condition of Children Index	18
Percentage of Families with Single Parent	27
Average Monthly TANF Payments	37
Welfare as a Percentage of Poverty-level Income	25
State Supplements of SSI	n/a
State Income Tax Liability of Typical Family in Poverty	33
Child Support Collections	38
Child Support Collections Per Dollar of Administrative Costs	48
Children in Foster Care	13
Welfare Spending Per Capita	48
Welfare Spending as a Percentage of Total Spending	47
Administrative Costs Per TANF Case	1

Technology · Section M

Percentage of Households with Computers	26
Percentage of Households with Internet Access	26
Zip codes with Broadband Service	37
High-tech Jobs	19
Dot-com Domain Names	34
State Government Website Ratings	23
Students per Computer	47

Kentucky

Population - Section A

Population 2001	25
Population Change 2000-2001	29
Population Change 1990-2001	28
Population 2015	39
Population 2025	27
Percentage 65 and Over	27
Percentage 17 and Under	39
Median Age	23
Percentage African American	24
Percentage Hispanic	44
Percentage in Poverty	17
Child Poverty Rate	16
Percentage Female	20
Birth Rates	33
Death Rates	6
Population Density	23
New Legal Immigrants 2000	33

Economies - Section B

Personal Income 2001	26
Gross State Product	40
Per Capita Personal Income	40
Personal Income from Wages and Salaries	29
Average Annual Pay	35
Average Hourly Earnings	22
Value Added in Manufacturing	14
Cost of Living	39
Average Annual Pay in Manufacturing	28
Average Annual Pay in Retailing	39
Labor Force	37
Unemployment Rate	21
Employment Rate	30
Government Employment	23
Manufacturing Employment	12
Fortune 500 Companies	29
Forbes 500 Companies	38
Tourism Spending Per Capita	43
Exports Per Capita	18
Housing Permits	33
Percentage Change in Home Prices	31
Net Farm Income	11
Financial Institution Assets	32
Bankruptcy Filings	12
Patents Issued	40
WC Disability Payment	27
UC Average Weekly Benefit	25
Economic Momentum	9
One-year Employment Change	2
Manufacturing Employment Change	12
Home Ownership	8
Gambling	25

Electricity Use Per Residential Customer	8
Cost Per Kwh	15
New Companies	43

Geography - Section C

Total Land Area	36
Federally Owned Land	28
State Park Acreage	42
State Park Visitors	31
Population Not Active	3
Hunters with Firearms	10
Registered Boats	28
State Spending for the Arts	24
Energy Consumption Per Capita	10
Toxic Chemical Release Per Capita	16
Hazardous Waste Sites	29
Polluted Rivers and Streams	28
Expired Surface Water Pollution Permits	42
Air Pollution Emissions	19

Government - Section D

Members of United States House	25
State Legislators	29
Legislators Per Million Population	26
Units of Government	25
Legislators Compensation	27
Female Legislators	47
Turnover in Legislatures	44
Term Limits	n/a
Legislative Session Length	32
Republicans in State Legislatures	36
Governor's Power Rating	24
Number of Statewide Elected Officials	9
State and Local Government Employees	24
State and Local Average Salaries	45
Local Employment	36
Local Spending Accountability	40
Registered Voters	18
Percentage of Population Voting	39
Statewide Initiatives	n/a
Campaign Costs Per Vote	50

Federal Impacts - Section E

Per Capita Federal Spending	21
Increase in Federal Spending	25
Per Capita Federal Grant Spending	18
Per Capita Federal Spending on Procurement	21

Per Capita Federal Spending on Payments to Individuals	19
Per Capita Federal Spending on Social Security and Medicare	10
Social Security Benefits	47
Federal Spending on Employee Wages and Salaries	17
Federal Grant Spending Per Dollar of State Tax Revenue	20
General Revenue from Federal Government	13
Federal Tax Burden Per Capita	40
Federal Spending Per Dollar of Taxes Paid	14
Highway Charges Returned to States	35
Terms of Trade	13
Federal Personal Income Taxes	42
Federal Share of Medicaid	11

Taxes - Section F

Tax Revenue	22
Per Capita Tax Revenue	39
Tax Effort	20
Tax Capacity	45
Percentage Change in Taxes	40
Property Taxes as a Percentage of Income	43
Property Taxes Per Capita	45
Property Tax Revenue as a Percentage of 3-tax Revenues	45
Sales Taxes as a Percentage of Income	23
Sales Taxes Per Capita	35
Sales Tax Revenue as a Percentage of 3-tax Revenues	22
Sales Tax Rate	9
Income Taxes as a Percentage of Income	8
Income Taxes Per Capita	15
Income Tax Revenue as a Percentage of 3-tax Revenues	5
Highest Personal Income Rate	22
Corporate Income Taxes	34
Motor Fuel Taxes	42
Tobacco Taxes	49
Taxes on High Income Families	15
Taxes in the Largest City in Each State	12
Progressivity of Taxes	31

Revenues and Finances - Section G

Per Capita Total Revenue	30
Per Capita General Revenue	37
Own-source General Revenue	41
Per Capita Non-tax Revenue	41

Per Capita Total Spending	41
General Spending as a Percentage of Income	20
Per Capita General Spending	40
Change in General Expenditures	12
State Government General Revenue	21
State Government General Spending	25
State Government General Fund Spending	8
State and Local Debt	12
Debt as a Percentage of Revenue	6
Per Capita Full Faith and Credit Debt	48
Bond Ratings	n/a
State Solvency Index	30
Pension Plan Assets	36
State Reserves	43
Capital Outlays and Interest	22
State Budget Process Quality	26
Relative State Spending "Needs"	33
Structural Deficits	5

Education - Section H

Math Proficiency, Eighth Grade	25
Science Proficiency, Eighth Grade	17
AFQT Ranks	42
SAT Scores	n/a
ACT Scores	22
Over-25 Population with a High School Diploma	48
Students in Private Schools	17
High School Completion Rates	33
Pupil-Teacher Ratio	14
Public School Enrollment	43
Library Holdings Per Capita	41
Children with Disabilities	15
Education Spending Per Capita	44
Education Spending as a Percentage of Total Spending	36
Spending Per Pupil	25
Average Teacher Salary	35
Sources of School Funds	39
State Aid Per Pupil	18
Higher Education Spending Per Capita	26
Higher Education Spending as a Percentage of Total Spending	18
Public Higher Education Enrollment	35
Per Pupil Support of Higher Education	5
Tuition and Fees	35
Average Professor Salary	32
Education Employees	8
R and D Spending	49
Library Operating Spending	40

Health - Section I

Immunization Rates	24
Infant Mortality Rates	21
State Health Rankings	39
Population Without Health Insurance	26
Abortions	40
Alcohol Consumption	47
Percentage of Adult Smokers	1
Percentage Obese	4
AIDS Cases	25
Physicians Per 100,000 Population	34
Hospital Beds Per 1,000 Population	12
Medicaid Recipients	6
Medicaid Recipients as a Percentage of Poverty Population	16
Health and Hospital Spending	43
Health and Hospital Spending as a Percentage of Total Spending	41
Per Capita Medicaid Spending	9
Medicaid Spending Per Aged Recipient	32
Medicaid Spending Per Child	14
Medicare Payment Per Hospital Day	38
Hospital Expense Per Inpatient Day	43
Population in HMOs	10

Crime - Section J

Crime Rate	43
Violent Crime Rate	41
Murder Rate	25
Property Crime Rate	41
Motor Vehicle Theft Rate	40
Violent Crime Rate Change	30
Prisoners	26
Change in Prisoners	29
Incarceration Rate	24
Juvenile Violent Crime Rate	32
Law Enforcement Employees	40
Corrections Employees	41
State Corrections Spending	35
Increase in State Corrections Spending	21
Law Enforcement Spending	38
Law Enforcement Spending as a Percentage of Total Spending	34

Transportation - Section K

Travel on Interstates	21
Interstate Mileage in Unacceptable Condition	29
Deficient Bridges	18

Traffic Deaths	14
Seat Belt Use	40
Vehicle-miles Traveled Per Capita	13
Workers Using Public Transportation	27
Road and Street Miles	8
Highway Employees	26
Public Transit Employees	28
Highway Spending Per Capita	19
Highway Spending as a Percentage of Total Spending	16

Welfare - Section L

Percentage of Births to Unwed Mothers	30
TANF Recipients as a Percentage of Population	16
Food Stamp Recipients as a Percentage of Population	4
SSI Recipients as a Percentage of Population	2
Change in TANF/AFDC Recipients	25
Condition of Children Index	37
Percentage of Families with Single Parent	27
Average Monthly TANF Payments	38
Welfare as a Percentage of Poverty-level Income	41
State Supplements of SSI	4
State Income Tax Liability of Typical Family in Poverty	2
Child Support Collections	22
Child Support Collections Per Dollar of Administrative Costs	31
Children in Foster Care	30
Welfare Spending Per Capita	8
Welfare Spending as a Percentage of Total Spending	2
Administrative Costs Per TANF Case	45

Technology - Section M

Percentage of Households with Computers	45
Percentage of Households with Internet Access	43
Zip codes with Broadband Service	42
High-tech Jobs	37
Dot-com Domain Names	43
State Government Website Ratings	44
Students per Computer	23

Louisiana

Population - Section A

Population 2001	22
Population Change 2000-2001	47
Population Change 1990-2001	41
Population 2015	26
Population 2025	24
Percentage 65 and Over	39
Percentage 17 and Under	7
Median Age	43
Percentage African American	2
Percentage Hispanic	36
Percentage in Poverty	5
Child Poverty Rate	5
Percentage Female	8
Birth Rates	11
Death Rates	2
Population Density	22
New Legal Immigrants 2000	32

Economies - Section B

Personal Income 2001	25
Gross State Product	32
Per Capita Personal Income	44
Personal Income from Wages and Salaries	37
Average Annual Pay	37
Average Hourly Earnings	11
Value Added in Manufacturing	32
Cost of Living	29
Average Annual Pay in Manufacturing	19
Average Annual Pay in Retailing	42
Labor Force	49
Unemployment Rate	10
Employment Rate	41
Government Employment	11
Manufacturing Employment	39
Fortune 500 Companies	40
Forbes 500 Companies	40
Tourism Spending Per Capita	16
Exports Per Capita	5
Housing Permits	41
Percentage Change in Home Prices	32
Net Farm Income	33
Financial Institution Assets	40
Bankruptcy Filings	17
Patents Issued	42
WC Disability Payment	48
UC Average Weekly Benefit	43
Economic Momentum	32
One-year Employment Change	29
Manufacturing Employment Change	20
Home Ownership	37
Gambling	7

Electricity Use Per Residential Customer	2
Cost Per Kwh	42
New Companies	34

Geography - Section C

Total Land Area	33
Federally Owned Land	31
State Park Acreage	44
State Park Visitors	50
Population Not Active	1
Hunters with Firearms	11
Registered Boats	15
State Spending for the Arts	20
Energy Consumption Per Capita	4
Toxic Chemical Release Per Capita	11
Hazardous Waste Sites	25
Polluted Rivers and Streams	1
Expired Surface Water Pollution Permits	2
Air Pollution Emissions	15

Government - Section D

Members of United States House	22
State Legislators	25
Legislators Per Million Population	27
Units of Government	46
Legislators Compensation	24
Female Legislators	39
Turnover in Legislatures	n/a
Term Limits	1
Legislative Session Length	31
Republicans in State Legislatures	42
Governor's Power Rating	41
Number of Statewide Elected Officials	9
State and Local Government Employees	7
State and Local Average Salaries	47
Local Employment	35
Local Spending Accountability	22
Registered Voters	14
Percentage of Population Voting	32
Statewide Initiatives	n/a
Campaign Costs Per Vote	33

Federal Impacts - Section E

Per Capita Federal Spending	23
Increase in Federal Spending	32
Per Capita Federal Grant Spending	15
Per Capita Federal Spending on Procurement	25

Per Capita Federal Spending on Payments to Individuals	18
Per Capita Federal Spending on Social Security and Medicare	14
Social Security Benefits	49
Federal Spending on Employee Wages and Salaries	32
Federal Grant Spending Per Dollar of State Tax Revenue	9
General Revenue from Federal Government	14
Federal Tax Burden Per Capita	46
Federal Spending Per Dollar of Taxes Paid	13
Highway Charges Returned to States	45
Terms of Trade	9
Federal Personal Income Taxes	45
Federal Share of Medicaid	6

Taxes - Section F

Tax Revenue	29
Per Capita Tax Revenue	41
Tax Effort	41
Tax Capacity	42
Percentage Change in Taxes	10
Property Taxes as a Percentage of Income	45
Property Taxes Per Capita	46
Property Tax Revenue as a Percentage of 3-tax Revenues	46
Sales Taxes as a Percentage of Income	5
Sales Taxes Per Capita	5
Sales Tax Revenue as a Percentage of 3-tax Revenues	4
Sales Tax Rate	37
Income Taxes as a Percentage of Income	40
Income Taxes Per Capita	39
Income Tax Revenue as a Percentage of 3-tax Revenues	40
Highest Personal Income Rate	37
Corporate Income Taxes	45
Motor Fuel Taxes	26
Tobacco Taxes	28
Taxes on High Income Families	35
Taxes in the Largest City in Each State	38
Progressivity of Taxes	2

Revenues and Finances - Section G

Per Capita Total Revenue	31
Per Capita General Revenue	32
Own-source General Revenue	36
Per Capita Non-tax Revenue	16

Per Capita Total Spending	33
General Spending as a Percentage of Income	13
Per Capita General Spending	29
Change in General Expenditures	46
State Government General Revenue	31
State Government General Spending	30
State Government General Fund Spending	14
State and Local Debt	35
Debt as a Percentage of Revenue	29
Per Capita Full Faith and Credit Debt	32
Bond Ratings	6
State Solvency Index	41
Pension Plan Assets	35
State Reserves	23
Capital Outlays and Interest	37
State Budget Process Quality	6
Relative State Spending "Needs"	47
Structural Deficits	22

Education - Section H

Math Proficiency, Eighth Grade	38
Science Proficiency, Eighth Grade	35
AFQT Ranks	49
SAT Scores	n/a
ACT Scores	25
Over-25 Population with a High School Diploma	43
Students in Private Schools	3
High School Completion Rates	45
Pupil-Teacher Ratio	32
Public School Enrollment	29
Library Holdings Per Capita	34
Children with Disabilities	25
Education Spending Per Capita	43
Education Spending as a Percentage of Total Spending	41
Spending Per Pupil	41
Average Teacher Salary	46
Sources of School Funds	30
State Aid Per Pupil	36
Higher Education Spending Per Capita	35
Higher Education Spending as a Percentage of Total Spending	37
Public Higher Education Enrollment	26
Per Pupil Support of Higher Education	32
Tuition and Fees	37
Average Professor Salary	39
Education Employees	19
R and D Spending	46
Library Operating Spending	27

Health - Section I

Immunization Rates	50
Infant Mortality Rates	5
State Health Rankings	50
Population Without Health Insurance	3
Abortions	31
Alcohol Consumption	10
Percentage of Adult Smokers	15
Percentage Obese	8
AIDS Cases	7
Physicians Per 100,000 Population	15
Hospital Beds Per 1,000 Population	9
Medicaid Recipients	12
Medicaid Recipients as a Percentage of Poverty Population	42
Health and Hospital Spending	3
Health and Hospital Spending as a Percentage of Total Spending	3
Per Capita Medicaid Spending	20
Medicaid Spending Per Aged Recipient	43
Medicaid Spending Per Child	44
Medicare Payment Per Hospital Day	17
Hospital Expense Per Inpatient Day	46
Population in HMOs	34

Crime - Section J

Crime Rate	4
Violent Crime Rate	6
Murder Rate	1
Property Crime Rate	6
Motor Vehicle Theft Rate	11
Violent Crime Rate Change	36
Prisoners	10
Change in Prisoners	13
Incarceration Rate	1
Juvenile Violent Crime Rate	7
Law Enforcement Employees	4
Corrections Employees	5
State Corrections Spending	45
Increase in State Corrections Spending	16
Law Enforcement Spending	19
Law Enforcement Spending as a Percentage of Total Spending	12

Transportation - Section K

Travel on Interstates	22
Interstate Mileage in Unacceptable Condition	8
Deficient Bridges	12

Traffic Deaths	1
Seat Belt Use	30
Vehicle-miles Traveled Per Capita	38
Workers Using Public Transportation	19
Road and Street Miles	10
Highway Employees	20
Public Transit Employees	24
Highway Spending Per Capita	29
Highway Spending as a Percentage of Total Spending	30

Welfare - Section L

Percentage of Births to Unwed Mothers	2
TANF Recipients as a Percentage of Population	28
Food Stamp Recipients as a Percentage of Population	2
SSI Recipients as a Percentage of Population	4
Change in TANF/AFDC Recipients	5
Condition of Children Index	49
Percentage of Families with Single Parent	1
Average Monthly TANF Payments	40
Welfare as a Percentage of Poverty-level Income	41
State Supplements of SSI	46
State Income Tax Liability of Typical Family in Poverty	9
Child Support Collections	35
Child Support Collections Per Dollar of Administrative Costs	22
Children in Foster Care	42
Welfare Spending Per Capita	36
Welfare Spending as a Percentage of Total Spending	34
Administrative Costs Per TANF Case	43

Technology - Section M

Percentage of Households with Computers	48
Percentage of Households with Internet Access	47
Zip codes with Broadband Service	28
High-tech Jobs	48
Dot-com Domain Names	38
State Government Website Ratings	43
Students per Computer	1

Maine

Population - Section A

Population 2001	40
Population Change 2000-2001	22
Population Change 1990-2001	46
Population 2015	34
Population 2025	42
Percentage 65 and Over	7
Percentage 17 and Under	47
Median Age	3
Percentage African American	47
Percentage Hispanic	49
Percentage in Poverty	26
Child Poverty Rate	33
Percentage Female	16
Birth Rates	49
Death Rates	22
Population Density	38
New Legal Immigrants 2000	43

Economies - Section B

Personal Income 2001	41
Gross State Product	44
Per Capita Personal Income	35
Personal Income from Wages and Salaries	40
Average Annual Pay	39
Average Hourly Earnings	14
Value Added in Manufacturing	28
Cost of Living	n/a
Average Annual Pay in Manufacturing	38
Average Annual Pay in Retailing	36
Labor Force	13
Unemployment Rate	40
Employment Rate	11
Government Employment	24
Manufacturing Employment	28
Fortune 500 Companies	n/a
Forbes 500 Companies	36
Tourism Spending Per Capita	32
Exports Per Capita	35
Housing Permits	24
Percentage Change in Home Prices	8
Net Farm Income	45
Financial Institution Assets	36
Bankruptcy Filings	44
Patents Issued	43
WC Disability Payment	40
UC Average Weekly Benefit	35
Economic Momentum	10
One-year Employment Change	13
Manufacturing Employment Change	46
Home Ownership	3
Gambling	38

Electricity Use Per Residential Customer	50
Cost Per Kwh	50
New Companies	18

Geography - Section C

Total Land Area	39
Federally Owned Land	44
State Park Acreage	29
State Park Visitors	37
Population Not Active	32
Hunters with Firearms	30
Registered Boats	31
State Spending for the Arts	37
Energy Consumption Per Capita	40
Toxic Chemical Release Per Capita	38
Hazardous Waste Sites	31
Polluted Rivers and Streams	50
Expired Surface Water Pollution Permits	15
Air Pollution Emissions	44

Government - Section D

Members of United States House	39
State Legislators	10
Legislators Per Million Population	6
Units of Government	10
Legislators Compensation	39
Female Legislators	10
Turnover in Legislatures	4
Term Limits	6
Legislative Session Length	2
Republicans in State Legislatures	33
Governor's Power Rating	18
Number of Statewide Elected Officials	48
State and Local Government Employees	15
State and Local Average Salaries	35
Local Employment	22
Local Spending Accountability	9
Registered Voters	n/a
Percentage of Population Voting	4
Statewide Initiatives	n/a
Campaign Costs Per Vote	49

Federal Impacts - Section E

Per Capita Federal Spending	20
Increase in Federal Spending	49
Per Capita Federal Grant Spending	13
Per Capita Federal Spending on Procurement	28

Per Capita Federal Spending on Payments to Individuals	20
Per Capita Federal Spending on Social Security and Medicare	18
Social Security Benefits	44
Federal Spending on Employee Wages and Salaries	20
Federal Grant Spending Per Dollar of State Tax Revenue	18
General Revenue from Federal Government	17
Federal Tax Burden Per Capita	37
Federal Spending Per Dollar of Taxes Paid	15
Highway Charges Returned to States	34
Terms of Trade	12
Federal Personal Income Taxes	35
Federal Share of Medicaid	15

Taxes - Section F

Tax Revenue	2
Per Capita Tax Revenue	11
Tax Effort	7
Tax Capacity	41
Percentage Change in Taxes	6
Property Taxes as a Percentage of Income	2
Property Taxes Per Capita	7
Property Tax Revenue as a Percentage of 3-tax Revenues	10
Sales Taxes as a Percentage of Income	26
Sales Taxes Per Capita	32
Sales Tax Revenue as a Percentage of 3-tax Revenues	40
Sales Tax Rate	19
Income Taxes as a Percentage of Income	11
Income Taxes Per Capita	17
Income Tax Revenue as a Percentage of 3-tax Revenues	25
Highest Personal Income Rate	6
Corporate Income Taxes	18
Motor Fuel Taxes	17
Tobacco Taxes	10
Taxes on High Income Families	6
Taxes in the Largest City in Each State	9
Progressivity of Taxes	11

Revenues and Finances - Section G

Per Capita Total Revenue	21
Per Capita General Revenue	13
Own-source General Revenue	17
Per Capita Non-tax Revenue	36

Per Capita Total Spending	24
General Spending as a Percentage of Income	9
Per Capita General Spending	18
Change in General Expenditures	21
State Government General Revenue	13
State Government General Spending	17
State Government General Fund Spending	11
State and Local Debt	27
Debt as a Percentage of Revenue	26
Per Capita Full Faith and Credit Debt	28
Bond Ratings	3
State Solvency Index	43
Pension Plan Assets	13
State Reserves	35
Capital Outlays and Interest	47
State Budget Process Quality	31
Relative State Spending "Needs"	2
Structural Deficits	9

Education - Section H

Math Proficiency, Eighth Grade	3
Science Proficiency, Eighth Grade	6
AFQT Ranks	13
SAT Scores	15
ACT Scores	n/a
Over-25 Population with a High School Diploma	12
Students in Private Schools	30
High School Completion Rates	1
Pupil-Teacher Ratio	47
Public School Enrollment	36
Library Holdings Per Capita	3
Children with Disabilities	6
Education Spending Per Capita	35
Education Spending as a Percentage of Total Spending	42
Spending Per Pupil	9
Average Teacher Salary	39
Sources of School Funds	20
State Aid Per Pupil	22
Higher Education Spending Per Capita	45
Higher Education Spending as a Percentage of Total Spending	46
Public Higher Education Enrollment	44
Per Pupil Support of Higher Education	18
Tuition and Fees	12
Average Professor Salary	40
Education Employees	4
R and D Spending	16
Library Operating Spending	30

Health - Section I

Immunization Rates	12
Infant Mortality Rates	49
State Health Rankings	10
Population Without Health Insurance	33
Abortions	29
Alcohol Consumption	26
Percentage of Adult Smokers	19
Percentage Obese	37
AIDS Cases	39
Physicians Per 100,000 Population	13
Hospital Beds Per 1,000 Population	26
Medicaid Recipients	20
Medicaid Recipients as a Percentage of Poverty Population	6
Health and Hospital Spending	39
Health and Hospital Spending as a Percentage of Total Spending	42
Per Capita Medicaid Spending	2
Medicaid Spending Per Aged Recipient	24
Medicaid Spending Per Child	1
Medicare Payment Per Hospital Day	36
Hospital Expense Per Inpatient Day	20
Population in HMOs	22

Crime - Section J

Crime Rate	46
Violent Crime Rate	48
Murder Rate	46
Property Crime Rate	44
Motor Vehicle Theft Rate	48
Violent Crime Rate Change	13
Prisoners	48
Change in Prisoners	30
Incarceration Rate	50
Juvenile Violent Crime Rate	43
Law Enforcement Employees	36
Corrections Employees	48
State Corrections Spending	3
Increase in State Corrections Spending	17
Law Enforcement Spending	47
Law Enforcement Spending as a Percentage of Total Spending	48

Transportation - Section K

Travel on Interstates	42
Interstate Mileage in Unacceptable Condition	44
Deficient Bridges	10

Traffic Deaths	35
Seat Belt Use	n/a
Vehicle-miles Traveled Per Capita	15
Workers Using Public Transportation	39
Road and Street Miles	7
Highway Employees	4
Public Transit Employees	41
Highway Spending Per Capita	18
Highway Spending as a Percentage of Total Spending	24

Welfare - Section L

Percentage of Births to Unwed Mothers	29
TANF Recipients as a Percentage of Population	15
Food Stamp Recipients as a Percentage of Population	11
SSI Recipients as a Percentage of Population	17
Change in TANF/AFDC Recipients	27
Condition of Children Index	12
Percentage of Families with Single Parent	13
Average Monthly TANF Payments	7
Welfare as a Percentage of Poverty-level Income	8
State Supplements of SSI	45
State Income Tax Liability of Typical Family in Poverty	18
Child Support Collections	15
Child Support Collections Per Dollar of Administrative Costs	8
Children in Foster Care	4
Welfare Spending Per Capita	3
Welfare Spending as a Percentage of Total Spending	1
Administrative Costs Per TANF Case	46

Technology - Section M

Percentage of Households with Computers	10
Percentage of Households with Internet Access	16
Zip codes with Broadband Service	37
High-tech Jobs	33
Dot-com Domain Names	31
State Government Website Ratings	34
Students per Computer	27

Maryland

Population - Section A

Population 2001	19
Population Change 2000-2001	16
Population Change 1990-2001	23
Population 2015	23
Population 2025	18
Percentage 65 and Over	40
Percentage 17 and Under	22
Median Age	19
Percentage African American	5
Percentage Hispanic	27
Percentage in Poverty	47
Child Poverty Rate	49
Percentage Female	7
Birth Rates	21
Death Rates	17
Population Density	5
New Legal Immigrants 2000	11

Economies - Section B

Personal Income 2001	15
Gross State Product	18
Per Capita Personal Income	5
Personal Income from Wages and Salaries	41
Average Annual Pay	8
Average Hourly Earnings	8
Value Added in Manufacturing	44
Cost of Living	33
Average Annual Pay in Manufacturing	9
Average Annual Pay in Retailing	9
Labor Force	10
Unemployment Rate	41
Employment Rate	10
Government Employment	14
Manufacturing Employment	43
Fortune 500 Companies	28
Forbes 500 Companies	22
Tourism Spending Per Capita	33
Exports Per Capita	44
Housing Permits	21
Percentage Change in Home Prices	17
Net Farm Income	31
Financial Institution Assets	41
Bankruptcy Filings	11
Patents Issued	23
WC Disability Payment	12
UC Average Weekly Benefit	23
Economic Momentum	19
One-year Employment Change	45
Manufacturing Employment Change	28
Home Ownership	25
Gambling	19

Electricity Use Per Residential Customer	17
Cost Per Kwh	7
New Companies	16

Geography - Section C

Total Land Area	42
Federally Owned Land	45
State Park Acreage	13
State Park Visitors	35
Population Not Active	29
Hunters with Firearms	46
Registered Boats	26
State Spending for the Arts	8
Energy Consumption Per Capita	43
Toxic Chemical Release Per Capita	37
Hazardous Waste Sites	20
Polluted Rivers and Streams	27
Expired Surface Water Pollution Permits	23
Air Pollution Emissions	35

Government - Section D

Members of United States House	18
State Legislators	8
Legislators Per Million Population	25
Units of Government	47
Legislators Compensation	15
Female Legislators	7
Turnover in Legislatures	15
Term Limits	n/a
Legislative Session Length	29
Republicans in State Legislatures	44
Governor's Power Rating	12
Number of Statewide Elected Officials	40
State and Local Government Employees	41
State and Local Average Salaries	10
Local Employment	34
Local Spending Accountability	2
Registered Voters	39
Percentage of Population Voting	17
Statewide Initiatives	n/a
Campaign Costs Per Vote	28

Federal Impacts - Section E

Per Capita Federal Spending	5
Increase in Federal Spending	27
Per Capita Federal Grant Spending	14
Per Capita Federal Spending on Procurement	3

Per Capita Federal Spending on Payments to Individuals	15
Per Capita Federal Spending on Social Security and Medicare	36
Social Security Benefits	15
Federal Spending on Employee Wages and Salaries	4
Federal Grant Spending Per Dollar of State Tax Revenue	42
General Revenue from Federal Government	43
Federal Tax Burden Per Capita	8
Federal Spending Per Dollar of Taxes Paid	18
Highway Charges Returned to States	18
Terms of Trade	28
Federal Personal Income Taxes	10
Federal Share of Medicaid	39

Taxes - Section F

Tax Revenue	30
Per Capita Tax Revenue	9
Tax Effort	16
Tax Capacity	13
Percentage Change in Taxes	22
Property Taxes as a Percentage of Income	33
Property Taxes Per Capita	19
Property Tax Revenue as a Percentage of 3-tax Revenues	32
Sales Taxes as a Percentage of Income	44
Sales Taxes Per Capita	39
Sales Tax Revenue as a Percentage of 3-tax Revenues	43
Sales Tax Rate	19
Income Taxes as a Percentage of Income	3
Income Taxes Per Capita	3
Income Tax Revenue as a Percentage of 3-tax Revenues	3
Highest Personal Income Rate	33
Corporate Income Taxes	29
Motor Fuel Taxes	13
Tobacco Taxes	10
Taxes on High Income Families	13
Taxes in the Largest City in Each State	8
Progressivity of Taxes	7

Revenues and Finances - Section G

Per Capita Total Revenue	26
Per Capita General Revenue	19
Own-source General Revenue	14
Per Capita Non-tax Revenue	40

Per Capita Total Spending 28
General Spending as a Percentage of
   Income 48
Per Capita General Spending 24
Change in General Expenditures 33
State Government General Revenue 27
State Government General Spending 31
State Government General Fund
   Spending 37
State and Local Debt 29
Debt as a Percentage of Revenue 24
Per Capita Full Faith and Credit Debt 13
Bond Ratings 1
State Solvency Index 35
Pension Plan Assets 8
State Reserves 9
Capital Outlays and Interest 27
State Budget Process Quality 11
Relative State Spending "Needs" 18
Structural Deficits 39

Education · Section H

Math Proficiency, Eighth Grade 19
Science Proficiency, Eighth Grade 22
AFQT Ranks 38
SAT Scores 8
ACT Scores n/a
Over-25 Population with a High
   School Diploma 27
Students in Private Schools 5
High School Completion Rates 26
Pupil-Teacher Ratio 16
Public School Enrollment 35
Library Holdings Per Capita 23
Children with Disabilities 29
Education Spending Per Capita 16
Education Spending as a Percentage
   of Total Spending 16
Spending Per Pupil 18
Average Teacher Salary 12
Sources of School Funds 5
State Aid Per Pupil 43
Higher Education Spending Per
   Capita 20
Higher Education Spending as a
   Percentage of Total Spending 21
Public Higher Education Enrollment 22
Per Pupil Support of Higher
   Education 20
Tuition and Fees 6
Average Professor Salary 3
Education Employees 39
R and D Spending 1
Library Operating Spending 10

Health · Section I

Immunization Rates 26
Infant Mortality Rates 16
State Health Rankings 28
Population Without Health
   Insurance 28
Abortions 37
Alcohol Consumption 34
Percentage of Adult Smokers 41
Percentage Obese 29
AIDS Cases 2
Physicians Per 100,000 Population 2
Hospital Beds Per 1,000 Population 45
Medicaid Recipients 29
Medicaid Recipients as a Percentage
   of Poverty Population 10
Health and Hospital Spending 46
Health and Hospital Spending as a
   Percentage of Total Spending 45
Per Capita Medicaid Spending 11
Medicaid Spending Per Aged
   Recipient 13
Medicaid Spending Per Child 4
Medicare Payment Per Hospital Day 50
Hospital Expense Per Inpatient Day 26
Population in HMOs 5

Crime · Section J

Crime Rate 11
Violent Crime Rate 2
Murder Rate 5
Property Crime Rate 14
Motor Vehicle Theft Rate 4
Violent Crime Rate Change 24
Prisoners 17
Change in Prisoners 42
Incarceration Rate 18
Juvenile Violent Crime Rate 4
Law Enforcement Employees 14
Corrections Employees 11
State Corrections Spending 20
Increase in State Corrections
   Spending 29
Law Enforcement Spending 9
Law Enforcement Spending as a
   Percentage of Total Spending 6

Transportation · Section K

Travel on Interstates 5
Interstate Mileage in Unacceptable
   Condition 13
Deficient Bridges 20

Traffic Deaths 38
Seat Belt Use 4
Vehicle-miles Traveled Per Capita 34
Workers Using Public
   Transportation 5
Road and Street Miles 20
Highway Employees 38
Public Transit Employees 14
Highway Spending Per Capita 47
Highway Spending as a Percentage
   of Total Spending 45

Welfare · Section L

Percentage of Births to Unwed
   Mothers 17
TANF Recipients as a Percentage
   of Population 31
Food Stamp Recipients as a
   Percentage of Population 44
SSI Recipients as a Percentage of
   Population 31
Change in TANF/AFDC Recipients 9
Condition of Children Index 21
Percentage of Families with Single
   Parent 13
Average Monthly TANF
   Payments 16
Welfare as a Percentage of Poverty-
   level Income 34
State Supplements of SSI 11
State Income Tax Liability of Typical
   Family in Poverty 35
Child Support Collections 16
Child Support Collections Per Dollar
   of Administrative Costs 25
Children in Foster Care 8
Welfare Spending Per Capita 29
Welfare Spending as a Percentage of
   Total Spending 28
Administrative Costs Per TANF Case 32

Technology · Section M

Percentage of Households with
   Computers 8
Percentage of Households with
   Internet Access 6
Zip codes with Broadband
   Service 16
High-tech Jobs 11
Dot-com Domain Names 8
State Government Website
   Ratings 27
Students per Computer 7

Massachusetts

Population - Section A

Population 2001	13
Population Change 2000-2001	35
Population Change 1990-2001	40
Population 2015	41
Population 2025	14
Percentage 65 and Over	12
Percentage 17 and Under	48
Median Age	12
Percentage African American	28
Percentage Hispanic	19
Percentage in Poverty	35
Child Poverty Rate	36
Percentage Female	2
Birth Rates	39
Death Rates	37
Population Density	3
New Legal Immigrants 2000	7

Economies - Section B

Personal Income 2001	10
Gross State Product	3
Per Capita Personal Income	2
Personal Income from Wages and Salaries	2
Average Annual Pay	3
Average Hourly Earnings	17
Value Added in Manufacturing	20
Cost of Living	3
Average Annual Pay in Manufacturing	2
Average Annual Pay in Retailing	5
Labor Force	14
Unemployment Rate	23
Employment Rate	28
Government Employment	48
Manufacturing Employment	29
Fortune 500 Companies	15
Forbes 500 Companies	4
Tourism Spending Per Capita	12
Exports Per Capita	8
Housing Permits	47
Percentage Change in Home Prices	1
Net Farm Income	47
Financial Institution Assets	11
Bankruptcy Filings	49
Patents Issued	3
WC Disability Payment	4
UC Average Weekly Benefit	1
Economic Momentum	50
One-year Employment Change	43
Manufacturing Employment Change	31
Home Ownership	46
Gambling	12

Electricity Use Per Residential Customer	44
Cost Per Kwh	47
New Companies	30

Geography - Section C

Total Land Area	45
Federally Owned Land	47
State Park Acreage	9
State Park Visitors	32
Population Not Active	35
Hunters with Firearms	43
Registered Boats	29
State Spending for the Arts	3
Energy Consumption Per Capita	49
Toxic Chemical Release Per Capita	47
Hazardous Waste Sites	12
Polluted Rivers and Streams	10
Expired Surface Water Pollution Permits	17
Air Pollution Emissions	31

Government - Section D

Members of United States House	13
State Legislators	6
Legislators Per Million Population	29
Units of Government	41
Legislators Compensation	7
Female Legislators	18
Turnover in Legislatures	43
Term Limits	n/a
Legislative Session Length	n/a
Republicans in State Legislatures	49
Governor's Power Rating	18
Number of Statewide Elected Officials	21
State and Local Government Employees	40
State and Local Average Salaries	9
Local Employment	19
Local Spending Accountability	31
Registered Voters	16
Percentage of Population Voting	11
Statewide Initiatives	9
Campaign Costs Per Vote	13

Federal Impacts - Section E

Per Capita Federal Spending	14
Increase in Federal Spending	41
Per Capita Federal Grant Spending	10
Per Capita Federal Spending on Procurement	9

Per Capita Federal Spending on Payments to Individuals	17
Per Capita Federal Spending on Social Security and Medicare	4
Social Security Benefits	17
Federal Spending on Employee Wages and Salaries	35
Federal Grant Spending Per Dollar of State Tax Revenue	47
General Revenue from Federal Government	38
Federal Tax Burden Per Capita	3
Federal Spending Per Dollar of Taxes Paid	41
Highway Charges Returned to States	36
Terms of Trade	34
Federal Personal Income Taxes	2
Federal Share of Medicaid	39

Taxes - Section F

Tax Revenue	27
Per Capita Tax Revenue	4
Tax Effort	9
Tax Capacity	8
Percentage Change in Taxes	18
Property Taxes as a Percentage of Income	17
Property Taxes Per Capita	9
Property Tax Revenue as a Percentage of 3-tax Revenues	20
Sales Taxes as a Percentage of Income	45
Sales Taxes Per Capita	44
Sales Tax Revenue as a Percentage of 3-tax Revenues	46
Sales Tax Rate	19
Income Taxes as a Percentage of Income	5
Income Taxes Per Capita	2
Income Tax Revenue as a Percentage of 3-tax Revenues	4
Highest Personal Income Rate	26
Corporate Income Taxes	6
Motor Fuel Taxes	23
Tobacco Taxes	1
Taxes on High Income Families	32
Taxes in the Largest City in Each State	21
Progressivity of Taxes	19

Revenues and Finances - Section G

Per Capita Total Revenue	12
Per Capita General Revenue	11
Own-source General Revenue	8
Per Capita Non-tax Revenue	32

Per Capita Total Spending	8
General Spending as a Percentage of Income	44
Per Capita General Spending	8
Change in General Expenditures	38
State Government General Revenue	10
State Government General Spending	10
State Government General Fund Spending	29
State and Local Debt	3
Debt as a Percentage of Revenue	1
Per Capita Full Faith and Credit Debt	4
Bond Ratings	3
State Solvency Index	49
Pension Plan Assets	17
State Reserves	14
Capital Outlays and Interest	4
State Budget Process Quality	7
Relative State Spending "Needs"	14
Structural Deficits	11

Education - Section H

Math Proficiency, Eighth Grade	5
Science Proficiency, Eighth Grade	2
AFQT Ranks	21
SAT Scores	6
ACT Scores	n/a
Over-25 Population with a High School Diploma	31
Students in Private Schools	14
High School Completion Rates	12
Pupil-Teacher Ratio	8
Public School Enrollment	44
Library Holdings Per Capita	3
Children with Disabilities	3
Education Spending Per Capita	30
Education Spending as a Percentage of Total Spending	47
Spending Per Pupil	4
Average Teacher Salary	10
Sources of School Funds	16
State Aid Per Pupil	16
Higher Education Spending Per Capita	47
Higher Education Spending as a Percentage of Total Spending	48
Public Higher Education Enrollment	49
Per Pupil Support of Higher Education	24
Tuition and Fees	16
Average Professor Salary	8
Education Employees	27
R and D Spending	4
Library Operating Spending	12

Health - Section I

Immunization Rates	15
Infant Mortality Rates	50
State Health Rankings	3
Population Without Health Insurance	46
Abortions	5
Alcohol Consumption	12
Percentage of Adult Smokers	48
Percentage Obese	49
AIDS Cases	15
Physicians Per 100,000 Population	1
Hospital Beds Per 1,000 Population	34
Medicaid Recipients	14
Medicaid Recipients as a Percentage of Poverty Population	20
Health and Hospital Spending	32
Health and Hospital Spending as a Percentage of Total Spending	37
Per Capita Medicaid Spending	4
Medicaid Spending Per Aged Recipient	8
Medicaid Spending Per Child	17
Medicare Payment Per Hospital Day	29
Hospital Expense Per Inpatient Day	3
Population in HMOs	2

Crime - Section J

Crime Rate	41
Violent Crime Rate	20
Murder Rate	41
Property Crime Rate	43
Motor Vehicle Theft Rate	17
Violent Crime Rate Change	35
Prisoners	30
Change in Prisoners	49
Incarceration Rate	41
Juvenile Violent Crime Rate	6
Law Enforcement Employees	3
Corrections Employees	46
State Corrections Spending	1
Increase in State Corrections Spending	9
Law Enforcement Spending	20
Law Enforcement Spending as a Percentage of Total Spending	31

Transportation - Section K

Travel on Interstates	6
Interstate Mileage in Unacceptable Condition	24
Deficient Bridges	3

Traffic Deaths	50
Seat Belt Use	45
Vehicle-miles Traveled Per Capita	44
Workers Using Public Transportation	3
Road and Street Miles	47
Highway Employees	39
Public Transit Employees	7
Highway Spending Per Capita	13
Highway Spending as a Percentage of Total Spending	21

Welfare - Section L

Percentage of Births to Unwed Mothers	45
TANF Recipients as a Percentage of Population	22
Food Stamp Recipients as a Percentage of Population	48
SSI Recipients as a Percentage of Population	12
Change in TANF/AFDC Recipients	22
Condition of Children Index	6
Percentage of Families with Single Parent	13
Average Monthly TANF Payments	14
Welfare as a Percentage of Poverty-level Income	20
State Supplements of SSI	22
State Income Tax Liability of Typical Family in Poverty	37
Child Support Collections	28
Child Support Collections Per Dollar of Administrative Costs	14
Children in Foster Care	19
Welfare Spending Per Capita	9
Welfare Spending as a Percentage of Total Spending	14
Administrative Costs Per TANF Case	30

Technology - Section M

Percentage of Households with Computers	17
Percentage of Households with Internet Access	13
Zip codes with Broadband Service	2
High-tech Jobs	2
Dot-com Domain Names	3
State Government Website Ratings	23
Students per Computer	14

Michigan

Population - Section A

Population 2001	8
Population Change 2000-2001	33
Population Change 1990-2001	39
Population 2015	50
Population 2025	8
Percentage 65 and Over	30
Percentage 17 and Under	16
Median Age	29
Percentage African American	15
Percentage Hispanic	31
Percentage in Poverty	33
Child Poverty Rate	29
Percentage Female	24
Birth Rates	36
Death Rates	21
Population Density	15
New Legal Immigrants 2000	12

Economies - Section B

Personal Income 2001	9
Gross State Product	26
Per Capita Personal Income	18
Personal Income from Wages and Salaries	12
Average Annual Pay	11
Average Hourly Earnings	1
Value Added in Manufacturing	7
Cost of Living	19
Average Annual Pay in Manufacturing	5
Average Annual Pay in Retailing	22
Labor Force	24
Unemployment Rate	12
Employment Rate	39
Government Employment	35
Manufacturing Employment	3
Fortune 500 Companies	11
Forbes 500 Companies	19
Tourism Spending Per Capita	45
Exports Per Capita	6
Housing Permits	25
Percentage Change in Home Prices	13
Net Farm Income	39
Financial Institution Assets	24
Bankruptcy Filings	26
Patents Issued	11
WC Disability Payment	18
UC Average Weekly Benefit	13
Economic Momentum	45
One-year Employment Change	34
Manufacturing Employment Change	15
Home Ownership	4
Gambling	9

Electricity Use Per Residential

Customer	41
Cost Per Kwh	31
New Companies	41

Geography - Section C

Total Land Area	22
Federally Owned Land	16
State Park Acreage	8
State Park Visitors	25
Population Not Active	31
Hunters with Firearms	15
Registered Boats	1
State Spending for the Arts	5
Energy Consumption Per Capita	37
Toxic Chemical Release Per Capita	30
Hazardous Waste Sites	5
Polluted Rivers and Streams	41
Expired Surface Water Pollution Permits	25
Air Pollution Emissions	9

Government - Section D

Members of United States House	8
State Legislators	23
Legislators Per Million Population	43
Units of Government	31
Legislators Compensation	3
Female Legislators	26
Turnover in Legislatures	1
Term Limits	15
Legislative Session Length	n/a
Republicans in State Legislatures	17
Governor's Power Rating	18
Number of Statewide Elected Officials	40
State and Local Government Employees	45
State and Local Average Salaries	11
Local Employment	17
Local Spending Accountability	48
Registered Voters	3
Percentage of Population Voting	16
Statewide Initiatives	6
Campaign Costs Per Vote	38

Federal Impacts - Section E

Per Capita Federal Spending	45
Increase in Federal Spending	26
Per Capita Federal Grant Spending	33
Per Capita Federal Spending on Procurement	41

Per Capita Federal Spending on

Payments to Individuals	32
Per Capita Federal Spending on Social Security and Medicare	12
Social Security Benefits	3
Federal Spending on Employee Wages and Salaries	49
Federal Grant Spending Per Dollar of State Tax Revenue	38
General Revenue from Federal Government	33
Federal Tax Burden Per Capita	16
Federal Spending Per Dollar of Taxes Paid	38
Highway Charges Returned to States	41
Terms of Trade	36
Federal Personal Income Taxes	20
Federal Share of Medicaid	34

Taxes - Section F

Tax Revenue	17
Per Capita Tax Revenue	16
Tax Effort	16
Tax Capacity	23
Percentage Change in Taxes	16
Property Taxes as a Percentage of Income	20
Property Taxes Per Capita	14
Property Tax Revenue as a Percentage of 3-tax Revenues	19
Sales Taxes as a Percentage of Income	35
Sales Taxes Per Capita	27
Sales Tax Revenue as a Percentage of 3-tax Revenues	32
Sales Tax Rate	9
Income Taxes as a Percentage of Income	22
Income Taxes Per Capita	19
Income Tax Revenue as a Percentage of 3-tax Revenues	22
Highest Personal Income Rate	36
Corporate Income Taxes	5
Motor Fuel Taxes	32
Tobacco Taxes	7
Taxes on High Income Families	10
Taxes in the Largest City in Each State	6
Progressivity of Taxes	35

Revenues and Finances - Section G

Per Capita Total Revenue	15
Per Capita General Revenue	16
Own-source General Revenue	13
Per Capita Non-tax Revenue	12

Per Capita Total Spending	16
General Spending as a Percentage of Income	25
Per Capita General Spending	17
Change in General Expenditures	26
State Government General Revenue	15
State Government General Spending	13
State Government General Fund Spending	22
State and Local Debt	23
Debt as a Percentage of Revenue	27
Per Capita Full Faith and Credit Debt	21
Bond Ratings	1
State Solvency Index	19
Pension Plan Assets	7
State Reserves	21
Capital Outlays and Interest	31
State Budget Process Quality	2
Relative State Spending "Needs"	33
Structural Deficits	6

Education - Section H

Math Proficiency, Eighth Grade	14
Science Proficiency, Eighth Grade	11
AFQT Ranks	25
SAT Scores	n/a
ACT Scores	12
Over-25 Population with a High School Diploma	23
Students in Private Schools	22
High School Completion Rates	21
Pupil-Teacher Ratio	10
Public School Enrollment	12
Library Holdings Per Capita	25
Children with Disabilities	37
Education Spending Per Capita	3
Education Spending as a Percentage of Total Spending	2
Spending Per Pupil	20
Average Teacher Salary	4
Sources of School Funds	48
State Aid Per Pupil	5
Higher Education Spending Per Capita	6
Higher Education Spending as a Percentage of Total Spending	9
Public Higher Education Enrollment	10
Per Pupil Support of Higher Education	39
Tuition and Fees	9
Average Professor Salary	1
Education Employees	36
R and D Spending	37
Library Operating Spending	19

Health - Section I

Immunization Rates	43
Infant Mortality Rates	12
State Health Rankings	29
Population Without Health Insurance	35
Abortions	26
Alcohol Consumption	34
Percentage of Adult Smokers	11
Percentage Obese	3
AIDS Cases	33
Physicians Per 100,000 Population	10
Hospital Beds Per 1,000 Population	33
Medicaid Recipients	25
Medicaid Recipients as a Percentage of Poverty Population	29
Health and Hospital Spending	21
Health and Hospital Spending as a Percentage of Total Spending	24
Per Capita Medicaid Spending	34
Medicaid Spending Per Aged Recipient	30
Medicaid Spending Per Child	49
Medicare Payment Per Hospital Day	27
Hospital Expense Per Inpatient Day	13
Population in HMOs	21

Crime - Section J

Crime Rate	27
Violent Crime Rate	13
Murder Rate	11
Property Crime Rate	26
Motor Vehicle Theft Rate	8
Violent Crime Rate Change	17
Prisoners	5
Change in Prisoners	35
Incarceration Rate	11
Juvenile Violent Crime Rate	39
Law Enforcement Employees	37
Corrections Employees	19
State Corrections Spending	11
Increase in State Corrections Spending	12
Law Enforcement Spending	16
Law Enforcement Spending as a Percentage of Total Spending	22

Transportation - Section K

Travel on Interstates	36
Interstate Mileage in Unacceptable Condition	6
Deficient Bridges	14

Traffic Deaths	33
Seat Belt Use	8
Vehicle-miles Traveled Per Capita	30
Workers Using Public Transportation	32
Road and Street Miles	48
Highway Employees	49
Public Transit Employees	19
Highway Spending Per Capita	44
Highway Spending as a Percentage of Total Spending	43

Welfare - Section L

Percentage of Births to Unwed Mothers	20
TANF Recipients as a Percentage of Population	13
Food Stamp Recipients as a Percentage of Population	20
SSI Recipients as a Percentage of Population	20
Change in TANF/AFDC Recipients	19
Condition of Children Index	29
Percentage of Families with Single Parent	13
Average Monthly TANF Payments	20
Welfare as a Percentage of Poverty-level Income	19
State Supplements of SSI	39
State Income Tax Liability of Typical Family in Poverty	7
Child Support Collections	1
Child Support Collections Per Dollar of Administrative Costs	17
Children in Foster Care	20
Welfare Spending Per Capita	24
Welfare Spending as a Percentage of Total Spending	23
Administrative Costs Per TANF Case	20

Technology - Section M

Percentage of Households with Computers	22
Percentage of Households with Internet Access	23
Zip codes with Broadband Service	12
High-tech Jobs	36
Dot-com Domain Names	30
State Government Website Ratings	19
Students per Computer	15

Minnesota

Population · Section A

Population 2001	21
Population Change 2000-2001	19
Population Change 1990-2001	20
Population 2015	32
Population 2025	21
Percentage 65 and Over	34
Percentage 17 and Under	14
Median Age	31
Percentage African American	34
Percentage Hispanic	34
Percentage in Poverty	44
Child Poverty Rate	45
Percentage Female	35
Birth Rates	29
Death Rates	48
Population Density	31
New Legal Immigrants 2000	18

Economies · Section B

Personal Income 2001	17
Gross State Product	12
Per Capita Personal Income	8
Personal Income from Wages and Salaries	4
Average Annual Pay	13
Average Hourly Earnings	19
Value Added in Manufacturing	9
Cost of Living	11
Average Annual Pay in Manufacturing	17
Average Annual Pay in Retailing	27
Labor Force	1
Unemployment Rate	42
Employment Rate	9
Government Employment	36
Manufacturing Employment	14
Fortune 500 Companies	3
Forbes 500 Companies	3
Tourism Spending Per Capita	31
Exports Per Capita	20
Housing Permits	13
Percentage Change in Home Prices	4
Net Farm Income	26
Financial Institution Assets	17
Bankruptcy Filings	39
Patents Issued	6
WC Disability Payment	10
UC Average Weekly Benefit	4
Economic Momentum	36
One-year Employment Change	28
Manufacturing Employment Change	24
Home Ownership	2
Gambling	27

Electricity Use Per Residential Customer	33
Cost Per Kwh	24
New Companies	42

Geography · Section C

Total Land Area	14
Federally Owned Land	15
State Park Acreage	14
State Park Visitors	39
Population Not Active	48
Hunters with Firearms	13
Registered Boats	4
State Spending for the Arts	7
Energy Consumption Per Capita	28
Toxic Chemical Release Per Capita	40
Hazardous Waste Sites	17
Polluted Rivers and Streams	8
Expired Surface Water Pollution Permits	4
Air Pollution Emissions	17

Government · Section D

Members of United States House	18
State Legislators	5
Legislators Per Million Population	23
Units of Government	9
Legislators Compensation	16
Female Legislators	11
Turnover in Legislatures	13
Term Limits	n/a
Legislative Session Length	13
Republicans in State Legislatures	18
Governor's Power Rating	12
Number of Statewide Elected Officials	40
State and Local Government Employees	22
State and Local Average Salaries	12
Local Employment	13
Local Spending Accountability	43
Registered Voters	13
Percentage of Population Voting	1
Statewide Initiatives	n/a
Campaign Costs Per Vote	39

Federal Impacts · Section E

Per Capita Federal Spending	46
Increase in Federal Spending	24
Per Capita Federal Grant Spending	35
Per Capita Federal Spending on Procurement	36

Per Capita Federal Spending on Payments to Individuals	41
Per Capita Federal Spending on Social Security and Medicare	41
Social Security Benefits	25
Federal Spending on Employee Wages and Salaries	46
Federal Grant Spending Per Dollar of State Tax Revenue	49
General Revenue from Federal Government	47
Federal Tax Burden Per Capita	11
Federal Spending Per Dollar of Taxes Paid	45
Highway Charges Returned to States	30
Terms of Trade	41
Federal Personal Income Taxes	14
Federal Share of Medicaid	39

Taxes · Section F

Tax Revenue	7
Per Capita Tax Revenue	5
Tax Effort	7
Tax Capacity	14
Percentage Change in Taxes	21
Property Taxes as a Percentage of Income	26
Property Taxes Per Capita	17
Property Tax Revenue as a Percentage of 3-tax Revenues	34
Sales Taxes as a Percentage of Income	22
Sales Taxes Per Capita	10
Sales Tax Revenue as a Percentage of 3-tax Revenues	30
Sales Tax Rate	4
Income Taxes as a Percentage of Income	7
Income Taxes Per Capita	7
Income Tax Revenue as a Percentage of 3-tax Revenues	12
Highest Personal Income Rate	9
Corporate Income Taxes	9
Motor Fuel Taxes	26
Tobacco Taxes	25
Taxes on High Income Families	9
Taxes in the Largest City in Each State	7
Progressivity of Taxes	16

Revenues and Finances · Section G

Per Capita Total Revenue	8
Per Capita General Revenue	6
Own-source General Revenue	6
Per Capita Non-tax Revenue	5

Per Capita Total Spending	4	**Health - Section I**		
General Spending as a Percentage of				
Income	18	Immunization Rates	18	
Per Capita General Spending	4	Infant Mortality Rates	43	
Change in General Expenditures	27	State Health Rankings	2	
State Government General Revenue	11	Population Without Health		
State Government General Spending	8	Insurance	48	
State Government General Fund		Abortions	23	
Spending	24	Alcohol Consumption	15	
State and Local Debt	14	Percentage of Adult Smokers	34	
Debt as a Percentage of Revenue	22	Percentage Obese	33	
Per Capita Full Faith and Credit Debt	8	AIDS Cases	43	
Bond Ratings	1	Physicians Per 100,000 Population	18	
State Solvency Index	18	Hospital Beds Per 1,000 Population	18	
Pension Plan Assets	32	Medicaid Recipients	37	
State Reserves	11	Medicaid Recipients as a Percentage		
Capital Outlays and Interest	10	of Poverty Population	5	
State Budget Process Quality	5	Health and Hospital Spending	28	
Relative State Spending "Needs"	16	Health and Hospital Spending as a		
Structural Deficits	9	Percentage of Total Spending	40	
		Per Capita Medicaid Spending	13	

Education - Section H

Math Proficiency, Eighth Grade	1	Medicaid Spending Per Aged
Science Proficiency, Eighth Grade	6	Recipient	5
AFQT Ranks	3	Medicaid Spending Per Child	8
SAT Scores	n/a	Medicare Payment Per Hospital Day	13
ACT Scores	2	Hospital Expense Per Inpatient Day	19
Over-25 Population with a High		Population in HMOs	19
School Diploma	3		
Students in Private Schools	20	**Crime - Section J**	
High School Completion Rates	6		
Pupil-Teacher Ratio	30	Crime Rate	33
Public School Enrollment	14	Violent Crime Rate	39
Library Holdings Per Capita	21	Murder Rate	39
Children with Disabilities	35	Property Crime Rate	32
Education Spending Per Capita	9	Motor Vehicle Theft Rate	30
Education Spending as a Percentage		Violent Crime Rate Change	31
of Total Spending	39	Prisoners	35
Spending Per Pupil	12	Change in Prisoners	16
Average Teacher Salary	19	Incarceration Rate	49
Sources of School Funds	31	Juvenile Violent Crime Rate	18
State Aid Per Pupil	7	Law Enforcement Employees	48
Higher Education Spending Per		Corrections Employees	44
Capita	23	State Corrections Spending	2
Higher Education Spending as a		Increase in State Corrections	
Percentage of Total Spending	38	Spending	31
Public Higher Education Enrollment	18	Law Enforcement Spending	33
Per Pupil Support of Higher		Law Enforcement Spending as a	
Education	9	Percentage of Total Spending	44
Tuition and Fees	15		
Average Professor Salary	12	**Transportation - Section K**	
Education Employees	14		
R and D Spending	21	Travel on Interstates	28
Library Operating Spending	14	Interstate Mileage in Unacceptable	
		Condition	39
		Deficient Bridges	49

Traffic Deaths	46
Seat Belt Use	20
Vehicle-miles Traveled Per Capita	21
Workers Using Public	
Transportation	15
Road and Street Miles	42
Highway Employees	18
Public Transit Employees	16
Highway Spending Per Capita	16
Highway Spending as a Percentage	
of Total Spending	27

Welfare - Section L

Percentage of Births to Unwed	
Mothers	46
TANF Recipients as a Percentage	
of Population	17
Food Stamp Recipients as a	
Percentage of Population	43
SSI Recipients as a Percentage of	
Population	43
Change in TANF/AFDC Recipients	47
Condition of Children Index	1
Percentage of Families with Single	
Parent	48
Average Monthly TANF	
Payments	15
Welfare as a Percentage of Poverty-	
level Income	5
State Supplements of SSI	14
State Income Tax Liability of Typical	
Family in Poverty	40
Child Support Collections	6
Child Support Collections Per Dollar	
of Administrative Costs	29
Children in Foster Care	28
Welfare Spending Per Capita	4
Welfare Spending as a Percentage of	
Total Spending	10
Administrative Costs Per TANF Case	29

Technology - Section M

Percentage of Households with	
Computers	7
Percentage of Households with	
Internet Access	8
Zip codes with Broadband	
Service	37
High-tech Jobs	10
Dot-com Domain Names	22
State Government Website	
Ratings	37
Students per Computer	42

Mississippi

Population - Section A

Population 2001	31
Population Change 2000-2001	36
Population Change 1990-2001	24
Population 2015	33
Population 2025	30
Percentage 65 and Over	32
Percentage 17 and Under	8
Median Age	44
Percentage African American	1
Percentage Hispanic	46
Percentage in Poverty	1
Child Poverty Rate	3
Percentage Female	6
Birth Rates	12
Death Rates	1
Population Density	32
New Legal Immigrants 2000	44

Economies - Section B

Personal Income 2001	33
Gross State Product	49
Per Capita Personal Income	50
Personal Income from Wages and Salaries	46
Average Annual Pay	47
Average Hourly Earnings	47
Value Added in Manufacturing	33
Cost of Living	37
Average Annual Pay in Manufacturing	50
Average Annual Pay in Retailing	48
Labor Force	48
Unemployment Rate	11
Employment Rate	40
Government Employment	5
Manufacturing Employment	5
Fortune 500 Companies	38
Forbes 500 Companies	39
Tourism Spending Per Capita	27
Exports Per Capita	38
Housing Permits	42
Percentage Change in Home Prices	39
Net Farm Income	14
Financial Institution Assets	35
Bankruptcy Filings	8
Patents Issued	50
WC Disability Payment	50
UC Average Weekly Benefit	50
Economic Momentum	15
One-year Employment Change	17
Manufacturing Employment Change	8
Home Ownership	6
Gambling	4

Electricity

Electricity Use Per Residential Customer	3
Cost Per Kwh	29
New Companies	36

Geography - Section C

Total Land Area	31
Federally Owned Land	26
State Park Acreage	47
State Park Visitors	41
Population Not Active	3
Hunters with Firearms	7
Registered Boats	16
State Spending for the Arts	31
Energy Consumption Per Capita	20
Toxic Chemical Release Per Capita	15
Hazardous Waste Sites	45
Polluted Rivers and Streams	6
Expired Surface Water Pollution Permits	34
Air Pollution Emissions	27

Government - Section D

Members of United States House	31
State Legislators	14
Legislators Per Million Population	16
Units of Government	26
Legislators Compensation	38
Female Legislators	46
Turnover in Legislatures	n/a
Term Limits	n/a
Legislative Session Length	29
Republicans in State Legislatures	45
Governor's Power Rating	34
Number of Statewide Elected Officials	9
State and Local Government Employees	3
State and Local Average Salaries	50
Local Employment	24
Local Spending Accountability	42
Registered Voters	n/a
Percentage of Population Voting	48
Statewide Initiatives	n/a
Campaign Costs Per Vote	11

Federal Impacts - Section E

Per Capita Federal Spending	11
Increase in Federal Spending	20
Per Capita Federal Grant Spending	12
Per Capita Federal Spending on Procurement	22

Federal (continued)

Per Capita Federal Spending on Payments to Individuals	4
Per Capita Federal Spending on Social Security and Medicare	15
Social Security Benefits	50
Federal Spending on Employee Wages and Salaries	24
Federal Grant Spending Per Dollar of State Tax Revenue	10
General Revenue from Federal Government	4
Federal Tax Burden Per Capita	50
Federal Spending Per Dollar of Taxes Paid	3
Highway Charges Returned to States	16
Terms of Trade	6
Federal Personal Income Taxes	49
Federal Share of Medicaid	1

Taxes - Section F

Tax Revenue	25
Per Capita Tax Revenue	48
Tax Effort	12
Tax Capacity	50
Percentage Change in Taxes	23
Property Taxes as a Percentage of Income	38
Property Taxes Per Capita	40
Property Tax Revenue as a Percentage of 3-tax Revenues	39
Sales Taxes as a Percentage of Income	6
Sales Taxes Per Capita	18
Sales Tax Revenue as a Percentage of 3-tax Revenues	10
Sales Tax Rate	1
Income Taxes as a Percentage of Income	39
Income Taxes Per Capita	40
Income Tax Revenue as a Percentage of 3-tax Revenues	39
Highest Personal Income Rate	32
Corporate Income Taxes	30
Motor Fuel Taxes	34
Tobacco Taxes	40
Taxes on High Income Families	28
Taxes in the Largest City in Each State	35
Progressivity of Taxes	9

Revenues and Finances - Section G

Per Capita Total Revenue	39
Per Capita General Revenue	39
Own-source General Revenue	47
Per Capita Non-tax Revenue	23

Per Capita Total Spending 36
General Spending as a Percentage of
   Income 5
Per Capita General Spending 34
Change in General Expenditures 4
State Government General Revenue 28
State Government General Spending 24
State Government General Fund
   Spending 9
State and Local Debt 47
Debt as a Percentage of Revenue 47
Per Capita Full Faith and Credit Debt 23
Bond Ratings 4
State Solvency Index 38
Pension Plan Assets 44
State Reserves 24
Capital Outlays and Interest 39
State Budget Process Quality 37
Relative State Spending "Needs" 48
Structural Deficits 19

Education - Section H

Math Proficiency, Eighth Grade 39
Science Proficiency, Eighth Grade 36
AFQT Ranks 50
SAT Scores n/a
ACT Scores 26
Over-25 Population with a High
   School Diploma 44
Students in Private Schools 25
High School Completion Rates 43
Pupil-Teacher Ratio 18
Public School Enrollment 15
Library Holdings Per Capita 41
Children with Disabilities 36
Education Spending Per Capita 37
Education Spending as a Percentage
   of Total Spending 31
Spending Per Pupil 44
Average Teacher Salary 48
Sources of School Funds 36
State Aid Per Pupil 37
Higher Education Spending Per
   Capita 19
Higher Education Spending as a
   Percentage of Total Spending 12
Public Higher Education Enrollment 20
Per Pupil Support of Higher
   Education 7
Tuition and Fees 31
Average Professor Salary 46
Education Employees 5
R and D Spending 24
Library Operating Spending 50

Health - Section I

Immunization Rates 8
Infant Mortality Rates 1
State Health Rankings 49
Population Without Health
   Insurance 9
Abortions 42
Alcohol Consumption 32
Percentage of Adult Smokers 13
Percentage Obese 1
AIDS Cases 11
Physicians Per 100,000 Population 49
Hospital Beds Per 1,000 Population 3
Medicaid Recipients 4
Medicaid Recipients as a Percentage
   of Poverty Population 18
Health and Hospital Spending 5
Health and Hospital Spending as a
   Percentage of Total Spending 2
Per Capita Medicaid Spending 15
Medicaid Spending Per Aged
   Recipient 47
Medicaid Spending Per Child 46
Medicare Payment Per Hospital Day 46
Hospital Expense Per Inpatient Day 50
Population in HMOs 48

Crime - Section J

Crime Rate 23
Violent Crime Rate 31
Murder Rate 2
Property Crime Rate 21
Motor Vehicle Theft Rate 29
Violent Crime Rate Change 41
Prisoners 22
Change in Prisoners 5
Incarceration Rate 2
Juvenile Violent Crime Rate 41
Law Enforcement Employees 20
Corrections Employees 24
State Corrections Spending 48
Increase in State Corrections
   Spending 40
Law Enforcement Spending 43
Law Enforcement Spending as a
   Percentage of Total Spending 41

Transportation - Section K

Travel on Interstates 47
Interstate Mileage in Unacceptable
   Condition 15
Deficient Bridges 19

Traffic Deaths 4
Seat Belt Use 41
Vehicle-miles Traveled Per Capita 6
Workers Using Public
   Transportation 42
Road and Street Miles 25
Highway Employees 12
Public Transit Employees 45
Highway Spending Per Capita 21
Highway Spending as a Percentage
   of Total Spending 18

Welfare - Section L

Percentage of Births to Unwed
   Mothers 1
TANF Recipients as a Percentage
   of Population 29
Food Stamp Recipients as a
   Percentage of Population 3
SSI Recipients as a Percentage of
   Population 1
Change in TANF/AFDC Recipients 8
Condition of Children Index 50
Percentage of Families with Single
   Parent 2
Average Monthly TANF
   Payments 50
Welfare as a Percentage of Poverty-
   level Income 41
State Supplements of SSI 38
State Income Tax Liability of Typical
   Family in Poverty 18
Child Support Collections 32
Child Support Collections Per Dollar
   of Administrative Costs 9
Children in Foster Care 45
Welfare Spending Per Capita 25
Welfare Spending as a Percentage of
   Total Spending 15
Administrative Costs Per TANF Case 49

Technology - Section M

Percentage of Households with
   Computers 50
Percentage of Households with
   Internet Access 50
Zip codes with Broadband
   Service 33
High-tech Jobs 49
Dot-com Domain Names 49
State Government Website
   Ratings 48
Students per Computer 2

Missouri

Population - Section A

Population 2001	17
Population Change 2000-2001	28
Population Change 1990-2001	30
Population 2015	31
Population 2025	19
Percentage 65 and Over	14
Percentage 17 and Under	25
Median Age	18
Percentage African American	19
Percentage Hispanic	39
Percentage in Poverty	29
Child Poverty Rate	30
Percentage Female	14
Birth Rates	31
Death Rates	14
Population Density	27
New Legal Immigrants 2000	23

Economies - Section B

Personal Income 2001	18
Gross State Product	28
Per Capita Personal Income	29
Personal Income from Wages and Salaries	19
Average Annual Pay	24
Average Hourly Earnings	21
Value Added in Manufacturing	24
Cost of Living	35
Average Annual Pay in Manufacturing	26
Average Annual Pay in Retailing	31
Labor Force	17
Unemployment Rate	31
Employment Rate	20
Government Employment	33
Manufacturing Employment	23
Fortune 500 Companies	13
Forbes 500 Companies	10
Tourism Spending Per Capita	28
Exports Per Capita	41
Housing Permits	30
Percentage Change in Home Prices	20
Net Farm Income	22
Financial Institution Assets	34
Bankruptcy Filings	20
Patents Issued	33
WC Disability Payment	20
UC Average Weekly Benefit	40
Economic Momentum	40
One-year Employment Change	48
Manufacturing Employment Change	39
Home Ownership	13
Gambling	13

Electricity Use Per Residential Customer	18
Cost Per Kwh	37
New Companies	35

Geography - Section C

Total Land Area	18
Federally Owned Land	13
State Park Acreage	21
State Park Visitors	17
Population Not Active	12
Hunters with Firearms	12
Registered Boats	13
State Spending for the Arts	12
Energy Consumption Per Capita	29
Toxic Chemical Release Per Capita	19
Hazardous Waste Sites	18
Polluted Rivers and Streams	22
Expired Surface Water Pollution Permits	12
Air Pollution Emissions	16

Government - Section D

Members of United States House	14
State Legislators	7
Legislators Per Million Population	24
Units of Government	12
Legislators Compensation	14
Female Legislators	23
Turnover in Legislatures	3
Term Limits	6.0
Legislative Session Length	10
Republicans in State Legislatures	19
Governor's Power Rating	34
Number of Statewide Elected Officials	21
State and Local Government Employees	28
State and Local Average Salaries	37
Local Employment	27
Local Spending Accountability	14
Registered Voters	10
Percentage of Population Voting	14
Statewide Initiatives	9
Campaign Costs Per Vote	22

Federal Impacts - Section E

Per Capita Federal Spending	12
Increase in Federal Spending	50
Per Capita Federal Grant Spending	22
Per Capita Federal Spending on Procurement	7

Per Capita Federal Spending on Payments to Individuals	14
Per Capita Federal Spending on Social Security and Medicare	13
Social Security Benefits	29
Federal Spending on Employee Wages and Salaries	22
Federal Grant Spending Per Dollar of State Tax Revenue	14
General Revenue from Federal Government	18
Federal Tax Burden Per Capita	30
Federal Spending Per Dollar of Taxes Paid	17
Highway Charges Returned to States	31
Terms of Trade	22
Federal Personal Income Taxes	29
Federal Share of Medicaid	23

Taxes - Section F

Tax Revenue	45
Per Capita Tax Revenue	37
Tax Effort	40
Tax Capacity	24
Percentage Change in Taxes	42
Property Taxes as a Percentage of Income	39
Property Taxes Per Capita	37
Property Tax Revenue as a Percentage of 3-tax Revenues	38
Sales Taxes as a Percentage of Income	21
Sales Taxes Per Capita	24
Sales Tax Revenue as a Percentage of 3-tax Revenues	19
Sales Tax Rate	36
Income Taxes as a Percentage of Income	27
Income Taxes Per Capita	27
Income Tax Revenue as a Percentage of 3-tax Revenues	19
Highest Personal Income Rate	22
Corporate Income Taxes	46
Motor Fuel Taxes	40
Tobacco Taxes	42
Taxes on High Income Families	29
Taxes in the Largest City in Each State	20
Progressivity of Taxes	32

Revenues and Finances - Section G

Per Capita Total Revenue	45
Per Capita General Revenue	44
Own-source General Revenue	44
Per Capita Non-tax Revenue	48

Per Capita Total Spending	46
General Spending as a Percentage of Income	43
Per Capita General Spending	48
Change in General Expenditures	11
State Government General Revenue	44
State Government General Spending	44
State Government General Fund Spending	40
State and Local Debt	43
Debt as a Percentage of Revenue	35
Per Capita Full Faith and Credit Debt	39
Bond Ratings	1
State Solvency Index	26
Pension Plan Assets	12
State Reserves	21
Capital Outlays and Interest	40
State Budget Process Quality	18
Relative State Spending "Needs"	12
Structural Deficits	17

Education - Section H

Math Proficiency, Eighth Grade	23
Science Proficiency, Eighth Grade	11
AFQT Ranks	27
SAT Scores	n/a
ACT Scores	7
Over-25 Population with a High School Diploma	21
Students in Private Schools	13
High School Completion Rates	4
Pupil-Teacher Ratio	39
Public School Enrollment	40
Library Holdings Per Capita	5
Children with Disabilities	9
Education Spending Per Capita	40
Education Spending as a Percentage of Total Spending	14
Spending Per Pupil	35
Average Teacher Salary	34
Sources of School Funds	6
State Aid Per Pupil	46
Higher Education Spending Per Capita	40
Higher Education Spending as a Percentage of Total Spending	33
Public Higher Education Enrollment	39
Per Pupil Support of Higher Education	33
Tuition and Fees	17
Average Professor Salary	19
Education Employees	30
R and D Spending	20
Library Operating Spending	25

Health - Section I

Immunization Rates	28
Infant Mortality Rates	21
State Health Rankings	32
Population Without Health Insurance	37
Abortions	41
Alcohol Consumption	26
Percentage of Adult Smokers	9
Percentage Obese	10
AIDS Cases	26
Physicians Per 100,000 Population	17
Hospital Beds Per 1,000 Population	15
Medicaid Recipients	15
Medicaid Recipients as a Percentage of Poverty Population	4
Health and Hospital Spending	23
Health and Hospital Spending as a Percentage of Total Spending	19
Per Capita Medicaid Spending	21
Medicaid Spending Per Aged Recipient	25
Medicaid Spending Per Child	42
Medicare Payment Per Hospital Day	15
Hospital Expense Per Inpatient Day	22
Population in HMOs	11

Crime - Section J

Crime Rate	12
Violent Crime Rate	14
Murder Rate	12
Property Crime Rate	11
Motor Vehicle Theft Rate	9
Violent Crime Rate Change	8
Prisoners	13
Change in Prisoners	10
Incarceration Rate	8
Juvenile Violent Crime Rate	12
Law Enforcement Employees	17
Corrections Employees	20
State Corrections Spending	46
Increase in State Corrections Spending	45
Law Enforcement Spending	36
Law Enforcement Spending as a Percentage of Total Spending	26

Transportation - Section K

Travel on Interstates	16
Interstate Mileage in Unacceptable Condition	10
Deficient Bridges	8

Traffic Deaths	22
Seat Belt Use	31
Vehicle-miles Traveled Per Capita	8
Workers Using Public Transportation	28
Road and Street Miles	12
Highway Employees	22
Public Transit Employees	17
Highway Spending Per Capita	24
Highway Spending as a Percentage of Total Spending	20

Welfare - Section L

Percentage of Births to Unwed Mothers	16
TANF Recipients as a Percentage of Population	12
Food Stamp Recipients as a Percentage of Population	12
SSI Recipients as a Percentage of Population	23
Change in TANF/AFDC Recipients	35
Condition of Children Index	26
Percentage of Families with Single Parent	27
Average Monthly TANF Payments	39
Welfare as a Percentage of Poverty-level Income	41
State Supplements of SSI	9
State Income Tax Liability of Typical Family in Poverty	14
Child Support Collections	19
Child Support Collections Per Dollar of Administrative Costs	38
Children in Foster Care	12
Welfare Spending Per Capita	31
Welfare Spending as a Percentage of Total Spending	17
Administrative Costs Per TANF Case	47

Technology - Section M

Percentage of Households with Computers	31
Percentage of Households with Internet Access	30
Zip codes with Broadband Service	37
High-tech Jobs	25
Dot-com Domain Names	33
State Government Website Ratings	22
Students per Computer	33

Montana

Population - Section A

Population 2001	44
Population Change 2000-2001	39
Population Change 1990-2001	22
Population 2015	7
Population 2025	44
Percentage 65 and Over	13
Percentage 17 and Under	26
Median Age	6
Percentage African American	50
Percentage Hispanic	40
Percentage in Poverty	14
Child Poverty Rate	17
Percentage Female	41
Birth Rates	44
Death Rates	30
Population Density	48
New Legal Immigrants 2000	47

Economies - Section B

Personal Income 2001	45
Gross State Product	48
Per Capita Personal Income	46
Personal Income from Wages and Salaries	50
Average Annual Pay	50
Average Hourly Earnings	32
Value Added in Manufacturing	48
Cost of Living	23
Average Annual Pay in Manufacturing	43
Average Annual Pay in Retailing	44
Labor Force	20
Unemployment Rate	44
Employment Rate	7
Government Employment	7
Manufacturing Employment	45
Fortune 500 Companies	n/a
Forbes 500 Companies	n/a
Tourism Spending Per Capita	9
Exports Per Capita	49
Housing Permits	45
Percentage Change in Home Prices	35
Net Farm Income	35
Financial Institution Assets	26
Bankruptcy Filings	31
Patents Issued	35
WC Disability Payment	43
UC Average Weekly Benefit	42
Economic Momentum	8
One-year Employment Change	4
Manufacturing Employment Change	3
Home Ownership	31
Gambling	29

Electricity Use Per Residential Customer	30
Cost Per Kwh	30
New Companies	10

Geography - Section C

Total Land Area	4
Federally Owned Land	9
State Park Acreage	36
State Park Visitors	42
Population Not Active	37
Hunters with Firearms	29
Registered Boats	43
State Spending for the Arts	47
Energy Consumption Per Capita	6
Toxic Chemical Release Per Capita	5
Hazardous Waste Sites	25
Polluted Rivers and Streams	4
Expired Surface Water Pollution Permits	8
Air Pollution Emissions	39

Government - Section D

Members of United States House	44
State Legislators	19
Legislators Per Million Population	5
Units of Government	6
Legislators Compensation	45
Female Legislators	20
Turnover in Legislatures	16
Term Limits	6
Legislative Session Length	23
Republicans in State Legislatures	23
Governor's Power Rating	12
Number of Statewide Elected Officials	16
State and Local Government Employees	13
State and Local Average Salaries	43
Local Employment	42
Local Spending Accountability	20
Registered Voters	4
Percentage of Population Voting	7
Statewide Initiatives	6
Campaign Costs Per Vote	12

Federal Impacts - Section E

Per Capita Federal Spending	8
Increase in Federal Spending	21
Per Capita Federal Grant Spending	5
Per Capita Federal Spending on Procurement	37

Per Capita Federal Spending on Payments to Individuals	5
Per Capita Federal Spending on Social Security and Medicare	28
Social Security Benefits	33
Federal Spending on Employee Wages and Salaries	13
Federal Grant Spending Per Dollar of State Tax Revenue	4
General Revenue from Federal Government	3
Federal Tax Burden Per Capita	45
Federal Spending Per Dollar of Taxes Paid	5
Highway Charges Returned to States	5
Terms of Trade	4
Federal Personal Income Taxes	46
Federal Share of Medicaid	5

Taxes - Section F

Tax Revenue	26
Per Capita Tax Revenue	45
Tax Effort	45
Tax Capacity	20
Percentage Change in Taxes	47
Property Taxes as a Percentage of Income	5
Property Taxes Per Capita	13
Property Tax Revenue as a Percentage of 3-tax Revenues	3
Sales Taxes as a Percentage of Income	46
Sales Taxes Per Capita	48
Sales Tax Revenue as a Percentage of 3-tax Revenues	49
Sales Tax Rate	n/a
Income Taxes as a Percentage of Income	28
Income Taxes Per Capita	33
Income Tax Revenue as a Percentage of 3-tax Revenues	20
Highest Personal Income Rate	18
Corporate Income Taxes	19
Motor Fuel Taxes	3
Tobacco Taxes	40
Taxes on High Income Families	30
Taxes in the Largest City in Each State	42
Progressivity of Taxes	4

Revenues and Finances - Section G

Per Capita Total Revenue	28
Per Capita General Revenue	22
Own-source General Revenue	35
Per Capita Non-tax Revenue	8

Per Capita Total Spending	35
General Spending as a Percentage of Income	6
Per Capita General Spending	28
Change in General Expenditures	34
State Government General Revenue	19
State Government General Spending	19
State Government General Fund Spending	15
State and Local Debt	33
Debt as a Percentage of Revenue	28
Per Capita Full Faith and Credit Debt	44
Bond Ratings	4
State Solvency Index	8
Pension Plan Assets	43
State Reserves	13
Capital Outlays and Interest	38
State Budget Process Quality	24
Relative State Spending "Needs"	29
Structural Deficits	33

Education - Section H

Math Proficiency, Eighth Grade	2
Science Proficiency, Eighth Grade	1
AFQT Ranks	9
SAT Scores	n/a
ACT Scores	4
Over-25 Population with a High School Diploma	11
Students in Private Schools	42
High School Completion Rates	10
Pupil-Teacher Ratio	32
Public School Enrollment	19
Library Holdings Per Capita	23
Children with Disabilities	42
Education Spending Per Capita	26
Education Spending as a Percentage of Total Spending	22
Spending Per Pupil	24
Average Teacher Salary	47
Sources of School Funds	21
State Aid Per Pupil	29
Higher Education Spending Per Capita	24
Higher Education Spending as a Percentage of Total Spending	20
Public Higher Education Enrollment	30
Per Pupil Support of Higher Education	46
Tuition and Fees	26
Average Professor Salary	48
Education Employees	13
R and D Spending	35
Library Operating Spending	42

Health - Section I

Immunization Rates	13
Infant Mortality Rates	39
State Health Rankings	24
Population Without Health Insurance	19
Abortions	20
Alcohol Consumption	9
Percentage of Adult Smokers	39
Percentage Obese	42
AIDS Cases	47
Physicians Per 100,000 Population	39
Hospital Beds Per 1,000 Population	5
Medicaid Recipients	35
Medicaid Recipients as a Percentage of Poverty Population	49
Health and Hospital Spending	25
Health and Hospital Spending as a Percentage of Total Spending	26
Per Capita Medicaid Spending	36
Medicaid Spending Per Aged Recipient	19
Medicaid Spending Per Child	7
Medicare Payment Per Hospital Day	39
Hospital Expense Per Inpatient Day	6
Population in HMOs	43

Crime - Section J

Crime Rate	31
Violent Crime Rate	28
Murder Rate	28
Property Crime Rate	31
Motor Vehicle Theft Rate	41
Violent Crime Rate Change	n/a
Prisoners	43
Change in Prisoners	6
Incarceration Rate	26
Juvenile Violent Crime Rate	9
Law Enforcement Employees	42
Corrections Employees	37
State Corrections Spending	24
Increase in State Corrections Spending	23
Law Enforcement Spending	35
Law Enforcement Spending as a Percentage of Total Spending	36

Transportation - Section K

Travel on Interstates	24
Interstate Mileage in Unacceptable Condition	25
Deficient Bridges	38

Traffic Deaths	2
Seat Belt Use	16
Vehicle-miles Traveled Per Capita	17
Workers Using Public Transportation	47
Road and Street Miles	34
Highway Employees	3
Public Transit Employees	31
Highway Spending Per Capita	8
Highway Spending as a Percentage of Total Spending	7

Welfare - Section L

Percentage of Births to Unwed Mothers	31
TANF Recipients as a Percentage of Population	19
Food Stamp Recipients as a Percentage of Population	16
SSI Recipients as a Percentage of Population	34
Change in TANF/AFDC Recipients	31
Condition of Children Index	34
Percentage of Families with Single Parent	13
Average Monthly TANF Payments	24
Welfare as a Percentage of Poverty-level Income	16
State Supplements of SSI	23
State Income Tax Liability of Typical Family in Poverty	6
Child Support Collections	42
Child Support Collections Per Dollar of Administrative Costs	35
Children in Foster Care	9
Welfare Spending Per Capita	42
Welfare Spending as a Percentage of Total Spending	42
Administrative Costs Per TANF Case	10

Technology - Section M

Percentage of Households with Computers	28
Percentage of Households with Internet Access	34
Zip codes with Broadband Service	45
High-tech Jobs	44
Dot-com Domain Names	44
State Government Website Ratings	25
Students per Computer	42

Nebraska

Population - Section A

Population 2001	38
Population Change 2000-2001	45
Population Change 1990-2001	38
Population 2015	28
Population 2025	37
Percentage 65 and Over	11
Percentage 17 and Under	13
Median Age	33
Percentage African American	32
Percentage Hispanic	21
Percentage in Poverty	33
Child Poverty Rate	28
Percentage Female	32
Birth Rates	15
Death Rates	43
Population Density	42
New Legal Immigrants 2000	36

Economies - Section B

Personal Income 2001	36
Gross State Product	25
Per Capita Personal Income	23
Personal Income from Wages and Salaries	27
Average Annual Pay	41
Average Hourly Earnings	37
Value Added in Manufacturing	25
Cost of Living	36
Average Annual Pay in Manufacturing	44
Average Annual Pay in Retailing	45
Labor Force	6
Unemployment Rate	49
Employment Rate	2
Government Employment	21
Manufacturing Employment	26.0
Fortune 500 Companies	5
Forbes 500 Companies	18
Tourism Spending Per Capita	35
Exports Per Capita	32
Housing Permits	26
Percentage Change in Home Prices	38
Net Farm Income	7
Financial Institution Assets	13
Bankruptcy Filings	34
Patents Issued	38
WC Disability Payment	31
UC Average Weekly Benefit	38
Economic Momentum	38
One-year Employment Change	25
Manufacturing Employment Change	30
Home Ownership	29
Gambling	37

Electricity Use Per Residential Customer	22
Cost Per Kwh	17
New Companies	39

Geography - Section C

Total Land Area	15
Federally Owned Land	36
State Park Acreage	22
State Park Visitors	6
Population Not Active	8
Hunters with Firearms	8
Registered Boats	38
State Spending for the Arts	27
Energy Consumption Per Capita	17
Toxic Chemical Release Per Capita	24
Hazardous Waste Sites	38
Polluted Rivers and Streams	15
Expired Surface Water Pollution Permits	3
Air Pollution Emissions	37

Government - Section D

Members of United States House	34
State Legislators	50
Legislators Per Million Population	31
Units of Government	3
Legislators Compensation	33
Female Legislators	31
Turnover in Legislatures	38
Term Limits	6
Legislative Session Length	8
Republicans in State Legislatures	n/a
Governor's Power Rating	10
Number of Statewide Elected Officials	21
State and Local Government Employees	5
State and Local Average Salaries	31
Local Employment	23
Local Spending Accountability	5
Registered Voters	n/a
Percentage of Population Voting	31
Statewide Initiatives	n/a
Campaign Costs Per Vote	6

Federal Impacts - Section E

Per Capita Federal Spending	22
Increase in Federal Spending	5
Per Capita Federal Grant Spending	24
Per Capita Federal Spending on Procurement	48

Per Capita Federal Spending on Payments to Individuals	8
Per Capita Federal Spending on Social Security and Medicare	33
Social Security Benefits	27
Federal Spending on Employee Wages and Salaries	23
Federal Grant Spending Per Dollar of State Tax Revenue	24
General Revenue from Federal Government	27
Federal Tax Burden Per Capita	28
Federal Spending Per Dollar of Taxes Paid	22
Highway Charges Returned to States	27
Terms of Trade	25
Federal Personal Income Taxes	31
Federal Share of Medicaid	28

Taxes - Section F

Tax Revenue	23
Per Capita Tax Revenue	24
Tax Effort	20
Tax Capacity	20
Percentage Change in Taxes	35
Property Taxes as a Percentage of Income	19
Property Taxes Per Capita	20
Property Tax Revenue as a Percentage of 3-tax Revenues	18
Sales Taxes as a Percentage of Income	29
Sales Taxes Per Capita	29
Sales Tax Revenue as a Percentage of 3-tax Revenues	25
Sales Tax Rate	19
Income Taxes as a Percentage of Income	31
Income Taxes Per Capita	28
Income Tax Revenue as a Percentage of 3-tax Revenues	31
Highest Personal Income Rate	17
Corporate Income Taxes	28
Motor Fuel Taxes	6
Tobacco Taxes	20
Taxes on High Income Families	20
Taxes in the Largest City in Each State	24
Progressivity of Taxes	17

Revenues and Finances - Section G

Per Capita Total Revenue	20
Per Capita General Revenue	23
Own-source General Revenue	22
Per Capita Non-tax Revenue	21

Per Capita Total Spending	14
General Spending as a Percentage of Income	33
Per Capita General Spending	32
Change in General Expenditures	37
State Government General Revenue	30
State Government General Spending	33
State Government General Fund Spending	27
State and Local Debt	37
Debt as a Percentage of Revenue	42
Per Capita Full Faith and Credit Debt	37
Bond Ratings	n/a
State Solvency Index	27
Pension Plan Assets	39
State Reserves	12
Capital Outlays and Interest	8
State Budget Process Quality	28
Relative State Spending "Needs"	2
Structural Deficits	2

Education - Section H

Math Proficiency, Eighth Grade	11
Science Proficiency, Eighth Grade	10
AFQT Ranks	17
SAT Scores	n/a
ACT Scores	4
Over-25 Population with a High School Diploma	5
Students in Private Schools	11
High School Completion Rates	9
Pupil-Teacher Ratio	39
Public School Enrollment	25
Library Holdings Per Capita	14
Children with Disabilities	12
Education Spending Per Capita	15
Education Spending as a Percentage of Total Spending	6
Spending Per Pupil	30
Average Teacher Salary	44
Sources of School Funds	8
State Aid Per Pupil	47
Higher Education Spending Per Capita	7
Higher Education Spending as a Percentage of Total Spending	6
Public Higher Education Enrollment	8
Per Pupil Support of Higher Education	16
Tuition and Fees	25
Average Professor Salary	25
Education Employees	11
R and D Spending	45
Library Operating Spending	29

Health - Section I

Immunization Rates	17
Infant Mortality Rates	20
State Health Rankings	15
Population Without Health Insurance	41
Abortions	24
Alcohol Consumption	29
Percentage of Adult Smokers	46
Percentage Obese	28
AIDS Cases	37
Physicians Per 100,000 Population	28
Hospital Beds Per 1,000 Population	4
Medicaid Recipients	27
Medicaid Recipients as a Percentage of Poverty Population	17
Health and Hospital Spending	41
Health and Hospital Spending as a Percentage of Total Spending	33
Per Capita Medicaid Spending	23
Medicaid Spending Per Aged Recipient	17
Medicaid Spending Per Child	29
Medicare Payment Per Hospital Day	10
Hospital Expense Per Inpatient Day	31
Population in HMOs	40

Crime - Section J

Crime Rate	16
Violent Crime Rate	35
Murder Rate	38
Property Crime Rate	16
Motor Vehicle Theft Rate	22
Violent Crime Rate Change	45
Prisoners	42
Change in Prisoners	25
Incarceration Rate	44
Juvenile Violent Crime Rate	44
Law Enforcement Employees	34
Corrections Employees	38
State Corrections Spending	14
Increase in State Corrections Spending	3
Law Enforcement Spending	37
Law Enforcement Spending as a Percentage of Total Spending	37

Transportation - Section K

Travel on Interstates	40
Interstate Mileage in Unacceptable Condition	17
Deficient Bridges	25

Traffic Deaths	32
Seat Belt Use	25
Vehicle-miles Traveled Per Capita	24
Workers Using Public Transportation	35
Road and Street Miles	36
Highway Employees	11
Public Transit Employees	27
Highway Spending Per Capita	12
Highway Spending as a Percentage of Total Spending	10

Welfare - Section L

Percentage of Births to Unwed Mothers	44
TANF Recipients as a Percentage of Population	27
Food Stamp Recipients as a Percentage of Population	34
SSI Recipients as a Percentage of Population	46
Change in TANF/AFDC Recipients	42
Condition of Children Index	10
Percentage of Families with Single Parent	40
Average Monthly TANF Payments	30
Welfare as a Percentage of Poverty-level Income	41
State Supplements of SSI	21
State Income Tax Liability of Typical Family in Poverty	18
Child Support Collections	8
Child Support Collections Per Dollar of Administrative Costs	42
Children in Foster Care	1
Welfare Spending Per Capita	22
Welfare Spending as a Percentage of Total Spending	13
Administrative Costs Per TANF Case	23

Technology - Section M

Percentage of Households with Computers	30
Percentage of Households with Internet Access	39
Zip codes with Broadband Service	43
High-tech Jobs	20
Dot-com Domain Names	42
State Government Website Ratings	40
Students per Computer	44

Nevada

Population · Section A

Population 2001	35
Population Change 2000-2001	1
Population Change 1990-2001	1
Population 2015	40
Population 2025	36
Percentage 65 and Over	44
Percentage 17 and Under	21
Median Age	38
Percentage African American	25
Percentage Hispanic	5
Percentage in Poverty	48
Child Poverty Rate	44
Percentage Female	49
Birth Rates	5
Death Rates	12
Population Density	43
New Legal Immigrants 2000	21

Economies · Section B

Personal Income 2001	32
Gross State Product	13
Per Capita Personal Income	17
Personal Income from Wages and Salaries	9
Average Annual Pay	23
Average Hourly Earnings	27
Value Added in Manufacturing	47
Cost of Living	8
Average Annual Pay in Manufacturing	22
Average Annual Pay in Retailing	4
Labor Force	35
Unemployment Rate	30
Employment Rate	21
Government Employment	50
Manufacturing Employment	48
Fortune 500 Companies	17
Forbes 500 Companies	25
Tourism Spending Per Capita	2
Exports Per Capita	48
Housing Permits	1
Percentage Change in Home Prices	44
Net Farm Income	43
Financial Institution Assets	25
Bankruptcy Filings	3
Patents Issued	30
WC Disability Payment	24
UC Average Weekly Benefit	27
Economic Momentum	1
One-year Employment Change	1
Manufacturing Employment Change	2
Home Ownership	44
Gambling	1

Electricity Use Per Residential Customer	23
Cost Per Kwh	45
New Companies	6

Geography · Section C

Total Land Area	7
Federally Owned Land	2
State Park Acreage	23
State Park Visitors	40
Population Not Active	36
Hunters with Firearms	25
Registered Boats	40
State Spending for the Arts	36
Energy Consumption Per Capita	26
Toxic Chemical Release Per Capita	2
Hazardous Waste Sites	49
Polluted Rivers and Streams	13
Expired Surface Water Pollution Permits	14
Air Pollution Emissions	43

Government · Section D

Members of United States House	34
State Legislators	47
Legislators Per Million Population	30
Units of Government	44
Legislators Compensation	41
Female Legislators	3
Turnover in Legislatures	14
Term Limits	1
Legislative Session Length	17
Republicans in State Legislatures	26
Governor's Power Rating	43
Number of Statewide Elected Officials	21
State and Local Government Employees	50
State and Local Average Salaries	6
Local Employment	11
Local Spending Accountability	32
Registered Voters	44
Percentage of Population Voting	44
Statewide Initiatives	9
Campaign Costs Per Vote	1

Federal Impacts · Section E

Per Capita Federal Spending	50
Increase in Federal Spending	31
Per Capita Federal Grant Spending	50
Per Capita Federal Spending on Procurement	31

Per Capita Federal Spending on Payments to Individuals	47
Per Capita Federal Spending on Social Security and Medicare	46
Social Security Benefits	12
Federal Spending on Employee Wages and Salaries	37
Federal Grant Spending Per Dollar of State Tax Revenue	50
General Revenue from Federal Government	50
Federal Tax Burden Per Capita	13
Federal Spending Per Dollar of Taxes Paid	47
Highway Charges Returned to States	19
Terms of Trade	50
Federal Personal Income Taxes	11
Federal Share of Medicaid	37

Taxes · Section F

Tax Revenue	41
Per Capita Tax Revenue	23
Tax Effort	50
Tax Capacity	1
Percentage Change in Taxes	2
Property Taxes as a Percentage of Income	37
Property Taxes Per Capita	34
Property Tax Revenue as a Percentage of 3-tax Revenues	33
Sales Taxes as a Percentage of Income	4
Sales Taxes Per Capita	2
Sales Tax Revenue as a Percentage of 3-tax Revenues	1
Sales Tax Rate	4
Income Taxes as a Percentage of Income	n/a
Income Taxes Per Capita	n/a
Income Tax Revenue as a Percentage of 3-tax Revenues	n/a
Highest Personal Income Rate	n/a
Corporate Income Taxes	n/a
Motor Fuel Taxes	11
Tobacco Taxes	30
Taxes on High Income Families	48
Taxes in the Largest City in Each State	47
Progressivity of Taxes	49

Revenues and Finances · Section G

Per Capita Total Revenue	35
Per Capita General Revenue	38
Own-source General Revenue	28
Per Capita Non-tax Revenue	28

Per Capita Total Spending	32	
General Spending as a Percentage of Income	42	
Per Capita General Spending	35	
Change in General Expenditures	1	
State Government General Revenue	48	
State Government General Spending	47	
State Government General Fund Spending	49	
State and Local Debt	5	
Debt as a Percentage of Revenue	2	
Per Capita Full Faith and Credit Debt	3	
Bond Ratings	3	
State Solvency Index	42	
Pension Plan Assets	9	
State Reserves	4	
Capital Outlays and Interest	5	
State Budget Process Quality	17	
Relative State Spending "Needs"	16	
Structural Deficits	50	

Education - Section H

Math Proficiency, Eighth Grade	29
Science Proficiency, Eighth Grade	30
AFQT Ranks	20
SAT Scores	n/a
ACT Scores	12
Over-25 Population with a High School Diploma	36
Students in Private Schools	47
High School Completion Rates	49
Pupil-Teacher Ratio	5
Public School Enrollment	17
Library Holdings Per Capita	36
Children with Disabilities	47
Education Spending Per Capita	48
Education Spending as a Percentage of Total Spending	45
Spending Per Pupil	43
Average Teacher Salary	14
Sources of School Funds	1
State Aid Per Pupil	50
Higher Education Spending Per Capita	48
Higher Education Spending as a Percentage of Total Spending	45
Public Higher Education Enrollment	28
Per Pupil Support of Higher Education	44
Tuition and Fees	46
Average Professor Salary	14
Education Employees	50
R and D Spending	27
Library Operating Spending	22

Health - Section I

Immunization Rates	46
Infant Mortality Rates	33
State Health Rankings	38
Population Without Health Insurance	12
Abortions	22
Alcohol Consumption	2
Percentage of Adult Smokers	6
Percentage Obese	37
AIDS Cases	15
Physicians Per 100,000 Population	47
Hospital Beds Per 1,000 Population	49
Medicaid Recipients	49
Medicaid Recipients as a Percentage of Poverty Population	45
Health and Hospital Spending	29
Health and Hospital Spending as a Percentage of Total Spending	27
Per Capita Medicaid Spending	50
Medicaid Spending Per Aged Recipient	40
Medicaid Spending Per Child	15
Medicare Payment Per Hospital Day	2
Hospital Expense Per Inpatient Day	40
Population in HMOs	24

Crime - Section J

Crime Rate	19
Violent Crime Rate	11
Murder Rate	3
Property Crime Rate	24
Motor Vehicle Theft Rate	2
Violent Crime Rate Change	38
Prisoners	31
Change in Prisoners	20
Incarceration Rate	12
Juvenile Violent Crime Rate	23
Law Enforcement Employees	13
Corrections Employees	16
State Corrections Spending	44
Increase in State Corrections Spending	46
Law Enforcement Spending	3
Law Enforcement Spending as a Percentage of Total Spending	1

Transportation - Section K

Travel on Interstates	30
Interstate Mileage in Unacceptable Condition	34
Deficient Bridges	48

Traffic Deaths	20
Seat Belt Use	18
Vehicle-miles Traveled Per Capita	42
Workers Using Public Transportation	13
Road and Street Miles	26
Highway Employees	44
Public Transit Employees	36
Highway Spending Per Capita	9
Highway Spending as a Percentage of Total Spending	6

Welfare - Section L

Percentage of Births to Unwed Mothers	9
TANF Recipients as a Percentage of Population	35
Food Stamp Recipients as a Percentage of Population	49
SSI Recipients as a Percentage of Population	44
Change in TANF/AFDC Recipients	46
Condition of Children Index	35
Percentage of Families with Single Parent	13
Average Monthly TANF Payments	44
Welfare as a Percentage of Poverty-level Income	41
State Supplements of SSI	31
State Income Tax Liability of Typical Family in Poverty	n/a
Child Support Collections	47
Child Support Collections Per Dollar of Administrative Costs	43
Children in Foster Care	47
Welfare Spending Per Capita	49
Welfare Spending as a Percentage of Total Spending	48
Administrative Costs Per TANF Case	4

Technology - Section M

Percentage of Households with Computers	23
Percentage of Households with Internet Access	20
Zip codes with Broadband Service	28
High-tech Jobs	45
Dot-com Domain Names	2
State Government Website Ratings	8
Students per Computer	5

New Hampshire

Population · Section A

Population 2001	41
Population Change 2000-2001	8
Population Change 1990-2001	21
Population 2015	24
Population 2025	41
Percentage 65 and Over	36
Percentage 17 and Under	32
Median Age	8
Percentage African American	43
Percentage Hispanic	43
Percentage in Poverty	50
Child Poverty Rate	47
Percentage Female	30
Birth Rates	47
Death Rates	31
Population Density	19
New Legal Immigrants 2000	37

Economies · Section B

Personal Income 2001	37
Gross State Product	10
Per Capita Personal Income	6
Personal Income from Wages and Salaries	39
Average Annual Pay	16
Average Hourly Earnings	38
Value Added in Manufacturing	12
Cost of Living	n/a
Average Annual Pay in Manufacturing	11
Average Annual Pay in Retailing	13
Labor Force	3
Unemployment Rate	35
Employment Rate	16
Government Employment	45
Manufacturing Employment	13
Fortune 500 Companies	n/a
Forbes 500 Companies	44
Tourism Spending Per Capita	11
Exports Per Capita	24
Housing Permits	23
Percentage Change in Home Prices	2
Net Farm Income	48
Financial Institution Assets	12
Bankruptcy Filings	47
Patents Issued	7
WC Disability Payment	2
UC Average Weekly Benefit	22
Economic Momentum	17
One-year Employment Change	12
Manufacturing Employment Change	18
Home Ownership	32
Gambling	35

Electricity Use Per Residential Customer	45
Cost Per Kwh	46
New Companies	20

Geography · Section C

Total Land Area	44
Federally Owned Land	33
State Park Acreage	33
State Park Visitors	8
Population Not Active	45
Hunters with Firearms	28
Registered Boats	35
State Spending for the Arts	42
Energy Consumption Per Capita	41
Toxic Chemical Release Per Capita	42
Hazardous Waste Sites	20
Polluted Rivers and Streams	45
Expired Surface Water Pollution Permits	27
Air Pollution Emissions	46

Government · Section D

Members of United States House	39
State Legislators	1
Legislators Per Million Population	1
Units of Government	19
Legislators Compensation	49
Female Legislators	12
Turnover in Legislatures	9
Term Limits	n/a
Legislative Session Length	6
Republicans in State Legislatures	4
Governor's Power Rating	34
Number of Statewide Elected Officials	48
State and Local Government Employees	39
State and Local Average Salaries	25
Local Employment	21
Local Spending Accountability	8
Registered Voters	33
Percentage of Population Voting	10
Statewide Initiatives	n/a
Campaign Costs Per Vote	23

Federal Impacts · Section E

Per Capita Federal Spending	47
Increase in Federal Spending	36
Per Capita Federal Grant Spending	38
Per Capita Federal Spending on Procurement	29

Per Capita Federal Spending on Payments to Individuals	43
Per Capita Federal Spending on Social Security and Medicare	34
Social Security Benefits	11
Federal Spending on Employee Wages and Salaries	44
Federal Grant Spending Per Dollar of State Tax Revenue	17
General Revenue from Federal Government	32
Federal Tax Burden Per Capita	6
Federal Spending Per Dollar of Taxes Paid	48
Highway Charges Returned to States	21
Terms of Trade	43
Federal Personal Income Taxes	4
Federal Share of Medicaid	39

Taxes · Section F

Tax Revenue	50
Per Capita Tax Revenue	32
Tax Effort	48
Tax Capacity	7
Percentage Change in Taxes	38
Property Taxes as a Percentage of Income	1
Property Taxes Per Capita	2
Property Tax Revenue as a Percentage of 3-tax Revenues	1
Sales Taxes as a Percentage of Income	48
Sales Taxes Per Capita	47
Sales Tax Revenue as a Percentage of 3-tax Revenues	47
Sales Tax Rate	n/a
Income Taxes as a Percentage of Income	42
Income Taxes Per Capita	42
Income Tax Revenue as a Percentage of 3-tax Revenues	42
Highest Personal Income Rate	n/a
Corporate Income Taxes	4
Motor Fuel Taxes	32
Tobacco Taxes	24
Taxes on High Income Families	41
Taxes in the Largest City in Each State	29
Progressivity of Taxes	46

Revenues and Finances · Section G

Per Capita Total Revenue	46
Per Capita General Revenue	43
Own-source General Revenue	39
Per Capita Non-tax Revenue	43

Per Capita Total Spending — 45

General Spending as a Percentage of Income — 50

Per Capita General Spending — 43

Change in General Expenditures — 41

State Government General Revenue — 38

State Government General Spending — 37

State Government General Fund Spending — 48

State and Local Debt — 13

Debt as a Percentage of Revenue — 3

Per Capita Full Faith and Credit Debt — 22

Bond Ratings — 3

State Solvency Index — 36

Pension Plan Assets — 29

State Reserves — 27

Capital Outlays and Interest — 43

State Budget Process Quality — 50

Relative State Spending "Needs" — 1

Structural Deficits — 41

Education - Section H

Math Proficiency, Eighth Grade — n/a

Science Proficiency, Eighth Grade — n/a

AFQT Ranks — 2

SAT Scores — 4

ACT Scores — n/a

Over-25 Population with a High School Diploma — 14

Students in Private Schools — 19

High School Completion Rates — 36

Pupil-Teacher Ratio — 35

Public School Enrollment — 18

Library Holdings Per Capita — 8

Children with Disabilities — 23

Education Spending Per Capita — 39

Education Spending as a Percentage of Total Spending — 21

Spending Per Pupil — 23

Average Teacher Salary — 31

Sources of School Funds — 11

State Aid Per Pupil — 34

Higher Education Spending Per Capita — 44

Higher Education Spending as a Percentage of Total Spending — 39

Public Higher Education Enrollment — 48

Per Pupil Support of Higher Education — 50

Tuition and Fees — 2

Average Professor Salary — 23

Education Employees — 15

R and D Spending — 10

Library Operating Spending — 17

Health - Section I

Immunization Rates — 4

Infant Mortality Rates — 41

State Health Rankings — 1

Population Without Health Insurance — 39

Abortions — n/a

Alcohol Consumption — 1

Percentage of Adult Smokers — 18

Percentage Obese — 39

AIDS Cases — 43

Physicians Per 100,000 Population — 23

Hospital Beds Per 1,000 Population — 38

Medicaid Recipients — 48

Medicaid Recipients as a Percentage of Poverty Population — 11

Health and Hospital Spending — 49

Health and Hospital Spending as a Percentage of Total Spending — 48

Per Capita Medicaid Spending — 29

Medicaid Spending Per Aged Recipient — 3

Medicaid Spending Per Child — 6

Medicare Payment Per Hospital Day — 28

Hospital Expense Per Inpatient Day — 5

Population in HMOs — 14

Crime - Section J

Crime Rate — 50

Violent Crime Rate — 46

Murder Rate — 46

Property Crime Rate — 50

Motor Vehicle Theft Rate — 46

Violent Crime Rate Change — n/a

Prisoners — 46

Change in Prisoners — 36

Incarceration Rate — 46

Juvenile Violent Crime Rate — 45

Law Enforcement Employees — 19

Corrections Employees — 47

State Corrections Spending — 26

Increase in State Corrections Spending — 2

Law Enforcement Spending — 44

Law Enforcement Spending as a Percentage of Total Spending — 39

Transportation - Section K

Travel on Interstates — 33

Interstate Mileage in Unacceptable Condition — 44

Deficient Bridges — 13

Traffic Deaths — 44

Seat Belt Use — n/a

Vehicle-miles Traveled Per Capita — 32

Workers Using Public Transportation — 43

Road and Street Miles — 13

Highway Employees — 9

Public Transit Employees — 43

Highway Spending Per Capita — 26

Highway Spending as a Percentage of Total Spending — 23

Welfare - Section L

Percentage of Births to Unwed Mothers — 48

TANF Recipients as a Percentage of Population — 39

Food Stamp Recipients as a Percentage of Population — 50

SSI Recipients as a Percentage of Population — 49

Change in TANF/AFDC Recipients — 41

Condition of Children Index — 2

Percentage of Families with Single Parent — 38

Average Monthly TANF Payments — 11

Welfare as a Percentage of Poverty-level Income — 13

State Supplements of SSI — 34

State Income Tax Liability of Typical Family in Poverty — n/a

Child Support Collections — 26

Child Support Collections Per Dollar of Administrative Costs — 10

Children in Foster Care — 43

Welfare Spending Per Capita — 13

Welfare Spending as a Percentage of Total Spending — 8

Administrative Costs Per TANF Case — 2

Technology - Section M

Percentage of Households with Computers — 2

Percentage of Households with Internet Access — 2

Zip codes with Broadband Service — 9

High-tech Jobs — 3

Dot-com Domain Names — 16

State Government Website Ratings — 14

Students per Computer — 12

New Jersey

Population · Section A

Population 2001	9
Population Change 2000-2001	24
Population Change 1990-2001	32
Population 2015	36
Population 2025	10
Percentage 65 and Over	19
Percentage 17 and Under	35
Median Age	9
Percentage African American	16
Percentage Hispanic	9
Percentage in Poverty	41
Child Poverty Rate	41
Percentage Female	10
Birth Rates	24
Death Rates	27
Population Density	1
New Legal Immigrants 2000	5

Economies · Section B

Personal Income 2001	8
Gross State Product	5
Per Capita Personal Income	3
Personal Income from Wages and Salaries	30
Average Annual Pay	4
Average Hourly Earnings	12
Value Added in Manufacturing	34
Cost of Living	1
Average Annual Pay in Manufacturing	3
Average Annual Pay in Retailing	3
Labor Force	31
Unemployment Rate	19
Employment Rate	32
Government Employment	37
Manufacturing Employment	35
Fortune 500 Companies	8
Forbes 500 Companies	8
Tourism Spending Per Capita	23
Exports Per Capita	17
Housing Permits	44
Percentage Change in Home Prices	9
Net Farm Income	40
Financial Institution Assets	33
Bankruptcy Filings	25
Patents Issued	9
WC Disability Payment	19
UC Average Weekly Benefit	3
Economic Momentum	34
One-year Employment Change	23
Manufacturing Employment Change	43
Home Ownership	41
Gambling	2

Electricity Use Per Residential Customer	40
Cost Per Kwh	40
New Companies	5

Geography · Section C

Total Land Area	46
Federally Owned Land	46
State Park Acreage	7
State Park Visitors	36
Population Not Active	16
Hunters with Firearms	45
Registered Boats	24
State Spending for the Arts	6
Energy Consumption Per Capita	42
Toxic Chemical Release Per Capita	43
Hazardous Waste Sites	1
Polluted Rivers and Streams	11
Expired Surface Water Pollution Permits	7
Air Pollution Emissions	26

Government · Section D

Members of United States House	9
State Legislators	35
Legislators Per Million Population	45
Units of Government	38
Legislators Compensation	8
Female Legislators	41
Turnover in Legislatures	n/a
Term Limits	n/a
Legislative Session Length	n/a
Republicans in State Legislatures	29
Governor's Power Rating	5
Number of Statewide Elected Officials	48
State and Local Government Employees	29
State and Local Average Salaries	2
Local Employment	25
Local Spending Accountability	10
Registered Voters	32
Percentage of Population Voting	40
Statewide Initiatives	n/a
Campaign Costs Per Vote	7

Federal Impacts · Section E

Per Capita Federal Spending	37
Increase in Federal Spending	48
Per Capita Federal Grant Spending	41
Per Capita Federal Spending on Procurement	32

Per Capita Federal Spending on Payments to Individuals	25
Per Capita Federal Spending on Social Security and Medicare	11
Social Security Benefits	1
Federal Spending on Employee Wages and Salaries	40
Federal Grant Spending Per Dollar of State Tax Revenue	39
General Revenue from Federal Government	48
Federal Tax Burden Per Capita	2
Federal Spending Per Dollar of Taxes Paid	50
Highway Charges Returned to States	43
Terms of Trade	49
Federal Personal Income Taxes	3
Federal Share of Medicaid	39

Taxes · Section F

Tax Revenue	18
Per Capita Tax Revenue	3
Tax Effort	6
Tax Capacity	8
Percentage Change in Taxes	39
Property Taxes as a Percentage of Income	4
Property Taxes Per Capita	1
Property Tax Revenue as a Percentage of 3-tax Revenues	4
Sales Taxes as a Percentage of Income	43
Sales Taxes Per Capita	30
Sales Tax Revenue as a Percentage of 3-tax Revenues	44
Sales Tax Rate	9
Income Taxes as a Percentage of Income	34
Income Taxes Per Capita	14
Income Tax Revenue as a Percentage of 3-tax Revenues	35
Highest Personal Income Rate	21
Corporate Income Taxes	10
Motor Fuel Taxes	46
Tobacco Taxes	2
Taxes on High Income Families	2
Taxes in the Largest City in Each State	2
Progressivity of Taxes	41

Revenues and Finances · Section G

Per Capita Total Revenue	11
Per Capita General Revenue	9
Own-source General Revenue	7
Per Capita Non-tax Revenue	27

Per Capita Total Spending	12
General Spending as a Percentage of Income	49
Per Capita General Spending	15
Change in General Expenditures	49
State Government General Revenue	20
State Government General Spending	29
State Government General Fund Spending	44
State and Local Debt	9
Debt as a Percentage of Revenue	16
Per Capita Full Faith and Credit Debt	15
Bond Ratings	3
State Solvency Index	16
Pension Plan Assets	18
State Reserves	40
Capital Outlays and Interest	36
State Budget Process Quality	9
Relative State Spending "Needs"	18
Structural Deficits	26

Education - Section H

Math Proficiency, Eighth Grade	n/a
Science Proficiency, Eighth Grade	n/a
AFQT Ranks	40
SAT Scores	12
ACT Scores	n/a
Over-25 Population with a High School Diploma	18
Students in Private Schools	8
High School Completion Rates	16
Pupil-Teacher Ratio	45
Public School Enrollment	41
Library Holdings Per Capita	18
Children with Disabilities	4
Education Spending Per Capita	4
Education Spending as a Percentage of Total Spending	5
Spending Per Pupil	2
Average Teacher Salary	5
Sources of School Funds	3
State Aid Per Pupil	26
Higher Education Spending Per Capita	38
Higher Education Spending as a Percentage of Total Spending	42
Public Higher Education Enrollment	45
Per Pupil Support of Higher Education	6
Tuition and Fees	4
Average Professor Salary	4
Education Employees	23
R and D Spending	13
Library Operating Spending	6

Health - Section I

Immunization Rates	30
Infant Mortality Rates	36
State Health Rankings	19
Population Without Health Insurance	22
Abortions	8
Alcohol Consumption	30
Percentage of Adult Smokers	41
Percentage Obese	36
AIDS Cases	6
Physicians Per 100,000 Population	8
Hospital Beds Per 1,000 Population	22
Medicaid Recipients	42
Medicaid Recipients as a Percentage of Poverty Population	35
Health and Hospital Spending	42
Health and Hospital Spending as a Percentage of Total Spending	44
Per Capita Medicaid Spending	24
Medicaid Spending Per Aged Recipient	10
Medicaid Spending Per Child	16
Medicare Payment Per Hospital Day	4
Hospital Expense Per Inpatient Day	41
Population in HMOs	13

Crime - Section J

Crime Rate	37
Violent Crime Rate	25
Murder Rate	26
Property Crime Rate	39
Motor Vehicle Theft Rate	16
Violent Crime Rate Change	37
Prisoners	14
Change in Prisoners	44
Incarceration Rate	32
Juvenile Violent Crime Rate	10
Law Enforcement Employees	2
Corrections Employees	36
State Corrections Spending	7
Increase in State Corrections Spending	15
Law Enforcement Spending	6
Law Enforcement Spending as a Percentage of Total Spending	7

Transportation - Section K

Travel on Interstates	46
Interstate Mileage in Unacceptable Condition	4
Deficient Bridges	9

Traffic Deaths	45
Seat Belt Use	15
Vehicle-miles Traveled Per Capita	46
Workers Using Public Transportation	2
Road and Street Miles	50
Highway Employees	27
Public Transit Employees	3
Highway Spending Per Capita	48
Highway Spending as a Percentage of Total Spending	47

Welfare - Section L

Percentage of Births to Unwed Mothers	39
TANF Recipients as a Percentage of Population	33
Food Stamp Recipients as a Percentage of Population	45
SSI Recipients as a Percentage of Population	29
Change in TANF/AFDC Recipients	16
Condition of Children Index	5
Percentage of Families with Single Parent	45
Average Monthly TANF Payments	19
Welfare as a Percentage of Poverty-level Income	26
State Supplements of SSI	37
State Income Tax Liability of Typical Family in Poverty	36
Child Support Collections	10
Child Support Collections Per Dollar of Administrative Costs	11
Children in Foster Care	41
Welfare Spending Per Capita	35
Welfare Spending as a Percentage of Total Spending	41
Administrative Costs Per TANF Case	38

Technology - Section M

Percentage of Households with Computers	13
Percentage of Households with Internet Access	7
Zip codes with Broadband Service	3
High-tech Jobs	12
Dot-com Domain Names	14
State Government Website Ratings	2
Students per Computer	23

New Mexico

Population - Section A

Population 2001	36
Population Change 2000-2001	32
Population Change 1990-2001	12
Population 2015	3
Population 2025	35
Percentage 65 and Over	37
Percentage 17 and Under	5
Median Age	40
Percentage African American	40
Percentage Hispanic	1
Percentage in Poverty	2
Child Poverty Rate	2
Percentage Female	29
Birth Rates	10
Death Rates	32
Population Density	45
New Legal Immigrants 2000	29

Economies - Section B

Personal Income 2001	38
Gross State Product	38
Per Capita Personal Income	47
Personal Income from Wages and Salaries	31
Average Annual Pay	40
Average Hourly Earnings	31
Value Added in Manufacturing	38
Cost of Living	12
Average Annual Pay in Manufacturing	27
Average Annual Pay in Retailing	30
Labor Force	47
Unemployment Rate	8
Employment Rate	43
Government Employment	3
Manufacturing Employment	46
Fortune 500 Companies	n/a
Forbes 500 Companies	34
Tourism Spending Per Capita	10
Exports Per Capita	47
Housing Permits	20
Percentage Change in Home Prices	50
Net Farm Income	24
Financial Institution Assets	44
Bankruptcy Filings	28
Patents Issued	27
WC Disability Payment	33
UC Average Weekly Benefit	44
Economic Momentum	3
One-year Employment Change	3
Manufacturing Employment Change	5
Home Ownership	15
Gambling	34

Electricity Use Per Residential Customer	46
Cost Per Kwh	32
New Companies	17

Geography - Section C

Total Land Area	5
Federally Owned Land	10
State Park Acreage	30
State Park Visitors	28
Population Not Active	24
Hunters with Firearms	44
Registered Boats	47
State Spending for the Arts	22
Energy Consumption Per Capita	13
Toxic Chemical Release Per Capita	6
Hazardous Waste Sites	31
Polluted Rivers and Streams	12
Expired Surface Water Pollution Permits	38
Air Pollution Emissions	33

Government - Section D

Members of United States House	34
State Legislators	38
Legislators Per Million Population	15
Units of Government	18
Legislators Compensation	50
Female Legislators	9
Turnover in Legislatures	46
Term Limits	n/a
Legislative Session Length	36
Republicans in State Legislatures	37
Governor's Power Rating	12
Number of Statewide Elected Officials	16
State and Local Government Employees	4
State and Local Average Salaries	44
Local Employment	45
Local Spending Accountability	50
Registered Voters	35
Percentage of Population Voting	36
Statewide Initiatives	n/a
Campaign Costs Per Vote	9

Federal Impacts - Section E

Per Capita Federal Spending	4
Increase in Federal Spending	11
Per Capita Federal Grant Spending	4
Per Capita Federal Spending on Procurement	2

Per Capita Federal Spending on Payments to Individuals	33
Per Capita Federal Spending on Social Security and Medicare	43
Social Security Benefits	45
Federal Spending on Employee Wages and Salaries	6
Federal Grant Spending Per Dollar of State Tax Revenue	19
General Revenue from Federal Government	12
Federal Tax Burden Per Capita	47
Federal Spending Per Dollar of Taxes Paid	1
Highway Charges Returned to States	22
Terms of Trade	2
Federal Personal Income Taxes	50
Federal Share of Medicaid	3

Taxes - Section F

Tax Revenue	5
Per Capita Tax Revenue	33
Tax Effort	12
Tax Capacity	43
Percentage Change in Taxes	19
Property Taxes as a Percentage of Income	49
Property Taxes Per Capita	49
Property Tax Revenue as a Percentage of 3-tax Revenues	50
Sales Taxes as a Percentage of Income	3
Sales Taxes Per Capita	7
Sales Tax Revenue as a Percentage of 3-tax Revenues	5
Sales Tax Rate	19
Income Taxes as a Percentage of Income	35
Income Taxes Per Capita	37
Income Tax Revenue as a Percentage of 3-tax Revenues	36
Highest Personal Income Rate	8
Corporate Income Taxes	26
Motor Fuel Taxes	35
Tobacco Taxes	37
Taxes on High Income Families	22
Taxes in the Largest City in Each State	30
Progressivity of Taxes	10

Revenues and Finances - Section G

Per Capita Total Revenue	13
Per Capita General Revenue	18
Own-source General Revenue	26
Per Capita Non-tax Revenue	7

Per Capita Total Spending — 19
General Spending as a Percentage of Income — 2
Per Capita General Spending — 16
Change in General Expenditures — 16
State Government General Revenue — 9
State Government General Spending — 6
State Government General Fund Spending — 1
State and Local Debt — 34
Debt as a Percentage of Revenue — 40
Per Capita Full Faith and Credit Debt — 36
Bond Ratings — 2
State Solvency Index — 3
Pension Plan Assets — 27
State Reserves — 6
Capital Outlays and Interest — 25
State Budget Process Quality — 8
Relative State Spending "Needs" — 50
Structural Deficits — 46

Education · Section H

Math Proficiency, Eighth Grade — 37
Science Proficiency, Eighth Grade — 34
AFQT Ranks — 41
SAT Scores — n/a
ACT Scores — 22
Over-25 Population with a High School Diploma — 39
Students in Private Schools — 38
High School Completion Rates — 41
Pupil-Teacher Ratio — 23
Public School Enrollment — 9
Library Holdings Per Capita — 27
Children with Disabilities — 5
Education Spending Per Capita — 11
Education Spending as a Percentage of Total Spending — 17
Spending Per Pupil — 31
Average Teacher Salary — 43
Sources of School Funds — 49
State Aid Per Pupil — 6
Higher Education Spending Per Capita — 1
Higher Education Spending as a Percentage of Total Spending — 2
Public Higher Education Enrollment — 5
Per Pupil Support of Higher Education — 14
Tuition and Fees — 41
Average Professor Salary — 37
Education Employees — 18
R and D Spending — 2
Library Operating Spending — 43

Health · Section I

Immunization Rates — 49
Infant Mortality Rates — 30
State Health Rankings — 42
Population Without Health Insurance — 2
Abortions — 27
Alcohol Consumption — 14
Percentage of Adult Smokers — 21
Percentage Obese — 34
AIDS Cases — 27
Physicians Per 100,000 Population — 32
Hospital Beds Per 1,000 Population — 48
Medicaid Recipients — 5
Medicaid Recipients as a Percentage of Poverty Population — 33
Health and Hospital Spending — 16
Health and Hospital Spending as a Percentage of Total Spending — 23
Per Capita Medicaid Spending — 10
Medicaid Spending Per Aged Recipient — 36
Medicaid Spending Per Child — 24
Medicare Payment Per Hospital Day — 23
Hospital Expense Per Inpatient Day — 16
Population in HMOs — 18

Crime · Section J

Crime Rate — 5
Violent Crime Rate — 3
Murder Rate — 19
Property Crime Rate — 8
Motor Vehicle Theft Rate — 21
Violent Crime Rate Change — 7
Prisoners — 37
Change in Prisoners — 15
Incarceration Rate — 38
Juvenile Violent Crime Rate — 19
Law Enforcement Employees — 18
Corrections Employees — 7
State Corrections Spending — 22
Increase in State Corrections Spending — 22
Law Enforcement Spending — 15
Law Enforcement Spending as a Percentage of Total Spending — 19

Transportation · Section K

Travel on Interstates — 14
Interstate Mileage in Unacceptable Condition — 31
Deficient Bridges — 45

Traffic Deaths — 9
Seat Belt Use — 2
Vehicle-miles Traveled Per Capita — 5
Workers Using Public Transportation — 30
Road and Street Miles — 16
Highway Employees — 21
Public Transit Employees — 22
Highway Spending Per Capita — 7
Highway Spending as a Percentage of Total Spending — 9

Welfare · Section L

Percentage of Births to Unwed Mothers — 2
TANF Recipients as a Percentage of Population — 5
Food Stamp Recipients as a Percentage of Population — 8
SSI Recipients as a Percentage of Population — 13
Change in TANF/AFDC Recipients — 30
Condition of Children Index — 46
Percentage of Families with Single Parent — 4
Average Monthly TANF Payments — 10
Welfare as a Percentage of Poverty-level Income — 15
State Supplements of SSI — 17
State Income Tax Liability of Typical Family in Poverty — 32
Child Support Collections — 50
Child Support Collections Per Dollar of Administrative Costs — 50
Children in Foster Care — 46
Welfare Spending Per Capita — 23
Welfare Spending as a Percentage of Total Spending — 24
Administrative Costs Per TANF Case — 48

Technology · Section M

Percentage of Households with Computers — 42
Percentage of Households with Internet Access — 45
Zip codes with Broadband Service — 35
High-tech Jobs — 21
Dot-com Domain Names — 26
State Government Website Ratings — 31
Students per Computer — 38

New York

Population - Section A

Population 2001	3
Population Change 2000-2001	42
Population Change 1990-2001	42
Population 2015	49
Population 2025	4
Percentage 65 and Over	24
Percentage 17 and Under	37
Median Age	23
Percentage African American	10
Percentage Hispanic	8
Percentage in Poverty	11
Child Poverty Rate	12
Percentage Female	3
Birth Rates	24
Death Rates	40
Population Density	7
New Legal Immigrants 2000	2

Economies - Section B

Personal Income 2001	2
Gross State Product	6
Per Capita Personal Income	4
Personal Income from Wages and Salaries	5
Average Annual Pay	2
Average Hourly Earnings	24
Value Added in Manufacturing	42
Cost of Living	7
Average Annual Pay in Manufacturing	12
Average Annual Pay in Retailing	8
Labor Force	45
Unemployment Rate	15
Employment Rate	36
Government Employment	19
Manufacturing Employment	38
Fortune 500 Companies	7
Forbes 500 Companies	5
Tourism Spending Per Capita	13
Exports Per Capita	19
Housing Permits	48
Percentage Change in Home Prices	7
Net Farm Income	25
Financial Institution Assets	4
Bankruptcy Filings	41
Patents Issued	14
WC Disability Payment	46
UC Average Weekly Benefit	10
Economic Momentum	48
One-year Employment Change	35
Manufacturing Employment Change	40
Home Ownership	50
Gambling	3

Electricity Use Per Residential Customer	47
Cost Per Kwh	1
New Companies	14

Geography - Section C

Total Land Area	30
Federally Owned Land	43
State Park Acreage	3
State Park Visitors	20
Population Not Active	10
Hunters with Firearms	31
Registered Boats	7
State Spending for the Arts	4
Energy Consumption Per Capita	47
Toxic Chemical Release Per Capita	44
Hazardous Waste Sites	4
Polluted Rivers and Streams	29
Expired Surface Water Pollution Permits	44
Air Pollution Emissions	8

Government - Section D

Members of United States House	3
State Legislators	4
Legislators Per Million Population	47
Units of Government	35
Legislators Compensation	2
Female Legislators	26
Turnover in Legislatures	40
Term Limits	n/a
Legislative Session Length	n/a
Republicans in State Legislatures	38
Governor's Power Rating	2
Number of Statewide Elected Officials	40
State and Local Government Employees	8
State and Local Average Salaries	3
Local Employment	2
Local Spending Accountability	11
Registered Voters	17
Percentage of Population Voting	41
Statewide Initiatives	n/a
Campaign Costs Per Vote	20

Federal Impacts - Section E

Per Capita Federal Spending	27
Increase in Federal Spending	46
Per Capita Federal Grant Spending	7
Per Capita Federal Spending on Procurement	44

Per Capita Federal Spending on Payments to Individuals	22
Per Capita Federal Spending on Social Security and Medicare	8
Social Security Benefits	4
Federal Spending on Employee Wages and Salaries	42
Federal Grant Spending Per Dollar of State Tax Revenue	13
General Revenue from Federal Government	20
Federal Tax Burden Per Capita	4
Federal Spending Per Dollar of Taxes Paid	42
Highway Charges Returned to States	15
Terms of Trade	21
Federal Personal Income Taxes	7
Federal Share of Medicaid	39

Taxes - Section F

Tax Revenue	1
Per Capita Tax Revenue	2
Tax Effort	1
Tax Capacity	12
Percentage Change in Taxes	46
Property Taxes as a Percentage of Income	9
Property Taxes Per Capita	4
Property Tax Revenue as a Percentage of 3-tax Revenues	23
Sales Taxes as a Percentage of Income	33
Sales Taxes Per Capita	11
Sales Tax Revenue as a Percentage of 3-tax Revenues	41
Sales Tax Rate	37
Income Taxes as a Percentage of Income	1
Income Taxes Per Capita	1
Income Tax Revenue as a Percentage of 3-tax Revenues	7
Highest Personal Income Rate	14
Corporate Income Taxes	2
Motor Fuel Taxes	16
Tobacco Taxes	2
Taxes on High Income Families	5
Taxes in the Largest City in Each State	11
Progressivity of Taxes	3

Revenues and Finances - Section G

Per Capita Total Revenue	3
Per Capita General Revenue	2
Own-source General Revenue	2
Per Capita Non-tax Revenue	13

Per Capita Total Spending	2
General Spending as a Percentage of Income	8
Per Capita General Spending	2
Change in General Expenditures	47
State Government General Revenue	7
State Government General Spending	9
State Government General Fund Spending	33
State and Local Debt	2
Debt as a Percentage of Revenue	4
Per Capita Full Faith and Credit Debt	6
Bond Ratings	6
State Solvency Index	28
Pension Plan Assets	2
State Reserves	29
Capital Outlays and Interest	2
State Budget Process Quality	20
Relative State Spending "Needs"	41
Structural Deficits	8

Education - Section H

Math Proficiency, Eighth Grade	19
Science Proficiency, Eighth Grade	22
AFQT Ranks	35
SAT Scores	18
ACT Scores	n/a
Over-25 Population with a High School Diploma	38
Students in Private Schools	6
High School Completion Rates	32
Pupil-Teacher Ratio	44
Public School Enrollment	47
Library Holdings Per Capita	7
Children with Disabilities	10
Education Spending Per Capita	7
Education Spending as a Percentage of Total Spending	48
Spending Per Pupil	1
Average Teacher Salary	3
Sources of School Funds	17
State Aid Per Pupil	12
Higher Education Spending Per Capita	49
Higher Education Spending as a Percentage of Total Spending	50
Public Higher Education Enrollment	46
Per Pupil Support of Higher Education	13
Tuition and Fees	14
Average Professor Salary	17
Education Employees	20
R and D Spending	23
Library Operating Spending	2

Health - Section I

Immunization Rates	15
Infant Mortality Rates	35
State Health Rankings	32
Population Without Health Insurance	14
Abortions	1
Alcohol Consumption	41
Percentage of Adult Smokers	26
Percentage Obese	32
AIDS Cases	1
Physicians Per 100,000 Population	3
Hospital Beds Per 1,000 Population	16
Medicaid Recipients	9
Medicaid Recipients as a Percentage of Poverty Population	28
Health and Hospital Spending	7
Health and Hospital Spending as a Percentage of Total Spending	21
Per Capita Medicaid Spending	1
Medicaid Spending Per Aged Recipient	2
Medicaid Spending Per Child	3
Medicare Payment Per Hospital Day	45
Hospital Expense Per Inpatient Day	36
Population in HMOs	6

Crime - Section J

Crime Rate	44
Violent Crime Rate	16
Murder Rate	24
Property Crime Rate	46
Motor Vehicle Theft Rate	39
Violent Crime Rate Change	43
Prisoners	4
Change in Prisoners	47
Incarceration Rate	27
Juvenile Violent Crime Rate	16
Law Enforcement Employees	1
Corrections Employees	1
State Corrections Spending	17
Increase in State Corrections Spending	47
Law Enforcement Spending	2
Law Enforcement Spending as a Percentage of Total Spending	13

Transportation - Section K

Travel on Interstates	45
Interstate Mileage in Unacceptable Condition	7
Deficient Bridges	7

Traffic Deaths	43
Seat Belt Use	10
Vehicle-miles Traveled Per Capita	50
Workers Using Public Transportation	1
Road and Street Miles	28
Highway Employees	29
Public Transit Employees	1
Highway Spending Per Capita	31
Highway Spending as a Percentage of Total Spending	48

Welfare - Section L

Percentage of Births to Unwed Mothers	12
TANF Recipients as a Percentage of Population	9
Food Stamp Recipients as a Percentage of Population	15
SSI Recipients as a Percentage of Population	6
Change in TANF/AFDC Recipients	28
Condition of Children Index	31
Percentage of Families with Single Parent	4
Average Monthly TANF Payments	2
Welfare as a Percentage of Poverty-level Income	9
State Supplements of SSI	24
State Income Tax Liability of Typical Family in Poverty	39
Child Support Collections	23
Child Support Collections Per Dollar of Administrative Costs	15
Children in Foster Care	6
Welfare Spending Per Capita	1
Welfare Spending as a Percentage of Total Spending	3
Administrative Costs Per TANF Case	13

Technology - Section M

Percentage of Households with Computers	33
Percentage of Households with Internet Access	28
Zip codes with Broadband Service	12
High-tech Jobs	18
Dot-com Domain Names	10
State Government Website Ratings	11
Students per Computer	15

North Carolina

Population - Section A

Population 2001	11
Population Change 2000-2001	10
Population Change 1990-2001	9
Population 2015	27
Population 2025	11
Percentage 65 and Over	33
Percentage 17 and Under	43
Median Age	33
Percentage African American	7
Percentage Hispanic	25
Percentage in Poverty	19
Child Poverty Rate	17
Percentage Female	22
Birth Rates	12
Death Rates	11
Population Density	17
New Legal Immigrants 2000	17

Economies - Section B

Personal Income 2001	13
Gross State Product	19
Per Capita Personal Income	32
Personal Income from Wages and Salaries	15
Average Annual Pay	25
Average Hourly Earnings	40
Value Added in Manufacturing	3
Cost of Living	25
Average Annual Pay in Manufacturing	33
Average Annual Pay in Retailing	24
Labor Force	40
Unemployment Rate	6
Employment Rate	45
Government Employment	31
Manufacturing Employment	7
Fortune 500 Companies	22
Forbes 500 Companies	29
Tourism Spending Per Capita	34
Exports Per Capita	21
Housing Permits	6
Percentage Change in Home Prices	30
Net Farm Income	3
Financial Institution Assets	3
Bankruptcy Filings	35
Patents Issued	25
WC Disability Payment	14
UC Average Weekly Benefit	17
Economic Momentum	28
One-year Employment Change	19
Manufacturing Employment Change	26
Home Ownership	18
Gambling	47

Electricity Use Per Residential Customer	15
Cost Per Kwh	18
New Companies	27

Geography - Section C

Total Land Area	29
Federally Owned Land	24
State Park Acreage	19
State Park Visitors	43
Population Not Active	19
Hunters with Firearms	33
Registered Boats	12
State Spending for the Arts	32
Energy Consumption Per Capita	33
Toxic Chemical Release Per Capita	21
Hazardous Waste Sites	15
Polluted Rivers and Streams	48
Expired Surface Water Pollution Permits	11
Air Pollution Emissions	11

Government - Section D

Members of United States House	9
State Legislators	15
Legislators Per Million Population	39
Units of Government	43
Legislators Compensation	31
Female Legislators	34
Turnover in Legislatures	17
Term Limits	n/a
Legislative Session Length	7
Republicans in State Legislatures	27
Governor's Power Rating	48
Number of Statewide Elected Officials	2
State and Local Government Employees	20
State and Local Average Salaries	29
Local Employment	16
Local Spending Accountability	37
Registered Voters	21
Percentage of Population Voting	35
Statewide Initiatives	n/a
Campaign Costs Per Vote	17

Federal Impacts - Section E

Per Capita Federal Spending	38
Increase in Federal Spending	19
Per Capita Federal Grant Spending	32
Per Capita Federal Spending on Procurement	39

Per Capita Federal Spending on Payments to Individuals	36
Per Capita Federal Spending on Social Security and Medicare	31
Social Security Benefits	35
Federal Spending on Employee Wages and Salaries	18
Federal Grant Spending Per Dollar of State Tax Revenue	23
General Revenue from Federal Government	16
Federal Tax Burden Per Capita	31
Federal Spending Per Dollar of Taxes Paid	30
Highway Charges Returned to States	37
Terms of Trade	26
Federal Personal Income Taxes	32
Federal Share of Medicaid	19

Taxes - Section F

Tax Revenue	31
Per Capita Tax Revenue	31
Tax Effort	27
Tax Capacity	35
Percentage Change in Taxes	15
Property Taxes as a Percentage of Income	40
Property Taxes Per Capita	39
Property Tax Revenue as a Percentage of 3-tax Revenues	41
Sales Taxes as a Percentage of Income	34
Sales Taxes Per Capita	37
Sales Tax Revenue as a Percentage of 3-tax Revenues	26
Sales Tax Rate	34
Income Taxes as a Percentage of Income	10
Income Taxes Per Capita	12
Income Tax Revenue as a Percentage of 3-tax Revenues	6
Highest Personal Income Rate	5
Corporate Income Taxes	12
Motor Fuel Taxes	10
Tobacco Taxes	48
Taxes on High Income Families	19
Taxes in the Largest City in Each State	18
Progressivity of Taxes	18

Revenues and Finances - Section G

Per Capita Total Revenue	27
Per Capita General Revenue	28
Own-source General Revenue	33
Per Capita Non-tax Revenue	24

Per Capita Total Spending	29
General Spending as a Percentage of Income	22
Per Capita General Spending	27
Change in General Expenditures	2
State Government General Revenue	23
State Government General Spending	27
State Government General Fund Spending	31
State and Local Debt	42
Debt as a Percentage of Revenue	41
Per Capita Full Faith and Credit Debt	35
Bond Ratings	2
State Solvency Index	7
Pension Plan Assets	21
State Reserves	46
Capital Outlays and Interest	33
State Budget Process Quality	41
Relative State Spending "Needs"	18
Structural Deficits	27

Education - Section H

Math Proficiency, Eighth Grade	13
Science Proficiency, Eighth Grade	25
AFQT Ranks	33
SAT Scores	19
ACT Scores	n/a
Over-25 Population with a High School Diploma	46
Students in Private Schools	34
High School Completion Rates	34
Pupil-Teacher Ratio	18
Public School Enrollment	33
Library Holdings Per Capita	41
Children with Disabilities	22
Education Spending Per Capita	33
Education Spending as a Percentage of Total Spending	30
Spending Per Pupil	39
Average Teacher Salary	22
Sources of School Funds	46
State Aid Per Pupil	8
Higher Education Spending Per Capita	18
Higher Education Spending as a Percentage of Total Spending	14
Public Higher Education Enrollment	31
Per Pupil Support of Higher Education	4
Tuition and Fees	48
Average Professor Salary	6
Education Employees	34
R and D Spending	28
Library Operating Spending	36

Health - Section I

Immunization Rates	3
Infant Mortality Rates	7
State Health Rankings	36
Population Without Health Insurance	17
Abortions	10
Alcohol Consumption	37
Percentage of Adult Smokers	10
Percentage Obese	11
AIDS Cases	17
Physicians Per 100,000 Population	29
Hospital Beds Per 1,000 Population	28
Medicaid Recipients	21
Medicaid Recipients as a Percentage of Poverty Population	30
Health and Hospital Spending	6
Health and Hospital Spending as a Percentage of Total Spending	6
Per Capita Medicaid Spending	19
Medicaid Spending Per Aged Recipient	33
Medicaid Spending Per Child	31
Medicare Payment Per Hospital Day	43
Hospital Expense Per Inpatient Day	32
Population in HMOs	32

Crime - Section J

Crime Rate	10
Violent Crime Rate	19
Murder Rate	15
Property Crime Rate	9
Motor Vehicle Theft Rate	31
Violent Crime Rate Change	25
Prisoners	11
Change in Prisoners	46
Incarceration Rate	31
Juvenile Violent Crime Rate	15
Law Enforcement Employees	30
Corrections Employees	8
State Corrections Spending	25
Increase in State Corrections Spending	42
Law Enforcement Spending	28
Law Enforcement Spending as a Percentage of Total Spending	25

Transportation - Section K

Travel on Interstates	44
Interstate Mileage in Unacceptable Condition	14
Deficient Bridges	17

Traffic Deaths	21
Seat Belt Use	5
Vehicle-miles Traveled Per Capita	16
Workers Using Public Transportation	41
Road and Street Miles	4
Highway Employees	32
Public Transit Employees	40
Highway Spending Per Capita	39
Highway Spending as a Percentage of Total Spending	39

Welfare - Section L

Percentage of Births to Unwed Mothers	19
TANF Recipients as a Percentage of Population	38
Food Stamp Recipients as a Percentage of Population	24
SSI Recipients as a Percentage of Population	18
Change in TANF/AFDC Recipients	9
Condition of Children Index	39
Percentage of Families with Single Parent	13
Average Monthly TANF Payments	34
Welfare as a Percentage of Poverty-level Income	41
State Supplements of SSI	1
State Income Tax Liability of Typical Family in Poverty	17
Child Support Collections	34
Child Support Collections Per Dollar of Administrative Costs	32
Children in Foster Care	34
Welfare Spending Per Capita	27
Welfare Spending as a Percentage of Total Spending	20
Administrative Costs Per TANF Case	35

Technology - Section M

Percentage of Households with Computers	43
Percentage of Households with Internet Access	42
Zip codes with Broadband Service	15
High-tech Jobs	23
Dot-com Domain Names	27
State Government Website Ratings	17
Students per Computer	10

North Dakota

Population - Section A

Population 2001	48
Population Change 2000-2001	50
Population Change 1990-2001	50
Population 2015	15
Population 2025	48
Percentage 65 and Over	5
Percentage 17 and Under	33
Median Age	14
Percentage African American	46
Percentage Hispanic	47
Percentage in Poverty	13
Child Poverty Rate	13
Percentage Female	42
Birth Rates	45
Death Rates	47
Population Density	47
New Legal Immigrants 2000	49

Economies - Section B

Personal Income 2001	49
Gross State Product	42
Per Capita Personal Income	37
Personal Income from Wages and Salaries	33
Average Annual Pay	48
Average Hourly Earnings	45
Value Added in Manufacturing	43
Cost of Living	34
Average Annual Pay in Manufacturing	45
Average Annual Pay in Retailing	46
Labor Force	12
Unemployment Rate	48
Employment Rate	3
Government Employment	4
Manufacturing Employment	42
Fortune 500 Companies	n/a
Forbes 500 Companies	16
Tourism Spending Per Capita	22
Exports Per Capita	37
Housing Permits	35
Percentage Change in Home Prices	45
Net Farm Income	30
Financial Institution Assets	10
Bankruptcy Filings	45
Patents Issued	36
WC Disability Payment	34
UC Average Weekly Benefit	34
Economic Momentum	14
One-year Employment Change	15
Manufacturing Employment Change	1
Home Ownership	28
Gambling	39

Electricity Use Per Residential Customer	19
Cost Per Kwh	25
New Companies	46

Geography - Section C

Total Land Area	17
Federally Owned Land	19
State Park Acreage	49
State Park Visitors	38
Population Not Active	32
Hunters with Firearms	6
Registered Boats	41
State Spending for the Arts	29
Energy Consumption Per Capita	2
Toxic Chemical Release Per Capita	10
Hazardous Waste Sites	50
Polluted Rivers and Streams	21
Expired Surface Water Pollution Permits	49
Air Pollution Emissions	40

Government - Section D

Members of United States House	44
State Legislators	26
Legislators Per Million Population	3
Units of Government	1
Legislators Compensation	36
Female Legislators	37
Turnover in Legislatures	39
Term Limits	n/a
Legislative Session Length	20
Republicans in State Legislatures	6
Governor's Power Rating	5
Number of Statewide Elected Officials	1
State and Local Government Employees	11
State and Local Average Salaries	32
Local Employment	47
Local Spending Accountability	34
Registered Voters	n/a
Percentage of Population Voting	9
Statewide Initiatives	9
Campaign Costs Per Vote	24

Federal Impacts - Section E

Per Capita Federal Spending	3
Increase in Federal Spending	1
Per Capita Federal Grant Spending	3
Per Capita Federal Spending on Procurement	35

Per Capita Federal Spending on Payments to Individuals	1
Per Capita Federal Spending on Social Security and Medicare	26
Social Security Benefits	42
Federal Spending on Employee Wages and Salaries	5
Federal Grant Spending Per Dollar of State Tax Revenue	5
General Revenue from Federal Government	1
Federal Tax Burden Per Capita	38
Federal Spending Per Dollar of Taxes Paid	2
Highway Charges Returned to States	4
Terms of Trade	3
Federal Personal Income Taxes	41
Federal Share of Medicaid	13

Taxes - Section F

Tax Revenue	11
Per Capita Tax Revenue	28
Tax Effort	35
Tax Capacity	24
Percentage Change in Taxes	37
Property Taxes as a Percentage of Income	15
Property Taxes Per Capita	27
Property Tax Revenue as a Percentage of 3-tax Revenues	15
Sales Taxes as a Percentage of Income	14
Sales Taxes Per Capita	19
Sales Tax Revenue as a Percentage of 3-tax Revenues	15
Sales Tax Rate	19
Income Taxes as a Percentage of Income	41
Income Taxes Per Capita	41
Income Tax Revenue as a Percentage of 3-tax Revenues	41
Highest Personal Income Rate	29
Corporate Income Taxes	15
Motor Fuel Taxes	23
Tobacco Taxes	26
Taxes on High Income Families	40
Taxes in the Largest City in Each State	37
Progressivity of Taxes	38

Revenues and Finances - Section G

Per Capita Total Revenue	18
Per Capita General Revenue	10
Own-source General Revenue	18
Per Capita Non-tax Revenue	6

Per Capita Total Spending	15
General Spending as a Percentage of Income	4
Per Capita General Spending	12
Change in General Expenditures	23
State Government General Revenue	8
State Government General Spending	11
State Government General Fund Spending	18
State and Local Debt	32
Debt as a Percentage of Revenue	34
Per Capita Full Faith and Credit Debt	41
Bond Ratings	n/a
State Solvency Index	4
Pension Plan Assets	50
State Reserves	7
Capital Outlays and Interest	9
State Budget Process Quality	36
Relative State Spending "Needs"	24
Structural Deficits	3

Education - Section H

Math Proficiency, Eighth Grade	5
Science Proficiency, Eighth Grade	2
AFQT Ranks	3
SAT Scores	n/a
ACT Scores	14
Over-25 Population with a High School Diploma	29
Students in Private Schools	39
High School Completion Rates	2
Pupil-Teacher Ratio	39
Public School Enrollment	10
Library Holdings Per Capita	16
Children with Disabilities	41
Education Spending Per Capita	14
Education Spending as a Percentage of Total Spending	33
Spending Per Pupil	50
Average Teacher Salary	49
Sources of School Funds	14
State Aid Per Pupil	49
Higher Education Spending Per Capita	3
Higher Education Spending as a Percentage of Total Spending	8
Public Higher Education Enrollment	4
Per Pupil Support of Higher Education	22
Tuition and Fees	33
Average Professor Salary	49
Education Employees	29
R and D Spending	36
Library Operating Spending	47

Health - Section I

Immunization Rates	11
Infant Mortality Rates	13
State Health Rankings	9
Population Without Health Insurance	38
Abortions	34
Alcohol Consumption	12
Percentage of Adult Smokers	37
Percentage Obese	31
AIDS Cases	50
Physicians Per 100,000 Population	27
Hospital Beds Per 1,000 Population	1
Medicaid Recipients	44
Medicaid Recipients as a Percentage of Poverty Population	40
Health and Hospital Spending	48
Health and Hospital Spending as a Percentage of Total Spending	49
Per Capita Medicaid Spending	25
Medicaid Spending Per Aged Recipient	7
Medicaid Spending Per Child	21
Medicare Payment Per Hospital Day	42
Hospital Expense Per Inpatient Day	44
Population in HMOs	49

Crime - Section J

Crime Rate	48
Violent Crime Rate	50
Murder Rate	48
Property Crime Rate	47
Motor Vehicle Theft Rate	45
Violent Crime Rate Change	6
Prisoners	50
Change in Prisoners	1
Incarceration Rate	48
Juvenile Violent Crime Rate	48
Law Enforcement Employees	46
Corrections Employees	49
State Corrections Spending	23
Increase in State Corrections Spending	1
Law Enforcement Spending	50
Law Enforcement Spending as a Percentage of Total Spending	50

Transportation - Section K

Travel on Interstates	37
Interstate Mileage in Unacceptable Condition	44
Deficient Bridges	30

Traffic Deaths	29
Seat Belt Use	44
Vehicle-miles Traveled Per Capita	12
Workers Using Public Transportation	45
Road and Street Miles	46
Highway Employees	10
Public Transit Employees	44
Highway Spending Per Capita	4
Highway Spending as a Percentage of Total Spending	4

Welfare - Section L

Percentage of Births to Unwed Mothers	43
TANF Recipients as a Percentage of Population	30
Food Stamp Recipients as a Percentage of Population	26
SSI Recipients as a Percentage of Population	45
Change in TANF/AFDC Recipients	48
Condition of Children Index	7
Percentage of Families with Single Parent	40
Average Monthly TANF Payments	26
Welfare as a Percentage of Poverty-level Income	32
State Supplements of SSI	2
State Income Tax Liability of Typical Family in Poverty	18
Child Support Collections	14
Child Support Collections Per Dollar of Administrative Costs	26
Children in Foster Care	25
Welfare Spending Per Capita	12
Welfare Spending as a Percentage of Total Spending	19
Administrative Costs Per TANF Case	7

Technology - Section M

Percentage of Households with Computers	37
Percentage of Households with Internet Access	38
Zip codes with Broadband Service	49
High-tech Jobs	32
Dot-com Domain Names	36
State Government Website Ratings	20
Students per Computer	47

Ohio

Population - Section A

Population 2001	7
Population Change 2000-2001	43
Population Change 1990-2001	45
Population 2015	46
Population 2025	7
Percentage 65 and Over	16
Percentage 17 and Under	28
Median Age	14
Percentage African American	17
Percentage Hispanic	41
Percentage in Poverty	24
Child Poverty Rate	20
Percentage Female	11
Birth Rates	24
Death Rates	15
Population Density	9
New Legal Immigrants 2000	16

Economies - Section B

Personal Income 2001	7
Gross State Product	24
Per Capita Personal Income	24
Personal Income from Wages and Salaries	16
Average Annual Pay	21
Average Hourly Earnings	4
Value Added in Manufacturing	6
Cost of Living	22
Average Annual Pay in Manufacturing	16
Average Annual Pay in Retailing	25
Labor Force	22
Unemployment Rate	16
Employment Rate	35
Government Employment	40
Manufacturing Employment	6
Fortune 500 Companies	9
Forbes 500 Companies	9
Tourism Spending Per Capita	46
Exports Per Capita	14
Housing Permits	32
Percentage Change in Home Prices	28
Net Farm Income	15
Financial Institution Assets	7
Bankruptcy Filings	13
Patents Issued	17
WC Disability Payment	21
UC Average Weekly Benefit	18
Economic Momentum	43
One-year Employment Change	36
Manufacturing Employment Change	14
Home Ownership	23
Gambling	14

Electricity Use Per Residential Customer	28
Cost Per Kwh	16
New Companies	48

Geography - Section C

Total Land Area	35
Federally Owned Land	40
State Park Acreage	15
State Park Visitors	9
Population Not Active	21
Hunters with Firearms	27
Registered Boats	8
State Spending for the Arts	17
Energy Consumption Per Capita	24
Toxic Chemical Release Per Capita	17
Hazardous Waste Sites	11
Polluted Rivers and Streams	25
Expired Surface Water Pollution Permits	16
Air Pollution Emissions	4

Government - Section D

Members of United States House	7
State Legislators	32
Legislators Per Million Population	46
Units of Government	29
Legislators Compensation	6
Female Legislators	28
Turnover in Legislatures	29
Term Limits	6
Legislative Session Length	n/a
Republicans in State Legislatures	9
Governor's Power Rating	5
Number of Statewide Elected Officials	35
State and Local Government Employees	33
State and Local Average Salaries	19
Local Employment	5
Local Spending Accountability	23
Registered Voters	15
Percentage of Population Voting	33
Statewide Initiatives	17
Campaign Costs Per Vote	27

Federal Impacts - Section E

Per Capita Federal Spending	39
Increase in Federal Spending	43
Per Capita Federal Grant Spending	37
Per Capita Federal Spending on Procurement	33

Per Capita Federal Spending on Payments to Individuals	26
Per Capita Federal Spending on Social Security and Medicare	16
Social Security Benefits	18
Federal Spending on Employee Wages and Salaries	43
Federal Grant Spending Per Dollar of State Tax Revenue	28
General Revenue from Federal Government	30
Federal Tax Burden Per Capita	27
Federal Spending Per Dollar of Taxes Paid	32
Highway Charges Returned to States	48
Terms of Trade	31
Federal Personal Income Taxes	27
Federal Share of Medicaid	29

Taxes - Section F

Tax Revenue	20
Per Capita Tax Revenue	20
Tax Effort	16
Tax Capacity	29
Percentage Change in Taxes	34
Property Taxes as a Percentage of Income	24
Property Taxes Per Capita	25
Property Tax Revenue as a Percentage of 3-tax Revenues	29
Sales Taxes as a Percentage of Income	38
Sales Taxes Per Capita	36
Sales Tax Revenue as a Percentage of 3-tax Revenues	36
Sales Tax Rate	19
Income Taxes as a Percentage of Income	9
Income Taxes Per Capita	9
Income Tax Revenue as a Percentage of 3-tax Revenues	9
Highest Personal Income Rate	11
Corporate Income Taxes	43
Motor Fuel Taxes	17
Tobacco Taxes	23
Taxes on High Income Families	16
Taxes in the Largest City in Each State	16
Progressivity of Taxes	27

Revenues and Finances - Section G

Per Capita Total Revenue	16
Per Capita General Revenue	25
Own-source General Revenue	25
Per Capita Non-tax Revenue	34

Per Capita Total Spending	22
General Spending as a Percentage of Income	31
Per Capita General Spending	25
Change in General Expenditures	28
State Government General Revenue	35
State Government General Spending	35
State Government General Fund Spending	21
State and Local Debt	40
Debt as a Percentage of Revenue	46
Per Capita Full Faith and Credit Debt	31
Bond Ratings	2
State Solvency Index	23
Pension Plan Assets	30
State Reserves	29
Capital Outlays and Interest	30
State Budget Process Quality	34
Relative State Spending "Needs"	28
Structural Deficits	3

Education · Section H

Math Proficiency, Eighth Grade	5
Science Proficiency, Eighth Grade	2
AFQT Ranks	24
SAT Scores	n/a
ACT Scores	8
Over-25 Population with a High School Diploma	19
Students in Private Schools	12
High School Completion Rates	25
Pupil-Teacher Ratio	25
Public School Enrollment	38
Library Holdings Per Capita	11
Children with Disabilities	31
Education Spending Per Capita	28
Education Spending as a Percentage of Total Spending	23
Spending Per Pupil	21
Average Teacher Salary	17
Sources of School Funds	12
State Aid Per Pupil	24
Higher Education Spending Per Capita	34
Higher Education Spending as a Percentage of Total Spending	36
Public Higher Education Enrollment	38
Per Pupil Support of Higher Education	29
Tuition and Fees	7
Average Professor Salary	21
Education Employees	35
R and D Spending	22
Library Operating Spending	1

Health · Section I

Immunization Rates	37
Infant Mortality Rates	16
State Health Rankings	27
Population Without Health Insurance	31
Abortions	16
Alcohol Consumption	36
Percentage of Adult Smokers	4
Percentage Obese	16
AIDS Cases	36
Physicians Per 100,000 Population	12
Hospital Beds Per 1,000 Population	24
Medicaid Recipients	36
Medicaid Recipients as a Percentage of Poverty Population	38
Health and Hospital Spending	17
Health and Hospital Spending as a Percentage of Total Spending	20
Per Capita Medicaid Spending	17
Medicaid Spending Per Aged Recipient	4
Medicaid Spending Per Child	26
Medicare Payment Per Hospital Day	33
Hospital Expense Per Inpatient Day	21
Population in HMOs	25

Crime · Section J

Crime Rate	24
Violent Crime Rate	29
Murder Rate	26
Property Crime Rate	22
Motor Vehicle Theft Rate	23
Violent Crime Rate Change	27
Prisoners	7
Change in Prisoners	45
Incarceration Rate	20
Juvenile Violent Crime Rate	29
Law Enforcement Employees	23
Corrections Employees	21
State Corrections Spending	15
Increase in State Corrections Spending	28
Law Enforcement Spending	21
Law Enforcement Spending as a Percentage of Total Spending	15

Transportation · Section K

Travel on Interstates	8
Interstate Mileage in Unacceptable Condition	33
Deficient Bridges	29

Traffic Deaths	36
Seat Belt Use	36
Vehicle-miles Traveled Per Capita	37
Workers Using Public Transportation	21
Road and Street Miles	22
Highway Employees	35
Public Transit Employees	15
Highway Spending Per Capita	33
Highway Spending as a Percentage of Total Spending	33

Welfare · Section L

Percentage of Births to Unwed Mothers	14
TANF Recipients as a Percentage of Population	21
Food Stamp Recipients as a Percentage of Population	29
SSI Recipients as a Percentage of Population	19
Change in TANF/AFDC Recipients	11
Condition of Children Index	25
Percentage of Families with Single Parent	7
Average Monthly TANF Payments	23
Welfare as a Percentage of Poverty-level Income	18
State Supplements of SSI	42
State Income Tax Liability of Typical Family in Poverty	11
Child Support Collections	2
Child Support Collections Per Dollar of Administrative Costs	23
Children in Foster Care	24
Welfare Spending Per Capita	20
Welfare Spending as a Percentage of Total Spending	16
Administrative Costs Per TANF Case	8

Technology · Section M

Percentage of Households with Computers	25
Percentage of Households with Internet Access	26
Zip codes with Broadband Service	10
High-tech Jobs	31
Dot-com Domain Names	28
State Government Website Ratings	21
Students per Computer	33

Oklahoma

Population - Section A

Population 2001	28
Population Change 2000-2001	38
Population Change 1990-2001	31
Population 2015	19
Population 2025	28
Percentage 65 and Over	17
Percentage 17 and Under	19
Median Age	29
Percentage African American	23
Percentage Hispanic	23
Percentage in Poverty	7
Child Poverty Rate	9
Percentage Female	28
Birth Rates	15
Death Rates	10
Population Density	35
New Legal Immigrants 2000	26

Economies - Section B

Personal Income 2001	29
Gross State Product	46
Per Capita Personal Income	39
Personal Income from Wages and Salaries	45
Average Annual Pay	43
Average Hourly Earnings	35
Value Added in Manufacturing	39
Cost of Living	44
Average Annual Pay in Manufacturing	42
Average Annual Pay in Retailing	40
Labor Force	38
Unemployment Rate	37
Employment Rate	14
Government Employment	10
Manufacturing Employment	32
Fortune 500 Companies	21
Forbes 500 Companies	11
Tourism Spending Per Capita	48
Exports Per Capita	46
Housing Permits	40
Percentage Change in Home Prices	26
Net Farm Income	21
Financial Institution Assets	27
Bankruptcy Filings	10
Patents Issued	31
WC Disability Payment	39
UC Average Weekly Benefit	29
Economic Momentum	7
One-year Employment Change	6
Manufacturing Employment Change	7
Home Ownership	20
Gambling	40

Electricity Use Per Residential Customer	10
Cost Per Kwh	20
New Companies	23

Geography - Section C

Total Land Area	19
Federally Owned Land	27
State Park Acreage	34
State Park Visitors	14
Population Not Active	5
Hunters with Firearms	24
Registered Boats	21
State Spending for the Arts	16
Energy Consumption Per Capita	12
Toxic Chemical Release Per Capita	34
Hazardous Waste Sites	38
Polluted Rivers and Streams	16
Expired Surface Water Pollution Permits	41
Air Pollution Emissions	23

Government - Section D

Members of United States House	27
State Legislators	22
Legislators Per Million Population	21
Units of Government	17
Legislators Compensation	10
Female Legislators	49
Turnover in Legislatures	35
Term Limits	1
Legislative Session Length	19
Republicans in State Legislatures	31
Governor's Power Rating	30
Number of Statewide Elected Officials	9
State and Local Government Employees	16
State and Local Average Salaries	46
Local Employment	32
Local Spending Accountability	27
Registered Voters	22
Percentage of Population Voting	25
Statewide Initiatives	17
Campaign Costs Per Vote	44

Federal Impacts - Section E

Per Capita Federal Spending	17
Increase in Federal Spending	15
Per Capita Federal Grant Spending	25
Per Capita Federal Spending on Procurement	23

Per Capita Federal Spending on Payments to Individuals	16
Per Capita Federal Spending on Social Security and Medicare	20
Social Security Benefits	37
Federal Spending on Employee Wages and Salaries	7
Federal Grant Spending Per Dollar of State Tax Revenue	27
General Revenue from Federal Government	21
Federal Tax Burden Per Capita	44
Federal Spending Per Dollar of Taxes Paid	10
Highway Charges Returned to States	47
Terms of Trade	14
Federal Personal Income Taxes	44
Federal Share of Medicaid	10

Taxes - Section F

Tax Revenue	33
Per Capita Tax Revenue	43
Tax Effort	29
Tax Capacity	45
Percentage Change in Taxes	25
Property Taxes as a Percentage of Income	47
Property Taxes Per Capita	47
Property Tax Revenue as a Percentage of 3-tax Revenues	44
Sales Taxes as a Percentage of Income	19
Sales Taxes Per Capita	33
Sales Tax Revenue as a Percentage of 3-tax Revenues	17
Sales Tax Rate	34
Income Taxes as a Percentage of Income	23
Income Taxes Per Capita	30
Income Tax Revenue as a Percentage of 3-tax Revenues	14
Highest Personal Income Rate	15
Corporate Income Taxes	42
Motor Fuel Taxes	41
Tobacco Taxes	36
Taxes on High Income Families	31
Taxes in the Largest City in Each State	26
Progressivity of Taxes	29

Revenues and Finances - Section G

Per Capita Total Revenue	47
Per Capita General Revenue	47
Own-source General Revenue	43
Per Capita Non-tax Revenue	31

Per Capita Total Spending   49
General Spending as a Percentage of
        Income   39
Per Capita General Spending   50
Change in General Expenditures   42
State Government General Revenue   39
State Government General Spending   49
State Government General Fund
        Spending   19
State and Local Debt   44
Debt as a Percentage of Revenue   36
Per Capita Full Faith and Credit Debt   47
Bond Ratings   4
State Solvency Index   44
Pension Plan Assets   34
State Reserves   25
Capital Outlays and Interest   45
State Budget Process Quality   19
Relative State Spending "Needs"   41
Structural Deficits   20

Education - Section H

Math Proficiency, Eighth Grade   25
Science Proficiency, Eighth Grade   22
AFQT Ranks   30
SAT Scores   n/a
ACT Scores   16
Over-25 Population with a High
        School Diploma   25
Students in Private Schools   45
High School Completion Rates   35
Pupil-Teacher Ratio   27
Public School Enrollment   5
Library Holdings Per Capita   36
Children with Disabilities   30
Education Spending Per Capita   38
Education Spending as a Percentage
        of Total Spending   1
Spending Per Pupil   37
Average Teacher Salary   45
Sources of School Funds   36
State Aid Per Pupil   32
Higher Education Spending Per
        Capita   25
Higher Education Spending as a
        Percentage of Total Spending   4
Public Higher Education Enrollment   17
Per Pupil Support of Higher
        Education   28
Tuition and Fees   49
Average Professor Salary   36
Education Employees   12
R and D Spending   47
Library Operating Spending   41

Health - Section I

Immunization Rates   32
Infant Mortality Rates   8
State Health Rankings   46
Population Without Health
        Insurance   5
Abortions   n/a
Alcohol Consumption   48
Percentage of Adult Smokers   2
Percentage Obese   13
AIDS Cases   30
Physicians Per 100,000 Population   45
Hospital Beds Per 1,000 Population   19
Medicaid Recipients   50
Medicaid Recipients as a Percentage
        of Poverty Population   50
Health and Hospital Spending   24
Health and Hospital Spending as a
        Percentage of Total Spending   12
Per Capita Medicaid Spending   37
Medicaid Spending Per Aged
        Recipient   42
Medicaid Spending Per Child   43
Medicare Payment Per Hospital Day   34
Hospital Expense Per Inpatient Day   48
Population in HMOs   32

Crime - Section J

Crime Rate   15
Violent Crime Rate   17
Murder Rate   20
Property Crime Rate   13
Motor Vehicle Theft Rate   24
Violent Crime Rate Change   21
Prisoners   19
Change in Prisoners   27
Incarceration Rate   4
Juvenile Violent Crime Rate   24
Law Enforcement Employees   12
Corrections Employees   33
State Corrections Spending   43
Increase in State Corrections
        Spending   26
Law Enforcement Spending   32
Law Enforcement Spending as a
        Percentage of Total Spending   8

Transportation - Section K

Travel on Interstates   41
Interstate Mileage in Unacceptable
        Condition   8
Deficient Bridges   5

Traffic Deaths   25
Seat Belt Use   31
Vehicle-miles Traveled Per Capita   7
Workers Using Public
        Transportation   44
Road and Street Miles   35
Highway Employees   16
Public Transit Employees   42
Highway Spending Per Capita   22
Highway Spending as a Percentage
        of Total Spending   11

Welfare - Section L

Percentage of Births to Unwed
        Mothers   15
TANF Recipients as a Percentage
        of Population   41
Food Stamp Recipients as a
        Percentage of Population   13
SSI Recipients as a Percentage of
        Population   21
Change in TANF/AFDC Recipients   12
Condition of Children Index   40
Percentage of Families with Single
        Parent   34
Average Monthly TANF
        Payments   18
Welfare as a Percentage of Poverty-
        level Income   33
State Supplements of SSI   40
State Income Tax Liability of Typical
        Family in Poverty   8
Child Support Collections   49
Child Support Collections Per Dollar
        of Administrative Costs   45
Children in Foster Care   10
Welfare Spending Per Capita   50
Welfare Spending as a Percentage of
        Total Spending   50
Administrative Costs Per TANF Case   9

Technology - Section M

Percentage of Households with
        Computers   44
Percentage of Households with
        Internet Access   44
Zip codes with Broadband
        Service   34
High-tech Jobs   30
Dot-com Domain Names   39
State Government Website
        Ratings   27
Students per Computer   27

Oregon

Population · Section A

Population 2001	27
Population Change 2000-2001	15
Population Change 1990-2001	11
Population 2015	10
Population 2025	26
Percentage 65 and Over	26
Percentage 17 and Under	36
Median Age	13
Percentage African American	41
Percentage Hispanic	14
Percentage in Poverty	20
Child Poverty Rate	24
Percentage Female	36
Birth Rates	35
Death Rates	33
Population Density	39
New Legal Immigrants 2000	19

Economies · Section B

Personal Income 2001	28
Gross State Product	22
Per Capita Personal Income	30
Personal Income from Wages and Salaries	21
Average Annual Pay	22
Average Hourly Earnings	9
Value Added in Manufacturing	17
Cost of Living	9
Average Annual Pay in Manufacturing	13
Average Annual Pay in Retailing	17
Labor Force	19
Unemployment Rate	3
Employment Rate	48
Government Employment	26
Manufacturing Employment	19
Fortune 500 Companies	36
Forbes 500 Companies	45
Tourism Spending Per Capita	29
Exports Per Capita	9
Housing Permits	16
Percentage Change in Home Prices	37
Net Farm Income	36
Financial Institution Assets	48
Bankruptcy Filings	9
Patents Issued	12
WC Disability Payment	6
UC Average Weekly Benefit	14
Economic Momentum	37
One-year Employment Change	27
Manufacturing Employment Change	19
Home Ownership	43
Gambling	21

Electricity Use Per Residential Customer	20
Cost Per Kwh	39
New Companies	12

Geography · Section C

Total Land Area	10
Federally Owned Land	7
State Park Acreage	28
State Park Visitors	2
Population Not Active	42
Hunters with Firearms	18
Registered Boats	27
State Spending for the Arts	48
Energy Consumption Per Capita	32
Toxic Chemical Release Per Capita	18
Hazardous Waste Sites	34
Polluted Rivers and Streams	42
Expired Surface Water Pollution Permits	1
Air Pollution Emissions	20

Government · Section D

Members of United States House	27
State Legislators	43
Legislators Per Million Population	33
Units of Government	21
Legislators Compensation	29
Female Legislators	4
Turnover in Legislatures	21
Term Limits	n/a
Legislative Session Length	3
Republicans in State Legislatures	20
Governor's Power Rating	30
Number of Statewide Elected Officials	21
State and Local Government Employees	42
State and Local Average Salaries	17
Local Employment	26
Local Spending Accountability	36
Registered Voters	36
Percentage of Population Voting	8
Statewide Initiatives	1
Campaign Costs Per Vote	35

Federal Impacts · Section E

Per Capita Federal Spending	41
Increase in Federal Spending	30
Per Capita Federal Grant Spending	19
Per Capita Federal Spending on Procurement	47

Per Capita Federal Spending on Payments to Individuals	34
Per Capita Federal Spending on Social Security and Medicare	32
Social Security Benefits	14
Federal Spending on Employee Wages and Salaries	39
Federal Grant Spending Per Dollar of State Tax Revenue	6
General Revenue from Federal Government	8
Federal Tax Burden Per Capita	25
Federal Spending Per Dollar of Taxes Paid	34
Highway Charges Returned to States	23
Terms of Trade	23
Federal Personal Income Taxes	24
Federal Share of Medicaid	24

Taxes · Section F

Tax Revenue	39
Per Capita Tax Revenue	29
Tax Effort	42
Tax Capacity	16
Percentage Change in Taxes	28
Property Taxes as a Percentage of Income	25
Property Taxes Per Capita	29
Property Tax Revenue as a Percentage of 3-tax Revenues	17
Sales Taxes as a Percentage of Income	50
Sales Taxes Per Capita	50
Sales Tax Revenue as a Percentage of 3-tax Revenues	50
Sales Tax Rate	n/a
Income Taxes as a Percentage of Income	2
Income Taxes Per Capita	4
Income Tax Revenue as a Percentage of 3-tax Revenues	2
Highest Personal Income Rate	4
Corporate Income Taxes	17
Motor Fuel Taxes	11
Tobacco Taxes	6
Taxes on High Income Families	14
Taxes in the Largest City in Each State	13
Progressivity of Taxes	30

Revenues and Finances · Section G

Per Capita Total Revenue	4
Per Capita General Revenue	8
Own-source General Revenue	15
Per Capita Non-tax Revenue	4

Per Capita Total Spending 7
General Spending as a Percentage of Income 10
Per Capita General Spending 9
Change in General Expenditures 10
State Government General Revenue 12
State Government General Spending 15
State Government General Fund Spending 7
State and Local Debt 28
Debt as a Percentage of Revenue 45
Per Capita Full Faith and Credit Debt 12
Bond Ratings 3
State Solvency Index 39
Pension Plan Assets 28
State Reserves 40
Capital Outlays and Interest 24
State Budget Process Quality 22
Relative State Spending "Needs" 11
Structural Deficits 12

Education - Section H

Math Proficiency, Eighth Grade 11
Science Proficiency, Eighth Grade 15
AFQT Ranks 5
SAT Scores 2
ACT Scores n/a
Over-25 Population with a High School Diploma 14
Students in Private Schools 32
High School Completion Rates 43
Pupil-Teacher Ratio 6
Public School Enrollment 37
Library Holdings Per Capita 27
Children with Disabilities 26
Education Spending Per Capita 19
Education Spending as a Percentage of Total Spending 43
Spending Per Pupil 17
Average Teacher Salary 13
Sources of School Funds 32
State Aid Per Pupil 10
Higher Education Spending Per Capita 13
Higher Education Spending as a Percentage of Total Spending 24
Public Higher Education Enrollment 16
Per Pupil Support of Higher Education 41
Tuition and Fees 20
Average Professor Salary 43
Education Employees 47
R and D Spending 26
Library Operating Spending 13

Health - Section I

Immunization Rates 39
Infant Mortality Rates 43
State Health Rankings 17
Population Without Health Insurance 25
Abortions 7
Alcohol Consumption 20
Percentage of Adult Smokers 44
Percentage Obese 24
AIDS Cases 28
Physicians Per 100,000 Population 31
Hospital Beds Per 1,000 Population 47
Medicaid Recipients 16
Medicaid Recipients as a Percentage of Poverty Population 22
Health and Hospital Spending 9
Health and Hospital Spending as a Percentage of Total Spending 11
Per Capita Medicaid Spending 33
Medicaid Spending Per Aged Recipient 31
Medicaid Spending Per Child 27
Medicare Payment Per Hospital Day 18
Hospital Expense Per Inpatient Day 4
Population in HMOs 15

Crime - Section J

Crime Rate 9
Violent Crime Rate 34
Murder Rate 39
Property Crime Rate 5
Motor Vehicle Theft Rate 18
Violent Crime Rate Change 47
Prisoners 29
Change in Prisoners 3
Incarceration Rate 33
Juvenile Violent Crime Rate 33
Law Enforcement Employees 41
Corrections Employees 18
State Corrections Spending 6
Increase in State Corrections Spending 8
Law Enforcement Spending 8
Law Enforcement Spending as a Percentage of Total Spending 14

Transportation - Section K

Travel on Interstates 25
Interstate Mileage in Unacceptable Condition 41
Deficient Bridges 37

Traffic Deaths 30
Seat Belt Use 3
Vehicle-miles Traveled Per Capita 31
Workers Using Public Transportation 12
Road and Street Miles 33
Highway Employees 25
Public Transit Employees 8
Highway Spending Per Capita 30
Highway Spending as a Percentage of Total Spending 42

Welfare - Section L

Percentage of Births to Unwed Mothers 34
TANF Recipients as a Percentage of Population 37
Food Stamp Recipients as a Percentage of Population 10
SSI Recipients as a Percentage of Population 35
Change in TANF/AFDC Recipients 40
Condition of Children Index 23
Percentage of Families with Single Parent 13
Average Monthly TANF Payments 22
Welfare as a Percentage of Poverty-level Income 11
State Supplements of SSI 20
State Income Tax Liability of Typical Family in Poverty 10
Child Support Collections 12
Child Support Collections Per Dollar of Administrative Costs 3
Children in Foster Care 15
Welfare Spending Per Capita 14
Welfare Spending as a Percentage of Total Spending 22
Administrative Costs Per TANF Case 27

Technology - Section M

Percentage of Households with Computers 5
Percentage of Households with Internet Access 5
Zip codes with Broadband Service 10
High-tech Jobs 6
Dot-com Domain Names 18
State Government Website Ratings 18
Students per Computer 19

Pennsylvania

Population - Section A

Population 2001	6
Population Change 2000-2001	46
Population Change 1990-2001	48
Population 2015	47
Population 2025	6
Percentage 65 and Over	2
Percentage 17 and Under	45
Median Age	4
Percentage African American	20
Percentage Hispanic	33
Percentage in Poverty	31
Child Poverty Rate	26
Percentage Female	5
Birth Rates	45
Death Rates	18
Population Density	10
New Legal Immigrants 2000	10

Economies - Section B

Personal Income 2001	6
Gross State Product	23
Per Capita Personal Income	15
Personal Income from Wages and Salaries	34
Average Annual Pay	18
Average Hourly Earnings	26
Value Added in Manufacturing	21
Cost of Living	16
Average Annual Pay in Manufacturing	20
Average Annual Pay in Retailing	26
Labor Force	34
Unemployment Rate	22
Employment Rate	29
Government Employment	49
Manufacturing Employment	15
Fortune 500 Companies	14
Forbes 500 Companies	12
Tourism Spending Per Capita	44
Exports Per Capita	34
Housing Permits	43
Percentage Change in Home Prices	27
Net Farm Income	18
Financial Institution Assets	15
Bankruptcy Filings	33
Patents Issued	21
WC Disability Payment	13
UC Average Weekly Benefit	8
Economic Momentum	46
One-year Employment Change	39
Manufacturing Employment Change	38
Home Ownership	7
Gambling	15

Electricity Use Per Residential Customer	32
Cost Per Kwh	9
New Companies	29

Geography - Section C

Total Land Area	32
Federally Owned Land	34
State Park Acreage	10
State Park Visitors	18
Population Not Active	28
Hunters with Firearms	14
Registered Boats	11
State Spending for the Arts	21
Energy Consumption Per Capita	22
Toxic Chemical Release Per Capita	23
Hazardous Waste Sites	3
Polluted Rivers and Streams	44
Expired Surface Water Pollution Permits	19
Air Pollution Emissions	7

Government - Section D

Members of United States House	5
State Legislators	2
Legislators Per Million Population	40
Units of Government	23
Legislators Compensation	4
Female Legislators	44
Turnover in Legislatures	45
Term Limits	n/a
Legislative Session Length	n/a
Republicans in State Legislatures	24
Governor's Power Rating	12
Number of Statewide Elected Officials	35
State and Local Government Employees	49
State and Local Average Salaries	14
Local Employment	18
Local Spending Accountability	30
Registered Voters	n/a
Percentage of Population Voting	30
Statewide Initiatives	n/a
Campaign Costs Per Vote	40

Federal Impacts - Section E

Per Capita Federal Spending	18
Increase in Federal Spending	40
Per Capita Federal Grant Spending	23
Per Capita Federal Spending on Procurement	26

Per Capita Federal Spending on Payments to Individuals	7
Per Capita Federal Spending on Social Security and Medicare	2
Social Security Benefits	9
Federal Spending on Employee Wages and Salaries	38
Federal Grant Spending Per Dollar of State Tax Revenue	33
General Revenue from Federal Government	25
Federal Tax Burden Per Capita	18
Federal Spending Per Dollar of Taxes Paid	29
Highway Charges Returned to States	17
Terms of Trade	29
Federal Personal Income Taxes	19
Federal Share of Medicaid	36

Taxes - Section F

Tax Revenue	35
Per Capita Tax Revenue	21
Tax Effort	12
Tax Capacity	32
Percentage Change in Taxes	44
Property Taxes as a Percentage of Income	29
Property Taxes Per Capita	28
Property Tax Revenue as a Percentage of 3-tax Revenues	22
Sales Taxes as a Percentage of Income	40
Sales Taxes Per Capita	38
Sales Tax Revenue as a Percentage of 3-tax Revenues	33
Sales Tax Rate	9
Income Taxes as a Percentage of Income	25
Income Taxes Per Capita	21
Income Tax Revenue as a Percentage of 3-tax Revenues	15
Highest Personal Income Rate	41
Corporate Income Taxes	13
Motor Fuel Taxes	4
Tobacco Taxes	10
Taxes on High Income Families	8
Taxes in the Largest City in Each State	3
Progressivity of Taxes	36

Revenues and Finances - Section G

Per Capita Total Revenue	24
Per Capita General Revenue	24
Own-source General Revenue	24
Per Capita Non-tax Revenue	29

Per Capita Total Spending	18
General Spending as a Percentage of Income	28
Per Capita General Spending	19
Change in General Expenditures	30
State Government General Revenue	26
State Government General Spending	26
State Government General Fund Spending	38
State and Local Debt	10
Debt as a Percentage of Revenue	8
Per Capita Full Faith and Credit Debt	11
Bond Ratings	3
State Solvency Index	11
Pension Plan Assets	3
State Reserves	39
Capital Outlays and Interest	28
State Budget Process Quality	25
Relative State Spending "Needs"	14
Structural Deficits	14

Education - Section H

Math Proficiency, Eighth Grade	n/a
Science Proficiency, Eighth Grade	n/a
AFQT Ranks	22
SAT Scores	19
ACT Scores	n/a
Over-25 Population with a High School Diploma	27
Students in Private Schools	2
High School Completion Rates	22
Pupil-Teacher Ratio	22
Public School Enrollment	49
Library Holdings Per Capita	35
Children with Disabilities	34
Education Spending Per Capita	18
Education Spending as a Percentage of Total Spending	25
Spending Per Pupil	14
Average Teacher Salary	6
Sources of School Funds	7
State Aid Per Pupil	27
Higher Education Spending Per Capita	37
Higher Education Spending as a Percentage of Total Spending	41
Public Higher Education Enrollment	50
Per Pupil Support of Higher Education	15
Tuition and Fees	3
Average Professor Salary	13
Education Employees	48
R and D Spending	17
Library Operating Spending	32

Health - Section I

Immunization Rates	6
Infant Mortality Rates	23
State Health Rankings	23
Population Without Health Insurance	44
Abortions	17
Alcohol Consumption	42
Percentage of Adult Smokers	16
Percentage Obese	19
AIDS Cases	10
Physicians Per 100,000 Population	7
Hospital Beds Per 1,000 Population	17
Medicaid Recipients	33
Medicaid Recipients as a Percentage of Poverty Population	27
Health and Hospital Spending	37
Health and Hospital Spending as a Percentage of Total Spending	34
Per Capita Medicaid Spending	30
Medicaid Spending Per Aged Recipient	18
Medicaid Spending Per Child	13
Medicare Payment Per Hospital Day	8
Hospital Expense Per Inpatient Day	37
Population in HMOs	11

Crime - Section J

Crime Rate	42
Violent Crime Rate	23
Murder Rate	20
Property Crime Rate	45
Motor Vehicle Theft Rate	33
Violent Crime Rate Change	5
Prisoners	9
Change in Prisoners	38
Incarceration Rate	35
Juvenile Violent Crime Rate	5
Law Enforcement Employees	38
Corrections Employees	23
State Corrections Spending	13
Increase in State Corrections Spending	36
Law Enforcement Spending	18
Law Enforcement Spending as a Percentage of Total Spending	21

Transportation - Section K

Travel on Interstates	34
Interstate Mileage in Unacceptable Condition	18
Deficient Bridges	4

Traffic Deaths	28
Seat Belt Use	24
Vehicle-miles Traveled Per Capita	43
Workers Using Public Transportation	7
Road and Street Miles	9
Highway Employees	33
Public Transit Employees	5
Highway Spending Per Capita	35
Highway Spending as a Percentage of Total Spending	41

Welfare - Section L

Percentage of Births to Unwed Mothers	23
TANF Recipients as a Percentage of Population	20
Food Stamp Recipients as a Percentage of Population	23
SSI Recipients as a Percentage of Population	14
Change in TANF/AFDC Recipients	17
Condition of Children Index	17
Percentage of Families with Single Parent	38
Average Monthly TANF Payments	8
Welfare as a Percentage of Poverty-level Income	27
State Supplements of SSI	41
State Income Tax Liability of Typical Family in Poverty	18
Child Support Collections	5
Child Support Collections Per Dollar of Administrative Costs	2
Children in Foster Care	22
Welfare Spending Per Capita	7
Welfare Spending as a Percentage of Total Spending	7
Administrative Costs Per TANF Case	26

Technology - Section M

Percentage of Households with Computers	35
Percentage of Households with Internet Access	31
Zip codes with Broadband Service	30
High-tech Jobs	26
Dot-com Domain Names	23
State Government Website Ratings	5
Students per Computer	27

Rhode Island

Population - Section A

Population 2001	43
Population Change 2000-2001	21
Population Change 1990-2001	43
Population 2015	48
Population 2025	43
Percentage 65 and Over	6
Percentage 17 and Under	46
Median Age	9
Percentage African American	30
Percentage Hispanic	13
Percentage in Poverty	31
Child Poverty Rate	38
Percentage Female	1
Birth Rates	41
Death Rates	35
Population Density	2
New Legal Immigrants 2000	34

Economies - Section B

Personal Income 2001	43
Gross State Product	21
Per Capita Personal Income	16
Personal Income from Wages and Salaries	42
Average Annual Pay	19
Average Hourly Earnings	48
Value Added in Manufacturing	35
Cost of Living	n/a
Average Annual Pay in Manufacturing	36
Average Annual Pay in Retailing	18
Labor Force	42
Unemployment Rate	27
Employment Rate	24
Government Employment	46
Manufacturing Employment	22
Fortune 500 Companies	18
Forbes 500 Companies	20
Tourism Spending Per Capita	38
Exports Per Capita	40
Housing Permits	49
Percentage Change in Home Prices	6
Net Farm Income	50
Financial Institution Assets	2
Bankruptcy Filings	29
Patents Issued	22
WC Disability Payment	11
UC Average Weekly Benefit	7
Economic Momentum	21
One-year Employment Change	5
Manufacturing Employment Change	6
Home Ownership	47
Gambling	30

Electricity Use Per Residential Customer	48
Cost Per Kwh	49
New Companies	15

Geography - Section C

Total Land Area	50
Federally Owned Land	50
State Park Acreage	50
State Park Visitors	5
Population Not Active	27
Hunters with Firearms	n/a
Registered Boats	45
State Spending for the Arts	9
Energy Consumption Per Capita	50
Toxic Chemical Release Per Capita	48
Hazardous Waste Sites	34
Polluted Rivers and Streams	31
Expired Surface Water Pollution Permits	33
Air Pollution Emissions	50

Government - Section D

Members of United States House	39
State Legislators	37
Legislators Per Million Population	8
Units of Government	45
Legislators Compensation	35
Female Legislators	25
Turnover in Legislatures	12
Term Limits	n/a
Legislative Session Length	5
Republicans in State Legislatures	48
Governor's Power Rating	49
Number of Statewide Elected Officials	35
State and Local Government Employees	31
State and Local Average Salaries	7
Local Employment	39
Local Spending Accountability	4
Registered Voters	12
Percentage of Population Voting	19
Statewide Initiatives	n/a
Campaign Costs Per Vote	14

Federal Impacts - Section E

Per Capita Federal Spending	16
Increase in Federal Spending	42
Per Capita Federal Grant Spending	11
Per Capita Federal Spending on Procurement	40

Per Capita Federal Spending on Payments to Individuals	12
Per Capita Federal Spending on Social Security and Medicare	5
Social Security Benefits	19
Federal Spending on Employee Wages and Salaries	15
Federal Grant Spending Per Dollar of State Tax Revenue	22
General Revenue from Federal Government	19
Federal Tax Burden Per Capita	19
Federal Spending Per Dollar of Taxes Paid	27
Highway Charges Returned to States	6
Terms of Trade	16
Federal Personal Income Taxes	21
Federal Share of Medicaid	35

Taxes - Section F

Tax Revenue	14
Per Capita Tax Revenue	13
Tax Effort	2
Tax Capacity	38
Percentage Change in Taxes	30
Property Taxes as a Percentage of Income	6
Property Taxes Per Capita	5
Property Tax Revenue as a Percentage of 3-tax Revenues	8
Sales Taxes as a Percentage of Income	37
Sales Taxes Per Capita	31
Sales Tax Revenue as a Percentage of 3-tax Revenues	38
Sales Tax Rate	1
Income Taxes as a Percentage of Income	19
Income Taxes Per Capita	18
Income Tax Revenue as a Percentage of 3-tax Revenues	33
Highest Personal Income Rate	1
Corporate Income Taxes	38
Motor Fuel Taxes	1
Tobacco Taxes	5
Taxes on High Income Families	3
Taxes in the Largest City in Each State	4
Progressivity of Taxes	21

Revenues and Finances - Section G

Per Capita Total Revenue	14
Per Capita General Revenue	20
Own-source General Revenue	19
Per Capita Non-tax Revenue	45

Per Capita Total Spending	20
General Spending as a Percentage of Income	30
Per Capita General Spending	21
Change in General Expenditures	48
State Government General Revenue	17
State Government General Spending	16
State Government General Fund Spending	12
State and Local Debt	7
Debt as a Percentage of Revenue	7
Per Capita Full Faith and Credit Debt	17
Bond Ratings	4
State Solvency Index	46
Pension Plan Assets	4
State Reserves	20
Capital Outlays and Interest	48
State Budget Process Quality	10
Relative State Spending "Needs"	4
Structural Deficits	24

Education - Section H

Math Proficiency, Eighth Grade	24
Science Proficiency, Eighth Grade	19
AFQT Ranks	29
SAT Scores	14
ACT Scores	n/a
Over-25 Population with a High School Diploma	41
Students in Private Schools	7
High School Completion Rates	24
Pupil-Teacher Ratio	49
Public School Enrollment	48
Library Holdings Per Capita	13
Children with Disabilities	1
Education Spending Per Capita	32
Education Spending as a Percentage of Total Spending	37
Spending Per Pupil	7
Average Teacher Salary	8
Sources of School Funds	4
State Aid Per Pupil	38
Higher Education Spending Per Capita	43
Higher Education Spending as a Percentage of Total Spending	43
Public Higher Education Enrollment	37
Per Pupil Support of Higher Education	42
Tuition and Fees	11
Average Professor Salary	28
Education Employees	17
R and D Spending	6
Library Operating Spending	11

Health - Section I

Immunization Rates	5
Infant Mortality Rates	36
State Health Rankings	13
Population Without Health Insurance	47
Abortions	4
Alcohol Consumption	15
Percentage of Adult Smokers	19
Percentage Obese	47
AIDS Cases	23
Physicians Per 100,000 Population	5
Hospital Beds Per 1,000 Population	39
Medicaid Recipients	11
Medicaid Recipients as a Percentage of Poverty Population	1
Health and Hospital Spending	45
Health and Hospital Spending as a Percentage of Total Spending	43
Per Capita Medicaid Spending	3
Medicaid Spending Per Aged Recipient	6
Medicaid Spending Per Child	11
Medicare Payment Per Hospital Day	35
Hospital Expense Per Inpatient Day	11
Population in HMOs	4

Crime - Section J

Crime Rate	32
Violent Crime Rate	33
Murder Rate	29
Property Crime Rate	30
Motor Vehicle Theft Rate	13
Violent Crime Rate Change	14
Prisoners	44
Change in Prisoners	43
Incarceration Rate	47
Juvenile Violent Crime Rate	21
Law Enforcement Employees	9
Corrections Employees	40
State Corrections Spending	5
Increase in State Corrections Spending	43
Law Enforcement Spending	24
Law Enforcement Spending as a Percentage of Total Spending	24

Transportation - Section K

Travel on Interstates	10
Interstate Mileage in Unacceptable Condition	27
Deficient Bridges	1

Traffic Deaths	47
Seat Belt Use	38
Vehicle-miles Traveled Per Capita	47
Workers Using Public Transportation	24
Road and Street Miles	17
Highway Employees	41
Public Transit Employees	13
Highway Spending Per Capita	49
Highway Spending as a Percentage of Total Spending	46

Welfare - Section L

Percentage of Births to Unwed Mothers	22
TANF Recipients as a Percentage of Population	1
Food Stamp Recipients as a Percentage of Population	18
SSI Recipients as a Percentage of Population	10
Change in TANF/AFDC Recipients	49
Condition of Children Index	16
Percentage of Families with Single Parent	7
Average Monthly TANF Payments	12
Welfare as a Percentage of Poverty-level Income	6
State Supplements of SSI	25
State Income Tax Liability of Typical Family in Poverty	18
Child Support Collections	39
Child Support Collections Per Dollar of Administrative Costs	23
Children in Foster Care	11
Welfare Spending Per Capita	6
Welfare Spending as a Percentage of Total Spending	4
Administrative Costs Per TANF Case	40

Technology - Section M

Percentage of Households with Computers	20
Percentage of Households with Internet Access	17
Zip codes with Broadband Service	6
High-tech Jobs	28
Dot-com Domain Names	29
State Government Website Ratings	35
Students per Computer	7

South Carolina

Population - Section A

Population 2001	26
Population Change 2000-2001	17
Population Change 1990-2001	15
Population 2015	30
Population 2025	25
Percentage 65 and Over	31
Percentage 17 and Under	30
Median Age	31
Percentage African American	3
Percentage Hispanic	37
Percentage in Poverty	7
Child Poverty Rate	6
Percentage Female	13
Birth Rates	22
Death Rates	9
Population Density	21
New Legal Immigrants 2000	35

Economies - Section B

Personal Income 2001	27
Gross State Product	43
Per Capita Personal Income	41
Personal Income from Wages and Salaries	28
Average Annual Pay	36
Average Hourly Earnings	49
Value Added in Manufacturing	8
Cost of Living	20
Average Annual Pay in Manufacturing	40
Average Annual Pay in Retailing	29
Labor Force	36
Unemployment Rate	18
Employment Rate	33
Government Employment	20
Manufacturing Employment	10
Fortune 500 Companies	39
Forbes 500 Companies	43
Tourism Spending Per Capita	24
Exports Per Capita	12
Housing Permits	9
Percentage Change in Home Prices	23
Net Farm Income	27
Financial Institution Assets	46
Bankruptcy Filings	40
Patents Issued	37
WC Disability Payment	28
UC Average Weekly Benefit	37
Economic Momentum	30
One-year Employment Change	30
Manufacturing Employment Change	41
Home Ownership	1
Gambling	26

Electricity Use Per Residential Customer	6
Cost Per Kwh	5
New Companies	24

Geography - Section C

Total Land Area	40
Federally Owned Land	32
State Park Acreage	31
State Park Visitors	30
Population Not Active	19
Hunters with Firearms	35
Registered Boats	10
State Spending for the Arts	23
Energy Consumption Per Capita	14
Toxic Chemical Release Per Capita	20
Hazardous Waste Sites	16
Polluted Rivers and Streams	38
Expired Surface Water Pollution Permits	13
Air Pollution Emissions	25

Government - Section D

Members of United States House	25
State Legislators	15
Legislators Per Million Population	22
Units of Government	34
Legislators Compensation	37
Female Legislators	48
Turnover in Legislatures	42
Term Limits	n/a
Legislative Session Length	10
Republicans in State Legislatures	15
Governor's Power Rating	43
Number of Statewide Elected Officials	4
State and Local Government Employees	14
State and Local Average Salaries	39
Local Employment	38
Local Spending Accountability	17
Registered Voters	29
Percentage of Population Voting	38
Statewide Initiatives	n/a
Campaign Costs Per Vote	18

Federal Impacts - Section E

Per Capita Federal Spending	30
Increase in Federal Spending	16
Per Capita Federal Grant Spending	27
Per Capita Federal Spending on Procurement	18

Per Capita Federal Spending on Payments to Individuals	27
Per Capita Federal Spending on Social Security and Medicare	27
Social Security Benefits	38
Federal Spending on Employee Wages and Salaries	21
Federal Grant Spending Per Dollar of State Tax Revenue	12
General Revenue from Federal Government	15
Federal Tax Burden Per Capita	39
Federal Spending Per Dollar of Taxes Paid	16
Highway Charges Returned to States	33
Terms of Trade	17
Federal Personal Income Taxes	40
Federal Share of Medicaid	12

Taxes - Section F

Tax Revenue	40
Per Capita Tax Revenue	44
Tax Effort	35
Tax Capacity	43
Percentage Change in Taxes	12
Property Taxes as a Percentage of Income	30
Property Taxes Per Capita	36
Property Tax Revenue as a Percentage of 3-tax Revenues	28
Sales Taxes as a Percentage of Income	27
Sales Taxes Per Capita	40
Sales Tax Revenue as a Percentage of 3-tax Revenues	23
Sales Tax Rate	19
Income Taxes as a Percentage of Income	26
Income Taxes Per Capita	32
Income Tax Revenue as a Percentage of 3-tax Revenues	23
Highest Personal Income Rate	12
Corporate Income Taxes	41
Motor Fuel Taxes	43
Tobacco Taxes	47
Taxes on High Income Families	18
Taxes in the Largest City in Each State	22
Progressivity of Taxes	6

Revenues and Finances - Section G

Per Capita Total Revenue	40
Per Capita General Revenue	34
Own-source General Revenue	37
Per Capita Non-tax Revenue	15

Per Capita Total Spending	27
General Spending as a Percentage of Income	15
Per Capita General Spending	26
Change in General Expenditures	7
State Government General Revenue	32
State Government General Spending	23
State Government General Fund Spending	16
State and Local Debt	25
Debt as a Percentage of Revenue	17
Per Capita Full Faith and Credit Debt	19
Bond Ratings	1
State Solvency Index	40
Pension Plan Assets	46
State Reserves	37
Capital Outlays and Interest	23
State Budget Process Quality	29
Relative State Spending "Needs"	33
Structural Deficits	29

Education - Section H

Math Proficiency, Eighth Grade	30
Science Proficiency, Eighth Grade	32
AFQT Ranks	47
SAT Scores	23
ACT Scores	n/a
Over-25 Population with a High School Diploma	35
Students in Private Schools	31
High School Completion Rates	36
Pupil-Teacher Ratio	27
Public School Enrollment	27
Library Holdings Per Capita	40
Children with Disabilities	7
Education Spending Per Capita	31
Education Spending as a Percentage of Total Spending	28
Spending Per Pupil	26
Average Teacher Salary	30
Sources of School Funds	27
State Aid Per Pupil	21
Higher Education Spending Per Capita	29
Higher Education Spending as a Percentage of Total Spending	28
Public Higher Education Enrollment	33
Per Pupil Support of Higher Education	19
Tuition and Fees	8
Average Professor Salary	30
Education Employees	26
R and D Spending	44
Library Operating Spending	34

Health - Section I

Immunization Rates	20
Infant Mortality Rates	6
State Health Rankings	48
Population Without Health Insurance	26
Abortions	33
Alcohol Consumption	15
Percentage of Adult Smokers	8
Percentage Obese	14
AIDS Cases	8
Physicians Per 100,000 Population	33
Hospital Beds Per 1,000 Population	27
Medicaid Recipients	10
Medicaid Recipients as a Percentage of Poverty Population	12
Health and Hospital Spending	4
Health and Hospital Spending as a Percentage of Total Spending	4
Per Capita Medicaid Spending	14
Medicaid Spending Per Aged Recipient	45
Medicaid Spending Per Child	34
Medicare Payment Per Hospital Day	21
Hospital Expense Per Inpatient Day	38
Population in HMOs	41

Crime - Section J

Crime Rate	13
Violent Crime Rate	5
Murder Rate	14
Property Crime Rate	15
Motor Vehicle Theft Rate	24
Violent Crime Rate Change	39
Prisoners	20
Change in Prisoners	40
Incarceration Rate	7
Juvenile Violent Crime Rate	14
Law Enforcement Employees	7
Corrections Employees	10
State Corrections Spending	39
Increase in State Corrections Spending	34
Law Enforcement Spending	31
Law Enforcement Spending as a Percentage of Total Spending	32

Transportation - Section K

Travel on Interstates	19
Interstate Mileage in Unacceptable Condition	41
Deficient Bridges	36

Traffic Deaths	3
Seat Belt Use	26
Vehicle-miles Traveled Per Capita	11
Workers Using Public Transportation	34
Road and Street Miles	5
Highway Employees	37
Public Transit Employees	39
Highway Spending Per Capita	37
Highway Spending as a Percentage of Total Spending	38

Welfare - Section L

Percentage of Births to Unwed Mothers	4
TANF Recipients as a Percentage of Population	36
Food Stamp Recipients as a Percentage of Population	14
SSI Recipients as a Percentage of Population	11
Change in TANF/AFDC Recipients	15
Condition of Children Index	45
Percentage of Families with Single Parent	13
Average Monthly TANF Payments	49
Welfare as a Percentage of Poverty-level Income	38
State Supplements of SSI	6
State Income Tax Liability of Typical Family in Poverty	18
Child Support Collections	36
Child Support Collections Per Dollar of Administrative Costs	20
Children in Foster Care	39
Welfare Spending Per Capita	17
Welfare Spending as a Percentage of Total Spending	12
Administrative Costs Per TANF Case	16

Technology - Section M

Percentage of Households with Computers	40
Percentage of Households with Internet Access	40
Zip codes with Broadband Service	18
High-tech Jobs	39
Dot-com Domain Names	41
State Government Website Ratings	26
Students per Computer	15

South Dakota

Population - Section A

Population 2001	46
Population Change 2000-2001	40
Population Change 1990-2001	37
Population 2015	13
Population 2025	46
Percentage 65 and Over	8
Percentage 17 and Under	9
Median Age	28
Percentage African American	45
Percentage Hispanic	45
Percentage in Poverty	40
Child Poverty Rate	47
Percentage Female	37
Birth Rates	22
Death Rates	38
Population Density	46
New Legal Immigrants 2000	48

Economies - Section B

Personal Income 2001	46
Gross State Product	33
Per Capita Personal Income	36
Personal Income from Wages and Salaries	48
Average Annual Pay	49
Average Hourly Earnings	50
Value Added in Manufacturing	27
Cost of Living	24
Average Annual Pay in Manufacturing	49
Average Annual Pay in Retailing	47
Labor Force	8
Unemployment Rate	50
Employment Rate	1
Government Employment	9
Manufacturing Employment	31
Fortune 500 Companies	27
Forbes 500 Companies	21
Tourism Spending Per Capita	18
Exports Per Capita	45
Housing Permits	18
Percentage Change in Home Prices	33
Net Farm Income	12
Financial Institution Assets	5
Bankruptcy Filings	42
Patents Issued	44
WC Disability Payment	42
UC Average Weekly Benefit	46
Economic Momentum	31
One-year Employment Change	14
Manufacturing Employment Change	45
Home Ownership	26
Gambling	31

Electricity Use Per Residential Customer	26
Cost Per Kwh	22
New Companies	37

Geography - Section C

Total Land Area	16
Federally Owned Land	18
State Park Acreage	27
State Park Visitors	3
Population Not Active	26
Hunters with Firearms	16
Registered Boats	42
State Spending for the Arts	34
Energy Consumption Per Capita	23
Toxic Chemical Release Per Capita	31
Hazardous Waste Sites	47
Polluted Rivers and Streams	19
Expired Surface Water Pollution Permits	31
Air Pollution Emissions	45

Government - Section D

Members of United States House	44
State Legislators	39
Legislators Per Million Population	7
Units of Government	2
Legislators Compensation	44
Female Legislators	38
Turnover in Legislatures	6
Term Limits	6
Legislative Session Length	34
Republicans in State Legislatures	5
Governor's Power Rating	12
Number of Statewide Elected Officials	21
State and Local Government Employees	30
State and Local Average Salaries	48
Local Employment	33
Local Spending Accountability	12
Registered Voters	2
Percentage of Population Voting	2
Statewide Initiatives	9
Campaign Costs Per Vote	31

Federal Impacts - Section E

Per Capita Federal Spending	7
Increase in Federal Spending	2
Per Capita Federal Grant Spending	8
Per Capita Federal Spending on Procurement	38

Per Capita Federal Spending on Payments to Individuals	2
Per Capita Federal Spending on Social Security and Medicare	30
Social Security Benefits	46
Federal Spending on Employee Wages and Salaries	12
Federal Grant Spending Per Dollar of State Tax Revenue	2
General Revenue from Federal Government	9
Federal Tax Burden Per Capita	35
Federal Spending Per Dollar of Taxes Paid	9
Highway Charges Returned to States	3
Terms of Trade	8
Federal Personal Income Taxes	36
Federal Share of Medicaid	16

Taxes - Section F

Tax Revenue	47
Per Capita Tax Revenue	46
Tax Effort	45
Tax Capacity	32
Percentage Change in Taxes	43
Property Taxes as a Percentage of Income	18
Property Taxes Per Capita	26
Property Tax Revenue as a Percentage of 3-tax Revenues	9
Sales Taxes as a Percentage of Income	15
Sales Taxes Per Capita	15
Sales Tax Revenue as a Percentage of 3-tax Revenues	7
Sales Tax Rate	37
Income Taxes as a Percentage of Income	n/a
Income Taxes Per Capita	n/a
Income Tax Revenue as a Percentage of 3-tax Revenues	n/a
Highest Personal Income Rate	n/a
Corporate Income Taxes	40
Motor Fuel Taxes	17
Tobacco Taxes	32
Taxes on High Income Families	46
Taxes in the Largest City in Each State	46
Progressivity of Taxes	48

Revenues and Finances - Section G

Per Capita Total Revenue	44
Per Capita General Revenue	45
Own-source General Revenue	48
Per Capita Non-tax Revenue	39

Per Capita Total Spending	47
General Spending as a Percentage of Income	32
Per Capita General Spending	44
Change in General Expenditures	43
State Government General Revenue	42
State Government General Spending	42
State Government General Fund Spending	32
State and Local Debt	31
Debt as a Percentage of Revenue	19
Per Capita Full Faith and Credit Debt	42
Bond Ratings	n/a
State Solvency Index	21
Pension Plan Assets	16
State Reserves	3
Capital Outlays and Interest	21
State Budget Process Quality	23
Relative State Spending "Needs"	24
Structural Deficits	32

Education - Section H

Math Proficiency, Eighth Grade	n/a
Science Proficiency, Eighth Grade	n/a
AFQT Ranks	11
SAT Scores	n/a
ACT Scores	8
Over-25 Population with a High School Diploma	1
Students in Private Schools	37
High School Completion Rates	5
Pupil-Teacher Ratio	39
Public School Enrollment	23
Library Holdings Per Capita	9
Children with Disabilities	38
Education Spending Per Capita	42
Education Spending as a Percentage of Total Spending	24
Spending Per Pupil	36
Average Teacher Salary	50
Sources of School Funds	15
State Aid Per Pupil	48
Higher Education Spending Per Capita	42
Higher Education Spending as a Percentage of Total Spending	34
Public Higher Education Enrollment	14
Per Pupil Support of Higher Education	45
Tuition and Fees	22
Average Professor Salary	50
Education Employees	25
R and D Spending	48
Library Operating Spending	39

Health - Section I

Immunization Rates	23
Infant Mortality Rates	45
State Health Rankings	16
Population Without Health Insurance	40
Abortions	44
Alcohol Consumption	20
Percentage of Adult Smokers	32
Percentage Obese	23
AIDS Cases	42
Physicians Per 100,000 Population	38
Hospital Beds Per 1,000 Population	2
Medicaid Recipients	26
Medicaid Recipients as a Percentage of Poverty Population	21
Health and Hospital Spending	47
Health and Hospital Spending as a Percentage of Total Spending	46
Per Capita Medicaid Spending	28
Medicaid Spending Per Aged Recipient	27
Medicaid Spending Per Child	32
Medicare Payment Per Hospital Day	41
Hospital Expense Per Inpatient Day	28
Population in HMOs	36

Crime - Section J

Crime Rate	49
Violent Crime Rate	47
Murder Rate	50
Property Crime Rate	49
Motor Vehicle Theft Rate	50
Violent Crime Rate Change	16
Prisoners	45
Change in Prisoners	11
Incarceration Rate	25
Juvenile Violent Crime Rate	42
Law Enforcement Employees	47
Corrections Employees	39
State Corrections Spending	42
Increase in State Corrections Spending	19
Law Enforcement Spending	48
Law Enforcement Spending as a Percentage of Total Spending	42

Transportation - Section K

Travel on Interstates	15
Interstate Mileage in Unacceptable Condition	37
Deficient Bridges	21
Traffic Deaths	8
Seat Belt Use	37
Vehicle-miles Traveled Per Capita	14
Workers Using Public Transportation	46
Road and Street Miles	41
Highway Employees	7
Public Transit Employees	49
Highway Spending Per Capita	3
Highway Spending as a Percentage of Total Spending	1

Welfare - Section L

Percentage of Births to Unwed Mothers	24
TANF Recipients as a Percentage of Population	44
Food Stamp Recipients as a Percentage of Population	27
SSI Recipients as a Percentage of Population	30
Change in TANF/AFDC Recipients	18
Condition of Children Index	20
Percentage of Families with Single Parent	40
Average Monthly TANF Payments	29
Welfare as a Percentage of Poverty-level Income	31
State Supplements of SSI	36
State Income Tax Liability of Typical Family in Poverty	n/a
Child Support Collections	21
Child Support Collections Per Dollar of Administrative Costs	1
Children in Foster Care	31
Welfare Spending Per Capita	39
Welfare Spending as a Percentage of Total Spending	33
Administrative Costs Per TANF Case	33

Technology - Section M

Percentage of Households with Computers	31
Percentage of Households with Internet Access	33
Zip codes with Broadband Service	48
High-tech Jobs	24
Dot-com Domain Names	45
State Government Website Ratings	8
Students per Computer	50

Tennessee

Population - Section A

Population 2001	16
Population Change 2000-2001	23
Population Change 1990-2001	14
Population 2015	16
Population 2025	15
Percentage 65 and Over	28
Percentage 17 and Under	40
Median Age	23
Percentage African American	11
Percentage Hispanic	38
Percentage in Poverty	12
Child Poverty Rate	11
Percentage Female	17
Birth Rates	24
Death Rates	3
Population Density	20
New Legal Immigrants 2000	25

Economies - Section B

Personal Income 2001	20
Gross State Product	31
Per Capita Personal Income	34
Personal Income from Wages and Salaries	24
Average Annual Pay	29
Average Hourly Earnings	39
Value Added in Manufacturing	11
Cost of Living	46
Average Annual Pay in Manufacturing	35
Average Annual Pay in Retailing	20
Labor Force	32
Unemployment Rate	32
Employment Rate	19
Government Employment	39
Manufacturing Employment	9
Fortune 500 Companies	30
Forbes 500 Companies	32
Tourism Spending Per Capita	25
Exports Per Capita	22
Housing Permits	19
Percentage Change in Home Prices	40
Net Farm Income	32
Financial Institution Assets	21
Bankruptcy Filings	1
Patents Issued	34
WC Disability Payment	23
UC Average Weekly Benefit	41
Economic Momentum	22
One-year Employment Change	16
Manufacturing Employment Change	10
Home Ownership	19
Gambling	n/a

Electricity Use Per Residential Customer	1
Cost Per Kwh	41
New Companies	25

Geography - Section C

Total Land Area	34
Federally Owned Land	22
State Park Acreage	20
State Park Visitors	11
Population Not Active	2
Hunters with Firearms	38
Registered Boats	19
State Spending for the Arts	49
Energy Consumption Per Capita	21
Toxic Chemical Release Per Capita	14
Hazardous Waste Sites	31
Polluted Rivers and Streams	33
Expired Surface Water Pollution Permits	39
Air Pollution Emissions	13

Government - Section D

Members of United States House	14
State Legislators	32
Legislators Per Million Population	37
Units of Government	39
Legislators Compensation	25
Female Legislators	40
Turnover in Legislatures	30
Term Limits	n/a
Legislative Session Length	14
Republicans in State Legislatures	32
Governor's Power Rating	5
Number of Statewide Elected Officials	45
State and Local Government Employees	36
State and Local Average Salaries	38
Local Employment	14
Local Spending Accountability	26
Registered Voters	30
Percentage of Population Voting	34
Statewide Initiatives	n/a
Campaign Costs Per Vote	32

Federal Impacts - Section E

Per Capita Federal Spending	19
Increase in Federal Spending	18
Per Capita Federal Grant Spending	21
Per Capita Federal Spending on Procurement	10

Per Capita Federal Spending on Payments to Individuals	21
Per Capita Federal Spending on Social Security and Medicare	17
Social Security Benefits	40
Federal Spending on Employee Wages and Salaries	34
Federal Grant Spending Per Dollar of State Tax Revenue	7
General Revenue from Federal Government	6
Federal Tax Burden Per Capita	32
Federal Spending Per Dollar of Taxes Paid	20
Highway Charges Returned to States	38
Terms of Trade	20
Federal Personal Income Taxes	33
Federal Share of Medicaid	17

Taxes - Section F

Tax Revenue	49
Per Capita Tax Revenue	49
Tax Effort	45
Tax Capacity	35
Percentage Change in Taxes	20
Property Taxes as a Percentage of Income	42
Property Taxes Per Capita	41
Property Tax Revenue as a Percentage of 3-tax Revenues	35
Sales Taxes as a Percentage of Income	8
Sales Taxes Per Capita	8
Sales Tax Revenue as a Percentage of 3-tax Revenues	2
Sales Tax Rate	1
Income Taxes as a Percentage of Income	43
Income Taxes Per Capita	43
Income Tax Revenue as a Percentage of 3-tax Revenues	43
Highest Personal Income Rate	n/a
Corporate Income Taxes	20
Motor Fuel Taxes	22
Tobacco Taxes	38
Taxes on High Income Families	45
Taxes in the Largest City in Each State	43
Progressivity of Taxes	45

Revenues and Finances - Section G

Per Capita Total Revenue	36
Per Capita General Revenue	49
Own-source General Revenue	50
Per Capita Non-tax Revenue	47

Per Capita Total Spending 31

General Spending as a Percentage of
Income 36

Per Capita General Spending 47

Change in General Expenditures 24

State Government General Revenue 47

State Government General Spending 46

State Government General Fund
Spending 35

State and Local Debt 46

Debt as a Percentage of Revenue 44

Per Capita Full Faith and Credit Debt 26

Bond Ratings 3

State Solvency Index 24

Pension Plan Assets 15

State Reserves 36

Capital Outlays and Interest 32

State Budget Process Quality 32

Relative State Spending "Needs" 38

Structural Deficits 43

Education - Section H

Math Proficiency, Eighth Grade 32

Science Proficiency, Eighth Grade 26

AFQT Ranks 25

SAT Scores n/a

ACT Scores 22

Over-25 Population with a High
School Diploma 45

Students in Private Schools 24

High School Completion Rates 22

Pupil-Teacher Ratio 21

Public School Enrollment 39

Library Holdings Per Capita 48

Children with Disabilities 20

Education Spending Per Capita 49

Education Spending as a Percentage
of Total Spending 38

Spending Per Pupil 45

Average Teacher Salary 32

Sources of School Funds 22

State Aid Per Pupil 45

Higher Education Spending Per
Capita 36

Higher Education Spending as a
Percentage of Total Spending 30

Public Higher Education Enrollment 40

Per Pupil Support of Higher
Education 31

Tuition and Fees 32

Average Professor Salary 29

Education Employees 41

R and D Spending 30

Library Operating Spending 48

Health - Section I

Immunization Rates 6

Infant Mortality Rates 4

State Health Rankings 44

Population Without Health
Insurance 32

Abortions 17

Alcohol Consumption 42

Percentage of Adult Smokers 17

Percentage Obese 9

AIDS Cases 19

Physicians Per 100,000 Population 20

Hospital Beds Per 1,000 Population 14

Medicaid Recipients 1

Medicaid Recipients as a Percentage
of Poverty Population 8

Health and Hospital Spending 13

Health and Hospital Spending as a
Percentage of Total Spending 7

Per Capita Medicaid Spending 18

Medicaid Spending Per Aged
Recipient 50

Medicaid Spending Per Child 41

Medicare Payment Per Hospital Day 25

Hospital Expense Per Inpatient Day 35

Population in HMOs 26

Crime - Section J

Crime Rate 6

Violent Crime Rate 4

Murder Rate 8

Property Crime Rate 10

Motor Vehicle Theft Rate 10

Violent Crime Rate Change 4

Prisoners 18

Change in Prisoners 8

Incarceration Rate 19

Juvenile Violent Crime Rate 35

Law Enforcement Employees 11

Corrections Employees 35

State Corrections Spending 41

Increase in State Corrections
Spending 38

Law Enforcement Spending 39

Law Enforcement Spending as a
Percentage of Total Spending 29

Transportation - Section K

Travel on Interstates 13

Interstate Mileage in Unacceptable
Condition 31

Deficient Bridges 34

Traffic Deaths 12

Seat Belt Use 29

Vehicle-miles Traveled Per Capita 9

Workers Using Public
Transportation 36

Road and Street Miles 23

Highway Employees 31

Public Transit Employees 33

Highway Spending Per Capita 43

Highway Spending as a Percentage
of Total Spending 31

Welfare - Section L

Percentage of Births to Unwed
Mothers 11

TANF Recipients as a Percentage
of Population 3

Food Stamp Recipients as a
Percentage of Population 7

SSI Recipients as a Percentage of
Population 9

Change in TANF/AFDC Recipients 44

Condition of Children Index 42

Percentage of Families with Single
Parent 7

Average Monthly TANF
Payments 45

Welfare as a Percentage of Poverty-
level Income 28

State Supplements of SSI 18

State Income Tax Liability of Typical
Family in Poverty n/a

Child Support Collections 37

Child Support Collections Per Dollar
of Administrative Costs 16

Children in Foster Care 23

Welfare Spending Per Capita 19

Welfare Spending as a Percentage of
Total Spending 9

Administrative Costs Per TANF Case 44

Technology - Section M

Percentage of Households with
Computers 41

Percentage of Households with
Internet Access 41

Zip codes with Broadband
Service 20

High-tech Jobs 42

Dot-com Domain Names 24

State Government Website
Ratings 1

Students per Computer 10

Texas

Population - Section A

Population 2001	2
Population Change 2000-2001	6
Population Change 1990-2001	8
Population 2015	11
Population 2025	2
Percentage 65 and Over	46
Percentage 17 and Under	4
Median Age	49
Percentage African American	18
Percentage Hispanic	3
Percentage in Poverty	9
Child Poverty Rate	10
Percentage Female	38
Birth Rates	2
Death Rates	20
Population Density	28
New Legal Immigrants 2000	4

Economies - Section B

Personal Income 2001	3
Gross State Product	17
Per Capita Personal Income	27
Personal Income from Wages and Salaries	11
Average Annual Pay	15
Average Hourly Earnings	46
Value Added in Manufacturing	30
Cost of Living	43
Average Annual Pay in Manufacturing	10
Average Annual Pay in Retailing	12
Labor Force	28
Unemployment Rate	7
Employment Rate	44
Government Employment	22
Manufacturing Employment	34
Fortune 500 Companies	12
Forbes 500 Companies	14
Tourism Spending Per Capita	30
Exports Per Capita	3
Housing Permits	11
Percentage Change in Home Prices	22
Net Farm Income	1
Financial Institution Assets	45
Bankruptcy Filings	43
Patents Issued	20
WC Disability Payment	30
UC Average Weekly Benefit	21
Economic Momentum	20
One-year Employment Change	31
Manufacturing Employment Change	35
Home Ownership	45
Gambling	11

Electricity Use Per Residential Customer	4
Cost Per Kwh	27
New Companies	32

Geography - Section C

Total Land Area	2
Federally Owned Land	20
State Park Acreage	4
State Park Visitors	48
Population Not Active	14
Hunters with Firearms	32
Registered Boats	5
State Spending for the Arts	50
Energy Consumption Per Capita	7
Toxic Chemical Release Per Capita	28
Hazardous Waste Sites	9
Polluted Rivers and Streams	35
Expired Surface Water Pollution Permits	22
Air Pollution Emissions	1

Government - Section D

Members of United States House	2
State Legislators	11
Legislators Per Million Population	49
Units of Government	33
Legislators Compensation	42
Female Legislators	33
Turnover in Legislatures	26
Term Limits	n/a
Legislative Session Length	12
Republicans in State Legislatures	14
Governor's Power Rating	34
Number of Statewide Elected Officials	21
State and Local Government Employees	19
State and Local Average Salaries	30
Local Employment	4
Local Spending Accountability	13
Registered Voters	7
Percentage of Population Voting	46
Statewide Initiatives	n/a
Campaign Costs Per Vote	30

Federal Impacts - Section E

Per Capita Federal Spending	42
Increase in Federal Spending	29
Per Capita Federal Grant Spending	39
Per Capita Federal Spending on Procurement	19

Per Capita Federal Spending on Payments to Individuals	45
Per Capita Federal Spending on Social Security and Medicare	47
Social Security Benefits	36
Federal Spending on Employee Wages and Salaries	26
Federal Grant Spending Per Dollar of State Tax Revenue	15
General Revenue from Federal Government	23
Federal Tax Burden Per Capita	22
Federal Spending Per Dollar of Taxes Paid	36
Highway Charges Returned to States	50
Terms of Trade	35
Federal Personal Income Taxes	18
Federal Share of Medicaid	26

Taxes - Section F

Tax Revenue	46
Per Capita Tax Revenue	40
Tax Effort	32
Tax Capacity	38
Percentage Change in Taxes	14
Property Taxes as a Percentage of Income	13
Property Taxes Per Capita	15
Property Tax Revenue as a Percentage of 3-tax Revenues	7
Sales Taxes as a Percentage of Income	11
Sales Taxes Per Capita	9
Sales Tax Revenue as a Percentage of 3-tax Revenues	8
Sales Tax Rate	7
Income Taxes as a Percentage of Income	n/a
Income Taxes Per Capita	n/a
Income Tax Revenue as a Percentage of 3-tax Revenues	n/a
Highest Personal Income Rate	n/a
Corporate Income Taxes	n/a
Motor Fuel Taxes	26
Tobacco Taxes	27
Taxes on High Income Families	44
Taxes in the Largest City in Each State	44
Progressivity of Taxes	43

Revenues and Finances - Section G

Per Capita Total Revenue	41
Per Capita General Revenue	46
Own-source General Revenue	40
Per Capita Non-tax Revenue	37

Per Capita Total Spending	43
General Spending as a Percentage of Income	40
Per Capita General Spending	42
Change in General Expenditures	8
State Government General Revenue	49
State Government General Spending	50
State Government General Fund Spending	47
State and Local Debt	20
Debt as a Percentage of Revenue	14
Per Capita Full Faith and Credit Debt	14
Bond Ratings	2
State Solvency Index	9
Pension Plan Assets	26
State Reserves	10
Capital Outlays and Interest	18
State Budget Process Quality	29
Relative State Spending "Needs"	46
Structural Deficits	40

Education - Section H

Math Proficiency, Eighth Grade	21
Science Proficiency, Eighth Grade	28
AFQT Ranks	33
SAT Scores	22
ACT Scores	n/a
Over-25 Population with a High School Diploma	46
Students in Private Schools	41
High School Completion Rates	48
Pupil-Teacher Ratio	31
Public School Enrollment	3
Library Holdings Per Capita	45
Children with Disabilities	40
Education Spending Per Capita	21
Education Spending as a Percentage of Total Spending	3
Spending Per Pupil	27
Average Teacher Salary	29
Sources of School Funds	18
State Aid Per Pupil	41
Higher Education Spending Per Capita	31
Higher Education Spending as a Percentage of Total Spending	23
Public Higher Education Enrollment	24
Per Pupil Support of Higher Education	21
Tuition and Fees	36
Average Professor Salary	21
Education Employees	6
R and D Spending	31
Library Operating Spending	45

Health - Section I

Immunization Rates	42
Infant Mortality Rates	41
State Health Rankings	37
Population Without Health Insurance	1
Abortions	19
Alcohol Consumption	24
Percentage of Adult Smokers	29
Percentage Obese	4
AIDS Cases	12
Physicians Per 100,000 Population	37
Hospital Beds Per 1,000 Population	32
Medicaid Recipients	30
Medicaid Recipients as a Percentage of Poverty Population	47
Health and Hospital Spending	20
Health and Hospital Spending as a Percentage of Total Spending	14
Per Capita Medicaid Spending	43
Medicaid Spending Per Aged Recipient	39
Medicaid Spending Per Child	35
Medicare Payment Per Hospital Day	7
Hospital Expense Per Inpatient Day	30
Population in HMOs	31

Crime - Section J

Crime Rate	7
Violent Crime Rate	12
Murder Rate	15
Property Crime Rate	7
Motor Vehicle Theft Rate	12
Violent Crime Rate Change	15
Prisoners	1
Change in Prisoners	33
Incarceration Rate	3
Juvenile Violent Crime Rate	30
Law Enforcement Employees	32
Corrections Employees	2
State Corrections Spending	40
Increase in State Corrections Spending	5
Law Enforcement Spending	25
Law Enforcement Spending as a Percentage of Total Spending	11

Transportation - Section K

Travel on Interstates	32
Interstate Mileage in Unacceptable Condition	28
Deficient Bridges	39

Traffic Deaths	18
Seat Belt Use	17
Vehicle-miles Traveled Per Capita	29
Workers Using Public Transportation	25
Road and Street Miles	11
Highway Employees	42
Public Transit Employees	18
Highway Spending Per Capita	34
Highway Spending as a Percentage of Total Spending	29

Welfare - Section L

Percentage of Births to Unwed Mothers	33
TANF Recipients as a Percentage of Population	24
Food Stamp Recipients as a Percentage of Population	21
SSI Recipients as a Percentage of Population	25
Change in TANF/AFDC Recipients	37
Condition of Children Index	38
Percentage of Families with Single Parent	27
Average Monthly TANF Payments	47
Welfare as a Percentage of Poverty-level Income	41
State Supplements of SSI	n/a
State Income Tax Liability of Typical Family in Poverty	n/a
Child Support Collections	33
Child Support Collections Per Dollar of Administrative Costs	13
Children in Foster Care	48
Welfare Spending Per Capita	47
Welfare Spending as a Percentage of Total Spending	44
Administrative Costs Per TANF Case	41

Technology - Section M

Percentage of Households with Computers	34
Percentage of Households with Internet Access	32
Zip codes with Broadband Service	20
High-tech Jobs	13
Dot-com Domain Names	17
State Government Website Ratings	6
Students per Computer	37

Utah

Population - Section A

Population 2001	34
Population Change 2000-2001	11
Population Change 1990-2001	4
Population 2015	9
Population 2025	34
Percentage 65 and Over	49
Percentage 17 and Under	1
Median Age	50
Percentage African American	42
Percentage Hispanic	12
Percentage in Poverty	24
Child Poverty Rate	31
Percentage Female	44
Birth Rates	1
Death Rates	46
Population Density	41
New Legal Immigrants 2000	30

Economies - Section B

Personal Income 2001	35
Gross State Product	34
Per Capita Personal Income	45
Personal Income from Wages and Salaries	3
Average Annual Pay	34
Average Hourly Earnings	33
Value Added in Manufacturing	36
Cost of Living	38
Average Annual Pay in Manufacturing	39
Average Annual Pay in Retailing	33
Labor Force	30
Unemployment Rate	20
Employment Rate	31
Government Employment	17
Manufacturing Employment	33
Fortune 500 Companies	37
Forbes 500 Companies	42
Tourism Spending Per Capita	21
Exports Per Capita	33
Housing Permits	8
Percentage Change in Home Prices	49
Net Farm Income	34
Financial Institution Assets	6
Bankruptcy Filings	2
Patents Issued	18
WC Disability Payment	26
UC Average Weekly Benefit	15
Economic Momentum	23
One-year Employment Change	46
Manufacturing Employment Change	44
Home Ownership	11
Gambling	n/a

Electricity Use Per Residential Customer	35
Cost Per Kwh	8
New Companies	3

Geography - Section C

Total Land Area	12
Federally Owned Land	4
State Park Acreage	26
State Park Visitors	24
Population Not Active	50
Hunters with Firearms	26
Registered Boats	37
State Spending for the Arts	15
Energy Consumption Per Capita	18
Toxic Chemical Release Per Capita	3
Hazardous Waste Sites	19
Polluted Rivers and Streams	37
Expired Surface Water Pollution Permits	49
Air Pollution Emissions	38

Government - Section D

Members of United States House	34
State Legislators	41
Legislators Per Million Population	20
Units of Government	27
Legislators Compensation	46
Female Legislators	24
Turnover in Legislatures	31
Term Limits	1
Legislative Session Length	42
Republicans in State Legislatures	2
Governor's Power Rating	1
Number of Statewide Elected Officials	35
State and Local Government Employees	25
State and Local Average Salaries	27
Local Employment	46
Local Spending Accountability	21
Registered Voters	20
Percentage of Population Voting	37
Statewide Initiatives	17
Campaign Costs Per Vote	47

Federal Impacts - Section E

Per Capita Federal Spending	48
Increase in Federal Spending	7
Per Capita Federal Grant Spending	42
Per Capita Federal Spending on Procurement	13

Per Capita Federal Spending on Payments to Individuals	50
Per Capita Federal Spending on Social Security and Medicare	49
Social Security Benefits	26
Federal Spending on Employee Wages and Salaries	14
Federal Grant Spending Per Dollar of State Tax Revenue	32
General Revenue from Federal Government	24
Federal Tax Burden Per Capita	41
Federal Spending Per Dollar of Taxes Paid	28
Highway Charges Returned to States	29
Terms of Trade	24
Federal Personal Income Taxes	39
Federal Share of Medicaid	7

Taxes - Section F

Tax Revenue	13
Per Capita Tax Revenue	34
Tax Effort	35
Tax Capacity	35
Percentage Change in Taxes	4
Property Taxes as a Percentage of Income	36
Property Taxes Per Capita	38
Property Tax Revenue as a Percentage of 3-tax Revenues	42
Sales Taxes as a Percentage of Income	12
Sales Taxes Per Capita	21
Sales Tax Revenue as a Percentage of 3-tax Revenues	18
Sales Tax Rate	33
Income Taxes as a Percentage of Income	15
Income Taxes Per Capita	23
Income Tax Revenue as a Percentage of 3-tax Revenues	16
Highest Personal Income Rate	28
Corporate Income Taxes	33
Motor Fuel Taxes	9
Tobacco Taxes	19
Taxes on High Income Families	26
Taxes in the Largest City in Each State	17
Progressivity of Taxes	24

Revenues and Finances - Section G

Per Capita Total Revenue	22
Per Capita General Revenue	29
Own-source General Revenue	30
Per Capita Non-tax Revenue	18

Per Capita Total Spending	26
General Spending as a Percentage of Income	14
Per Capita General Spending	31
Change in General Expenditures	5
State Government General Revenue	24
State Government General Spending	22
State Government General Fund Spending	23
State and Local Debt	15
Debt as a Percentage of Revenue	15
Per Capita Full Faith and Credit Debt	30
Bond Ratings	1
State Solvency Index	31
Pension Plan Assets	22
State Reserves	45
Capital Outlays and Interest	12
State Budget Process Quality	3
Relative State Spending "Needs"	18
Structural Deficits	28

Education - Section H

Math Proficiency, Eighth Grade	21
Science Proficiency, Eighth Grade	14
AFQT Ranks	15
SAT Scores	n/a
ACT Scores	8
Over-25 Population with a High School Diploma	4
Students in Private Schools	49
High School Completion Rates	17
Pupil-Teacher Ratio	1
Public School Enrollment	2
Library Holdings Per Capita	32
Children with Disabilities	45
Education Spending Per Capita	17
Education Spending as a Percentage of Total Spending	9
Spending Per Pupil	49
Average Teacher Salary	38
Sources of School Funds	33
State Aid Per Pupil	35
Higher Education Spending Per Capita	2
Higher Education Spending as a Percentage of Total Spending	1
Public Higher Education Enrollment	7
Per Pupil Support of Higher Education	37
Tuition and Fees	50
Average Professor Salary	34
Education Employees	37
R and D Spending	32
Library Operating Spending	21

Health - Section I

Immunization Rates	40
Infant Mortality Rates	47
State Health Rankings	4
Population Without Health Insurance	18
Abortions	43
Alcohol Consumption	50
Percentage of Adult Smokers	50
Percentage Obese	41
AIDS Cases	33
Physicians Per 100,000 Population	44
Hospital Beds Per 1,000 Population	46
Medicaid Recipients	41
Medicaid Recipients as a Percentage of Poverty Population	39
Health and Hospital Spending	36
Health and Hospital Spending as a Percentage of Total Spending	31
Per Capita Medicaid Spending	45
Medicaid Spending Per Aged Recipient	28
Medicaid Spending Per Child	22
Medicare Payment Per Hospital Day	14
Hospital Expense Per Inpatient Day	12
Population in HMOs	9

Crime - Section J

Crime Rate	20
Violent Crime Rate	44
Murder Rate	34
Property Crime Rate	17
Motor Vehicle Theft Rate	34
Violent Crime Rate Change	44
Prisoners	39
Change in Prisoners	9
Incarceration Rate	43
Juvenile Violent Crime Rate	31
Law Enforcement Employees	44
Corrections Employees	30
State Corrections Spending	4
Increase in State Corrections Spending	32
Law Enforcement Spending	26
Law Enforcement Spending as a Percentage of Total Spending	23

Transportation - Section K

Travel on Interstates	1
Interstate Mileage in Unacceptable Condition	11
Deficient Bridges	35

Traffic Deaths	41
Seat Belt Use	14
Vehicle-miles Traveled Per Capita	26
Workers Using Public Transportation	20
Road and Street Miles	27
Highway Employees	45
Public Transit Employees	10
Highway Spending Per Capita	17
Highway Spending as a Percentage of Total Spending	15

Welfare - Section L

Percentage of Births to Unwed Mothers	50
TANF Recipients as a Percentage of Population	45
Food Stamp Recipients as a Percentage of Population	46
SSI Recipients as a Percentage of Population	50
Change in TANF/AFDC Recipients	39
Condition of Children Index	3
Percentage of Families with Single Parent	50
Average Monthly TANF Payments	17
Welfare as a Percentage of Poverty-level Income	17
State Supplements of SSI	47
State Income Tax Liability of Typical Family in Poverty	15
Child Support Collections	30
Child Support Collections Per Dollar of Administrative Costs	39
Children in Foster Care	50
Welfare Spending Per Capita	38
Welfare Spending as a Percentage of Total Spending	37
Administrative Costs Per TANF Case	5

Technology - Section M

Percentage of Households with Computers	2
Percentage of Households with Internet Access	14
Zip codes with Broadband Service	31
High-tech Jobs	14
Dot-com Domain Names	7
State Government Website Ratings	10
Students per Computer	9

Vermont

Population - Section A

Population 2001	49
Population Change 2000-2001	26
Population Change 1990-2001	35
Population 2015	29
Population 2025	50
Percentage 65 and Over	25
Percentage 17 and Under	44
Median Age	5
Percentage African American	48
Percentage Hispanic	48
Percentage in Poverty	29
Child Poverty Rate	34
Percentage Female	23
Birth Rates	50
Death Rates	26
Population Density	30
New Legal Immigrants 2000	45

Economies - Section B

Personal Income 2001	48
Gross State Product	37
Per Capita Personal Income	26
Personal Income from Wages and Salaries	36
Average Annual Pay	31
Average Hourly Earnings	30
Value Added in Manufacturing	10
Cost of Living	n/a
Average Annual Pay in Manufacturing	21
Average Annual Pay in Retailing	28
Labor Force	4
Unemployment Rate	43
Employment Rate	8
Government Employment	25
Manufacturing Employment	17
Fortune 500 Companies	n/a
Forbes 500 Companies	n/a
Tourism Spending Per Capita	5
Exports Per Capita	2
Housing Permits	28
Percentage Change in Home Prices	14
Net Farm Income	42
Financial Institution Assets	31
Bankruptcy Filings	48
Patents Issued	2
WC Disability Payment	8
UC Average Weekly Benefit	26
Economic Momentum	25
One-year Employment Change	18
Manufacturing Employment Change	42
Home Ownership	30
Gambling	45

Electricity Use Per Residential Customer	43
Cost Per Kwh	33
New Companies	19

Geography - Section C

Total Land Area	43
Federally Owned Land	41
State Park Acreage	35
State Park Visitors	44
Population Not Active	44
Hunters with Firearms	2
Registered Boats	48
State Spending for the Arts	25
Energy Consumption Per Capita	36
Toxic Chemical Release Per Capita	50
Hazardous Waste Sites	42
Polluted Rivers and Streams	43
Expired Surface Water Pollution Permits	46
Air Pollution Emissions	49

Government - Section D

Members of United States House	44
State Legislators	12
Legislators Per Million Population	2
Units of Government	7
Legislators Compensation	40
Female Legislators	13
Turnover in Legislatures	22
Term Limits	n/a
Legislative Session Length	14
Republicans in State Legislatures	30
Governor's Power Rating	50
Number of Statewide Elected Officials	21
State and Local Government Employees	9
State and Local Average Salaries	26
Local Employment	44
Local Spending Accountability	49
Registered Voters	6
Percentage of Population Voting	6
Statewide Initiatives	n/a
Campaign Costs Per Vote	25

Federal Impacts - Section E

Per Capita Federal Spending	29
Increase in Federal Spending	17
Per Capita Federal Grant Spending	6
Per Capita Federal Spending on Procurement	24

Per Capita Federal Spending on Payments to Individuals	40
Per Capita Federal Spending on Social Security and Medicare	29
Social Security Benefits	28
Federal Spending on Employee Wages and Salaries	30
Federal Grant Spending Per Dollar of State Tax Revenue	16
General Revenue from Federal Government	5
Federal Tax Burden Per Capita	24
Federal Spending Per Dollar of Taxes Paid	26
Highway Charges Returned to States	8
Terms of Trade	10
Federal Personal Income Taxes	25
Federal Share of Medicaid	20

Taxes - Section F

Tax Revenue	8
Per Capita Tax Revenue	17
Tax Effort	16
Tax Capacity	20
Percentage Change in Taxes	27
Property Taxes as a Percentage of Income	3
Property Taxes Per Capita	6
Property Tax Revenue as a Percentage of 3-tax Revenues	6
Sales Taxes as a Percentage of Income	41
Sales Taxes Per Capita	45
Sales Tax Revenue as a Percentage of 3-tax Revenues	42
Sales Tax Rate	19
Income Taxes as a Percentage of Income	21
Income Taxes Per Capita	24
Income Tax Revenue as a Percentage of 3-tax Revenues	34
Highest Personal Income Rate	2
Corporate Income Taxes	37
Motor Fuel Taxes	26
Tobacco Taxes	15
Taxes on High Income Families	17
Taxes in the Largest City in Each State	19
Progressivity of Taxes	13

Revenues and Finances - Section G

Per Capita Total Revenue	23
Per Capita General Revenue	14
Own-source General Revenue	23
Per Capita Non-tax Revenue	38

Per Capita Total Spending   17

General Spending as a Percentage of Income   11

Per Capita General Spending   14

Change in General Expenditures   15

State Government General Revenue   3

State Government General Spending   2

State Government General Fund Spending   13

State and Local Debt   24

Debt as a Percentage of Revenue   23

Per Capita Full Faith and Credit Debt   24

Bond Ratings   2

State Solvency Index   37

Pension Plan Assets   40

State Reserves   34

Capital Outlays and Interest   49

State Budget Process Quality   48

Relative State Spending "Needs"   8

Structural Deficits   29

Education · Section H

Math Proficiency, Eighth Grade   5

Science Proficiency, Eighth Grade   2

AFQT Ranks   8

SAT Scores   7

ACT Scores   n/a

Over-25 Population with a High School Diploma   7

Students in Private Schools   18

High School Completion Rates   13

Pupil-Teacher Ratio   50

Public School Enrollment   28

Library Holdings Per Capita   1

Children with Disabilities   28

Education Spending Per Capita   6

Education Spending as a Percentage of Total Spending   8

Spending Per Pupil   8

Average Teacher Salary   28

Sources of School Funds   46

State Aid Per Pupil   2

Higher Education Spending Per Capita   10

Higher Education Spending as a Percentage of Total Spending   16

Public Higher Education Enrollment   43

Per Pupil Support of Higher Education   47

Tuition and Fees   1

Average Professor Salary   38

Education Employees   3

R and D Spending   33

Library Operating Spending   31

Health · Section I

Immunization Rates   1

Infant Mortality Rates   40

State Health Rankings   6

Population Without Health Insurance   41

Abortions   12

Alcohol Consumption   19

Percentage of Adult Smokers   29

Percentage Obese   48

AIDS Cases   38

Physicians Per 100,000 Population   6

Hospital Beds Per 1,000 Population   30

Medicaid Recipients   3

Medicaid Recipients as a Percentage of Poverty Population   2

Health and Hospital Spending   50

Health and Hospital Spending as a Percentage of Total Spending   50

Per Capita Medicaid Spending   6

Medicaid Spending Per Aged Recipient   48

Medicaid Spending Per Child   9

Medicare Payment Per Hospital Day   48

Hospital Expense Per Inpatient Day   27

Population in HMOs   38

Crime · Section J

Crime Rate   45

Violent Crime Rate   49

Murder Rate   48

Property Crime Rate   42

Motor Vehicle Theft Rate   49

Violent Crime Rate Change   19

Prisoners   47

Change in Prisoners   28

Incarceration Rate   45

Juvenile Violent Crime Rate   47

Law Enforcement Employees   50

Corrections Employees   43

State Corrections Spending   8

Increase in State Corrections Spending   18

Law Enforcement Spending   46

Law Enforcement Spending as a Percentage of Total Spending   47

Transportation · Section K

Travel on Interstates   49

Interstate Mileage in Unacceptable Condition   25

Deficient Bridges   11

Traffic Deaths   49

Seat Belt Use   33

Vehicle-miles Traveled Per Capita   2

Workers Using Public Transportation   38

Road and Street Miles   18

Highway Employees   5

Public Transit Employees   30

Highway Spending Per Capita   11

Highway Spending as a Percentage of Total Spending   14

Welfare · Section L

Percentage of Births to Unwed Mothers   32

TANF Recipients as a Percentage of Population   10

Food Stamp Recipients as a Percentage of Population   22

SSI Recipients as a Percentage of Population   22

Change in TANF/AFDC Recipients   43

Condition of Children Index   9

Percentage of Families with Single Parent   27

Average Monthly TANF Payments   5

Welfare as a Percentage of Poverty-level Income   10

State Supplements of SSI   28

State Income Tax Liability of Typical Family in Poverty   41

Child Support Collections   18

Child Support Collections Per Dollar of Administrative Costs   36

Children in Foster Care   14

Welfare Spending Per Capita   5

Welfare Spending as a Percentage of Total Spending   5

Administrative Costs Per TANF Case   25

Technology · Section M

Percentage of Households with Computers   14

Percentage of Households with Internet Access   15

Zip codes with Broadband Service   31

High-tech Jobs   7

Dot-com Domain Names   25

State Government Website Ratings   41

Students per Computer   23

Virginia

Population - Section A

Population 2001	12
Population Change 2000-2001	14
Population Change 1990-2001	16
Population 2015	17
Population 2025	12
Percentage 65 and Over	42
Percentage 17 and Under	41
Median Age	27
Percentage African American	8
Percentage Hispanic	26
Percentage in Poverty	42
Child Poverty Rate	45
Percentage Female	25
Birth Rates	24
Death Rates	19
Population Density	14
New Legal Immigrants 2000	8

Economies - Section B

Personal Income 2001	12
Gross State Product	15
Per Capita Personal Income	12
Personal Income from Wages and Salaries	8
Average Annual Pay	12
Average Hourly Earnings	28
Value Added in Manufacturing	22
Cost of Living	18
Average Annual Pay in Manufacturing	29
Average Annual Pay in Retailing	23
Labor Force	16
Unemployment Rate	45
Employment Rate	6
Government Employment	18
Manufacturing Employment	36
Fortune 500 Companies	10
Forbes 500 Companies	7
Tourism Spending Per Capita	17
Exports Per Capita	29
Housing Permits	10
Percentage Change in Home Prices	12
Net Farm Income	29
Financial Institution Assets	30
Bankruptcy Filings	18
Patents Issued	32
WC Disability Payment	17
UC Average Weekly Benefit	24
Economic Momentum	11
One-year Employment Change	33
Manufacturing Employment Change	22
Home Ownership	15
Gambling	24

(Utilities continued)

Electricity Use Per Residential Customer	9
Cost Per Kwh	11
New Companies	26

Geography - Section C

Total Land Area	37
Federally Owned Land	21
State Park Acreage	38
State Park Visitors	47
Population Not Active	32
Hunters with Firearms	21
Registered Boats	20
State Spending for the Arts	35
Energy Consumption Per Capita	38
Toxic Chemical Release Per Capita	33
Hazardous Waste Sites	13
Polluted Rivers and Streams	20
Expired Surface Water Pollution Permits	21
Air Pollution Emissions	14

Government - Section D

Members of United States House	12
State Legislators	27
Legislators Per Million Population	41
Units of Government	49
Legislators Compensation	23
Female Legislators	42
Turnover in Legislatures	n/a
Term Limits	n/a
Legislative Session Length	41
Republicans in State Legislatures	11
Governor's Power Rating	34
Number of Statewide Elected Officials	44
State and Local Government Employees	26
State and Local Average Salaries	21
Local Employment	30
Local Spending Accountability	25
Registered Voters	27
Percentage of Population Voting	50
Statewide Initiatives	n/a
Campaign Costs Per Vote	5

Federal Impacts - Section E

Per Capita Federal Spending	2
Increase in Federal Spending	6
Per Capita Federal Grant Spending	49
Per Capita Federal Spending on Procurement	1

(Federal Impacts continued)

Per Capita Federal Spending on Payments to Individuals	23
Per Capita Federal Spending on Social Security and Medicare	42
Social Security Benefits	32
Federal Spending on Employee Wages and Salaries	3
Federal Grant Spending Per Dollar of State Tax Revenue	45
General Revenue from Federal Government	49
Federal Tax Burden Per Capita	12
Federal Spending Per Dollar of Taxes Paid	12
Highway Charges Returned to States	20
Terms of Trade	48
Federal Personal Income Taxes	13
Federal Share of Medicaid	38

Taxes - Section F

Tax Revenue	43
Per Capita Tax Revenue	22
Tax Effort	35
Tax Capacity	18
Percentage Change in Taxes	7
Property Taxes as a Percentage of Income	31
Property Taxes Per Capita	24
Property Tax Revenue as a Percentage of 3-tax Revenues	25
Sales Taxes as a Percentage of Income	42
Sales Taxes Per Capita	41
Sales Tax Revenue as a Percentage of 3-tax Revenues	37
Sales Tax Rate	44
Income Taxes as a Percentage of Income	14
Income Taxes Per Capita	11
Income Tax Revenue as a Percentage of 3-tax Revenues	10
Highest Personal Income Rate	27
Corporate Income Taxes	31
Motor Fuel Taxes	39
Tobacco Taxes	50
Taxes on High Income Families	36
Taxes in the Largest City in Each State	31
Progressivity of Taxes	33

Revenues and Finances - Section G

Per Capita Total Revenue	29
Per Capita General Revenue	31
Own-source General Revenue	21
Per Capita Non-tax Revenue	25

Per Capita Total Spending	37
General Spending as a Percentage of Income	46
Per Capita General Spending	33
Change in General Expenditures	13
State Government General Revenue	34
State Government General Spending	34
State Government General Fund Spending	42
State and Local Debt	30
Debt as a Percentage of Revenue	21
Per Capita Full Faith and Credit Debt	27
Bond Ratings	1
State Solvency Index	15
Pension Plan Assets	24
State Reserves	16
Capital Outlays and Interest	35
State Budget Process Quality	42
Relative State Spending "Needs"	24
Structural Deficits	37

Education - Section H

Math Proficiency, Eighth Grade	16
Science Proficiency, Eighth Grade	17
AFQT Ranks	37
SAT Scores	10
ACT Scores	n/a
Over-25 Population with a High School Diploma	21
Students in Private Schools	29
High School Completion Rates	28
Pupil-Teacher Ratio	48
Public School Enrollment	34
Library Holdings Per Capita	27
Children with Disabilities	19
Education Spending Per Capita	23
Education Spending as a Percentage of Total Spending	13
Spending Per Pupil	38
Average Teacher Salary	23
Sources of School Funds	13
State Aid Per Pupil	31
Higher Education Spending Per Capita	27
Higher Education Spending as a Percentage of Total Spending	25
Public Higher Education Enrollment	19
Per Pupil Support of Higher Education	30
Tuition and Fees	19
Average Professor Salary	7
Education Employees	24
R and D Spending	3
Library Operating Spending	20

Health - Section I

Immunization Rates	29
Infant Mortality Rates	25
State Health Rankings	18
Population Without Health Insurance	34
Abortions	13
Alcohol Consumption	38
Percentage of Adult Smokers	27
Percentage Obese	26
AIDS Cases	13
Physicians Per 100,000 Population	14
Hospital Beds Per 1,000 Population	36
Medicaid Recipients	46
Medicaid Recipients as a Percentage of Poverty Population	34
Health and Hospital Spending	27
Health and Hospital Spending as a Percentage of Total Spending	25
Per Capita Medicaid Spending	49
Medicaid Spending Per Aged Recipient	38
Medicaid Spending Per Child	37
Medicare Payment Per Hospital Day	31
Hospital Expense Per Inpatient Day	39
Population in HMOs	29

Crime - Section J

Crime Rate	38
Violent Crime Rate	36
Murder Rate	23
Property Crime Rate	38
Motor Vehicle Theft Rate	38
Violent Crime Rate Change	23
Prisoners	12
Change in Prisoners	39
Incarceration Rate	17
Juvenile Violent Crime Rate	38
Law Enforcement Employees	35
Corrections Employees	4
State Corrections Spending	21
Increase in State Corrections Spending	27
Law Enforcement Spending	23
Law Enforcement Spending as a Percentage of Total Spending	17

Transportation - Section K

Travel on Interstates	7
Interstate Mileage in Unacceptable Condition	30
Deficient Bridges	27

Traffic Deaths	40
Seat Belt Use	21
Vehicle-miles Traveled Per Capita	28
Workers Using Public Transportation	11
Road and Street Miles	3
Highway Employees	30
Public Transit Employees	32
Highway Spending Per Capita	28
Highway Spending as a Percentage of Total Spending	28

Welfare - Section L

Percentage of Births to Unwed Mothers	35
TANF Recipients as a Percentage of Population	43
Food Stamp Recipients as a Percentage of Population	35
SSI Recipients as a Percentage of Population	26
Change in TANF/AFDC Recipients	20
Condition of Children Index	14
Percentage of Families with Single Parent	34
Average Monthly TANF Payments	33
Welfare as a Percentage of Poverty-level Income	12
State Supplements of SSI	10
State Income Tax Liability of Typical Family in Poverty	18
Child Support Collections	31
Child Support Collections Per Dollar of Administrative Costs	6
Children in Foster Care	44
Welfare Spending Per Capita	41
Welfare Spending as a Percentage of Total Spending	38
Administrative Costs Per TANF Case	31

Technology - Section M

Percentage of Households with Computers	18
Percentage of Households with Internet Access	12
Zip codes with Broadband Service	23
High-tech Jobs	4
Dot-com Domain Names	11
State Government Website Ratings	15
Students per Computer	27

Washington

Population - Section A

Population 2001	15
Population Change 2000-2001	13
Population Change 1990-2001	10
Population 2015	8
Population 2025	13
Percentage 65 and Over	43
Percentage 17 and Under	20
Median Age	33
Percentage African American	35
Percentage Hispanic	16
Percentage in Poverty	23
Child Poverty Rate	27
Percentage Female	39
Birth Rates	33
Death Rates	41
Population Density	25
New Legal Immigrants 2000	9

Economies - Section B

Personal Income 2001	14
Gross State Product	14
Per Capita Personal Income	13
Personal Income from Wages and Salaries	13
Average Annual Pay	10
Average Hourly Earnings	3
Value Added in Manufacturing	31
Cost of Living	13
Average Annual Pay in Manufacturing	7
Average Annual Pay in Retailing	6
Labor Force	25
Unemployment Rate	2
Employment Rate	49
Government Employment	12
Manufacturing Employment	30
Fortune 500 Companies	20
Forbes 500 Companies	23
Tourism Spending Per Capita	37
Exports Per Capita	1
Housing Permits	14
Percentage Change in Home Prices	18
Net Farm Income	28
Financial Institution Assets	37
Bankruptcy Filings	15
Patents Issued	15
WC Disability Payment	7
UC Average Weekly Benefit	2
Economic Momentum	26
One-year Employment Change	47
Manufacturing Employment Change	50
Home Ownership	42
Gambling	20

Electricity Use Per Residential Customer	16
Cost Per Kwh	48
New Companies	1

Geography - Section C

Total Land Area	20
Federally Owned Land	12
State Park Acreage	12
State Park Visitors	4
Population Not Active	48
Hunters with Firearms	40
Registered Boats	18
State Spending for the Arts	43
Energy Consumption Per Capita	19
Toxic Chemical Release Per Capita	41
Hazardous Waste Sites	7
Polluted Rivers and Streams	17
Expired Surface Water Pollution Permits	5
Air Pollution Emissions	18

Government - Section D

Members of United States House	14
State Legislators	24
Legislators Per Million Population	34
Units of Government	28
Legislators Compensation	12
Female Legislators	1
Turnover in Legislatures	32
Term Limits	n/a
Legislative Session Length	24
Republicans in State Legislatures	28
Governor's Power Rating	29
Number of Statewide Elected Officials	4
State and Local Government Employees	43
State and Local Average Salaries	8
Local Employment	40
Local Spending Accountability	19
Registered Voters	34
Percentage of Population Voting	27
Statewide Initiatives	6
Campaign Costs Per Vote	48

Federal Impacts - Section E

Per Capita Federal Spending	26
Increase in Federal Spending	37
Per Capita Federal Grant Spending	30
Per Capita Federal Spending on Procurement	14

Per Capita Federal Spending on Payments to Individuals	35
Per Capita Federal Spending on Social Security and Medicare	40
Social Security Benefits	8
Federal Spending on Employee Wages and Salaries	11
Federal Grant Spending Per Dollar of State Tax Revenue	37
General Revenue from Federal Government	36
Federal Tax Burden Per Capita	5
Federal Spending Per Dollar of Taxes Paid	40
Highway Charges Returned to States	28
Terms of Trade	42
Federal Personal Income Taxes	6
Federal Share of Medicaid	39

Taxes - Section F

Tax Revenue	32
Per Capita Tax Revenue	15
Tax Effort	9
Tax Capacity	15
Percentage Change in Taxes	36
Property Taxes as a Percentage of Income	23
Property Taxes Per Capita	16
Property Tax Revenue as a Percentage of 3-tax Revenues	24
Sales Taxes as a Percentage of Income	1
Sales Taxes Per Capita	1
Sales Tax Revenue as a Percentage of 3-tax Revenues	3
Sales Tax Rate	4
Income Taxes as a Percentage of Income	n/a
Income Taxes Per Capita	n/a
Income Tax Revenue as a Percentage of 3-tax Revenues	n/a
Highest Personal Income Rate	n/a
Corporate Income Taxes	n/a
Motor Fuel Taxes	14
Tobacco Taxes	4
Taxes on High Income Families	43
Taxes in the Largest City in Each State	39
Progressivity of Taxes	47

Revenues and Finances - Section G

Per Capita Total Revenue	9
Per Capita General Revenue	17
Own-source General Revenue	12
Per Capita Non-tax Revenue	10

Per Capita Total Spending   5

General Spending as a Percentage of Income   29

Per Capita General Spending   13

Change in General Expenditures   36

State Government General Revenue   22

State Government General Spending   18

State Government General Fund Spending   30

State and Local Debt   6

Debt as a Percentage of Revenue   13

Per Capita Full Faith and Credit Debt   7

Bond Ratings   2

State Solvency Index   32

Pension Plan Assets   10

State Reserves   19

Capital Outlays and Interest   6

State Budget Process Quality   33

Relative State Spending "Needs"   18

Structural Deficits   36

Education - Section H

Math Proficiency, Eighth Grade   n/a

Science Proficiency, Eighth Grade   n/a

AFQT Ranks   5

SAT Scores   1

ACT Scores   n/a

Over-25 Population with a High School Diploma   1

Students in Private Schools   35

High School Completion Rates   26

Pupil-Teacher Ratio   4

Public School Enrollment   16

Library Holdings Per Capita   25

Children with Disabilities   44

Education Spending Per Capita   13

Education Spending as a Percentage of Total Spending   32

Spending Per Pupil   22

Average Teacher Salary   18

Sources of School Funds   42

State Aid Per Pupil   14

Higher Education Spending Per Capita   17

Higher Education Spending as a Percentage of Total Spending   26

Public Higher Education Enrollment   13

Per Pupil Support of Higher Education   36

Tuition and Fees   21

Average Professor Salary   15

Education Employees   49

R and D Spending   14

Library Operating Spending   7

Health - Section I

Immunization Rates   33

Infant Mortality Rates   47

State Health Rankings   11

Population Without Health Insurance   24

Abortions   6

Alcohol Consumption   33

Percentage of Adult Smokers   27

Percentage Obese   40

AIDS Cases   24

Physicians Per 100,000 Population   25

Hospital Beds Per 1,000 Population   50

Medicaid Recipients   19

Medicaid Recipients as a Percentage of Poverty Population   15

Health and Hospital Spending   10

Health and Hospital Spending as a Percentage of Total Spending   9

Per Capita Medicaid Spending   47

Medicaid Spending Per Aged Recipient   35

Medicaid Spending Per Child   48

Medicare Payment Per Hospital Day   19

Hospital Expense Per Inpatient Day   2

Population in HMOs   28

Crime - Section J

Crime Rate   8

Violent Crime Rate   27

Murder Rate   34

Property Crime Rate   3

Motor Vehicle Theft Rate   3

Violent Crime Rate Change   26

Prisoners   27

Change in Prisoners   24

Incarceration Rate   40

Juvenile Violent Crime Rate   13

Law Enforcement Employees   45

Corrections Employees   34

State Corrections Spending   9

Increase in State Corrections Spending   33

Law Enforcement Spending   22

Law Enforcement Spending as a Percentage of Total Spending   27

Transportation - Section K

Travel on Interstates   11

Interstate Mileage in Unacceptable Condition   22

Deficient Bridges   28

Traffic Deaths   42

Seat Belt Use   6

Vehicle-miles Traveled Per Capita   41

Workers Using Public Transportation   9

Road and Street Miles   44

Highway Employees   24

Public Transit Employees   4

Highway Spending Per Capita   27

Highway Spending as a Percentage of Total Spending   36

Welfare - Section L

Percentage of Births to Unwed Mothers   42

TANF Recipients as a Percentage of Population   7

Food Stamp Recipients as a Percentage of Population   32

SSI Recipients as a Percentage of Population   27

Change in TANF/AFDC Recipients   32

Condition of Children Index   13

Percentage of Families with Single Parent   13

Average Monthly TANF Payments   13

Welfare as a Percentage of Poverty-level Income   7

State Supplements of SSI   43

State Income Tax Liability of Typical Family in Poverty   n/a

Child Support Collections   7

Child Support Collections Per Dollar of Administrative Costs   21

Children in Foster Care   32

Welfare Spending Per Capita   15

Welfare Spending as a Percentage of Total Spending   21

Administrative Costs Per TANF Case   39

Technology - Section M

Percentage of Households with Computers   4

Percentage of Households with Internet Access   3

Zip codes with Broadband Service   14

High-tech Jobs   8

Dot-com Domain Names   5

State Government Website Ratings   7

Students per Computer   33

West Virginia

Population · Section A

Population 2001	37
Population Change 2000-2001	49
Population Change 1990-2001	49
Population 2015	42
Population 2025	38
Percentage 65 and Over	3
Percentage 17 and Under	50
Median Age	1
Percentage African American	37
Percentage Hispanic	50
Percentage in Poverty	4
Child Poverty Rate	8
Percentage Female	15
Birth Rates	48
Death Rates	5
Population Density	29
New Legal Immigrants 2000	46

Economies · Section B

Personal Income 2001	39
Gross State Product	50
Per Capita Personal Income	49
Personal Income from Wages and Salaries	49
Average Annual Pay	44
Average Hourly Earnings	20
Value Added in Manufacturing	40
Cost of Living	41
Average Annual Pay in Manufacturing	25
Average Annual Pay in Retailing	49
Labor Force	50
Unemployment Rate	9
Employment Rate	42
Government Employment	13
Manufacturing Employment	37
Fortune 500 Companies	n/a
Forbes 500 Companies	46
Tourism Spending Per Capita	50
Exports Per Capita	39
Housing Permits	50
Percentage Change in Home Prices	42
Net Farm Income	46
Financial Institution Assets	42
Bankruptcy Filings	19
Patents Issued	48
WC Disability Payment	36
UC Average Weekly Benefit	39
Economic Momentum	35
One-year Employment Change	42
Manufacturing Employment Change	34
Home Ownership	5
Gambling	23

Electricity Use Per Residential Customer	21
Cost Per Kwh	26
New Companies	45

Geography · Section C

Total Land Area	41
Federally Owned Land	30
State Park Acreage	16
State Park Visitors	13
Population Not Active	6
Hunters with Firearms	1
Registered Boats	39
State Spending for the Arts	14
Energy Consumption Per Capita	5
Toxic Chemical Release Per Capita	8
Hazardous Waste Sites	42
Polluted Rivers and Streams	24
Expired Surface Water Pollution Permits	9
Air Pollution Emissions	34

Government · Section D

Members of United States House	34
State Legislators	31
Legislators Per Million Population	12
Units of Government	24
Legislators Compensation	30
Female Legislators	35
Turnover in Legislatures	27
Term Limits	n/a
Legislative Session Length	36
Republicans in State Legislatures	43
Governor's Power Rating	2
Number of Statewide Elected Officials	21
State and Local Government Employees	32
State and Local Average Salaries	41
Local Employment	43
Local Spending Accountability	44
Registered Voters	31
Percentage of Population Voting	49
Statewide Initiatives	n/a
Campaign Costs Per Vote	15

Federal Impacts · Section E

Per Capita Federal Spending	13
Increase in Federal Spending	39
Per Capita Federal Grant Spending	9
Per Capita Federal Spending on Procurement	46

Per Capita Federal Spending on Payments to Individuals	3
Per Capita Federal Spending on Social Security and Medicare	1
Social Security Benefits	34
Federal Spending on Employee Wages and Salaries	27
Federal Grant Spending Per Dollar of State Tax Revenue	11
General Revenue from Federal Government	2
Federal Tax Burden Per Capita	49
Federal Spending Per Dollar of Taxes Paid	4
Highway Charges Returned to States	7
Terms of Trade	5
Federal Personal Income Taxes	48
Federal Share of Medicaid	2

Taxes · Section F

Tax Revenue	16
Per Capita Tax Revenue	42
Tax Effort	20
Tax Capacity	49
Percentage Change in Taxes	45
Property Taxes as a Percentage of Income	41
Property Taxes Per Capita	44
Property Tax Revenue as a Percentage of 3-tax Revenues	43
Sales Taxes as a Percentage of Income	13
Sales Taxes Per Capita	26
Sales Tax Revenue as a Percentage of 3-tax Revenues	14
Sales Tax Rate	9
Income Taxes as a Percentage of Income	33
Income Taxes Per Capita	35
Income Tax Revenue as a Percentage of 3-tax Revenues	32
Highest Personal Income Rate	19
Corporate Income Taxes	16
Motor Fuel Taxes	7
Tobacco Taxes	42
Taxes on High Income Families	27
Taxes in the Largest City in Each State	32
Progressivity of Taxes	25

Revenues and Finances · Section G

Per Capita Total Revenue	34
Per Capita General Revenue	30
Own-source General Revenue	42
Per Capita Non-tax Revenue	35

Per Capita Total Spending	34
General Spending as a Percentage of Income	7
Per Capita General Spending	36
Change in General Expenditures	44
State Government General Revenue	18
State Government General Spending	21
State Government General Fund Spending	5
State and Local Debt	36
Debt as a Percentage of Revenue	30
Per Capita Full Faith and Credit Debt	50
Bond Ratings	4
State Solvency Index	47
Pension Plan Assets	47
State Reserves	5
Capital Outlays and Interest	44
State Budget Process Quality	38
Relative State Spending "Needs"	30
Structural Deficits	15

Education - Section H

Math Proficiency, Eighth Grade	27
Science Proficiency, Eighth Grade	19
AFQT Ranks	43
SAT Scores	n/a
ACT Scores	17
Over-25 Population with a High School Diploma	50
Students in Private Schools	43
High School Completion Rates	19
Pupil-Teacher Ratio	37
Public School Enrollment	42
Library Holdings Per Capita	27
Children with Disabilities	2
Education Spending Per Capita	34
Education Spending as a Percentage of Total Spending	20
Spending Per Pupil	13
Average Teacher Salary	41
Sources of School Funds	41
State Aid Per Pupil	9
Higher Education Spending Per Capita	33
Higher Education Spending as a Percentage of Total Spending	27
Public Higher Education Enrollment	27
Per Pupil Support of Higher Education	34
Tuition and Fees	44
Average Professor Salary	41
Education Employees	21
R and D Spending	29
Library Operating Spending	46

Health - Section I

Immunization Rates	14
Infant Mortality Rates	16
State Health Rankings	41
Population Without Health Insurance	20
Abortions	38
Alcohol Consumption	49
Percentage of Adult Smokers	3
Percentage Obese	2
AIDS Cases	33
Physicians Per 100,000 Population	19
Hospital Beds Per 1,000 Population	6
Medicaid Recipients	7
Medicaid Recipients as a Percentage of Poverty Population	26
Health and Hospital Spending	40
Health and Hospital Spending as a Percentage of Total Spending	32
Per Capita Medicaid Spending	7
Medicaid Spending Per Aged Recipient	26
Medicaid Spending Per Child	36
Medicare Payment Per Hospital Day	49
Hospital Expense Per Inpatient Day	42
Population in HMOs	39

Crime - Section J

Crime Rate	47
Violent Crime Rate	37
Murder Rate	43
Property Crime Rate	48
Motor Vehicle Theft Rate	44
Violent Crime Rate Change	n/a
Prisoners	41
Change in Prisoners	4
Incarceration Rate	42
Juvenile Violent Crime Rate	46
Law Enforcement Employees	49
Corrections Employees	50
State Corrections Spending	36
Increase in State Corrections Spending	14
Law Enforcement Spending	49
Law Enforcement Spending as a Percentage of Total Spending	49

Transportation - Section K

Travel on Interstates	12
Interstate Mileage in Unacceptable Condition	19
Deficient Bridges	6
Traffic Deaths	11
Seat Belt Use	47
Vehicle-miles Traveled Per Capita	18
Workers Using Public Transportation	37
Road and Street Miles	1
Highway Employees	6
Public Transit Employees	29
Highway Spending Per Capita	15
Highway Spending as a Percentage of Total Spending	12

Welfare - Section L

Percentage of Births to Unwed Mothers	28
TANF Recipients as a Percentage of Population	8
Food Stamp Recipients as a Percentage of Population	1
SSI Recipients as a Percentage of Population	3
Change in TANF/AFDC Recipients	26
Condition of Children Index	41
Percentage of Families with Single Parent	13
Average Monthly TANF Payments	36
Welfare as a Percentage of Poverty-level Income	30
State Supplements of SSI	n/a
State Income Tax Liability of Typical Family in Poverty	5
Child Support Collections	13
Child Support Collections Per Dollar of Administrative Costs	18
Children in Foster Care	16
Welfare Spending Per Capita	10
Welfare Spending as a Percentage of Total Spending	6
Administrative Costs Per TANF Case	24

Technology - Section M

Percentage of Households with Computers	46
Percentage of Households with Internet Access	46
Zip codes with Broadband Service	47
High-tech Jobs	47
Dot-com Domain Names	50
State Government Website Ratings	35
Students per Computer	27

Wisconsin

Population - Section A

Population 2001	18
Population Change 2000-2001	25
Population Change 1990-2001	27
Population 2015	35
Population 2025	20
Percentage 65 and Over	23
Percentage 17 and Under	24
Median Age	19
Percentage African American	29
Percentage Hispanic	29
Percentage in Poverty	43
Child Poverty Rate	35
Percentage Female	33
Birth Rates	40
Death Rates	36
Population Density	24
New Legal Immigrants 2000	24

Economies - Section B

Personal Income 2001	19
Gross State Product	27
Per Capita Personal Income	20
Personal Income from Wages and Salaries	20
Average Annual Pay	27
Average Hourly Earnings	18
Value Added in Manufacturing	2
Cost of Living	28
Average Annual Pay in Manufacturing	24
Average Annual Pay in Retailing	34
Labor Force	2
Unemployment Rate	26
Employment Rate	25
Government Employment	42
Manufacturing Employment	2
Fortune 500 Companies	16
Forbes 500 Companies	26
Tourism Spending Per Capita	42
Exports Per Capita	23
Housing Permits	12
Percentage Change in Home Prices	24
Net Farm Income	23
Financial Institution Assets	20
Bankruptcy Filings	36
Patents Issued	13
WC Disability Payment	15
UC Average Weekly Benefit	20
Economic Momentum	27
One-year Employment Change	11
Manufacturing Employment Change	17
Home Ownership	21
Gambling	32

Electricity Use Per Residential Customer	36
Cost Per Kwh	10
New Companies	47

Geography - Section C

Total Land Area	25
Federally Owned Land	25
State Park Acreage	24
State Park Visitors	19
Population Not Active	43
Hunters with Firearms	5
Registered Boats	6
State Spending for the Arts	44
Energy Consumption Per Capita	31
Toxic Chemical Release Per Capita	35
Hazardous Waste Sites	10
Polluted Rivers and Streams	26
Expired Surface Water Pollution Permits	36
Air Pollution Emissions	22

Government - Section D

Members of United States House	18
State Legislators	32
Legislators Per Million Population	36
Units of Government	14
Legislators Compensation	9
Female Legislators	22
Turnover in Legislatures	36
Term Limits	n/a
Legislative Session Length	n/a
Republicans in State Legislatures	16
Governor's Power Rating	30
Number of Statewide Elected Officials	21
State and Local Government Employees	34
State and Local Average Salaries	16
Local Employment	7
Local Spending Accountability	47
Registered Voters	n/a
Percentage of Population Voting	15
Statewide Initiatives	n/a
Campaign Costs Per Vote	41

Federal Impacts - Section E

Per Capita Federal Spending	49
Increase in Federal Spending	23
Per Capita Federal Grant Spending	34
Per Capita Federal Spending on Procurement	42

Per Capita Federal Spending on Payments to Individuals	38
Per Capita Federal Spending on Social Security and Medicare	25
Social Security Benefits	10
Federal Spending on Employee Wages and Salaries	50
Federal Grant Spending Per Dollar of State Tax Revenue	44
General Revenue from Federal Government	40
Federal Tax Burden Per Capita	21
Federal Spending Per Dollar of Taxes Paid	37
Highway Charges Returned to States	26
Terms of Trade	32
Federal Personal Income Taxes	23
Federal Share of Medicaid	32

Taxes - Section F

Tax Revenue	4
Per Capita Tax Revenue	8
Tax Effort	3
Tax Capacity	24
Percentage Change in Taxes	33
Property Taxes as a Percentage of Income	11
Property Taxes Per Capita	11
Property Tax Revenue as a Percentage of 3-tax Revenues	21
Sales Taxes as a Percentage of Income	31
Sales Taxes Per Capita	28
Sales Tax Revenue as a Percentage of 3-tax Revenues	39
Sales Tax Rate	19
Income Taxes as a Percentage of Income	4
Income Taxes Per Capita	8
Income Tax Revenue as a Percentage of 3-tax Revenues	11
Highest Personal Income Rate	15
Corporate Income Taxes	21
Motor Fuel Taxes	2
Tobacco Taxes	17
Taxes on High Income Families	12
Taxes in the Largest City in Each State	10
Progressivity of Taxes	12

Revenues and Finances - Section G

Per Capita Total Revenue	5
Per Capita General Revenue	15
Own-source General Revenue	11
Per Capita Non-tax Revenue	26

Per Capita Total Spending	13
General Spending as a Percentage of Income	17
Per Capita General Spending	11
Change in General Expenditures	22
State Government General Revenue	16
State Government General Spending	14
State Government General Fund Spending	6
State and Local Debt	22
Debt as a Percentage of Revenue	39
Per Capita Full Faith and Credit Debt	10
Bond Ratings	4
State Solvency Index	6
Pension Plan Assets	6
State Reserves	40
Capital Outlays and Interest	17
State Budget Process Quality	44
Relative State Spending "Needs"	4
Structural Deficits	16

Education · Section H

Math Proficiency, Eighth Grade	n/a
Science Proficiency, Eighth Grade	n/a
AFQT Ranks	1
SAT Scores	n/a
ACT Scores	1
Over-25 Population with a High School Diploma	20
Students in Private Schools	9
High School Completion Rates	17
Pupil-Teacher Ratio	29
Public School Enrollment	31
Library Holdings Per Capita	20
Children with Disabilities	21
Education Spending Per Capita	8
Education Spending as a Percentage of Total Spending	15
Spending Per Pupil	11
Average Teacher Salary	21
Sources of School Funds	28
State Aid Per Pupil	13
Higher Education Spending Per Capita	11
Higher Education Spending as a Percentage of Total Spending	22
Public Higher Education Enrollment	12
Per Pupil Support of Higher Education	40
Tuition and Fees	23
Average Professor Salary	9
Education Employees	31
R and D Spending	42
Library Operating Spending	15

Health · Section I

Immunization Rates	10
Infant Mortality Rates	30
State Health Rankings	11
Population Without Health Insurance	48
Abortions	30
Alcohol Consumption	5
Percentage of Adult Smokers	25
Percentage Obese	16
AIDS Cases	40
Physicians Per 100,000 Population	26
Hospital Beds Per 1,000 Population	29
Medicaid Recipients	38
Medicaid Recipients as a Percentage of Poverty Population	31
Health and Hospital Spending	35
Health and Hospital Spending as a Percentage of Total Spending	35
Per Capita Medicaid Spending	26
Medicaid Spending Per Aged Recipient	11
Medicaid Spending Per Child	25
Medicare Payment Per Hospital Day	30
Hospital Expense Per Inpatient Day	8
Population in HMOs	17

Crime · Section J

Crime Rate	35
Violent Crime Rate	45
Murder Rate	30
Property Crime Rate	35
Motor Vehicle Theft Rate	36
Violent Crime Rate Change	10
Prisoners	21
Change in Prisoners	n/a
Incarceration Rate	23
Juvenile Violent Crime Rate	n/a
Law Enforcement Employees	26
Corrections Employees	17
State Corrections Spending	10
Increase in State Corrections Spending	7
Law Enforcement Spending	10
Law Enforcement Spending as a Percentage of Total Spending	16

Transportation · Section K

Travel on Interstates	48
Interstate Mileage in Unacceptable Condition	44
Deficient Bridges	41

Traffic Deaths	34
Seat Belt Use	28
Vehicle-miles Traveled Per Capita	23
Workers Using Public Transportation	26
Road and Street Miles	39
Highway Employees	28
Public Transit Employees	20
Highway Spending Per Capita	14
Highway Spending as a Percentage of Total Spending	19

Welfare · Section L

Percentage of Births to Unwed Mothers	36
TANF Recipients as a Percentage of Population	46
Food Stamp Recipients as a Percentage of Population	42
SSI Recipients as a Percentage of Population	33
Change in TANF/AFDC Recipients	6
Condition of Children Index	11
Percentage of Families with Single Parent	34
Average Monthly TANF Payments	31
Welfare as a Percentage of Poverty-level Income	23
State Supplements of SSI	19
State Income Tax Liability of Typical Family in Poverty	34
Child Support Collections	4
Child Support Collections Per Dollar of Administrative Costs	7
Children in Foster Care	21
Welfare Spending Per Capita	21
Welfare Spending as a Percentage of Total Spending	30
Administrative Costs Per TANF Case	6

Technology · Section M

Percentage of Households with Computers	27
Percentage of Households with Internet Access	28
Zip codes with Broadband Service	18
High-tech Jobs	35
Dot-com Domain Names	37
State Government Website Ratings	46
Students per Computer	44

Wyoming

Population - Section A

Population 2001	50
Population Change 2000-2001	44
Population Change 1990-2001	34
Population 2015	1
Population 2025	49
Percentage 65 and Over	38
Percentage 17 and Under	17
Median Age	14
Percentage African American	44
Percentage Hispanic	20
Percentage in Poverty	36
Child Poverty Rate	39
Percentage Female	47
Birth Rates	41
Death Rates	25
Population Density	49
New Legal Immigrants 2000	50

Economies - Section B

Personal Income 2001	50
Gross State Product	8
Per Capita Personal Income	19
Personal Income from Wages and Salaries	47
Average Annual Pay	42
Average Hourly Earnings	7
Value Added in Manufacturing	45
Cost of Living	16
Average Annual Pay in Manufacturing	37
Average Annual Pay in Retailing	43
Labor Force	7
Unemployment Rate	47
Employment Rate	4
Government Employment	2
Manufacturing Employment	49
Fortune 500 Companies	n/a
Forbes 500 Companies	n/a
Tourism Spending Per Capita	4
Exports Per Capita	43
Housing Permits	39
Percentage Change in Home Prices	34
Net Farm Income	38
Financial Institution Assets	28
Bankruptcy Filings	27
Patents Issued	41
WC Disability Payment	32
UC Average Weekly Benefit	36
Economic Momentum	4
One-year Employment Change	8
Manufacturing Employment Change	25
Home Ownership	24
Gambling	46

Electricity Use Per Residential Customer	31
Cost Per Kwh	6
New Companies	4

Geography - Section C

Total Land Area	9
Federally Owned Land	8
State Park Acreage	25
State Park Visitors	12
Population Not Active	39
Hunters with Firearms	19
Registered Boats	49
State Spending for the Arts	26
Energy Consumption Per Capita	1
Toxic Chemical Release Per Capita	9
Hazardous Waste Sites	47
Polluted Rivers and Streams	46
Expired Surface Water Pollution Permits	35
Air Pollution Emissions	42

Government - Section D

Members of United States House	44
State Legislators	43
Legislators Per Million Population	4
Units of Government	5
Legislators Compensation	47
Female Legislators	43
Turnover in Legislatures	18
Term Limits	1
Legislative Session Length	40
Republicans in State Legislatures	3
Governor's Power Rating	34
Number of Statewide Elected Officials	9
State and Local Government Employees	1
State and Local Average Salaries	40
Local Employment	15
Local Spending Accountability	29
Registered Voters	41
Percentage of Population Voting	5
Statewide Initiatives	n/a
Campaign Costs Per Vote	37

Federal Impacts - Section E

Per Capita Federal Spending	9
Increase in Federal Spending	4
Per Capita Federal Grant Spending	2
Per Capita Federal Spending on Procurement	20

Per Capita Federal Spending on Payments to Individuals	37
Per Capita Federal Spending on Social Security and Medicare	37
Social Security Benefits	23
Federal Spending on Employee Wages and Salaries	8
Federal Grant Spending Per Dollar of State Tax Revenue	1
General Revenue from Federal Government	7
Federal Tax Burden Per Capita	15
Federal Spending Per Dollar of Taxes Paid	23
Highway Charges Returned to States	11
Terms of Trade	7
Federal Personal Income Taxes	12
Federal Share of Medicaid	22

Taxes - Section F

Tax Revenue	12
Per Capita Tax Revenue	19
Tax Effort	48
Tax Capacity	3
Percentage Change in Taxes	17
Property Taxes as a Percentage of Income	10
Property Taxes Per Capita	12
Property Tax Revenue as a Percentage of 3-tax Revenues	5
Sales Taxes as a Percentage of Income	16
Sales Taxes Per Capita	13
Sales Tax Revenue as a Percentage of 3-tax Revenues	13
Sales Tax Rate	37
Income Taxes as a Percentage of Income	n/a
Income Taxes Per Capita	n/a
Income Tax Revenue as a Percentage of 3-tax Revenues	n/a
Highest Personal Income Rate	n/a
Corporate Income Taxes	n/a
Motor Fuel Taxes	47
Tobacco Taxes	45
Taxes on High Income Families	50
Taxes in the Largest City in Each State	50
Progressivity of Taxes	44

Revenues and Finances - Section G

Per Capita Total Revenue	2
Per Capita General Revenue	3
Own-source General Revenue	5
Per Capita Non-tax Revenue	2

Per Capita Total Spending	3
General Spending as a Percentage of Income	3
Per Capita General Spending	3
Change in General Expenditures	35
State Government General Revenue	4
State Government General Spending	5
State Government General Fund Spending	39
State and Local Debt	21
Debt as a Percentage of Revenue	50
Per Capita Full Faith and Credit Debt	46
Bond Ratings	n/a
State Solvency Index	2
Pension Plan Assets	25
State Reserves	33
Capital Outlays and Interest	3
State Budget Process Quality	27
Relative State Spending "Needs"	33
Structural Deficits	45

Education - Section H

Math Proficiency, Eighth Grade	16
Science Proficiency, Eighth Grade	9
AFQT Ranks	18
SAT Scores	n/a
ACT Scores	8
Over-25 Population with a High School Diploma	7
Students in Private Schools	50
High School Completion Rates	30
Pupil-Teacher Ratio	45
Public School Enrollment	7
Library Holdings Per Capita	2
Children with Disabilities	13
Education Spending Per Capita	2
Education Spending as a Percentage of Total Spending	35
Spending Per Pupil	15
Average Teacher Salary	36
Sources of School Funds	23
State Aid Per Pupil	20
Higher Education Spending Per Capita	8
Higher Education Spending as a Percentage of Total Spending	31
Public Higher Education Enrollment	2
Per Pupil Support of Higher Education	17
Tuition and Fees	42
Average Professor Salary	46
Education Employees	1
R and D Spending	43
Library Operating Spending	16

Health - Section I

Immunization Rates	22
Infant Mortality Rates	28
State Health Rankings	26
Population Without Health Insurance	10
Abortions	46
Alcohol Consumption	11
Percentage of Adult Smokers	34
Percentage Obese	34
AIDS Cases	49
Physicians Per 100,000 Population	48
Hospital Beds Per 1,000 Population	10
Medicaid Recipients	45
Medicaid Recipients as a Percentage of Poverty Population	46
Health and Hospital Spending	1
Health and Hospital Spending as a Percentage of Total Spending	5
Per Capita Medicaid Spending	44
Medicaid Spending Per Aged Recipient	14
Medicaid Spending Per Child	23
Medicare Payment Per Hospital Day	32
Hospital Expense Per Inpatient Day	7
Population in HMOs	47

Crime - Section J

Crime Rate	34
Violent Crime Rate	40
Murder Rate	44
Property Crime Rate	34
Motor Vehicle Theft Rate	47
Violent Crime Rate Change	1
Prisoners	49
Change in Prisoners	32
Incarceration Rate	30
Juvenile Violent Crime Rate	37
Law Enforcement Employees	8
Corrections Employees	14
State Corrections Spending	16
Increase in State Corrections Spending	n/a
Law Enforcement Spending	12
Law Enforcement Spending as a Percentage of Total Spending	33

Transportation - Section K

Travel on Interstates	3
Interstate Mileage in Unacceptable Condition	34
Deficient Bridges	40

Traffic Deaths	5
Seat Belt Use	n/a
Vehicle-miles Traveled Per Capita	1
Workers Using Public Transportation	31
Road and Street Miles	14
Highway Employees	2
Public Transit Employees	37
Highway Spending Per Capita	2
Highway Spending as a Percentage of Total Spending	3

Welfare - Section L

Percentage of Births to Unwed Mothers	38
TANF Recipients as a Percentage of Population	50
Food Stamp Recipients as a Percentage of Population	38
SSI Recipients as a Percentage of Population	48
Change in TANF/AFDC Recipients	1
Condition of Children Index	32
Percentage of Families with Single Parent	40
Average Monthly TANF Payments	6
Welfare as a Percentage of Poverty-level Income	37
State Supplements of SSI	44
State Income Tax Liability of Typical Family in Poverty	n/a
Child Support Collections	9
Child Support Collections Per Dollar of Administrative Costs	30
Children in Foster Care	29
Welfare Spending Per Capita	45
Welfare Spending as a Percentage of Total Spending	49
Administrative Costs Per TANF Case	14

Technology - Section M

Percentage of Households with Computers	24
Percentage of Households with Internet Access	24
Zip codes with Broadband Service	44
High-tech Jobs	50
Dot-com Domain Names	46
State Government Website Ratings	50
Students per Computer	49

Index

A

AARP, 3
Abortions, 230
Acquired immunodeficiency syndrome (AIDS), 234. *See also* Health and health-care
AFDC. *See* Aid to Families with Dependent Children
Age. *See* Population
Agriculture. *See* Farming and agriculture income
AIDS. *See* Acquired immunodeficiency syndrome
Aid to Families with Dependent Children (AFDC), 288,
Alabama, 5, 314-315
Alaska, 3, 5, 6, 11, 13, 316-317
Alcohol consumption, 233
American Demographics, 7
Annie B. Casey Foundation, 3
Arizona, 3, 318-319
Arkansas, 320-321
Armed forces qualification test, 196
Arts. *See* Cultural attractions and recreation

B

Banks. *See* Financial institution assets
Benefits
disability, 63
federal payments to individuals, 124
federal share of, 135
Medicare, 125
Social Security, 125-126
state pensions, 184
unemployment, 64
Birth rates. *See* Social issues
Bridges. *See* Transportation
Broadband, 306

Budget Processes in the States, 10
Bureau of Labor Statistics, 1, 10
"Business climate," 9
Business issues. *See also* Decisionmaking; Economic issues; Taxes; Trade
bankruptcy filings, 61
business location, 6-7, 8
costs, 7-8
federal procurement, 123
Forbes 500 companies, 54
Fortune 500 companies, 53
government regulation, 9-10
manufacturing, 7, 8, 44, 46, 52, 67
multistate firms, 8
new companies, 72
pro-business attitudes, 9
productivity, 7
retailing, 7, 47
taxes, 10, 11
transportation, 7, 9
travel expenses, 7
utility costs, 9, 71
wages and salaries, 7-8, 41-43, 46-47

C

California, 3, 4, 5, 322-323
Capital punishment, 4. *See also* Crime; Law enforcement
Center for Budget and Policy Priorities, 11
Children. *See also* Decisionmaking; Education; Social issues; Welfare
child support collections, 295-296
Condition of Children Index, 289
with disabilities, 205
environment for, 3
foster care, 297
infant mortality rates, 227
poverty rate, 29
Children's Defense Fund, 3

Choose a College Town for Retirement (Lubow), 3
Colorado, 5, 324-325
Common Cause, 13
Computers
internet access, 305
ownership, 304
in schools, 310
Connecticut, 13, 326-327
Construction industry, 1
Corporation for Enterprise Development, 9
Corrections. *See* Crime; Law enforcement
Cost of living index, 6, 45
County Business Patterns, 1, 10
Crime. *See also* Decisionmaking
crime rates, 250-255
employees, 260-261
juvenile, 259
prisons and prisoners, 256-257
safety from, 6
spending on, 262-265
Cultural attractions and recreation. *See also* Decisionmaking; Environment
boats, 84
government support of, 9
hunting, 83
opportunities for, 3-4
retirement and, 3
spending for the arts, 85
state parks, 80-81

D

Death rates. *See* Social issues
Decisionmaking. *See also* Information resources
business or home location, 1, 6-7
children's issues, 3
commercial issues, 9-10

crime and law enforcement issues, 5-6
cultural and recreational issues, 3-4
education issues, 2, 3, 11
employment issues, 7
environmental issues, 5
governmental, policy, and regulation
   issues, 4-5, 8, 10-11
healthcare issues, 5
investment issues, 4
labor issues, 7
real estate issues, 4
retirement issues, 3
social issues, 6
taxation and cost issues, 2, 5-12
transportation issues, 9, 11
welfare issues, 11
Deficits and debt. *See* Local and regional
   factors; States
Delaware, 328-329
Democratic Party. *See* Political issues
Department of Commerce, 2, 7, 10
Department of Labor, 10
Development Report Card for the States, 9
Disabilities, children with, 205
District of Columbia, xiii. *See also indi-*
   vidual tables
Domain names, 308
Drugs, control of, 4

E

Economic issues. *See also* Business
   issues; Employment; Income;
   Revenues and finances; State expenditures; Taxes; Trade
   bankruptcy filings, 61
   cost of living, 6, 45
   employment, 1-2, 49-52
   gross state product, 39
   growth rates, 1-2, 4, 5, 6, 65, 66
   housing, 1, 4
   income, 38, 40-43, 46-47
   information resources, 1-2
   ratios of men to women, 6
   state capital outlays and interest, 186
   state credit risks, 10
Education. *See also* Decisionmaking;
   Libraries
   armed forces qualification test, 196
   computer use in, 310
   higher education enrollment, 214
   high school graduates, 199, 201
   policies, 11
   private schools, 200
   proficiency, 194-195
   public schools and universities, 2, 3,

203, 205, 214, 216-217
   pupil-teacher ratios, 202
   salaries, 209, 217
   spending on, 3, 206-208, 212-213, 215
   test scores, 196-198
   tuition and fees, 216
   university systems, 3, 9
   voucher programs, 2
Employment. *See also* Decisionmaking;
   Economic issues; Income
   changes in, 66-67
   economic factors, 1-2
   education, 218
   government, 51, 108-110
   high-tech, 307
   highway and transit, 278-279
   labor force, 48
   law enforcement and corrections,
      261-262
   local, 110
   manufacturing, 52, 67
   new companies and, 72
   ratios of men to women, 6
   unemployment and employment rates,
      49-50
Energy. *See* Utilities
Environment. *See also* Decisionmaking;
   Cultural attractions and recreation
   federal government lands, 79
   hazardous waste sites, 89
   pollution, 5, 89-91
   state parks, 79-80
   toxic chemical releases, 87

F

Farming and agriculture income, 59
Federal government
   grants, 122, 128
   spending, 110-128, 131, 213
   wages and salaries, 127
Fifty Healthiest Places to Live and Retire
   (Ford), 3
Financial institution assets, 60
Financing State Government in the
   1990s, 10
Florida, 2, 3, 5, 6, 330-331
Food stamps. *See* Welfare
Forbes 500 companies, 54
Fortune 500 companies, 53
Fuel taxes, 157

G

Gambling, 69
Georgia, 332-333
Governing, 13

Government. *See also* Decisionmaking; Federal government; Local and
   regional factors; States
   best institutions, 12-13
   corruption in, 12-13
   employees and employment, 51, 108,
      110
   House of Representatives, 96
   interference by, 4-5, 9
   land owned by, 79
   management of, 10
   political parties in, 105
   state legislatures, 97-98, 100-105
   term limits, 103
   units of, 99
   website rating, 309
Governors. *See* States
Gross state product (GSP). *See* States
Guns, 4, 83

H

Hawaii, 2, 6, 334-335
Hazardous waste. *See* Pollution and hazardous waste
Health and healthcare. *See also* Decisionmaking; Medicaid; Medicare; Social
   issues
   abortions, 230
   AIDS, 234
   alcohol consumption, 231
   compensation for temporary
      disability, 63
   hospital beds, number of, 236
   immunization/vaccination rates, 226
   infant mortality rates, 227
   insurance, 229
   physicians, 235
   population not physically active, 82
   population overweight, 233
   smokers, 232
   spending on, 239-245
   state health rankings, 228
   statistics, 5
Health maintenance organizations
   (HMOs), 248
High Costs of High Costs, The (Regional
   Financial Associates), 8
Highways. *See* Transportation
HMOs. *See* Health maintenance organizations
Housing, 68. *See also* Real estate

I

Idaho, 336-337
Illinois, 3, 338-339

Immigration, 34

Immunization. *See* Health and healthcare

Incarceration. *See* Crime

Income. *See* Economic issues; Employment; Taxes

  education spending as percentage of, 207, 213

  farm, 59

  government employees, 109

  highway spending as percentage of, 280

  income taxes and, 134, 152

  legislatures, 100

  personal, 38, 40-41

  poverty level, 294

  property taxes and, 145

  sales taxes and, 148

  state and local taxes and, 140, 144

  tax burden and, 159

  of teachers, 209

Index of Condition of Children, 289

Index of Juvenile Violent Crime, 259

Index of State Budget Process Quality, 187

Index of State Economic Momentum, 1, 7, 65

Indiana, 340-341

Information resources. *See also* Decisionmaking

  business, 6-10

  cultural and recreation, 3-4

  economic issues, 1

  government, 10-13

  retirement, 3

  taxation, 2, 5, 8, 10, 11, 12

  welfare, 11

Insurance, health, 229

Internet, 305-306, 308-310

Investments, 4. *See also* Business issues; Decisionmaking; Economic issues

Iowa, 3, 5, 342-343

K

Kansas, 344-345

Kentucky, 8, 346-347

Kids Count Data Book, 3

KPMG Peat Marwick, 8

L

Labor. *See* Employment

Law enforcement. *See also* Crime

  employment in, 261-262

  spending on, 263-265

Legislatures. *See* Government; States

Libraries, 204, 220

Line-item veto, 12

Living costs. *See* Economic issues

Local and regional factors. *See also* Decisionmaking

  business location, 6-7

  capital outlays and interest, 186

  debt and solvency, 179-181, 183

  economic growth, 1-2

  employment, 110

  expenditures, 188, 174

  government spending, 111

  schools, 2

  taxes, 2, 141

Louisiana, 348-349

M

Maine, 4, 350-351

Maryland, 11, 352-353

Massachusetts, 354-355

Medicaid, 11, 135, 237-238, 241-243

Medicare, 125, 244

Michigan, 356-357

Minnesota, 3, 358-359

Mississippi, 13, 360-361

Missouri, 362-363

Montana, 3, 364-365

Murder. *See* Crime

N

National Conference of State Legislatures, 10, 12

National Governors' Association, 10

Nebraska, 366-367

Nevada, 1, 5, 6, 368-369

New Hampshire, 370-371

New Jersey, 372-373

New Mexico, 4, 374-375

New York

  bonds, 4

  construction industry, 1

  cultural attractions, 3

  living costs, 6

  rankings, 376-377

  tax burdens, 2, 5, 8

  tax competitiveness study, 8

North Carolina, 8, 378-379

North Dakota, 380-381

No Child Left Behind Act (NCLB), 2

O

Office of Federal Housing Enterprise Oversight, 4

Ohio, 2, 3, 382-383

Oklahoma, 384-385

Oregon, 1, 2, 386-387

Overdrive, 11

P

Patents, 62

Pennsylvania, 3, 388-389

Physicians, 235. *See also* Health and healthcare

Political issues, 105, 114. *See also* Government; Voters and voting

Pollution and hazardous waste. *See also* Environment

  air, 91

  hazardous waste sites, 88

  rivers, streams, and surface water, 89-90

  statistics use, 5

  toxic chemical release, 87

  in the West, 5

Population. *See also* Immigration; Race

  age 17 and under, 24

  age 65 and over, 23

  change in, 1, 19-21

  density of, 33

  labor force as percentage of, 48

  median age, 25

  percentage distribution, 18

  percentage overweight, 233

  not physically active, 82

  in poverty, 28

  projections, 21-22

  totals, 18-22

Poverty. *See also* Medicaid; Welfare

  assistance, 11

  income tax liability in poverty, 294

  population, 28

  rate for children, 29

  welfare as percentage of poverty-level income, 292

Prisons and prisoners. *See* Crime

Private schools. *See* Education

Public libraries, 204, 220

Public schools. *See* Education

R

Race, 26, 27

Ranking. *See individual tables*

Rape. *See* Crime

Real estate. *See also* Decisionmaking; Housing

  costs/prices of, 6, 58

  home ownership, 68

  housing permits, 57

  investment in, 4

Recreation. *See* Cultural attractions and recreation

Regional Financial Associates, 8

Republican Party. *See* Political issues

Research and development, 219

Retirement, 3. *See also* Decisionmaking
Retirement Places (Savageau), 3
Revenues and finances
    budget process, 10, 181
    capital outlays and interest, 186
    debt and solvency, 179-181, 183
    expenditures, 172-175, 177, 178
    government bond ratings, 182
    pension plans, 184
    relative spending needs, 188
    reserves, 185
    revenues, 168-171, 176, 180,
Rhode Island, 390-391

S

Scholastic Aptitude Test (SAT), 197
Schools. *See* Education
Seat belts. *See* Transportation
Site Selection, 10
Social issues. *See also* Decisionmaking; Education; Health and healthcare; Welfare
    birth rates, 31
    child support collections, 295-296
    death rates, 32, 227, 273
    female legislators, 101
    foster care, 297
    opposite-sex partners, 6
    single parents, 290
Social Security, 125-126
South Carolina, 3, 392-393
South Dakota, 4, 394-395
Sports, 3-4
State Budget & Tax News, xii
State expenditures
    capital outlays and interest, 186
    changes in, 175
    corrections and law enforcement, 263-266
    education spending, 206-208, 212-213, 215, 219
    general, 173-174, 177-178
    reserves as a percentage of spending, 185
    spending needs, 188
    total, 172
    transportation, 280-281
    welfare, 298-299
State Policy Reports, xii, 4, 11
States. *See also* Government; Taxes
    bond ratings, 182
    debt and solvency, 179-181, 183, 185, 189
    economic momentum, 1, 7, 65
    elected officials, 107
    federal grants and revenues, 122, 128-129, 135
    governors, 103, 106, 115
    gross state product, 39

health rankings, 228
highway charges returned to, 132
income taxes, 152-155, 294
initiatives, 114
land owned by federal government, 79
legislatures, 97-98, 100-105
management of, 10, 187
parks, 80-81
pensions, 184
revenues, 168-171, 176, 180
SSI supplements, 293
total land area, 78
units of government, 99
Supplemental security income (SSI). *See* Welfare

T

Taxes. *See also* Business issues; Decision-making; Economic issues
    bonds, 4
    business/corporate, 8, 10-11, 156
    capacity, 143
    effective use of, 12
    effort, 142
    fairness of, 10
    federal spending and, 128
    fuels, 157
    future rates, 5
    as government intrusiveness, 4-5
    income, 134, 152-155
    inheritance, 162
    liability in poverty, 294
    progressivity, 10, 161
    property, 145-147
    retirement and, 3
    sales, 148-152
    tax burdens, 2, 130, 159
    tobacco, 158
Teachers. *See* Education
Temporary Assistance for Needy Families (TANF), 285, 288, 291, 300
Tennessee, 2, 396-397
Term limits, 12, 103
Texas, 2, 5, 398-399
Tobacco, 158, 232
Tourism, 55
Trade, 56
Transportation. *See also* Decisionmaking
    best, 9, 11-12
    bridges, 272
    highway charges returned to states, 132
    interstate highways, 270-271
    road and street miles, 277
    seat belts, 274
    spending on, 280-281

traffic deaths, 273
use of public transportation, 276
vehicle-miles traveled, 275

U

Unemployment compensation (UC), 10, 64. *See also* Workers' compensation
United States (totals). *See individual tables*
Urban Institute, 12
Utah, 400-401
Utilities
    costs, 71
    energy consumption, 86
    rates, 9
    use of, 70

V

Vaccination. *See* Health and healthcare
Vermont, 402-403
Virginia, 404-405
Voters and voting, 114-115, 155

W

Washington, D.C. *See* District of Columbia
Washington (state), 1, 406-407
WC. *See* Workers' compensation
Welfare. *See also* Decisionmaking
    Aid to Families with Dependent Children, 288
    births to unwed mothers, 284
    federal share of, 135
    food stamp recipients, 286
    population in poverty, 28-29
    poverty level, 292
    spending on, 298-299
    SSI, 287, 293
    state aid, 11
    Temporary Assistance for Needy Families, 285, 288, 291, 300
West Virginia, 6, 408-409
Wisconsin, 2, 410-411
Workers' compensation (WC), 63. *See also* Unemployment compensation
Wyoming, 5, 13, 412-413